To the memory of

JOHN RHINESMITH McCLURE
1934–1964

Poet, teacher, friend

WHO
LIVED
WHERE
IN EUROPE

WHO LIVED WHERE IN EUROPE

A Biographical Guide to Homes and Museums

John Eastman

Facts On File Publications
New York, New York • Oxford, England

Who Lived Where in Europe: A Biographical Guide to Homes and Museums

Library of Congress Cataloging in Publication Data
Eastman, John.
    Who lived where in Europe.

    Includes index.
    1. Historic buildings—Europe—Guide-books.
2. Historical museums—Europe—Guide-books.   3.
Dwellings—Europe—Guide-books.   4. Europe—
Description and travel—1971–   —Guide-books.   I. Title.
D910.5.E17 1984   914   82-18200
ISBN 0-87196-749-9

Printed in the United States of America

10 9 8 7 6 5 4 3 2 1

Book Composition by Logidec
Book Printing by the Maple-Vail Manufacturing Group

CONTENTS

PICTURE CREDITS

While great care has been taken to acknowledge the correct sources for the illustrations reproduced in this book, original ownership of several of the pictures is obscure, and I extend apologies to anyone whose copyright may have been unknowingly infringed.

ACKNOWLEDGEMENTS

A book of this type is usually done by committee these days. I am fortunate in not having had to deal with a committee but with a notable group of supportive friends and associates, all of whom helped make this book possible.

Heading the list, not for the first time, must be Susan Woolley Stoddard, who planned and shared with me a European itinerary that included many of the homes listed in the following pages. Not only a superb travel partner, Sue is a constantly invigorating companion whose enthusiasm and support, helpful suggestions and practical mastery of a thing called a "word processor" are vital ingredients of this book. It is impossible to overestimate the value of her participation.

Also vital was the generous aid and patience of Peter L. Ginsberg, Robert B. Hutchins, Prof. John M. Murphy, Dr. Eleanora Schoenebaum and Robin Smith. I made frequent use of the extensive facilities of the Dwight B. Waldo Library at Western Michigan University in Kalamazoo. My friend William J. Mills offered "extensive facilities" of his own—his charming cabin in the backwoods of northern Michigan, where these words are written.

My special thanks go to Judith Linn for expert picture research and to copy editor Valerie Pitt. I am also grateful to the following individuals and organizations who took time to offer aid or hunt down and clarify obscure bits of information: Erika Faisst, Swiss National Tourist Office; Elisabeth Halvarsson-Stapen, Swedish Consulate General Information Service; Uta Hoffmann, German Information Center; Geneviève Hureau, Services Culturels Français; James McBride, Arnold Schoenberg Institute, Los Angeles; Bedford Pace, British Tourist Authority; Sylvia Panarites, Belgian National Tourist Office; Alexandra Reynolds, AC&R Public Relations, Inc., New York; Else Rothe, Danish Information Office; Maria Siff, National Tourist Office of Spain; Irene Varvayanis, Norwegian Information Office; Claus Wolf, Cultural Attaché, Embassy of the German Democratic Republic; Kathryn Woolley, Kalamazoo, Michigan; and Karin Zechner, Austrian Press and Information Service.

INTRODUCTION

We were both stationed in West Germany during the late 1950s. My friend John McClure (to whose memory this book is dedicated) rode the train down from Wiesbaden and I rode up from Pirmasens to share a weekend pass in Heidelberg. While climbing up to the old castle that overlooks the town, we must have been talking about "doing" some museums in nearby Frankfurt, because I remember his exact words: "I like Goethe, but I don't care to see chairs dusted by his great backside."

To McClure, always rigorously unkind to his heroes, the homes and memorabilia of notable historical figures were all more or less irrelevant "backsides" to their words or acts—words and acts for which he may have been conservative in his praise, but which he always took seriously. Often, I suspect, he viewed famous homes and exhibits as arranged for someone's material enrichment, as betrayals, somehow, of the dignity and creativity of the life in question. So I went to Goethe's house by myself, saw his well-dusted chairs among other things, and have, of course, never regretted it.

One's approach to a historic figure who has at some time stimulated one's thoughts or interests is a distinctly individual matter. To McClure, the value he derived from a "hero" was to be found in that person's words and works. They told him all he wanted to know. To me, on the other hand, a further connection has always seemed desirable. The words and works that I appreciate have more often stirred than quenched my curiosity. I want to view the scene of this personal creativity or act. Many people, I know, share McClure's preference in the matter. And there are many who share mine. Though he didn't go to Frankfurt with me, McClure did understand my viewpoint, and he would understand this book; he might laugh, but he would understand.

In focusing on the great personalities of European history, we are talking about "who" and "where." Though the "who" is gone, the name and life have left certain indelible marks on earth. The "where," in most cases, survives—to a greater or lesser degree. Exploring the "where" as a historical artifact can be a means of knowing the "who"—sometimes the best means, providing as close a proximity as we can have to the actual lifetimes of those who stood remarkably above (or below) the common run of humanity.

The title of this book is slightly misleading, in that not every European country is included. Nations of the Eastern bloc that are politically dominated by the Soviet Union, as well as the Soviet Union itself, have been omitted. Certainly these countries do not lack rich pasts peopled by distinguished historical figures, nor are they inherently less interesting. But because their official policies often inhibit free access, information and movement, and thus tend to discourage travel on anything approaching the scale that Western European nations welcome, I have reluctantly left them out. It is a pity that current political realities must be reflected in the organization of a book of this type; on any absolute scale of values, a country's style of government must ordinarily rank as one of its less important, more ephemeral features (though some readers may, of course, disagree with this assessment). Perhaps a future edition can reflect more sensible conditions and bring the book's title closer to being. The only exception to the stated omissions is the German Democratic Republic (East Germany), which is included in Chapter 4 because of its geographical and historical unity with what is now the Federal Republic of Germany.

For the 19 European nations included, I have attempted to select the most outstanding names, concentrating on those figures whose works or influence have carried beyond strictly national borders; persons whose lives have, to some extent, entered the common fund of all nations and peoples, whether in the arts, politics, war or science. Any such selection must, of course, be arbitrary and vulnerable to the criticism that goes with the territory. Probably no two authors limited to some three hundred names would select or omit exactly alike. I can only plead that name selections are not intended to imply degrees of relative importance, since other factors—including the presence or absence of actual homes or locatable sites—also entered into my choices. My perspective as an American writer viewing Europe from the outside carries obvious advantages and disadvantages; but as an American of distant European ancestry (like most Americans), I have tried to treat European historical figures within the context of a supranational cultural heritage. The general organization of the book follows the pattern of my previous volume on the United States titled *Who Lived Where*.

The aims of this book are thus twofold: to catalog and present data on the residences of more than three hundred persons whose lives had major effects on European society and history; and to enable travelers, students of history and biography and anyone else so inclined, to find and view for themselves the homes or sites associated with these famous persons. For the combined aims of creating a reference work and a practical tour guide, several basic items of information are included, where possible, for each home discussed:
—Year of construction
—Year of destruction, if pertinent
—Dates of occupance by the noted inhabitant
—1984 status of the home or site, including street address and access information.

In some instances, the loss or inaccessibility of records prevents the inclusion of one or more of these items. When exact years of construction or destruction are unknown, however, the general period can often be assigned from the architecture of the dwelling itself or of subsequent constructions on the site. Dates of occupance are usually well documented by biographers, though imprecise or conflicting information is not uncommon; in such cases, I have generally relied upon the most recent accounts.

For purposes of this book, European history is represented in the conventionally accepted time periods. Most home sites of classical and early Christian notables are found in Chapter 8, specifically the sections on Greece and Italy. Medieval, Renaissance and modern periods are well represented by historical homes or sites throughout all chapters. The biographical span thus extends from Homer, who may have lived in the ninth century B.C., to Joan Miró, who died in 1983—almost 30 centuries of human existence.

Most of the European nations treated in this book have at some time in their histories been major world powers of stunning magnitude and affluence. Several have dominated massive political empires; Rome and Britain ruled more territories and peoples under their proficient administrative systems than any other powers known to humankind, empires which lasted longer than most modern nations have existed. To these two power centers we owe most of the spread of what we call Western civilization. In addition the enormous Macedonian empire of Alexander the Great, while focused mainly in the East, nevertheless spread vital elements of Greek culture throughout the known world. Austrian and German states formed the Holy Roman Empire, temporal legatee of the Palatine Hill; Hapsburgs and Bourbons dominated the great central European monarchies and empires for centuries. The Netherlands, Portugal and Spain also had their glorious moments in the sun. From the bursting vitality of Scandinavia came the Norse raiders who colonized and settled much of Europe. Louis XIV and Napoleon, each in their own time, created a France of unsurpassed vigor and influence. The German empires of Frederick the Great and Wilhelm II shifted the European mosaic of nations—while the ravaging Hitler regime bore political effects whose outcome is yet uncertain.

The 20th century saw the final breakup of the old colonial empires as Europe entered a new age bereft of its fruits of conquest. Torn by two world wars of unprecedented destruction, genocidal mania and gratuitous violence, Europe again picked up its pieces, as it so often has; realigned, as it so often has; and struggled into an unfamiliar role as a buffer region between new intimidating superpowers to the east and west. While most Western European nations are parliamentary democracies of fair to excellent stability, European memories are long. No large Western European nation today may be said to remotely equal the "great days" of its past in terms of power and influence. Indeed, a few of them are in sad decline compared with the "golden ages" they amply memorialize. Yet, while most of them struggle with economic problems, several enjoy unprecedented standards of living along with the highest literacy rates and best health-care facilities in the world.

Throughout Europe the traveler may view carefully maintained monuments, ruins, museums and shrines that attest to days of power and glory and to the desire to identify with those days. For historically aware Europeans (and there are very many of them), the experience of past world leadership forms a background of consciousness that is important for the visitor to realize. Greatness once achieved does not altogether disperse when fortunes decline; it becomes an internalized identity, a part of who you are. This consciousness may account for the impression that some Europeans give—that there is nothing very much that can startle them. The "news" isn't really very new, after all; and a bemused, at times almost parental, tolerance toward those visitors who too obviously believe that history began either yesterday or 10 centuries ago is often readily apparent. Despite the presence of advanced technology and modern industrialized cities, this basic rectitude gained from glorious traditions and the awareness of long, eventful pasts runs very deep. It is what gives vigor and stability to some of the world's shakiest-seeming social and political institutions; gives deliberately unstated rules and codes the

power of humane law; and, on the individual level, gives an easy grace of maturity and character.

There are, of course, profound cultural and geographical differences both in Europe as a whole and within each country. Yet the cliche that Europe or any European nation is a land of contrasts (so is my backyard) misses a more important point. These highly visible differences in peoples, landscapes, climates, architecture and history pale to insignificance when compared with the common background of shared assumptions about humanity, about the world, and about Europe's place in it. The basic viewpoints and underlying agreements that were necessary, even in order for Europeans to contest among themselves in the ways they did, are more mutual and profound (though mostly unstated) than any contrasts that might be identified. Because this fact may not be readily apparent as we narrow our view to specific countries, it is worth stating loud and clear at the outset.

Yet, despite significant economic steps and various other efforts to lower national barriers, the old dream of a European union based on volition, not conquest, seems as remote from realization as ever. For all the pain and displacements brought by war, political philosophies remain generally conservative and nationalistic, tied to the old power-politics ways of thinking that have so often failed to provide a durable security. European unity, if it comes, will probably be forced by expedience, not by rationalistic planning, simply because the nature of nations is to react more often than to act to benefit themselves. A constant push toward European unity is, of course, provided by the current East-West superpower contest. Soon, if geopolitical history is a guide, both Eastern and Western European blocs will begin challenging their alliances and looking to their own interests to a far greater degree than we have seen. For Europe, and possibly for the world, such a development could carry enormous consequences. Few perceptive prophets would venture to predict that Europe has permanently vacated center stage.

Most historical pilgrims will be astonished at the number of notable homes that survive in Europe, despite centuries of destructive wars, natural disasters and periods of widespread vandalism toward certain historical reminders. Modern excavations have exposed the palatial halls of Nero, the houses of Augustus and Constantine, the Roman prison of St. Peter and St. Paul. Religious or political revolutions, those implosions that are often more destructive than cannons from without, wreaked massive violence in the England of Henry VIII and during the French Revolution, as people vented long-suppressed rage against church and nobility, furiously laying waste to any structure that was even faintly reminiscent of the hated past. Throughout Europe, however, numerous castles do survive from the feudal age, and many of them remain superbly functional as hotels or tourist attractions. Many historic homes in Germany, the Low Countries and England even survived the raining bombs of World War II; and numerous others that were destroyed in that conflict have been meticulously reconstructed on their sites.

Such reconstructions and survivals owe much to the general European philosophy of preservation. Though rarely codified and largely unstated, it has remained supremely functional over the centuries. It consists of the simple fact that seldom in normal periods is a building demolished merely for the sake of replacing it with something new. While road construction, subway excavations and high-rise structures have occasionally displaced historic dwellings (especially during the last several decades), such events remain relatively rare and controversial. Most European structures were and are built to last; the materials used consist mainly of stone, brick, stucco and timber beams. Permanence is part of the European structural philosophy (else why bother?) and "built-in" obsolescence or plans for replacement are not in the blueprints. The typical European city dwelling has usually been occupied by at least several generations of owners or renters; and many town and village houses, dating from or predating the medieval period, still hold families. Tearing things down is not and has never been a typically European thing to do, particularly in times of relative stability.

Europeans are famous for their skill in reconstructing lost or damaged historic buildings. Some of the better-known houses detailed in the following pages stand in their second or third incarnations on the same site, faithful in every detail to the original structure and often including many of the original materials. Another common European style of preservation is to extend or incorporate older dwellings into later structures for functional purposes. The palace at Versailles is a prime example (though in this case Louis XIV himself did most of the extending). Most royal palaces that remain intact represent in fact, many centuries of additions, reconstructions and restorations. Numerous "town houses," particularly in Paris, likewise enclose walls, courtyards and chambers of progenitor structures on their sites.

Where demolition or destruction have occurred, materials of a historic building often turn up in newer structures; thus they may come to possess something of the historical mystique of the original. In Paris, for instance, the stones of the infamous Bastille were placed deliberately underfoot, forming the river arch of the Pont de la Concorde crossing the Seine. In Rome, according to H. V. Morton, "If a magician waved his wand over any famous Roman palace and commanded the stones which compose it to fly back to their original buildings, there would be some curious scenes. The Farnese Palace would melt away to help fill the gap in the Colosseum, a part of it would come to rest on the Quirinal . . . and piles of stone would descend into Trajan's Forum, the Baths of Diocletian and the Baths of Caracalla." In Europe stone and brick seldom travel far from their original wall sites. Village houses near castle ruins can often be traced in their materials to the former towers on the hill.

While the science of archaeology and the art of restoration have resurrected, preserved or rebuilt numerous remnants of Europe's historic panorama, the specific nature of this activity has not been universally applauded. Science and art are in conflict on this ground too. "Too much restoration," writes art critic Alexander Eliot, "takes the life out of a place more surely than ever the attrition of the centuries will." Any experienced house pilgrim can cite examples of Eliot's concern: the polished-up dwelling, faithful down to every last nail, tile and furnishing, but a place in which its memorialized occupant would not in 10 lifetimes have set foot. Such places more nearly resemble embalmments, dressed-up and cosmeticized corpses, than the dwellings of real people. Such places subvert their stated intentions by sterilizing the surroundings of their famous dwellers—and, inevitably, the dwellers themselves—out of all human recognition. One may well wonder if the real intentions of such scrubbing for the sake of "authenticity" are always as zealous as claimed; for "cleaning up" the image of a historical gadfly, who may still arouse discomfort or controversy if presented too "literally," is a familiar ploy of propaganda or avoidance.

British art critic Osbert Lancaster calls this sterile school of restoration "learned vandalism," and particularly cites American archaeology in Greece. "The average archaeologist, being almost invariably totally deficient in visual sense," he writes, "is about as safe a person to have around . . . as a bomber pilot or by-pass builder." In view of archaeology's total achievements, such savage judgments probably overkill the target; yet few knowledgeable observers would disagree that resurrecting the tangible past is a complex matter—too complex to leave entirely to the hands and tools of professional diggers or restorers. Without the participation of multiple disciplines steeped in past ways of thinking and seeing, the results are bound to be 20th-century reflections, finally telling us more about restorative technology than about the object of restoration. For some professionals, that's quite enough to shoot for. Nobody can ever *really* know what a past time was like, they argue; and modern science helps preclude less authentic notions about the past by admitting only what is "in the ground" and working exclusively with that. But narrow specialties, as we know, give narrowly specialized views. The matter of restoring a cultural microcosm (which is what any good house restoration should aspire to be) is territory, if ever there was, for the Renaissance man or woman, the cultural historian who is also a generalist—a rare creature these days and getting rarer.

For the typical visitor to a historic house, such controversies may seem too esoteric to matter. Serious pilgrims bring their own visualizations, create their own auras of a place—and who is to judge their "authenticity"? Far more important to most of us are matters of meaning, significance, tribute; matters beyond the concerns and capacities of archaeology or construction skills to decide. Yet an awareness of some of the scholarly thorn-bushes that exist on these topics may lend the traveler a useful dose of skepticism—always healthy medicine—to carry along with the camera.

What qualifies as a home? Generally, for the purposes of this book, a *home* is any currently existing structure, whether house, hotel or apartment dwelling, where the eminent person resided for any extensive length of time. *Extensive* usually means at least a year, though some addresses of shorter durations are included if the place has some outstanding association with the person's life or career. Not listed as homes (with some significant exceptions) are academic lodgings and transient military quarters.

A *site* is the home address minus the eminent person's residence, which may have been destroyed or moved elsewhere; the site is usually occupied by another building.

Most famous homes that admit the public are careful *restorations* according to original plans and designs, and incorporate a large amount of original materials along with some elements necessarily replaced because of destruction or decay. Most restorations begin from a basically intact "skeleton," then are "fleshed out" by specialists in historical architecture working from the accumulated data. *Reconstructions* are entirely rebuilt from the ground up, using original plans but little or no original materials. *Preservations*, the least common structures, maintain both original design and materials.

The text portion of this book focuses upon (a) homes open to the public, (b) surviving homes that remain privately owned and (c) museums that display biographical collections.

Most houses or palaces of well-known Europeans that now function as museums are owned and staffed by either national or municipal governments. Relatively rare is the house-museum that remains under the private control of individuals or organizations. The admission information listed for buildings open to the public was accurate in 1984; but since this type of information is subject to frequent change, travelers planning to visit a place should always check locally for days and hours of admission. Often, for many smaller museums that do not widely publicize admission information, local inquiry is the *only* way to find it out. Bear in mind that the distance unit in continental Europe is the kilometer; in Great Britain and Ireland, it is the mile.

For the vast majority of homes and sites, visitors must content themselves with exterior views, for such places remain privately owned and do not admit the public. (Any address not specifically stated as open to the public may be assumed to be privately owned and *not* open to the public.) They are usually, though not invariably, marked by signs or plaques. One may find the selectivity of houses chosen to be marked interesting and revealing in itself. People and cultures obviously like to memorialize those notables who make them look good—and prefer to ignore the others. Some omissions are puzzling. A system of discreet markers on Rome's Palatine Hill might clarify certain aspects of this once "prime residential" area considerably. The Nazi era in Germany is not, of course, a matter for historic plaques (except for a few in memory of the victims), nor is Mussolini's Italy. Without a stake in such preferences or avoidances, however, the following pages include a certain number of addresses that fit the "ignorable" category; these are places in which one definitely won't see plaques or markers but which, in my opinion, deserve inclusion in a book of this sort. Selective history can be habit-forming for individuals and countries alike; definite address records help keep us honest.

In occasional instances, however, information is not as definite as I would like. Numbered street addresses often do not exist in small villages or towns, and address directions must often refer to nearby orientation points such as the village church, square or main street. In a few cases, numbered addresses have been withheld by request; anyone sufficiently inclined can seek them out by local inquiry.

Unless described as reconstructions or sites, addresses in the following pages may be generally assumed to represent original dwellings of the people concerned. Authenticity is often difficult to establish for lesser known structures that remain privately owned, as the majority do. One must sometimes make large assumptions from architectural details or neighborhood surroundings—educated guesses, in short, that may in some instances prove wrong.

Though I have visited a number of the homes and museums included, especially in the larger European cities, it was obviously impossible for one person to view each house or site and still complete a book of this magnitude. Thus I have gratefully relied upon the best qualified extensions I could find. I have gathered address information from various published sources, including biographies and memoirs, general and specialized travel guides, tourist literature, architectural guides, government publications, maps and journalistic accounts. Private contacts and correspondence have helped unearth and clarify obscure addresses. Strenuous efforts have been made to check and update information from older sources and to provide the highest possible degree of accuracy, without which a book of this type cannot fulfill its purpose. In occasional instances, certain information was dropped entirely because, though possibly valid, its precision or veracity resisted all attempts at clarification. Despite my attempts to cover all bases, however, the profusion of secondary data and sources restrains me from claiming one hundred percent accuracy. From any reader or authority who may knowledgeably offer corrections or additions, I cordially invite correspondence.

The Blue Guide series of guidebooks to individual countries are especially valuable to travelers interested in history. Authors in several European countries—most notably Great Britain, France and West Germany—have also provided excellent specialized guidebooks (most of which are mentioned in the following chapters) to literary or artistic homes and sites within their countries. Specialized guidebooks to Western Europe in general include the *Guide to Literary Europe* (1966), edited by Margaret Crosland; *A Religious Guide to Europe* (1975), by Daniel M. Madden; and *Music Lover's Europe* (1983), by Kenneth Bernstein. These books cover only the high points of their concerns and make no claim for comprehensiveness. Until now, there has never been a comprehensive attempt to catalog the homes of European notables in one volume under the exclusive rubric of biography. Such an attempt is long overdue. Yet, when confronted with the intimidating roster of historic figures who have decorated the European scene, such an effort can finally give only an inkling of the richness and variety that await the biographical traveler.

As we get closer to the historical figures that attract or intrigue us, either through biographies or their own works, such people achieve more human dimensions and lose some of the mythic larger-than-life qualities that fame automatically confers. This process of fleshing out a recognizable person from a "name" is one of the pleasures of reading biography; and the degree of this accomplishment is a measure of the biographer's success. A work of successful biography is an act that not only honors the famous dead by forsaking platitudes about them, but produces psychological and intellectual wealth for the living. Biography is thus creative in its constant reshaping and refocusing (yes, and "retooling") of persons who, as pioneers or examples, have shaped and focused aspects of the world we know today. A notable person's fame endures only as long as there remains something left of a life that we can use or identify with, here and now.

History "repeats" itself, of course, with dismaying frequency, and humanity's failure to learn from such repetitions seems safely predictable. Yet within such repetitions the differences that make one period absolutely foreign to another are startling. Since most of the forces that have shaped and rule our lives go without saying and are therefore largely hidden from us, we have, in some sense, forgotten more than Socrates ever knew. Surely Socrates or Aristotle would not recognize the jaded world of Nietzsche or Sartre. Gauguin would only bewilder Giotto, Louis XIV would not comprehend even so imperious a figure as Charles de Gaulle, Beethoven might prefer his deafness to the tones explored by Schönberg, and Galileo and Newton would be *almost* as befuddled by Einstein as are most nonphysicists today. Dietrich Bonhoeffer might use some of the same words as St. Augustine but they would hardly mean the same things, and discussion between the two would quickly bog down. All of these people are like islands connected by submerged ridges, hiding the progression of thought, the paths and links between them. Others of different eras would probably find themselves less "islanded" by the passage of time. Most writers could probably relate because of their constant replenishment from (and parasitism of) their literary forebears. Soldiers could converse despite profound changes in weaponry, for the study of war is the same; and the thought and slogans of political revolutionaries through history would be largely interchangeable.

The question of who in the historical roster could still shine in a transplanted time and place is not just a bemusing game. In a more comprehensive sense, it is actually the challenge posed by any outstanding life to a biographer as the latter tries to recreate a complex person and period for the equally complex requirements of modern readers. Some of Europe's historic notables would probably have surged to the forefront in any age, while many others more distinctively personified their own times and places. During the Middle Ages, birth in a castle was the only avenue to political

power, while a life of learning was usually impossible unless it stemmed from simultaneous dedication to celibacy and the church. The attempt to define such background elements and give them proper weight is a part of that biographical process: bringing a portrait to life—*our* life. To make an icon live is the biographer's eminent feat.

Yet even a biographer's success can only take us so far. Biography is necessarily told as a story. But our experience of the actual places associated with a life often shatters our neat "story notions" about both person and places. Actually confronting the scenes of a life we have known only from a book—face to face with our hero or villain's garden, parlor or prison—we at last approach the hard surface underlying the stylistic construction of words. On the spot of the daily events of this life, we can sense the less tangible relics: the conversations, laughters, griefs, boredoms, angers, days of great works and great nothings. Being on the spot defies the subtle disbeliefs we carry that are engendered by (and despite) the best biographies, the truest stories. One moves from a mental picture to the solid bric-a-brac of a personal space that lies exposed at last behind its artfully crafted curtains. One approaches, at last, a human being.

Finally, of course, anyone who finds this book interesting or useful is one who doesn't need lectures on the worth or value of visiting a historic home. Each traveler will have selective preferences; not everybody cares about Napoleon or Shakespeare or politicians or painters. For some visitors, the interest will be curiosity alone; for others, visiting such a home may represent a culmination of years of study and interest, a high point of European travel.

My wish for you as an explorer of the following pages is that the information presented may guide, aid and expand your acquaintance with a heritage that all of us, in some measure, share; and that these pages may encourage and assist your personal journey toward a historic figure who has, perhaps, enlarged your own life or view of humanity, or may yet do so. In the pursuit of such a quest is expressed the spirit of those fortunate souls in Paradise who, in Dante's final chorus, sounded the unsurpassable refrain of tribute and discovery: "Lo, here is one who shall increase our loves."

WHO
LIVED
WHERE
IN EUROPE

Chapter 1
AUSTRIA AND SWITZERLAND

AUSTRIA

In its complex history, this central European country embodies a virtual microcosm of the European past. Through its crossroads location has moved a vast panorama of the peoples and events that have shaped the continental map since Roman times. It was, and is, a junction of Europe.

Agricultural tribes were densely settled in Austria by 3000 B.C. The Romans, who found aggressive Germanic tribes in control about the time of Christ, created the Roman provinces of Pannonia and Noricum and founded the present cities of Bregenz, Innsbruck and Salzburg. Vindobona, later Vienna, became one of Rome's most important northern outposts.

With the decline of Roman strength came the great migrations from eastern Europe. Goths, Huns, Celts, Slavs and Magyars ravaged, ruled, and dispersed in wave upon violent wave of what gentle professors call "historical movement." These episodes were not wars so much as human tides that simply "rolled over" the backwash of the previous wave, giving the population a profoundly mixed genetic ancestry that is still evident today. Austrians have no ethnographic "nationality" in the sense that Italians, Germans, French or Scandinavians can claim.

From the 10th century, however, the German influence remained dominant in language, culture and politics. The Ostmark (loosely translated as "eastern unit" of the German Empire) was established in 976 under the rule of the Babenberg family and soon achieved near-sovereignty in the empire. It was known as Österreich, which remains the German name of the country. The Babenberg dynasty, overthrown in 1246, was replaced by another family line whose progenitor, a Swiss nobleman named Count Rudolf of Hapsburg, became German emperor. Via numerous subdivisions among descendants, territorial acquisitions by marriage, and exchanges of property, the House of Hapsburg ruled Austria for 640 years. Its generally conservative monarchs, the lack of forceful personalities among them, and their anxiety to avoid family feuds, probably account for the duration of this dynasty through countless power shifts, intrigues, and predatory ventures spawned by the European courts.

Eventually, the strongly Catholic Hapsburg monarchs also ruled the Netherlands and Spain, while the Holy Roman Empire—created on the ashes of the pagan Pax Romana—became a virtually hereditary Hapsburg monarchy. "No other ruling family was so 'European,' " wrote Adam Wandruszka, "or became in the course of historical development so much an embodiment. . . of a universal and supranational principle of monarchy." From this 16th-century apex of power and influence, the Holy Roman Empire and Austria with it became torn by religious controversy as the European states contended for supremacy in their styles of Christian worship. Wars, coalitions, and geopolitical deals with rival European powers marked the 18th and 19th centuries. Even as Napoleon terminated the Holy Roman Empire in 1806, however, Hapsburg rule continued. In 1848, amid popular uprisings, Franz Josef I came to the throne and reigned for 68 years. The dual monarchy of Austria-Hungary, created under his rule, lasted from 1867 to 1918. Bismarck's power politics forced a close alliance with Germany that was maintained through World War I. While defeat in war had never previously affected the essential unity of the Hapsburg domain, the notorious Versailles Treaty changed all that. Out of it came the new nation of Czechoslovakia, a separate Hungary, a recreated Poland. Austria's last monarch, Charles I, abdicated in 1918. Hapsburg rule was dead, and a republic was declared.

The present national borders of the Republic of Austria thus date only from 1919. The next two decades, marked by internal political crises, ended with the authoritarian rule of Chancellor Engelbert Dollfuss. A wave of Nazi terrorism forced the nation to its knees in 1938 as Hitler occupied Austria and emotionally declared the *Anschluss* (the German term for the incorporation of Austria into Germany) to be a "restoration" of the medieval Ostmark.

For the first time since its 10th-century beginnings, Austria lost every shred of political independence. Barbaric pogroms devastated its Jewish citizens; the death camp of Mauthausen near Linz added its living fuel to the Holocaust; and entire populations were shifted around the country to suit the needs of the Nazi war machine. The country's human and economic losses during World War II were appalling.* Vienna, heavily bombarded by the Allies and occupied by Soviet troops in 1945, remained under four-power control until Allied occupation of the country ended in 1955.

Since then, Austria's predominantly Socialist parliamentary democracy (the "second republic") has proven one of the most stable in Europe. Politically, World War II purged the country's spirit; from a backward, faction-ridden nation, Austria evolved to a position of political tolerance. Today in East-West superpower disputes, Austria

takes great care to preserve a policy of "active neutrality," a position that maintains the country's historical importance in diplomacy. Its internationalist outlook has given it strong influence in the United Nations.

The country consists of nine provinces. Landlocked and sharing borders with seven nations, Austria encompasses a total area of 83,854 square kilometers. The population, about the size of London's, approaches eight million. Some 99 percent of the people are German-speaking and about 90 percent are Roman Catholic. A scenic mountainous country, Austria's landscape is dominated by the eastern Alps but levels out to gentle hills in the easternmost portion. Forests cover almost half of Austria, while the Danube (*Donau* in German) which spans some 220 miles of the northern part of the country on its route from Bavaria to the Black Sea, is its major river. Nationalized industry employs about one-fifth of the labor force; and agriculture, primarily mixed farming, about one-third. Tourism annually covers Austria's balance-of-trade deficit.

Vienna, Austria's capital and the seat of the old Hapsburg monarchy, is by far its largest city—about one-fourth of the population lives there. The city's strategic location on the Danube and its experience in multinational commerce continue to give it importance as a major European center of east-west trade and communications.

Among Austria's famous residents in earlier times were some of the world's great composers—Beethoven, Brahms, Haydn, Liszt, Mahler, Mozart, Schubert, and both Johann and Richard Strauss, among others. Why did so many gifted musicians flourish in Austria? Aside from the traditional Austrian preference for music above other forms of artistic expression, one major reason was the relative stability of the patronage system. Royal or wealthy sponsors not only supported individual composers but placed great emphasis on the place of music in both entertainment and religious worship. This employment of musical genius was the bright creative side of Hapsburg decadence—even though, until the 19th century, composers were treated as hardly more than talented servants (much as Shakespeare was in London) rather than as "creative artists."

Today Austria's carefully nurtured image as a Straussian never-never land of "wine, women and song" has worn a bit thin. Too much has happened in the Vienna woods, as it were. Yet mu-

---

*Both world wars had Austrian roots. It was the 1914 assassination of the Austrian crown prince, Archduke Franz Ferdinand, which led directly to World War I. And it was Adolf Hitler, a native Austrian obsessed with the twin goals of German nationalism and anti-Semitism, who precipitated World War II.

sic—of all kinds—remains a dominant part of the culture, and numerous homes of the great composers survive, some of them as municipally owned museums and some as privately owned homes marked by tablet. An excellent guidebook to Austria's musical heritage is *The Music Guide to Austria and Germany* (1975), by Elaine Brody and Claire Brook.

AUDEN, WYSTAN HUGH (1907–1973). The English-born poet (he became an American citizen) bought a yellow-clay house at **Kirchstetten** in 1957 and resided there with his longtime companion, Chester Kallman, for part of each year until his death. A former farmhouse, it remains privately owned on Audenstrasse.

Auden died at the Altenburgerhof, a hotel where he was temporarily rooming in **Vienna**. It is now a private office building at Walfischgasse 5.

Auden tomb: Village cemetery, **Kirchstetten**.

(See Chapter 5, ENGLAND; also Chapter 8, ITALY.)

BEETHOVEN, LUDWIG VAN (1770–1827). German by birth, the composer resided in **Vienna** from 1792 until his death. During this 35-year period the restless genius moved 79 times, occupying some 44 dwellings in or near the city. Always lugging his pots and pans and piano to a new lodging, which soon satisfied him no better than the previous one, on at least one occasion he

BEETHOVEN'S HOME IN 1802. This 1927 view of Probusgasse 6 in the **Vienna** suburb of Heiligenstadt shows the house where the composer worked on his Second Symphony and finally realized that his deafness was incurable. It has been a Beethoven museum since 1970.

signed leases on two dwellings and actually moved into a third. Completely deaf by 1824, slovenly in habit and a mean tyrant in his personal relationships, Beethoven struck many observers as more than a little unhinged as he ranted and shouted his solitary way around Vienna. Visitors to his lodgings were horrified to notice the general litter—partly eaten meals and unemptied chamber pots were scattered amid the music manuscripts. Obviously, somewhere beyond all that Beethoven dwelled on a titanic plane. Beneath his increasingly coarse exterior, as we know, compulsively flowed the sounds that only he could hear.

One of his first residences (1792–95) was a palace owned by Prince Lichnowsky, an early patron. It stood at Alsnerstrasse 30.

In 1802 Beethoven lodged during the summer and fall at Probusgasse 6 in the suburb of Heiligenstadt. "In no Beethoven house is one so near the spirit of the immortal," wrote Max Graf, for there Beethoven finally lost all hope of regaining his hearing and wrote his *Heiligenstadt Testament*, a journal addressed to his brothers. ("Unfortunately," wrote musicologist Richard Anthony Leonard, "it is such a wallowing in self-pity that it almost destroys a modern reader's sympathy.") He also worked on his Second Symphony there. This small low house is now a Beethoven museum; it was opened on the composer's bicentennial in 1970. (See below for admission information.)

At the Theater an der Wien, the composer occupied a second-floor apartment with his brother Karl at intervals from 1803 to 1805. There he worked on his opera *Fidelio* (1805), which was first performed to a hostile audience in the theater. First performances of his First, Second, Third, Fifth and Sixth symphonies and his Violin Concerto also occurred in this theater which still stands at Linke Wienzeile 6 and presents light opera.

During the summers of 1803 and 1804 Beethoven lived at Döblinger Hauptstrasse 92, which came to be known as "Eroica House" because he finished his Third Symphony ("the Eroica") there; it was a composition which, according to Leonard, "ended the reign of eighteenth-century music." A new story has been added to the house and the facade widened. In Beethoven's time, vineyards surrounded the structure. Visitors may see Beethoven's death mask, and a collection of portraits and personal items. (See below for admission information.)

Beethoven's residence of longest duration, which he occupied at intervals from 1804 to 1815, was the home of Baron Pasqualati. The house stands on a remnant of the old city fortifications at Mölkerbastei 8. The baron kept rooms in readiness for Beethoven's use when he could find no other accommodation. There the composer worked on *Fidelio*, as well as his Fourth, Fifth and Seventh symphonies, his Violin Concerto and several other works. This house, Austria's best-known Beethoven museum, displays numerous items associated with the composer, including a lock of his hair, and the door from the apartment where he died. (Houses at Probusgasse 6, Döblinger Hauptstrasse 92 and Mölkerbastei 8, all municipally owned, open Tuesday—Friday 10:00—4:00, Saturday 2:00—6:00, Sunday 9:00—1:00; 6370665; free.) Beethoven's apartment at Laimgrubengasse 22, where he resided in 1822 and 1823, may also be viewed. (Open May—September, Sunday 10:00—12:00; admission.)

The Beethoven-Grillparzer House at Grinzingerstrasse 64, Heiligenstadt, was the composer's summer lodging in 1808; he finished his Sixth Symphony there. Another lodger at this time was 17-year-old Franz Grillparzer, who would become Austria's greatest dramatic poet. This two-story house remains privately owned. Other privately owned Beethoven lodgings survive at Seilerstätte 21 (1815); Pfarrplatz 2, Heiligenstadt, a 17th-century double house where he stayed but wrote no music (1817); and the former "Flower Pot" inn at Ballgasse 6 (1819—20).

Beethoven completed his Ninth Symphony at Ungargasse 5 (corner of Beatrixgasse 8), his lodgings from autumn 1823 to spring 1824. This four-story building has shops on the street floor.

Beethoven's last residence, from 1825, was Schwarzspanierstrasse 15, originally a convent of Spanish Benedictines. There the composer died in his third-floor, six-room apartment during a thunderstorm, shaking his fist at the raging elements. A marker identifies the site of this house which was demolished in 1903.

Beethoven fled the city during most summers and frequently took lodgings in nearby villages. In **Baden**, where he spent about 12 summers, his 1816 lodgings stand at Breitnerstrasse 26, a large three-story house. In 1821 and 1823 he lived at Rathausgasse 10, while sketching out most of his Ninth Symphony and completing his *Missa Solemnis*. Two rooms in this two-story house have been made into a Beethoven museum and contain memorabilia of the composer. (Open May 1—October 31, Friday—Wednesday 9:00—11:00, 3:00—5:00; November 1—April 30, Tuesday, Saturday 3:00—5:00, Thursday 9:00—11:00; admission.)

At **Mödling**, another favorite haunt of the composer, Beethoven lived at Haupstrasse 79, a two-story structure with shop fronts, during 1818 and 1819. (Apply for admission at City Museum, Museumsplatz 2; 02236-4159.) At Achsenaugasse 6, an ivy-covered two-story house, he composed his *Missa Solemnis* (Mass in D) in 1820.

Contact the Beethoven Society at Pfarrplatz 3, **Vienna**, for further information.

Beethoven tomb: Central Cemetery, **Vienna**.

Exhibits: Austria has many biographical exhibits relating to the composer's life and works and most of them contain items of memorabilia and autographed manuscripts. In **Vienna**, manuscripts (including the "Eroica" copy on which the angry, disillusioned composer erased the name of Napoleon from the dedication) may be seen at the Museum of the Association of Friends of Music, Bösendorferstrasse 12; musical manuscripts of Bach, Bruckner, Haydn, Mozart and Schubert are also displayed there. City bus tours, sponsored by this organization, guide visitors to Vienna's main musical landmarks from May 1 to September 30. (Open September 1—June 30, Monday, Wednesday, Friday 9:00—1:00; 658681; admission.) Beethoven's Erard piano may be seen at the Music Instrument Collection in the Ephesus Museum (see the entry on Johannes Brahms, *Exhibits*, later in this chapter). The Alsergrund District Museum at Währingerstrasse 43 also displays mementos of Bruckner, Mozart, and Johann Strauss, as well as of Beethoven. (Open daily 10:00—12:00; 423575; admission.) In the Kunsthistorisches Museum may be seen Beethoven's clavier, especially made for him in 1803 (see the entry on Pieter Bruegel later in this chapter).

In **Baden**, the municipal Rollett Museum at Weikersdorfer Platz 1 displays memorabilia associated with the composer's local residence. (Inquire locally for hours of admission.)

The Municipal Museum at Museumsplatz 2 in **Mödling** also has a Beethoven display. (Inquire locally for hours of admission: 02236-4159.)

(See Chapter 4, WEST GERMANY.)

BRAHMS, JOHANNES (1833–1897). The German composer made his permanent home in **Vienna** from 1866 and occupied several residences. His last home, from 1872, was a third-floor apartment at Karlsgasse 4 (also called Brahmsgasse), where he entertained many of Europe's most notable composers and musicians in his three rooms. Here Brahms indulged his taste for somewhat hostile practical jokes by seating visitors in his trick rocking chair, which unceremoniously tipped them over, to the accompaniment of his loud guffaws. The composer died at this dwelling of liver cancer. Parts of the house were incorporated as a wing of the Technical University on Karlsplatz. An earlier occasional dwelling before Brahms moved permanently to Vienna (1863–65) was the Deutscheshaus (see the entry on Wolfgang Amadeus Mozart later in this chapter).

At **Mürzzuschlag**, a favorite country retreat, the composer wrote his Fourth Symphony in 1884. The two-story stone house he occupied remains privately owned.

Brahms tomb: Central Cemetery, **Vienna**.

Exhibits: The City Museum at Kammerhofgasse A in **Gmunden** displays a Brahms collection including letters, photos, portraits, and personal objects. (Inquire locally for admission information: 07612–3381.)

In **Bad Ischl**, the Haenel-Pancera-Familien-Museum at Concordiastrasse 3 shows Brahms scores. (Open May 1—September 30, daily 9:00—5:00; admission.)

The Music Instrument Collection in the Ephesus Museum, located in the Neue Hofburg, Heldenplatz, **Vienna**, contains an 1840 piano given to Brahms by the performer-composer couple, Clara Wieck and Robert Schumann. (Open Monday—Thursday 10:00—3:00, Sunday 9:00—1:00; admission.) A memorial room of Brahms memorabilia is displayed in the Haydn Museum at Haydngasse 19 (see the entry on Franz Joseph Haydn later in this chapter).

(See Chapter 4, WEST GERMANY.)

BRUCKNER, ANTON (1824–1896). An organist and fervently religious composer of church and symphonic music, Bruckner was born at **Ansfelden**, where his father was the village schoolmaster. Bruckner's birthplace and home until 1837 is now the Bruckner Memorial Museum; it displays a collection of memorabilia. (Inquire locally for admission information.)

Bruckner attended school (1837–40) at the 1715 Augustinian monastery in **St. Florian** and later lived there as abbey organist during the years 1845–56. The west wing of the abbey contains the Bruckner Memorial Room, part of the Augustinian monastery collections, and displays memorabilia of the composer's residence there. (Open by arrangement: Bruckner Gedenkräume, 4490 St. Florian, Stift.)

At **Steyr**, the Parish House of the Parish Church (Stadtpfarrkirche) bears a marker relating to Bruckner's residence there from 1886 to 1894. He composed his Sixth Symphony in this house, which remains privately owned.

In 1894 Emperor Franz Josef I gave the aged composer a gardener's house in the elegant Belvedere Gardens, Prinz Eugenstrasse 27, **Vienna**. The one-story stone lodge stands behind the Upper Belvedere palace. It was Bruckner's last home and the place where he died. It is not open to visitors. (Belvedere Gardens open Tuesday—Thursday, Saturday 10:00—4:00, Friday 10:00—1:00, Sunday 9:00—12:00; 724538; admission.)

Contact the International Bruckner Society at Bösendorferstrasse 12 for further information; 658681.

Bruckner tomb: Stiftskirche, St. Florian Abbey, **St. Florian**.

Exhibits: See Ludwig van Beethoven, *Exhibits*, earlier in this section.

A Bruckner Room in the Mesnerhaus at **Steyr** also displays memorabilia. (Inquire locally for admission information.)

BRUEGEL, PIETER (1525–1569).
Exhibit: The Bruegel Room of the Kunsthistorisches Museum, the National Museum of Fine Arts in **Vienna**, displays half of the noted Flemish painter's total works including *The Hunters' Return*. The museum is located at Burg Ring 5 (Maria-Theresien Platz 1). (Open Tuesday—Friday 10:00—3:00, Saturday—Sunday 9:00—1:00; 934541; admission.)

(See Chapter 4, BELGIUM.)

DÜRER, ALBRECHT (1471–1528).
Exhibits: In **Vienna**, the Dürer collection at the Kunsthistorisches Museum is the world's largest

display of the German Renaissance artist's works (see the entry on Pieter Bruegel above). Another outstanding Dürer collection of drawings (including the famed *Praying Hands*) is displayed at the Albertina Museum, Augustinerstrasse 1. (Open Monday, Tuesday, Thursday 10:00—4:00, Wednesday 10:00—6:00, Friday 10:00—2:00, Saturday—Sunday 10:00—1:00 (closed Sunday July—August; 524232; admission.)

(See Chapter 4, WEST GERMANY.)

FREUD, SIGMUND (1856–1939). The psychiatrist and founder of psychoanalysis, one of the most influential figures of the 20th century, was born in what is now the town of Príbor, Czechoslovakia, where his birthplace still stands. A resident of **Vienna** from 1860 until he fled Nazi bar-

THE BIRTHPLACE OF PSYCHOANALYSIS. Sigmund Freud's longtime office dwelling in **Vienna**, until the Nazi takeover forced his departure, was Berggasse 19. He occupied the mezzanine floor above the entrance and the floor above. From this building, shown in a recent photograph, came the discoveries that made modern psychiatry a hugely influential force in 20th-century thought, art, and literature.

barism in 1938, Freud opened his private medical practice in a large stone building at Rathausstrasse 7 in 1886. Later that year, having married Martha Bernays, he transferred home and office to the Kaiserliches Stiftungshaus, a new building erected on the ruins of the Ring-Theater which had burned down with great loss of life in 1881. Because of superstitions thus associated with the site, the Freuds were among the building's first tenants and remained there until 1891. This structure stands at Maria-Theresienstrasse 8.

From 1891 until his final departure from his homeland, Freud occupied a home and office suite on the second floor of Berggase 19, which today is the Freud Memorial Museum. In these rooms Freud began developing "free association" techniques, gradually building his theory of the unconscious mind and the nature of repression from his own clinical observations. There also he produced the works that became the foundation of modern psychiatry: *The Interpretation of Dreams* (1900), *Totem and Taboo* (1918), and *The Ego and the Id* (1927) among others. After the Austrian *Anschluss* of 1938, with the Gestapo watching the apartment and even searching it on occasion, Freud allowed photographer Edmund Engelman to take pictures of the furnished rooms so that in later years they could be restored as a museum. The Nazis hung a swastika above the entrance to the building but gave the aged, cancer-ridden doctor permission to remove his furniture and personal possessions. At war's end, Engelman found the

FREUD'S CONSULTING ROOM AT BERGGASSE 19. In this chamber, Freud researched and practiced "the talking cure" for 47 years, building his psychoanalytic theories of consciousness. The "ancestor" of all psychiatrists' couches is seen in this 1964 view of the room, restored with some of Freud's possessions.

apartment being used as a knitting factory. With the aid of his priceless photographs, the planned restoration was accomplished in 1971 and visitors may now see Freud's consulting rooms filled with personal bric-a-brac, furnishings, and memorabilia. Locked within these silent walls, one senses, reside memories of profound emotional events from the 47 years Freud spent practicing the "talking cure." For our own day, these chambers represent one of those pebble-in-the-pond areas that have radiated waves to every aspect of our thought, art and literature. (Open Monday—Friday 9:00—1:00, Saturday—Sunday 9:00—3:00; 311596; admission.)

Freud's summer house, which he occupied at intervals from 1934 to 1937, stands at Strassergasse 47 in nearby **Grinzing**.

(See Chapter 6, LONDON.)

GOERING, HERMANN WILHELM
(1893–1946). The German Nazi leader inherited Mauterndorf Castle overlooking the village of **Mauterndorf** from his Jewish godfather, Hermann von Epstein, in 1939. Epstein, a wealthy patron of the family and Goering's mother's lover for some 15 years, often hosted the Goerings during Hermann Goering's boyhood, and Goering also spent frequent periods there in later life. He staged a pompous entry during the Austrian *Anschluss* in 1938. In 1945, he spent his last days of relative freedom there, though under house arrest and a death sentence by the S.S., as World War II ended; and from there went into Allied captivity to await the Nuremberg Trials. Built on the ruins of a Roman citadel, the 16th-century castle affords a spectacular view. (Open July—September, Wednesday—Monday 10:00—12:00, 3:00—5:00; admission.)

Much earlier, in 1923 and 1924, Goering recovered at **Innsbruck** from a serious leg wound received during Hitler's Munich *putsch*. To avoid arrest in Germany for his participation in the failed coup, he sought refuge at the Tyrol Hotel in Bruneckerstrasse, where he resided in an ostentatious style supported by Nazi sympathizers. It was also during this period that Goering became a morphine addict, a dependency from which he underwent periodic strenuous withdrawals but was never finally withdrawn until his 1945 capture.

(See Chapter 4, EAST GERMANY, WEST GERMANY.)

GOETHE, JOHANN WOLFGANG VON
(1749–1832).
Exhibit: The **Vienna** Goethe Museum at Augustinerstrasse 1 displays portraits, drawings, manuscripts, and various editions of the German poet, scientist and philosopher's work. (Open Monday—Tuesday, Thursday—Friday 10:00—1:00; closed Sunday July—August; admission.)

(See SWITZERLAND in this chapter; also Chapter 2, FRANCE; also Chapter 4, EAST GERMANY, WEST GERMANY; also Chapter 8, ITALY.)

HAYDN, FRANZ JOSEPH (1732–1809). The "father of the symphony," who composed 104 symphonies (and established the classical form of orchestral movements), 80 string quartets, and numerous operas and oratorios, lived in Austria almost all his life. Haydn's thatch-roofed birthplace at **Rohrau**, probably built by his father in 1728, was his home until 1738. His composer brother, Michael Haydn, was also born there in 1737. The original house burned down in 1899; the present Haydn Museum on the site is, according to Haydn scholar H. C. Robbins Landon, "more a remembrance than actual relic," bearing only "some vague resemblance" to the birthplace. It displays memorabilia, scores, early editions of his works, and paintings of the composer. (Open March 15—November 15, Tuesday—Saturday 9:00—5:00; admission.)

In **Vienna** the composer occupied an unheated

HAYDN'S BIRTHPLACE. This earliest home of the "father of the symphony" was built by the composer's father in 1728. The present structure in the village of **Rohrau** is not the original dwelling shown in this 19th-century painting but a "vague resemblance" erected on the site.

attic room at Michaelerplatz 1220, (Kohlmarkt 11) from 1749 to 1755. This 1720 house, slightly altered, remains privately owned. Haydn was 17 when he moved there. With his adolescent voice breaking, he had been cast out of the boys' choir at St. Stephen's Cathedral, where he had lived in the Capellhaus (demolished 1803) since 1740. Fortunately for Haydn, his father had refused permission for him to be emasculated in order to preserve his clear soprano voice. Haydn wrote his first mass and first opera in his attic room. The Italian poet, Pietro Metastasio, occupied a lower apartment and died there in 1782.

From 1761 to 1790, as an employee of Prince Nicolaus Esterhazy, Haydn spent the winter months in Vienna at Esterhazy Palace, which survives on Wallnerstrasse.

The magnificent palace called Esterhaz, built by Prince Nicolaus at **Eisenstadt** in 1766, remained Haydn's home until the prince's death in 1790. As choir master there, Haydn directed all musical arrangements and personnel, conducted rehearsals and performances, and composed an enormous number of works—some 60 symphonies, 40 string quartets, masses, operas, sonatas, and incidental music. "My prince was always satisfied with my work," he reported. "Cut off from the rest of the world, I had nothing to worry about, and I was compelled to be original." In huge contrast to most of the Romantic composers who later expanded and built on his work, Haydn had an exceedingly amiable disposition. His job carried little prestige—a *kapellmeister* had no social status—and so the agreeable genius wore the blue palace uniform of a servant throughout his employment. For relaxation, Haydn hunted and fished in the forests and marshes surrounding the palace. Parts of the palace burned in 1768 and 1776 during his tenure. Today Esterhaz serves as the provincial capital of Burgenland. Its Haydn Room, where the composer conducted, was the great hall of state. (Open Tuesday—Sunday, 9:00—5:00; admission.) Haydn's own residence (1766–88) while serving at the palace is now the Haydn Museum at Joseph Haydngasse 21, displaying memorabilia, musical instruments, letters and manuscripts, as well as material relating to the later composer, Franz Liszt (see the entry on Liszt later in this section). (Open Easter Sunday—October 31, daily 9:00—12:00, 1:00—5:00; admission.)

After returning from two enormously successful trips to England in 1795, Haydn bought his last home, now the municipally owned Haydn Museum at Haydngasse 19 in **Vienna**. There, elderly and exhausted, he completed with difficulty his last two magnificent oratorios, *The Creation* (1798) and *The Seasons* (1801), after which he composed no more. Senile, but given many honors in his last years, he died at the house five days after one of Napoleon's invading soldiers came to pay his respects and sing an aria from *The Creation*: it was an episode that delighted Haydn despite his fierce Austrian patriotism. Today the two-story house displays numerous relics of the composer, including his death mask, a baton and clavichord he used, and autographed manuscripts and scores. (Open Tuesday—Friday 10:00—4:00, Saturday 2:00—6:00, Sunday 9:00—1:00; 561307; free.)

Contact the Haydn Society at Friesenplatz 7-2-15 for further information (6296222).

Haydn tomb: Bergkirche, **Eisenstadt**.

Exhibits: Haydn memorabilia may also be seen at the Museum of the Mariahilf District, Gumpendorferstrasse 4, in **Vienna**. (Open Sunday 9:30—12:00, other times by appointment; 5799965; admission.) The State Museum of Lower Austria at Herrengasse 9 also displays Haydn material. (Open Tuesday—Friday 9:00—5:00, Saturday 9:00—2:00, Sunday 9:00—12:00; 635711; admission.)

Also see Ludwig van Beethoven, *Exhibits*, earlier in this chapter.

(See Chapter 6, LONDON.)

HITLER, ADOLF (1889–1945). At the height of the Nazi demagogue's power, earnest efforts were made to identify and memorialize all of his early homes in Austria. This particular form of adulation brought little encouragement from the fuehrer, who liked to talk about his origins but preferred them not to be too closely inspected. Today most Austrians are eager to comply, while most of Hitler's family dwellings still stand, they are privately owned and unmarked. His birthplace was the Gasthof zum Pommer at **Braunau** on the Austro-German border. "This place of birth," wrote William L. Shirer, "was to prove significant, for early in his life, as a mere youth, Hitler became obsessed with the idea that there should be no border between these two German-speaking peoples." The two-story former inn survives at Salzburger Vorstadt 15. The son of an Austrian customs official whose original name was Schicklgruber and his second cousin, Klara Poelzl, Hitler lived there until age three. During the late 1930s, the structure became a revered banner-

BIRTHPLACE OF ADOLF HITLER. The Gasthof zum Pommer at **Braunau** was Hitler's home until age three. This 1945 view, taken just after World War II ended, eloquently summarizes the Nazi leader's contribution to civilization, with the figure of the solitary amputee passing by. Note the projecting flagpoles that once held swastika banners. Formerly a place of pilgrimage for devout Nazis, the building was being used as the town library at war's end and has since been converted to a school for retarded children.

draped shrine of the Nazi movement. Hitler himself made a highly emotional visit during his takeover of Austria on March 12, 1938. During World War II the six-room structure was the town library, then held a technical school. In 1976 it was converted into a school for retarded children.

Though Hitler described himself in *Mein Kampf* as a child of poverty and privation, his childhood circumstances were never less than adequate. At **Lambach**, where the family lived from 1897 to 1899, he attended classes at the 17th-century Benedictine monastery and dreamed of becoming a priest. The family first resided on the third floor of Lambach 58, which became the Gasthof Leingartner, opposite the monastery. Later, they moved to a farmhouse attached to a mill on eight acres where they lived on the second floor. Biographers have attached various significance to the fact that on his daily route to school Hitler passed a stone arch displaying prominent swastikas in the abbot's coat of arms.

From 1899 to 1905 the family lived in a small house with a half-acre garden adjacent to a cemetery in **Leonding**, a suburb of Linz, where his father had retired and where he died in 1903. Hitler attended high school while living there but dropped out in 1905 without graduating. Biographer Werner Maser reported that in 1938 an American wanted to buy this house to exhibit in the United States but was refused. Called "the Hitler House," it became the object of devoted pilgrimage and is now a funeral parlor. Plans during the 1970s to turn it into a museum were shelved after local protests. It is somehow appropriate that it remains a funeral parlor.

During summers from 1903 to 1907, the youth (who today would be diagnosed as having "a behavior problem") spent vacations in his mother's childhood home at **Spital 36**, the ancestral village of both his parents on route 41 near the Czech border. This house and its nextdoor neighbor were owned at this time by Hitler's uncle, Anton Schmidt. In 1942 Hitler's minister of armaments, Albert Speer, drove through the village and noticed a large plaque on this "handsome house," marking it as the fuehrer's boyhood home. When Speer mentioned it, Hitler flew into a rage and ordered the plaque removed immediately. "Apparently he had some motive for erasing this part of his youth," concluded Speer. The "motive" was probably Hitler's desire to guard a family secret—the illegitimate birth of his father.

In **Linz**, a third-floor apartment at Humboldtstrasse 31 became the home of Hitler, his mother, and his step-sister Paula (who survived him) from 1905 to 1907. Refusing to learn a trade or further his education, he spent an indolent period there that he often described as "the happiest days of my life." Linz, he determined in 1937, would become his retirement home and tomb, and as late as 1944 he spent hours poring over architectural plans for the new buildings he planned to erect there.

In 1907 the Hitlers moved to Blütengasse 9 in the Urfahr quarter of Linz, where they occupied a three-room apartment on the second floor of the stone building, also a pilgrimage site. Klara Poelzl Hitler, still a relatively young woman, died there of breast cancer in late 1907; and her son, determined to become an artist, fled to Vienna.

Vienna, where Hitler resided from 1907 to 1913—most of the time in utter destitution—was a bitter turning point. The Academy of Fine Arts promptly rejected him as a talentless student, and he eked out a solitary hand-to-mouth existence for a time as a painter of Vienna scenes and postcards (they were strangely lifeless attempts) which he peddled in the streets and taverns. It was during these formative years that he absorbed his first strong dose of anti-Semitism: the fabled city of waltzes and *gemütlichkeit* was a hotbed of racial fanaticism in the declining days of the Hapsburg monarchy. Apparently, Hitler's character and opinions never advanced beyond this stage. In 1907, with his only friend August Kubizek—who later wrote *The Young Hitler I Knew* (1955)—Hitler lived in a tiny second-floor room at Stumpergasse 29 (gone) in southwest Vienna. From 1910 to 1913 he bunked with over 500 other down-and-outers at Meldmannstrasse 27, a dormitory for destitute men. This was his last Austrian home.

(See Chapter 4, EAST GERMANY, WEST GERMANY, BELGIUM; also Chapter 5, ENGLAND.)

KAFKA, FRANZ (1883–1924). The Bohemian novelist spent his last weeks and died of tuberculosis at the Sanatorium Dr. Hoffman, Hauptstrasse 187 in **Kierling**. Until a few hours before his death, he worked on proofs of his short-story collection *A Hunger Artist* (1924).
(See Chapter 4, EAST GERMANY.)

KEPLER, JOHANNES (1571–1630). The sun, not the Earth, is the center of the solar system, and this German astronomer and mathematician was the first to prove it. His reputed home in **Graz**, where he taught from 1594 to 1600, stands marked at Stempfergasse 6. Though he certainly lived in this street (1597–1600), at least one biographer doubts that this particular house was Kepler's; if so, it has been considerably modified.

As district mathematician in **Linz** from 1612 to 1626, Kepler lodged with his family at several undetermined addresses. His final home in the city stood at Rathausgasse 5.

Exhibit: In **Graz**, the Kepler Room of the Joanneum Provincial Museum of Cultural History and Applied Art, Neutorgasse 45, displays material relating to the scientist. (Open daily 9:00—12:00; admission.)
(See Chapter 4, WEST GERMANY.)

LISZT, FRANZ (1811–1886). Though the virtuoso pianist and composer was Hungarian by birth, his birthplace and home until 1821 stands within the present political boundary of Austria at **Raiding**. Now the Franz Liszt Museum, located at Lisztstrasse 42, it displays photos, letters, and

FRANZ LISZT'S EARLIEST HOME. The 1811 birthplace of the composer survives in **Raiding**, a town located in Hungarian territory at the time. This 1937 view shows the courtyard entrance to the building on the left, where Liszt resided with his parents until 1821.

memorabilia. (Open March 1—October 31, daily; other times by appointment; 02619–2059/92; admission.)

In **Vienna**, the young Liszt lived with his family in a second-floor flat at Krügerstrasse 1014 from 1821 to 1823. Only the exterior walls remain of the Schottenhof at Freyung 6, Liszt's periodic city lodging from 1869 until his death.

Exhibit: The Haydn Museum at **Eisenstadt** displays material relating to Liszt, whose father was an official in the service of Prince Esterhazy (see the entry on Franz Josef Haydn earlier in this section.)

At **Bad Ischl**, the Haenel-Pancera-Familien-Museum displays Liszt scores (see the entry on Johannes Brahms, *Exhibits*, earlier in this section.)

(See SWITZERLAND in this chapter; also Chapter 3, PARIS; also Chapter 4, EAST GERMANY, WEST GERMANY; also Chapter 8, ITALY.)

MAHLER, GUSTAV (1860–1911). Regarded as a bridge between 19th and 20th-century music and the last great figure of German Romanticism—full of titanic struggles and megalomania—Mahler first achieved eminence as a conductor. Today he is known for such compositions as his lyrical *Das Lied von der Erde* ("Song of the Earth") (1908) and his heroic symphonies, which, in Promethean intensity, tried to pick up where Beethoven's Ninth left off. All of his dwellings still in existence remain privately owned.

A Bohemian native, born in the Czech village of Kalist, Mahler made his permanent home in Austria after 1897. By 1894, however, he had built a small summer house on the lakeshore of Attersee at **Steinbach**. He retired there for periods of solitude, working in a hut with windows on three sides, completing his Second Symphony there and composing his Third. He used the house until 1906.

Mahler's **Vienna** home from 1898 stands partially reconstructed at Auenbruggergasse and Rennweg. A four-story building dating from 1891, it suffered extensive damage during the latter days of World War II but the original facade and staircase survive. Mahler gave up the family apartment there in 1907 but held the lease on it until 1909. From 1907 until his last year his occasional Vienna lodging was the 1906 villa of his in-laws at Wollergasse 10.

From 1901 until 1907 he spent summers away from his conducting duties with the Vienna State Opera at **Maiernigg**, on the lakeshore of the Wörthersee. At the Villa Mahler, the large castle-like house he built whose stone walls front the waves, he composed his Fourth through Eighth symphonies. The scenery there is spectacular. "Don't bother looking," he reputedly told a visitor, the young conductor Bruno Walter, "I have already composed it" (referring to the first movement of his Sixth Symphony). After the death of his daughter Maria there in 1907, Mahler sold the house.

The composer lived in the South Tyrol region from 1908 to 1910 at **Altschluderbach**. There, in an 11-room house with wide verandahs and a workhouse in the woods, he wrote *Das Lied von der Erde* and his Ninth and Tenth symphonies.

For further information, contact the International Mahler Society, Bösendorferstrasse 12, **Vienna**: 7259084.

Mahler tomb: Grinzing Cemetery, **Vienna**.

(See Chapter 4, EAST GERMANY, WEST GERMANY.)

MARCUS AURELIUS (121–180). The Roman emperor, Stoic philosopher, author of the noble *Meditations*, and savage persecutor of Christians died in **Vienna**. At the time it was a small Roman outpost called Vindobona, and the emperor was commanding troops against invading Marcomanni tribes from Bohemia. The traditional spot of his death is the Hoher Markt, where ruins of the Roman settlement exist beneath the busy square. Excavations may be seen at Hoher Markt 3. (Open Tuesday—Sunday 9:00—1:00; free.)

(See Chapter 8, ITALY.)

MARIE ANTOINETTE (1755–1793). The 15th child of Holy Roman Empress Maria Theresa and Emperor Francis I, Marie Antoinette became a highly influential queen of France when her husband ascended the throne as Louis XVI in 1774. As a German-speaking daughter of Hapsburg royalty, she early acquired a slanted view of the world which her sheltered life and defective education did nothing to correct. She spent the years until her 1770 marriage in the opulent splendor of two surviving palaces. In **Vienna**, her winter home was the imperial residence called the Hofburg. A vast melange of structural styles and shapes, it includes parks and courtyards and is located at the large open square of the Heldenplatz. The massive Alte Hofburg, directly east of the square, contained the main Hapsburg residences from 1276 to 1918. It grew outward from the 13th-century Schweizerhof, which now houses the Schatzkammer (imperial treasury), and displays the Hapsburg crown jewels and crown of the Holy Roman Empire, a gold table service, coronation garments, and the cradle of Napoleon II (see below). (Open Monday—Saturday 8:30—4:30, Sunday 8:30—1:00; 575554; admission.) The apartments where Marie Antoinette's mother, Maria Theresa, died in 1780 were housed in the Reichkanzleitrakt in the northeastern sector of the Hofburg complex. Now the official residence of Austria's president, this building may be viewed from the outside. It was built in 1730. The well-preserved apartments of the last important Hapsburg ruler, Emperor Franz Josef I (died 1916), are open to the public. Entrance to the Alte Hofburg may be gained at Michaelerplatz.

The summer home of the young princess was Schönbrunn Palace in Vienna's southwestern suburbs at Schönbrunner Schlossstrasse. Completed in 1750, it was Vienna's answer to Versailles and one of Europe's finest baroque palaces. Little changed since Empress Maria Theresa decorated it, 40 of its 1,441 splendidly furnished rococo rooms are open to public view, including the apartments where Napoleon I lodged briefly in 1805 and 1809. His son, the so-called Napoleon II who never reigned, lived under virtual house arrest at Schönbrunn throughout much of his short life; the Napoleon Room, where he died at age 21 in 1832, may be seen. There is also a collection of historical coaches (1562–1919) on view. Six-year-old Wolfgang Amadeus Mozart stunned the empress and her court when he gave a piano recital at Schönbrunn. He solemnly told Princess Marie Antoinette, only slightly older than himself, "when I grow up I shall marry you." Both of them were to marry less than satisfactorily, in fact, and both were to die in tragic circumstances (see the entry on Mozart later in this section). Today the Palace Theater, where Marie Antoinette acted in skits and Mozart performed, presents light opera performances in July and August. In June 1961, the castle was the setting for U.S. President John F. Kennedy's and Soviet Premier Nikita Khruschev's summit conference. (Open daily, 9:00—12:00, 1:00—5:00; 833646; free; admission for public tours to state rooms and coach collection; park open daily 6:00 a.m. to dusk.)

At **Innsbruck**, another favorite Hapsburg retreat was the Hofburg which was altered by Maria Theresa in 1770. Elaborate royal furnishings include numerous tapestries, portraits, and the type of baroque ornamentation characteristic of Hapsburg Austria. (Open May 16—October 15, daily 9:00—12:00, 2:00—5:00; October 16—May 15, Monday—Saturday 10:00—12:00, 2:00—4:00; admission.)

(See Chapter 2, FRANCE; also Chapter 3, PARIS.)

MENDEL, JOHANN GREGOR (1822–1884). The famous biologist, an Augustinian monk whose cross-hybrid experiments with peas ushered in the modern science of genetics, lived in what is now Brno, Czechoslovakia, for most of his quiet life. From 1851 to 1853, however, he lodged as a philosophy student at Invalidenstrasse 10 in

GETREIDEGASSE 9, A WORLD MUSICAL LANDMARK. Wolfgang Amadeus Mozart was born in this **Salzburg** house in 1756 and lived there with his family until 1773. The floor above the sign in this photograph held the Mozart family apartment, and today displays memorabilia of the composer.

Vienna while attending the University of Vienna. This building, which was and still is owned by the Order of St. Elizabeth, has changed little though the street level has since been raised.

MOZART, WOLFGANG AMADEUS

(1756–1791). The great musical genius was a native of Salzburg, where dour Leopold Mozart early recognized his fun-loving son's prodigious gifts and devoted the rest of his life to cultivating, state-managing, and generally trying to harness a spirit as earthy as a peasant's and as irrepressible as a river.

Salzburg, a city Mozart hated in later life and which studiously ignored him while he lived, thrives on his memory and music today. Mozart's birthplace, a 15th-century five-story building surrounding a small central court at Getreidegasse 9, is now a museum. Memorabilia, portraits, Mozart's first clavichord, and the 1780-built grand piano he used for composition and performances during his last decade are on display. Also on view are his first half-sized violin, letters, musical autographs, locks of hair, and miniature models of set-

A view of Mozart's birthplace as it looks today.

tings for his operas. The third-floor museum was Mozart's family home until 1773. (Open May 15—June 30, September, daily 9:00—7:00; July 1—August 31, daily 8:00—8:00; October 1—May 14, daily 9:00—6:00; admission.)

From 1773 to 1787 the Salzburg family home was the 17th-century Tanzmeisterhaus at Makartplatz 8, though Mozart himself had settled in Vienna by 1781. Leopold Mozart rented eight rooms on the upper floor. This building was about two-thirds destroyed during an air raid on October 16, 1944; only Mozart's "music room" survived. The house, now restored to its original appearance, displays 18th-century instruments and autographed manuscripts. Leopold Mozart died there, alone and embittered, in 1787. (Open June 30—September 1, concerts July—August, Monday—Saturday 5:00, 7:30 p.m.; 748973; admission.)

The Zauberflötenhäuschen, a tiny structure in which the composer reputedly wrote *The Magic Flute* (1791), stands in the gardens of the Mozarteum at Schwarzstrasse 26. This wooden hut, one

ENTRANCE TO MOZART'S BIRTHPLACE. This recent close-up view of Getreidegasse 9 shows the original 15th-century doorway through which the young prodigy must have passed many times. By 1773, when he last walked out this door, he had already performed in royal courts across Europe.

of Mozart's last lodgings, was part of the Starhemberg Freihaus estate in Vienna when impresario Emanuel Schikaneder installed Mozart there to complete the opera. "There the masterpiece took shape," wrote Richard Anthony Leonard, "Mozart pausing only for occasional drinking bouts with Schikaneder and his troupe." There too, in July 1791, Mozart received the anonymous stranger who commissioned him to write what proved to be his final unfinished work: the *Requiem* (1791). Weak from mental and physical exhaustion, the vision of the stranger who would not tell his name began to obsess Mozart with the thought that the Devil had commissioned him to write his own death music. The hut, twice moved since 1877, was restored in 1950. (Open May—October, daily 9:00—12:00, 3:00—6:00; 74492; admission.) All of Mozart's Salzburg homes are owned by the International Mozart Foundation.

From 1781 until his death, Mozart occupied some 12 addresses in **Vienna** (see Name Index and Gazetteer). His first lodging in the city was the Deutscheshaus, a 1667-built structure that housed the Knights of the Teutonic Order. Mozart's six-week stay there was marked by conflict with his employer, the Archbishop Hieronymus von Colloredo, who called the young composer a "scoundrel, knave, and scurvy fellow" and had him thrown bodily out of his rooms. Today the hall and chapel of the Teutonic Knights at Singerstrasse 7 displays relics and regalia of the Holy Roman Empire. Johannes Brahms also once occupied an apartment there (see the entry on Brahms earlier in this section). (Open Tuesday, Thursday, Saturday, Sunday 10:00—12:00; 5211656; admission.)

Mozart's first married home with Constanze Weber (1782) consisted of second-floor rooms in "the Red Sabre," a house which stood at Wipplingerstrasse 19. At Schulerstrasse 8 (also numbered Domgasse 5), the couple lived from 1784 to 1787. This narrow stucco building, called "the Figarohaus" because Mozart composed his comic opera *The Marriage of Figaro* (1786) there and began *Don Giovanni* (1787), is a Mozart museum today; it displays manuscripts, portraits, and mementos of his visitors Franz Josef Haydn and Ludwig van Beethoven (see the entries on Beethoven and Haydn earlier in this section). The second-story apartment rented by Mozart projects over the street. (Open Tuesday—Friday 9:00—4:00, Saturday 2:00—6:00, Sunday 9:00—1:00; 5240722; free.)

Always exceedingly impractical, even with the little money Mozart was able to earn from his vast output of music, the couple led a bare poverty existence in a succession of ever cheaper lodgings. Constanze, incessantly pregnant (only two of their six children survived to adulthood), was ill much of the time. Mozart composed his opera *Cosi fan tutte* (1790) and his last three symphonies at Währingerstrasse 16, his home in 1788 and 1789. The house has since been destroyed.

If ever a joyous, brilliant man was undone by unrelenting circumstances, that man was Mozart. At the family's last address, a visitor found them dancing vigorously for warmth in the almost bare rooms as they had no wood for fuel. Totally exhausted, Mozart worked feverishly but vainly to complete his *Requiem* before his final collapse and death at age 35. His final address, from 1790, was Rauhensteingasse 8. On the site of the original building, which was demolished in 1844, is the Mozarthof, a privately owned structure.

In **Baden**, where Constanze Mozart went in 1791 to bear their last son, Mozart composed one of his final works—the motet *Ave Verum Corpus*. The couple lived at Renngasse 4, a three-story private structure now called the Mozart Hof.

Mozart tomb (unmarked): St. Mark's Cemetery, **Vienna**.

Exhibits: The best memorial to any composer is, of course, the music. In **Salzburg**, Mozart Memorial Week is the last week in January (call 73155 for information.) Mozart is also the focus of the world-renowned Salzburg Summer Festival (July 25—August 30), which attracts international orchestras and soloists. One must plan far in advance in order to attend these musical events, as the small city has few spare beds during these periods (contact any Austrian National Tourist Office for reservations). The Mozarteum at Schwarzstrasse 26, operated by the International Mozart Foundation, contains a music school, two concert halls, and the Mozart Archive which displays numerous autographs, scores and letters. Chamber music is presented on Saturdays in the gardens. (Open Monday—Friday 10:00—12:00, 3:00—5:00; closed September; 73155; admission.)

In **Vienna**, the Alsergrund District Museum, located not far from a Mozart address of 1788–89 (Währingerstrasse 16), and the Museum of the Association of Friends of Music display Mozart items and manuscripts (for both addresses, see the

ingstrasse 18 in 1869 and there composed his operetta *Die Fledermaus* (1874). This house no longer stands.

With income from *Die Fledermaus* and other works, Strauss built a palatial Venetian-style mansion during the 1870s. It was his last home. The street where he lived, known as Igelgasse, has been renamed Johann-Straussgasse, but the original house at number 4 was destroyed during the latter days of World War II. Nazi and Soviet occupiers of Vienna stripped the city of most of its Strauss memorabilia. Beyond the museum, mentioned previously, and its contents, little of Strauss remains—except, of course, the ubiquitous music in the city that he made virtually synonymous with the waltz.

For further information, contact the Johann Strauss Society, Rathaus, Rathausplatz; 42800.

Strauss tomb: Central Cemetery, **Vienna**.

Exhibit: In **Vienna**, the Alsergrund District Museum displays some Strauss mementos. (See the entry on Ludwig van Beethoven, *Exhibits*, earlier in this section.)

STRAUSS, RICHARD (1864–1949). This German composer, no relation to Johann Strauss, developed the tone poem to its highest artistic peak. He lived in **Vienna** as director of the Vienna State Opera (1919–24), and during these years resided at Mozartplatz 4. As a reward for his services, the Austrian government, which made Strauss an honorary citizen in 1945, granted him a parcel of land in the botanical gardens near the Upper Belvedere Palace (see the entry on Anton Bruckner earlier in this section). Strauss built a costly home on the property, importing a wooden ceiling from Italy and antique furnishings. From 1924 until about 1940, he resided there at frequent intervals. The house remains at Jacquingasse 10.

Exhibit: At **Bad Ischl**, the Haenel-Pancera-Familien Museum displays Strauss scores (see the entry on Johannes Brahms, *Exhibits*, earlier in this section).

For further information, contact the International Richard Strauss Society, Vienna State Opera, Opernring 2, **Vienna**; 527636.

(See Chapter 4, EAST GERMANY, WEST GERMANY.)

VIVALDI, ANTONIO (1678–1741). A resident of **Vienna** during his last, poverty-stricken years, the Italian composer died in lodgings that stood until 1858 in the block bounded by Krügerstrasse, Walfischgasse and Kärntnerstrasse.

(See Chapter 8, ITALY.)

WAGNER, RICHARD (1813–1883). The German composer, whose operas were as monumental as his sybaritic ego and appalling bigotry, resided briefly in **Vienna** at various times. Probably his lengthiest stay was in a yellow country house at suburban Penzing in 1863 and 1864; the period marked one of the lowest points in Wagner's life, however, despite this lavish apartment at Hadikgasse 72. He was laboring on the text of *Die Meistersinger* (1868), and creditors were hounding him. Finally he fled from Austria to escape debtors' prison.

For further information, contact the Austrian Richard Wagner Society at Schwindgasse 19/14; 657293.

(See SWITZERLAND in this chapter; also Chapter 3, PARIS; also Chapter 4, EAST GERMANY, WEST GERMANY; also Chapter 6, LONDON; also Chapter 8, ITALY.)

SWITZERLAND

As the "roof tree" of Europe, Switzerland rises above the continent in more ways than one. This landlocked nation of about seven million has been peaceful, prosperous, and self-contained for so long that only determined readers of history can view its traumatic periods. Today, as for centuries (in contrast to most European nations), the Swiss are not fond of engaging in periodic war. After almost 700 years of fiercely guarded democracy and no involvement in a foreign war since 1515, the canny Swiss know they can depend on the rest of the world to provide them with an international role. The existence of neutral Switzerlands and Swedens are vital, they know, as international observation decks, clearinghouses and breathing spaces for peoples who manifestly don't share Swiss feelings on the topic.

The Swiss deal in heavy ironies as well as industries. They observe with some amusement that while no nation has reason to spy on Switzerland itself, the country probably contains more foreign spies per capita than any other. It is a veritable watering hole for professional peekers from all the Western and Eastern powers, an international refuge for intrigue. It is also, of course, a supranational headquarters for financial and humanitarian activities. Switzerland accepts the heavy responsibilities of a neutral nation in a world of determined team players by welcoming both the outcast refugee and the purposeful agent with equal aplomb, as long as each abides by the house rules. In Switzerland behavioral decency reigns, whatever the state of the heart.

It is impractical for the Swiss themselves to become team players in world politics. Since the nation itself is quadrilingual (with French, German and Italian areas plus the Grisons, where Romansch is spoken); since 20 percent of the population is foreign-born; and since so many equally disparate elements mix so well in Switzerland, a typical Swiss will politely listen to team logic, and just as politely reject it. Nevertheless he or she will be thankful that others buy into such logic so fervently, since it is to a large extent the team philosophy that sustains Bern banks and Geneva commerce. The Swiss are a frankly materialistic people, though probably less so than the Germans. For the Swiss, it has been said, the mere gaining of money—anybody's money—far outmotivates the idea of spending it. It is materialism in its most abstract form. Socially, you cannot go much higher in Switzerland than to become a banker; it gives you a "secret clearance" passport to the world financial community, with prerogatives analogous at least to those of an American Pentagon janitor—and even more prestigious.

A Celtic tribe, the Helvetii, occupied today's Switzerland before 500 B.C. Their lineal descendants, known as the "aristocracy of Switzerland," are brawny physical specimens who still herd cattle in the hills above Lake Lucerne.

Julius Caesar organized the Roman province of Helvetia in 58 B.C., and Rome ruled the country for about 500 years, building towns and roads and improving agriculture. On the heels of Roman withdrawal, two Germanic tribes—the Burgundians from the west and the Alemanni from the north—invaded and established the Sarine River border that still linguistically divides Switzerland's French- and German-speaking peoples.

Charlemagne brought the country into the Holy Roman Empire, where it existed as a loose collection of feudal states until 1291. In that year modern Switzerland originated when three small states (cantons)—Uri, Schwyz and Unterwalden—founded the Swiss Confederation. During the following centuries, the Swiss named themselves after the founding canton of Schwyz and enlarged

their union by both conquest and diplomacy, becoming famed as tough, belligerent fighters. As mercenary troops they achieved a European reputation as "tamers of kings." (The Swiss Guards at the Vatican represent a vestige of this era.) Switzerland's subsequent policy of neutrality was laid in the 15th century by a brilliant mediator, St. Nicholas of Flue, the country's patron saint. The union remained stable in size from 1513 until 1803, when Napoleon added six new cantons to the original 13. Switzerland achieved its present borders in 1815, and there are now 25 cantons.

Today's Swiss government, based mainly on a large civil service, works like a well-oiled machine. Civil power moves from the bottom up, not from the top down. A new president assumes office each year. Most Swiss, in any given year, probably cannot tell you his name; communal and cantonal policies remain immeasurably more important to them than national politics. Indeed universal suffrage dates only from 1972, when Swiss women (somewhat unwillingly) were made eligible to vote.

Swiss unity consists not in mutual agreement on methods, goals, philosophy, religion or social values, but in mutual agreement to disagree on all these things. Swiss actor Walter Morath even described his homeland as "the land of brotherly hate." "We love foreigners because we detest ourselves so much," he said. As another observer, Herbert Kubly, pointed out, "By tacitly agreeing to disagree, the Swiss turn religious, cultural and linguistic differences, which cause riots and insurrections in a country like Belgium, into stabilizing forces in their union."

Geneva, not a part of the Swiss nation until 1815, became a notable center of the Reformation when French exile John Calvin established his religious dictatorship there. "His method," wrote Herbert Kubly, "was to renovate human character by force," and he ruled Geneva more ironhandedly than any pope ever dared rule Rome. Calvin's theology gave the stamp of approval to frank materialism; riches, he taught, signified divine reward. Encouraging business enterprise and acumen became distinctively Swiss pursuits. From Geneva's harsh theocracy, the reformed-church doctrine spread to the Netherlands, Scotland and North America along with the philosophical basis for the modern industrial world: capitalism, as much a religious philosophy as an economic one.

If the guilt-implanted work ethic and its striving for material wealth brought prosperity to Switzerland and the Western world, however, the spiritual price was—and continues to be—high. Switzerland's rates of mental illness and suicide rank among the world's highest. While violence is comparatively rare, sex crimes (often indicative of a repressive, guilt-obsessed society) are disproportionately numerous. The Swiss are quick to describe themselves as an unhappy people. One Zurich observer blames "the disparity between human instinct and human convention." No other people so relentlessly concerns itself with providing for the future; some 12 percent of the national income goes into insurance of one sort or another.

Yet their philanthropy and charity have also given the Swiss a consistent, well-deserved reputation as world humanitarians, a role symbolized best, perhaps, by the presence of the International Red Cross, whose headquarters are in Geneva. Nobody can say that the Swiss, as neutral peacemakers, haven't tried. From the quickly subverted League of Nations to numerous United Nations agencies and disarmament conferences, Switzerland has hosted meetings and encouraged communication between generations of world leaders, refusing to become discouraged at their massive records of failure. The "Geneva Convention" even attempted to make nations restrain themselves to make war, if they must, by certain "humane" rules. These activities continue unabated, though the Swiss themselves are Calvinistically quick to point out that international tensions have seldom drawn anything but benefit to Switzerland's own solid economy. Few peoples are more pragmatic (or driven) in both generosity and self-service; few are more conservative in thinking or more liberal in social action; and few agonize over their contrasts, attributes and deficiencies more than the Swiss themselves.

Four areas of topography comprise the matchless Swiss landscape: lakes and Alps (about 60 percent), forests, high-altitude pasture land, and cultivated acreage. Though Switzerland is one of the world's most highly industrialized countries, cattle and dairy production are also dominant activities. Tourism, of course, ranks as a major source of income though, as Swiss playwright Friedrich Dürrenmatt observes, "In our modern industrial country, the simpering milkmaid and the alphorn are about as valid national images as the gangster and gun-toting cowboy are in America." But the alpine scenery of southern Switzerland, old sea bottoms broken and upthrust into some of the most rugged mountains on earth, is indeed a valid and imposing national image. Bern, the capital, ranks fourth in size after Zurich, Basel and Geneva. In religion, for all of its rigorous this-worldly ethic, the country is about equally divided between the Protestant and Roman Catholic faiths.

The nature of man was a topic that engaged two native Swiss thinkers as different as Rousseau and Jung, both to the discomfort of their peers. Switzerland is, of course, best known as an oasis for the politically badgered and war-weary, a shelter in the time of storm for notable residents whose opinions or presence were too threatening for their home countries to tolerate. Not only Calvin found refuge in Geneva but also for a time Voltaire, a man as unlike the pious religionists as one can imagine. Other refugees included people as diverse in aim and accomplishment as Erasmus, Richard Wagner, Charlie Chaplin and Thomas Mann. Some found in Switzerland a home that was simply more desirable than their own— Hermann Hesse, for instance, Rilke, Brecht, even Stravinsky for a time. Likewise Nietzsche, Einstein and James Joyce accomplished major works in Switzerland, far from their places of origin.

Most of these residents, whether native or adopted, are represented by surviving houses and, frequently, by museums commemorating their lives in this welcoming, careful country.

BRECHT, BERTOLT (1898–1956). The German playwright returned to Europe from America after World War II and resided in Switzerland from 1947 to 1949. In **Zurich** his first home (1947) was Gartenstrasse 38. In 1949 he occupied a room at Hottingerstrasse 25, a place he called the "Au bien être" ("well-being") house.

Most of his Swiss period was spent at **Feldmeilen**, where he inhabited the loft of the farmhouse at Buenishoferstrasse 14. Brecht wrote no important works in these places.

(See Chapter 4, EAST GERMANY, WEST GERMANY, DENMARK, FINLAND, SWEDEN.)

BYRON, GEORGE GORDON, LORD (1788–1824). In June 1816 the English poet, accompanied by his new friend Percy Bysshe Shelley, went to view the Château of Chillon on an islet in Lake Geneva (see the entry on Shelley later in this section). Two days later the pair lodged in **Ouchy** at the Hôtel de l'Ancre where they had first registered some weeks before; with his characteristic flair for self-dramatization, the 28-year-old Byron had entered himself in the hotel register as 100 years old. There Byron, inspired after their lake voyage, wrote his poem *The Prisoner of Chillon* (1816). The building is marked.

The Villa Diodati, where Byron resided from June to October of 1816, stands in **Cologny**. There, residing next door to Shelley and his mistress, Mary Godwin, Byron carried on an unenthusiastic affair with Godwin's half-sister, Claire Clairmont, and she became pregnant. There he also completed the third canto of *Childe Harold's Pilgrimage* and wrote his "Sonnet to Lake Leman." The house majordomo complained that after the poet's departure it took him two days to burn all the papers that Byron left behind. The three-story house on the Lake Geneva shore is privately owned and may be visited only by prearrangement and personal recommendation.

(See Chapter 4, BELGIUM; also Chapter 5, ENGLAND; also Chapter 6, LONDON; also Chapter 7, SCOTLAND; also Chapter 8, GREECE, ITALY.)

CALVIN, JOHN (1509–1564). The French theologian and founder of Calvinism resided permanently in **Geneva** from 1541 and made it "the Rome of the Protestants," the principal center of Reformation activity for the French-speaking world. Calvin became virtual dictator of the city, decreed strict laws and burned heretic Miguel Serveto at the stake. His last home from 1543 was demolished in 1706 but rebuilt later in the 18th century. It stands at 11 Rue Calvin.

Calvin tomb (reputed): Plaispalais Cemetery, **Geneva**.

Exhibits: The chair in which Calvin sat while preaching may be seen in the 13th-century St. Peter's Cathedral, Rue St-Pierre, **Geneva**, where he addressed Sunday audiences from 1536, the year it became a Protestant church. (Open daily 9:00—12:00; also June—September, 1:30—7:00, October—May 2:00—5:00; donation.)

The John Calvin Auditorium (also known as the John Knox Chapel, Notre Dame, and the National Protestant Church of Geneva) is the 14th-century church at 6 Place Cornavin where Calvin and others conducted weekly meetings from 1557. He was the pastor there from 1562. Regular services

are still conducted by several different denominations. Alcoves in the 1959-restored hall display exhibits and memorabilia relating to Calvin and the Reformation. (Open March—October, daily 2:00—5:00; November—February, daily 2:00—4:00; donation.)

The Museum of the History of the Reformation at the Public and University Library, Promenade des Bastions, also displays exhibits illustrating this important period in Geneva history. (Open Monday—Friday 9:00—12:00, 2:00—5:00, Saturday 9:00—12:00; free.)

(See Chapter 2, FRANCE; also Chapter 3, PARIS.)

CHAPLIN, SIR CHARLES SPENCER "CHARLIE" (1889–1977). The English film comic, one of the most creatively gifted performers of any age, was virtually expelled from the United States, his adopted home, because of his liberal politics and unconventional sex life. Switzerland, as usual, was more than glad to welcome a genius and Chaplin made his permanent home there from 1952. He bought the 20-room Manoir de Bain on a 37-acre estate with broad lawns and orchard at the Lake Geneva village of **Corsier**. He and his wife, Oona O'Neill, raised their large family on the estate while Chaplin completed his final film work and enjoyed a contented and prosperous old age.

Chaplin tomb: Village cemetery, **Corsier**.

(See Chapter 4, WEST GERMANY; also Chapter 6, LONDON.)

CONRAD, JOSEPH (1857–1924). In **Geneva**, while undergoing a treatment of medicinal baths in 1894, the Polish-English writer worked on his novel *Almayer's Folly* (1895). He lived in a pension at 25 Rue de la Roseraie, a house that bears a tablet commemorating his presence despite his loud remarks about the "marvelous banality" of Geneva.

(See Chapter 5, ENGLAND; also Chapter 6, LONDON.)

COWARD, SIR NOËL PIERCE (1899–1973). One of the most versatile men of the English theater, Coward bought his summer home Les Avants, an 1899 chalet high above Montreux and Lake Geneva, in 1959 and returned there each year through 1972. The chalet with its four gardens on about five acres stands in the resort village of **Les Avants**.

(See Chapter 5, ENGLAND; also Chapter 6, LONDON.)

DOSTOEVSKI, FEODOR MIKHAILOVICH (1821–1881). The great Russian novelist lived, he said, "as on an uninhabited island" in **Geneva** during 1867 and 1868. He resided in a modest furnished apartment behind the Hôtel des Bergues, corner of the Rue Berthelier and the Rue Guillaume Tell. The hotel's address is 33 Quai des Bergues.

(See Chapter 4, EAST GERMANY, WEST GERMANY; also Chapter 8, ITALY.)

DOYLE, SIR ARTHUR CONAN (1859–1930).

Exhibits: At the 16th-century Château of **Lucens** near Moudon, the Conan Doyle Foundation displays a reconstruction of the London drawing room of Doyle's fictional hero, detective Sherlock Holmes. Personal possessions of Doyle are also exhibited. (Open April 1—October 30, Tuesday—Sunday 9:00—6:00; November 1—December 15, March, Tuesday—Sunday 10:00—5:00; admission.)

The spectacular Reichenbach Falls, where Doyle killed off Holmes in 1893 (but ultimately resurrected him) may be seen by funicular about one kilometer southeast of **Meiringen**.

(See Chapter 5, ENGLAND; also Chapter 6, LONDON; also Chapter 7, SCOTLAND.)

EINSTEIN, ALBERT (1879–1955). At **Bern**, while working as a minor bureaucrat in the Swiss patent office, Einstein developed the four epochal ideas that would revolutionize the entire field of physics and forever change science's view of the universe: the special theory of relativity, the equation relating mass and energy, the theory of Brownian movement, and the photon theory of light. From 1903 to 1905, part of the period spanning this activity, he lived at Kramgasse 49. Today his residence is the Einstein House Museum and displays memorabilia, photographs and documents relating to the German physicist. (Inquire locally for admission information.)

(See Chapter 4, EAST GERMANY.)

ELIOT, GEORGE. See MARY ANN EVANS.

ERASMUS, DESIDERIUS (1466?–1536). **Basel**, a hotbed of Protestant reform, was not well disposed toward Catholic peacemakers. Because the great Dutch scholar, humanist and monk was not a religious extremist, his Christian enemies from both camps made life extremely unpleasant for him in this city which he made his home from 1521 to 1529 and during his last year. His lodging during most of this period, and the place where he died in a first-floor room, was a small house called "Zur Luft." It survives at Baumleingasse 18 and is now known as the Erasmus House. His rooms have been preserved essentially as they were, though a shop now occupies the ground floor. (Inquire locally for admission information.)

THE ERASMUS HOUSE. In **Basel** the great Dutch humanist made his last home at Baumleingasse 18. One of his rooms above the ground-floor shop is marked by the window on the right.

Erasmus tomb: Cathedral, **Basel**.

Exhibit: The Historical Museum in the Barfusserplatz at **Basel** displays Erasmus memorabilia, including his sword and various other mementos. (Open Tuesday—Sunday 10:00—12:00, 2:00—5:00; admission. Free Saturday—Sunday, Wednesday afternoon.)

(See Chapter 3, PARIS; also Chapter 4, WEST GERMANY, BELGIUM, THE NETHERLANDS; also Chapter 5, ENGLAND.)

EVANS, MARY ANN ("GEORGE ELIOT") (1819–1880). Grief-stricken, the English novelist came to **Geneva** in 1849 after her beloved father's death and stayed for a year in the home of M. and Mme. D'Albert Durade, where she soon felt herself "living in a soft nest placed high up in an old tree." This house stands at 18 Rue de la Pélisserie.

(See Chapter 5, ENGLAND; also Chapter 6, LONDON; also Chapter 8, ITALY.)

GOETHE, JOHANN WOLFGANG VON (1749–1832).

Exhibit: Any student or devotee of the German philosopher—Europe's "last Renaissance man"—will want to visit the Goetheanum just north of **Dornach**. This international headquarters of the Universal Anthroposophical Society, a sect that philosopher Rudolf Steiner founded and based on Goethe's scientific theories, is an immense concrete structure. Performances of Goethe's plays, among other activities, are presented. (Open daily, 9:00—12:00, 2:30—6:00; admission.)

(See AUSTRIA in this chapter; also Chapter 3, FRANCE; also Chapter 4, EAST GERMANY, WEST GERMANY; also Chapter 8, ITALY.)

HESSE, HERMANN (1877–1962). The German novelist and poet spent much of his life in Switzerland and resided there permanently after 1912. His earlier lodgings in **Basel**, where he worked in antiquarian bookshops, included unidentified rooms in the Mullerweg (1881–86).

In **Bern** he occupied the 17th-century Wittighofen Palace, actually a country house, from 1912 to 1919 and there wrote *Demian* (1919).

From 1919 to 1931 Hesse's home was the Casa Camuzzi at **Montagnola**, about five kilometers west of Lugano on the Collina d'Oro peninsula ridge. In his four-room, second-story apartment in this 19th-century baroque structure he wrote his novels *Siddhartha* (1922) and *Steppenwolf* (1927). "Hesse's twelve years in the Casa Camuzzi," wrote biographer Joseph Mileck, "were no doubt the most trying, but also the happiest, and certainly the most memorable years of his life." Hesse himself wrote that "in this house I enjoyed and suffered from the most intense loneliness, gained comfort from writing and painting much, and became more fondly familiar with the place than with any other since childhood."

Having married for the third time in 1931, Hesse designed and built his final permanent home on a nearby wooded slope overlooking Lake Lugano. In this two-story Casa Bodmer, or Casa Hesse, the gift of his patron-friend Hans C. Bodmer, the novelist did his final writing, received notification of his 1946 Nobel Prize, gardened on the slopes, and finally died of leukemia.

Hesse's frequent residence during Novembers from 1923 to 1951 was the Hotel Verenahof-Ochsen at the health resort of **Baden**, where he went for relief of chronic sciatica, rheumatism and nervous breakdowns. Portions of his novels *Narcissus and Goldmund* (1930) and *The Glass Bead Game* (1943) were written there. Still a popular spa hotel, the building stands on the left bank of the Limmat River.

Hesse tomb: St. Abbondio Cemetery, **Gentileno**.

(See Chapter 4, WEST GERMANY.)

JOYCE, JAMES (1882–1941). The expatriate Irish novelist, a giant of 20th-century literature, made **Zurich** his home at two different periods. From 1915 to 1920 he resided first at the Gasthof Hoffnung, Reitergasse 16; then at Seefeldstrasse 54; later at Seefeldstrasse 73; and finally at Universitatstrasse 29. Joyce completed *A Portrait of the Artist as a Young Man* (1916) at the first address. He wrote *The Exiles* (1918) and worked on *Ulysses* (1922) in the subsequent lodgings.

A longtime resident of Paris, Joyce by 1940 was plagued by ill health and a foreboding sense of doom as Europe erupted into war. He spent months negotiating official permission to reside again in neutral Switzerland and finally obtained it. Back in Zurich he survived for only a month, however. His last lodging was a two-room apartment at the Pension Delphin, Muhlebacherstrasse 69.

Joyce tomb: Fluntern Cemetery, **Zurich**.

(See Chapter 2, FRANCE; also Chapter 3, PARIS; also Chapter 7, IRELAND; also Chapter 8, ITALY.)

JUNG, CARL GUSTAV (1875–1961). The founder of analytic psychology and a profoundly influential thinker and therapist, Jung was born in the village rectory at **Kesswil**, the son of a Swiss Reformed pastor.

When he was barely six months old, the family moved to **Laufen** and occupied the vicarage there until 1879. It stood near the 16th-century Laufen Castle on the brink of the Rhine falls.

Jung's family home for the next 21 years was the vicarage at **Kleinhüningen**, a village three kilometers north of Basel. The 18th-century house still stands in the village.

As a medical doctor in **Zurich**, Jung resided from 1900 to 1909 at his place of work and research, the Burghölzli Psychiatric Hospital at Lenggstrasse 31. After his 1903 marriage to Emma Rauschenbach, the couple occupied a three-room flat in the main building. Still a public psychiatric hospital, the Burghölzli displays no marker indicating its epochal significance in the history of psychology; its doctors do not even practice Jungian therapy.

Jung designed and built his final home at Seestrasse 22B in **Küsnacht** near Zurich in 1909. Located on the shore of Lake Zurich, this house was the center of Jung's research, writing and psychiatric practice for the rest of his life. He liked towers and turrets, as can be seen; over the main entrance he engraved a quotation from Erasmus, borrowed from the Greeks: "Called or not called, God shall be there." The legend, as Laurens van der Post wrote, seemed "not only an exposition of the motivic theme of his life but also a sacred exorcism of darkness and evil." The house, surrounded by a large garden, is still owned by the Jung family and does not admit visitors.

In **Bollingen**, also on Lake Zurich, Jung built himself a stone house in 1922, using it often as a solitary retreat as well as for weekends with his colleague and mistress, Antonia Wolff. Among other things, wrote one biographer, the house symbolized a "spiritual split" from his wife and coworker Emma Jung. Jung enlarged and altered the house frequently over the years—it was his "sand castle," said his son—and his tower annex became his private "spiritual oasis," a haven of thought and meditation. In his Kusnacht home, wrote van der Post, "Jung *did*. But in the house of stone at Bollingen, he could just *be*." He cherished its utmost simplicity, believing that "if a man of the sixteenth century came to it, he would feel utterly at home." During excavations for the house foundation on a promontory where Jung and his family had often camped and picnicked, the site yielded the grave of a French soldier buried there during the Napoleonic wars; Jung ceremoniously reburied the bones. He also planted most of the trees that surround the two-story house. In the stone walls and on surrounding rocks he carved images, quotations and alchemical symbols, "signatures of the unconscious" that held great meaning for him.

Jung tomb: Village cemetery, **Küsnacht**.

KNOX, JOHN (1505–1572).
Exhibit: The Scottish Protestant reformer preached to a small English congregation in **Geneva** from 1556 to 1558. His address during this period remains unknown. He delivered his fiery sermons, however, at the John Calvin Auditorium before Calvin himself occupied that pulpit (see the entry on Calvin, *Exhibits*, earlier in this section).
(See Chapter 7, SCOTLAND.)

LENIN, VLADIMIR (1870–1924). The Russian

FROM SPIEGELGASSE TO THE KREMLIN. Vladimir Lenin lived in this crowded **Zurich** tenement (his rooms are marked by the arrow) just before the 1917 Russian Revolution that brought him to power and established the Soviet Union.

revolutionary leader spent the three years immediately before the 1917 upheaval in Moscow that brought him to power and established the USSR, in Switzerland. He lived in **Zurich** for slightly more than a year (1916–17) with his wife Nadezhda Krupskaya in crowded rooms at Spiegelgasse 14. A nearby sausage factory inflicted vile odors on the neighborhood and Lenin spent as little time there as possible, preferring to work in the Central Library at Zähringerplatz 6.

(See Chapter 3, PARIS; also Chapter 4, EAST GERMANY, WEST GERMANY, FINLAND; also Chapter 6, LONDON.)

LISZT, FRANZ (1811–1886). In 1835 and 1836 the Hungarian composer rented an apartment in **Geneva** with his married mistress, Countess Marie d'Agoult, with whom he had "eloped" from Paris. The couple eventually had three children but never married. The building where they resided is marked at 22 Rue Etienne-Dumont.

(See AUSTRIA in this chapter; also Chapter 3, PARIS; also Chapter 4, EAST GERMANY, WEST GERMANY; also Chapter 8, ITALY.)

MANN, THOMAS (1875–1955). Back in Europe in 1953 after a wartime exile in the United States, the German novelist preferred to reside permanently in Switzerland rather than return to Germany. He bought his last home in 1954 at **Kilchberg** on Lake Zurich. It stands at Alte Landstrasse 39.

From 1934 to 1938, as an exile from Nazi Germany, Mann had resided in **Küsnacht**, also near Zurich, at Schiedhaltenstrasse 33, a two-story dwelling where he worked on his tetralogy *Joseph and his Brothers* (1933–43) and *The Beloved Returns* (1939).

Mann tomb: Village cemetery, **Kilchberg**.

Exhibit: The Thomas Mann Archive, which displays some 600 of the writer's manuscripts and letters, his recreated study and library, plus numerous items of memorabilia, is housed in the 18th-century **Zurich** dwelling that belonged to poet Johann Jakob Bodmer, whom Goethe visited in 1775 and 1779. It stands at Schonberggasse 14. (Open Wednesday, Saturday 2:00—4:00; admission.)

(See Chapter 4, WEST GERMANY; also Chapter 8, ITALY.)

NAPOLEON I (1769–1821).

Exhibit: The Napoleonic Museum in the 16th-century Arenenberg Castle about one kilometer west of **Ermatingen** displays much material relating to the Corsican-French Bonaparte family, rulers of Europe during portions of the 19th century. This castle was the residence (1830–37) of Queen Hortense, daughter of the Empress Joséphine and mother of Napoleon III, who spent much of his childhood there. Most furnishings and memorabilia relate to these later Bonapartes, but items concerning the first nepotistic emperor of the French are also displayed. (Open May 1—September 30, Tuesday—Sunday 9:00—12:00, 1:30—6:00; April, October, Tuesday—Sunday 10:00—12:00, 1:30—5:00; rest of year, open to 4:00; admission.)

(See AUSTRIA in this chapter; also Chapter 2, FRANCE; also Chapter 3, PARIS; also Chapter 4, EAST GERMANY, BELGIUM; also Chapter 8, ITALY, SPAIN.)

NIETZSCHE, FRIEDRICH WILHELM (1844–1900). As a professor at the University of **Basel**, the German philosopher and poet resided from 1870 to 1875 in a rooming house that survives at Schutzengraben 45. He wrote his philosophical essay *The Birth of Tragedy* (1872) while living there.

"Loving not man nor woman neither, and praying that Man might be surpassed," wrote Will Durant, Nietzsche sought the alpine solitude of a small house at **Sils Maria** and spent summers there from 1881 to 1888. There he wrote his poetic masterpiece *Thus Spake Zarathustra* (1883). "It was partly this setting," wrote Jean-Daniel Candaux, "which made him urge men to live dangerously. He wanted to see men become, like mountains, 'neighbors of the sun, the eagle and the snow.' " (Toward women, Nietzsche bore only fear and contempt.) His cottage beside the Hôtel Edelweiss displays his bed, oil lamp, his death mask, a poem manuscript and other memorabilia. (Inquire locally for admission information.)

(See Chapter 4, EAST GERMANY, WEST GERMANY.)

PICASSO, PABLO (1881–1973).

Exhibit: At **Lucerne** the Picasso Museum in the Am Rhyn House displays an important collection of the artist's works, including paintings, drawings and sculptures. This 17th-century building stands at Furrengasse 21. (Open Tuesday—Sunday 10:00—5:00; admission.)

(See Chapter 2, FRANCE; also Chapter 3, PARIS; also Chapter 8, SPAIN.)

RILKE, RAINER MARIA (1875–1926). The Bohemian-born poet's last home from 1921 was the small Château de Muzot, located a short distance north of **Sierre**. The old, towered structure was bought for him by a patron, Swiss millionaire Werner Reinhardt. Rilke wrote his last, best-known works there, including the *Duino Elegies* (1923) and *The Sonnets to Orpheus* (1923). The château does not admit visitors.

Rilke tomb: Village churchyard, **Raron**.

Exhibits: In **Sierre** the Rilke Room at the Hôtel Château-Bellevue, Rue du Bourg, displays memorabilia, letters and editions of the poet's works. (Inquire locally for admission information.) Mementos are also exhibited in the Château de Villa, now a restaurant, in the Rue du Château.

(See Chapter 2, FRANCE; also Chapter 3, PARIS; also Chapter 4, WEST GERMANY.)

ROUSSEAU, JEAN-JACQUES (1712–1778). A native of **Geneva**, the philosopher became disillusioned with Switzerland at several key times in his life. Rousseau was born at 40 Grand-Rue, where his mother died 10 days after his birth. The facade on this house has been rebuilt. In 1717 Rousseau's watchmaker father moved himself and his sons to a house at 28 Rue de Coutance, which survived until 1958. It remained Rousseau's home until 1722, and he lived there again from 1724 to 1728, when he abandoned the city in disgust. Rousseau proved "an embarrassing figure in this strict Calvinist community," wrote Phyllis Méras, "writing as he had about man's being innately good when churchmen were preaching of original sin." The city banned and burned his *Émile* and *The Social Contract* in 1762.

Rousseau's subsequent stays in Switzerland were mostly brief and stressful. Civic authorities, upset by his seldom-withheld challenges to the conventional wisdoms of the day, often drove him out of his temporary havens. In 1730 he came to **Vevey** for the first time and "acquired a love for this town which has pursued me throughout all my travels." He used Vevey and adjacent Clarens as background for his novel *The New Hélouïse* (1761). Rousseau's lodging was the "Auberge de la Clef," which survives north of the market

BIRTHPLACE OF ROUSSEAU. Marked by a plaque, this house at 40 Grand-Rue in the old section of **Geneva** was the philosopher's home for his first five years.

square and is marked with a plaque. The town was the 1699 birthplace of his benefactor, Mme. de Warens, whose marital home until 1726 also stands northeast of the square.

Forced to escape France after his "educational romance" *Émile* (1762) was banned there, Rousseau returned to Switzerland expecting to settle in a "land of liberty." He soon discovered that Swiss authorities were no more lenient than the French toward honest mind-speakers, and he was hounded from one refuge to the next. He came first to 5 Rue de la Plaine in **Yverdon**, where he stayed a month.

Forced to move on once more, he went next to **Môtiers** and was able to settle there for three years (1762–65). Scottish journalist James Boswell visited him there and asked him point-blank if he was a Christian (a question over which many people agonized concerning Rousseau). The philosopher's answer was charming; after a long pause, wrote Boswell, "He struck his breast and replied, 'Yes, I pique myself upon being one.' " Local church folk, however, didn't believe it. Inflamed by their pastor, they mobbed and stoned Rousseau's house, and again he took to the road. Their progeny decided he wasn't such a bad fellow, however, and his house in (of course) the Rue Jean-Jacques-Rousseau is now a museum displaying copies of his works and exhibits on his life and achievements. (Inquire locally for admission information.)

Rousseau's next stop, for a few weeks in 1765 before traveling to England, was the Île St-Pierre in Lake Bienne. He recalled this brief period in his *Confessions* (1781–88) as one of the happiest of his life. No longer an island but a strip of land dividing the lake, St-Pierre may be approached on foot from **Erlach** or by boat from **Bienne** or **La Neuveville**. The inn where Rousseau and his mistress, Thérèse Lavasseur, stayed was formerly a Cluniac priory founded in 1120. Today it displays the original room they occupied (redecorated in 1945) with its original furnishings. Goethe and Kant were among those who made pilgrimages here in tribute to the philosopher. This was his last Swiss lodging. (Open daily.)

Exhibits: Rousseau hadn't been safely dead very long when Switzerland decided that he had been a great man after all. Calvinistic **Geneva**, however, delayed adulation for about a century. Today a museum honors him in the Public and University Library. Displays include rare editions of his works and letters; manuscripts of *Émile*, *The Social Contract* (1762) and *Confessions*; his watch, teapot and coffee pot; and his death mask (See the entry on John Calvin, *Exhibits*, earlier in this section.)

At **Neuchâtel**, the Municipal Library in the Place Numa Droz owns more Rousseau manuscripts than any other archive in the world, thanks to a local benefactor who had treated Rousseau decently and bequeathed this material to the library. (Inquire locally for admission information.)

(See Chapter 2, FRANCE; also Chapter 3, PARIS; also Chapter 5, ENGLAND; also Chapter 8, ITALY.)

SHELLEY, PERCY BYSSHE (1792–1822). The English Romantic poet traveled to Switzerland in the spring of 1816 with his mistress and later wife, Mary Godwin. They installed themselves from May to August in a small, two-story chalet called the Villa de Montalègre or Maison Chappuis in **Cologny** near the lodging of Lord Byron who had joined them (see the entry on Byron earlier in this section). The most notable writing of this period

was done by Godwin, who began her classic horror tale *Frankenstein* (1818) after Byron proposed one night that they all write ghost stories. The villa, destroyed in 1883, was promptly rebuilt using the original materials and lasted until 1970, when Prince Victor Emmanuel of Italy bought the property. He demolished the house and built a new villa. Today only the original foundations and cellar plus a few outbuildings remain on the site. The former carriage house is now a private residence off route N5 on the Lake Geneva shore.

(See Chapter 5, ENGLAND; also Chapter 6, LONDON; also Chapter 8, ITALY.)

STEVENSON, ROBERT LOUIS (1850–1894). During periods in 1881 and 1882 the tubercular Scottish author stayed in the health resort town of **Davos**. He finished his novel *Treasure Island* (1883) in the Am Stein chalet above the Hôtel Buol in 1882.

(See Chapter 2, FRANCE; also Chapter 5, ENGLAND; also Chapter 7, SCOTLAND.)

STRAVINSKY, IGOR (1882–1971). The Russian-born composer made his home in Switzerland during World War I (1914–20). In 1913 at **Clarens**, a suburb of Montreux, he composed *The Rite of Spring* (1913) in the Hôtel du Chatelard near the railroad station.

At **Morges** on Lake Geneva, Stravinsky and his family resided at the Villa Rogivue in the Avenue des Pâquis from 1915 to 1917. From 1917 to 1920 they lived in the Maison Bornand at Place St-Louis 2. At the latter address Stravinsky wrote *The Soldier's Tale* (1918) and his ballet *Pulcinella* (1920).

(See Chapter 2, FRANCE; also Chapter 3, PARIS.)

TELL, WILHELM. Evidence for the actual existence of this mountain archer and keen-eyed apple shooter is thin at best. His name first occurs in late-15th-century chronicles, and similar tales exist in Danish, Icelandic and English folk hero literatures. Each culture builds its own symbolic figures, if not by amplifying the exploits of actual persons, then by creating figures to reflect a people's aspirations. Tell fits a familiar patriotic mold in an age-old variation of the David and Goliath story. In that mold, he's more alive in Switzerland today than in the 14th century. His modern fame results primarily from Schiller's drama *Wilhelm Tell* (1804) and Rossini's 1829 opera of the same name. The several Tell chapels marking the sites associated with his legend were all erected or named for him generations after his supposed death in 1350. In the village of **Bürglen** the 1582 Tell Chapel is said to occupy the site of the Swiss patriot's house.

Exhibits: These consist mostly of tablets and markers identifying spots that figured significantly in the Tell chronicles. The Tell Monument in the central square of **Altdorf** marks the spot where the archer, responding to an order from the Austrian tyrant Gessler, shot the apple from his son's head (historians have been unable to discover any Gessler, much less Tell, in the old charters of this settlement). Schiller's play is periodically performed in the town.

A 1638 Tell Chapel in the Hohle Gasse, about two kilometers north of **Küssnacht**, marks where Gessler is said to have received the fatal "other arrow" from Tell's quiver (no apple this time). Paintings inside the chapel display details of the episode. (Inquire locally for admission information.)

In **Bürglen** the Tell Museum in the Romanesque tower adjoining the church exhibits a collection of material relating to the village's "native son" (this museum is not the place to dispute that statement). (Open June 1—October 31, daily 9:30—11:30, 2:00—5:00; admission.)

VERNE, JULES (1828–1905). The French science fiction writer sought refuge in 1870 and 1871 in **Sion**, where he lived on the top story of the Maison Jordan in the Rue de l'Église.

(See Chapter 2, FRANCE; also Chapter 3, PARIS.)

VOLTAIRE, FRANÇOIS-MARIE AROUET (1694–1778). "When I powder my wig, I powder the whole republic," Voltaire said of what was then the independent city-state of **Geneva**. Exiled from both Prussia and Paris in 1755 for his refusal to stop reminding people of the hypocrisies of his age, the French philosopher bought a 1730 country house he called "Les Délices" and settled there with his niece, Mme. Denis, until 1765. Voltaire employed a large staff of servants and workmen, "planting, sowing and building incessantly," he reported. There he wrote his best-known book, *Candide* (1759), and his *Philosophical Dictionary* (1764), among many other works, including plays. Because Calvinistic Geneva prohibited the theater, Voltaire finally left the city and moved a few kilometers across the border to France, where he

LES DÉLICES, VOLTAIRE'S SWISS ESTATE. Hounded from France, the philosopher lived in **Geneva** for a decade (1755–65) with his niece-mistress, Mme. Denis, cultivating his grounds and his muse. Inside the house, the wax figure of Voltaire is seen seated at his original desk and wears Voltaire's actual clothing. The house, open to the public, is now the Voltaire Museum and Institute.

built another estate (to which Genevans flocked, of course, to see his plays). Now owned by the City of Geneva, Les Délices, located at 25 Rue des Délices, became the Voltaire Museum and Institute in 1954. Numerous items of memorabilia and Voltaire possessions on display include portraits, letters, manuscripts, rare editions and furniture from his last estate at Ferney in France. (Open Tuesday—Saturday 2:00—5:00, Sunday 10:00—12:00, 2:00—5:00; free.)

Exhibit: The elaborately carved paneling from Voltaire's drawing room at Les Délices may be seen at the Museum of Art and History, 2 Rue Charles-Galland in **Geneva**. (Open Monday 2:00—6:00, Tuesday—Sunday 10:00—12:00, 2:00—6:00; free.)

(See Chapter 2, FRANCE; also Chapter 3, PARIS; also Chapter 4, EAST GERMANY.)

WAGNER, RICHARD (1813–1883). Exiled from his native Germany because of his implication in the 1848 insurrection there, the opera composer lived in **Zurich** from 1849 to 1858. From 1849 to 1853 he and his wife, Minna Planer, resided in a small apartment at Zeltweg 11. In 1853 they moved to larger quarters at Zeltweg 13, where Wagner wrote *Das Rheingold* (1870), and stayed until 1857, when a rich patron rescued the composer's fortunes. Silk merchant Otto Wesendonck built the "Asyl" house for Wagner on his estate overlooking Lake Zurich, offering him this small dwelling adjacent to the Villa Wesendonck for life at a nominal rent. But Wesendonck's generosity was ill repaid when the composer fell in love with his wife. Not surprisingly, this period marked the end of Wagner's first marriage and his scenic lodging (1858). Wagner composed most of his opera *Tristan and Isolde* (1865) there. Though Wagner's house is gone, the Villa Wesendonck is now the Rietberg Museum at Gablerstrasse 15, displaying Asian, African and American antiquities and art. (Open Tuesday—Sunday 10:00—5:00; admission.)

From 1866 to 1872 the composer resided, again with a friend's wife (Cosima von Bülow, marrying her in 1870), in **Lucerne**. Their stay at Tribschen, a lovely villa overlooking Lake Lucerne in the Tribschenstrasse, was due to the patronage of Bavarian King Ludwig II ("the mad king"), who came here one midnight emotionally distraught over an impending war with Prussia; Wagner talked him out of abdication. The composer ac-

complished some of his best-known work here, including the operas *Die Meistersinger* (1868), *Siegfried* (1870) and *Götterdämmerung* (1876). Now known as the Richard Wagner Museum, the house displays original scores, Wagner's piano, pictures, posters and other memorabilia as well as a collection of old instruments. (Open April 16—September 14, Monday—Saturday 9:00—12:00, 2:00—6:00, Sunday 10:30—12:00, 2:00—6:30; September 15—April 15, Tuesday, Thursday, Saturday—Sunday, same hours as above; admission.)

(See AUSTRIA in this chapter; also Chapter 2, FRANCE; also Chapter 3, PARIS; also Chapter 4, EAST GERMANY, WEST GERMANY; also Chapter 6, LONDON; also Chapter 8, ITALY.)

Chapter 2
FRANCE

"France," wrote Sanche de Gramont, "was not geographically predestined to be a nation, as were such spatially defined units as the British Isles, Italy, and the Iberian peninsula. It is the creation of history more than geography."

Just as Germany idealizes the booted masculine image of the fatherland, France identifies with the feminine—la belle France. Romantic, seductive, an irresistible sex object among nations and yet bosomly and earth-motherly enough to die for— one of French manhood's highest skills for centuries—France sees itself as unequivocally female. To some observers, this self-perception explains almost everything about the French; to others, it only begs the question. The vision of such a France is more than occasionally shared by foreign visitors; it was no Parisian or Provençal who declared himself "as happy as God in France," but a German (who undoubtedly thought he should know).

France is also a mental creation, an intellectual framework held together by various crosspieces labeled "honor," "glory," "destiny" and other similar abstractions. Probably no European nation at once personalizes and deifies its history to the extent of France or labors so hard to mold that history into a verification of its self-assumptions. These assumptions begin from a certitude of divine favor as revealed by perfect proportions of landscape and climate. France, believe the French, comes as close to Biblical Eden in all its parts as humanity has any reasonable right to expect. The French love the idea of order, precision, and balance in the make-up of their country. One French geographer likened the shape of France to an almost perfect hexagon, with three borders on the sea and three on land. Despite the fact that only patriotic eyes suffering severe cataracts could detect such an outline, the mythical hexagon nevertheless came to represent France's sacred emblem of itself, a symbol weighted with romanticism.

Yet the French tendency toward self-congratulation hardly betrays an overwhelming self-confidence. Precisely because France is *not* a self-contained geographical unit but, as Gramont points out, "a quilt of regions stitched over many centuries and after many wars," the romanticized vision of one idealized fabric represents yearning rather than fact.

This intense nationalism is the child of the 1789 French Revolution, that bloody struggle which supplanted the tyranny of a decadent nobility with the terrorism of street mobs and citizen executioners. The Revolution—not a revolution at all in terms of permanent reforms but more of a civil war—divided the French people into either heroes or traitors. It was one of the biggest spontaneous outbursts of hate that Europe has ever seen. With the country awash in high principles (and the blood of those whose principles were judged not high enough), French patriotism was born from the kind of defensive psychology that always accompanies doctrinaire rigidity. Anxious to convert other European nations to their new political gospel, the revolutionaries applied their ideals of "liberty, equality, fraternity" to other "enslaved" peoples, embroiling France in constant wars with its neighbors from 1792 to 1815. Hatred of the enemy, not a common idea in most European warfare up to that point, governed the French eagerness to justify and protect the nation's new-found identity. The Revolution's most enduring legacy was the patriotic citizen-soldier; most wars in the world since 1800 have been fought by such patriots.

Emperor Napoleon I skillfully wove this free-floating patriotism into his own banner. His cynical manipulation of revolutionary ideals to legitimize his own dictatorship looks squalid to almost everyone except the French. Ironically, he gave France a system of laws, the Code Napoléon, that has proven highly durable. He not only brought the nation to ruin, however; he sacrificed more Frenchmen in his various military adventures than died in both World Wars. Yet the French revere him today because he embodied the real nub of the revolutionary ideal: to be not only right, but powerful.

It was Julius Caesar who first won firm control of the Roman province of Gaul in 52 B.C., and his *Gallic Wars* remains the classic military account of the first-recorded war on French soil. Later, the fifth-century Franks, originally mercenary soldiers employed to defend the frontiers of the declining Roman Empire, achieved mastery over both the Gallic tribes and the Romans; they established the first united French kingdom and gave their own name to the region that would, some 12 centuries later, constitute modern France.

The rise of France to aggressive self-awareness was preceded by centuries of feudal warfare, English invasions and control, and hostilities and shifts of alliance among the country's various states. To trace this history requires a taste for complex geopolitics, in which the Roman papal authority and other European monarchies played important parts. Feudal France owed loyalty to diverse kings and nobles, not to a nation as such. Thus the historical roster of dynasties that "governed France"—the Carolingians, Capets, Valois and earlier Bourbons—mainly represent the monarchs who controlled the Île de France, the central region surrounding Paris. These monarchs had to contend with subordinate feudal lordships in order to enlarge and consolidate the kingdom, and eventually they succeeded. The French borders

defined by the Treaty of Utrecht in 1713 remain approximately the same today. High points of this period, which began with the Merovingian Clovis in 486 and fell with the witless head of Louis XVI in 1793, included the reigns of Charlemagne, of Francis I, and of the "sun king," Louis XIV, the shining apex of French royalty. After the Revolution, two Napoleons, two restored Bourbons and Louis-Philippe of the House of Orléans were on-again, off-again rulers until Napoleon III was deposed in 1870. The Third Republic and French democracy emerged under the presidency of Adolphe Thiers in that year.

Major battles of World War I—a war, historians generally agree, for which France bears large responsibility—were fought on French soil. French generalship, anything but brilliant, threw away the lives of some 1,400,000 young Frenchmen in pointless sorties and sacrifices, an expenditure ranking among the genuine "war crimes" of all time. Though it culminated in Allied victory, for France World War I was a colossal defeat in terms of human and economic loss. Understandably, the French were in no mood for another war and only reluctantly allied with a not-much-less reluctant Britain to challenge Hitler's conquest of the continent. Rapidly overwhelmed by the Nazi blitzkrieg in 1940, the country "sat out" most of World War II under its German conquerors and the collaborationist Vichy regime headed by World War I hero Gen. Henri Petain. Because of a strong Resistance movement and the "Free French" forces of Gen. Charles de Gaulle, World War II became a civil war for France, with many French genuinely puzzled over which side merited their patriotism since French leaders on both sides claimed it. Postwar politics, marked by frequent cabinet crises and the kind of street-barricade scenarios with which the French frequently memorialize their Revolution, were stabilized by the autocratic "reign" of President Charles de Gaulle. He was probably the only man in France who had sufficient moral authority to end France's obsolete and expensive colonial policies, particularly in Algeria. In 1958 de Gaulle ushered in France's Fifth Republic with a new constitution which placed dominant power in the presidency.

Historically, it is probably fair to generalize that with rare exceptions the French have not been well served by their political masters. And yet, wrote Maurice Druon, "the two sovereigns who in all her history did France the most harm, Charlemagne with his conquest of the west and Napoleon with his European hegemony, are the very two to whose memory the French are most attached." It seems to be a national hallmark: the veneration of those leaders who have cost France the most in terms of human lives and social disruption.

Of course any nation's politics form an astonishing mixture of comedy, tragedy and rare good sense if viewed closely enough. The French, if somewhat more egocentric about their behavior, are certainly not unique in this regard. This egocentricity—the certitude that French mores, language and civilization are inherently superior—extends politically to their refusal to become one of the European "crowd," a coolly aloof attitude that often sends foreign diplomats into paroxysms of foot-stomping frustration. Such serenely perverse qualities are somehow refreshing in a world that is overanxious to pigeonhole nations into "us" and "them." Only one prediction is safe: that France will continue to subvert all international pigeonholing to the best of its practiced ability.

In religion, France remains predominantly Roman Catholic; the Protestant minority consists of under two percent of the population. But religion has never been a major issue in France. Though church and state were not separated until 1905, the church has always been more of a civic institution than a spiritual center. "The French as a people," wrote Gramont, "can best be qualified as moderately agnostic." Anticlerical episodes are frequent in its history, but the country made up for its lack of religious fervor with the emotional fervor of its various intellectual and social ideals, preaching these with a violence comparable to the Crusades.

Surrounded on three sides by seacoasts and bordered by the Alps and the Pyrenees in the south, France enjoys a large variety of climate and landscape. While almost one-quarter of the country is forested, vineyard France—those sunny hills that produce the most famous wines in the world—is best known. The Loire River divides the southern Mediterranean portion of the country, one of Europe's most popular winter resort areas, from the temperate north. Distinctive regions of the country—Normandy, Brittany, the Dordogne, Provence, the Loire Valley, the Riviera, among others—reveal different facets of French landscape, culture and peoples.

Administratively, France is divided into 95 departments, which are roughly equivalent to English counties: in the following pages the department name is placed in parentheses after the name of the town in order to facilitate location. Paris, of course, is the capital and largest city by far (see Chapter 3). France's oldest and second largest city, and its largest port, is Marseille.

The French language, that Romance tongue most distant from its Latin prototype, is used by almost 100 million people outside France.

Probably no other country in the world so devotedly honors its men and women of achievement by naming streets and squares after them. Any town of moderate size has its Rue Victor-Hugo, its Avenue Charles-de-Gaulle and Place Georges-Clemenceau. Writers, especially, outshine statesmen in the urban nomenclature ("literature is to the French what the playing fields of Eton are to the English," wrote one observer), for in France the intellectual is, in a way that is foreign to most Western nations, a *public* figure. As the birthplace of the Gothic in architecture, Impressionism and Surrealism in painting, and Romanticism in literature, France has, of course, numerous writers and artists to honor, and many of them are superbly memorialized; the homes of Balzac, Dumas, Flaubert, Hugo, Monet, Renoir, Rousseau, Sand and Voltaire stand well preserved, among others. In the field of music, visitors will find the residences of Berlioz, Debussy and Chopin marked if not always enshrined. The effects of the scientific work of Marie Curie and Louis Pasteur—and of France's idol of rationalism, Descartes—have been felt all over the world; only Descartes and Pasteur, however, are represented by dwellings open to the public.

Both world wars took heavy tolls of historical homes. Indeed, wars and the Revolution, much more than planned schemes of "urban renewal," have been the main disruptive elements on the landscapes of the past. Despite the frantic ravages of the French Revolution, however, many royal homes survive and have been restored; the foremost example, of course, is Versailles.

Two people outshine all others in the number of memorials devoted to them, and both lives form vital components of French self-identity to this day. Ironically, neither was French by birth, as French borders were then defined. Joan of Arc has come to represent many things to many causes and interests; and Napoleon I, himself more Italian than French, brought France not only military greatness but chaos through his own personal ambition. A large part of being French is tied up in the lives and legends of these two adopted French leaders; and visitors eager to discover something of what "being French" means could do worse than begin their journeys by visiting the former homes of these two extraordinary figures. Most French royal châteaus are now operated by the Service des Monuments Historiques, while the majority of local museums are municipally owned.

Good guidebooks to France include the Michelin "Green Guides" and American Express Guides to various regions. However, English language coverage of the country as a whole is spotty and incomplete. One of the best all-around English guides for motorists, though somewhat dated, is the *AA Road Book of France* (1969). Among the few specialized English language guidebooks is Barbara Whelpton's *Painters' Provence* (1970). In French, the *Guide Littéraire de la France* (1964) and the *Guide Artistique de la France* (1968), both compiled by the Librairie Hachette, are superb classics of guidebook literature.

NOTE: Two designations often encountered when seeking the residences of French notables are the words *hôtel* and *château*. Hôtel now usually signifies a commercial inn, as in the English usage, but its earlier meaning—and one still used—was that of a private town house (whereas "Hôtel de Ville" is always the town hall). Thus a hôtel in France is not invariably a place where you can expect to bunk in for the night.

Châteaus are country houses, usually elaborate, often palatial. Towns and villages grew around seventeenth-century (and earlier) châteaus, and the name of such a château usually provides the name of the town as well.

Reliable admission information on homes and museums open to the public and located in France's smaller towns and villages is not well publicized or easily accessible except in the communities themselves. Visitors will generally find such places open on most days, however, though hours of admission may vary widely. Serious pilgrims should always consult the regional Tourist Information Centers (*Syndicats d'Initiative*) for updated information before jaunting forth.

ABÉLARD, PETER (1079–1142). The scholastic philosopher, theologian, teacher and tragic lover

of Hélouïse was born at **Le Pallet** (Loire-Atlantique), his home until about 1095. Hélouïse gave birth there to their son, Peter Astrolabe, in about 1119. Only turf-covered ruins of the small castle owned by Abélard's father which overlooked the village survive on a hill locally known as *la butte d'Abélard* (route 149).

Always in conflict with church authorities because of his rationalistic approach to dogma, Abélard nevertheless drew an immense popular following. After 1119, however, the year he was savagely emasculated at the hands of four thugs hired by Hélouïse's protective uncle, Canon Fulbert, with whom she lived, Abélard spent the rest of his life as a contentious monk at various abbeys.

Immediately after his recovery from the attack, Abélard took vows as a monk at the Benedictine basilica of St-Denis in **St-Denis** (Seine-St-Denis) which housed the tombs of French kings. He soon horrified his superiors with the heretic suggestion that the obscure St. Denis, for whom the abbey was named, had not been buried there at all. Abélard resided there until 1123 when, after a final falling-out with the other monks, he founded his own Abbey of the Paraclete (see below). The present monastic buildings south of the basilica in St-Denis were rebuilt in the 18th century. Abélard would recognize most of the present basilica, a brooding presence which dates from the 12th and 13th centuries. St-Denis today is a somewhat derelict northern suburb of Paris.

After being condemned for such audacious errors as trying to divide the indivisible godhead, Abélard was confined to the "penetentiary monastery" of St-Médard Abbey at **Soissons** (Aisne) for a short time in 1121. About 400 monks lived there. Only fragments of this abbey remain above ground in the Rue de Bouvines.

In 1123 he founded the Abbey of the Paraclete where he taught until 1125. He handed over the property to Hélouïse and her sisterhood for a convent in 1129 and visited frequently thereafter. Hélouïse brought Abélard's body back there for burial, where it remained on the site until 1817. The abbey itself, situated on the Arduzon River, lasted until 1792. "If the Paraclete is no longer the religious house intended by its founder," wrote Elizabeth Hamilton in *Hélouïse* (1967), "neither is it a museum nor an historical curiosity. It is a home and one lived in with graciousness and dignity by persons who esteem the past." She refers to a private château built in 1685 on the site of the origi-nal Paraclete abbey, where Hélouïse served as ab-bess until her own death. It is located about eight kilometers southeast of **Nogent-sur-Seine** (Aube) off route 442. A summer residence on the river, formerly a mill, stands on the site of Abélard's oratory. (See the entry on Hélouïse later in this chapter.)

In 1125, Abélard was assigned as abbot of St-Gildas de Rhuys Abbey near Vannes. As in many medieval monasteries, the monks were hardly holy men—Abélard complained of thieves and as-sassins among them—but he stayed until 1133. He probably wrote his autobiographical *Historia Calamitatum* (ca. 1134) there. The site of the abbey, located on a rockbound coastal peninsula, is now occupied by a convent in the village of **St-Gildas-de-Rhuys** (Morbihan) about 32 kilometers south of Vannes on route 780.

Hounded by St. Bernard of Clairvaux for his ag-gressive challenges to clerical authority, Abélard was given sanctuary by Peter the Venerable, abbot of **Cluny** (Saône-et-Loire), in 1141 while prepar-ing to appeal his case before the pope in Rome. This monastery, one of the intellectual capitals of Europe in the 12th century, held the largest church in Christendom until the 1626 erection of St. Peter's in Rome. Only a few walls and frag-ments, enough to indicate its size, survive; the present monastery buildings in the Rue Munici-pale are mostly 15th- to 18th-century structures. Abélard rapidly declined in health during this period. An ancient lime tree called "Abélard" in the cloister garden is pointed out as the spot where the harried philosopher sat pining for the only place he considered home, the Paraclete. (Open April—September, Wednesday—Monday 9:00—11:30, 2:00—6:00; October—March, Wednesday—Monday 10:00—11:00, 2:00—4:00; admission.)

Instead of setting off for Rome as he had hoped, Abélard was sent for recovery to the monastery of St-Marcel about two kilometers east of **Chalon-sur-Saône** (Saône-et-Loire). The 12th-century church of the Cluniac Sisters of St. Joseph with its convent occupies the present site. Abélard died there, probably of Hodgkins disease, after a resi-dence of several months. (See Chapter 3, PARIS.)

BALZAC, HONORÉ DE (1799–1850). Many of Balzac's novels contain descriptions of **Tours** (In-dre-et-Loire), his native city. His birthplace and home until 1807, a row-house tenement at 39 Rue Nationale, was destroyed by fire in 1940. Novelist Henry James deplored its squalid surroundings during a worshipful visit in 1899 but regretted that the house was not open to the public.

At **Vendôme** (Loir-et-Cher), Balzac attended school and resided from 1807 to 1813 at what is now the Lycée Ronsard in the Rue St-Jacques.

A frequent and favorite abode of the novelist at intervals throughout his life from about age four is now the Balzac Museum on route D17 in the vil-lage of **Saché** (Indre-et-Loire). This gray stone château belonged to Jean de Margonne, the lover of Balzac's mother. Margonne remained a lifelong friend of the novelist, setting aside apartments in the house for his use, and Balzac accomplished much writing there. Visitors may see his bedroom with its original furnishings plus a collection of Balzac manuscripts, revised proofs, portraits and first editions. (Open March 15—September 30, daily 9:00—12:00, 2:00—7:00; October 1—March 14, Thursday—Tuesday 9:00—12:00, 2:00—5:30; closed December—January; Saché 10; admission.)

The northeastern Parisian suburb of **Villepari-sis** (Seine-et-Marne) became the home of Balzac's parents in 1820, though the house where they re-sided was not purchased by them until 1824. The young writer occupied an attic room in the three-story dwelling and from 1820 to 1822 paid his parents 1,200 francs per year for his keep. There Balzac met the woman who became his first mis-tress, 45-year-old Mme. Laure de Berny; the liai-son lasted 15 years. This private house survives in dilapidated condition, albeit with a marker, in the Rue de Meaux.

"A bird cage" was how novelist Victor Hugo described Balzac's country house, the Villa des Jardies, in the southwestern Parisian suburb of **Ville d'Avray** (Hauts-de-Seine). Balzac en-thusiastically bought the dwelling in 1837, but "no man could have chosen a less suitable site for a house," wrote one biographer. Rainstorms eroded much of his five acres into a gully behind the house. With his impractical business sense, Balzac became obsessed with the notion of estab-lishing a pineapple plantation there. Bereft of top-soil, however, the ground produced nothing—not even a tree grew there—and was, by all accounts, a dismal patch of desert. Balzac imported tons of topsoil and poured some 100,000 francs into the property to no avail; by 1841 he was bankrupt and creditors were seizing the furniture. Balzac finally sold the house and land for only 17,500 francs. Later the house belonged to republican politician Léon Gambetta, who died there in 1882. Marked, it stands near the railroad station.

(See Chapter 3, PARIS.)

BECKET, ST. THOMAS À (ca. 1118–1170). Fleeing to exile as a result of the dispute with Henry II that eventually was to cause his death and martyrdom, the English Archbishop of Canterbury lived in France from 1164 to 1170. During the first two years, he resided at the Cistercian abbey of **Pontigny** (Yonne). Only the abbey church, dating from 1150, remains of the monastery, which was largely destroyed during the French Revolution.

When Henry II threatened to expel the Cistercian brotherhood from England for sheltering his recalcitrant archbishop, Becket withdrew to **Sens** (Yonne), where he lived until his fateful return to England at the sixth-century Abbey of Ste-Colombe. This abbey, rebuilt since it was destroyed in 1793, stands on route N5 about two kilometers north of Sens.

Exhibit: The treasury in the Cathedral of St-Étienne, Place de la République at **Sens**, displays a faded chasuble worn by Becket as well as a less authenticated mitre (open daily; admission). In the same cathedral, the Chapel of St. Thomas of Canterbury exhibits a 12th-century stone sculpture said to have been removed from a Becket residence in Sens. This figure, several biographers believe, may well represent the most authentic portrait of the saint that exists.

(See Chapter 5, ENGLAND; also Chapter 6, LONDON.)

BERLIOZ, HECTOR (1803–1869). The birthplace of the Romantic composer is now the Berlioz Museum at 69 Rue de la République in **La-Côte-St-André** (Isère), which since 1935 has exhibited collections on his life and work. The stone house with a sloping roof, built by Berlioz' grandfather and inherited by his physician father, was the composer's home until 1821 though he returned for brief visits throughout his life. (Inquire locally for admission information.)

(See Chapter 3, PARIS; also Chapter 6, LONDON; also Chapter 8, ITALY.)

BERNADETTE OF LOURDES, ST. (1844–1879). The peasant girl Bernadette Soubirous, whose 18 visions of the Virgin Mary in 1858 were officially sanctioned by the Roman Catholic Church in 1862, achieved sainthood status in 1933, much more rapidly than most contenders. It has been suggested that perhaps this was because one of her visions seemed to confirm the dogma of the Immaculate Conception, which had been proclaimed by Pope Pius IX only four years before. Pilgrimages to **Lourdes** (Hautes-Pyrénées), her birthplace, began in 1864 though not until a decade later did the town begin to achieve renown as a healing shrine. Today Lourdes is visited by more pilgrims than any other shrine in Christendom except Rome (more than four million per year).

Bernadette was born at Boly Mill, a combined house and mill that was her mother's dowry. The mill, which was operated by her father, is now a marked structure in the Rue Bernadette-Soubirous. (Open Easter—October, daily 8:00—7:00; free.) While her family resided there until 1854, Bernadette herself lived there only at intervals; during intervening periods she lived with her nurse, Marie Laguës, at the nearby village of **Bartrès**. The old sheepfold they used as a house survives on private land. Bernadette lived there again in 1857 and 1858, just before her visions.

In Lourdes her family moved to Le Cachot ("the dungeon"), so-called because it had formerly been the town prison, in 1857 after the milling business failed. The family of six occupied one basement room in this two-story building at 15 Rue des Petits-Fossés. This was Bernadette's home at the time of her visionary experiences. Le Cachot is operated by the Congregation of Sisters of Charity. Several Masses are said there daily (open Easter—October 15, daily 10:00—12:00, 2:00—5:00; donation). In 1860, suffering from tuberculosis, Bernadette entered the Hospice of the Sisters of Charity but constant streams of visitors, plus the manual work required of her, worsened her condition.

As Sister Marie-Bernarde she entered the Convent of St-Gillard-de-Nevers at **Nevers** (Nièvre), her last home, in 1866. There, through years of increasing ill health, she was disciplined more severely than the average nun "so as not to encourage her pride" (certainly the least of her problems). Today the saint's body is displayed in a bronze and crystal coffin in the convent's Chapel of St. Joseph, Rue St-Gildard. Sick pilgrims also journey there in large numbers, guided by a staff of 40 Chevaliers of Bernadette. (Open daily; donation.)

Exhibits: Many a merchant of **Lourdes** has the saint to thank for material if not spiritual prosperity. Bernadette, in contrast, always refused money and gifts from pilgrims. Today sainthood spells thriving commerce to Lourdes; its souvenir industry (more than 700 shops) must be one of the world's largest. As for the cures, according to Father Jean Raymond, director of the Lourdes information bureau, they have numerically declined in recent years. Today the emphasis is on spiritual rather than physical healing. Day and night, however, petitioners still come to pray at the soot-blackened riverside grotto where the visions occurred. The Miraculous Grotto of Massabielle is a 47-acre sanctuary adjoining the 1889 Church of the Rosary, reached via the Esplanade des Processions, and nearby is the fountain from the curative spring that appeared near the site of the visions. A 60-yard wall of spigots dispenses water from the spring (which tests the same as Lourdes drinking water). A nearby underground basilica with a ramp for wheelchairs is jokingly called "Bernie's Drive-in." The visit of Pope John Paul II in 1983, marking the 125th anniversary of Bernadette's visions, was marred by a bomb explosion at the grotto just before his arrival; a cast-iron statue of Pontius Pilate was the only casualty of the anti-clerical group responsible. The Museum of Our Lady of Lourdes displays memorabilia of the peasant girl who found her celebrity status the worst "trial" of all. (Open daily; admission.) Signs and literature indicating the locations of all possible sites associated with the saint are impossible to miss in Lourdes.

BERNHARDT, SARAH (1844–1923). Probably the foremost tragedienne of the 19th century, the actress resided for most of her life in Paris. During almost every summer from 1887 to 1922, however, she lived at her large estate on Belle-Isle off the Brittany coast in the Bay of Biscay. Located 16 kilometers southwest of Quiberon (Morbihan), this rocky island provided the solitary grandeur she needed to renew her energies plus a place to raise her constant menagerie of animals and entertain her numerous guests. Bernhardt acquired a crumbling 17th-century fortress on the island's northwest extremity. Through the years she renovated it into a palatial mansion, adding numerous cottages and outbuildings. She also acquired the nearby château of Penhoët with its red-tiled roof to add to her domain. German occupation troops demolished these buildings when they vacated in October 1944 and few reminders of Bernhardt's opulent estate survive. The site, near the present Fort Sarah Bernhardt, is located two kilometers beyond the village of **Sauzon** on route D25.

(See Chapter 3, PARIS.)

BLUEBEARD. See GILLES DE RAIS.

CALVIN, JOHN (1509–1564). One of the leading religious reformers, from whose work most English-speaking Protestantism stems, Calvin was born Jean Cauvin at **Noyon** (Oise). It was his home until about 1520. "Even in his youth he was severe and dignified," wrote Charles Francis Potter, "so much so that his fellow Latin students nicknamed him 'the Accusative.'" Calvin's birthplace at 6 Place Aristide-Briand had disappeared by 1614, according to one source, but was reconstructed on the site in 1930 by the Society for the History of French Protestantism. Destroyed in World War II, the house was reconstructed by the City of Noyon in 1955. Handhewn beams from

BIRTHPLACE OF JOHN CALVIN. The father of "Calvinism," the stern creed from which many English-speaking Protestant denominations derived, was born at **Noyon** in 1509. Though the original dwelling shown in this old engraving has been twice reconstructed on the site, many of the materials survived and may still be seen in the house, now a museum devoted to the reformer.

the original 16th-century house as well as original ironwork and "one-way" glass in the front wall, made from the bottoms of glass bottles, were discovered and used in this reconstruction. Calvin's birth site was the large, flagstoned room on the main floor. An adjacent room hosts Sunday morning services. The house displays no original furnishings but many documents, engravings and 16th-century editions of Calvin's works. (Open daily; admission.)

At **Orléans** (Loiret), where he studied law at the University of Orléans from 1525 to 1529, Calvin lived at 10 Rue du Gros-Anneau.

In 1529 and 1530 he studied and began preaching at the University of **Bourges** (Cher). His residence was the old Augustinian convent in the Rue Mirabeau.

Exhibit: The **Noyon** Regional Museum in the Rue de l'Eveche displays a collection of Calvin memorabilia. (Inquire locally for admission information.)

(See Chapter 1, SWITZERLAND; also Chapter 3, PARIS.)

CAMUS, ALBERT (1913–1960). Conscious humanity confronting an unintelligible universe was the theme of this writer's work. The Algerian-born novelist, Resistance leader and 1957 Nobel Prize-winner made his last home, from 1957, in the tiny village of **Lourmarin** (Vaucluse). His large house in the later named Rue Albert-Camus, where he did much of his writing, remains privately owned. Camus bought this property with his Nobel Prize money.

Camus tomb: Village Cemetery, **Lourmarin**.
(See Chapter 3, PARIS.)

CASALS, PABLO (1876–1973). The cellist and composer, forced to flee his native Spain in 1936 with the onset of the Spanish Civil War, took up residence in **Prades** (Pyrénées-Orales), a town in the Pyrenees as close to Spain as he could get. From 1936 to 1940 he lived in the Grand Hotel at 102 Route Nationale. As France fell to German invasion and the Nazi-installed Vichy regime, the hotel management began complaining that the "noise" of Casals' cello was disturbing other guests, and the hotel finally locked him out.

Casals spent the duration of World War II and later (1941–49) in a modest two-story house in the town, the Villa Colette, where he occupied

two cubicles on the second floor. Comfort and privacy were minimal. "His bedroom-studio was so small," wrote biographer H.L. Kirk, "that when he was awake the only place his cello was not in danger of being tripped over was on the bed."

From 1949 to 1955, when he moved permanently to Puerto Rico, Casals rented the gardener's cottage on the grounds of the Château Valroc, a dwelling he christened "El Cant del Ocells" ("The Song of the Birds"), engraving the words in ceramic tile over the entrance.

(See Chapter 3, PARIS; also Chapter 8, SPAIN.)

CÉZANNE, PAUL (1839–1906). When Cézanne's wealthy father, a hat-maker, deeming his son an altogether useless profligate, cut his allowance Emile Zola supported the painter for several years (see the entry on Zola later in this chapter). Despite the elder Cézanne's "corrective" action, the world lost another hat-maker in the son. The notable painter's birthplace and final home was **Aix-en-Provence** (Bouches-du-Rhône), an area rich in scenic landscapes that Cézanne, in some sense, defined for our eyes through his shimmering canvases. The address where he was born is variously given as 55 Cours Mirabeau (corner of Rue Fabrot) or 28 Rue de l'Opéra; the latter was probably a temporary lodging and his actual birthplace,

THE CÉZANNE FAMILY ESTATE. Located a short distance west of **Aix-en-Provence**, the Jas de Bouffan provided a frequent refuge and work place for Paul Cézanne over a period of 40 years. Financial distress compelled him to sell it in 1899.

while the former was his childhood home—a flat above his father's hat shop—until 1844. As a resident boarder from 1852 to 1856 he attended the Lycée Bourbon, now the Lycée Mignet, in the Rue Cardinale, where he met his lifelong friend, the novelist Zola. The family's subsequent town house stood at 14 Rue Matheron.

The Jas de Bouffan ("Place of the Winds"), an 18th-century red-tile-roofed mansion on 37 acres surrounded by low walls, was purchased by Cézanne's father in 1859 for family summers and weekends. For the next 40 years the estate remained the one stable factor in the artist's existence. He spent more time painting there than in any other single place and returned often to absorb the color and scenery of house and grounds. He installed a studio there in 1862. By 1899, to his profound distress, he could no longer maintain the estate and was forced to sell it. Located about one and one-half kilometers west of the city, the mansion remains privately owned on the Roquefavour road.

In 1899 Cézanne moved into 23 Rue Boulegon where he arranged an attic studio. It was his last home and he died at this address in 1906. In 1901, however, he bought about an acre of land north of the city and built a small two-story studio, the Pavillon des Lauves. Almost daily for the rest of his life he went there by carriage or by foot to paint in the first-floor main room. "Any studio of Cézanne's," wrote Barbara Whelpton, "was everything that a romantic novel writer could hope for. . . always in disorder and full of the traditional dust and muddle." Now a museum at 9 Avenue Paul-Cézanne, the Cézanne Studio displays only two of his drawings and a gouache but an abundance of memorabilia and possessions, including his easel and palette, chair, hat and cloak, photographs, letters and several of the actual objects that he painted in his still lifes, including wineglasses, bottles and human skulls. The building has been restored, not by the city—which during Cézanne's lifetime largely ignored him—but by American admirers of the painter. (Open June—September, Wednesday—Monday 10:00—12:00, 2:30—6:00; October—May, Wednesday—Monday 10:00—12:00, 2:00—5:00; 42-21-06-53; admission.)

From 1870 to 1885 Cézanne spent much time in the nearby coastal village of l'Estaque, one of his favorite haunts, where he resided in whatever fisherman's cottage was available for rent. "The sun is so dreadful," he wrote, "that silhouettes are not only black and white but also blue, red, brown-violet."

Cézanne tomb: St-Pierre Cemetery, **Aix-en-Provence**.

Exhibits: The Granet Museum in the Place St-Jean, **Aix-en-Provence**, displays no significant work of the artist but, in a room devoted to "Cézanne and His Friends," exhibits a few of his drawings and watercolors. (Open Wednesday—Monday 10:00—12:00, 2:00—6:00; 42-38-14-70; admission.)

Suggested routes to Cézanne sites in and around Aix are signposted.

(See Chapter 3, PARIS.)

CHARLEMAGNE (742–814). One of the greatest kings in Christendom and papally designated Emperor of the West from A.D. 800, Charlemagne vastly enlarged his Frankish kingdom by conquest to include most of France, Germany and northern Italy. An effective administrator, he revived Latin culture, established schools throughout his empire and patronized the arts and sciences. Probably the illegitimate son of Pepin the Short, king of the Franks, Charlemagne's birthplace remains unknown. As king of Nuestria, which occupied the Seine region, his capital was located at **Noyon** (Oise), and there he was crowned king of the Franks in 768. None of his palaces, not even ruins, survive. As biographer Friedrich Heer points out, "Charlemagne's palace was his court, not a building. During most of his reign it was itinerant, following him as he travelled through his empire." A frequent residence, however, was his villa at **Thionville** (Moselle), where he called an assembly and partitioned his empire in favor of his three sons in 806.

(See Chapter 4, WEST GERMANY, THE NETHERLANDS; also Chapter 8, ITALY.)

CHOPIN, FRÉDÉRIC FRANÇOIS (1810–1849). The Polish-born Romantic composer lived mainly in Paris from 1831. During his eight-year affair with novelist George Sand, however, he spent five summers (1841–46) at the latter's country château in **Nohant** (see the entry on Sand later in this chapter). Some memorabilia of the composer is displayed there.

(See Chapter 3, PARIS; also Chapter 8, SPAIN.)

CLEMENCEAU, GEORGES (1841–1929). Nick-named "the Tiger" because of his ferocious political wit, the World War I prime minister (1917–20) held France together during the latter part of that period and made possible its recovery and resurgence. Results of the 1919 Paris Peace Conference led to popular disillusionment, however, and Clemenceau spent most of his last decade in retirement.

The son of a physician, his birthplace was recently occupied by a bakery at **Mouilleron-en-Pareds** (Vendée), a marked house located between the village cemetery and church. Nearby, on route N137 at **Féaule**, the Château de l'Aubraie was the ancestral estate which Clemenceau inherited from his grandfather in 1860. Farm buildings fronted the 16th-century manor house and a moat surrounded it. Until 1897, when Clemenceau's father died there, the estate was a regular and frequent retreat for the young physician-journalist.

From 1843 until 1860 the family resided at **Nantes** (Loire-Atlantique) in the Rue Crébillon.

Clemenceau made his summer retirement home after 1921 in a seaside cottage at **St-Vincent-sur-Jard** (Vendée), where he gardened in sandy soil and watched the world move toward a new war. Now the Clemenceau House-Museum, it displays the original furnishings as they appeared at the time of his death. (Inquire locally for admission information.)

Clemenceau tomb: Village cemetery, **Le Colombier** (Vendée).

Exhibit: The Museum of the Two Victories at **Mouilleron-en-Pareds**, Clemenceau's native village, displays memorabilia relating to the statesman's life and career. (Inquire locally for admission information.)

(See Chapter 3, PARIS.)

COLETTE, SIDONIE GABRIELLE (1873–1954). The writer who refused to distinguish between "normal" and "abnormal" sexuality and wrote sensitively erotic novels under her pen name "Colette," was born at **St-Sauveur-en-Puisaye** (Yonne). Her home until 1890, the house survives in the Rue des Vignes. Colette fondly described the happiness of her childhood there in *La Maison de Claudine* (1922) and *Sido* (1929). Her father's unwise financial speculations compelled the sale of this house at public auction in 1890, one of the rare sad events of her young life. The two-story dwelling with its large windows is marked by a plaque.

In 1926 the novelist bought a house in **St-Tropez** (Var) that she named La Treille Muscate ("The Muscat Vine"). Located just outside the village, it was surrounded by a small vineyard and pine grove. Colette grew roses and tangerines there during summers until she sold the property in 1938. It remains privately owned.

(See Chapter 3, PARIS.)

CURIE, MARIE SKLODOWSKA (1867–1934). The Polish-born chemist, who with her husband Pierre discovered radium, resided for most of her life in Paris. Immediately after Pierre Curie's death in 1906, however, she rented a house with garden at 6 Rue du Chemin de Fer in **Sceaux** (Hauts-de-Seine), her husband's native village. Though at first she intended to make Sceaux her final home, she abandoned the plan in 1912 when her work made a move back to Paris expedient.

Curie tomb: Village cemetery, **Sceaux**.

(See Chapter 3, PARIS.)

DEBUSSY, CLAUDE-ACHILLE (1862–1918). France's leading impressionist composer was born in a room above his parents' china chop, a tiny hole-in-the-wall place at 38 Rue au Pain, **St-Germain-en-Laye** (Yvelines), now marked by a plaque. He lived there until 1864.

During the summer of 1879, Debussy was engaged at **Chenonceaux** (Indre-et-Loire) as a pianist at the Château de Chenonceau (see the entry on Jean-Jacques Rousseau later in this chapter). There the young performer came into contact with a larger, more stimulating world of music than he had previously known; an experience, wrote biographer Edward Lockspeiser, that "I do not think we can over-rate."

(See Chapter 3, PARIS; also Chapter 5, ENGLAND; also Chapter 8, ITALY.)

DE GAULLE, CHARLES (1890–1970). A professional soldier, France's autocratic president (1959–69), and World War II leader of the Free French allies, de Gaulle was a native of **Lille** (Nord). His two-story birthplace in the ancient Flemish quarter of the city stands marked at 9 Rue Princesse. The house belonged to his maternal grandparents and his father, a teacher, soon removed the family to Paris.

CHARLES DE GAULLE AT HIS ESTATE. In 1958, just before becoming French president, the World War II hero posed outside the office tower he added to his country mansion at **Colombey-les-Deux-Églises**. De Gaulle permitted few invasions of his privacy there; even the world statesmen he assiduously cultivated were mostly excluded. In 1969 he retired there permanently.

On route N19 at **Colombey-les-Deux-Églises** (Haute-Marne), de Gaulle bought the Château de la Boisserie (originally La Brasserie, "The Brewery") in 1933 and made this wooded estate his permanent home. The climate had been recommended for his daughter Anne, who suffered from Down's syndrome and died in 1948. None of his family resided there during World War II (his wife, Yvonne, brought him the keys in London in 1940). During the war years the property suffered considerable damage, but the general made prompt repairs at the end of the war. Between 1946 and 1959 he spent an uneasy retirement on the estate, impatiently awaiting his nation's call for a savior, a role he considered himself eminently qualified to fulfill. He finally retired there again, in 1969, and died at the château a year later.

At Colombey, de Gaulle maintained an aloof distance from village people and events, and jealously guarded his privacy with firmly locked gates. The only world leader he ever invited to his estate was German Chancellor Konrad Adenauer, who came in 1958. A small portion of the 15-room house was opened to the public in 1979. De Gaulle added a hexagonal tower to the two-story stone mansion and maintained his office in the tower's ground floor. Visitors may view it behind a sealed barrier and also see the family dining room plus de Gaulle furnishings and souvenirs. (Open Wednesday—Monday 10:00—1:00, 2:00—5:00; admission.)

De Gaulle tomb: Village cemetery, **Colombey-les-Deux-Églises**.

(See Chapter 3, PARIS; also Chapter 6, LONDON.)

DESCARTES, RENÉ (1596–1650). For dividing the world into subject and object, we have Descartes to thank; he has probably been the world's most influential philosopher as far as method is concerned. "I think, therefore I am," he declared (French philosophy students satirize him by saying *coito ergo sum*—"I copulate, therefore I am"). The dualistic mode of thought, so important in science, has long been regarded by most Western cultures as the only "normal" way of viewing things; only recently are its inadequacies becoming apparent in both philosophy and science.

Descartes' birthplace is generally accepted as the farmhouse of his great-grandmother which is marked in the village of **La Haye-Descartes** (Indre-et-Loire). Some sources, however, maintain that a ditch along route N10 between Dangé and Châtellerault (Vienne) was his actual emergency birthplace.

In **Châtellerault** his later boyhood home at 126 Rue de Bourbon is well authenticated. The house, owned by his grandparents, had passed to his parents. It now contains a small museum of Descartes memorabilia. (Inquire locally for admission information.)

From 1606 to 1614 Descartes attended and resided at the Jesuit Collège de la Flèche at **La Flèche** (Sarthe). This institution, also known as Collège Henri IV, was replaced by a military preparatory school after the Jesuits were expelled in 1702, and Napoleon I organized it as a military school in 1803. Today it functions as the Prytanée Militaire. The restored chapel and college rooms may be viewed. (Open daily; guided tours 9:00—11:00, 2:00—5:00; admission.)

(See Chapter 3, PARIS; also Chapter 4, THE NETHERLANDS, SWEDEN.)

DUMAS, ALEXANDRE (*père*) (1802–1870). This massive (and massively prolific) writer, best known for his swashbuckling historical romances, was born in the two-story house now numbered 54 Rue Alexandre-Dumas in **Villers-Cotterêts** (Aisne). It was his home until his soldier father's death in 1806.

A "mass-production" writer who employed a corps of collaborators to research his novels, Dumas turned out some 300 volumes of fiction, plays and nonfiction. He produced his most popular novels, including *The Count of Monte Cristo* (1844) and *The Three Musketeers* (1844), at **St-Germain-en-Laye** (Yvelines) where he rented the Villa Médicis in 1843 and 1844. The building, now known as the Pavillon Henri-IV and a popular hotel since 1836, is a remnant of the 16th-century Château-Neuf built for Henry II and Henry IV. It stands at the southeast corner of the Jardin Anglais. French President Adolphe Thiers died there in 1877.

At nearby **Port-Marly** on route N13 stands the only house built by Dumas, who made and squandered immense sums. Le Château de Monte Cristo, named for his own favorite of his works, was one of the oddest houses ever constructed. The three-story towered structure was a mongrelized mixture displaying the gaudiest elements of at least a dozen Western and oriental architectural styles—a heavily ornate combination of French villa, rococo château and Arabian-nights fantasy. The rooms also reflected a variety of styles and furnishings. Dumas spent a fortune on the house, added a park and zoo, and orchestrated a gigantic housewarming party in 1848. He maintained a constant open house for friends and predators alike but his largesse soon bankrupted him and creditors seized the property by 1850.

Finally impoverished in 1870 and sorely afflicted, probably by syphilis, the writer stumbled to the country home of his son Alexandre in **Puys** (Seine-Maritime), announcing that he had come there to die. And there, to the astonishment of a literary world that had come to think of him as immortal, he did die. Information is lacking as to the existence and exact location of this residence.

Dumas tomb: Village cemetery, **Villers-Cotterêts**.

Exhibit: In his birthplace village of **Villers-Cotterêts**, the Alexandre Dumas Museum at 24 Rue Démoustier displays memorabilia and manuscripts of this titanic man, writer and irrepressible lover of life; and also of Dumas *fils*, his son. (Inquire locally for admission information.)

(See Chapter 3, PARIS.)

DUMAS, ALEXANDRE (*fils*) (1824–1895). See the entry on Alexandre Dumas *père* above.

(See Chapter 3, PARIS.)

EDWARD VIII (1894–1972). Immediately after his 1936 abdication as king, Britain's Edward (renamed duke of Windsor) married Wallis Warfield Simpson in the privately owned Château de Candé which stands five kilometers northwest of **Montbazon** (Indre-et-Loire). Thereafter the couple made their permanent home in France, except during the war years.

Their summer residence from 1938 to 1949 was the Château de la Croë, a villa built in about 1930 on 12 walled acres facing the Mediterranean Sea at **Cap d'Antibes** (Alpes-Maritimes). The couple undertook numerous repairs and alterations there, and the duke established his private quarters in a penthouse he named "Fort Belvedere," after his beloved former bachelor home near Windsor, England. In the late 1970s this private property, abandoned for almost 30 years, remained empty and weed-grown, as desolate, one might say, as the functional life of an ex-king.

From 1952 until the duke's death, the Windsors maintained a 26-acre summer estate they called "The Mill" (le Moulin de la Tuilerie) near the village of **Gif-sur-Yvette** (Essonne), about 20 kilometers southwest of Paris. The duke converted the large 17th-century millhouse to an English country mansion, installing furnishings brought from Fort Belvedere in England and roomfuls of his trophies and souvenirs. A retinue of 31 servants waited on the couple (the duke admitted that he had never learned to dress himself) and maintained the mixed farmland-forest acreage. The duchess never shared her husband's fondness for this estate, however, and sold it immediately after his death.

(See Chapter 3, PARIS; also Chapter 5, ENGLAND; also Chapter 6, LONDON; also Chapter 7, SCOTLAND.)

FLAUBERT, GUSTAVE (1821–1880). The novelist was a native of **Rouen** (Seine-Maritime) where his birthplace, the 1755 Hôtel-Dieu, stands at 51 Rue de Lecat. His father was surgeon-in-chief at this 15-ward hospital, an 18th-century building that now displays a Flaubert museum. As children, Flaubert and his sister would secretly climb to a ground-floor window from the garden to watch their father perform autopsies. The room where Flaubert was born and the billiard room, which the future novelist converted into a make-shift theater, may be seen as well as mementoes of his family, who lived there until 1844. (Guided tours Tuesday—Saturday, 9:00—12:00, 2:00—6:00; admission.)

THE BIRTH ROOM OF GUSTAVE FLAUBERT. In **Rouen**, this residence chamber of the local hospital, where the novelist's father was a surgeon, is displayed as a Flaubert museum.

The writer's permanent home from 1844 until his death was a riverside house at **Croisset** (Seine-Maritime). Bought by Flaubert senior as a refuge for the invalid Gustave, who was subject to epileptic-like seizures, the low white house dated from 1804 and was originally a farm belonging to the Benedictine order. Local tradition maintains that author l'Abbé Prevost wrote his *Manon Lescaut* (1731) in an earlier house on the property. Flaubert did most of his writing there, including his best-known novel *Madame Bovary* (1857). When Prussian troops occupied the village during the Franco-Prussian War in 1870, Flaubert buried his manuscripts in the garden for safekeeping. Among his visitors were Guy de Maupassant and George Sand (see the entries on Maupassant and Sand later in this chapter). In dire financial straits because of his futile attempts to rescue a son-in-law

from bankruptcy, Flaubert died of a stroke at the house. Immediately after his death, his niece sold the house and it was destroyed to make way for a distillery. More recently, biographer Philip Spencer wrote that "if Flaubert could revisit the scene of his labors, it would give him a delicious sense of the grotesque to know that. . . on the precise spot where he once wrote *Bovary*, there is now a huge and prosperous paper-factory." Today the only surviving portion of the estate is the 18th-century garden pavilion alongside the river, little used by Flaubert himself except to fish from its wrought-iron balcony, but the place where he installed his devoted friend, critic Louis Bouilhet, in the tiny room used as a study. Several large windows open upon the Seine and the garden of the house. Visitors may view Flaubert memorabilia including the large round table where he labored over his perfect sentences. The Pavillon Flaubert Museum stands at 18 Quai Gustave-Flaubert. (Open daily 10:00—12:00, 2:00—6:00; guided tours, but schedules vary so check beforehand; admission.)

Flaubert tomb: Monumental Cemetery, **Rouen**.

Exhibits: Flaubert's library, formerly at Croisset, is now preserved in the Town Hall of nearby **Canteleu** (Seine-Maritime; open daily, weekdays).

The manuscript of *Madame Bovary* is displayed in the Municipal Library of **Rouen** (open daily).

(See Chapter 3, PARIS.)

FRANCIS I (1494–1547). Ninth king in the House of Valois, which ruled France for more than two centuries, François d'Angoulême reigned for 32 years. Though an eager warrior, he is chiefly remembered as a patron of the arts—a king who imported the Italian Renaissance to France in the persons of Benvenuto Cellini and Leonardo da Vinci, among others (see the entry on Leonardo later in this chapter).

His birthplace was the castle of **Cognac** (Charente), owned by his father, Charles d'Angoulême. Today the remnants of that castle form part of a distillery warehouse in the city.

Francis spent a turbulent childhood at the château of **Romorantin-Lanthenay** (Loir-et-Cher), where ruins of the 15th-century castle owned by his family stood. In 1517 Francis commissioned Leonardo da Vinci to build a new palace astride the river Sauldre for the king's mother, Louise of Savoy; when she died, however, the project was abandoned. The royal château, of which the main residential building and a round tower remain, now contains district administrative offices and is not open to the public.

At **Amboise** (Indre-et-Loire) a castle has stood on the present site of the Château d'Amboise since A.D. 496. In 1500 Louise of Savoy and her son were assigned royal lodgings there and this fortress palace remained their home through the first three years of Francis' reign as king (1500–18). Thereafter he visited the residence at intervals but seldom resided after Leonardo's death there in 1519. Later at Amboise (1560) occurred the bloody Amboise Conspiracy in which 57 Protestant noblemen were executed under the eyes of Francis II and his queen, the later Mary, Queen of Scots (see the entry on Mary later in this chapter). Louis XIII was the last monarch to live there. The castle later served as a state prison. Most of it was demolished in the 19th century, and World War II bombs damaged the remnants. Thus the present château represents only fragments of the extensive fortress that hosted French royalty from

1434—and still does, in the person of the current Bourbon pretender, Henri d'Orléans, the Count of Paris, who maintains the palace as his official residence and established the Fondation St-Louis to preserve it. The King's Apartments, dating from 1491, are approached by a ramp from the town center. It is said that Francis, as an unruly teenager, once upset the castle routine by letting a wild boar loose in the tapestried halls, then knifing it to death on the great staircase. (Open March 16—October 31, guided tours daily 9:00—12:00, 2:00—7:00; November 1—March 15, daily 9:00—12:00, 2:00—5:30; admission.)

At **Blois** (Loir-et-Cher), the château dating originally from the 13th century became the "Versailles of the Renaissance" when Francis I built the wing named after him (1515–24); it remains the finest part of the quadrilateral castle. His first wife, Claude de France, daughter of Louis XII, had grown up in the Louis XII wing which now contains an art museum. In the Francis I wing

THE PALACE OF FONTAINEBLEAU. Francis I had his personal emblems stamped on every portion of the massive Renaissance palace he built at **Fontainebleau** (note the huge F's on two of the roof towers of the Fran-

cis I Gallery, finished in 1544). Louis XIV and Napoleon also used the palace extensively during their reigns, and it remains one of Europe's most splendid windows into the royal past of France.

may be seen the lavish rooms of Queen Catherine de Médicis (she died there in 1589) and the second-floor chambers of Henri III, in which occurred the 1588 murder of his rival, the Duc de Guise. The feudal State Room is the oldest part of the castle and served as the council hall where the States-General of 1576 and 1588 met. In 1810 the castle was being used as a barracks; restoration, begun in 1845, has resulted in one of France's most finely preserved royal châteaus. It is approached via the Place du Château. (Open February 1—March 15, daily 9:00—12:00, 2:00—5:30; March 16—September 30, to 6:30; October 1—January 31, to 5:00; admission.)

Though the castle of **Fontainebleau** (Seine-et-Marne) has existed as a royal residence from the 12th century, its present appearance owes most to Francis I who assembled a group of Italian artists to create the Renaissance palace. One of the few extant rooms of his original palace is the 210-foot-long Francis I Gallery, completed in 1544. The king's salamander emblem is conspicuous in the decoration. His royal suite in the Henry II Gallery was later occupied by the mistress and later second wife of Louis XIV, Mme. de Maintenon, and is identified by her name today. "Like many of his descendants," wrote Robert Hughes, "Francis I was a licentious monarch. Unlike them, however, he was also a clean one," as demonstrated by the series of massive bath chambers decorated with "cheerfully obscene designs of pagan deities clambering into the tub with one another." The palace consists of many distinct buildings, mostly two-story stone structures built around five courtyards and erected at various times. Henri IV and Louis XIII made large additions. Louis XIV, Marie Antoinette and Napoleon I, who restored the palace after its furnishings were scattered during the French Revolution, were among later monarchs who lived there in splendor (see the entries on Louis XIV, Marie Antoinette and Napoleon I later in this chapter). Much later, during World War II, Fontainebleau became the headquarters of German Field Marshal Walther von Brauchitsch, was liberated by American General George S. Patton in 1944 and served as NATO headquarters in Europe. Today the Louis XV wing of the palace houses the American School of Fine Arts. The forest of Fontainebleau, some 48,000 acres and formerly a royal hunting preserve, surrounds the palace and town. Entrance to the palace is gained from the Place Gén.-De-Gaulle. (Open Wednesday—Monday 10:00—12:30, 2:00—5:00; August—September, to 6:00; 6422-34-39; admission.)

Francis built another huge palace—the largest of the Loire Valley palaces—at **Chambord** (Loir-et-Cher) on the river Cosson. Not content with the abundance of royal châteaus throughout France that hosted his peripatetic court, the king desired to create his own distinctive residence, and did so. "Chambord had no excuse," wrote biographer Francis Hackett, "except that it really represented the scale of indulgence at which Francis aimed. It was, in short, to be a true domicile of absolute monarchy, of a size and a seclusion that later was held desirable for lunatic asylums." Francis demolished a royal hunting lodge at Chambord in 1519 and employed 1,800 workmen for 15 years to build his dream palace. With the help of Leonardo da Vinci, he may even have supervised the architecture. Basically of feudal design, Chambord consists of a central keep, six round towers, 440 rooms and a 14,000-acre park; the whole is enclosed by a 32-kilometer wall (the longest in France). The palace roof "looks as if Francis had said to the assembled masons, do, each of you, that which you like best to do," wrote Vivian Rowe. As a result, Chambord is one of the finest Renaissance structures in the world. By 1539 the castle was sufficiently finished to receive Holy Roman Emperor Charles V. Having completed this magnificent tribute to his own majesty, however, Francis himself seldom actually resided there; no more than a total of 36 days, according to one source. His successors made much more use of it. Louis XIV was the last monarch to stay frequently, and the dramatist Molière wrote two plays there (see the entry on Molière later in this chapter). Today, however, Francis I's ubiquitous salamander emblem still plainly indicates the claim of its builder. His bedchamber displays a 16th-century gold-embroidered bedspread, and nearby is the Hunting Room, hung with tapestries recording the king's expeditions into the surrounding forests. The palace fell into neglect and disrepair after the Revolution. It has been owned by the state since 1932 and, since 1948, has been the headquarters of the National Hunting Reserve. The decoratively sculptured apartments have been restored with period furnishings and exhibit paintings of their royal inhabitants. (Open April 1—September 30, Wednesday—Monday 9:00—11:45, 2:00—6:30; October 1—March 31, Wednesday—Monday 10:00—11:45, 2:00—4:00; admission.)*

The château at **Villers-Cotterêts** (Aisne), begun in 1522 for Francis I on the site of an earlier royal palace destroyed by the English in 1429, was completed in 1545. Though it has now been converted to a senior citizens' home, parts of the interior may be visited. There Francis delivered a famous edict in 1539 regarding domestic civil affairs. (Open daily, 8:30—10:30, 2:00—5:00; admission.)

Another occasional residence of the king was the famous Château of Chenonceau, where his bedroom is displayed (see the entry on Jean-Jacques Rousseau later in this chapter).

Francis died (probably of syphilis) in the palace of **Rambouillet** (Yvelines), which belonged to one of his officers. Later royalty often visited the residence. Most of the present castle dates from the 18th century and was restored by Napoleon III, but the 14th-century round tower in which Francis died may still be seen. Since 1897 the château has served as the official summer mansion of French presidents. (Open when president not in residence, Wednesday—Monday 10:00—12:00, 2:00—4:00 or 6:00; admission.)

Francis I tomb: Basilica, **St-Denis** (Seine-St-Denis).

(See Chapter 3, PARIS; also Chapter 8, SPAIN.)

GARIBALDI, GIUSEPPE (1807–1882). The Italian patriot who unified Italy through military conquest was actually a native of **Nice** (Alpes-Maritimes), which at that time was a part of the independent province of Savoy. His birthplace as well as the street in which it stood were demolished in 1897 to make way for the enlargement of Port Lympia, the harbor. Water covers the site on the harbor's north side.

At intervals from 1815 through the 1830s, Garibaldi resided at his parental home, "Aburarum House," at 3 Quai Lunel. Shops now occupy the ground floor of what one biographer called "a rabbit warren of a place."

Exhibit: The Masséna Museum at 65 Rue de France in **Nice**, operated by the City of Nice, displays souvenirs and various items relating to Garibaldi. (Open Tuesday—Sunday 10:00—12:00, 2:00—5:00; 93–88–11–34; admission.)

(See Chapter 8, ITALY.)

---

* *Son et lumière* (sound and light or audiovisual) performances illustrating castle history have become popular evening features at many Loire castles, including Amboise, Blois, Chambord and Chenonceau. Performances are given only on selected evenings during spring and summer. For further information, contact French tourist information centers.

GAUGUIN, PAUL (1848–1903). At **Orléans** (Loiret), one of the painter's boyhood homes, where he lived with his mother and an uncle during the years 1855–59, stood at 25 Quai Tudelle.

Gauguin first devoted himself entirely to painting in 1886 at **Pont-Aven** (Finistère); he returned to this Brittany village several times, the last time in 1894. The place was highly significant to his work, for there he found time and energy to develop his own postimpressionist style, a step toward abstract art. His main residence during these visits was the Gloanec Inn, now known as the Hôtel des Ajoncs-d'Or.

The house that Gauguin shared with the painter Vincent van Gogh in 1888 at **Arles** (Bouches-du-Rhône) was destroyed by bombing in 1944 (see the entry on van Gogh later in this chapter).

Exhibit: Numerous markers in hilly **Pont-Aven** point out sites and scenes associated with the "Pont-Aven school" of painters led by Gauguin. The Bois d'Amour, a wooded park beside the River Aven, contains signposts indicating places that inspired these painters and became immortalized on canvas.

(See Chapter 3, PARIS; also Chapter 4, DENMARK.)

GILLES DE RAIS. ("BLUEBEARD") (1404–1440). This soldier, homosexual sadist and notorious child murderer never went by the name "Bluebeard" during his lifetime (if he had a beard at all, it was probably red) but may have been the villain on whom author Charles Perrault based his 1697 folktale of the unfriendly husband of seven fatally curious brides. According to some accounts, however, Gilles de Rais was an even less savory character; some 140 boys and girls, mostly abandoned or kidnapped peasant children, allegedly fell victim to his lust. On the other hand, wrote Vivian Rowe, "to the careful investigator of the evidence, there can be very much doubt indeed whether there was even one victim." As a marshal of France, Gilles de Rais owned a number of vast estates, fought beside Joan of Arc against the English and was a generous patron of the arts until he turned to sorcery and murder. His three major castle residences in the lower Loire Valley (Loire-Atlantique) are grass-grown ruins today, but remnants may still be seen.

Gilles de Rais was born in the 11-towered castle of Champtocé, his home at intervals until 1433, and may have committed his first child murders there about 1426. Only a solitary tower of this castle remains alongside the Loire about five kilometers west of **Ancenis** on route N23.

His favorite retreat from about 1436 was a 12th-century castle owned by his wife, Catherine de Thouars. This was **Tiffauges**, the legendary principal site of his crimes. Biographer D. B. Wyndham Lewis wrote that "its remains afflict the sensitive beholder very strongly with that *malaise* radiated by ancient stones soaked in iniquity—the Tower of London has the same aura—and still whispering, as it were, of devilries they have witnessed." These ruins, including a 12th-century square keep, cover about eight acres on a high eminence overlooking the valleys of the rivers Crûme and Sèvre.

From 1433, Gilles de Rais also lodged at Machecoul Castle, now ivy-clad ruins in **Machecoul** (route D13). A large fireplace, it is said, was used for cremating (unsuccessfully) the evidence of his crimes, and some 40 children's bodies were recovered there. Gilles de Rais was arrested at Machecoul for heresy and murder in 1440.

"Only the Nuremberg trials, perhaps, can match the horrifying nature of the charges and the intensity of passion they aroused," wrote biographer Jean Benedetti. The accused murderer was imprisoned, tried and condemned at the moated castle of La Tour Neuve, now known as the Ducal Castle, in **Nantes**. Almost every French king from Charles VIII to Louis XIV spent time in this castle (see the entry on Louis XIV later in this chapter). Henri IV signed the Edict of Nantes there in 1598. While the present building dates mainly from 1466, remnants of the old castle remain in the courtyard and the moat has been reestablished. Entrance is via the Rue du Château. (Open Wednesday—Monday 10:00—12:00, 2:00—6:00; admission; Saturday—Sunday, free.)

GOETHE, JOHANN WOLFGANG VON (1749–1832).

As a young student in 1770 and 1771, the German dramatist, poet, and novelist resided in **Strasbourg** (Bas-Rhin) at 36 Rue du Vieux-Marché. It is said that he tried to overcome the vertigo from which he suffered by regularly climbing the 470-foot tower of the Cathedral of Notre-Dame that dominates the city.

Exhibits: At **Sessenheim** (Bas-Rhin), the Goethe Memorial Museum commemorates his period in Alsace with memorabilia. (Inquire locally for admission information.)

The Garinet Museum at 13 Rue Pasteur in **Châ-**lons-sur-Marne (Marne) also displays exhibits on Goethe. (Inquire locally for admission information.)

(See Chapter 1, AUSTRIA, SWITZERLAND; also Chapter 4, EAST GERMANY, WEST GERMANY; also Chapter 8, ITALY.)

GOYA Y LUCIENTES, FRANCISCO JOSÉ DE (1746–1828).

The Spanish painter whose bitter visions of war's insanity have rarely been surpassed lived as a voluntary exile in **Bordeaux** (Gironde) from 1824 until his death. He occupied three dwellings during that period: first at 38 Cours de Tourny (1824); then at 10 Rue de la Croix-blanche (1824–26); and finally, his last home, where he died, at 57 Cours de l'Indépendence (1827–28).

Exhibit: The Goya Museum in **Castres** (Tarn), located in the Town Hall, displays the painter's largest tableau and many of his etchings. (Open Tuesday—Saturday 9:00—12:00, 2:00—6:00, Sunday 10:00—12:00; admission.)

(See Chapter 8, SPAIN.)

GUTENBERG, JOHANNES (1398–1468).

Credited with the invention of movable type, the German goldsmith and printer lived and worked in **Strasbourg** (Bas-Rhin) from 1434 to 1444, making the city a main printing center of medieval Europe. His residence was the "Inn of the Crossed Swords," which probably stood somewhere in the vicinity of the Place Gutenberg where his statue now stands.

(See Chapter 4, WEST GERMANY.)

HÉLOUÏSE (1101–1164).

"It has been said of Hélouïse and Abélard," wrote Elizabeth Hamilton, "that without them the twelfth century would have been dull." The brilliant woman whose tragic romance with scholar-priest Peter Abélard resulted in her becoming a nun, spent many of her early years at the Benedictine convent of **Argenteuil** (Val d'Oise). She returned there, at Abélard's behest, after their secret marriage, and she took the nun's habit there. Argenteuil was her home from 1119 to 1129. The only trace of the convent is an old chapel on the grounds of a private house. A clinic also occupies part of the site.

Abélard, who founded the Abbey of the Paraclete near **Nogent-sur-Seine** (Aube) in 1123, gave the Paraclete property to Hélouïse and her sisterhood in 1129; this convent became her lifelong home thereafter (see the entry on Peter Abélard earlier in this chapter). There she wrote her famous letters to Abélard, communications that sound surprisingly modern in tone and concern. Though she remained devoted to him, the pair never lived together as husband and wife.

Exhibit: The Old **Argenteuil** Museum at 5 Rue Pierre-Guierme displays pictures and memorabilia of one of history's less enthusiastic brides of the church. (Inquire locally for admission information.)

(See Chapter 3, PARIS.)

HUGO, VICTOR (1802–1885). Countless streets and squares throughout France memorialize Hugo's name.* A "Renaissance man" of the 19th century, this noted novelist and liberal politician was born at **Besançon** (Doubs), where he lived during his first year. His birthplace structure stands marked at 138 Grande-Rue and is now a bistro.

Exhibits: **Villequier** (Seine-Maritime) was the scene of the 1843 boating accident in which Hugo's eldest daughter, Léopoldine Vacquerie, was drowned with her husband and two others. The Vacquerie house on the quay, where Hugo grieved for his daughter, is now the Victor Hugo Museum and contains some original furnishings, memorabilia, letters and portraits. (Inquire locally for admission information.)

At **Besançon** the Historical Museum, 94-96 Grande-Rue, displays memorabilia of the town's famous son. (Inquire locally for admission information.)

(See Chapter 3, PARIS; also Chapter 4, BELGIUM, LUXEMBOURG; also Chapter 5, ENGLAND.)

JOAN OF ARC, ST. (1412–1431). Among historians, this visionary peasant girl turned soldier remains almost as controversial a figure five centuries after her martyrdom as she was at the time of her execution in Rouen. "Was she a nationalist or an armed nun," pondered Sanche de Gramont, "a mental case or a visionary touched by grace, a martyr or a charlatan, the first lady general or, as the Soviet encyclopedia sees her, a Communist freeing her people? Three thousand books have been written about her, some of whose authors apparently hope they too will hear voices." To the

Roman Catholic church—which condemned her to death for, among other things, wearing men's clothing, then reversed its opinion 25 years later—she is a saint. Whatever may be the final verdict on her actions and their significance, she was obviously a much more complex person than the simple Norman peasant girl that some mythologizers have tried to make of her. One thing Joan was not, however, was French; nor did she ever consider herself to be, for her native province of Lorraine was not annexed to the kingdom until more than three centuries after her death. Still, she continues to be used as a shining example for just about anything that the French (and others too) need shining examples for.

Her birthplace at **Domremy-la-Pucelle** (Vosges), a gray-stone four-roomed cottage in the village, survives and has long been an object of pilgrimage. In recent years some 400,000 annual visitors have journeyed to the scene. The daughter of Jacques d'Arc, himself the leading man of the community, Joan performed mostly indoor domestic chores at her home until 1429, when her impelling "voices" took charge of her life and cast her in the unlikely role of savior of the English-beleaguered French monarchy. While her birthplace, which faces the Meuse bridge within a grassy enclosure, has been restored numerous times, first in 1481, it remains basically the same structure she knew. Her collateral descendants lived there as late as the 19th century, when the Vosges department acquired and again restored it. (Open daily; admission.)

Joan's subsequent dwellings were mainly fortress castles or prisons. In 1429 at **Chinon** (Indre-et-Loire), she convinced the wavering dauphin, later crowned Charles VII because of Joan's intervention, that he was the true king of France—her voices had told her so—and persuaded him to let her lead his troops to the relief of Orléans. The site of this notable peptalk was the Great Hall of the 11th-century Château of Milieu, Charles's residence, which today is the central of three castle ruins overlooking the town. Henri II had died there in 1189, and the castle was often rebuilt and extended. The tower in which Joan lodged for six weeks on the first floor is part of the Château of Caudray, which lies west of the central castle. From there Joan marched to Orléans and her destiny. In the "Tour de l'Horloge," or watchtower, of the château the Jeanne d'Arc Museum displays relics and memorabilia. The castles surmounting

---

* Though runners-up for this distinction include politicians Georges Clemenceau and Charles de Gaulle, in few other countries will one find such universal street-naming in honor of writers (except, of course, for the Soviet satellites' adulation of Karl Marx)—a revealing indication of French intellectual priorities.

HOME OF JOAN OF ARC. The stone cottage birthplace of one of France's most venerated historical figures remains essentially unchanged at **Domremy-la-Pucelle**. When she left here in 1429 it was at the behest of inner "voices" that impelled her to turn soldier and come to the aid of a weak monarch, an action that led first to her trial on charges of heresy, and then to her canonization—only one anomaly of many in the still-controversial life of the maid.

the town are approached via the Rue du Puy-des-Bancs. The *son et lumière* (audiovisual) performance of "Jeanne de France" is presented there on summer evenings. (Open March 15—September 30, daily 9:00—12:00, 2:00—7:00; October 1—March 14, Thursday—Tuesday 9:00—12:00, 2:00—5:30; closed December—January; admission.)

Following her triumphant lifting of the year-long English siege of **Orléans** (Loiret), an event annually celebrated there on May 8, Joan resided in the city during April and May of 1429. The "Jeanne d'Arc House" in the Place Charles-De-Gaulle, where she is said to have lodged, displays exhibits relating to Joan and the type of weapons and warfare she employed. (Open May 1—October 31, Tuesday—Sunday 10:00—12:00, 2:00—6:00; November 1—April 31, Tuesday—Sunday 2:00—6:00; admission.)

The warlike maiden moved rapidly after that,

defeating the English in various battles, hounding a reluctant Charles VII to his coronation at Reims, dodging the king's jealous courtiers and military experts (worse enemies, ultimately, than the English), and finally being captured by Burgundians at Compiègne and sold by them to the English, who regarded her as a witch. In **Rouen** (Seine-Maritime), she was imprisoned in chains in the castle of Philip-Augustus. Foundations of the tower in which she was held in 1430 and 1431 are marked in the Rue Jeanne d'Arc.

Exhibits: "Each generation," wrote Gramont, "has reinvented a Joan to suit its times." Next to Napoleon, nobody in France is so widely memorialized with museums and site markers as the maid. The Jeanne d'Arc Museum adjacent to her birthplace in **Domremy-la-Pucelle** displays material on her life. (Open daily; admission.) Also near Domremy, about two kilometers south, is the Basilica of the Bois-Chênu, erected in the 19th century on one of the spots where, at age 13, Joan began hearing those imperative "voices." (Inquire locally for admission information.) About three kilometers north of the village stands the forest chapel at **Bermont** where Joan prayed each Saturday before a 14th-century statue of the Madonna.

More relics of the maid are displayed at the Jeanne d'Arc Museum in the 16th-century Town Hall at **Riom** (Puy-de-Dôme). (Inquire locally for admission information.)

The house of the States-General at 44 Place St-Maurice in **Chinon** also displays relics (see the entry on Richard I, Coeur de Lion later in this chapter).

Joan's military career ended at **Compiègne** (Oise) when she was pulled off her horse near the present railroad station (Rue de la Gare) and imprisoned temporarily in the 12th-century Tour Jeanne d'Arc (also called the Tour Beauregard) in the Rue Jeanne d'Arc.

In **Rouen**, the 1204 Joan of Arc Tower in the Rue du Donjon displays the dismal room where she was questioned and verbally harassed by princes of the church. (Open Friday—Wednesday 10:00—12:00, 2:00—5:00; admission.) The approximate spot where she was burned at the stake on May 30, 1431, is marked by the Cross of the Rehabilitation in the Place du Vieux Marché. Excavations have uncovered the actual pillory foundation a short distance north of the monument. An adjacent museum in the square celebrates her life in a series of waxwork groups. (Open April 1—October 30, daily 9:00—7:00; November 1—March 31, daily 10:00—12:00, 2:00—7:00; admission.)

Of the numerous biographies and treatments of Joan of Arc by objective scholars and revisionists alike, W. S. Scott's *Jeanne d'Arc* (1974) is notable for its detailed itineraries and maps, useful for anyone wishing to retrace the maid's steps.

(See Chapter 5, ENGLAND.)

JOYCE, JAMES (1882–1941). The avant-garde novelist's final home in France (he had lived for 20 years in Paris) was the Hôtel de la Paix in the village of **St-Gérand-le-Puy** (Allier), where he took his family in 1939 and from which he fled the German invasion of France in 1940. The hôtel stands in the Route Nationale.

(See Chapter 1, SWITZERLAND; also Chapter 3, PARIS; also Chapter 7, IRELAND; also Chapter 8, ITALY.)

KAZANTZAKIS, NIKOS (1885–1957). The Greek novelist and poet, an inveterate world traveler, spent most of his final years from 1949 in **Antibes** (Alpes-Maritimes), where he occupied the Villa Manolita at 8 Rue du Bas-Castelet.

(See Chapter 8, GREECE.)

LAFAYETTE, MARIE JOSEPH GILBERT, MARQUIS DE (1757–1834). Aristocrat, major-general in the American Revolution and liberal influence in French politics throughout his long public career, the soldier-statesman was born in the Château of **Chavaniac** (Haute-Loire), his home until 1768 and frequent summer residence thereafter. Purchased and restored by the Lafayette Memorial Fund in 1916, the house became a convalescent home for French soldiers during World War I and later an orphanage. Thirteen bedrooms of the château carry the names of the 13 original United States, which would probably never have achieved independence without French aid.

Following his forced exile from France in 1799, Lafayette purchased the 16th-century château and 800-acre estate of La-Grange-Bléneau as his permanent home. The inheritance of his wife, the remarkable Adrienne d'Ayen Lafayette, paid for it. Though he farmed 500 of the acres and introduced American corn and tobacco to France as well as modern fertilization methods, Lafayette's fields and orchards never produced much profit. He isolated himself from Napoleonic intrigues in his twin-turreted, moated castle, and returned to public life only after the emperor's downfall in 1815. Today the privately owned château retains his library. It stands south off route N4, two kilometers south of **Rozay-en-Brie** (Seine-et-Marne).

(See Chapter 3, PARIS.)

LA SALLE, ROBERT CAVELIER, SIEUR DE (1643–1687). The explorer of North America, who claimed the Mississippi River Valley for France in 1682 and named it Louisiana after Louis XIV, was a native of **Rouen** (Seine-Maritime), his home until 1658. His family, prosperous wholesale merchants, probably lived somewhere in the Rue du Gros Horloge. World War II bombing destroyed the church of St-Herbland where he was baptized.

From 1660 to 1663 La Salle attended and resided at the Collège Henri IV at **La Flèche** (see the entry on René Descartes earlier in this chapter), originally intending to become a Jesuit priest.

Having achieved a poor record as student and teacher, he was released from his vows in 1667. (See Chapter 3, PARIS.)

LAWRENCE, DAVID HERBERT (1855–1930). The controversial English novelist, several of whose books were banned in England, spent his last tubercular months (1929–30) in **Bandol** (Var) where he wrote his last work, *Apocalypse* (1931), in the Villa Beau Soleil, a six-room house overlooking the sea; and in the health resort town of **Vence** (Alpes-Maritimes) where he died in a house called the Villa Robermond (later known as the Villa Aurella). It was demolished in 1968.

(See Chapter 5, ENGLAND; also Chapter 6, LONDON; also Chapter 8, ITALY.)

LEONARDO DA VINCI (1452–1519). The greatest artistic figure of the Italian Renaissance was brought to France in 1516 by Francis I, who installed him as "First Painter, Engineer and Architect to the King" near his palace at **Amboise** (Indre-et-Loire; see the entry on Francis I earlier in this chapter). Leonardo's projected engineering tasks for the king were so enormous that none of them got off his drawing board; he also worked on plans for expanding the châteaus of Amboise and Chambord. After 1517, when he suffered a stroke, he worked on scientific studies for a flying machine. But "of all his work in those last years," wrote biographer Robert Wallace, "it can at best be said that Leonardo puttered about at the things that interested him most." Even crippled and half-paralyzed, however, he forged centuries ahead of his time with his creative ideas and inspirations of this period. Le Clos-Lucé, the 15th-century three-story brick manor where Leonardo spent these final years and died, has been restored with period furnishings and displays drawings, models, reproductions and representative collections of his life and work. Only the manor kitchen remains much as the artist knew it; during winter evenings he spent hours there near the fire. Underground remnants of a tunnel that connected the house with the Château of Amboise also survive. Count Hubert de Saint-Bris operates the manor, which stands at the eastern end of the Rue Victor-Hugo. (Guided tours daily, 9:00—12:00, 2:00—7:00; closed January; admission.)

Leonardo da Vinci tomb (reputed): Chapel of St-Hubert, Château of Amboise, **Amboise**.

(See Chapter 3, PARIS; also Chapter 8, ITALY.)

LOUIS XIV (1638–1715). Embodying the age of absolutism in his resplendent power and person, the "sun king" demanded brilliant reflections of his glory in all his surroundings. Both he and his age regarded kingship as a matter of "divine right": a deliberate act of God rather than an accident of birth. For many centuries the sense of profound individual responsibility inculcated by this belief helped restrain the behavior of even the most vain and tyrannous of European monarchs.

Louis was born at the royal Château of **St-Germain-en-Laye** (Yvelines) where his father, Louis XIII, died in 1643. This palace was actually the Château-Neuf, not the surviving 16th-century Château-Vieux, and it remained his favorite residence and seat of the French court until the palace of Versailles was built. The Château-Neuf, built by Henri IV, stood below the present palace until 1776 when it was demolished. The only surviving portions are the Pavillon Henri-IV, where Louis XIV was baptized and the Treaty of St-Germaine was signed between the Allies and the Austrian monarchy in 1919 (see the entry on Alexandre Dumas, *père*, earlier in this chapter); and the Pavillon Sully. The Château-Vieux, rebuilt by Francis I from 1539 to 1548 on the site of the 12th-century palace of Louis VI and incorporating the 1368 keep built by Charles V, had been the childhood home of Mary, Queen of Scots (see the entry on Mary later in this chapter) and also provided a 1689 refuge for the exiled English king, James II, who died there in 1701. The Château-Vieux was used by French royalty as a summer residence from the 12th century on. Inside the château, the Salle de Mars was used by Louis XIV for grand receptions and theatrical productions, for which Molière and his company often performed (see the entry on Molière later in this chapter); and the king also occupied a suite of rooms. It was there, apparently, that Louis had his first extramarital affair with one Mlle. de la Motte-Housancourt. Later, as king, he installed his mistress, Mme. de Montespan, in ground-floor rooms of the queen's wing. Revolutionists stripped the château of furnishings, and it became in turn a military school, barracks and prison. Napoleon III converted it to a museum, vastly altering the interior, and today this surviving palace overlooking a bend of the Seine houses the Museum of National Antiquities. It displays items dating from prehistoric, Roman and Merovingian Gallic periods. (Open Wednesday—Monday

9:45—12:00, 1:30—5:15; admission.)

The Château of **Fontainebleau** was a favorite hunting resort of the king; he often stayed there during the month of October. Louis XIII had been born there in 1601 and many mementos of both him and Louis XIV are on view. The Salon de St-Louis in the 13th-century keep of Louis IX's original palace was the bedchamber of kings until the 17th century. It is said that Louis XIV signed the 1685 Revocation of the Edict of Nantes, which led to a Huguenot bloodbath in France, in the first-floor salon of Mme. de Maintenon, his second (morganatic) wife. These finely furnished apartments occupy the original suite of Francis I.

Louis stayed at the Château of **Chambord** nine times, but seldom after 1685. His first-floor apartments exhibit tapestries, paintings and furnishings of the Restoration (1821) period. Also on the first floor may be seen the hall where the king summoned premiere performances of two comedies by Molière in 1669 and 1671. On both occasions the quaking playwright viewed the monarch's icy solemnity with distress but finally managed to make him laugh—an achievement that automatically made a play a "hit" in those days. (See the entry on Francis I earlier in this chapter for the châteaus of Fontainebleau and Chambord.)

The immense 14th-century moated Château of Vincennes, rectangular in outline with nine square towers (only one of which survives), was not a frequent residence of the king and his court during Louis's reign, though all French kings from Louis VII to Louis XVI occupied it for greater or lesser intervals. Louis XIV used it mainly as a base for hunting parties but deserted it after his move to Versailles. He did, however, spend his unwilling honeymoon with Queen Marie-Thérèse there in 1660. This castle of dark forbidding aspect has seen much history, including the birth of Charles V (1337) and the deaths of Louis X (1316), Charles IV (1328), Henry V of England (1422), Charles IX (1574) and Cardinal Mazarin (1661). During and after the reign of Louis XIII, the 170-foot keep housed important state prisoners, including Denis Diderot, the Marquis de Sade and the Comte de Mirabeau (see the entry on Sade later in this chapter). A porcelain factory, cadet school and arsenal successively occupied portions of the castle, which was converted to a fortress in 1840. The Dutch spy Mata Hari was executed by a firing squad there in 1917. Its bloodiest episode,

however, occurred in 1944. Three days before German troops evacuated the castle, having used it as a supply depot, they shot 26 hostages against the interior of the ramparts. Restoration of the château, located in the Avenue de Paris in **Vincennes** (Val-de-Marne), proceeds sporadically. (Open Wednesday—Monday, 10:00—12:00, 2:00—5:00; admission.)

More volumes have been written about the Château of Versailles, the splendor of its buildings and gardens and the opulent lifestyles of its residents, than any other European castle. Younger by far than most French royal palaces and more than the monument to his own reign intended by Louis XIV, this "crown jewel of Europe" symbolizes the pomp and power of monarchy in days when kings were seen as being chosen by God. In 1624 Louis XIII had built a "small" hunting lodge on a low hill—a two-story manor of 20 rooms flanked by two wings—on the former site of a windmill. He used it as a hermitage. His son made only fleeting appearances there as king until 1661 when he chose the site ("a thankless place," wrote Saint-Simon, "without a view, without water, without soil") as a refuge for his court and France's civil government from the unpredictable tempers of Paris. He chose Versailles rather than Vincennes, according to biographer John B. Wolf, "to show the world that the King of France could build in the open. His soldiers were his defense; he needed neither walls nor moat to guarantee his security." The immediate impetus for construction, however, may have been the king's jealousy of an extravagant château built by his minister of finance, Nicolas Fouquet, at Vaux-le-Vicomte (Seine-et-Marne). Fouquet's pocketing of royal funds for his château (which survives) gave Louis sufficient excuse to banish him and hire Fouquet's architect, Louis Le Vau, and his landscapist, André Le Nôtre, for the work at Versailles.

The work began in 1669 but continued throughout Louis's reign, impoverishing France (about $1.5 billion, six out of every ten francs collected in taxes, was spent but Louis burned the accounts) and employing some 36,000 workers. The remodeled château of Louis XIII, set within 15,000 acres of gardens, groves and lawns, became the nucleus of the complex which centered on the innermost courtyard (Cour de Marbre). The present vast outlines of the château and gardens were mostly complete by 1688. The total 634-yard length of the château includes 150-yard-long north and south wings, built to house the royal family and princes of the blood. Some 2,000 rooms housed 1,000 favored noblemen plus their retinues, while the daily population of the château numbered about 10,000. The court routine at Versailles was precise and inflexible, embodying countless rules of etiquette whose mastery was the sole occupation of the courtiers, all of whom were roomed and boarded by the king. "Court etiquette was a life study," wrote W. H. Lewis. Matters of correct seating and precedence virtually outshone all other concerns, and a personal *faux pas*, or a frown from the king, was ample cause for banishment from the court and the loss of its all-important status. By surrounding himself with his nobles and making them utterly dependent upon his favors, Louis virtually eliminated noble opposition in France. The palace atmosphere, naturally enough, was constantly fraught with subtle intrigues, devious politics and tense conformity to the rigidly stratified "pecking order."

Versailles became the ideal model for almost all European courts, and for two centuries foreign monarchs judged their own performance on how well they emulated the pomp if not the palace of Versailles. Louis himself wrote a sort of guidebook to the gardens, specifing the "proper" route to view them to best advantage, and he sometimes conducted such tours. According to W. H. Lewis, however, "Louis rarely strolled at Versailles, for even he seems to have felt the oppression of those vast formal spaces in which the gravel burnt through the shoes in summer, and through which oozed black mud in winter." Of the gardens, said Saint-Simon, "One admired and avoided them."

A modern observer, Margaret Crosland, raises more modern concerns: "The dirtiness of Versailles must have been terrible and solemn. . . . the thing that strikes me, if we think of the Versailles of the period, is the luxury and the lack of comfort. Why should there be such a lack of comfort among people who were so clever with water and light? Because comfort consisted of beauty. They washed only their eyes, so to speak." So the draughts, dirt and odors in this grandest palace of them all were not very important nuisances.

One would never know of such problems at Versailles today, of course. Louis XIV's personal suites are located in the oldest, central portion of the château on the north side of the first floor. The king's bedchamber overlooks the inner courtyard at the central point of the palace. His nightly retirement and morning ablutions in this room

THE HEART OF 17TH-CENTURY EUROPE. Today, as during the reign of Louis XIV, the halls and courts of the Palace of **Versailles** swarm with people. The central court with its original pavement, shown in this 1984 view, was a highly restricted area when Louis XIV and, later, Marie Antoinette lived here. The oldest, central portion of the palace, shown in the background, was also its nerve center. The king's private chambers were located behind the three topmost windows—the "center of the center." Standing on the balcony here in 1789, Marie Antoinette and Louis XVI tried to appease a furious Revolutionary mob, but their efforts were too litlle and too late.

were ceremonial occasions ruled by rigid etiquette and requiring the presence of valets, mirror holders, wigmakers, numerous other "gentlemen of the bedchamber" and favored courtiers. The king also lunched daily in this room. Seated at a square table in front of the middle window, he was observed not only by a favored audience of courtiers but by a moving queue of just about anyone decently dressed who had driven out from Paris for the occasion. W. H. Lewis thought the occasions rare when Louis ever tasted hot food, so lengthy were his meal preparations and so distant lay the palace kitchens from his chamber. Louis XIV died in this room, and Louis XVI, ill-fated husband of Marie Antoinette, was the last monarch to sleep there. The nearby Salon de Mercure was the king's card room during his reign, and he lay in state there for eight days following his death. In the nearby council chamber, several times enlarged and dating in its present form from 1753, the king met his ministers three mornings a week; the apparent informality of these sessions contrasted starkly with the general tenor of life at Versailles. Today in this chamber is displayed the desk on which the Treaty of Versailles, recognizing American independence, was signed in 1783.

THE BEDROOM OF LOUIS XIV. Most 17th-century European kingdoms revolved to a greater or lesser extent around this central chamber in the Palace of **Versailles**. Fawning courtiers crowded the "sun king's" every waking moment. Two of his most important daily rituals occurred in this room: his morning ablutions and his evening retirement, each aided by squads of servants whose meticulous duties toward the king's person were governed by a fantastically rigid etiquette. Privacy was clearly not a royal priority. After a 72-year reign, Louis XIV died in this huge canopied bed.

On the rare occasions when Louis dined privately, it was in the king's antechamber on the opposite (south) side of the central palace. Nearby are the apartments of Mme. de Maintenon, furnished by the king in 1682 for the mistress who would become his second wife the following year. Her bedchamber, which also became the king's working retreat and where most state business was transacted, probably saw more of him during the afternoons and evenings than any other palace room; in his later years he even breached etiquette to dine there twice a week. The king's unfortunate first wife, Marie-Thérèse, died in the queen's chamber in 1683. All of these rooms, as well as many others, contain notable art works and furnishings, though relatively few of the originals that decorated Versailles.

Probably the palace's best-known room is the Gallery of Mirrors, the 235-foot-long hall begun in 1678 whose mirrors reflect the light from the 17 windows that overlook the park at the back of the château. This long room has witnessed numerous important historical ceremonies. William I of Prussia was crowned German emperor there in 1871. The peace treaty ending World War I was signed there by Clemenceau, Orlando, Lloyd George and Woodrow Wilson in 1919. In 1982 the European economic summit conference of Western leaders met in this chamber. During the

reign of Louis XIV it was the scene of fetes and grand receptions that became the gossip of Europe.

After the death of Louis XIV, interior alterations and redecorations proceeded under Louis XV. Notables born in the palace include Louis XV, Louis XVI, Louis XIII and Charles X. Louis XV and Mme. de Pompadour, his mistress, also died there. Royal residence ended at Versailles with the mob arrest of Louis XVI and Marie Antoinette in 1789 (see the entry on Marie Antoinette later in this chapter). By 1792 the lavish rooms had been stripped almost bare by revolutionaries. King Louis-Philippe preserved the château from destruction in the 19th century by converting it to an art museum (the art was appallingly bad), and much of the interior was rudely destroyed and transformed, though the royal chambers themselves were left intact.

In 1923 American financier John D. Rockefeller, Jr., donated money to begin restoration; the proceedings were interrupted during World War II when German and then Allied troops occupied the palace. Immediately after the war, prominent Nazi war criminals were held at the palace to await transportation to the Nuremberg trials. The Rockefeller family resumed a fund-raising drive for restoration of the palace, and some $75 million has been spent since 1950. Restoration at Versailles is continuous; more than 60 rooms are now open to the public and some original furnishings have been located and returned.

"To understand Versailles fully," wrote Christopher McIntosh, "it is necessary to appreciate that the whole complex is a kind of symbolic Utopia in which one theme is constantly emphasized: that of a solar deity around which everything revolves, just as the state revolves around the king."

Behind the château the immense gardens of Versailles, today basically reflecting the changes wrought by Louis XV and Louis XVI, form a geometric landscape of planned vistas, tree-lined walks, groves, ponds, terraces, statuary and fountains. North of the Grand Canal, a 20-minute walk from the palace, is the Grand Trianon, a "miniature" pink and green marble palace of 72 rooms built for Louis XIV in 1687. Even the sun king tired of the incessant formality of the court life he had instituted and he erected this scaled-down palace for his own pleasure: "I have made Versailles for the court, Marly for my friends and Trianon for myself," he said. The Grand Trianon was erected on the site of an earlier pavilion built for Mme. de Montespan, the king's mistress for 12 years and mother of eight of his children. The Salon des Glaces, the Chambre de Monseigneur later used by Louis-Philippe, the Salon de la Chapelle and the Salle des Princes made up the first suite of Louis XIV. The apartments of Mme. de Maintenon, subsequently occupied by Mme. de Pompadour, mistress of Louis XV, and later by Napoleon I, display furnishings of the latter dweller (see the entry on Napoleon later in this chapter). Since the 1966 restoration of the Grand Trianon (first restored in 1925), it has hosted visiting prime ministers and heads of state. In 1982, when Ronald Reagan stayed there, six antiaircraft missiles ringed the park to "protect" the American president (from Communist-trained pigeons, according to one theory). So Versailles still has its exotic moments.

In **Versailles** (Yvelines) the palace is approached via the 17th-century Place d'Armes and the visitors' entrance, the Vestibule Gabriel off the outer courtyard (Cour Royale). The entire complex of château, parks and gardens needs more than a day for even cursory inspection; crowds become especially heavy between Easter and late September. Since certain suites are off-limits to unescorted individuals, more of the château can be seen via group tours; these may be either previously reserved or assembled on the spot and are conducted in French and English. (State apartments open daily 10:00—5:00; group tours 12:30—2:30; call 6-950-38-32 for information and reservations; admission; gardens open dawn to dusk; free.)

The king's need for "quiet retreats" from Versailles is understandable, but though far smaller, most of them came to rival Versailles in terms of opulent splendor. One such was the Château of Marly which consisted of a large palace plus 12 smaller lodges and was elaborately landscaped. Construction began about 1679 and was largely completed by 1685, though work continued for many years. It was a singular mark of favor to be invited to Marly with the king, and courtiers intrigued and competed for the honor. Etiquette was somewhat relaxed there; the sun king apparently enjoyed food battles at his table, tossing pieces of bread at his guests. On one occasion, an observer wrote, a maid of honor "was slightly hurt by the impact of some pieces of fruit thrown by the king, and she retorted by hurling at his head a whole dish of dressed salad"—thus the sport of kings. "Marly had some of the characteristics of a mod-

ern motel," wrote John B. Wolf, "but on a scale fit for a king." Louis XIV became increasingly fond of Marly, and his visits grew longer and more frequent as he aged. At Marly in 1715 he was seized by the blood poisoning that was to kill him three weeks later at Versailles. Stripped during the Revolution, the building housed a cotton mill by 1800, and the château was demolished for its materials in 1808. Remnants of the famed hydraulic "Machine de Marly," built in 1681 to lift water from the Seine to the fountains and pools of Versailles, were finally dismantled in 1967 and only vestiges of the former arbors and park remain. A few stones and a hummock mark the palace site at **Marly-le-Roi** (Yvelines) on route D7.

Louis XIV tomb (site): Basilica, **St-Denis** (Seine-St-Denis).

Exhibit: Memorabilia of the king's longtime mistress and second wife, Mme. de Maintenon, may be seen in the Château of **Maintenon** (Eure-et-Loire), a palace given to her by Louis XIV in 1674. Parts of the structure date from the 13th century. Restored from damage suffered in 1940, the property is owned by the Noailles family, heirs of Mme. de Maintenon. (Open Wednesday—Monday 2:00—5:30; admission.)

(See Chapter 3, PARIS.)

MARIE ANTOINETTE (1755–1793). In 1770 the Austrian Hapsburg princess married France's Bourbon dauphin, who as Louis XVI succeeded to the throne in 1774, and thus sealed an alliance between the two countries. Because of a genital defect and extreme shyness about it, the king was unable to consummate their marriage until 1777 when he finally consented to undergo a simple operation. The royal couple remained oblivious of the gathering storm clouds, harbingers of the 1789 Revolution. As queen, Marie Antoinette aroused fierce hostility in the populace for her extravagance and flippant passion for luxury while the nation went bankrupt, earning the nickname "Mme. Deficit."

Her betrothed received the princess in 1770 at the then unfinished palace of **Compiègne** (see the entry on Napoleon I later in this chapter). After 1786 the royal couple often resided there. The apartments of Marie-Antoinette display the furniture designed for these rooms by Jacob-Desmalter.

The Château of **Versailles** was her chief residence both before and after she became queen (see the entry on Louis XIV above). In the first-floor

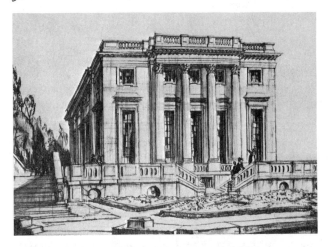

MARIE ANTOINETTE'S FAVORITE RESIDENCE. The Petit Trianon at **Versailles** was originally built for Louis XV and his mistress, Mme. de Pompadour. This little palace stands in the gardens of Versailles Palace and displays many of Marie Antoinette's furnishings.

queen's chamber of the central building, where Queen Marie-Thérèse died in 1683 and Queen Marie Leczinska died in 1768, Marie Antoinette bore her children. She used the Petits Appartements nearby as her private suite, where she slept, received friends, conferred with her dressmaker and sat for portraits. The Salon des Nobles was her official reception chamber and in the next-door antechamber she dined in public. Three of her Swiss guards died in her defense in the adjacent guardroom on October 6, 1789, when the revolutionary mob burst in. All of these rooms have been finely restored to their lavish prerevolutionary appearance and display articles and furnishings that belonged to the queen as well as portraits, tapestries and statuary. From the balcony of the king's chamber, the palace's central room, Marie Antoinette and her husband showed themselves to the courtyard mob on that fateful October day. The time was long past, however, when a condescending appearance would placate the rage swelling from the Cour de Marbre and from the country as a whole. The royal pair were escorted to Paris to face the real world for the first time in their absurdly sheltered lives.

In the immense gardens of Versailles Marie Antoinette also kept two "country retreats" where she often escaped the ceremonial rigors of the palace. The Petit Trianon, a small two-story palace built between 1762 and 1768 for Louis XV and Mme. de Pompadour, was a favorite residence; it also housed Mme. du Barry and, later, Napoleon's sister, Pauline Borghese. It has been recently renovated, and visitors may see the furnishings Marie

Antoinette selected for her informal surroundings. Nearby stands the 1780 theater where the queen and her "company of lords" indulged her fondness for acting in amateur dramatics. (Petit Trianon and theater open daily 2:00—6:00.) The queen was resting in a grotto beside the nearby octagonal Belvedere pavilion in 1789 when told that a Paris mob had stormed Versailles.*

Further north of the Petit Trianon stands the mock-rustic Hameau, a sort of toy farm-village where the queen liked to play milkmaid. She seldom did more than languidly churn butter, though, leaving the real work of the place to real peasants. Her "farmhouse" displays several stylish rooms.

At **Fontainebleau**, another frequent royal residence, Marie Antoinette's apartments were in a 16th-century portion of the château. She used the present music room as her card room. The bedroom was occupied by every French queen from Marie de Médicis to the Empress Eugénie; it is sometimes called "the chamber of the six Maries" for that reason.

In the Château of **Rambouillet**, which Marie Antoinette found unbearably dull ("a Gothic toadhole"), she occupied the east wing while Louis XVI took the west. The queen's dairy on the grounds, a two-room pavilion, was erected in 1787 so that her majesty could play farmgirl. (For the châteaus of Fontainebleau and Rambouillet, see the entry on Francis I earlier in this chapter.)

"Madame, it is only a bagatelle," said Marie Antoinette's brother-in-law, the Comte d'Artois (later Charles X), who built the Bagatelle, a little domed villa, in 64 days as the result of a wager with the queen that he could do so. The count spent far more than the 100,000-livre bet to indulge his fancy. He presented the finished house to Marie Antoinette in 1777 and she used it for stopovers between Paris and Versailles. Nineteenth-century alterations modified the exterior and hid the dome, but the interior with its salon, billiard room and music room display the carved paneling and Pompeian style popular at the end of the 18th century. During the Revolution it

---

* Probably the most unusual visit to Versailles ever recorded was that of two sober respectable English schoolteachers in 1901. Annie Moberly and Eleanor Jourdain lost their bearings in the Trianon area of the gardens and experienced what they believed was a psychic time regression. They claimed to have observed buildings, persons and landscape features of the gardens which after painstaking documentary research they later dated to the year 1789. They published their account, *An Adventure*, in 1911. The matter has never been satisfactorily explained and remains part of the endlessly intriguing lore of Versailles.

became a tavern and later a private residence. The City of Paris acquired it in 1905. In addition to waterfalls and romantic grottoes, its 60-acre park contains one of Europe's most famous rose gardens, dating from the 18th century. It is at its most spectacular in mid-June. The Bagatelle stands in the Place de Bagatelle at **Neuilly-sur-Seine** (Yvelines) on Paris's western outskirts. (Open daily, 8:30—7:30; admission.)

Marie Antoinette tomb: Basilica, **St-Denis** (Seine-St-Denis.)

(See Chapter 1, AUSTRIA; also Chapter 3, PARIS.)

MARQUETTE, JACQUES (1637–1675). The Jesuit missionary to North America, codiscoverer with Louis Jolliet of the Mississippi River, was a native of **Laon** (Aisne) which was his home to age nine. The exact site of his wealthy family's large house remains unknown.

Marquette resided and underwent his training at the Jesuit college of **Reims** (Marne), a building that now houses part of the general hospital, from 1646 to 1654 and from 1659 to 1661.

A succession of novitiate and academic dwellings became Marquette's lodgings until his 1666 departure to New France. From 1654 to 1656 he studied at the 1602 monastery located in the Rue St-Dizier at **Nancy** (Meurthe-et-Moselle).

MARX, KARL (1818–1883).

Exhibit: In **Montreuil** (Pas-de-Calais) at the Museum of Living History, a room is devoted to exhibits of the Socialist philosopher and his collaborator Friedrich Engels: the Château of Montreau, 21 Boulevard Théophile-Sueur. (Inquire locally for admission information.)

(See Chapter 3, PARIS; also Chapter 4, EAST GERMANY, WEST GERMANY, BELGIUM; also Chapter 6, LONDON.)

MARY, QUEEN OF SCOTS (1542–1587). Born in Scotland and ruler there from 1561 until her forced abdication in 1567, Mary Stuart was raised in the French royal court from the age of six and reigned as queen of France for a year (1559–60) when her first husband became King Francis II.

The Château du Grand Jardin in **Joinville** (Haute-Marne) belonged to her mother's family, the powerful Guise family; it was a place "much beloved of Mary," wrote biographer Antonia Fraser. Only ruins of the castle overlooking the town now remain.

The Château of **St-Germain-en-Laye** became one of Mary's frequent childhood homes, as did the châteaus of **Amboise**, **Blois** and **Villers-Cotterêts**; she spent her 1558 honeymoon in the latter (see the entry on Francis I earlier in this chapter for accounts of these palaces). The castle of **Fontainebleau** was also a familiar residence during the constant peripatetic movements of the French court (see the entry on Napoleon I later in this chapter.)

In **Orléans** (Loiret) Francis II died in 1560 of a brain tumor. The former Hôtel Groslot in the Place de l'Étape is the present Hôtel de Ville (town hall), an extensively altered Renaissance mansion dating from about 1550. For weeks while the king declined, Mary waited on him in his darkened chamber there. After his death, she remained there for several weeks in mourning. (Guided tours daily, 10:00—6:00; admission.)

(See Chapter 3, PARIS; also Chapter 5, ENGLAND; also Chapter 7, SCOTLAND.)

MATISSE, HENRI (1869–1954). The noted painter, leader of the Fauvists whose brilliant colors and free forms characterized their work, made his permanent home from 1917 in **Nice** (Alpes-Maritimes). He occupied several hotel apartments until 1921, then rented a balconied suite on the top floor of an ochre-colored building in the Place Félix-Faure which remained his home until 1938. From 1938 to 1943, and again from 1948 until his death, Matisse resided in the Hôtel Regina, which stood in the northern suburb of **Cimiez**.

Earlier at **Issy-les-Moulinoux** (Hauts-de-Seine), Matisse lived in the square two-story house at 92 Avenue de Clamart (1909 to 1913) amid a pastoral setting of pond and lawns. He used a prefabricated shed as a garden studio there.

During the war years and after, between 1943 and 1948, the painter made his home at the Villa Le Rêve in **Vence** (Alpes-Maritimes) where he had moved for fear of possible air raids on Nice.

Matisse tomb: Cimiez Cemetery, **Cimiez**.

Exhibits: In **Le Cateau** (Nord) the Matisse Museum in the Town Hall displays works donated by the artist to the town of his birth, including drawings, etchings and sculpture. (Open Friday—Sunday 3:00—6:00; admission.)

The Matisse Museum at 164 Avenue des Arènes-de-Cimiez in **Cimiez** has the foremost display in France on this painter's life and work. Thirty canvases plus drawings, engravings, sculpture and sketches represent successive stages of

Matisse's artistic development. His personal effects, furniture and private art collection are also shown. (Open May—September, daily 10:00—12:00, 2:30—6:30; October—April, daily 10:00—12:00, 2:00—5:00; 93–81–59–57; free.)

At **Vence** the famous jewel-like Chapel of the Rosary in the Route de St-Jeannet was designed and decorated by the artist between 1947 and 1951. "I think it is my masterpiece," he said, "the result of a lifetime devoted to the search for truth." Though an agnostic, Matisse intended the chapel as a gift for the adjacent Dominican convent; the nuns had nursed him through a long illness. The white interior, spare in its simplicity and restraint, is patterned with small stained-glass windows. A gallery displays some of the artist's sketches for his finished designs. (Open Tuesday, Thursday 10:00—11:30, 2:30—5:30; or by arrangement, Foyer Lacordaire, Avenue H. Matisse, Vence; closed November; 93–58–03–26; free.)

(See Chapter 3, PARIS.)

MAUGHAM, WILLIAM SOMERSET (1874–1965).
Anthony Burgess called him "the last of the literary tycoons." V. S. Pritchett believed him "a man wounded and aloof who ... sought consolation in excelling in his profession." The English novelist and playwright made his permanent home from 1927 in the Villa Mauresque at **St-Jean-Cap-Ferrat** (Alpes-Maritimes), where he welcomed such guests as Sir Winston Churchill, H. G. Wells and the Duke and Duchess of Windsor. Rich beyond most writers' dreams with a staff of six servants and four gardeners for his 20-acre estate, he rigidly patterned his working life, yearning for literary acclaim as well as money and popularity. Apart from frequent travel and a long sojourn in the United States during World War II, Maugham remained with his successive secretary-companions Gerald Haxton and Alan Searle in the aristocratic splendor of his Moorish villa. He wrote most of his later works there and resented the intrusion of curious tourists. Increasingly senile, Maugham tired of life long before he died in his villa at 91. The mansion stands near the south cape of the peninsula.

(See Chapter 3, PARIS; also Chapter 5, ENGLAND; also Chapter 6, LONDON.)

MAUPASSANT, GUY DE (1850–1893).
One of France's major writers, best known for his classic short stories, Maupassant was a native of Normandy, where he also often resided in later life.

The Château of Miromesnil, the opulent brick and stone mansion where he was born, survives off route N27 in the village of **Tourville-sur-Arques** south of Dieppe (Seine-Maritime). The room where he was born is located just below the west turret. Built during the 1770s the mansion, which was owned by his wealthy family, was the writer's home until the age of three. Later he made two pilgrimages there while working on his first novel, *Une Vie* (1883). (Open May 1—October 15, daily 2:00—6:00; admission.) His nearby boyhood home at **Fecamp**, owned by his grandparents, is also sometimes claimed as his birthplace. It Stands at 82 Quai Guy-de-Maupassant. He used the town as background for some of his fiction.

Maupassant's subsequent Norman homes were located in and near **Étretat**. The first dwelling he remembered (1854–59) was the rented Château Blanc on the Grainville-Ymanville road. Les Verguies, owned by his mother, was a villa in the Avenue de Verdun with orchards and gardens; it was his home at intervals from 1861 into the 1870s. At Étretat in 1883 Maupassant built "La Guillette", a two-story villa with wings joined by a balcony, on a plot also owned by his mother. It is located in what is now the Rue Guy-de-Maupassant. The name of the villa is a feminine diminutive of his own, and the house represented the profits from *Une Vie* and several short stories. Maupassant surrounded it with a large garden, planted trees and flowers, and raised poultry. He wrote most of his best-known stories there.

(See Chapter 3, PARIS.)

MILL, JOHN STUART (1806–1873).
The English philosopher and economist resided in **Avignon** (Vaucluse) for much of his later life. Harriet Taylor Mill, his beloved wife, died in 1858 at the Hôtel de Europe, a 16th-century building at 12 Place Crillon and still a hostelry, where Mill had brought her in vain hopes of improving her health. Just after her death he bought a five-room cottage with a tile roof. The Hermitage de Monloisier stands near the cemetery of St-Véran about five kilometers south-east of Avignon. It was approached by a long drive bordered by sycamore and mulberry trees. Mill installed some furniture from the hotel room in which Harriet Mill died and he lived there for long intervals until his own death.

Mill tomb: St-Véran Cemetery, **Avignon**.

(See Chapter 5, ENGLAND; also Chapter 6, LONDON.)

MOLIÈRE, JEAN BAPTISTE POQUELIN DE (1622–1673).

Exhibit: France's greatest comic and satiric dramatist toured widely as a "road actor" in the provinces during the 1640s and 1650s, a period virtually unknown to biographers in any detail. "Almost every town in southern France of any size," wrote one of them, "has naturally wished to claim a piece of him and is ready to contend even for the honor of having pelted him from the stage."

One such town was **Pézenas** (Hérault) where his company performed at several different times in the 16th-century Hôtel d'Alfonce in the Rue Conti. The Vulliod St-Germain Museum at 3 Rue A.-P.-Allies displays memorabilia of Molière and his troupe. (Inquire locally for admission information.)

(Also see the entry on Francis I, Château of Chambord, earlier in this chapter.)

(See Chapter 3, PARIS.)

MONET, CLAUDE (1840–1926). Leader of the impressionists, and one of the greatest of all landscape painters, Monet analyzed the play and changes of light in his glowing canvases in order to record precisely what the eye sees. The painter's boyhood home in **Le Havre** (Seine-Maritime) was an uncle's house at 13 Rue Fontenelle, razed after World War II to provide a parking lot.

At **Chailly-en-Bière** (Seine-et-Marne), the Cheval Blanc in the village center is the two-story stone-fronted inn where Monet resided and painted in 1864 and 1865. The stables where he produced his immense canvas *Le Déjeuner sur l'herbe* have been converted to garages, but the inn remains basically unchanged.

From 1871 to 1878 the artist resided in **Argenteuil** (Val d'Oise) with his family. These were difficult years when his work was rejected and he stubbornly slashed his canvases to keep them from the hands of creditors. He rented houses at 2 Pierre-Guienne (1871–74) and in the nearby Boulevard St-Denis. The present status of these dwellings is uncertain. *Monet at Argenteuil* (1982), by Paul Hayes Tucker, describes this crucial place and period for the artist's work.

Monet's last home, from 1883, was the Norman village of **Giverny** (Eure). At first he rented the two-story, pink-stucco farmhouse which became his home but by 1890 he was able to buy the property. "He settled in," wrote Bennett Schiff, "with a kind of bourgeois ferocity, the opposite side of, but just as inflexible as, his artistic tenacity." Over the years he built two studios plus a greenhouse and cultivated flowers in dense profusion ("I perhaps owe having become a painter to flowers"). He also bought two acres across the road and enlarged a small pond there to create his "water garden," whence came his famed artistic preoccupation with water lilies. Monet's country house and gardens became one of his most vital lavish works of art. He not only achieved fame, wealth and fulfillment at Giverny but also played frequent host to such friends as Georges Clemenceau, Auguste Rodin, Pierre Renoir and Paul Cézanne (see entries on each of these men in this chapter). After his death Monet's garden estate fell into neglect and disrepair. By 1966, when his son left the property to the Institute of France, the estate was completely derelict and the gardens a jungle. The Academie des Beaux-Arts assumed joint responsibility with the Claude Monet Foundation for restoration and meticulously completed the job in 1980. Today visitors may experience Monet's "harem of nature" just as the artist created it. Flowers abound in riotous splendor. "There is a way of feeling here that it is raining flowers," wrote Schiff. "To walk through the garden is to be in a painting." In Monet's largest studio, a cavernous skylighted structure, he spent his last 13 years painting the panels of his *Décorations des Nymphéas*, an immense water-garden landscape. Original furnishings, Monet's collection of Japanese prints and carefully recreated household items may be viewed in the blue-tiled kitchen, sunshine-yellow dining room and other rooms. An underpass beneath the road connects the house to the water garden, where water lilies again bloom. The Monet house and gardens border route D5E. (Open April 1—November 1, Tuesday—Sunday 10:00—12:00, 2:00—6:00; admission.) An excellent accompaniment to a visit is the book *Monet at Giverny* (1975), by Claire Joyes.

Monet tomb: Village churchyard, **Giverny**.

(See Chapter 3, PARIS.)

MONTAIGNE, MICHEL EYQUEM DE (1533–1592). He was an aristocrat, public official and masterly creator of the personal essay as a literary form. Montaigne's birthplace and ancestral estate was the Château de Montaigne, a castle that still dominates the vineyards he cultivated on the north bank of the River Dordogne. The château, purchased by Montaigne's great-grandfather in

1477, remains privately owned and still bottles Château de Michel de Montaigne, a dry white wine from the grapes of his original stock vines. Montaigne retired there from 1571 to 1580 to write and enjoy a life of comfortable leisure with his books and vineyards. "He loved his manor," wrote biographer Donald M. Frame, "but he often grew bored there." After 1585 the château became his permanent home, and he died there. The central portion of the castle was rebuilt to a different pattern following an 1885 fire but Montaigne's tower study, where he wrote most of his *Essays*, survives and may be viewed along with its rafter timbers on which he carved Greek and Latin quotations. The Château de Montaigne is located three kilometers north of **La Mothe-Montravel** (Gironde) on route 936. (Inquire locally for admission information.)

Montaigne tomb: Faculty of Letters, University of Bordeaux, **Bordeaux** (Gironde).

Exhibit: The Bordeaux Library in the Rue Mably, **Bordeaux**, displays some of Montaigne's personal books and manuscripts. (Inquire locally for admission information.)

NAPOLEON I (1769–1821). "He ruined me; but what a gentleman he was!" Like a woman enchanted with a ruffian, France's affair continues with the "little corporal" who conquered most of Europe and then lost it, along with the blood of more Frenchmen than died in both World Wars—1,700,000 according to his own estimate. "His reign was disastrous," wrote Sanche de Gramont, "but it left France an inexhaustible reservoir of epic memories." Today the blood is forgotten and no historical figure is so widely memorialized in France; almost anyplace the talented Corsican soldier lingered for a night, whether in victory or defeat, displays a marker if not a museum. The man who subverted the aims of the French Revolution to his own greed for power also knew how to manipulate French public opinion. And still does.*

Born Napolione Buonaparte on the recently French-conquered island of Corsica, he was, like most Corsicans, of Italian descent and spoke no

---

* It is intriguing, though, how relatively few public squares or avenues (favorite places for honoring French notables) are named after him. It is easy to forget, while observing the numerous sometimes maudlin expressions of French hero worship, that the French themselves—not outside enemies—deposed Napoleon. Twice. They worshipped him as a winner but angrily forsook him in the end. Living with his decorated memory has proven a far more pleasant experience for France (and Europe) than dealing with the tyrannous, destructive man himself.

NAPOLEON'S BIRTHPLACE. In **Ajaccio**, Corsica, the first home of the French emperor and European conqueror survives as a museum in the Rue St-Charles. Napoleon grew up here but ultimately turned his back on Corsica and never returned after 1792.

French until adolescence. **Ajaccio**, which Napoleon made capital of the island in 1811 at his mother's request, reveres his birthplace, which stands in the Rue St-Charles. Today Napoleon would still recognize both street and house. He was born on the first floor of the large, oblong, stuccoed structure and lived there until the age of nine. During his early military career he frequently returned to the house for visits. By 1792, however, he had chosen his alliance and it was not with Corsica; he was banished from the island for leading the revolutionary attempt to wrest political control from local partisans. British soldiers were quartered in the house during their occupation of 1794–95 (one of them, it is said, later became one of Napoleon's guards during his last exile on St. Helena). Now a museum, the National Museum of the House of the Bonapartes displays furnishings acquired by the family after the house was pillaged in 1793, plus other memorabilia, documents and portraits. (Open summer, Wednesday—Monday 9:00—11:00, 2:00—5:30; rest of year, Wednesday—Monday 10:00—11:30, 2:00—5:00; admission.)

Above the city stands Les Milelli, the Buonaparte farm where Napoleon spent many boyhood days. There in 1792 he wrote an impulsive manifesto for Corsican independence just before switching sides to lead the local revolutionists. The farm is now the site of a summer music festival, and the family house is undergoing restoration. Napoleon's 1792 opportunism does not diminish his luster in Ajaccio, which has been governed by a small but highly vocal Bonapartist party for most years since 1924. The island of Corsica, still part of France, lies in the Mediterranean 240 kilometers south of Nice.

From 1779 to 1784 the youth attended the Royal Military School of **Brienne-le-Château** (Aube). The first time he pronounced his name there, other students laughed at his Italian accent and mimicked him. Moody, taciturn, trigger-tempered, he kept to his studies, occupying a six-foot-square cell containing a narrow camp bed and small washstand. The experience gave him a lifelong preference for spartan accommodations and field tents. In later life, he lavishly favored and promoted some of his old schoolmates. The Napoleonic Museum in the Rue de l'École-Militaire, site of the school, displays manuscripts and letters relating to this period of his youth. (Inquire locally for admission information.)

After his later graduation from the Military School in Paris, Napoleon joined his artillery regiment as a lieutenant at **Valence** (Drôme), where he lodged in 1785–86 and again in 1791 in rented cafe rooms at 48 Grand-Rue. In his oak-furnished study next to the noisy billiard room, he absorbed himself in books—history, military science, economics—and wrote discursive essays.

Two dwellings briefly housed Napoleon in **Nice** (Alpes-Maritimes). As a brigadier general of artillery in 1794 he lived at 6 Rue Bonaparte, while writing his report of a spying trip to Genoa, and was arrested there following the downfall of Robespierre in Paris. He also proposed to his landlord's daughter there. In 1796, just after his marriage to Joséphine de Beauharnais and en route to command the invasion of Italy, he resided in front of the opera house in the Rue St-François-de-Paule. "My darling," wrote the lovestruck groom to his bride back in Paris, "my emotion thunders in my ears like a volcano. . . I would like to tear out my heart with my teeth." Both houses carry markers.

Joséphine acquired the Château de Malmaison in **Rueil-Malmaison** (Hauts-de-Seine) in 1799.

The estate became the couple's favorite country refuge until 1804 when they assumed imperial titles and occupied official residences. "All through the Consulate," wrote Jacques Levron, "the château was Bonaparte's place of rest. . . . He relaxed there. . . became pleasant and human, playing like a child. He delighted to see Joséphine walking along the paths." Joséphine continued to spend much time there after becoming empress and retired permanently to her château after the couple's 1809 divorce. Napoleon returned to Malmaison just before the Battle of Waterloo to stand silently in Joséphine's bedroom. Malmaison also became one of his last French residences when, after his abdication in Paris, he spent a few days there before surrendering to the English vessel that took him to permanent exile. Later owners of the estate included Queen Maria-Christina of Spain and Napoleon III. Banker Daniel Osiris gave it to the nation in 1906 as a Napoleonic museum. Built in 1662 on the site of a leper house and enlarged in 1800, the manor notably reflects the tastes and presence of the empress in rooms and grounds. Among the superb collections of memorabilia, possessions and furnishings on display are Napoleon's throne from Fontainebleau (see below), his library, original furnishings from his bedroom (a reconstruction of his Tuileries bedroom in Paris *), the camp bed on which he died at St. Helena, his death mask, clothing, manuscripts and numerous portraits and gifts. Joséphine's apartments contain personal souvenirs, original furnishings and the bed in which she died in 1814 during Napoleon's exile on Elba. Other items relate to Joséphine's children, Queen Hortense and Eugène de Beauharnais. Fifteen acres of the original 500 remain; they are planted with some of the 250 different kinds of rose that Joséphine cultivated. The coach house displays her carriage, as well as a gala coach used by Napoleon and the cart from which he fled Waterloo. In the Osiris Pavilion are displayed numerous caricatures, medallions and snuffboxes portraying the emperor. A summer house he used as a study also stands on the grounds. (Open Wednesday—Monday 10:00—12:00, 1:30—5:00; admission.)

Napoleon and Joséphine were residing at the royal castle of **St-Cloud** (Hauts-de-Seine) during

---

* A creature of precise habit and lover of standardized surroundings, as are most military men, Napoleon insisted on installing exact duplicates of his Tuileries chambers in his other palatial dwellings—so this bedroom "reconstruction" was probably as much his own intention as that of later restorers.

the 1804 coup that made him first consul, the dictator of France and king in all but name. In the earlier 16th-century palace in St-Cloud had occurred the 1589 assassination of Henri III. In 1658 the palace had become the property of Philippe, Duc d'Orléans ("Monsieur"), the flagrantly homosexual brother of Louis XIV. He had the structure pulled down and erected a new hill-top château. Queen Marie Antoinette acquired the estate in 1785 and modified the rooms and gardens (see the entry on Marie Antoinette earlier in this chapter). Perhaps because of its association with his triumph in subjugating France to his dominion, Napoleon frequently returned to the castle, restoring the interior and filling the rooms with heavy Empire furniture. There in 1810 he celebrated his expedient second marriage to Archduchess Marie Louise of Austria, "the kind of womb I want to marry." His last visit was in 1813. Napoleon III was baptized there—as was Napoleon's son, "L'Aiglon," the ill-fated king of Rome—and the palace became Napoleon III's favorite summer residence; it was from there that he departed in 1870 to defeat and exile. Destroyed by artillery fire during the Franco-Prussian War, the palace ruins stood until 1891. Today only the 1,000-acre public park with its elaborate cascades and fountains survives.

As emperor, Napoleon frequently resided in the homes of the old regime, castles once occupied by the hated Bourbon dynasty. The Château of **Fontainebleau** owes almost as much of its present aspect to Napoleon as to its creator, Francis I (see the entry on Francis I earlier in this chapter). Napoleon spent some 12 million francs on alterations and restoration. In 1811, after the French annexation of the papal states, he imprisoned Pope Pius VII in the first-floor apartments traditionally occupied by France's queen mother. He signed his first abdication at Fontainebleau on April 6, 1814, bidding farewell to his guard in the Cour du Cheval Blanc. A year later, in that same courtyard, he reviewed his grenadiers after his escape from Elba and led them on to Paris. Napoleon's apartments are located in a wing built by Louis XV abutting the Francis I Gallery and display numerous relics of the emperor—his bed, camp bed, desk, the table on which he signed his abdication, and the hat he wore on his return from Elba. His study, map room and bedroom have all been accurately restored. The English garden created for him reminded him of Malmaison (see above), and made

A WING OF THE GRAND TRIANON. Napoleon I made this small palace in the **Versailles** gardens his frequent residence.

Fontainebleau his favorite among the royal châteaus.

At **Versailles** Napoleon's residence was the Grand Trianon in the extensive gardens behind the palace (see the entry on Louis XIV earlier in this chapter), and the Empire furnishings he installed remain there. The Salon des Colonnes contains his gilded bed from the Tuileries. Napoleon and his wife, Marie Louise, occupied the earlier apartments of Mme. de Maintenon. His mother, "Madame Mère," also settled in the Grand Trianon during his reign and refurnished it. The nearby Voitures Museum displays Napoleon and Marie Louise's marriage coach. In 1978 Napoleon seemed a convenient symbol for Breton terrorists intent on registering a violent protest against "French oppression." Their bomb in a south-wing gallery that displayed paintings from the Napoleonic era caused much irreparable damage. (The Bretons were not, of course, so brave in 1811.)

Several other royal palaces served as important Napoleonic residences, though for briefer periods. The palace of **Compiègne** (Oise) dates from the reign of Louis XV, but its site held a royal estate for more than 12 centuries before that. The castle's projected "new" design in 1740 would have made it as massive as Versailles, but shortage of money prevented such expansion; finished by 1785, it occupies only five acres. Marie Antoinette was a frequent resident. Napoleon restored and redecorated the palace as a residence after its use as an officers' school. There in 1810 he met his new empress Marie Louise, after marrying her by proxy in Austria, and the couple frequently resided there during the Empire's final years. Their rooms contain original furniture that was made for them. The palace, with its cold forbidding exterior, later became a favorite of Napoleon III and Empress Eugènie; it offers a unique view of court life during the Second Empire period. (Open Wednesday—Monday 10:00—12:00, 1:30—5:30; admission.)

Emulating the style of his Bourbon predecessors, Napoleon resided several times at the Château of **Rambouillet** where he engaged in day-long hunts in the surrounding forest. He didn't especially enjoy hunting; he stalked deer but didn't shoot them and usually ended the day with a bruised shoulder from carrying his gun the wrong way. After his disaster at Waterloo, he took refuge at the château for a brief period before giving himself up to the English. (See the entry on Francis I earlier in this chapter for information on Rambouillet.)

Napoleon's last residence on the French mainland was the 1771 Hôtel de Marine, now a naval headquarters near the dockyard at **Rochefort** (Charente-Maritime). His last lodging in France was the nearby offshore **Île d'Aix**, where he stayed three days before embarking on July 15, 1815, to his final exile on St. Helena. The "House of the Emperor," maintained by the Fondation Gourgaud on this tiny speck of land, displays a small collection of relics. (Inquire locally for admission information.)

Exhibits: Beside the places where he lived, France is full of Napoleonic reminders. Some of the monuments and statues encountered at odd places are astonishing examples of "iconographic hyperbole"; the classic togas and laurel crowns that decorate his statues also help to sanitize the image of a bloodthirsty tyrant. But along with the numerous memorials that either make the emperor look ridiculous or commercialize his charisma, there exist some important displays that help reveal who he was and what he did.

In his birthplace of **Ajaccio** (Corsica), the Napoleon Museum in the Town Hall, Place Maréchal Foch, displays memorabilia of his family's history and residence in Corsica. (Open Monday—Saturday, summer 9:00—12:00, 2:30—6:00; rest of year, Monday—Saturday 9:00—12:00, 2:00—5:00; admission.) Also on Corsica, the Ethnographic Museum of Corsica, located in the 1378 governors' palace at **Bastia**, shows Napoleonic items, including a copy of his ubiquitous death mask. (Open Monday—Saturday, summer

9:00—12:00, 3:00—6:00; rest of year, Monday—Saturday 9:00—12:00, 2:00—5:00; admission.)

In **Auxonne** (Côte-d'Or), where Napoleon resided in regimental barracks from 1788 to 1791 and attended artillery school, the Bonaparte Museum in the Rue Lafayette exhibits memorabilia of his stay in the town. (Inquire locally for admission information.)

Adjacent to the Château of Malmaison at **Rueil-Malmaison** (see above) is the National Museum of the Château of Bois-Preau, Avenue de l'Impératrice Joséphine. Bonaparte portraits, clothing, items from St. Helena and gifts adorn this building bought by Joséphine in 1810 and given to the nation by American art collector Edward Tuck in 1926. (Open same hours as Château of Malmaison.)

The Noisot Napoleonic Museum in the Parc Noisot at **Fixin** (Côte-d'Or) displays paintings, engravings and medals relating to the emperor. (Inquire locally for admission information.)

At **Cap d'Antibes** (Alpes-Maritimes), the Naval and Napoleonic Museum occupies the former Batterie du Grillon on the southwestern tip of the peninsula. Collections include displays relating to Napoleon's dramatic return from Elba in 1815. (Open June 15—September 15, Wednesday—Monday 10:00—12:00, 3:00—7:00; September 16—June 14, Wednesday—Monday 10:00—12:00, 2:00—5:00; closed November—December 15; admission.)

A marker at nearby **Golfe-Juan** commemorates Napoleon's landing from Elba with some 1,000 men. The "Route Napoleon," the mountainous road he followed to Paris from this harbor, is marked with roadside tablets, monuments and plaques on houses where he slept. The march on Paris, with royalist troops flocking to his side and "Long live the Emperor!" echoing from the hamlets he passed, was the most splendid experience of his life, he later said. Route N85 now covers much of the lower road.

(See Chapter 1, AUSTRIA, SWITZERLAND; also Chapter 3, PARIS; also Chapter 4, EAST GERMANY, BELGIUM; also Chapter 8, ITALY, SPAIN.)

NOSTRADAMUS (1503–1566). Born Michel de Nostredame, the physician and astrologer who possessed an uncanny ability to prophesy world events that would occur hundreds of years after his death is not easily dismissed as a charlatan. He later Latinized his name to Nostradamus. After practicing medicine during the plague years in southern France, he achieved a massive reputation for his curative methods.

After years of wandering he settled in 1544 at **Salon-de-Provence** (Bouches-du-Rhône) where he practiced medicine, spent hours studying astrology and staring into a water-filled brass bowl, and began recording his visions in his top-floor study. Eventually he produced his book of cryptic versified predictions entitled *Centuries* (1555). His house, now a Nostradamus museum in the Place Nostradamus, displays exhibits relating to the seer. (Inquire locally for admission information.)

Nostradamus tomb: Church of St-Laurent, **Salon-de-Provence**.

Exhibit: In **St-Remy-de-Provence** (Bouches-du-Rhône), the Pierre de Brun Alpilles Museum displays souvenirs of Nostradamus, who was born in this town. The museum is located in the Rue de Parège. (Open Wednesday—Monday; admission.)

PASTEUR, LOUIS (1822–1895). The chemist whose research led to acceptance of the modern germ theory of disease and vaccine therapy was born in **Dôle** (Jura). "Had Pasteur lived in the thirteenth century," wrote Rene Dubos, "his silhouette would adorn the stained glass windows of our cathedrals.... For, as much as a scientist, he was the priest of an idea, an apostle and a crusader." His birthplace at what is now 43 Rue Pasteur was purchased and given to the town by American financier John D. Rockefeller. Now restored, this family house overlooking the canal displays old tanning techniques and equipment as well as numerous documents and memorabilia of Pasteur, for the chemist's father operated a tannery in the house. The family lived there until 1827. (Inquire locally for admission information.)

Pasteur's own home from 1827 until his death is also a museum; it is located at 83 Rue de Courcelles in **Arbois** (Jura). Though usually active in Paris and elsewhere, he often returned for holidays and lengthy visits to rest or work on various scientific projects, the last time in 1894. In 1883 he established a laboratory in his home to test his theories and studies on fermentation. Visitors see the home as he left it, with its original furnishings; his office, library and laboratory may be viewed and there are numerous mementos of the scientist. (Inquire locally for admission information.) Pas-

teur established his first laboratory in an old cafe which is marked at 32 Route de Dôle.

Pasteur died in the Château of Villeneuve-l'Étang, a branch of the Pasteur Institute still used for medical research, about three kilometers west of **St-Cloud** (Hauts-de-Seine) on route N307.

(See Chapter 3, PARIS.)

PATRICK, ST. (ca. 389–ca. 461). The Romano-British evangelizer of Ireland lived for several years (ca. 415) as a monk on tiny **St-Honorat Island**, one of the Lérins Islands near Cannes (Alpes-Maritimes). This spot is one of the more probable sites thought to have sheltered this saint whose life remains thickly obscured by Celtic mists and outlandish miracle tales. Today Cistercian monks continue to maintain the fourth-century Monastery of St-Honorat, of which remnants of Patrick's time survive. Walking and bathing are permitted on the island. (Boat service from Cannes, Antibes and Golfe-Juan; contact Campagnie Esterel-Chanteclair, Gare Maritime des Îles, Cannes; 39–11–82.)

(See Chapter 7, IRELAND.)

PETRARCH, FRANCESCO (1304–1374). Sometimes called "the first modern man," the Italian poet and scholar, a founder of Renaissance humanism, spent much of his lifetime in southern France. He came to the papal court of Avignon (Vaucluse) with his parents in 1313 and resided there and in nearby **Carpentras** at unknown addresses until 1320 and from 1326 to 1347. In the latter year he established his home at **Fontaine-de-Vaucluse**. He loved the romantic serenity of the area, describing it in his writings and even climbing mountains in the vicinity—a most unusual pursuit for medieval scholars. There too he composed his influential *Canzoniere* (1327–74), 366 lyrical poems inspired by the idealized "Laura," whom he worshipped from a chaste distance. Today nothing remains of Petrarch's house which was situated near the spectacular fountain that draws over a million visitors a year to this busy commercial resort. "The sentimental visitor today," wrote Morris Bishop, "must use imagination to recall the beauty of Petrarch's solitude. ... There is no peace." Occupying the house site, where the poet lived and wooed his pedestaled maiden until 1353, is a small museum which displays Petrarch's works and prints, brochures and exhibits on his life. (Open daily, 9:00—12:00, 2:00—7:00; 90–20–32–22; admission.)

Exhibit: Most scholars believe that Petrarch's unattainable Laura was not a real person but a literary personification of the poet's aspirations and psychological conflicts. Others think she was Laure de Sade, a 19-year-old married woman and ancestor of the Marquis de Sade (see the entry on Sade later in this chapter). Petrarch was specific enough on certain details, claiming he first saw and fell in love with Laura in the Church of St. Claire at **Avignon** on April 6, 1327. A marker identifies the site of the church at 22 Rue du Roi René.

(See Chapter 8, ITALY.)

PICASSO, PABLO (1881–1973). Probably the world's foremost 20th-century artist, the Spanish-born Picasso lived and worked in France for most of his long, vigorous life. His constantly evolving style and technical virtuosity made him as much a prodigy as Mozart. "Painting is stronger than I am," he once remarked. "It makes me do what it wants." There was virtually no medium of art he did not master and use profusely—in addition to his canvases he made drawings, collages, prints, lithographs, pottery, and sculpture in every sort of material.

From the 1920s Picasso often lived and painted in southern France. There he "felt the Greeks in the ground," wrote Robert Hughes. "His Mediterranean images are the last appearance, in serious art, of the symbols of that once Arcadian coast." Not until 1955, however, did he buy property there: a large 1880 villa in **Cannes** (Alpes-Maritimes) called La Californie, where he lived with his mistress and later wife, Jacqueline Rogue. A heavily stylized, ornately pretentious structure built about 1900, the house was not selected for its exterior charms. To Picasso, wrote biographer Roland Penrose, "his house had always been his workshop and a place to store his belongings rather than something to be admired for its elegance and comfort." La Californie, where Picasso resided at intervals until 1958, remains in the Avenue de la Californie.

In 1958, as residential developments encroached on his hilltop solitude, Picasso bought the 17th-century Château de Vauvenargues, about 15 kilometers east of **Aix-en-Provence** (Bouches-du-Rhône) on route D10, situated on a spur of rock overlooking the Infernet Valley. The

proportions of the château set in its rugged terrain reminded him of a Spanish castle. "I've bought Cézanne's view," he marveled. He owned about 2,000 forested acres surrounding the château, entitling him to claim the landed title Marquis of Vauvenargues. Though he owned the château until his death, Picasso spent little time there after 1960. It remains inaccessible to the public.

The artist's last home, from 1961, was Notre-Dame-de-Vie, another large hilltop villa near **Mougins** (Alpes-Maritimes). Well screened by trees and shrubs, the house stands opposite a 17th-century chapel, the Notre-Dame-de-Vie Hermitage, in a high scenic meadow bordered by cypresses. There, on the last day of his life, Picasso worked in his studio until dawn. Signs give directions to the chapel off route D35 east of the town.

Picasso tomb: Park, Château de Vauvenargues, **Aix-en-Provence**.

Exhibits: In the 16th-century Grimaldi Castle at **Antibes** (Alpes-Maritimes), the Picasso Museum displays the artist's versatile output of a single season—autumn 1946. It includes paintings, lithographs, drawings and ceramics. Many of the works were created in the castle itself; Picasso used it as a studio for four months. In gratitude for the work space provided, he donated his entire production of the season to the town as well as numerous ceramics he later created at nearby Vallauris. Picasso's happiness during this period is evident in the exuberant vitality of the works on display. The Château Grimaldi is located in the old town section. (Open Wednesday—Monday 10:00—12:00, 3:00—5:00; closed November; 93–33–67–67; admission.)

Vallauris, the town Picasso made a world center of ceramics, also has a Picasso Museum: the National Museum of War and Peace. The artist decorated this 12th-century deconsecrated chapel in 1952 with his powerful painting *War and Peace* which covers the entire walls and ceiling. The museum stands at the top of the main street. (Open daily 10:00—12:00, 2:00—5:00; admission.)

(See Chapter 1, SWITZERLAND; also Chapter 3, PARIS; also Chapter 8, SPAIN.)

PROUST, MARCEL (1871–1922). At what is now 4 Rue du Docteur-Proust in **Illiers-Combray** (Eure-et-Loir), the novelist spent frequent childhood intervals, episodes which are meticulously described in his mammoth opus, *Remembrance of Things Past* (1913–27). Illiers was the "Combray" of the novel. An indispensable guide for any Proust pilgrim in Illiers is George D. Painter's *Marcel Proust* (1959) which describes both the physical and psychological landscape of the writer's earliest memories and associations. Proust spent regular periods there until about 1884 and returned occasionally until 1900. The two-story house (its front now a shop) with its rear garden was the property of his Aunt Léonie Amiot and now exhibits mementos of the author. (Open Wednesday—Monday, afternoons only; admission.)

Proust came often to **Cabourg** (Calvados) during his adolescence and later life to seek sea-air relief from his asthma. Volume two of his novel, *Within a Budding Grove*, concerns life in this resort town. The Grand Hôtel (no longer a commercial hotel), where Proust resided, survives in the Boulevard des Anglais facing the sea.

(See Chapter 3, PARIS.)

RABELAIS, FRANÇOIS (1494?–1553). Author of some of the rowdiest, randiest, most boisterous satires ever written, this monk-physician-scholar's traditional birthplace was his family house near **Seuilly-la-Divinière** (Indre-et-Loire).

La Devinière, the two-story 15th-century stone farmhouse (now restored), had been brought by his mother to her marriage with Rabelais' father, a prominent lawyer, and the writer spent much of his boyhood there. The ground-floor rooms are oak-beamed, and the house displays documents and memorabilia relating to Rabelais. It stands north of the village on route D117. (Open March 15—September 30, daily 9:00—12:00, 2:00—7:00; October 1—March 14, Thursday—Tuesday to 5:30; closed December—January; admission.)

Another boyhood home stood in nearby **Chinon** at 15 Rue de la Lamproie on the site of the present house there. The small gated courtyard is probably the only relic of the Rabelais dwelling.

The Town Hall in **Fontenay-le-Comte** (Vendée), on the Rue Clemenceau, occupies the site of the Franciscan convent of Puy-St-Martin where Rabelais lived and trained as a monk from about 1520 to 1524. Protestants destroyed the monastery in 1568.

Rabelais fled from arrest to **Metz** (Moselle) in 1546 when Book III of *Gargantua and Pantagruel* (1532–64) was condemned in France for its at-

tacks on the church (Metz did not become part of France until 1648). He stayed for a year, reputedly at what is now 38 En Jurue, the main street of the former Jewish district of the town. There, it is said, he began Book IV of his "Gargantuan" satire, *Le Quart Livre* (1552).

(See Chapter 3, PARIS; also Chapter 8, ITALY.)

RENOIR, PIERRE AUGUSTE (1841–1919). The painter's birthplace in **Limoges** (Haute-Vienne) remains at 35 Boulevard Gambetta; it was his home until age four.

Afflicted during his final decades with rheumatoid arthritis, Renoir sought relief in southern France. From 1903 to 1909 he resided in the present Town Hall at **Cagnes-sur-Mer** (Alpes-Maritime). He rented a large apartment in this building, which stands in the Avenue de l'Hôtel-de-Ville.

From 1909 until his death the artist lived at Les Collettes, the present Renoir Museum in the Avenue des Collettes in nearby **Cagnes-Ville**. This simple villa sits in a large garden of olive trees and it was there that Renoir painted by means of arm movements—his brushes tied to his arthritic fingers. "He painted nonstop," wrote Georges Besson, "pell-mell—flowers, fruit, landscapes, nymphs, naiads, goddesses, garlanded necks, bounding bodies, expressed with a harmony ever more bold and vibrant." Visitors see Renoir's last home and studio exactly as it existed during his later years. His easel, wheelchair, clothing, drawings, sculptures, two small canvases, prints, letters, photographs and family furnishings are among the items displayed. "This quiet house is wrapped in a serene nostalgia," wrote John Ardagh. "It attracts, so it seems, not numbers of impatient sightseers, but only the discerning and caring visitor." (Open June 1—October 15, Wednesday—Monday 2:30—6:00; 93–20–61–07; admission.)

Renoir tomb: Village Churchyard, **Essoyes** (Aube).

(See Chapter 3, PARIS.)

THREE VIEWS OF LES COLLETTES. Olive trees surround the villa of Pierre Renoir at **Cagnes-Ville**, where he resided from 1909 until his death ten years later. Renoir, crippled with arthritis, did much of his last painting in these gardens, using brushes tied to his fingers. The serenity of house and gardens is immediately felt by visitors and reflects the harmonic vision of this great artist.

RICHARD I, COEUR DE LION (1157–1199). Richard Plantagenet, Duke of Aquitaine and king of England from 1189, spent little time in England but devoted most of his considerable energies to leading the Third Crusade and defending his Norman and Anjou territories. By language and preference he was French, and was probably raised in the royal courts of his mother, Eleanor of Aquitaine, at Poitiers (Vienne) and Bordeaux (Gironde). Older parts of the Aquitaine palace in the Rue des Cordeliers at **Poitiers** mostly antedate the residence of Richard by a century or so. In the 13th-century hall on this site, which incorporates the present Palace of Justice, Charles VII became king of France in 1422, and Joan of Arc answered interrogators in 1429. Nothing remains of the Bordeaux palace.

As a warrior in almost constant motion throughout his life, the violent Richard settled in few places long enough to qualify as "homes" in the normal sense. One Anjou family property with which he was long familiar was the Château of Loches, a well-preserved complex of 11th-century masonry in **Loches** (Indre-et-Loire). A castle has occupied this site from the sixth century. The English King John, Richard's brother, ceded the château to King Philip Augustus in 1192, but Richard seized it back by surprise attack in 1194. From 1205 it became a royal residence, sheltering Queen Marie de Médicis, Charles VII and his mistress Agnès Sorel, Charles VIII, Louis XI and Louis XII. Joan of Arc arrived there in 1429; in the Vieux Logis of the castle, she persuaded the reluctant dauphin to accept the crown as Charles VII (see the entry on Joan of Arc earlier in this chapter). During the reign of Louis XI the castle became a state prison. Today Loches remains one of the most impressive examples of a medieval stronghold in Europe. Interior features and artworks reflect the period of the 15th-century Valois monarchy. Entry is via the Porte Royale from the Mail de la Poterie. (Open March 15—September 30, daily 9:00—12:00, 2:00—7:00; October 1—March 14, Wednesday—Monday 9:00—12:00, 2:00—5:30; closed December—January; admission.)

England's treasury, raided and drained by Richard throughout his reign, paid for the Château Gaillard which he built at **Les Andelys** (Eure) in 1197. In contrast to most European castles, which have been enlarged and revamped over the centuries, this massive fortress above the town is the product of just one hectic year of construction. It became the key defensive stronghold of Normandy, blocking the French passage to Rouen from Paris. Now ruins, this high scenic bastion was Richard's favorite residence during his last two years and from there he dominated the kingdom he most cared about. Philip Augustus finally subdued the fortress in 1204, and Henri IV demolished much of it in 1603; only one tower of the original five remains. The wall and keep ruins are gigantic and impressive and are approached via the Allée du Roi de Rome. (Guided tours Easter—October 31, Wednesday—Monday 10:00—12:00, 2:00—6:00; admission.)

Though only superficially wounded in his siege of Chalus in 1199, after threatening to hang every man, woman and child in the town, Richard died of gangrenous infection after a butcher of a surgeon had removed the arrowhead from his shoulder. According to tradition he died in **Chinon** (Indre-et-Loire) at the building now known as the "House of the States-General," 44 Place St-Maurice. The house is now a museum and displays portraits and antiques. (Open June 1—August 31, Wednesday—Monday 10:00—12:00, 3:00—7:00; September 1—May 31, Wednesday—Monday 10:00—12:00, 2:00—5:00; closed January; admission.)

Richard I tomb (site): Abbey of Fontevraud, **Fontevraud-L'Abbaye** (Maine-et-Loire).

(See Chapter 1, AUSTRIA; also Chapter 4, WEST GERMANY; also Chapter 5, ENGLAND; also Chapter 6, LONDON.)

RICHELIEU, ARMAND JEAN DU PLESSIS, DUC DE (1585–1642). France's most powerful 17th-century statesman, the "scheming cardinal" and master intriguer who controlled a weak king and the country's foreign and domestic affairs for a generation, had a profound affect on the nation's politics and culture. Of noble birth, his ancestral home was the now long-gone Château of Richelieu in **Richelieu** (Indre-et-Loire) in which he lived at intervals until 1594. Much later, during the height of his power, he built a new château on the site of the old one. Begun during the 1620s, the work was only half-finished during the cardinal's lifetime. Protected by moats and bastions, the castle anticipated the pattern of the later Versailles (see the entry on Louis XIV earlier in this chapter). Numerous artworks, statuary and fountains graced the huge estate. Beginning in 1631

Richelieu also directed the building of the town: the first planned town in France, it was designed in a rectangular, severely classical style. Richelieu's castle was demolished for building materials in 1805 and its lavish contents were scattered all over France. Its site centers the present 1,174-acre Parc du Château, entered from route D749 south of the town. A few parts of the former precincts remain, including a domed pavilion, an orangery, wine cellar and canals. The formal gardens and straight tree-lined avenues have been maintained, as have the 17th-century pattern and architecture of the town itself. (Park open daily, 10:00—12:00, 2:00—7:00; admission July—September, free rest of year.)

The ambitious Richelieu, who used the church as a means of gaining political power and influence, seldom actually functioned in a priestly office. An exception was when he assumed the bishopric of **Luçon** (Vendée) in 1608. Though he hated the routine of his churchly duties—"my house is my prison," he said—for a while he devoted himself to correcting abuses and converting Protestants, as was expected of any good bishop. By 1610 he was weary of it all and, though he held the see until 1624, he seldom returned thereafter. The bishop's palace which he occupied was "a ramshackle affair resembling a little island lost in a sea of mud," according to one biographer. Parts of it survive adjacent to the 13th-century cathedral in Luçon. St. Vincent de Paul stayed there in 1633 and 1649.

Exhibit: In **Richelieu**, the Museum of the 17th Century in the Town Hall displays documents and other items pertaining to the cardinal and his lavish château. (Open July 1—August 31, Wednesday—Monday 10:00—12:00, 1:00—6:00; September 1—June 30, Monday, Wednesday—Friday 10:00—12:00, 2:00—4:00; admission.)

(See Chapter 2, PARIS.)

RILKE, RAINER MARIA (1875–1926). At **Meudon** (Hauts-de-Seine) the German poet and novelist served the sculptor Auguste Rodin as secretary at the latter's Villa des Brillants in 1905 and 1906 (see the entry on Rodin later in this chapter). Rilke published his monograph *Das Rodin-Buch* in 1907.

(See Chapter 1, SWITZERLAND; also Chapter 3, PARIS; also Chapter 4, WEST GERMANY.)

ROBESPIERRE, MAXIMILIEN DE (1758–1794). One of France's more sordid figures, the instigator of the Reign of Terror, Robespierre began his career as a highly idealistic lawyer with a distinct aversion to capital punishment. A native of **Arras** (Pas-de-Calais), his birthplace remains privately owned in the Rue des Rapporteurs. Succeeding dwellings stood in the Rue des Jésuites and the Rue du Collège.

(See Chapter 3, PARIS.)

RODIN, AUGUSTE (1840–1917). "To compare him with Michelangelo is not, in the end, impertinent," wrote Robert Hughes, "for Rodin was one of the last artists to live and work in the belief that making sculpture. . . was a moral act, that it could express one's whole sense of being in the world." At **Meudon** (Hauts-de-Seine), Rodin's country estate, the Villa des Brillants, is now a museum annex of the Rodin Museum in Paris, containing plaster work and rough sketches for some of his best-known sculpture. Rodin lived there from 1897 with his longtime mistress, Marie-Rose Beuret, whom he finally married at the villa in 1917, the year of his death. The three-story high-roofed stone and brick mansion overlooks the Seine at 19 Avenue Auguste-Rodin. Rainier Maria Rilke, the German poet-novelist, served Rodin as secretary there in 1905 and 1906 (see the entry on Rilke earlier in this chapter). (Open Saturday—Monday 1:30—6:00; admission.)

Rodin tomb: Villa des Brillants, **Meudon**.

(See Chapter 3, PARIS; also Chapter 4, BELGIUM.)

ROSSINI, GIOACCHINO (1782–1868). One of the Italian composer's last and most popular operas, *William Tell* (1829), was mostly written at Petit-Bourg, a château loaned to him by a banker friend in 1828. It stands alongside the Seine south of Paris, just north of **Evry** (Essone). Rossini also spent time there in 1830 and 1832.

(See Chapter 3, PARIS; also Chapter 6, LONDON; also Chapter 8, ITALY.)

ROUSSEAU, JEAN-JACQUES (1712–1778). The Swiss-born philosopher and political theorist resided in France for most of his life. From 1722 to 1724, the boy resided as a paying guest at the rectory of Pastor Lambercier at **Bossey** (Haute-Savoie). Jean-Daniel Candaux wrote that Rousseau's "stay at Bossey is famous because Jean-Jacques underwent two important experiences there. He first became aware of social injustice: he was accused of having broken and burnt a comb and, in spite of his protestations of innocence, he was punished. . . . The other experience was that of sex, for Jean-Jacques felt great pleasure when Mlle. Lambercier, the pastor's young sister, spanked his bottom." The rectory still stands in the village.

In 1728 Rousseau fled Geneva and came to **Annecy** (Haute-Savoie), where he met his benefactress and future mistress, Mme. de Warens. A monument commemorating their meeting stands near the site of her house (demolished in 1784) near the Canal du Thiou, where Rousseau lived until 1731.

From 1731 to 1742 the couple lived at long intervals at **Chambéry** (Savoie). The house they occupied in the town, now marked, is located off 54 Place St-Léger. From 1738 they resided at Les Charmettes, a rented 17th-century cottage about one kilometer south in the Chemin des Charmettes. Rousseau began his first serious reading and study there. The municipality displays some original furnishings, period pieces, prints, documents and other memorabilia in the house. (Inquire locally for admission information.)

Appointed as a tutor in 1746, Rousseau taught the son of Mme. Dupin at the 16th-century Château de Chenonceau which spans the River Cher at **Chenonceaux** (Indre-et-Loire). This magnificent palace, one of France's most famous and best preserved, was acquired by Francis I in 1526 in settlement of a debt. It became the frequent residence of Queen Catherine de Médicis who expanded it and laid out a large park and garden (see the entry on Francis I earlier in this chapter). "We enjoyed ourselves much in that beautiful place," recalled Rousseau. "I grew fat as a monk." (Open March 16—September 30, daily 9:00—7:00, *Son et Lumière* performances in evenings; October 1—November 30, February 1—March 15, daily 9:00—5:00; December 1—January 31, daily 9:00—12:00, 2:00—4:00; admission.)

In 1756 Rousseau retired to the country cottage—the Hermitage—built for him by his patroness, Mme. d'Epinay, in the garden of her château. There he proceeded to live the "simple life," giving away most of his possessions and renouncing his previously comfortable existence. He began writing his novel *The New Héloïse* (1761) there but broke with Mme d'Epinay in 1757. Composer André Grétry died there in 1813. Only remnants of the Hermitage survive on route D125 at **Mont-morency** (Val-d'Oise). Rousseau immediately moved to nearby quarters offered by the Duc de Luxembourg, where he lived until 1767 and produced his best-known works, including *Émile* (1762) and *The Social Contract* (1762). Known as "Montluis," the château at what is now 5 Rue Jean-Jacques-Rousseau contains the Rousseau Museum and exhibits manuscripts and memorabilia. (Inquire locally for admission information.)

The philosopher died at **Ermenonville** (Oise) in a pavilion of the château owned by the Marquis de Girardin. Girardin, a devout admirer of Rousseau, had laid out an idyllic English-style park surrounding the château which was intended to demonstrate Rousseau's idea of the environment best suited to the "natural man." The château, wooded islands, streams and text-engraved rocks, plus a columned temple of philosophy—though not Rousseau's pavilion—still exist. Among the notables who made pilgrimages there in tribute were Benjamin Franklin and Napoleon I. (Park open daily, 9:00—5:00 or 7:00; admission.)

(See Chapter 1, SWITZERLAND; also Chapter 3, PARIS; also Chapter 5, ENGLAND; also Chapter 8, ITALY.)

SADE, DONATIEN ALPHONSE FRANÇOIS, MARQUIS DE (1740–1814). In complete contrast to Rousseau, Sade believed that humans are criminal by nature (a position with perhaps more evidence in its favor than Rousseau's), and his violent sexual acts and fantasies, as spelled out in his novels, stories and plays (some of which are still banned), reflect this conviction. Sade "chose cruelty rather than indifference," wrote Simone de Beauvoir. "This is probably why he finds so many echoes today, when the individual knows that he is more the victim of men's good consciences than of their wickedness."

Sade's ancestral estate was the Château of Saumane above the village at **Lacoste** (Vaucluse), where he resided at intervals from 1747. There occurred many of the debaucheries, orgies and erotic spectacles, held with the compliance of Sade's wife and her sister, that led to his imprisonment at Vincennes in 1778. The château was plundered by revolutionists in 1792 and sold by Sade in 1796. Only ruins survive.

From 1778 to 1784 Sade was imprisoned at the Château of **Vincennes** (see the entry on Louis XIV earlier in this chapter).

His last, rather comfortable home from 1803 was the lunatic asylum of Charenton at **Charenton-le-Pont** (Val-de-Marne). There he occupied a small apartment in the second story of the right wing, collected a library of 300 books and directed other inmates in performances of his own plays (he usually chose the villain's part for himself). The asylum, which stood alongside the Seine, is long gone.

(See Chapter 3, PARIS.)

SAND, GEORGE (1804–1876). The prolific novelist and feminist spent most of her childhood and adolescence at her ancestral estate in **Nohant** (Indre). She returned at frequent intervals throughout her life, living there with her first husband, Baron Dudevant, and her later lovers Alfred de Musset and Frédéric Chopin (see the entry on Chopin earlier in this chapter). There she also wrote her first novel, *Indiana* (1832), worked on many others and finally died. The 18th-century mansion is now the George Sand House-Museum (locally known as "The Château"), and displays numerous memorabilia and furnishings of the writer as well as of her many famous guests, including Balzac, Chopin, Flaubert, Dumas *fils* and Franz Liszt. The original appearance of the small 1864 theater where she and her friends staged dramas has been preserved. (Open April

GEORGE SAND'S LIFELONG HOME. Known as "The Château," the novelist's ancestral mansion at **Nohant** was the scene of much of her work and also hosted some of Europe's most notable writers, painters, and musicians.

1—September 30, Wednesday—Monday 9:00—11:45, 2:00—6:00; October 1—March 31, Wednesday—Monday 10:00—11:45, 2:00—4:00; admission.)

The nearby village of **La Châtre** is the heart of George Sand country, a landscape made famous in her novels. She wrote part of *Lélia* (1833) at lodgings in the Rue des Pavillons.

Another nearby retreat, from 1858 to 1864, was Algira, a cottage given her at **Gargilesse-Dampierre**. Escorted tours are guided by Mme. Sand, a descendant of the writer. Mementos and manuscripts are on display. (Open April 1—September 30, daily 9:00—12:00, 3:00—7:00; admission.)

Sand tomb: Chapel cemetery, **Nohant**.

Exhibit: At **La Châtre**, the George Sand and Black Valley Museum, 71 Rue Venôse, is housed in Chauvigny Castle. Portraits, letters, first editions and mementos of Sand and her notable friends are the highlights of this collection. (Open Palm Sunday—October 15, Friday—Wednesday 9:30—11:30, 2:00—5:30, except closed Sunday morning; October 16—Palm Sunday, Wednesday, Sunday 3:00—6:00; admission.)

(See Chapter 3, PARIS; also Chapter 8, ITALY, SPAIN.)

SCHWEITZER, ALBERT (1875–1965). Alsace, Schweitzer's birthplace and European home, belonged to Germany when he was born, and the philosopher, physician, humanitarian and winner of the 1954 Nobel Peace Prize always considered himself German. The Lutheran vicarage where he was born survives in the village of **Kaysersberg** (Haute-Rhin); it is now the Schweitzer Museum and displays memorabilia. (Inquire locally for admission information.)

Another vicarage at nearby **Gunsbach** became his home when he was only a few months old. The present family dwelling dates from 1926 and Schweitzer returned there for infrequent intervals after establishing his Lambaréné mission in Gabon, Africa, in 1912; the longest such interval was a period after World War I (1918–24).

Schweitzer studied and taught at St. Thomas College, University of Strasbourg, in **Strasbourg** (Bas-Rhin) during the 1890s and from 1905 to 1912; he also served as Lutheran pastor of St. Nicholas Church. He resided in rooms at St. Thomas College, Quai St-Thomas.

World War I interrupted his missionary activities. Both Schweitzer and his wife, Hélène Bresslau, were interned as German nationals upon their return from Africa in 1917 and both suffered extreme illness at their first place of confinement: a camp located at 136 Rue Belleville in **Bordeaux** (Gironde). They were held there only briefly, but "those three weeks," wrote James Brabazon, "were a tragic turning point for both of them, for never again was Hélène fully fit to work beside her husband in Africa."

Confined during the next year in a former monastery at **St-Rémy-de-Provence** (Bouches-du-Rhône), Schweitzer vaguely recognized his room and soon realized he had seen it in a painting by van Gogh, who had spent some of his last months incarcerated in the same chamber (see the entry on Vincent van Gogh later in this chapter).

(See Chapter 3, PARIS; also Chapter 4, WEST GERMANY, THE NETHERLANDS.)

SIBELIUS, JEAN (1865–1957). In 1905 and 1906 the Finnish symphonic composer lived at the Henri-IV Pavilion in **St-Germain-en-Laye** (see the entry on Alexandre Dumas, *père*, earlier in this chapter).

(See Chapter 1, AUSTRIA; also Chapter 3, PARIS; also Chapter 4, FINLAND.)

STEVENSON, ROBERT LOUIS (1850–1894).

Exhibit: One of the Scottish writer's most engaging books is *Travels with a Donkey in the Cévennes* (1879), recently issued in new editions. Stevenson began his 12-day, 193-kilometer hike through the Cévennes Mountains with his donkey Modestine from **Le Monastier-sur-Gazeille** (Haute-Loire) in September 1878. "Everybody here thought him a lunatic because such a thing was unheard of at the time," said Mayor Marcel Bocquin in 1984. Today the Robert Louis Stevenson Trail, not an easy walk, draws numerous dedicated hikers to retrace the scenic, sparsely populated route traversed by the author. Trail markers begin in Le Monastier and end at St-Jean-du-Gard, where Stevenson sold Modestine for 35 francs. In the lobby of Le Monastier's town hall may be seen a wall display that details Stevenson's route. (Contact Syndicat d'Initiative, Le Monastier.)

(See Chapter 1, SWITZERLAND; also Chapter 5, ENGLAND; also Chapter 7, SCOTLAND.)

STRAVINSKY, IGOR (1882–1971). From 1924 to 1931 the Russian-born composer, who became a naturalized French citizen in 1934, lived in the Villa des Roses at 167 Boulevard Carnot on scenic Mount Boron, **Nice** (Alpes-Maritimes). His *Oedipus Rex* (1927) and *Symphony of Psalms* (1930) were written during this period.

(See Chapter 1, SWITZERLAND; also Chapter 3, PARIS.)

TOULOUSE-LAUTREC, HENRI DE (1864–1901). Portrayer of Montmartre night life in his posters and illustrations and an important influence on Picasso and advertising art, Toulouse-Lautrec was born of a wealthy family in **Albi** (Tarn). His birthplace was the Hôtel du Bosc, a mansion owned by a great-aunt at what is now 14 Rue de Toulouse-Lautrec. It was his home until 1872 and frequent vacation residence thereafter. There in 1878 he suffered a fracture of his left thigh after a simple fall from a chair and the following year broke his right leg in another fall. These injuries, probably the result of a bone disease, stunted his leg growth and crippled him for life, giving him a dwarfish appearance.

Near **Coursan** (Aude), the Château of Céleyran, which remains in the Route de Salles-d'Aude, belonged to his maternal grandparents. The painter spent many childhood years on this estate.

About two kilometers southeast of **Naucelle-Gare** (Aude), via signs, stands another childhood home: the Château of Bosc, owned by his paternal grandparents, is still retained by the family. A huge stone-towered castle with an interior courtyard, it displays memorabilia of the painter. (Guided tours Easter—October 15, Sunday—Monday, Thursday; admission.)

At **Neuilly-sur-Seine** (Hauts-de-Seine) near Paris, the alcoholic artist in 1899 underwent three months of drying out at the clinic of Dr. Sémelaigne, located at 16 Avenue de Madrid.

Toulouse-Lautrec's mother purchased the Château of Malromé in the village of **St-André-du-Bois** (Gironde) in 1883, an estate that the painter made his frequent holiday home. He died there of advanced alcoholism and untreated syphilis at a very aged 36.

Toulouse-Lautrec tomb: Churchyard, **Verdelais** (Gironde).

Exhibit: Probably the largest collection of Toulouse-Lautrec art is displayed at the Toulouse-Lautrec Museum, located in the Palais de la Berbie at **Albi**. It includes paintings, drawings and lithographs. (Open summer, daily 9:00—12:00, 2:00—6:00; rest of year, daily 10:00—12:00, 2:00—5:00; admission.)

(See Chapter 3, PARIS.)

VAN GOGH, VINCENT (1853–1890). "We cannot look at a wheatfield, sunflower or a cypress tree except through his eyes," wrote Robert Payne of the Provence region where the painter produced some of his most luminous works, "and all of southern France belongs to him." In 1888 van Gogh arrived at **Arles** (Bouches-du-Rhône) and sequestered himself in the right wing of a two-story yellow-fronted house. There he experimented with color. "Instead of trying to reproduce exactly what I have before my eyes," he wrote his brother Théo in letters that have since become literary classics, "I use color more arbitrarily in order to express myself with more force." As a result, his canvases, both landscapes and still lifes, shimmer and pulse with feverish energy. Théo had financed his brother's move to Arles, and van Gogh invited his friend Paul Gauguin there for companionship and to share the exquisite sunlight. Their friendship rapidly disintegrated as van Gogh began suffering episodes of paranoia and bizarre behavior. On one occasion, he attacked Gauguin with a razor; and it was in this house that he impulsively mutilated himself by cutting off part of his left ear and giving it to a prostitute who had favored Gauguin over himself (see the entry on Gauguin earlier in this chapter). From that point on, he was lucid only at intervals. During his 15 months at Arles, however, van Gogh painted more brilliantly than at any time in his relentlessly compulsive life; he produced more than 300 canvases, including his famed *Sunflowers* and *Self-Portrait*. The site of the yellow house, bombed out in 1944, is marked at 21 Place Lamartine.

During a lucid period in 1889, van Gogh admitted himself to an asylum, the priory of St-Paul-de-Mausole at nearby **St-Rémy-de-Provence**, for care and rest. The yellow stone garden house of this former 12th-century monastery became his cell, and he completed another vast quantity of canvases, drawings and watercolors there—including some interiors and scenes of the view from his window. A later inmate in the same chamber was Albert Schweitzer (see the entry on Schweitzer earlier in this chapter). Van Gogh's room with its original furnishings remains basically intact in the former monastery, still a convalescent home as it basically was then. Special permission must be sought from the custodian to view the room. (Monastery open November 1—March 31, daily 8:00—7:00; donation.)

Van Gogh's last home, in 1890, was Gustave Ravoux's cafe in **Auvers-sur-Oise** (Val-d'Oise). From this inn he went out one Sunday afternoon to the nearby fields and shot himself in the chest. He died a day later at the inn, which is still a cafe, now called Chez Van Gogh. Visitors may see the upstairs room where the painter's devoted brother Théo sat with van Gogh during his last hours.

Van Gogh tomb: Village cemetery, **Auvers-sur-Oise**.

(See Chapter 3, PARIS; also Chapter 4, BELGIUM, THE NETHERLANDS; also Chapter 5, ENGLAND.)

VERNE, JULES (1828–1905). The writer's prophetic science fiction, enormously popular in his own day, has been adapted into numerous successful films. A native of **Nantes** (Loire-Atlantique), Verne was born at 3 Rue Olivier-de-Clisson in his grandparents' apartment. The house stood on an island in the River Loire in 1828 but the Loire has since shifted course and placed it high on the shoreline. Shortly after his birth, Verne's family moved to 2 Quai Jean-Bart; it was their home until 1840 and his father also practiced law in the building. Verne began studying law himself at their next home, 6 Jean-Jacques-Rousseau, from which he departed for Paris in 1848. Much later, as a well-known author, he returned to Nantes for a year (1877–78) and resided at 1 Rue Suffren, an apartment he had rented in 1874 for his worrisome son.

The village of **Le Crotoy** (Somme), Verne's home from 1869 to 1872, was where he wrote one of his best-known novels, *Twenty Thousand Leagues Under the Sea* (1870). His house remains at what is now 9 Rue Jules-Verne.

Verne's permanent residence from 1872 was **Amiens** (Somme). From 1878 to 1890 he lived at what is now 44 Boulevard Jules-Verne. His last home from 1890, and the place where he died, is the three-story house he rented at 2 Rue Charles-Dubois.

Verne tomb: La Madeleine Cemetery, **Amiens**.

Exhibits: At **Nantes**, the Jules Verne Museum at 3 Rue de l'Hermitage displays memorabilia, letters, furniture, portraits and a collection of the writer's works. (Open Wednesday—Monday 10:00—12:30, 2:00—5:00; admission.)

The Museum of Regional Art and History at 36 Rue Victor-Hugo in **Amiens** contains a room devoted to Verne. (Inquire locally for admission information.)

(See Chapter 1, SWITZERLAND; also Chapter 3, PARIS.)

VOLTAIRE, FRANÇOIS-MARIE AROUET (1694–1778). "To name Voltaire," said Victor Hugo, "is to characterize the entire eighteenth century." "He was for his country," wrote Will Durant, "both Renaissance and Reformation, and half the Revolution." When all is said, he was probably France's greatest man and a durable inspiration to freedom-lovers everywhere.

Exiled from Paris by royalty in 1716, in what was to become the standard authoritarian remedy for his biting, unwelcome wit (e. g., "Christianity must be divine since it has lasted 1,700 years despite the fact that it is so full of villainy and nonsense"), Voltaire spent some eight years "guesting" for longer or shorter periods at various châteaus as a darling of the aristocracy. One of these residences was the Château of Sully, the 14th-century feudal palace at **Sully-sur-Loire** (Loiret). This rectangular towered structure, damaged in 1940 but since restored, retains its original timbered roof—still in fine shape after more than 600 years. In its first-floor hall, Voltaire watched his plays performed. The château stands alongside the Loire at the junction of routes D948 and D951. (Open for guided tours April 1—September 30, daily 9:00—11:45, 2:00—6:00; November, daily 10:00—11:45, 2:00—4:30; admission.)

Voltaire wrote part of his epic poem *La Henriade* (1723) at the now abandoned Château of La Rivière-Bourdet in **Quevillon** (Seine-Maritime). The 17th-century castle stands on route D67 at the village entrance.

At **Maisons-Laffitte** (Yvelines) in 1724, Voltaire was a guest at the Château of Maisons; there he suffered from smallpox (which he claimed to have cured by drinking 120 pints of lemonade) and had to flee his bed when it somehow caught fire. The 17th-century château displays little of note on Voltaire but does have some notable interior decorations and furnishings. (Open May—September, Wednesday, Saturday 3:30, Sunday

3:00 and 4:30; October—May, Sunday 3:30; admission.)

One of the philosopher's important dwellings was the Château Cirey-sur-Blaise, owned by the learned Marquise du Châtelet, his mistress and collaborator from 1733 to 1748. Rebuilt and enlarged by the couple, the château provided frequent refuge during those years from the inclement political weather in Paris. Voltaire performed scientific experiments in his laboratory there, and the lovers competed with each other in scholarly activities, occupying most of their daytimes with study and research and welcoming numerous guests in the evenings. "Very soon Cirey became the Paris of the French mind," wrote Durant. "The aristocracy and the bourgeoisie joined in the pilgrimage to taste Voltaire's wine and wit, and see him act in his own plays." Among the many historical and polemical works he produced there, Voltaire also wrote his philosophical tale *Zadig* (1748). Voltaire left Cirey when the marquise took another lover. The château is located six kilometers from **Doulevant-le-Château** (Haute-Marne) on route D2.

By 1758 Voltaire had achieved a worldwide reputation. But while he was worshipped by the multitudes, he was harassed, as ever, by the royalty and churchmen whom he studiously offended. The philosopher sought refuge in the tiny, free Republic of Geneva, buying the estate of Ferney, which today lies within the French border just across from Geneva, Switzerland. He designed and built a château and resided there with his niece and mistress, Marie-Louise Denis, from 1765 to 1778. At Ferney, Voltaire did all of his later writing, including numerous vitriolic pamphlets attacking both Catholicism and Calvinism. He received countless visitors, built houses and factories on his estate to provide for people who sought his protection, instituted social reforms and aided countless individual victims of injustice who came to his attention. The village of **Ferney-Voltaire** (Ain), located on route N5, grew around his estate. Privately owned, the Château of Ferney contains numerous memorabilia and possessions of the philosopher. (Open July—August, Saturday 2:00—5:00; contact Syndicat d'Initiative, Ferney-Voltaire, for information.)

(See Chapter 1, SWITZERLAND; also Chapter 3, PARIS; also Chapter 4, EAST GERMANY.)

WAGNER, RICHARD (1813–1883). In 1841 in

Meudon (Hauts-de-Seine) the German composer worked on his opera *The Flying Dutchman* (1843) at 27 Avenue du Château.

(See Chapter 1, AUSTRIA, SWITZERLAND; also Chapter 3, PARIS; also Chapter 4, EAST GERMANY, WEST GERMANY; also Chapter 6, LONDON; also Chapter 8, ITALY.)

WILLIAM THE CONQUEROR (WILLIAM I) (1027–1087). The feudal Duke William's claim to the throne of England was, and is, controversial but he led the 1066 Norman invasion that deposed the Saxon monarchy and ultimately transformed the entire face, language and culture of Great Britain. Known as "William the Bastard" because of his royal father's coupling with a peasant girl he did not wed, William was born at Falaise Castle in **Falaise** (Calvados). Only ruins, though impressive ones, survive of the massive fortress which was the favorite residence of the first dukes of Normandy. The ramparts dominating the town were once flanked by 14 towers. The square keep and oldest visible walls actually date from the 12th and 13th centuries, after William's time, a circumstance that does not prevent tour guides from pointing out the window where Duke Robert "the Devil" first spied the fair Arlette washing clothes in a stream below the castle; and the cell in which their son William was born. William spent his childhood and youth at Falaise, inherited the Norman throne as Duke William II in 1035 at the age of eight, and emerged from Falaise to become one of the century's greatest warriors. Until he invaded England, most of William's numerous battles were successfully undertaken to subdue revolts against his ducal control. Falaise remained a functional stronghold until the late 16th century. (During World War II, in 1944, a pincer movement by the Allied forces trapped the German Seventh Army at Falaise; the town had served as a German observation post.) The St. Prix Chapel in the castle displays a memorial tablet listing the names of 315 men who accompanied William to England in 1066. The castle is approached via the Place Guillaume-le-Conquérant. (Guided tours, April 1—September 30, Wednesday—Monday 9:00—12:00, 2:00—6:00; November 3—March 31, Monday, Wednesday—Saturday, same hours; closed October; admission.)

In 1060 William erected a château at **Caen** (Calvados) which remained his favorite seat for the rest of his life. The ruined ramparts high above the city date from this period but most surviving portions of the castle itself represent later expansions during the 12th through 15th centuries when England held Caen. The castle, accessible from the Porte sur la Ville, suffered extensive damage during World War II but restoration has preserved its prewar aspect. In addition to the 12th-century keep and the public gardens within the walls, visitors may also see the Fine Arts Museum, Normandy Museum and St-Georges Chapel. (Castle grounds open summer, daily 7:00 a.m.—9:30 p.m.; free.)

William prepared for the English invasion at the Château of Bonneville, **Bonneville-sur-Touques** (Calvados) where he spent some seven months in 1066. This was also the probable spot where Harold of England had earlier sworn fealty to William in 1064. The breaking of that oath, when Harold assumed the English throne, provided the impetus for William's invasion. Only a few wall remnants of the castle survive off route N834. (Open March 1—November 30, Saturday—Sunday 2:00—6:00; admission.)

Following his fall from a horse at Mantes in 1087 during a raid on the town, William was brought to the hilltop monastery of St-Gervais in **Rouen** (Seine-Maritime); there he suffered for weeks from a slowly spreading peritonitis and finally died. The monastery stood on the present site of the 19th-century Church of St-Gervais in the Rue St-Gervais.

William I tomb (site): Church of St-Étienne, **Caen**.

Exhibits: Coastal markers recall the gathering of William's 696-ship invasion fleet at **Dives-sur-Mer** (Calvados) and its departing point at the port of **St-Valéry-sur-Somme** (Somme), where he awaited a favorable east wind.

The most unique historical record of the invasion is, of course, the 11th-century Bayeux Tapestry. Sometimes called "Queen Matilda's Tapestry," it was wrongly attributed as the handiwork of William's queen during the 18th century; the actual artisans remain unknown. This 231-foot-long embroidery, stitched with colored wools on a linen background, was probably commissioned in England by William's half-brother, Bishop Odo of Bayeux, several years after the Conquest. Protected by glass and special lighting, this notable historic work may be seen in the former Bishop's Palace located south of Notre-Dame Cathedral in **Bayeux** (Calvados). A recorded commentary in

English is available. (Open June 1—September 15, daily 9:00—7:00; September 16—October 15, daily 9:00—12:00, 2:00—6:30; October 16—May 31, daily 9:00—12:00, 2:00—6:00; admission.)

(See Chapter 5, ENGLAND; also Chapter 6, LONDON.)

WORDSWORTH, WILLIAM (1770–1850). The English poet journeyed to France "to learn French" during—of all times—the French Revolution. Seeing some of the conditions that brought about that uprising, he soon became an enthusiastic supporter of the Revolution. He roomed in Orléans (Loiret, 1791–92) in the house of a hatter, located at the intersection of the Rue Royale and the Rue du Tabour. It was probably there that he met and fell in love with Annette Vallon, who bore him a child. For various reasons they did not marry, and Wordsworth returned to England in 1792. He supported Vallon and their daughter for years afterward, and there are still Wordsworth descendants in France. His Orléans lodging is long gone.

(See Chapter 5, ENGLAND.)

YEATS, WILLIAM BUTLER (1865–1939). The ailing Irish poet spent his last two winters in the Mediterranean climate of France's Alpes-Maritimes. At **Menton** he lodged during 1937 and 1938 in the Hôtel Carlton at what is now 6 Avenue Général-de-Gaulle.

Yeats's last home (1938–39) was a suite in the now long-gone Hôtel Idéal Séjour at **Roquebrune-Cap-Martin**, where he died.

(See Chapter 5, ENGLAND; also Chapter 6, LONDON; also Chapter 7, IRELAND.)

ZOLA, ÉMILE (1840–1902). The novelist and pioneer of literary naturalism had several boyhood homes in **Aix-en-Provence** (Bouches-du-Rhône); they included unknown addresses in the Impasse Sylvacanne, Rue Roux-Alphéran and Rue Mazarine. From 1852 to 1856 he boarded with his friend Paul Cézanne at the Lycée Bourbon, now the Lycée Mignet, in the Rue Cardinale (see the entry on Cézanne earlier in this chapter). Zola carried few pleasant memories of Aix in later life and disparaged it under the name "Plassans" in several novels. The town has reciprocated by studiously memorializing the civil engineering accomplishments of his father, Italian-born François Zola, rather than his own literary works.

From the profits of his novel *L'Assommoir* (1877), Zola bought a country house on an island of the Seine in the village of **Médan** (Yvelines) in 1878 and for the rest of his life spent about six months of each year there. He never stopped enlarging, planting and transforming the estate, which he called Le Paradou. Eventually it grew to considerable size. Alexandrine Meley, his wife, would ceremonially plant the first trees, stakes and foundation stones for new gardens, greenhouses, marble stables and other structures. Zola wrote most of his best-known works there, including *Nana* (1880) and *Germinal* (1885). After his death, Mme. Zola gave the estate to the Assistance Publique for use as an orphanage, a purpose it has served ever since.

Nearby, in the village of **Cheverchemont**, Zola installed his longtime mistress, Jeanne Roserot, in a house he bought for her in 1888 at 64 Rue du Général-Leclerc. She raised their two children within sight of Zola's villa—from which he watched them, it is said, through a telescope.

(See Chapter 3, PARIS; also Chapter 6, LONDON.)

Chapter 3
FRANCE: PARIS

Because almost every French notable as well as many other famous Europeans resided in Paris at some time in their lives, this world capital and largest French city merits a separate chapter. A population of more than eight million makes greater Paris the world's sixth largest city; for convenience, however, this chapter treats only central Paris, that densely populated area of 106 square kilometers (41 square miles) containing about 2.5 million people. Its borders, now marked by the ring road of the Boulevard Périphérique, follow the outline of the city's 19th-century defensive walls. Homes of notables who lived in outlying suburbs of Paris are included in Chapter 2.

As many observers have noted, Parisians regard Paris as the center of all true culture, progress and civilization—anyone who can't see this self-evident fact is simply to be pitied. From Henry James, that reserved American expatriate, Paris evoked a virtual emotional outburst: "Paris is the greatest temple ever built to material joys and the lust of the eyes."

From the 13th-century opening of the Sorbonne, Paris has attracted students, travelers and artists of every talent and description. No world city has made creative spirits feel so at home. Paris introduced new ways of seeing—through the eyes of impoverished Left Bank painters, whose works now decorate places that they themselves could not have entered. In Paris emerged new ways of thinking, of intellectually framing the world, through the minds of philosophers such as Des-

cartes, Rousseau, Camus and Sartre. Such literary expatriates as James Joyce, Henry Miller, Ernest Hemingway, Oscar Wilde, Richard Wright and James Baldwin not only found freedom in Paris to pursue their own visions but found in it a place of refuge from the religious, sexual and racial repressions that crippled their less permissive homelands. "It is not what France gives you," said American-Parisian Gertrude Stein, "it's what she doesn't take away." Emerson, another American, would have agreed: "England built London for its own use, but France built Paris for the world." And the world has gathered a rich harvest from the streets, quays and quarters of Paris. Even the Nazi masters of the city ignored Hitler's order to destroy it in 1944 when Allied forces approached. Earth without a Paris would be a cold world for humanity.

Yet the course of Parisian civilization has hardly run as broad and smooth as the Champs Élysées. Under World War II German occupation, Paris marked time. "The French," wrote Sanche de Gramont "suffered from such an intense sense of guilt that they felt obliged to act out, as though in some penitential charade, the opinion the Germans had of them as a futile, frivolous people." The end of the occupation saw a massive heaping of self-immolation upon injury. In an old revolutionary reflex Parisians divided themselves into condemners and condemned, indulging in their own bloodbath against accused collaborators, and treating other nations to the astonishing spectacle of how well they had learned their methods of "justice" from the Germans. This self-inflicted wound probably hurt Paris as a community more than any other action of the war.

The city of Paris originated on the Île de la Cité, the boat-shaped island in the River Seine which still forms the hub of the city. As early as the third century B.C., a Gallic tribe called the Parisii had settled there, fortifying the island and prospering by fishing and river trade. The settlement was first mentioned by Julius Caesar in 53 B.C. He called it "Lutetia" and made it a meeting place for delegates from conquered Gaul. Roman Lutetia Parisiorum grew on the South Bank in the present area of the Latin Quarter but the colony remained governed from the island. In 360, when Julian the Apostate was proclaimed Roman emperor in his villa on the present site of the Palace of Justice, the name "Paris" was applied to the town. The Frankish king Clovis made Paris a Christian capital in 508. Under Capetian monarch Philip-Augustus in 1194, Paris became the political and administrative center of the Île de France, the district which included the city and its surrounding area. The Île de France gradually brought under its control the numerous feudal states from which modern France evolved. Thus the nation is simply a historical extension, through many wars and centuries, of this region surrounding Paris.

Likewise "much of French history," wrote one observer, "is simply Paris history presented as a *fait accompli* to the provinces." In Paris was established the principle of French monarchy, which continued through six royal houses and more than 40 kings and emperors until 1870. After the invading Franks reestablished the town center on the Île de la Cité in the sixth century, the island remained the royal, legal and ecclesiastical nucleus of Paris for some 700 years. The aforementioned Philip-Augustus not only built the Louvre as a fortress in 1190 but also established the famed medieval University of Paris (1208), predecessor of the Sorbonne. On the Île de la Cité rises the 13th-century cathedral of Notre Dame, scene of numerous French coronations and state marriages and funerals. The supremacy of Paris as the dominant economic, intellectual and governmental center of France has never been challenged.

The French Revolution, that volatile mix of high ideals, reign of terror, civil war and cynical betrayal, was a Parisian phenomenon that began as a street riot in 1789 and spread like napalm to the provinces. Ruthlessly determined to sever everything remotely connected to the royalist past, revolutionists even invented a Revolutionary calendar that dated year one from 1792, when the First Republic was proclaimed, and which remained in effect until 1806. The street insurrection has been a characteristic Parisian form of civil protest ever since. Anticlerical Paris mobs were noted for butchering monks and priests, most notably during the shortlived Communard Insurrection of 1871. What the French Revolution finally gave to the world was not a pattern for implementing its ideals—*liberté, égalité, et fraternité*—but a rhetoric and rationale of anarchy. It provided patterns for civil insurrection, guerrilla warfare, terrorism as a political tool, *coup* tactics of government and the predominance of the citizen-soldier as a military weapon. It gave a fierce new paranoiac notion of patriotism. And in the final analysis it corrected none of the profound evils that had inspired it: in the words of a gloating Napoleon, "It did not displace any interests, while awakening many."

Even now Paris without its periodic uprisings, most often inspired by students, would not be the Paris we know. But today (such has been their predictable regularity) Paris mob scenes seem almost dutiful or ceremonial in nature: it is a rare year—one might almost say an unpatriotic one—in which the city does not indulge itself in at least one modest riot, never complete without the fondly erected street barricades. "If you're not part of the solution, you're part of the problem," is not 20th-century protest coinage but 18th-century French rhetoric. Parisians have seldom lacked the readiness to define "us" from "them," and this constant readiness may be the Revolution's most durable result.

Paris locations are commonly identified by referring to the Right Bank and Left Bank of the curving Seine. To anyone unfamiliar with the city, however, these are confusing designations—they have meaning only if one faces in the correct direction. The correct direction is west, the downstream course of the Seine. Paris locations in this chapter thus follow the traditional nomenclature of Parisians, being identified as either on the Right (i.e., north) or Left (i.e., south) Bank, or on one of the two Seine islands within the city: the Île de la Cité and the Île St-Louis. The Right Bank is the traditional center of Paris commerce and government, while the Left Bank achieved renown for its student, artistic and cafe society population. (Though the Left Bank is still a popular residence for foreign artists, Paris no longer provides the main focus for their work; jet travel has efficiently wiped out the symbolic value of solitary artists "holed up" against an uncaring world.) Both urban banks are much more equal in civic importance than is the case in London, where the Thames north bank far outranks the boroughs south of the river. The Seine is also much less of a social boundary than the Thames and more of a simple geographical fact. (In the following pages, the boldfaced bank designation applies to all addresses within.)

Central Paris, the exclusive focus of this chapter, is divided into 20 municipal districts called *arrondissements*. The arrondissement number, identified in any city map or directory, is part of a formal Paris address. These numbered districts spiral outward from the Île de la Cité; it is a pleasing pattern of urban districting in a Western culture that usually prefers square-and-rectangle thinking. Each district has its own distinctive flavor. Within and often overlapping them are found the quarters familiar to tourists and armchair travelers: the Latin Quarter, St-Germain, Montparnasse, Montmartre and many others. In streets parallel to the Seine, houses are numbered from east to west. In streets at right angles to the river numbering begins from the end nearest the Seine. Paris guidebooks are numerous and, for the most part, excellent. The "bible" for all seekers of historical Paris streets and buildings is Jacques Hillairet's two-volume *Dictionnaire Historique des Rues de Paris* (1963). An excellent specialized biographical guidebook is Brian N. Morton's *Americans in Paris* (1984).

Since 1977 Paris has been governed by a mayor and city council, rather than nationally, which has vastly improved the administration of the city. Paris demolishes few buildings; it is full of 17th- and 18th-century structures that have been built to last and which are superbly functional. War has been the major destructive element, though there was more disruption during the First than the Second World War. Numerous dwellings and apartment lodgings of notables still exist but while many of them are marked with tablets, only a few stand open to the public. These latter house-museums are mainly operated by the City of Paris. A massive cleanup program begun during the 1960s has transformed the faded, gray buildings and squares of central Paris and today their pristine appearance resembles that of earlier decades. Paris' plumbing, water supply, housing and even currency have also been improved. Today Paris is one of the best administered urban complexes in the world, far ahead of such cities as New York, London, or Tokyo in the science of civic planning and engineering. Thus the inherent Parisian assumption of superiority is harder than ever to discount—for anyone, that is, who would choose to.

NOTE: The word *bis* following an address number in the following pages indicates a fractional address; for example, the address 1bis is equivalent to 1a or 1 1/2.

Also bear in mind the former as contrasted to the modern usage of the word *hôtel*, as explained in the introduction to Chapter 2.

ABÉLARD, PETER (1079–1142). About 1112, as a popular canon and lecturer at Notre Dame School, this philosopher-theologian provoked his superiors with his rationalistic challenges to dogma. He soon withdrew many of his students to the Abbaye Ste-Genevieve, nucleus of the University of Paris, where he lived, taught and verbally sniped at his former mentors until 1119. He also returned briefly in 1136. Most of these abbey buildings were reconstructed in the 18th century but a relic of the original abbey exists as part of the Lycée Henry-IV Tower at 23 Rue Clovis, **Left Bank**.

On the **Île de la Cité**, the traditional site of the 12th-century house where Abélard and Hélouïse lived is marked at 9 Quai aux Fleurs, the home of Hélouïse's uncle, Canon Fulbert. (Some sources give the address as 10 Rue Chanoinesse.) The house stood until 1849. Abélard, a charismatic 39-year-old scholar, moved there in about 1118, ostensibly to tutor the 16-year-old Hélouïse but actually to seduce her, an act he quickly accomplished. Hélouïse, willing to be Abélard's mistress but not his wife, soon became pregnant. Fulbert insisted on their marriage and the ceremony was secretly performed so as not to hinder Abélard's future in the church. When news of their child got out, however, Fulbert revealed the marriage, Hélouïse hotly denied it, and Abélard spirited her off to a convent. Convinced that Abélard had dealt treacherously with his niece, Fulbert hired four thugs to wreak a terrible revenge. At Abélard's unknown nearby lodgings, they invaded his bedroom with a razor and, as Abélard wrote," cut off those parts of my body whereby I had done that which was the cause of their complaint." News of the castration stunned Paris. Fulbert was fined all of his earthly goods. Though he visited her frequently in later years, Abélard and Hélouïse spent the rest of their sad lives apart, both living in holy orders. After their deaths they were buried together. (See the entry on Hélouïse later in this chapter.)

Abélard tomb: Père-Lachaise Cemetery.
(See Chapter 2, FRANCE.)

AQUINAS, ST. THOMAS (1225–1274). On the **Left Bank** at 14 Rue Soufflot a tablet marks the site of the Dominican convent where this Italian scholar and philosopher studied, taught and resided during three separate intervals (1245–48, 1252–59 and 1268–72). During the latter period he undoubtedly worked on his major treatise, *Summa Theologica* (1265–74): it remains the philosophical cornerstone and synthesis of Roman Catholic doctrines. Like so many French abbeys, the convent was suppressed and destroyed during

the Revolution in 1790. Its entrance stood at 156 Rue St-Jacques.

(See Chapter 4, WEST GERMANY; also Chapter 8, ITALY.)

BALZAC, HONORÉ DE (1799–1850). Both realist and romantic in more than 90 novels and tales, Balzac was a compulsive writer whose fictional characters often became more real to him than living people. His series *La Comédie Humaine*, in which he attempted to depict every facet of French society, includes more than 50 volumes. Balzac resided permanently (though restlessly) in Paris from 1814. Until 1819 he lived with his family at what is today 122 Rue du Temple on the **Right Bank**, attending a private boarding school. At 9 Rue Lesdiguières he rented an attic room he described as "a hole worthy of the stews of Venice" and there began writing in earnest (1819–20); the original house was moved to the Boulevard Henri-IV, where it may still exist.

His address from 1826 to 1828 was on the **Left**

THE HOUSE OF BALZAC. With his mistress Louise Breugnol, the prolific novelist lived in this house at 47 Rue Raynouard in Passy for seven years. It is now owned by the City of Paris and displays memorabilia of the writer.

Bank at 17 Rue Visconti. There he operated a print shop, which ruined him financially, and occupied three squalid rooms above it. The Romantic painter Eugène Delacroix later occupied a studio there (1838–43; composer Frédéric Chopin and writer George Sand were among those who came to pose for him). At 1 Rue Cassini, Balzac's three-room lodging from 1828 to 1835, the writer experienced his first literary success with his novel *Les Chouans* (1829); he also wrote *Eugénie Grandet* (1833) and *Le Père Goriot* (1834) there. The house was destroyed during the 1890s.

Back on the **Right Bank**, the years 1835 to 1838 were spent hiding from creditors at 13 Avenue d'Iéna, where he admitted visitors only by password. From 1840 to 1847 he lived with his mistress, Louise Breugnol, at 47 Rue Raynouard in **Passy**. "It was a splendid house for this man who could never make ends meet and where creditors would go to any length to try and make him pay up," wrote Anne Roche. "He kept a ladder handy,

BALZAC'S ESCAPE PASSAGE. Constantly harassed by creditors, Balzac often made use of this alley, the Rue Berton, behind his Passy house when these unwelcome guests appeared at his door. The ivy-covered walls of the passage, essentially unchanged today, became one of his most familiar views of the neighborhood and no doubt heard many a sputtered expletive as he hastened to elude the bill collectors.

down which he slid to the Rue Berton [number 24] and would only come back when he learnt the hunt was off." One of many Balzac dwellings in Paris, this house was chosen by the City of Paris in 1908 as a repository for the writer's few surviving possessions. Now the Balzac Museum, it displays a desk and chair, the coffee pot that fueled him through long nights of writing, and various documents and portraits. Among the novels that Balzac produced there were *La Cousine Bette* (1846) and *Le Cousin Pons* (1847). The ivy-covered space behind the house in the Rue Berton remains one of the few such courtyards in Passy. (Open Wednesday—Sunday 10:00—6:00; 224-56-38; admission.)

Balzac's last home, from 1847, stood at what is now 12 Rue Balzac on the **Right Bank**; a mansion, he bought and richly furnished it for his mistress and later wife, Eveline Hanska, who savagely criticized his choice of dwellings. Balzac's ever-present mother supervised the choice of furnishings and decoration. There the newly married couple, returning from a journey to the Ukraine in May 1850, had to engage a locksmith to open the door—Balzac had lost the key. Gravely ill, he died there three months later. His widow stayed, cleared the debt on the house and sold it years later. It was demolished in 1890.

Balzac tomb: Père-Lachaise Cemetery.
(See Chapter 2, FRANCE.)

BAUDELAIRE, CHARLES PIERRE (1821–1867). A gifted poet, Baudelaire sought beauty in the perverse and morbid and was prosecuted for obscenity on the appearance of his highly influential *Les Fleurs du Mal* (1857). A native of Paris, Baudelaire never resided for long anywhere else, yet he settled in no permanent home, instead dwelling briefly in hotels or other lodgings—some 32 identified places—all over the city (see Name Index and Gazetteer). His birthplace stood at 15 Rue Hautefeuille, **South Bank**.

On the **Île St-Louis** the present Hôtel de Lauzun, a 1657 structure, was Baudelaire's lodging in 1843 and again in 1845. Now owned by the City of Paris at 17 Quai d'Anjou, the building is used for official receptions and tours must be prearranged. The apartments rented to Baudelaire and later to novelist and poet Théophile Gautier are on the south side, now used as a storage area for the Carnavalet Museum, and remain inaccessible to visitors. The first and second floors, however, display lavish furnishings of the Louis XIV period.

Guided tours are usually scheduled for Tuesday afternoons. (Apply to Centre d'accueil, Hôtel de Ville, Place de l'Hôtel-de-Ville; or Ministry of Cultural Affairs, 3 Rue de Valois.) The Hôtel du Quai Voltaire, still known as a good "literary hotel" at 19 Quai Voltaire, was Baudelaire's lodging at intervals from 1856 to 1858 and the place where he completed *Les Fleurs du Mal*. Later occupants included Richard Wagner, Oscar Wilde and Jean Sibelius (see the entries on these men later in this chapter). In 1858 and 1859 Baudelaire lodged at the Grand Hôtel de Charny, 22 Rue Beautreillis, which displays woodcarvings in the style of Louis XIII beneath the carriage entrance.

During the years 1859–64 Baudelaire often stayed at the Hôtel de Dieppe, still at 22 Rue d'Amsterdam, **Right Bank**. The poet's last year was spent in a private hospital at 1 Rue du Dôme, where he died.

Baudelaire tomb: Montparnasse Cemetery.

(See Chapter 4, BELGIUM.)

BERLIOZ, HECTOR (1803–1869). Though born elsewhere in France, this major 19th-century composer resided at some dozen addresses in Paris from 1821 and made the city his permanent home. His first lodging was 79 Rue St-Jacques, **Left Bank**, which he occupied from 1821 to 1824.

At 96 Rue de Richelieu, **Right Bank**, where he resided from 1827 to 1830, he composed his *Symphonie Fantastique* (1830). His first home after marrying actress Harriet Smithson in 1833 was 24 Rue du Mont-Cenis in Montmartre, a house later occupied by painter Maurice Utrillo and since rebuilt. The couple lived there until 1836. Other significant Right Bank addresses, all quite close together, included 34 Rue de Londres, where he composed his *Romeo and Juliet* symphony (1839) and which was his home from 1836 to 1843; 41 Rue de Provence, the apartment of his mistress, Marie Recio (1844–47); his own legal address for the same period at 43 Rue Blanche, where he worked on his cantata *The Damnation of Faust* (1846); and his last home, from 1856, at 4 Rue de Calais. The latter address, where Berlioz died, is his only Paris home that is definitely known to survive.

Berlioz tomb: Montmartre Cemetery.

(See Chapter 2, FRANCE; also Chapter 6, LONDON; also Chapter 8, ITALY.)

BERNHARDT, SARAH (1844–1923). Even into old age Bernhardt remained "the divine Sarah," an actress without peer in her time. A Paris native,

she resided in the city for most of her life. "As many streets in Paris claim Bernhardt's birthplace as towns in Greece claim Homer," wrote Cornelia Otis Skinner, one of her biographers. Four separate addresses are given by various sources, including 125 Rue du Faubourg-St-Honoré on the **Right Bank**; and 22 Rue de la Michodière and 5 Rue de l'École-de-Médecine, now the Institute of Modern Languages, on the **Left Bank**. The latter building, a 1694 structure where her unwed mother, Julie Van Hard, probably occupied an apartment, is Bernhardt's generally accepted birthplace and bears a marker.

At age four, and again from 1859 to 1864, she lived with her mother at 265 Rue St-Honoré, **Right Bank**; she made her acting debut during this period. Julie Van Hard died at the residence in 1876. The house is gone. Near the corner of Rue Duphot and Rue St-Honoré, Bernhardt lived with Prince Henri de Ligne in a three-room apartment and bore their son, the later stage producer Maurice Bernhardt, in 1864; she lived there until 1868. In 1868 and 1869 she resided at 16 Rue Auber and in the latter year rescued her young son and grandmother from a fire which demolished the building. Her home during the years 1876 to 1898 was a mansion she built at the corner of Rue Fortuny and Avenue de Villiers. Her lifestyle grew quite opulent, especially after 1881, with a large retinue of servants and a menagerie of animals. Her last home, from 1898, was 56 Boulevard Péreire, a small elegant building with lavish furnishings and her initials carved over the gate. In March 1923, too ill to work in a film studio, she performed her last role there—for the silent movie *La Voyante* (1923). She finished it only four days before she died. This house was demolished in 1963.

The Théâtre Sarah Bernhardt, which she renovated in 1899 and where she performed exclusively in Paris for the last 23 years of her life, survives at 2 Place du Châtelet, **Right Bank**. In this cavernous structure she maintained a five-room apartment on two floors, gave stylish dinners for her salon of admirers and spent much time preparing for (and recuperating from) her stage performances. During World War II the Nazi occupiers of Paris changed the name of the theater back to its original designation of Théâtre des Nations after learning that Bernhardt was half Jewish. The theater was again graced with her name after the war but today is known as the Théâtre de la Ville. It offers regular stage performances.

Bernhardt tomb: Père-Lachaise Cemetery.
(See Chapter 2, FRANCE.)

BLAIR, ERIC ARTHUR. ("GEORGE ORWELL") (1903–1950). The influential socialist novelist, essayist and critic spent several years as a vagabond doing odd jobs for a living, as he recalled in *Down and Out in Paris and London* (1933). In 1929, while "down and out" in Paris, he lodged at a cheap hotel located at 6 Rue du Pot de Fer, **Left Bank**.

(See Chapter 5, ENGLAND; also Chapter 6, LONDON; also Chapter 7, SCOTLAND.)

CALVIN, JOHN (1509–1564). The French Protestant reformer, whose doctrine of predestination found eager acceptance in the austere dogmas of Puritanism and Presbyterianism, received much of his education in Paris. At the Collège de Montaigu, founded in 1314, Calvin studied and resided during the 1520s. The site of this building is occupied by the 1850 Bibliothèque Ste-Geneviève on the north side of the Place du Panthéon, **Left Bank**. Desiderius Erasmus and St. Ignatius of Loyola were earlier students there. Nearby, at 21 Rue Valette, are incorporated ruins of the 1397 Collège Fortet where Calvin studied in 1531, just two years before he was obliged to flee Paris because of his proposal to create a new theology based on the New Testament. A tower of this old house, reputedly Calvin's domicile, is called the "Tour de Calvin."

(See Chapter 1, SWITZERLAND; also Chapter 3, FRANCE.)

CAMUS, ALBERT (1913–1960). The Algerian-born novelist whose works reflected his existentialist philosophy tempered with a humanitarian outlook lived in Paris at intervals from 1940. During World War II he became active in the French Resistance and eluded capture throughout the war. Camus occupied the long-time suite of novelist André Gide at 1bis Rue Vaneau, **Left Bank** during the latter part of the war (1944–45); Gide died there in 1951. From 1946 to 1949 Camus resided at 18 Rue Séguier.

(See Chapter 3, FRANCE.)

CASALS, PABLO (1876–1973). From 1904 to 1914, the period when he was making an international name for himself as a concert performer, the Spanish cellist and composer made Paris his haven between concert tours. He resided at 20 Villa Molitor in the suburban district of **Auteuil**. This small house, located at the end of a private street off the Rue Molitor, "bubbled with conversations and rehearsals," in the words of one biographer.

(See Chapter 2, FRANCE; also Chapter 8, SPAIN.)

CELLINI, BENVENUTO (1500–1571). From 1540 to 1544 the Florentine goldsmith, sculptor, and one of the world's great autobiographers was the guest of Francis I, that royal importer of the Italian Renaissance to France (see the entry on Francis I later in this chapter). Cellini was one of the king's prize acquisitions, and the artist created some of his most notable works under his patronage. Francis assigned Cellini a workshop-lodging in the western portion of the 13th-century Hôtel de Nesle, called the Petit-Nesle. In order to claim his residence, however, Cellini—an excellent swordsman with a hair-trigger temper—had to evict the provost of Paris as well as other lodgers, actions that involved him in characteristic violent escapades. The building itself, demolished in 1663, had a reputation for being "haunted": the 14th-century Queen Jeanne, wife of Philip V, was said to have ordered several murders to be committed there. The site is covered by the east wing of the French Institute, seat of the prestigious French Academy at 21-25 Quai de Conti, **Left Bank**.

(See Chapter 8, ITALY.)

CÉZANNE, PAUL (1839–1906). Perhaps the greatest figure in modern French painting, this postimpressionist artist lived in Paris frequently but for relatively brief periods during his career (see Name Index and Gazetteer). From 1865 to 1867 his lodging was a fourth-floor attic room in the Grand Hôtel de Charny (see the entry on Charles Baudelaire earlier in this chapter).

On the **Left Bank** Cézanne lodged in a two-story house at 120 Rue de Vaugirard in 1874 and 1875.

At intervals from 1875 to 1888 the painter roomed in another two-story flat at 15 Quai d'Anjou on the **Île St-Louis**.

Exhibit: Room 13 of the Jeu de Paume Museum is the main Paris repository of Cézanne paintings and several of his most representative canvases may be seen there (see the entry on Paul Gauguin, *Exhibit*, later in this chapter.)

(See Chapter 3, FRANCE.)

CHOPIN, FRÉDÉRIC FRANÇOIS (1810–1849). "Paris," wrote the Polish-born composer, "is whatever one chooses to make of it. In Paris you can amuse yourself or be bored, laugh or cry, do whatever you like, nobody so much as looks at you." A resident of Paris from 1831 in a succession of nine **Right Bank** lodgings, Chopin has been called "the first [composer] who understood what the piano could do." He composed in all of his lodgings, mostly works for solo piano. Chopin resided until 1832 at 27 Boulevard Poissonnière. From 1833 to 1836 he lived at 5 Rue de la Chaussée-d'Antin, a house that had earlier sheltered Wolfgang Amadeus Mozart (see the entry on Mozart later in this chapter). The present structure on this site is not the original.

"Chopin," wrote Richard Anthony Leonard, "was the sybarite of composers. He loved luxurious surroundings, elegant clothes, aristocratic people. When he chose an apartment, it had to be in the best neighborhood, away from bad smells, smoke, or the sound of blacksmiths." From 1839 to 1840 he lived at 5 Rue Tronchet. The famous love of his life was, of course, novelist-feminist George Sand (see the entry on Sand later in this chapter) and from 1840 to 1842 the pair lived at 16 Rue Pigalle, occupying adjoining houses that stood in the garden of the present dwelling. From 1842 to 1846 the couple occupied adjacent apartments at 5 (Chopin) and 9 (Sand) Square d'Orléans; Chopin continued to reside there after their separation until his last year. His final brief address was 12 Place Vendôme, a 17th-century building, where after years of advancing tuberculosis he died.

Chopin tomb: Père-Lachaise Cemetery.

Exhibit: The Adam Mickiewicz Museum at 6 Quai d'Orléans, **Île St-Louis**, was a 19th-century meeting place of expatriate Polish artists and writers, including Chopin. Memorabilia of the composer, along with those of other famous Poles, include manuscripts, portraits and his death mask. (Open Thursday 3:00—6:00 by appointment; closed July 14—September 15; 354–35–61; free.)

(See Chapter 2, FRANCE; also Chapter 8, SPAIN.)

CLÉMENCEAU, GEORGES (1841–1929). Almost every French city of any size has its boulevard or avenue named after "the Tiger" of France. Twice prime minister and one of the nation's strongest, most aggressive leaders, Clémenceau foresaw the resurgence of German militarism after World War I—an event that his own intransigence toward the defeated nation at the Paris Peace

GEORGES CLEMENCEAU IN HIS GARDEN. The French statesman lived at one Paris address, 8 Rue Franklin, from 1883 until his death. This rear view of the house, in which his four-room apartment is now a Clemenceau museum, probably dates from about 1920.

Conference of 1919 did much to guarantee. From 1883, through his rise in French politics, right up to the end of his life, Clémenceau occupied one Paris lodging, a modest four-room apartment at 8 Rue Franklin, **Right Bank**. Today this suite is the Clémenceau Museum: it displays his library and original furnishings and exhibits on his life and career (including the quill pen he preferred over a fountain pen). (Open Tuesday, Thursday, Saturday—Sunday 2:00—5:00; 520–43–51; admission.)

(See Chapter 2, FRANCE.)

COLETTE, SIDONIE GABRIELLE (1873–1954). A novelist whose works wryly probed the nature of romance and the female heart, she used the single pen name "Colette" from 1916. Colette's first married home in 1893 with Henri Gauthier-Villars was a three-room apartment that still survives at 28 Rue Jacob, **Left Bank** (the novelist Stendhal [Henri Beyle] had been a guest at this address in 1808). Colette's first erotic novels were issued under her husband's pseudonym "Willy"; this virtual literary bondage lasted until 1904.

From 1927 until 1931 the author lived in a suite at the Palais-Royal, the **Right Bank** complex of historic buildings and galleries begun by Cardinal Richelieu at the Place du Palais-Royal (see the entry on Richelieu later in this chapter). The apartment was located underground beneath the palace colonnades. Later, in 1938, she moved back into the building and until her death lived in a large sunny apartment directly above her earlier one. There, through World War II, she hid her Jewish third husband, Maurice Goudeket, from Gestapo-infested Paris while appearing to live alone. This building, still containing private apartments, fronts on 9 Rue de Beaujolais. Colette wrote her last works there, including *Gigi* (1945), and died there. Another Right Bank lodging, between 1931 and 1938, was a top-floor suite at the Hôtel Claridge, 74 Avenue des Champs-Élysées. A cosmetics shop, which Colette owned and operated for about a year (1932–33), stood at 6 Rue de Miromesnil.

Colette tomb: Père-Lachaise Cemetery.
(See Chapter 2, FRANCE.)

CURIE, MARIE SKLODOWSKA (1867–1934). The Polish-born chemist who, with her husband Pierre, pioneered the earliest research into radioactivity and discovered the elements polonium and radium was a Paris dweller from 1891. Her first residence, shared with her sister and brother-in-law, was 92 Avenue Jean-Jaurès in the suburb of **La Villette**. The Curies' first married home (1895–1900), a three-room apartment, stands at 24 Rue de la Glacière, **Left Bank**. They resided from 1900 until Pierre Curie's accidental death in 1906 in the same area, at 108 Boulevard Kellermann, where a plaque marks the site.

Marie Curie's home from 1912 until her death survives at 36 Quai de Béthune, **Île St-Louis**. Her large apartment on the third floor of this 18th-century house lacked carpets or curtains, as she preferred.

Exhibits: **Left Bank** sites associated with the Curies and their work (though not "exhibits" in the usual sense) include the School of Physics and Chemistry at 42 Rue Lhomond, site of their 1898 discovery of radium and scene of their experimental work until 1900, though the actual building where they worked is gone; the Curie laboratory at 12 Rue Cuvier where they worked from 1900 to 1914; the Rue Dauphine, where Pierre Curie met death under the wheels of a loaded wagon; and the Curie Institute, built for Marie Curie in 1914 at 11 Rue Pierre-et-Marie-Curie (also numbered 26 Rue d'Ulm).
(See Chapter 2, FRANCE.)

DANTE ALIGHIERI (1265–1321). From about 1309 to 1311 the Italian poet, one of the world's great literary masters, resided in Paris, attending lectures at the University of Paris and working on the beginning portions of *The Divine Comedy* (1321). According to tradition, he resided somewhere in the present Rue de Bièvre, **Left Bank**. There is no question that he inhabited this general area of the city.
(See Chapter 8, ITALY.)

DEBUSSY, CLAUDE-ACHILLE (1862–1918). The composer, whose impressionistic music was a profound reaction against the Romantic bombast of Richard Wagner (see the entry on Wagner later in this chapter), was a **Right Bank** resident for almost his entire life. Debussy lived with his parents (1867–68) at 11 Rue de Vintimille. He studied for 11 years at the Paris Conservatory of Music, located at that period in the Faubourg Poissonière. His parental homes during most of those years were 59bis Rue Pigalle and a fourth-floor apartment in the Rue Clapeyron. His "soul home," however, was the residence of his benefactress, Mme. Vasnier, with whom he had an early love affair. The Vasniers provided a cultural milieu for his talent and also a room for his private use at their 28 Rue de Constantinople address.

Following a period in Rome (1887–88), Debussy lived uncomfortably with his parents at 27 Rue de Liège. Then from 1888 to 1893, at 42 Rue de Londres, he occupied an attic room with his longtime mistress (to whom he was constantly unfaithful), Gabrielle "Gaby" Dupont. He wrote his piano piece *Clair de Lune* there. While living with Gaby in a better though still modest apartment at 10 Rue Gustave-Doré (1893–99), he began his opera *Pelléas et Mélisande* (1902), his most ambitious work.

Forsaking Gaby, who had managed his impoverished domestic affairs for a decade, the composer married dressmaker Rosalie "Lily" Texier in 1899. They lived in a fifth-floor apartment at 58 Rue Cardinet for the duration of their marriage; Debussy walked out one day in 1903. There, three months after his desertion, Lily shot herself but recovered from her two wounds. (Gaby had also shot herself nonfatally during one of his affairs.)

Debussy's last home from 1905, with his second wife Emma Bardac, remains at 24 Square de l'Avenue Foch, surrounded by a high iron fence. Racked by cancer, he completed his last work and died there as World War I broke over Paris and the German bombardment crashed outside his windows.

Debussy tomb: Passy Cemetery.
(See Chapter 2, FRANCE; also Chapter 5, ENGLAND; also Chapter 8, ITALY.)

DE GAULLE, CHARLES (1890–1970). The nationalistic aspirations and lofty rhetoric of the "Free French" leader of World War II—later the first president of the Fifth Republic (1959–69)—frequently exasperated those of his allies who preferred talking politics on a less mystical plane. De Gaulle spent much of his boyhood in Paris, where his father taught at the Jesuit College of the Immaculate Conception; the family lived in one of the large college buildings at 389 Rue Vaugirard, **Left Bank**. His first married home with Yvonne Vendroux in 1921 was a flat at 4 Boulevard des Invalides. De Gaulle lectured at the Military Academy of St-Cyr during this period. An apartment he occupied in 1957–58 is now the Institut Charles de Gaulle, containing archival materials. It is located at 5 Rue de Solferino. (Call 555–12–60 for information.)

During his long, impatient retirement from public life (1946–57), de Gaulle used the Hôtel Lapérous, 40 Rue La Pérouse, **Right Bank**, for his Paris pied-à-terre; he usually spent Wednesdays in the city.

From 1959 to 1969, as president of the Republic, de Gaulle occupied the Élysée Palace, official residence of French presidents since 1873 and a royal domicile before that (see the entry on Napoleon I later in this chapter). Not a few observers noted that President de Gaulle's magisterial presence marked him among the most imperial of personages ever to have lived there. (Also see the entry on Edward VIII later in this chapter.)

(See Chapter 2, FRANCE; also Chapter 6, LONDON.)

DESCARTES, RENÉ (1596–1650). The philosopher, an obsessed lifelong seeker of intellectual certainty ("I think therefore I am") and the inventor of analytical geometry, occupied a house at the site of 14 Rue Rollin, **Left Bank** in 1644 and 1647–48.

Descartes tomb: Church of St-Germain-des-Prés.

Exhibit: The Museum of Mankind in the west wing of the Chaillot Palace, Place du Trocadéro, **Left Bank**, displays a skull purported to be that of Descartes and apparently taken during one of several transfers of his tomb. (Open April—September, daily 10:00—6:00; October—March, daily 10:00—5:00; 505–70–60; admission.)

(See Chapter 2, FRANCE; also Chapter 4, THE NETHERLANDS, SWEDEN.)

DUMAS, ALEXANDRE (*père*) (1802–1870). Hundreds of volumes—plays, travel, biography, novels—flowed from the "writing factory" operated by Dumas *père*, a man whose mistresses described him as "a force of nature." Gargantuan in appearance as well as in appetites and achievement, Dumas had a ready reply for bigots who remarked on his African ancestry and Creole accent: "My father was a mulatto, my grandmother was a Negress, and my great-grandparents were monkeys. My pedigree begins where yours ends."

Dumas came to Paris in 1823 and took a small apartment at 1 Place Boïeldieu, **Right Bank**. There he met dressmaker Catherine Labay, who bore their son, Alexandre Dumas *fils*, in 1824 (see below).

Dumas occupied numerous Paris apartments throughout his career. At 25 Rue de l'Université, **Left Bank**, he lived with his mistress, Mélanie Waldor, in 1830. **Right Bank** addresses included 97 Rue d'Amsterdam (1854–61), 112 Rue de Richelieu (1862), 70 Rue St-Lazare (1864) and toward the end of his irrepressible life, 107 Boulevard Malasherbes.

(See Chapter 2, FRANCE.)

DUMAS, ALEXANDRE (*fils*) (1824–1895). Bearing a physical resemblance to his dynamic, beloved father but far more conservative in temperament and lifestyle, the playwright son of Dumas *père* was born at 1 Place Boïeldieu (see above entry). He bought a house at 98 Avenue de Villiers, **Right Bank**, in 1862 and remained there until his final months. The garden was so small that Dumas *père* teased, "You ought to open the window of your salon to give your garden some air." The house in which he last resided and died stood at 11 Rue Ampère.

Dumas tomb: Montmartre Cemetery.

(See Chapter 2, FRANCE.)

EDWARD VIII (1894–1972). The British king, whose love for an American divorcee resulted in a political crisis and his 1936 abdication after only a year on the throne, thereafter resided mainly in France. After marrying Wallis Warfield Simpson, the "woman I love," the duke of Windsor, as he was now known, became a prestigious figure on the international celebrity circuit and spent the next 35 years in spectacular idleness.

From 1938 the duke and duchess occupied **Right Bank** winter dwellings in Paris; they held their hedge-surrounded house at 24 Boulevard

Suchet until 1946 but did not live in it during World War II. From 1946 to 1949 they inhabited the largest suite at the elegant Ritz Hotel, 15 Place Vendôme. They rented the house at 85 Rue de la Faisanderie from 1949 to 1953. Their last Paris home, from 1953, was 4 Route du Champ d'Entrainement in suburban **Neuilly**, a small château in a two-acre park surrounded by a high spiked fence. The City of Paris, the owner of this house, leased it to the Windsors for a token rent of $50 per year. Free French leader Charles de Gaulle had directed his forces and awaited the liberation of Paris there in 1944 and 1945 (see the entry on de Gaulle earlier in this chapter).

(See Chapter 2, FRANCE; also Chapter 5, ENGLAND; also Chapter 6, LONDON; also Chapter 7, SCOTLAND.)

ERASMUS, DESIDERIUS (1466?–1536). The Dutch humanist scholar attended the Collège de Montaigue in 1495 and 1496 (see the entry on John Calvin earlier in this chapter).

(See Chapter 1, SWITZERLAND; also Chapter 4, WEST GERMANY, BELGIUM, THE NETHERLANDS; also Chapter 5, ENGLAND.)

FLAUBERT, GUSTAVE (1821–1880). One of the great literary names of the 19th century, Flaubert was a hugely influential stylist; probably no other major writer has ever devoted so much perfectionism and labor to the craft. He occupied several lodgings at intervals in Paris from 1842. He was living at 42 Boulevard du Temple, **Right Bank**, when his masterpiece, *Madame Bovary* (1857), was published. This was his winter home from 1856 to 1869. From 1869 to 1875 he lived in a fourth-floor flat at 4 Rue Murillo; and his last Paris home from 1875 was 240 Rue du Faubourg-St-Honoré.

(See Chapter 2, FRANCE.)

FRANCIS I (1494–1547). The Palace of the Louvre, surrounding three sides of the Square du Carrousel on its 40-acre **Right Bank** site, is not only the most important public building in Paris but one of France's most magnificent palaces, containing what is probably the world's greatest art museum. The site of a seventh-century fortress, it was made an official residence by Charles V in the 14th century. Francis, who made the palace his Paris residence, rebuilt the west and south sides (1515–47), and every important French monarch up to Napoleon III extended and added to its dimensions. The oldest part of the complex, de-

signed by Pierre Lescot for Francis, is the southwest corner of the Cour Carré, also called the Cour du Louvre, now containing the Pavillon des Arts and the Caryatid Gallery (see the entry on Louis XIV later in this chapter). Francis began the Louvre's notable collections and the buildings were opened as a national art gallery in 1793. (Open daily 9:45—5:15; 260–32–14; admission; Sunday free.)

(See Chapter 2, FRANCE; also Chapter 8, SPAIN.)

FRANKLIN, BENJAMIN (1706–1790). As the popular American ambassador to France from 1776 to 1785, Franklin was responsible for enlisting French aid during the American Revolution— an alliance that turned the tide toward victory for the former British colonies. His massive scientific and diplomatic reputation had preceded him (Queen Marie Antoinette called him "l'ambassadeur électrique") and he became a symbol throughout France for the libertarian ideals of the "common man," ideals that would soon cause the eruption of France's own bloody revolution.

Franklin's residence, the Hôtel de Valentinois, stood at 62 Rue Raynouard, corner of Rue Singer, **Right Bank**. Atop this building Franklin erected the first lightning rod seen in France. He acted as brilliant host at numerous banquets there, including Fourth of July parties commemorating American independence. France, he said, "is the civilest nation upon earth," and he enjoyed Parisian society, wine and women and played his grandfatherly statesman role to the hilt, indulging all the while in some extremely hard-nosed diplomacy. Franklin's city office may have stood at 26 Rue de Penthièvre.

(See Chapter 5, ENGLAND; also Chapter 6, LONDON.)

GAUGUIN, PAUL (1848–1903). A Paris native, the stockbroker turned painter, one of the postimpressionist masters, was born at 56 Rue Notre-Dame-de-Lorette, **Right Bank**, a building identified by marker. Painter Eugène Delacroix had his studio at number 58, the next-door lodging, at this time. As the Second Republic fell, the politically liberal Gauguin family, fearing arrest or worse, fled from their Paris apartment to Peru in 1849.

Later, as a rising businessman, Gauguin lived in a small apartment at 28 Place St-Georges, **Right Bank**, with his Danish-born wife, Mette-Sophie Gad. The office where he worked as a broker's agent from 1871 to 1883 stood at 1 Rue Laffitte.

The family homes until 1884, by which time Gauguin was painting full-time with no steady income, included 74 Rue Falguière, **Left Bank**, a flat in a three-story building (1877–80); and an unidentified address in the Rue Carcel (1880–84), where he painted in the garden of his residence. During the 1870s he occupied a room and studio at 8 Rue de la Grande-Chaumière.

After 1884, when Mette-Sophie Gauguin gave up on her husband's "whim for painting" and took their children to Denmark, Gauguin's Paris lodgings were shabby, briefly held hovels. In 1885 he brought his son Clovis to 10 Rue Cail, **Right Bank**, where they lived on the generosity of friends for a year. During 1886 and 1887 he resided at 257 Rue Lecourbe, **Left Bank**. After the painter's first return from Tahiti, in 1890 and 1891, he occupied a second-floor room in the three-story brick and stone house at 14 Rue Alfred-Durand-Claye. Gauguin's last Paris lodging (1893–94) was a second-floor studio at 6 Rue Vercingétorix, where he decorated the deep-yellow walls with native hatchets and boomerangs and exhibited himself in outlandish dress.

Exhibit: Numerous Gauguin paintings, his Tahitian carvings and other items are displayed in room 15 of the Jeu de Paume Museum (also called the Museum of Impressionism) in the Place de la Concorde, **Right Bank**. (Open Wednesday—Monday 9:45—5:15; 260-12-07; admission.)

(See Chapter 2, FRANCE; also Chapter 4, DENMARK.)

HEINE, HEINRICH (1797–1856). Exiled from his native Germany, the lyric poet and satirist spent his last 25 years in Paris, the city he preferred above all others. He changed hotel and room lodgings frequently until his 1841 marriage to Mathilde Mirat. A turbulent pairing, the marriage was full of crises—a state of affairs that seemed vital for them both. Near the time of his marriage Heine lived at 25 Rue des Grands Augustins, **Left Bank**, a former dwelling of writer Jean de la Bruyère (1676–91) and historian Augustin Thierry (1820–30).

Other surviving residences include his 1834 dwelling at 3 Rue Cité Bergère, **Right Bank**; 64 Rue de Passy, a summer residence; 50 Rue d'Amsterdam, where he lived in a second-floor apartment from 1848 to 1851; and his last home, from 1854, marked by a plaque at 3 Avenue Matignon.

Heine died after a long illness in his fifth-floor apartment there.

Heine tomb: Montmartre Cemetery.

(See Chapter 4, WEST GERMANY; also Chapter 6, LONDON.)

HÉLOUÏSE (1101–1164). The beloved of theologian and priest Peter Abélard was seduced by him in 1118 at the home of her uncle, Canon Fulbert. She secretly married Abélard after the birth of their son, Peter Astrolabe, and, unwillingly but according to Abélard's wishes, became a nun. The famous exchange of letters between them gave their story romantically tragic if not operatic dimensions.

Probably a Paris native, Hélouïse was one of Abélard's most brilliant students, but the theologian later admitted that his private tutorship in her uncle's house began with ulterior motives. Canon Fulbert's house, scene of the seduction, stood at 9 Quai aux Fleurs, **Île de la Cité** (see the entry on Peter Abélard earlier in this chapter).

Hélouïse tomb: Père-Lachaise Cemetery.

(See Chapter 2, FRANCE.)

HEMINGWAY, ERNEST MILLER (1899–1961). As a correspondent for the *Toronto Star*, the American writer settled in Paris—"a fine place to be quite young in," he later assessed—in 1922 and made it his base for most of a decade. He and his first wife, Hadley Richardson, occupied a fourth-floor apartment at 74 Rue du Cardinal-Lemoine, **Left Bank**, in 1922 and 1923. This was the period when he met American expatriate Gertrude Stein, who entertained numerous avant-garde writers and painters at her house, 27 Rue de Fleurus, which still survives. From 1924 to 1926 the Hemingways lived in a second-floor apartment at 113 Notre-Dame-des-Champs, where the author wrote several of his "Nick Adams" stories and completed *The Sun Also Rises* (1926). With his second wife, Pauline Pfeiffer, Hemingway resided in a large apartment at 6 Rue Férou, from 1926 to 1928 and worked on *A Farewell to Arms* (1929). This was his last Paris dwelling of any duration.

Several of Hemingway's favorite cafes in the Boulevard du Montparnasse are still operating: La Closerie des Lilas at 171, Le Sélect at 99 and Le Dôme at 108, among others.

Hemingway's Paris (1978) by Robert E. Gajdusek provides an interesting chronicle of the writer's years in the city.

(See Chapter 8, ITALY, SPAIN.)

HUGO, VICTOR (1802–1885). Romantic novelist, lyric poet and political activist, Hugo was France's most notable 19th-century writer. His opposition to the Second Empire and Napoleon III led to his long exile in England, where he wrote most of his best-known works. Hugo's earliest memories were of a house that stood at 24 Rue de Clichy, **Right Bank**, and which was his home from 1803 to about 1808. Much later in his life (1874–78), he occupied 21 Rue de Clichy, a house which survives today.

From 1808 to 1813 Hugo's family lived in a large ground-floor apartment at 12 Rue des Feuillantines, **Left Bank**, a house that occupied part of a former 1622 convent. A school stands on this site today. Hugo's Paris dwellings until his 1852 exile were numerous. Among those that survive are 30 Rue du Dragon, where he occupied an attic

OLD AND RECENT VIEWS OF 6 PLACE DES VOSGES. Novelist Victor Hugo occupied a second-floor suite in this house from 1832 to 1848 (in the modern photograph, the house faces the end of the street). During his residence it became one of the city's foremost gathering places for intellectuals, political liberals, and writers. It houses the Victor Hugo Museum today.

apartment with a cousin (1821–22); and, on the **Right Bank**, 9 Rue Jean Goujon (1830–32), where he completed *The Hunchback of Notre Dame* (1831). From 1832 to 1848, and now famous, the author "held court" and wrote several novels at 6 Place des Vosges, a second-floor suite in what was then the Hôtel de Rohan-Guémenée. Insurgents who invaded the apartment in 1848 scrupulously respected his possessions, so esteemed was Hugo as a liberal writer. Since 1903 this building has housed the Victor Hugo Museum, operated by the City of Paris, which displays numerous Hugo drawings (he was also an accomplished artist), his own designed furniture and woodwork, as well as manuscripts, family memorabilia and portraits. One feature is the reconstructed dining room from Hauteville House, his home during his exile on the Channel Island of Guernsey. Hugo's library may also be seen there but by appointment only. (Museum open Tuesday—Sunday 10:00—5:40; 272–10–16; admission; Sunday free.)

Hugo's last home from 1878 stood at 124 Avenue Victor-Hugo. He died there. The present house on the site is of later construction.

Hugo tomb: Panthéon.

(See Chapter 2, FRANCE; also Chapter 4, BELGIUM, LUXEMBOURG; also Chapter 5, ENGLAND.)

IGNATIUS OF LOYOLA, ST. (1491–1556). The Basque founder of the militant, controversial Order of the Society of Jesus (Jesuits) lived in Paris from 1528 to about 1537. During this period he attended the Collège de Montaigu (see the entry on John Calvin earlier in this chapter) and the Collège Ste-Barbe in the nearby Rue Cujas, **Left Bank**. The latter public educational institution, founded in 1460, is France's oldest.

In 1534 (three years before he became a priest) St. Ignatius and six companions took the first Jesuit vows in a crypt beneath a Montmartre chapel. The site of this epochal event in the history of Roman Catholicism is the Chapelle du Martyre at 9 Rue Yvonne-le-Tac, **Right Bank**, also the reputed site of the third-century martyrdom of St. Denis.

(See Chapter 8, ITALY, SPAIN.)

JAMES, HENRY (1843–1916). "Henry James writes fiction as if it were a painful duty," commented Oscar Wilde on the American novelist's complex, endlessly qualified sentences. From 1875 to 1877 James occupied a third-floor apartment at 29 Rue Cambon, **Right Bank**, where he worked on his novel *The American* (1877), and from which he jaunted forth to "observe Paris."

(See Chapter 5, ENGLAND; also Chapter 6, LONDON; also Chapter 8, ITALY.)

JEFFERSON, THOMAS (1743–1826). During his period as American ambassador to France, from 1784 to 1789, the future third president of the United States resided at three Paris dwellings. None of them survive. His last, where he lived from 1785 to 1789, stood until 1842 at the corner of the Avenue des Champs-Élysées and the Rue de Berri, **Right Bank**; today a tablet marks the site of the mansion, the Hôtel de Langeac. Jefferson enjoyed his extensive grounds and garden there, experimenting with corn and grape crops. A frequent guest was American painter John Trumbull who worked at the house on Jefferson's portrait for the famed *Declaration of Independence* canvas which hangs in the U.S. Capitol, Washington, D. C. It was Trumbull who introduced the diplomat to the English wife of painter Richard Cosway, 27-year-old Maria Cosway, with whom the widowed Jefferson had a year-long affair. *Thomas Jefferson's Paris* (1976), by Howard C. Rice, Jr., provides a fascinating description of the city as Jefferson knew it.

JOHN XXIII (1881–1963). As papal nuncio to France from 1945 to 1953, Angelo Roncalli, who became pope in 1958, occupied the nuncio's palace at 10 Avenue du Président-Wilson, **Right Bank**.

(See Chapter 8, ITALY.)

JOYCE, JAMES (1882–1941). The expatriate Irish novelist "came to Paris to stay a week and remained for twenty years," wrote biographer Richard Ellmann. Joyce, who occupied some dozen addresses, spent most of that period (1920–40) in greater or lesser degrees of poverty, though he was not timid in finding and badgering patrons to support himself and his family while he produced some of the century's most complex experimental fiction. These "angels," mostly women, made it possible for him to be poor "only through determined extravagance," wrote one cynical observer.

The "twentieth address," he said, at which he worked on *Ulysses* (1922), one of the great novels of the 20th century, was 9 Rue de l'Université, **Left Bank**, his home in 1920 and 1921. Joyce's lengthiest Paris address (1925-31) was 2 Square Robiac, a cul-de-sac off 192 Rue de Grenelle, where he worked on *Finnegans Wake* (1939) and convalesced from several eye operations (he had undergone eye surgery some 25 times by 1930).

From 1932 to 1934 the Joyces occupied a furnished flat at 42 Rue Galilée, **Right Bank**. They lived in a fifth-floor apartment at 7 Rue Edmond-Valentine, **Left Bank**, from 1934 to 1939. Joyce's last Paris address (1939) was 34 Rue des Vignes, **Right Bank**. *James Joyce in Paris: His Final Years* (1965), by Gisèle Freund and V. B. Carleton, provides an interesting photo record.

Any Joyce devotee in Paris will want to make a stop at the famed English-language bookshop Shakespeare and Co., 37 Rue de la Bûcherie, **Left Bank**. Between World Wars I and II, it became a popular meeting place for literary expatriates, including Ezra Pound, Henry Miller and Ernest Hemingway (see the entry on Hemingway earlier in this chapter). With the collaboration of longtime owner Sylvia Beach, James Joyce often read his book proofs there, and the store published the first edition of *Ulysses*. Its address during Joyce's period in Paris was 12 Rue de l'Odéon. (Open daily, 12:00—12:00.)

(See Chapter 1, SWITZERLAND; also Chapter 2, FRANCE; also Chapter 7, IRELAND; also Chapter 8, ITALY.)

LAFAYETTE, MARIE JOSEPH GILBERT, MARQUIS DE (1757–1834). A father of the French Revolution and author of its Declaration of Rights, this soldier-aristocrat was too royalist for the revolutionaries and too revolutionary for the royalists—in short, too liberal and sensible a statesman for the times in which he lived. In consequence he spent seven years in exiled imprisonment between the American Revolution, in which he fought as a major general, and the advent of Napoleon in France.

A frequent Paris resident from 1768, as a boy Lafayette lived with his mother and grandfather in the Luxembourg Palace, described by one biographer as "a kind of apartment house for the *noblesse*" (see the entry on Napoleon I later in this chapter). Portions of the luxurious town house of the Noailles family—his patrons and, from 1774 when he married Adrienne d'Ayen, his in-laws—are incorporated in the present Hôtel St-James et Albany, 202 Rue de Rivoli, **Right Bank**, the site of his home until 1782. Two of the hotel's restaurants, Le Noailles and the Lafayette Bistrot, are named in honor of the soldier.

Following his 1782 return from America Lafayette lived at 81 Rue de Bourbon until 1791; its site is the present 123 Rue de Lille, **Left Bank**. This mansion became a focal point for Americans in Europe; Lafayette designated Mondays as "American Day," and he acted as host to Benjamin Franklin and John and Abigail Adams, among numerous others. Inside his front entrance he kept a large framed copy of the American Declaration of Independence. He saved space alongside, it is said, for the revolutionary French document he envisioned. From there, after the fall of the Bastille, he took command of the Paris National Guard.

Back in Paris from his Austrian exile in 1799, Lafayette used the **Left Bank** mansion of his friend, the Countess of Tessé, for his residence. He recovered from a broken leg there in 1803. His wife, Adrienne, died at the house in 1807. The Hôtel Tessé remains at the corner of the Rue de Lille and the Quai Voltaire.

"His arousing of the Chamber after Waterloo lost us everything," said a crushed Napoleon of the suddenly vocal Lafayette, not knowing that through years of foreign exile and political silence on his country estate, the soldier had never abandoned his dream of a French democracy. Lafayette's last Paris home, which family members bought for him in 1827 and from which he attended his last debates in the Chamber of Deputies, stood at 8 Rue d'Anjou, **Right Bank**. The small house was staffed with servants from Lafayette's country estate, and the aged warrior-statesman died there.

Lafayette tomb: Picpus Cemetery.

Exhibit: The Army Museum at Les Invalides contains a room devoted to Lafayette (see the entry on Napoleon I, *Exhibits*, later in this chapter).

(See Chapter 2, FRANCE.)

LA SALLE, ROBERT CAVELIER, SIEUR DE (1643–1687). The explorer, who named and claimed Louisiana for the French in 1682, lodged at an unknown address in the Rue de la Grande Truanderie, **Right Bank**, in 1678 while enlisting royal support for his North American expedition. He occupied the same residence during 1684 before sailing to America on his final journey.

(See chapter 2, FRANCE.)

LENIN, VLADIMIR (1870–1924). "What the devil made us go to Paris," wondered the revolutionary leader and founder of the Soviet Union during his exile from prerevolutionary Russia. He regarded the city as "in many ways a nasty hole." Yet, as biographer Robert Payne points out, it was a city he always came back to during his continental wanderings. Lenin, his wife Nadezhda Krupskaya, his mother-in-law and his sister occupied two successive apartments during the years 1908 to 1912, both of which—small as they were—became focal points for the Russian exile community in Paris. The first stood at 24 Rue Beaunier (1908–09), **Left Bank**; the second even smaller, cheaper lodging at 4 Rue Marie-Rose (1909–12), is now the Lenin Museum and contains exhibits on Lenin's life and work. (Contact museum for admission information.) An addition to the crowded household at the latter address was Lenin's mistress, Elizabeth Armand. Lenin himself spent much of his Paris exile reading revolutionary texts in the National Library at 58 Rue de Richelieu, **Right Bank**.

(See Chapter 1, SWITZERLAND; also Chapter 4, EAST GERMANY, WEST GERMANY, BELGIUM, FINLAND; also Chapter 6, LONDON.)

LEONARDO DA VINCI (1452–1519).

Exhibit: Probably the world's most famous painting, endlessly copied and parodied, is the Italian Renaissance artist's *A Portrait*, better known as the *Mona Lisa*. Leonardo painted it in Florence during the years 1500 to 1504, and his French patron Francis I bought it as one of the first artworks for the Louvre. It still hangs there, along with several other Leonardo canvases, in the Italian Schools gallery (see the entry on Francis I earlier in this chapter).

(See Chapter 2, FRANCE; also Chapter 8, ITALY.)

LISZT, FRANZ (1811–1886). The Hungarian piano virtuoso and composer resided in Paris for greater and lesser periods at various addresses. His first lodging was the Hôtel d'Angleterre, which stood at 13 Rue du Mail, **Right Bank**, his home at intervals from 1823 to 1878. One residence that survives is 9 Rue de Montholon which he inhabited exclusively from 1827 to about 1831. Liszt supported himself and his mother by giving piano lessons there. One of his virtuoso "tricks" was to play a complicated piece of music with a glass of water balanced on the back of each hand and not spill a drop. (Also see the entry on George Sand later in this chapter.)

(See Chapter 1, AUSTRIA, SWITZERLAND;

also Chapter 4, EAST GERMANY, WEST GERMANY; also Chapter 8, ITALY.)

LOUIS XIV (1638–1715). The "sun king," epitome of royal splendor and absolutism of the old regime, was Europe's longest-reigning monarch (72 years). Third of the French Bourbon dynasty, his main Paris residence as boy king from 1643 to 1652 was the Palais Royal, the palace willed to Louis XIII by Cardinal Richelieu (see the entry on Richelieu later in this chapter). A miniature fort was built in the grounds for him to play in. In 1651 his bedroom at the palace was invaded by rioters, members of the Fronde uprising, who wanted to see for themselves that the king had not escaped the palace through their blockade. "One may hazard the guess," wrote historian W. H. Lewis, "that for the rest of his long life not a week passed without his recalling his greatest humiliation.... The Versailles idea, which was to insulate Louis and his successors from all contact with their subjects, was born that night." His mother, Anne of Austria, ruled as regent in the Palais Royal during this period.

No lover of Paris since his rage at having to flee it twice during the Fronde—and living as a virtual prisoner there betweentimes—Louis spent as little time in the city during his reign as possible and virtually none at all after the 1682 removal of the royal court to Versailles. From 1652 until a fire broke out in 1671, the royal residence was the palace of the Louvre, the portion that today surrounds the Cour du Louvre, or Cour Carée, now a part of the world's greatest art museum (see the entry on Francis I earlier in this chapter). There in 1661 Louis took the reins of government into his own hands following the death of his chief minister, Cardinal Mazarin, and never let go of them until his own death. The king's bedchamber and the state room were located in the present Salle des Sept Cheminées, main room of the first-floor Pavillon du Roi. These interiors were demolished in the 19th century, but the carved paneling that decorated them may be viewed in the Chambre à Alcove of the first-floor Colonnade Galleries. The oldest room in the Louvre is the ground-floor Salle des Caryatides, used for ceremonies and banquets; Louis attended a play by Molière there in 1658. The first-floor Salle Etrusque, the king's antechamber, was the center of palace business.

From 1671 to 1682 Louis resided in the palace of the Tuileries (see the entry on Napoleon I later in this chapter).

Exhibit: The Salle Henri IV of the Army Museum at Les Invalides displays an armored suit made for Louis XIV (see the entry on Napoleon I, *Exhibits*). (See Chapter 2, FRANCE.)

MARIE ANTOINETTE (1755–1793). The last Bourbon queen of France, despised for her frivolity as well as her total ignorance of and indifference to the French public, resided in the palace of the Tuileries with her husband, Louis XVI, during their reign (see the entry on Napoleon I later in this chapter). Her last three years were spent as a prisoner in the erupting Paris of the Revolution, an event which her own actions and inactions had done much to precipitate. The royal family, brought from Versailles in August 1789, was confined in the Tuileries until August 1792 when mobs overran the building and massacred everyone there except for the family.

They were taken to the Temple Tower, from which Louis XVI departed to the guillotine on January 21, 1793. Marie Antoinette remained there, subject to constant scrutiny and harassment, until August. Their son, the dauphin (Louis XVII), is believed to have died there in 1795. The tower, which dated from 1265 as part of a fortress of the Knights Templar, was occupied as the palace of the Grand Prior of the Knights of St. John from 1313. It stood at the present site of the Square du Temple, **Right Bank**, and was demolished by Napoleon I.

Marie Antoinette was transferred to the Conciergerie, one of the world's notorious prisons, which still stands at 1 Quai de l'Horloge, **Île de la Cité**, occupying a gloomy lower part of the enormous Palace of Justice. The Conciergerie was originally part of the great 13th-century royal palace built by Philippe IV. Torture and death became frequent occurrences there, especially during the Reign of Terror when almost 300 prisoners were murdered in 1792 alone. Figures vary with sources, but as many as 2,600 prisoners may have been sent from the Conciergerie to the guillotine in 1793 and 1794. Other famous prisoners included Mme. du Barry, Charlotte Corday, Georges Jacques Danton, André Chénier, Robespierre and Marshal Ney (see the entry on Robespierre later in this chapter). Marie Antoinette's cell, her last residence from August to October 1793, is now a chapel dedicated to her memory. In a nearby chapel a small collection of relevant items is displayed, including a guillotine blade, the crucifix found in the queen's cell, documents and

WHERE PARIS BEGAN. The immense Palace of Justice complex alongside the Seine on the **Île de la Cité** covers the site of the first Roman palace and the home of the first French kings. The two medieval towers at the right represent the oldest surviving portions. Just left of them, the large entrance is the gateway to the Conciergerie, where Revolutionary prisoners, including Marie Antoinette, awaited the guillotine.

portraits. (Open daily 10:00—11:25, 1:30—5:25; winter, closed Tuesday; 354–30–06; admission.)

Exhibits: Room 70 of the Carnavalet Museum displays memorabilia of Louis XVI and his family during their imprisonment in the Temple (see the entry on Napoleon I, *Exhibits*, later in this chapter).

As a condemned prisoner Marie Antoinette displayed more regal qualities than she had shown in her previous 19 years as queen. Courageous dignity and glacial nerve replaced the banal frivolity and cruel flippancy that had so antagonized the French populace. Basically, however, it was not their own deeds or lack of them that condemned the royal pair to death but what they symbolized: the hated power and privilege of the nobility that had paralyzed the country and stalemated desperately needed reforms. Swept away with them was the entire system of government that had ruled France for centuries. Marie Antoinette's last ride, in an open tumbril from the Conciergerie to what is now the Place de la Concorde, **Right Bank**—Paris's largest and central square—was not a long one. The square's placid name does not hide the facts of its history. Surrounded by cannons and thousands of jeering people, the guillotine stood on the site of the southern fountain adjacent to the Obelisk of Luxor (which was erected there in 1836 to squelch arguments about whose statue should adorn the site of the blade). It is said that by the end of the Terror in 1795 oxen refused to cross the square because of the odor of blood from this carnage.

INSIDE THE CONCIERGERIE. The Gothic-vaulted dungeon of the Palace of Justice, where Marie Antoinette and Robespierre spent their last days during the Terror, still evokes a chill. All it costs to get in today is a few francs; all it costs to get out is the motion of one's feet, not the sacrifice of one's head.

In the Square Louis XVI, Boulevard Haussmann, stands the Expiatory Chapel built by order of Louis XVIII on the site of the former Madeleine Cemetery, where lie victims of the Terror. Remnants of the royal bodies were removed from the cemetery in 1815. Statues of the couple and a bas-relief of the body removal are displayed inside the classical-style mausoleum. (Open daily 10:00—12:00, 2:00—5:00; admission.)

(See Chapter 1, AUSTRIA; also Chapter 2, FRANCE.)

MARX, KARL (1818–1883). The German economic philosopher and socialist theoretician resided in Paris for two years (1843–45) at 38 Rue Vaneau, from which he was expelled from France for his political writings. In Paris, Marx's ideas assumed definite shape as he worked with his supporter-collaborator Friedrich Engels there in 1844. During a stealthy return visit in 1849 he hid from French police for two months at 45 Rue de Lille. Both of these **Left Bank** dwellings are gone.

(See Chapter 2, FRANCE; also Chapter 4, EAST GERMANY, WEST GERMANY, BELGIUM; also Chapter 6, LONDON.)

MARY, QUEEN OF SCOTS (1542–1587). The Scottish-born Mary Stuart, who was queen of France for a year (1559–60) as the wife of Francis II and later monarch of Scotland, resided in the royal palace of the Louvre during her brief reign (see the entry on Francis I earlier in this chapter). In the present Salle des Caryatides, the oldest room in the present museum, Mary was officially betrothed at age 15 to the 14-year-old dauphin in 1558. Their opulent marriage ceremony was performed in the Cathedral of Notre Dame on April 24 of that year.

From 1553 until her French coronation, a frequent residence was the Hôtel de Guise, the magnificent mansion of the powerful Guise family who were related to Mary Stuart on her mother's side. It remained in the Guise family until 1696. The house occupied the site and portions of four previous mansions, parts of which were incorporated into the present Hôtel de Soubise, built in 1712. This building, located at 60 Rue des Francs-Bourgeois, **Right Bank**, has housed the National Archives of France since 1808. Exhibited there is the country's finest collection of historical documents, letters and wills. All of France's most notable royalty, leaders and writers are represented in what one observer called "an intriguing scrapbook of the French nation." (Open Wednesday—Monday 2:00—5:00; 277–11–30; admission.)

(See Chapter 2, FRANCE; also Chapter 5, ENGLAND; also Chapter 7, SCOTLAND.)

MATISSE, HENRI (1869–1954). The Fauvist painter, and one of modern art's notable stylists, lodged in Paris from the 1890s to 1917. His first married home with Amélie Parayre, from 1895 to about 1900, was 10 Quai St-Michel, **Left Bank**. He again occupied a studio there from 1913 to about 1916.

From 1906 to 1909 Matisse taught numerous students at his studio in the Hôtel Biron, a building acquired by the state for the use of artists in 1901 and which also held the residence and studio of sculptor Auguste Rodin (see the entry on Rodin later in this chapter).

Exhibit: Numerous representative works of the artist are displayed in the National Museum of

Modern Art, located in the Centre Georges Pompidou, Plateau Beaubourg, **Right Bank**. (Open Monday, Wednesday—Friday 12:00—10:00, Saturday—Sunday 10:00—10:00; 277–12–33; admission.)

(See Chapter 2, FRANCE.)

MAUGHAM, WILLIAM SOMERSET (1874–1965). The English novelist's first memories were of the Champs-Élysées in 19th-century Paris. His birthplace was the present British Embassy at 35-39 Rue du Faubourg-St-Honoré, **Right Bank**. Built in 1723 as the Hôtel de Charost, the mansion was acquired in 1803 by Pauline Borghese, sister of Napoleon I; she sold it to the Duke of Wellington in 1814. Charles Dickens resided there briefly during a Paris visit; Hector Berlioz (1833) and William Makepeace Thackeray (1836) were both married there; and Bertrand Russell lived there in 1894 (see the entries on Napoleon, Wellington, Berlioz and Russell in this chapter). Maugham's father, a solicitor employed at the embassy, had installed his pregnant wife in makeshift obstetrical quarters there because of a proposed French law requiring military service of anyone born on French soil (which, of course, the embassy was not). Many of the Borghese furnishings remain in this building, which is open only to those who have business with government offices of the United Kingdom (phone 266–91–42).

Maugham's infant home was a large third-floor apartment at what is now 25 Avenue Franklin D. Roosevelt, **Right Bank**. Orphaned in 1882, the lad was shipped off to England to be raised by an unwelcoming uncle.

(See Chapter 2, FRANCE; also Chapter 5, ENGLAND; also Chapter 6, LONDON.)

MAUPASSANT, GUY DE (1850–1893). Author of some of the world's best-known short stories, Maupassant maintained **Right Bank** residences from 1869 until his death. From about 1871 to 1876, while working as a clerk in the naval ministry, he lived in a ground-floor room at 2 Rue Moncey. "It was so small," wrote biographer Francis Steegmuller, "that guests, upon arrival, were handed folding chairs which were at other times kept in a closet." From 1876 to 1881 the writer occupied three rooms at 17 Rue Clauzel (controversy still exists over whether the present marker on number 19 was misplaced or actually identifies the former number 17).

By 1884 Maupassant was successful enough to move into a luxurious suite on the ground floor of

10 Rue de Montchanin (today the Rue Jacques-Bingen), a house built by his cousin. It remained his Paris home until 1889. One of his last residences (1890–92) was a five-room apartment at 24 Rue du Boccador near the Hôtel George V. There in 1890 he finished his last novel, *Notre Coeur* (1890).

Mentally ravaged as a result of untreated syphilis, Maupassant spent his final months often straitjacketed in the luxurious sanitarium of Dr. Esprit Blanche, where he died. This mansion, now the Turkish Embassy, stands at 17 Rue d'Ankara. Previous patients there included poet Gerard de Nerval and composer Charles Gounod.

Maupassant tomb: Montparnasse Cemetery.

(See Chapter 2, FRANCE.)

MIRÓ, JOAN (1893–1983). The Spanish surrealist painter spent most of his winters in Paris from 1919 to 1942. His first lengthy residence and studio (1920–27) was 45 Rue Blomet (Left Bank), where he finished his canvas *The Farm* (1922). "As I was very poor," the artist recalled, "I could only afford one dinner a week; the other days I had to manage on dry figs and I chewed gum." Years later he revisited the address and found "a very fine lilac in the courtyard. The house was being demolished and a big dog sprang out at me." His first married home in 1929 with Pilar Juncosa was 3 Rue François-Mouthon.

At 22 Rue Tourlaque (Right Bank), he occupied an apartment and studio from 1927 to 1929.

(See Chapter 8, SPAIN.)

MOLIÈRE, JEAN BAPTISTE POQUELIN DE (1622–1673). A native of Paris and dweller there for most of his life, the great comic playwright left few tangible traces. None of his known residences survive.

Most biographers agree that his birthplace site is 96 Rue St-Honoré (corner of 2 Rue Sauval, **Right Bank**). The 15th-century three-story house where the lad named Jean Poquelin apprenticed in his father's ground-floor upholstery shop was marked by a corner post of carved wooden monkeys, and thus became known as the "monkey house." In 1655 it also became the birthplace of a playwright regarded as Molière's closest successor, Jean François Régnard. This now long-gone house was certainly Molière's boyhood dwelling (his birthplace has also been claimed as 31 Rue du Pont-Neuf).

From 1633 to 1658 the playwright's main Paris address probably remained his father's later house, which stood further east in the Rue St-Honoré near the old market arcades.

Poquelin and his acting company founded their first theater, the Illustre, in a former tennis court at 12 Rue Mazarine in 1643. He took the stage name "Molière" at this time to avoid embarrassing his father (acting was then a less than respectable occupation) and kept the name throughout his life. He probably resided at number 10 Rue Mazarine with the Béjart family; actress Armande Béjart became his wife in 1662, and Madeleine Béjart, probably her sister, was his lifelong companion and mistress.

Molière's last home, again shared with his wife, stood at 40 Rue de Richelieu, where he was brought dying after he collapsed while performing in his play *Le Malade imaginaire* (1673). The nearby ornate Molière Fountain at the corner of the Rue Molière memorializes the playwright.

Molière tomb: Père Lachaise Cemetery.

Exhibit: The Théâtre Français, better known as the Comédie Française, at 2 Rue de Richelieu (Place André Malraux, **Right Bank**) displays in its foyer museum (12 Galerie du Théâtre-Française) the chair in which the playwright was fatally stricken during his last performance. This famous theater specializes in presenting works of classical French dramatists, including Molière comedies (phone 296-10-20).

(See Chapter 2, FRANCE.)

MONET, CLAUDE (1840–1926). None of Monet's fellow impressionists, wrote critic Robert Hughes, were "able to go so far in the direction of displaying reality as a collection of tiny, discrete stillnesses." A native of Paris, Monet was born at 45 Rue Laffitte, **Right Bank**, where he spent his first five years. In adulthood he resided steadily in Paris for one formative decade (ca. 1859–68), during which he came into contact with painters, poets and writers. This richly creative milieu influenced his own genius and led to the first impressionist exhibition in 1874. He occupied lodgings at 35 Rue Rodier in 1859 and at 28 Rue Pigalle in 1860.

On the **Left Bank**, Monet lived with fellow artist Frédéric Bazille (1865–66) at 6 Rue de Furstenberg, the small studio built in 1857 by romantic painter Eugène Delacroix, who died there in 1863. Now known as the Delacroix Museum, the apartment-studio displays mementos of that artist. (Open Wednesday—Monday 9:45—5:15; 354-04-87; admission.)

CLAUDE MONET'S EARLY HOME AND STUDIO. Today 6 Rue de Furstenberg is better known as the Delacroix Museum, as artist Eugène Delacroix lived and painted there from 1857 to 1863. In 1865, however, years before he achieved his own reputation, Monet lived there with a fellow painter, absorbing the rich creative atmosphere of a city that has always been kind to artists.

Monet's last, brief Paris dwelling (1877–78) was a small apartment at 26 Rue d'Edimbourg, **Right Bank**.

Exhibits: *Impression, Sunrise* was the name of the Monet painting that attracted derisive critical attack in 1874; the label "impressionists" was soon attached to the exhibiting group, which included Renoir, Manet and Pissarro. As so often happens with derogatory labels, this one soon lost its negative connotations. The exhibition was presented at 35 Boulevard des Capucines, **Right Bank** (see the entry on Pierre Renoir later in this chapter).

The Marmottan Museum at 2 Rue Louis-Boilly displays probably the largest Monet collection in the world, donated by the artist's son. Among the canvases exhibited here are *Sunrise* and many of the painter's water-lily studies. (Open Tuesday—Sunday 10:00—6:00; 224-07-02; admission.)

The Jeu de Paume Museum displays a Monet collection in Room 10 (see the entry on Paul Gauguin, *Exhibit*, earlier in this chapter). Located south across the Tuileries gardens, the Orangerie portion of this museum holds the monumental series *Décorations des Nymphéas*, which occupied Monet's final years at Giverny.

(See Chapter 2, FRANCE.)

MOZART, WOLFGANG AMADEUS (1756–1791). In 1778 the young Austrian musical genius came to Paris for concert recitals, bringing his mother, Anna Pertl Mozart, with him. They lodged in the Hôtel des Quatre Fils Aymon in the Rue du Sentier, **Right Bank**, now a wholesale warehouse district; and there, to Mozart's intense anguish, Anna Mozart died. "Never," he wrote his father back in Salzburg, "had I seen anyone die—and the first time it must be my mother." For several months after her death the grieving composer resided at 5 Rue de la Chausée-d'Antin, a later dwelling of Frédéric Chopin (see the entry on Chopin earlier in this chapter). The present building on the site is not the original.

Earlier, in 1763, the child prodigy had resided with his impresario father in the Hôtel de Beauvais at 68 Rue François-Miron for several months while performing in various aristocratic salons as a kind of marvelous freak. According to Kenneth Bernstein in *Music Lover's Europe* (1983), this building's first occupant "was Catherine Bellier, alias One-Eyed Kate, the first woman in the life of Louis XIV (he was sixteen and she was about forty). The palace was so grateful for her kindnesses that she and her husband were given noble titles and the land for this mansion." The ornate 17th-century building housed the Bavarian Embassy at the time. Queen Christina of Sweden was a later tenant.

(See Chapter 1, AUSTRIA; also Chapter 4, WEST GERMANY; also Chapter 6, LONDON.)

NAPOLEON I (1769–1821). The military leader who led France in the successful conquest of Europe and created an empire on the ashes of the French Revolution began his rise and consolidated his rule in Paris.

Corsican-born Napoleon Buonaparte received his officer's training in the École Militaire, an elite college for French soldiers, in 1784 and 1785. "He is taciturn, with a love for solitude," reported his superiors, "is moody, overbearing, and extremely egotistical." Founded by Louis XV and opened in 1756, the school was closed in 1787 and used as a military depot and barracks. Today it is once again a military staff college, formally titled the École Supérieure de Guerre. Enlarged in 1856 the vast building, with its long classical facade, central domed portico and huge courtyard, covers some 29 acres. "Where its neighbor, Les Invalides, is an officer in ceremonial dress," wrote Christopher McIntosh, "the École Militaire is a sergeant major bawling out across the Champ-de-Mars to the Eiffel Tower." It stands at 7 Place Joffre, **Left Bank**. The chapel where Napoleon was confirmed is open daily to the public. Guided tours through other parts of the building must be prearranged in writing. (Contact General Director, École Militaire, 1 Place Joffre, Paris 75007.)

Just before his marriage in 1795, Napoleon—a rather undisciplined career officer whose future looked unpromising at this point—took dismal lodgings in a rear room facing the Seine at 10 Rue de la Huchette, **Left Bank**.

The rising, crude-mannered young general courted Joséphine de Beauharnais, a beautiful widowed Creole noblewoman six years his senior, in her home at 6 Rue Chantereine. The villa, rented by Joséphine in 1795, stood at the end of a long path surrounded by gardens. The couple spent their wedding night there and shared their bed, Napoleon later complained, with Joséphine's aggressive pug terrier. After Napoleon's Italian and Egyptian campaigns in 1799, he bought the house. In this, his first real home in Paris, he hatched the coup of the 18th Brumaire that would make him first consul and the master of France. The couple vacated the house for more lordly dwellings in 1800. Napoleon III had the dwelling demolished in 1859 to accommodate his building plans. Even the street has disappeared; the site is now covered by bank buildings in the Rue de la Victoire, **Right Bank**.

Napoleon's first official residence as first consul was the Petit-Luxembourg, a 16th-century mansion standing adjacent to the Luxembourg Palace, 15 Rue de Vaugirard, **Left Bank**. The Luxembourg, used as a prison during the Revolution, held Georges Jacques Danton and Thomas Paine among its notable cellmates and became the seat of the Directory that elevated Napoleon to power. Much altered and enlarged, it now houses the French senate. The Petit-Luxembourg, where Napoleon occupied ground-floor chambers for three crucial months of 1800, is now the official residence of the senate's president; there is no public admission. (Luxembourg Palace open for tours, Sunday 9:30—11:00, 2:00—4:00; 329–12–62; free.)

The Tuileries Palace, Napoleon's Paris residence from 1800 to 1815, was the north-south-aligned building that once "squared off" the Louvre; it connected the present west ends of the Pavillon de Marsan and the Pavillon de Flore wings and flanked the east side of the Avenue du Gén.-Lemonnier. The main entrance to its courtyard ran through the surviving Arc de Triomphe du Car-

THE TUILERIES PALACE, HOME OF NAPOLEON. The Tuileries, together with the Louvre, was the central residence of French royalty in Paris for several centuries. This 17th-century view, looking east from the Place de la Concorde, reveals the rigidly formalized landscape gardens that were so popular in France during the age of Louis XIV, who lived in the palace about the time this engraving was made. The actual layout of the Tuileries Gardens has changed little. No remnant of the palace itself survives.

SITE OF THE TUILERIES TODAY. From the Tuileries Gardens may be seen the Arc de Triomphe du Carrousel, eastern entrance to the palace that once connected the two wings of the Louvre (left and right sides in this photograph).

rousel, built in 1806 to commemorate the emperor's victories. Begun in 1564 on the site of tile kilns ("tuileries"), the palace served as a residence for most French royalty from the time of Catherine de Médicis to Napoleon III. The Empress Joséphine's private chambers occupied the ground floor of the south wing facing west on the present avenue, the former apartment of Marie Antoinette; from these same chambers was instituted the Reign of Terror when the notorious Committee of Public Safety met there in 1792. Napoleon's apartment was directly above Joséphine's in the former king's suite; a reconstruction of his bedroom may be seen at the Château of Malmaison (see the entry on Napoleon I, Chapter 2). Burned by Communard mobs in 1871, the palace's charred walls stood until 1884. The **Right Bank** site, now an extension of the famed Tuileries gardens, is marked with 19 bronze female statues by Aristide Maillol.

The Élysée Palace at 55-57 Rue du Faubourg-St-Honoré, **Right Bank**, official dwelling of

French presidents since 1873, was Napoleon's last home in Paris. He fled there after the Battle of Waterloo in 1815, watched his support crumble in the Chamber of Deputies and signed his second abdication there. Napoleon had given the palace to Joséphine, now his ex-wife, as her city residence, but she gave it up in 1812 and Napoleon had used it occasionally thereafter as a weekend residence. Other notable residents of the palace included Mme. de Pompadour, Joachim Murat and Napoleon's nemesis, the Duke of Wellington. Napoleon's nephew, Napoleon III, lived there as president from 1848 to 1852 when he became emperor. During state visits, Queen Victoria resided there in 1855 and Elizabeth II in 1957. President Charles de Gaulle occupied the palace during his term of office (see the entries on de Gaulle and the Duke of Wellington in this chapter). Built as the Hôtel d'Évreux in 1718, the building has been much altered and enlarged. It is not open to the public.

Exhibits: On March 6, 1796, the new commander of the Army of Italy married Joséphine de Beauharnais at 3 Rue d'Antin, **Right Bank**, a surviving building which then served as town hall of the second arrondissement. The wedding party waited there in a dismal room for the groom, who finally arrived amid much officious clatter two hours late for the five-minute civil ceremony.

Napoleon's coronation as emperor by Pope Pius VII on December 2, 1804, occurred at Notre Dame Cathedral. The present cathedral has stood for

NAPOLEON'S LAST HOME IN PARIS. This pastoral view of the Élysée Palace belies the traumatic events that have occurred there as well as the dramatic figures who have inhabited it, people such as the Duke of Wellington and Charles de Gaulle as well as Napoleon. Since 1873 it has served as the official dwelling of French presidents.

more than six centuries at Place du Parvis Notre-Dame, **Île de la Cité**, the earlier site of a Roman temple to Jupiter. The Cathedral treasury, located in the sacristy, displays souvenirs in memory of Napoleon's coronation—a ceremony at which he seized the crown from the pope and crowned himself. (Treasury open daily 10:00—5:00; 354-22-63; admission; cathedral open daily 8:00—7:00; free.)

The Carnavalet Museum (Musée Historique de la Ville de Paris) illustrates Paris history from the 16th to 19th centuries at 23 Rue de Sévigné, **Right Bank**. Room 74 on the ground floor displays personal mementos of Napoleon and his huge family. This 16th-century mansion was the home of one of France's notable literary women, Mme. de Sévigné, who lived there from 1677 to her death in 1696. Her apartments, in the southeast corner of the first floor, are also displayed. (Open Tuesday—Sunday 10:00—5:40; 272-21-13; admission; Sunday free).

Les Invalides, the 17th-century building that contains four museums plus Napoleon's tomb, is an essential stop for anyone interested in the emperor's career. The Army Museum therein displays memorabilia and numerous personal possessions, including a hat, gray coat, and sword, Napoleon's field tent and furniture, and the mounted skin of his white horse "Vizier." Visitors may also see Napoleon's death mask; a reconstruction of his death chamber at Longwood House, St. Helena; and other items related to his exile there. Les Invalides is approached via the Esplanade des Invalides, **Left Bank**. (Open April 1—September 30, daily 10:00—6:00; October 1—March 31, daily 10:00—5:00; 551-92-84; admission.)

Napoleon I tomb: Dome church, Les Invalides.

(See Chapter 1, AUSTRIA, SWITZERLAND; also Chapter 2, FRANCE; also Chapter 4, EAST GERMANY, BELGIUM; also Chapter 8, ITALY.)

ORWELL, GEORGE. See ERIC ARTHUR BLAIR.

PASTEUR, LOUIS (1822–1895). Most modern medical theory is based on the work of Pasteur, the chemist and immunologist whose research confirmed the germ theory of disease and who went on to develop vaccines to counter specific disease organisms. Just as important, he introduced the modern era of scientific medicine by as-

HOME OF LOUIS PASTEUR. The Pasteur Institute in the Rue du Docteur-Roux is now surrounded by institute buildings. In this structure occurred some of the most notable breakthroughs in 19th-century medicine. A Pasteur museum here displays exhibits on the great scientist.

signing his trained associates to attack killer diseases by systematic methodology.

Pasteur lived and worked in Paris from 1842 to 1847 and then again from 1857 until his death, teaching and directing research at several institutions. The École Normale Supérieure at 45 Rue d'Ulm, **Left Bank**, was the center of his activities from 1843 to 1888. There he performed the sometimes hazardous experiments that led to his epochal discovery of fermentation, the development of the pasteurization process, and the formulation of a rabies vaccine. During his work with rabies, scores of people who had been bitten by animals crowded his tiny laboratory seeking treatment; most of them survived as a result of Pasteur's radical methods. Though half-crippled by a stroke in 1868, he continued his energetic teaching and experimentation into old age. He lived to see a dream come true with the founding of the Pasteur Institute in 1888, which was built with the help of donations from all over the world. This still-thriving, much enlarged institute continues to lead world research in preventive medicine. Its headquarters remain at 25 Rue du Docteur-Roux. Today Pasteur's house, which is now surrounded by institute buildings, is the Pasteur Museum; it displays exhibits on both his scientific career and personal life. Furnishings, personal possessions, his laboratory instruments as well as numerous documents and photographs reveal aspects of one of humanity's great creditors. (Open Monday—Friday 2:30—5:00, closed August; 541–52–66; admission.)

(See Chapter 2, FRANCE.)

PICASSO, PABLO (1881–1973). The Spanish-born Picasso, a prodigious and versatile genius in almost every art medium, centered his life in Paris for half a century (1904–54)—a period which encompassed both world wars and numerous changes in the artist's surroundings and personal creative direction. His earliest **Right Bank** studio-dwellings, before he settled permanently in the city, included 49 Rue Gabrielle (1900) and 130 Boulevard de Clichy (1901). In 1904 he moved into the Bateau-Lavoir, a low wooden subterranean building at 13 Place Émile-Goudeau. Painters Georges Braque, Juan Gris, Amedeo Modigliani and Pierre Renoir, as well as poets Guillaume Apollinaire and Max Jacob also lived there at various times. It was Picasso's home until 1909. There, in 1907, he created *Les Demoiselles d'Avignon*, said to be the first Cubist painting. This structure, often called the "birthplace of modern art," where Picasso and Braque created Cubism—"a new mode of describing space"—burned in 1970, but has since been rebuilt and remains occupied by artists.

From 1909 to 1912 Picasso worked and resided at 11 Boulevard de Clichy, **Right Bank**; and from 1912 to 1918 at 5bis Rue Schoelcher and at 242 Boulevard Raspail, both on the **Left Bank**. With his first wife, Olga Koklova, he occupied 23 Rue de la Boétie, **Right Bank**, from 1918 to 1937—the longest period he spent in one dwelling. After the couple's never-finalized divorce, Picasso continued to use the studio space at this address for a storehouse until he was evicted in 1951 by a postwar government faced with a crucial housing shortage.

A rented studio in the 17th-century Hôtel d'Hercule at 7 Rue des Grands-Augustins, **Left Bank**, was Picasso's last Paris home (1937–54). There he painted his best-known canvas, *Guernica* (1937), perhaps the most eloquent artistic protest against war ever produced. The interior of this building, despite the efforts of the late culture minister André Malraux to preserve it as a Picasso memorial, has been converted to municipal offices.

Exhibits: The recently opened Picasso Museum in the 17th-century Hôtel Aubert-de-Fontenay, (also known as Hôtel Sale) at 5 Rue Thorigny, **Right Bank**, displays the artist's large personal collection of paintings and sculpture. Much of it passed to the French government after Picasso's death in lieu of taxes on his estate. Though none of his most famous works are here, the exhibit provides a unique view of Picasso's artistic evolution—through his blue, rose, Cubist and later periods—as well as some astonishing childhood creations; it provides a broad view of his work that is impossible to survey in any other museum. To Picasso, this collection also represented his carefully hoarded "bank account," a lifelong increasing treasure of "Picasso's Picassos" that he kept beside him like a tangible insurance policy. Works by other artists are also on display from Picasso's private collection. (Contact museum for admission information.)

The National Museum of Modern Art also exhibits paintings that are representative of Picasso's various artistic phases (see the entry on Henri Matisse, *Exhibit*, earlier in this chapter).

(See Chapter 1, SWITZERLAND; also Chapter 2, FRANCE; also Chapter 8, SPAIN.)

PROUST, MARCEL (1871–1922). A novelist intrigued by various interpretations of reality, Proust's acutely introspective seven-part *Remembrance of Things Past* (1913–27), remains an influential work. Except for childhood visits to relatives, he resided for almost his entire life on the **Right Bank**, becoming increasingly reclusive as his health declined and his writing more and more obsessed him. A plaque marks his birthplace site at 96 Rue de la Fontaine in **Auteuil**, a district at the extreme southwestern edge of Paris. This was an uncle's home, which Proust often visited in later life.

His parental home until 1900 was 9 Boulevard Malesherbes; then, from 1900 to 1906, he lived at 45 Rue de Courcelles (corner of Rue de Monceau), where his parents died. He remembered this large house most especially for its "echo and a staircase."

Almost the whole of Proust's lengthy opus was written at 102 Boulevard Haussmann, his home from 1906 to 1919. He rarely ventured outside during those years. Plagued by serious asthma and neurotic episodes he concentrated feverishly "in search of lost time," lining the bedroom-study that had become the center of his life with cork to shut out noise, working nights, sleeping days, all the while fed and cared for by a devoted housekeeper. Proust's last address from 1919 was 44 Rue Hamelin, where he died.

Proust tomb: Père-Lachaise Cemetery.

(See Chapter 2, FRANCE.)

RABELAIS, FRANÇOIS (1494?–1553). "Few books in history are more well," wrote Kenneth Rexroth of Rabelais' *Gargantua and Pantagruel* (1532–64), "no characters in all literature less sick, than those genial giants and their companions." Only an ex-monk could have satirized the church so deftly and bawdily as did this Renaissance scholar, physician and lay brother of two successive orders, the Franciscans and Benedictines.

Rabelais died at an address in the Rue des Jardins-St-Paul, **Right Bank**; the site has been variously identified as numbers 2, 8 and 34. His last words, according to legend: "The farce is finished. I go to seek a vast perhaps." He was apparently buried in the now vanished church of St-Paul-des Champs, which stood near the present 17th-century church of St-Paul-St-Louis in the nearby Rue St-Antoine.

(See Chapter 2, FRANCE; also Chapter 8, ITALY.)

RENOIR, PIERRE AUGUSTE (1841–1919). The impressionist painter resided at a number of Paris addresses from 1844 to about 1900. His boyhood home from 1844 to 1854 stood in a street that no longer exists, the Rue de la Bibliothèque, located on the site of the present Place du Carrousel at the Louvre, **Right Bank**, formerly a labyrinth of narrow streets encircled by the royal palaces. The area was cleared to form the present square in 1854.

Renoir's surviving lodgings include 12 Rue Cortot, **Right Bank**, a 17th-century house in which he rented two attic rooms and a stable as studio space in 1875 and 1876. At 17 Rue St-Vincent, where Renoir lodged briefly in 1875, the Museum of Montmartre now displays period and local mementos of the Montmartre district. The artists Maurice Utrillo and Raoul Dufy also number among those who lodged in the building at various times. (Open Monday—Saturday 2:30—5:30, Sunday 11:00—5:30; admission.)

From 1894 to 1898 Renoir lived at the Château des Brouillards, 9 Allée des Brouillards (off the Rue Girardon, **Left Bank**), a large block of buildings in which he occupied Pavilion 6. This was the 1894 birthplace of his son, the noted film director Jean Renoir.

Again on the **Right Bank** in 1897 and 1898 the painter occupied a studio at 64 Rue de la Rochefoucauld (corner of Rue La Bruyère). His last Paris residence was 27 Boulevard Rochechouart. (Also see the entry on Pablo Picasso earlier in this chapter.)

Exhibit: Several of Renoir's best-known canvases, including *Le Moulin de la Galette*, are exhibited in Room 11 of the Jeu de Paume Museum (see the entry on Paul Gauguin, *Exhibit*, earlier in this chapter).

(See Chapter 2, FRANCE.)

RICHELIEU, ARMAND JEAN DU PLESSIS, DUC DE (1585–1642).

The cardinal and statesman, chief minister of Louis XIII, dominated the king and all of France for almost two decades, making royal authority absolute and crushing Protestant political opposition. Richelieu claimed to be a Paris native and his birthplace probably stood at 2–4 Rue du Bouloi, **Right Bank**, until demolished in 1880.

As chief minister from 1624 Richelieu occupied the 17th-century mansion at 21 Place des Vosges until he built his own immense palace. This was the Palais-Cardinal. Today, with its extensive enlargements, buildings and galleries, it is known as the Palais-Royal, Place du Palais-Royal. Built during the years 1634 to 1639, the palace—where the prelate resided in opulent splendor until his death—was bequeathed to Louis XIII, whose son, Louis XIV, lived there during boyhood (see the entry on Louis XIV earlier in this chapter). Cardinal Mazarin, Richelieu's successor as chief minister, occupied Richelieu's old apartments. Various royal relatives lived there until the Revolution, when the palace area became the center of numer-

THE PALAIS-ROYAL. One of Europe's most powerful 17th-century statesmen, the Duc de Richelieu built this massive palace in the 1630's as his personal domain. This engraving represents a 19th-century view of a complex that has undergone extensive enlargements, rebuilding, and adaptations. Among others who lived there were Louis XIV, Cardinal Mazarin, Louis-Philippe, Jérôme Bonaparte, and writers Colette and Jean Cocteau. Government offices, apartment dwellings, and shops now occupy most of these buildings surrounding the Place du Palais-Royal.

ous rallies and demonstrations; Marat called it the "nucleus of the Revolution." As the "Palais-Égalité," it was used for government offices until the building was returned to the Orléans family in 1814. King Louis-Philippe lived there until 1832, and Jérôme Bonaparte resided there during the Second Empire. After riot damage during the Commune, much of the palace was rebuilt during the 1870s. Later noted residents included the authors Colette and Jean Cocteau (see the entry on Colette earlier in this chapter). Today this complex of residential buildings, government offices, shops, cafes and gardens represents a mixture of 17th- to 19th-century structures. The Council of State and the Ministry of Cultural Affairs now occupy the palace proper, and there is no public admission.

Richelieu tomb: Church of Ste-Ursule de la Sorbonne.

(See Chapter 2, FRANCE.)

RILKE, RAINER MARIA (1875–1926).

"Paris stood for whatever there was of continuity in his life," wrote E. M. Butler of the German lyric poet. Rilke, whose work has aroused increasing interest since his death, resided in Paris at several **Left Bank** addresses during intervals from 1902 to 1914. His first Paris address was 11 Rue Toullier, the setting of his novel *The Notebooks of Malte Laurids Brigge* (1910). In 1906 and 1907 he lodged at 29 Rue Cassette. He lived at 17 Rue Campagne-Première in 1908 and again in 1913 and 1914, when it became his last Paris address.

Rilke resided longest (1908–11) at the Hôtel Biron, 77 Rue de Varenne, which was acquired by the state for the use of artists in 1901. It is now the Rodin Museum. Rilke idolized the sculptor and had previously served as Rodin's secretary there in 1905 and 1906 (see the entry on Auguste Rodin later in this chapter).

(See Chapter 1, SWITZERLAND; also Chapter 2, FRANCE; also Chapter 4, WEST GERMANY.)

ROBESPIERRE, MAXIMILIEN DE (1758–1794).

Though his power was far from absolute, Robespierre's leadership of the notorious Committee of Public Safety, which organized the Reign of Terror during the Revolution and virtually ruled France for a year, has made his name synonymous with the bloodiest excesses of that period. A brilliant lawyer, Robespierre was also a fanatical idealist—that most deadly breed of man—and, unlike his compatriots, he saw the Terror as a means of bringing about the creation of Rousseau's "ideal" state. In the end, this unsavory character was beheaded on the same guillotine to which he had sent hundreds of other French citizens; and Paris cheered his passing, just as it had cheered the executions of his victims.

Robespierre's first Paris dwelling (1789–91) was a two-room apartment at 64 Rue de Saintonge, **Right Bank**, where he lodged with one Villiers, a young playwright. This building was demolished after a long period of vacancy in 1934. In 1791 Robespierre moved to a house owned by the Duplay family, with whom he lodged until his 1794 arrest. In a first-floor room on the west side of the house, he prepared his inflammatory Convention speeches and plotted the strategy that made the streets of Paris flow red. Located at 398 Rue Honoré, the stone house, now incorporated into the facade of another building, was recently occupied by the unsinister Chez Robespierre nightclub, then by a restaurant. On the day of Robespierre's death, the tumbril carrying him to the guillotine paused in front of the house while a citizen splashed a bucket of animal blood on the door (according to another version, a child smeared blood on the door with a brush).

Earlier, fleeing arrest, Robespierre sought shelter in the Hôtel de Ville, or Paris town hall, Place de l'Hôtel-de-Ville. National guardsmen stormed the building and in the melee Robespierre was either shot or shot himself; he was then dragged wounded to the Conciergerie (see the entry on Marie Antoinette earlier in this chapter). The present Hôtel de Ville, center of Paris municipal government, dates only from 1874 and replicates on a larger scale the 16th-century building burned down by the Communards in 1871. The public relations office, where information on Paris as well as the building itself may be obtained, is located in the entrance vestibule at 29 Rue de Rivoli.

Robespierre tomb (unmarked): Errancis Cemetery, Parc de Monceau.

(See Chapter 2, FRANCE.)

RODIN, AUGUSTE (1840–1917). Probably the greatest sculptor of the 19th century, Rodin was a man of few inhibitions. "Flesh, both his own and others',"wrote critic Robert Hughes, "was a source of inexhaustible fascination to him." A Paris native, Rodin was born at what is now 7 Rue de l'Arbalète, **Left Bank**. The house, now gone, was his home until the 1860s.

THE RODIN MUSEUM. The sculptor's statuary also adorns the extensive park behind the Hôtel Biron, where Rodin lived and worked from 1908 until his death in 1917.

Rodin's longtime workplace, the Dépôt des Marbres, stood at 182 Rue de l'Université until the 1930s; in three consecutive studios there from 1880 until his death, he created (with the help of a large staff) his most notable sculptures.

From 1908 until his death the sculptor occupied ground-floor quarters and studio at the Hôtel Biron, 77 Rue de Varenne, a 1728 mansion and former convent acquired by the state for the use of artists in 1901. It stood on a 17-acre estate. Henri Matisse and Rainer Maria Rilke were among others who also resided there (see the entries on Matisse and Rilke earlier in this chapter). Today this building houses the Rodin Museum which contains the sculptor's major works, including *The Kiss* and *The Thinker*. Busts, statuary and drawings are exhibited on two floors and a garden provides an ideal setting for many of Rodin's sculptures. (Open Wednesday—Monday 10:00—6:00; 705–01–34; admission.)

(See Chapter 2, FRANCE; also Chapter 4, BELGIUM.)

ROSSINI, GIOACCHINO (1782–1868). The Italian operatic composer made his permanent home in Paris from 1824. As director of the Théâtre des Italiens (1824–25), he lodged at 28 Rue Taitbout, **Right Bank**; and later (1830 *et seq.* 1837) in attic rooms of the theater itself in the Boulevard des Italiens, which fire destroyed in 1838, along with a large collection of his music. From 1857 to 1860 Rossini lived at 2 Rue de la Chaussée-d'Antin in a large second-floor apartment where he entertained lavishly.

Rossini's last homes were in **Passy**. He rented a 17th-century villa at 24 Rue de la Pompe from

1856 to 1860. The Villa Rossini, where he spent summers from 1860, stood at 2 Avenue Ingres. It was here that he died. Erected on a parcel of land sold to him at discount by the City of Paris, the house became a noted rendezvous for artists and musicians. A new owner demolished it after Rossini's death.

(See Chapter 2, FRANCE; also Chapter 6, LONDON; also Chapter 8, ITALY.)

ROUSSEAU, JEAN-JACQUES (1712–1778). Rousseau believed in the intrinsic goodness of humanity and the world; it was the optimistic base on which he built his political theory, and the reason why he is considered an important precursor of the Romantic movement. Swiss-born, Rousseau resided in Paris at lengthy intervals from 1742. In 1745 at the Hôtel St-Quentin which stood in the Rue Victor-Cousin, **Left Bank**, he met his lifelong mistress, Thérèse Levasseur, by whom he had five children (all of whom he placed in orphanages).

The couple later resided in attic rooms at 57 Rue des Petits-Champs, **Right Bank**. Their residence of longest duration (1770–78) was probably a house that stood at what is now 52 Rue Jean-Jacques-Rousseau.

Rousseau tomb: Panthéon.

(See Chapter 1, SWITZERLAND; also Chapter 2, FRANCE; also Chapter 5, ENGLAND.)

RUSSELL, BERTRAND, LORD (1872–1970). "My career in diplomacy," wrote the noted philosopher and pacifist, "was brief and inglorious. I loathed the work and the people." Russell's residence and assignment as honorary attaché in 1894 was the British Embassy, 35–39 Rue du Faubourg-St-Honoré, **Right Bank** (see the entry on William Somerset Maugham earlier in this chapter).

(See Chapter 5, ENGLAND; also Chapter 6, LONDON; also Chapter 7, WALES.)

SADE, DONATIEN ALPHONSE FRANÇOIS, MARQUIS DE (1740–1814). The word *sadism*, the infliction of pain for the purposes of sexual gratification, derives from the name of this noble-born author whose own debauchery and licentious novels outraged even a libertine age. As late as 1957 French courts denied publication of his works; his profound psychological insights, years ahead of Freud, have only recently brought him

serious attention as one of France's literary prophets. Sade spent about 30 years of his life imprisoned, often by *lettre de cachet* (a royal order for indefinite detention without trial) sponsored by his own scandalized family. A Paris native, Sade was born at the now vanished Hôtel de Condé, which stood at 5–9 Rue de Condé, **Left Bank**; it was his home until 1744 (some sources give the birth site as number 20 on this street). The Théâtre de France stands in the former garden of the Condé palace.

Cellars belonging to the infamous Bastille, that fortress prison which became a hated symbol of tyranny to revolutionists, may survive beneath the present paving stones that indicate the outline of the building in the Place de la Bastille, **Right Bank**. Originally a bastion defending the city's eastern entrance, the Bastille was massively enlarged with towers, thick walls and a wide moat. It served Henri IV as the royal treasury, then, from the reign of Louis XIII, as a state prison for political offenders. Famous prisoners included the mysterious "Man in the Iron Mask" (1698–1703) and Voltaire (see the entry on Voltaire later in this chapter). Revolutionary mobs stormed the fortress on July 14, 1789, and released the few prisoners it then contained. The building was razed to the ground that same year. Part of its masonry went for construction of the upper part of the Pont de la Concorde across the Seine—so, it is said, that Parisians could tread underfoot the symbol of royal oppression. The main keep of the Bastille stood on the west side of the square across the end of the Rue St-Antoine. Sade successively occupied two octagonal tower cells there from 1784 to 1789 and it was there that he wrote two of his most profligate fantasies, *Justine* (1791) and *The 120 Days of Sodom*, unpublished until 1931. The latter work, he claimed, was "the most impure tale that has been written since the world began." According to one story, he incited mobs to storm the Bastille from his tower window and thus became a brief hero of the Revolution after his release. A model of the Bastille may be seen at the Carnavalet Museum (see the entry on Napoleon I, *Exhibits*, earlier in this chapter).

In 1796 and 1797 Sade and his last and longtime mistress, actress Marie-Constance Quesnet, dwelled somewhere in the Rue de la Réunion—leaving there eventually because they could not pay the rent.

(See Chapter 2, FRANCE.)

SAND, GEORGE (1804–1876). A Paris native, the novelist, feminist and catalyst for a wide circle of literary and artistic intimates was born Amandine Aurore Dupin at 15 Rue de la Meslay, **Right Bank**.

Sand, who adapted her pseudonym from the name of her early lover, novelist Jules Sandeau, maintained Paris residences throughout her life and several survive. At 21 Rue de la Seine, **Left Bank**, she lived with a half-brother in 1831 and published her first stories. "Traditionally it was here," wrote Anne Roche, "that she first appeared dressed as a man . . . her own experiences form the basis of her early novels." This building now houses the Akademia, an art gallery founded by Raymond Duncan, brother of dancer Isadora Duncan, and now operated by his daughter.

Sand lived with Sandeau and, later, her mother at 19 Quai Malaquais from 1832 to 1836; wrote *Lélia* (1833) there; and there began her affair with writer Alfred de Musset. A decade later (1844), the house became the brithplace of novelist Anatole France.

The Hôtel de la France at 15 Rue Laffitte, **Right Bank**, where George Sand resided in 1836, no longer stands. There she shared quarters with Franz Liszt and his mistress, and met Chopin, whose mistress she became. She occupied an apartment adjacent to Chopin's at 16 Rue Pigalle (now gone) from 1839 to 1842, then resided next door to him at 9 Square d'Orléans from 1842 to 1846 (see the entries on Frédéric Chopin and Franz Liszt earlier in this chapter). In 1848 she lived at 8 Rue de Condé, **Left Bank**, with her son, Maurice Dudevant. Her last Paris residence (1870s) was 5 Rue Gay-Lussac.

(See Chapter 2, FRANCE; also Chapter 8, ITALY, SPAIN.)

SARTRE, JEAN-PAUL (1905–1980). The existentialist philosopher, playwright and 1964 Nobel Prize winning novelist was born in Paris and lived there most of his life. A distant cousin of Albert Schweitzer (see the entry on Schweitzer below), Sartre was born at 2 Rue Mignard, **Right Bank**, and was raised in his maternal grandparents' home at 1 Rue Le Goff, **Left Bank** (1911–17, 1920–22). His lifelong companion, author Simone de Beauvoir, wrote that "he has spent his adult life in a series of hotel rooms in which there is nothing of his own, not even a copy of his latest work, and which surprise visitors by their bareness." Some of the

couple's **Left Bank** lodgings included the Hôtel de Blois in the Rue Gay-Lussac (1930s); the Hôtel Mistral, 24 Rue Cels, during the early 1940s; and the Hôtel de la Louisiane, 60 Rue de la Seine, to 1944. In 1945 Sartre installed his mother in a fourth-floor apartment at 42 Rue Bonaparte and made it his Paris base—though he seldom spent much time there—until Algerian terrorists set off a bomb in the hallway in 1962. An anticolonial activist and constant fighter for left-wing causes, Sartre's prestige was such that he could not provoke authorities into arresting him for his antigovernment polemics: "One does not arrest Voltaire," pronounced President de Gaulle. Sartre's last home, from 1962, was a tenth-floor suite in the highrise apartment building at 222 Boulevard Raspail.

The likeliest "birthplace" of the existentialist movement was a cafe table, something Sartre always preferred to a desk. The Café de Flore at 172 Boulevard St-Germain was where he and Beauvoir "more or less set up house" during the 1940s, she wrote. They worked there during the day and socialized there in the evenings. Today, according to one recent observer, "times have changed and only the wealthier literati can afford to hold court regularly. . . . most of the customers belong to the most trendy international set" (people with whom Sartre himself wasted no time).

Sartre tomb: Montparnasse Cemetery.

(See Chapter 8, ITALY.)

SCHWEITZER, ALBERT (1875–1965). German Lutheran theologian, philosopher, organist and missionary-physician, Schweitzer studied at the Sorbonne from 1896 to 1899 and resided in a small room at an unknown address in the Rue de la Sorbonne, **Left Bank**.

(See Chapter 2, FRANCE; also Chapter 4, WEST GERMANY, THE NETHERLANDS.)

SIBELIUS, JEAN (1865–1957). The Finnish composer resided in the Rue de Richelieu, **Right Bank**, in 1912; and, at an unknown date, at 19 Quai Voltaire, **Left Bank**, former lodgings of Charles Baudelaire and later Richard Wagner (see the entries on Baudelaire and Wagner in this chapter).

(See Chapter 1, AUSTRIA; also Chapter 2, FRANCE; also Chapter 4, FINLAND.)

STRAVINSKY, IGOR (1882–1971). The Russian-born Stravinsky, probably the 20th-century's major classical composer, resided in France from 1920 to 1939. From 1921 to 1924 he lived and worked in a two-room studio at the Maison Pleyel, a piano factory at 22 Rue de Rochechouart, **Right Bank**. His last French home (1934–39) was 125 Rue de la Faubourg-St-Honoré.

(See Chapter 1, SWITZERLAND; also Chapter 2, FRANCE.)

STRINDBERG, AUGUST (1849–1912). In 1895 and 1896 the Swedish playwright and novelist resided at 62 Rue d'Assas, **Right Bank**.

(See Chapter 4, SWEDEN.)

TOULOUSE-LAUTREC, HENRI DE (1864–1901). Toulouse-Lautrec, master of poster and lithographic art, and the supreme depicter of Montmartre night life and cafe society—its dancers, pleasure seekers and prostitutes—lived on the **Right Bank** from 1872 and maintained studios there from 1886. Crippled by leg injuries in childhood, he made light of his dwarfish appearance and difficult movements. Toulouse-Lautrec spent much of his boyhood at the Hôtel Pérey, 5 Cité du Rétiro, a mansion owned by family relatives. From 1887 to 1894 he roomed with a physician friend, Dr. Henri Bourges, first at 19, then at 21 Rue Fontaine. He moved to 30 Rue Fontaine in 1895 and lived there until 1897. His last Paris home and studio from 1897 stood at 5 Avenue Frochot. An earlier studio was 7 Rue Tourlaque (also known as 27 Rue Caulaincourt, 1886–97); he also resided in a ground-floor apartment there in 1894 and 1895. The Moulin Rouge, Toulouse-Lautrec's favorite revue, where he spent hours sketching the scenes around him on napkins, survives in the Place Blanche off the Boulevard de Clichy.

(See Chapter 2, FRANCE.)

TROTSKY, LEON (1879–1940). The influential Russian revolutionary who built the Red Army but was ultimately expelled from the Communist Party by Stalin, spent several years in Paris both before and after the 1917 Russian Revolution. From 1914 he espoused his political views in the expatriate Russian colony of Paris until expelled from France for antiwar activity in 1916. One address where he resided with his wife, Natalia Sedova, was 46 Rue Gassendi, **Left Bank**.

VAN GOGH, VINCENT (1853–1890). The Dutch painter, a frustrated evangelist, failed at ev-

erything he tried except his self-taught art (light literally pulses and glows from his canvases), but he achieved little recognition even for that during a lifetime of acute psychological distress. In 1886, just before settling at Arles for the last highly productive but tragic phase of his life, he resided with his brother Théo in a third-floor apartment at 54 Rue Lepic, **Right Bank**.

Exhibit: The Jeu de Paume Museum displays a number of van Gogh's feverish, brilliant canvases (see the entry on Paul Gauguin, *Exhibit*, earlier in this chapter).

(See Chapter 2, FRANCE; also Chapter 4, BELGIUM, THE NETHERLANDS; also Chapter 6, LONDON.)

VERNE, JULES (1828–1905). The "father of science fiction" briefly occupied several Paris addresses during the 1850s and 1860s. From 1857 to about 1860 he resided in a fifth-floor apartment at 18 Boulevard Poissonnière, **Right Bank**.

(See Chapter 1, SWITZERLAND; also Chapter 2, FRANCE.)

VOLTAIRE, FRANÇOIS-MARIE AROUET (1694–1778). "My trade is to say what I think," said France's universal literary genius. That "trade" became a merciless thorn inflicting the sedate political and religious hides of his time. Again and again the satirist-philosopher stung the mighty with his razor wit and ridicule: indeed, few in history have been so able, by disposition and intellect, to afflict the comfortable and comfort the afflicted as was "the laughing philosopher," and he is considered an intellectual forebear of the French Revolution. A Paris native, Voltaire was born on the **Left Bank**—somewhere, it is thought, in the area below the Pont St-Michel. "The exact place is unknown, which is a pity," wrote biographer Theodore Besterman in 1969, "for it is more than likely that the home is still standing." Voltaire lived there until age seven.

From 1701 until about 1711 his home was the Palace Arouet, a ten-room house owned by his lawyer father in the Boulevard du Palais, **Île de la Cité**. The site is now covered by portions of the Palace of Justice complex.

The only defense the young Arouet's powerful victims could muster against his verbal weaponry was that last resort of fearful authorities everywhere: imprisonment. Thus, Voltaire spent two periods in the Bastille for his temerity (1717–18 and 1726; see the entry on the Marquis de Sade earlier in this chapter). He began an epic poem, the *Henriade* (1723), while confined there and also adopted—for unknown reasons—the pen name of Voltaire.

During his 14-year liaison (1733–48) with mathematician-physicist the Marquise Gabrielle du Châtelet, the pair often resided at the Hôtel Lambert, a fine 1650 mansion at 1–3 Quai d'Anjou, **Île St-Louis**. Voltaire called it "a house made for a king who would be a philosopher." It was bought for the couple by the marquise's accommodating husband.

VOLTAIRE'S "HOUSE MADE FOR A KING." At 1–3 Quai d'Anjou alongside the Seine on the **Île St-Louis**, the philosopher and his mistress, Mme. du Châtelet, resided at intervals for 14 years.

After Gabrielle's death in 1749, Voltaire resided at a number of **Right Bank** lodgings during his visits to the city, including 21 Rue Molière (1750, site only) and the Hôtel de la Fontaine Martel, 20 Rue de Valois (1753).

The **Left Bank** house where Voltaire received the adulation of Paris, and spent his last weeks and died, survives at 27 Quai Voltaire—the four-story mansion of the Marquis de Villette. Benjamin Franklin was among those who visited the

philosopher there. Years before, in 1723, Voltaire had briefly lodged in the same house.

Voltaire tomb (site): Panthéon.

(See Chapter 1, SWITZERLAND; also Chapter 2, FRANCE; also Chapter 4, EAST GERMANY.)

WAGNER, RICHARD (1813–1883). The German operatic composer lived in Paris for two fairly lengthy intervals at widely separate times. The first period (1839–42) with his wife, Minna Planer, was full of futility and "privations so cruel," wrote one biographer, "that he spoke of them forty years later with tears." He lived at 25 Boulevard des Italiens, **Right Bank**, in 1840 and 1841, working feverishly to complete his opera *Rienzi* (1842), emerging every fourth day for exercise.

In 1841 and 1842 Wagner worked on *The Flying Dutchman* (1843) while lodging at 14 Rue Jacob, **Left Bank**, a later address of political philosopher Pierre-Joseph Proudhon.

Wagner's next stay in Paris (1860–62) also marked a low point in his career: the failure of his *Tannhäuser* at the Paris Opera, an event called "the most notorious fiasco in the history of opera." He first lived in the Rue Newton, **Right Bank**; then, in 1861 and 1862, completed the libretto of *Die Meistersinger* (1868) in 30 days at the Hôtel du Quai Voltaire, still at 19 Quai Voltaire, **Left Bank**. He later called these weeks the happiest of his life. Among others who lodged in this hotel, famed for its literary associations, were Charles Baudelaire, Oscar Wilde and Jean Sibelius (see the entries on Baudelaire, Sibelius and Wilde in this chapter).

(See Chapter 1, AUSTRIA, SWITZERLAND; also Chapter 2, FRANCE; also Chapter 4, EAST GERMANY, WEST GERMANY; also Chapter 6, LONDON; also Chapter 8, ITALY.)

WELLINGTON, ARTHUR WELLESLEY, DUKE OF (1769–1852). The Irish soldier who defeated Napoleon at Waterloo entered Paris in the style of a conqueror in 1814, occupying the Élysée Palace (see the entry on Napoleon I earlier in this chapter). He soon bought what is now the British Embassy from Napoleon's sister, Princess Pauline Borghese, and made it his residence until 1816 (see the entry on William Somerset Maugham earlier in this chapter).

(See Chapter 4, BELGIUM; also Chapter 5, ENGLAND; also Chapter 6, LONDON; also Chapter 7, IRELAND; also Chapter 8, SPAIN.)

WILDE, OSCAR (1854–1900). His literary career shattered after two years of imprisonment for a victimless crime, the Irish-born playwright and poet fled England in 1897 and wandered the continent. From 1898 he made his permanent home in Paris. There, under the assumed name of Sebastian Melmoth, he led an impoverished hotel existence. Though deserted by his family and all but a few devoted homosexual companions, Wilde retained his wit and refused to indulge in self-pity at his degrading circumstances. "I am dying beyond my means," he quipped as he sank into a coma in his room at the Hôtel d'Alsace, 13 Rue des Beaux-Arts, **Left Bank**, where he had lodged on credit from 1898. Even so, he deplored the furnishings. "This wallpaper is killing me," he murmured before he died. "One of us has got to go." The same 18th-century building stands today, but Wilde would not recognize it as the cheap, run-down hotel he knew. Converted in 1967 to a luxurious hostel known simply as L'Hôtel, it now attracts many notable guests from the worlds of show business, fashion and advertising.

On temporary occasions before 1898, Wilde also lodged at the Hôtel du Quai Voltaire (see the entry on Charles Baudelaire earlier in this chapter.)

Wilde tomb: Père-Lachaise Cemetery.

(See Chapter 5, ENGLAND; also Chapter 6, LONDON; also Chapter 7, IRELAND.)

BIRTHPLACE OF ÉMILE ZOLA. The 19th-century novelist lived at 10bis Rue St-Joseph only briefly in 1840. A marker on the building commemorates the event.

ZOLA, ÉMILE (1840–1902). A native of Paris, the novelist was born at 10bis Rue St-Joseph, **Right Bank**, but lived there only briefly during infancy. From 1858 until his death he occupied residences in the city, though only during winters from 1878 on (see Name Index and Gazetteer).

His first Paris address as a young man, in 1858, was 63 Rue Monsieur-le-Prince, **Left Bank**, which he shared with his mother and grandfather. In 1861 and 1862 he shared the house at 11 Rue Soufflot with students and prostitutes. From 1866 to 1870, by which time he had published his first novel, Zola and his mother shared the apartment of Alexandrine Meley at 10 Rue de Vaugirard. He and Alexandrine were married in 1870.

Zola's last residence was 21bis Rue de Bruxelles, **Right Bank**, where he had lived during winters from 1889. There, during the night of September 28, 1902, he and his wife were overcome by carbon monoxide fumes from a blocked chimney. Zola died there, but Mme. Zola recovered in a hospital. Since Zola's open letter *J'Accuse* (1898) denouncing the French army in the celebrated Dreyfus affair had gained him many enemies, it was suspected—though never proved—that anti-Dreyfusards had deliberately blocked the chimney. Zola wrote this letter, probably his most famous work, at the Café Durand, which stood at 2 Place de la Madeleine.

Zola tomb: Panthéon.

(See Chapter 2, FRANCE; also Chapter 6, LONDON.)

CHAPTER 4
GERMANY, THE LOW COUNTRIES, SCANDINAVIA

GERMANY

The *country* Germany exists only in a geographical sense. Hitler's enduring legacy is the existence of two German *nations*, one aligned with the Eastern, the other with the Western bloc of nations that smashed the Third Reich in 1945: the German Democratic Republic (East Germany) and the Federal Republic (West Germany). In Europe, only Ireland presents a similar distinction between geographical borders and political division.

No other European country in modern times has compelled so many efforts at "explanation," attempts highlighted by anomaly and quandary. Ruminations speculating on what Germany is up to, why it proceeded to do what it did, and what it will do next, have formed a more or less constant current of curiosity, bewilderment, alarm, horror, propaganda and admiration throughout the 20th century.

Some of the influences that have so distinctively shaped Germany seem fairly straightforward, cause-and-effect outcomes of historical events. Other influences, less tangible, apparently emanate from the psychological characteristics of Germans themselves. Individualism, to take one example, is not a strongly held value. Germans like to be led; they cherish a sense of well-laid direction; they like plans to match performances and (especially) vice versa. Spontaneity of action or demeanor is not a high priority, though meticu-

lous rehearsals often seek to achieve the effect of it in life and politics. The "group ethic" is generally deemed not only superior to personal choice in such matters but somehow more valid in an absolute sense. To Germans, "soul symbols" of one sort or another convey messages of an emotional intensity that an English or French observer may find absurd. Anyone who listens to much German music, classical or popular, knows something of the yearning paeans and ponderous sentiments that appeal to the German soul. Storm and stress fire the imagination (literally in the *Sturm und Drang* literary movement in late 18th-century Germany).

Outsiders have often confused the turbulence of such German emotionalism with deep, driven feeling—which it is not necessarily. Germans have seldom drawn a clear line between drama and melodrama, between soul and stage productions, between living quarters and theater set. The love of uniforms (i.e., costume), representing a gold-braided "official capacity" for every minor public functionary, the fascination with tongue-rolling titles and honorary doctorates, mark a people mightily impressed by (and anxious to impress with) the skin aspect of things. Such a people, who take the *Sturm und Drang* play profoundly seriously, are capable of high drama and rich entertainment; and, too often, of injury to those who have no empathy with the action.

To some observers, such intense concern for the way things look is a form of overcompensation, tied to the German quest for self-identity. For historically, too, the lines are chaotic even for the complex European past. Far from embodying the ridiculous notion of "Aryan" purity, dreamed up by Hitler, Germans, like all other Europeans, have always been culturally and racially mixed, with especially heavy infusions of Latin and Slavic peoples. The so-called Germanic type—blond, blue-eyed, rawboned, fair-complexioned—is only a north German characteristic not essentially different from that of other northern European stock. Nationalism came late to Germany, long after most other European countries had comfortably settled into discrete political units. But when it came, it arrived with a typically exaggerated force and fervor that little resembled the slower growth to nationhood of its neighbors. The present political division of the country is a far more normal state of affairs in German history than national unity. In Germany the great European westward migrations left hundreds of minor principalities, a complex mosaic of jealous peoples and shifting borders that ruled German politics and culture for most of recorded history. Only in the sense that these political fragments shared a similar language and a common geographical region did the word "German" achieve any unitary significance whatever. Thus while major upheavals were shaping the modern national outlines of Europe, this patchwork of petty German states dwelt in a kind of oblivious backwater.

The historical components go back to the Romans, who occupied the Rhineland in the first century. Germanic tribes—Goths, Vandals, Angles, Saxons, Jutes—spread throughout Western Europe as the Roman Empire collapsed. Frankish control succeeded to the empire of Charlemagne, whom Germans claim as their own political ancestor. In 962 began the Holy Roman Empire (though not called that until the 12th-century reign of Frederick Barbarossa). While Barbarossa and his successors viewed themselves as the ordained successors of the Roman Caesars, the actual result was the first German empire, made up of contending dynasties and factions. The Austrian House of Hapsburg achieved dominant control in the 15th century as another cleavage developed—a religious one—with the advent of reformer Martin Luther. Religious strife erupted in the Thirty Years War (1618–48), which set north German Protestants and their allies against the Catholic south, a conflict that developed into a struggle against Hapsburg power. At the end of this period, the most destructive in German history up to this date, most other European nations had sorted out which brand of Christianity they wanted; but Germany, with a bare Lutheran majority, remained religiously split. More than 300 separate units of government picked up the pieces left by ravaging Spanish, French, and Scandinavian armies—and fragmentation supplanted the dreams of a united empire.

One German state slowly arose from the general chaos. Prussia, founded by the 13th-century Order of Teutonic Knights, became a kingdom dominated by the Hohenzollern family in 1701. It was a dynasty that included Frederick the Great, its most notable monarch, and it lasted until the 1918 abdication of Kaiser Wilhelm II. What were seen as the rugged "Prussian virtues" of courage, discipline, and hard work, politically based on a large aristocratic class, rapidly achieved dominion over neighboring German states. Paradoxically, Prussia's 1807 defeat by Napoleon I, who demolished scores of petty German states and forever ended the anachronistic dream of a Germanic Holy Roman Empire, eventually enabled Prussia to emerge as leader of the German Confederation which was established by the 1815 Congress of Vienna. The Confederation came very close to achieving national unity in 1848 as a constitutional German monarchy under the king of Prussia, but Prussia itself rejected the scheme as too democratically dangerous. What Prussia wanted, as embodied in the "might makes right" philosophy of Chancellor Otto von Bismarck, was Prussian dominance of Germany. Bismarck achieved this in 1871 with the proclamation of the German Empire (the "Second Reich").

Decades later, the projected world empire of Kaiser Wilhelm II never materialized, though German colonies were established in Africa and the Pacific. Not counting territories it annexed before and during World War II, Germany was never larger than in the period 1871 to 1914. The kaiser's bungling, aggressive foreign policy was partly provoked by Germany's huge expansion of population and industry, partly by power politics elsewhere in Europe. Increasing national tensions resulted in an arms race, with Germany boxed in and reduced to one ally, Austria-Hungary. (It is interesting to note that against Germany, the "armed strength deters aggression" philosophy so familiar to our own day provoked only national desperation and its terrible consequences.) Thus exploded World War I, a four-year blood orgy. More than nine million men—some two million of them German—were slain. Germany signed the 1918 Armistice before the country was invaded, and a Socialist revolution ended the German monarchy. The democratic Weimar Republic, established in 1919, attempted to deal not only with the harsh terms of the Treaty of Versailles but with massive runaway inflation and political chaos inspired by the devastated economy.

Thus arose, after years of increasingly virulent political turmoil, the National Socialist Party and Adolf Hitler. Hitler did not take the German government by force or coup but by ballot. He was legally endorsed as chancellor in 1933 with 92 percent of the vote (it was Germany's last election for 13 years). Nor were his plans and programs secret; indeed, he had gone to great lengths to spell them out. There can be no question that he plainly represented what a majority of Germans wanted, and events of the succeeding years of his regime more than justify that presumption. Organized opposition to the regime was never more than weak and halfhearted at best. Germans found in Hitler a personification of Germany itself; to them he was a massively efficient solution to their old identity problem. Hitler's own ambitions rested firmly on his profound contempt for people and for the German people most of all. And, perversely, the German people arose to confirm his view of them, and finally outnumbered by far all of his millions of victims.

This suicidal mania of Germans, as manifested in their clear choice of a leader who did not find it necessary to hide his preference for the "death's head" (symbols of death were rife in Nazi Gemany), is what scares people about Germany. If Germany wanted to go the route of the devil, let it, but it insisted on sharing its mania with peoples who had made no such choice. The Munich Agreement of 1938 represented a vast failure of the Christian philosophy of turning the other cheek. And even today, one must still wonder how deep the purging of war has gone. It is easy, for example, to reform one's attitudes toward Jews in a society where few exist anymore. The question that Germany has taught us to ask is, can we trust such species of "reform"—in Germans or ourselves? For Germany's value to the 20th century is mainly one of example. It has shown us depths of the human psyche that we would rather

not, but must, know. A Germany in the world has left us no further excuses.

Most popular travel guides to West Germany (practically none exist in English for East Germany) contain extremely selective history. World War II, the Nazi regime, the Holocaust are largely and studiously ignored. The approach of this chapter is opposite to that unstated "let bygones be bygone" philosophy. Those 12 years of German history are so vital to remember that to let bygones be bygone is a hideously irresponsible act. No sane person wants to see boulders and tablets commemorating Hitler, and nobody will—but honoring is not the same as taking notice. These pages, therefore, take notice of specific places where a few of the top Nazis lived and murderously worked, in the belief that taking such notice is essential to any true account of Germany and its people. It is less discomforting to think of Hitler and his men as monsters from hell transplanted to Munich and Berlin than as human beings of mostly bourgeois habit and conventional upbringing. But viewing the mostly unimpressive buildings and sites associated with them quickly spoils this evasion. They were men, say these places; they were men, and beware.

Hitler's war against the Jews was the war he unquestionably won. From a prewar population of over half a million, German Jews today number only about 35,000. Because Hitler won this war, Germany remains a shattered country in those aspects of civilized life that it had previously represented to the world. By the end of Germany's determined attempt to slay itself, only a careful restructuring of political institutions by the occupying powers enabled the country to look beyond the chaos it had finally won. Given this aid, Germany efficiently picked up the pieces; today German standards of living and its economy rank among the world's healthiest. But there were pieces it could not pick up. Vital elements of its population had fled the suicide mentality, a human wealth that immeasurably enriched their destination countries. Many other Germans lie buried in the human ash heaps of Dachau, Auschwitz, Buchenwald, Flensburg. "Nothing can mitigate them," said West German President Gustav Heinemann in 1970, "no rhetoric can dissipate them, they cannot and must not be relegated to oblivion."

It is easy today to view the German "economic miracle" as proof or symbol of the country's healing and restoration, but more perceptive observers know that the German phoenix has yet to rise from its human ash heaps, that Germany has yet to restore the soul that gave us Goethe, Schiller, Beethoven, Heine, Schopenhauer, Einstein, Mann. It will take more than wreaths laid at Dachau, ceremonies at Buchenwald—and considerably more than Krupp or Volkswagen can supply—for such a restoration to occur. Indeed, whether it can happen at all is by no means certain. There is, of course, a new generation. More than half of all living Germans were born since the end of World War II. They do not accept blame for their parents' sins, nor should they, and many of them are not afraid to ask fiercely embarrassing questions in exactly the right places.

Germany has adapted well, in the West, to a democratic form of government, and in the East likewise to a form of communism; both are highly industrialized prosperous nations. But a hallmark of German history has been this very ease of adaptation to outside influence, whatever its particular features. The sparse history of German unity has given the country little experience at developing an integrated, viable center from which to direct its life and culture. Thus Germany's capacity to function as a responsible adult in the world community has yet to be tested. And, understandably, not a few nations are prepared to do anything in their power to prevent such testing.

The contributions of German art and thought to world civilization have been vast. In philosophy, science, and music, especially, the country's influence was unsurpassed. Both Protestantism and socialism are German inventions. The present pattern of Christendom emerged from German pulpits with Martin Luther's revolutionary defiance of an ingrown, callous papacy. Karl Marx emerged from Germany with his dreams for a social system in which people could control their own economic destinies; ultimately half the world was converted to his view, or rather to a corrupt version of it. Kant (who spent most of his life in east Prussia, now Poland, and is therefore not included in these pages), Hegel, Nietzsche, and Schopenhauer created the foundations of 20th-century philosophy. Kepler and Einstein gave us entirely new views and concepts of the universe, while the works of Bach, Beethoven, Brahms, Mendelssohn, Schumann, and Wagner remain the dominant core of the classical music tradition. Few

countries have so internalized their own distinctive literature as has Germany with Goethe's *Faust*, with Heine's lyrics, with Schiller's odes. The mystical, irrational side of the German psyche is amply evident in the writings of the brothers Grimm and Hermann Hesse; Thomas Mann's concerns with the artist in a bourgeois society reflect another facet of the same Germanic obsession. Whatever Germany itself has done or may do to this matchless cultural treasure, the rest of the world well knows its priceless value.

As a result of World War II thousands of German refugees resettled in various parts of the country, thoroughly mixing the provincial populations. Prussians and Bavarians (or, perhaps more accurately, north Germans and south Germans) were quite unalike in temperament, appearance, and dialects. The north German qualities of seriousness, hard work, firm discipline, and militant respect for authority contrasted sharply with the more Latin, fun-loving, easygoing attitudes of the south. Styles of architecture, with baroque curlicues in the south and stern simplicity in the north, also mark this difference. While this provincial disparity can still be seen, the enormous scale of population diffusion and resettlement has made German society much more homogeneous than ever before. The country is also far smaller today than before World War II: the entire eastern half of Prussia went to Poland in 1945, and Alsace-Lorraine was returned to France. Birth rates are virtually static, and Hitler's excuse of *lebensraum* in seeking territory for a crowded population has been rendered inert by Germany's political division and postwar shift of peoples. Germany today is far too small and divided to harbor dreams of European domination. So today the old dream of unity—despite the fact that two German nations exist and despite the loss of a whole generation of its best creative minds—is closer in some respects to actuality than ever before.

EAST GERMANY

Formed in 1949 by the Soviet Military Administration, the German Democratic Republic (DDR) includes the former provinces of Mecklenburg, Brandenburg, Saxe-Anhalt, Thuringia, and Saxony. These provinces were abolished as governing units, and 15 districts (including East Berlin) were established under the rigid unitary control of the German Socialist Unity Party, which controls all state, economic and civil affairs by means of its Central Council. No free election has ever legitimized this regime, so this part of Germany has actually had no self-government since the election that established Hitler in 1933. The DDR's status as a sovereign state is as euphemistic as its name—few other nations of the Eastern bloc are Soviet "satellites" to quite the abject degree of East Germany. The Soviet attitude to Germany, both East and West, is deeply, profoundly mistrustful. From the Soviet point of view, a divided Germany helps ensure against any resurgent threat to the Soviet Union.

Thus, as in all totalitarian regimes, the tightly centralized political control is essentially based on fear and contempt of the people, and many elements of the previous Nazi regime still exist, albeit under different banners, labels, and institutions. The army still goosesteps, press censorship is rigid, the police are dominant and pervasive, civil liberties are restricted, and all social and economic activities are directed from above. Visitors find, as a result, that the East Germans often make enormously complicated procedures out of what would elsewhere be quite simple tasks or requests. Their well-learned habit of covering themselves in any given situation not only inhibits them from taking any action that doesn't require rehearsals or forms in triplicate, but frequently angers and frustrates outsiders who can't see the fear behind the officious masks. In the words of one observer, "Life is terribly earnest."

Thus, be patient in East Germany; bear with the absurd paperwork; don't do things to alarm the easily shaken authorities; be careful where you aim your camera; don't, in short, rock the precarious ship of state. The nation is not so raw and fumbling in hosting tourists as several years ago, but don't expect much "European sophistication."

Treading softly, then, one finds that East Germany has much to offer that has nothing to do with its anachronistic politics. It's much smaller than West Germany—some 107,000 square kilometers—and is mostly agricultural and flat. The Erzgebirge and Harz mountain ranges provide topographical relief in the south and west, and Baltic Sea resorts line the northern coast. East Germany, including both East and West Berlin, contains roughly a third of the total German population, about 18 million. Despite the disadvantages of an imposed economic policy and a severe labor shortage caused by a massive postwar exodus of laborers, the nation has become Europe's fifth strongest industrial power; most exports go to Communist bloc countries, and its standard of living ranks highest among those nations. East Berlin is the largest city and capital of the DDR.

Berlin, of course, is a special situation. Not an old city as European capitals go, it dates only from the 13th century. It was the center of the German Empire in 1871 and remained Germany's capital and largest city until the end of World War II. The period between the two world wars saw a remarkable flourishing of the arts, especially theater and film, until Adolf Hitler smothered all such creativity.

Divided into four sectors (American, British, French, and Soviet) by the 1945 Potsdam Conference, the city is today divided into two, with the western three sectors making up West Berlin, and the Soviet sector forming walled-off East Berlin. West Berlin lies 168 kilometers inside East German territory. Though not a constituent part of the Federal Republic (West Germany) and still technically governed by the Western allies, West Berlin is actually a "welfare case" supported by West Germany.

As a divided symbol of Germany itself, Berlin remains an international sore spot. Its postwar crises have raised cold war temperatures more than once. When the Soviets closed Western road access to the city in 1948 (the Berlin Blockade), the action amounted to a siege of West Berlin and resulted in the Berlin Airlift—an 18-month air shuttle of food and supplies that kept the city alive. East Berlin workers' strikes in 1953 brought in Soviet tanks to squelch the revolt. And DDR erection of the infamous Berlin Wall in 1961 made the barrier between the two cities physically tangible. It also slowed to a trickle the stream of East Germans fleeing to the West, an exodus which was slowly gutting the DDR economic recovery. The Wall has since become a starkly eloquent symbol of totalitarian repression to the world. And it has become Germany's own "wailing wall," a place where numerous East Germans attempting escape to West Berlin have been brutally gunned down.

There is no immediate prospect of the Wall's removal; certainly the Soviets intended it as permanent. Thus separated, the two Berlins continue to grow away from each other. The contrast between them has become supremely apparent. Colorful, loud, and bawdy, West Berlin doesn't hold much in reverence. East Berlin's more somber values, on the other hand, are reflected in the plodding uniformity of its facades, the studious planning that goes into its ceremonies and displays. East Berlin churches, however, are now freer to criticize the regime than a few years ago.

It is remarkable how many historic residences survived World War II. Germans, both East and West, are great reconstructors, however, and numerous historic dwellings have been rebuilt or restored. Allied bombing raids concentrated on the largest cities, of course. Dresden was gratuitously wiped out in February 1945, but today is again one of East Germany's loveliest cities. Weimar and Leipzig, two ancient cities of vast historical importance, are not as culturally sophisticated as they once were, but there is still much to see. East Germany puts much effort into "laundering" certain of its historical figures by relating them somehow to Marxist doctrine—"putting them to work," in a sense. Such treatment may be seen in the numerous Goethe exhibits and, more recently, in the homes of Frederick the Great and Martin Luther. The ingenuity of these revisionistic treatments are often quite fascinating in their own right, showing (in less subtle fashion than in the West) how the past may be enlisted to serve the present.

BACH, JOHANN SEBASTIAN (1685–1750). Primarily known during his lifetime as an organist and choirmaster, Bach did not achieve recognition as a towering genius of composition until his music was rediscovered in the 19th century. Since then his prestige and popularity have built like "a mighty fortress," with an astonishing splendor of works that range from delicate crystals to massive temples of sound. He was born at **Eisenach** in a house on the present site of Lutherstrasse 35; it was his home until 1695, by which time both his parents had died.

From 1695 to 1700 he resided with an elder brother, Johann Christian, at the latter's two-story cottage in **Ohrdruf**. A house which is said to be this one survives in the Bachstrasse near Kirchstrasse; its ground floor is now a shop.

In 1703 Bach became church organist at **Arnstadt**, where he lodged at the foot of the Leather Market in a house called the "Golden Crown" until 1707. Shops also occupy this structure.

Bach's first great creative period emerged at **Weimar**, where he was employed as organist and chamber musician to the Duke of Saxe-Weimar from 1708 to 1717. There he produced some of his most brilliant organ preludes and fugues. At least until 1713, and possibly until 1717, he resided in a building that was much later attached to the Parkhotel Erbprinz. The composer's eldest son by his first wife, Maria Barbara, was born there in 1710: composer Wilhelm Friedemann Bach. Of the couple's seven children born at Weimar, only four survived, among them Carl Philipp Emanuel Bach, born in 1714. The site of Bach's daily musical activities was the 1650 castle rebuilt under Goethe's supervision in 1790 (see the entry on Johann Wolfgang von Goethe, *Exhibits*, later in this section).

Bach's last home from 1723 was **Leipzig**, where he served as director of music at St. Thomas School and produced his greatest works, the *St. Matthew Passion* (1729) and the *Mass in B minor* (1733–38). His musical output was prodigious, and much of it has been lost. "In the space of about twenty years," wrote Richard Anthony Leonard, "he composed about two hundred and sixty-five cantatas, an average of one a month." These sacred pieces were written for regular Sunday services at St. Thomas Church, performances which Bach himself rehearsed and directed. One would never know from the wealth and splendor of the music he produced in Leipzig that this entire period of his life was burdened by personal griefs and petty harassments of the most humiliating sort. His music was disparaged by his bigoted employers, who treated him with less courtesy than most hack musicians earned. Six of the 13 children he had by his second wife, Anna Magdalena Wilcke, died at ages ranging from one day to five years. Among those who survived was another notable composer son, Johann Christian Bach, born at Leipzig in 1735. The large family lived in the south wing of St. Thomas School, which stood directly behind the church until the early 20th century. Occupying dark, unsanitary quarters in the ancient building, Bach wrote his music in a cramped workroom surrounded by classroom noise and the constant grind of a nearby mill wheel. The mortality rate of his children decreased remarkably after the structure's renovation and addition of two stories in 1732. Despite increasing blindness from probable glaucoma and two butchered eye operations that painfully destroyed what little vision he had, Bach composed sacred music almost to the last.

Bach tomb: St. Thomas Church, **Leipzig**.

Exhibits: (Inquire locally for admission information.)

In **Eisenach**, the "Bach House" at Frauenplan 21 was long thought to be the composer's birthplace. Though it is sometimes still claimed as such, its authenticity is not accepted by most Bach scholars. The house dates from Bach's time, however, and displays period furnishings and exhibits relating to the composer and his family. A collection of 16th- to 19th-century musical instruments is also featured.

The Bach Memorial Museum at Bahnhofstrasse 2a in **Arnstadt** contains material illustrating Bach's period in this city.

At **Köthen**, where Bach lived at an unknown address from 1717 to 1723, the Town Museum, Museumstrasse 4-5, displays a Bach Memorial Room.

The Bach Museum at Menckestrasse 23 in **Leipzig** displays documents, portraits, manuscripts, and numerous other items pertaining to the composer.

In **East Berlin** the German State Library at Unter den Linden and Charlottenstrasse displays Bach's own score of the *St. Matthew Passion* among its musical treasures.

BISMARCK, OTTO VON (1815–1898). The Prussian *Junker* aristocrat, first chancellor of the Second Reich (1867–90), unifier of the German states into an empire, and powerful advocate of "blood and iron" in Germany's dealings with other nations, was a native of **Schönhausen**. An Elbe estate had been held there by his family since 1562. Though raised on another Bismarck estate that is now in Polish territory, Bismarck returned to occupy his ancestral Schönhausen in 1845 but only occasionally resided there after his 1867 appointment as chancellor. Other family members and descendants continued to reside there, however, until Countess Sibylle von Bismarck shot herself at age 81 as Russian troops approached in 1945. They burned the manor to the ground, and nothing is now to be seen of what might be called the birthplace of German nationalism. The present village occupies lands of the former Bismarck estate.

Though his duties as chancellor required his frequent presence in Berlin, Bismarck disliked the city. From 1862 until 1890 his official residence as Prussian and federal chancellor was the Reich Chancellery in **East Berlin** (see the entry on Adolf Hitler later in this section). It is said that Bismarck buried his favorite horse and dog in the same Chancellery garden where Hitler spent his last days.

(See WEST GERMANY in this chapter.)

BONHOEFFER, DIETRICH (1906–1945). The martyred Lutheran theologian, whose "nonreligious" alternatives to traditional Christian interpretations influenced an entire generation of church scholars, was active in the Nazi resistance and fell victim to Gestapo executioners during the last days of World War II. Born in Breslau (now Wroclow, Poland), he lived in Berlin from 1912 until his 1943 imprisonment.

Wangenstrasse 14 was his parental home in **West Berlin** from 1916 to 1935. The two-story house where the large family of children grew up occupied an acre of garden. His last home, from 1936, was Marienburger Allee 43, again with his parents; Bonhoeffer never married though was engaged when he was captured. This home is now a religious study center. In 1932 Bonhoeffer took a room in suburban **Wedding** while teaching a confirmation class at nearby Zion Church. This rooming house stands at Oderbergerstrasse 61.

In **East Berlin** Bonhoeffer was confined in Tegel Prison at the northern end of the Tegeler See in 1943 and 1944. During four months of 1944 and 1945, he was held in the detention cellars of Himmler's Gestapo headquarters (see the entry on Heinrich Himmler, *Exhibits*, later in this section). Though he underwent a series of inquisitions there, he was apparently not tortured.

(See WEST GERMANY in this chapter; also Chapter 6, LONDON.)

BRAHE, TYCHO (1546–1601). In 1598 and 1599 the Danish astronomer was an unhappy exile from his native land, which in fact he never saw again. He resided in **Lutherstadt Wittenberg**, where he had attended the university some 30 years before, at the house formerly owned by Protestant reformer Philipp Melanchthon, who died in 1560. This house stands at Collegienstrasse 60.

(See SWEDEN in this chapter.)

BRECHT, BERTOLT (1898–1956). From 1924 to the early 1930s the playwright resided at Spichernstrasse 16 in **West Berlin**. This was the period in which he wrote *The Threepenny Opera* (1928) and *Rise and Fall of the Town Mahagonny* (1929).

Brecht returned to Germany from America after World War II. From 1949 to 1953 he made his **East Berlin** home at Berliner Allee 190 with his wife, actress Helene Weigel, and novelist Anna Seghers. The building now houses a political club. The couple's last home in the city, from 1953, was an apartment suite at Chausseestrasse 125, now the Brecht-Weigel Memorial. They occupied three rooms on the first floor in the rear. Today the ground floor is a Brecht archive and displays manuscripts of his works. (Open Tuesday—Wednesday, Friday 10:00—12:00, Thursday 10:00—12:00, 5:00—7:00, Saturday 9:30—12:00, 12:30—2:00; 2829916; free.)

At **Buckow**, a Berlin suburb, Brecht purchased a lakeside plot with two houses in 1952 and often resided there until his death. Today known as the Brecht-Weigel House-Museum, the dwelling in which he lived has original furnishings and memorabilia of the playwright on display. It is located in the Märkische Schweiz. (Open Tuesday, Thursday—Friday 10:00—12:00, 1:30—3:30; free.)

Brecht tomb: Dorotheenstadt and Friedrichswerder Cemetery, **East Berlin**.

Exhibits: In **East Berlin** the theatrical collection of the March Museum at Märkischer Platz displays Brecht memorabilia. (Open Tuesday, Thursday—Sunday 9:00—4:00; Wednesday 9:00—7:00; admission.) Founded by Brecht in 1954, the Berliner Ensemble at Bertolt-Brecht-Platz staged his plays under his own direction until his death and has since been operated by his widow, Helene Weigel. This is probably the only theater in the world where one may see Brecht plays performed exactly as he intended. The building is the former Theater am Schiffbauerdamm. (Closed July—August; 2825871.)

(See WEST GERMANY, DENMARK, FINLAND, SWEDEN in this chapter; also Chapter 1, SWITZERLAND.)

DOSTOEVSKI, FEODOR MIKHAILOVICH (1821–1881). The Russian writer made his home in **Dresden** from 1869 to 1871, years when he labored on his novels *The Eternal Husband* (1870) and *The Possessed* (1871–72). He and his growing family rented three rooms in the English quarter of the city at Victoriastrasse 5, now Dostojewskistrasse. It is long since gone.

(See WEST GERMANY in this chapter; also Chapter 1, SWITZERLAND; also Chapter 8, ITALY.)

EINSTEIN, ALBERT (1879–1955). It is difficult to view the few Einstein sites in and near Berlin without raw cynicism. This towering genius, perhaps the greatest scientist who ever lived, embellished German scholarship by his mere presence. Yet he would doubtless have ended in one of Hitler's efficient crematoriums had he stayed in his native land. Admire Einstein memorials in other countries, but remember here that, in the long run, much more significant than Germany's treatment of Einstein was Einstein's thorough dismissal of Germany.

He occupied a bachelor apartment in **West Berlin** at Wittelsbacherstrasse 13 in 1914, the year he became director of the Kaiser Wilhelm Institute for Physics and separated permanently from his first wife, Mileva Maritsch, and this remained his home until 1917. The institute has been succeeded by the Max Planck Institute in the Dahlem area of the city. From 1917 until his 1932 flight from Germany, the physicist occupied a fifth-floor apartment with his second wife, Elsa Löwenthal, at Nördlingerstrasse 8 (formerly Haberlandstrasse 5).

In 1929, after a ludicrous charade in which the government withdrew its loudly announced offer to give him a house, Einstein bought land and built a cottage in the East Berlin suburb of **Caputh**, where he spent summers until 1932. Furious at Einstein's denunciation of Germany in 1933, Nazis confiscated the property, and stormtrooper thugs raided it to search for reputed hidden weapons. They found a breadknife. Now designated a national memorial, the house stands at Waldstrasse 7, not open to the public.

(See WEST GERMANY in this chapter; also Chapter 1, SWITZERLAND.)

FREDERICK II, THE GREAT (1712–1786). The Prussian king not only became one of Europe's most powerful warrior monarchs but also an intellectual patron of the arts, prolific writer (always in French), musician, composer, and epitome of the "enlightened despot." Among the brilliant minds and creative spirits he cultivated at his court was the philosopher Voltaire, a close friend until their mutual disillusionment (see the entry on Voltaire later in this section).

Frederick, third king of the Prussian House of Hohenzollern, was born in the Royal Palace, also called the City Palace (Stadtschloss), in **East Berlin**, the son of King Frederick Wilhelm I and Princess Sophia Dorothea of Hanover. This massive baroque structure, a Berlin landmark for centuries, served the Hohenzollern margraves, electors, kings and emperors as chief residence from the year 1470 to Kaiser Wilhelm II's abdication in 1918 (see the entry on Wilhelm II later in this section). The palace grew in size and opulence from the 17th to 19th centuries. After World War I, it housed the Museum of Arts and Crafts. Fires resulting from the Allied air attack of February 3, 1945, burned out the immense walls. The building could have been restored, but its demolition was completed in 1951—except for one 1713 baroque portion, which is now the central government building of the State Council. The main palace site is now the Marx-Engels-Platz, formerly known as the Schlossplatz, a large open space for parades and political rallies; the State Council building adorns its south side.

In **West Berlin** the Palace of Charlottenburg was a main residence of Prussian royalty from its 1695 beginnings as a country house. Massive wings were added to its large central portion during the 18th century; Frederick added the east wing to balance the orangery wing on the west, which was completed in 1749. Unlike his successors, the king seldom resided for long intervals in the palace but used it mainly for large family and social gatherings. His reception rooms and private apartments on the first floor of the east wing display his collection of snuffboxes, tapestries and French paintings. His library contains some of his books from the palace of Sans-Souci at Potsdam (see below). Fire bombs gutted the palace interior in 1943, but faithful reconstruction has restored both interior and exterior. Today the palace with its royal apartments, portraits, and other works of art functions mainly as Berlin's museum center and memorial to the Prussian Hohenzollerns who dominated the city for more than 400 years. The Berlin Senate hosts official receptions in the State Apartments. Among the collections housed in the Charlottenburg are the Museum of Decorative Arts, the Museum of Prehistory and Protohistory, and the Islamic and Egyptian museums. The pal-

ace is located in the Spandauer Damm at Luisenplatz 19. (Guided tours, Tuesday—Sunday 9:00—5:00; admission.)

SANS-SOUCI, THE TERRACED PALACE OF FREDERICK THE GREAT. The Prussian king built this magnificent garden-estate at **Potsdam** in 1745, and it became the favorite of his several palaces. Voltaire was a resident guest of the king for two years (1750–52).

The royal palace (Stadtschloss) at **Potsdam** was a favorite residence of the king's father, and Frederick spent much time there before he became king in 1740. Originally built in 1670, the rococo palace was reconstructed in 1750. Frederick used it mainly as a winter residence, and he lay in state there after his death. The king chose Potsdam as his permanent residence in 1744; the city soon grew into one of the major imperial seats of Europe. In 1745 Frederick began building his own palace, Sans-Souci, an elaborate one-storied terraced structure for which he drew the plans and laid out the gardens. By 1747 he was able to move there; it became the favorite of his several Potsdam palaces and his last home. Primarily an art museum today, displaying 17th-century masters, Sans-Souci also exhibits original furnishings and memorabilia; a concert room where the king played flute concerts may also be seen. Nymph and cherub types of statuary abound. Both palaces stand, alongside two others and many pavilions, in the 600-acre Sanssouci Park by the River Havel. (Palaces open summer, daily 9:00—5:00; admission.)

Frederick was given an old manor house at **Rheinsberg** by his father, and in 1734 he converted it into a small symmetrical castle he called "Remusberg." This castle remained his most frequent residence as crown prince until 1740, when he became king. It does not admit the public.

Exhibits: In **East Berlin** note the equestrian statue of Frederick the Great in the Unter den Linden, long a familiar Berlin landmark but banished by Communist authorities in 1950. Restored to its pedestal in 1980, "Comrade Fritz" again surveys the city, much different than the one he knew in life.

The Musical Instruments Museum at Bundesallee 1-12 in **West Berlin** displays two ivory flutes that were owned and played by Frederick. (Open Tuesday, Thursday—Friday 9:00—5:00; Wednesday 11:00—9:00; Saturday, guided tours 11:00; Sunday 10:00—2:00; admission.)

(See WEST GERMANY in this chapter.)

GOEBBELS, JOSEPH (1897–1945). Few top Nazis rivaled his power over German domestic life or his cynical contempt for Germans. "It is quite amazing what people will believe," he marveled as propaganda minister of the Third Reich. Even during the last stages of World War II, as destruction rained daily on Berlin, his diaries noted with astonishment the compliant trust of bombed-out Berliners in their decrepit leadership.

From 1931, when he married Magda Quandt, he occupied her luxurious seven-room flat in a building that stood at Reichkanzlerplatz 2 (later named Adolf-Hitler-Platz and now Theodor-Heuss-Platz), **West Berlin**. This remained their home until 1933, when Goebbels became propaganda minister. The apartment was a favorite refuge of Hitler himself, who often came there to relax with the delighted couple during the period just before and after he became German chancellor. He was dining there the night of the 1933 Reichstag fire, the effects of which enabled him to consolidate his power. The building has been replaced at the north side of the square.

In the Lake Wannsee area, Goebbels bought a wooded estate on 62-acre Schwanenwerder Island in 1934 and added adjacent property in 1936. The two-story English-style country house had been expropriated from a Jewish millionaire, and Goebbels paid a cheap price for it. He rebuilt other existing houses on the property and also added a private cinema. During the Nazi heyday he entertained famous guests there, including the Duke and Duchess of Windsor, and competed with the Goerings in hosting elaborate lawn parties (see the entry on Hermann Wilhelm Goering

below). Goebbels liked to treat his guests to rides aboard his luxurious yacht, the *Baldur*, on the lake. His large family stayed on the estate, well removed from the bombing targets in Berlin, until the final weeks of the war. A bridge connects the island to the mainland. The former Goebbels estate plus adjacent properties are now convalescent homes operated by various charitable organizations.

In **East Berlin** Goebbels's official residence from 1933 was a former palace of the Prussian court marshals, which stood at Wilhelmstrasse 72 (now Otto-Grotewohl-Strasse), part of the German Food Ministry complex. The palace wasn't as spacious or luxurious as Goering's, however, so Goebbels rebuilt it from the ground up in 1938—and remodeled it twice more before he was through. Eventually it contained 40 rooms plus a comfortable air-raid bunker 60 feet beneath the building, where the entire household spent increasing amounts of time as bombs pounded Berlin. The building, plundered during the final days of the war, was leveled. The site is now lawn and is part of the huge vacant space adjacent to the Berlin Wall that once held the seat of Nazi government in this street. Goebbels also maintained private residential quarters plus a luxurious office suite in his nearby workplace, the Propaganda Ministry building; his bachelor apartment was convenient for the numerous affairs he conducted with various actresses and secretaries. Formerly known as the Prince Leopold Palace, this two-story building stood at Wilhelmplatz 8–9 (now Thälmannplatz) directly opposite the new Reich Chancellery (see the entry on Adolf Hitler later in this section). After bombs destroyed much of the ministry in 1945, Goebbels wrote in his diary that he would have preferred to lose his home and all that he owned. The last week in the lives of Joseph and Magda Goebbels and their six beautiful children was spent in Hitler's cramped underground bunker behind the Chancellery. One of Hitler's final acts was to appoint Goebbels, his last loyal chieftain, as German chancellor to succeed him. During the final hours in the bunker, Goebbels made futile attempts to negotiate a safe-conduct pass from the oncoming Russian army. There after Hitler's suicide, the squalid couple poisoned their unsuspecting children and killed themselves in a final act worthy of their lives.

In 1938 Goebbels built a large one-story country house on Lake Bogensee, located about 65 kilometers northeast of Berlin. Even with adroit financial juggling, he could not pay for it, so funds were provided by the German film industry to purchase and "lease" the property to him. He installed every known modern convenience in his "House on the Bogensee," which he used mainly as a weekend retreat. Surrounded by pine and fir forest, the house is now a Communist party boarding school in the Lake Liepnitz Nature Preserve. It stands several kilometers west of **Lanke** on the lake.

Exhibit: "The soul of the German people can again express itself," Goebbels yelled as students heaped some 20,000 books on the burning pyre. The barbaric ceremony occurred after a torchlight parade on May 10, 1933. Its site doesn't look like a cemetery, but it is; Germany destroyed its massive intellectual heritage and cultural soul that night in a scene unwitnessed in the Western world since medieval times. The spot does not display a tombstone, though it should, or even a marker mourning the event. This **East Berlin** site of Germany's cultural immolation, directed by Goebbels, is the Bebelplatz, the square on the Unter den Linden between Humboldt University on one side and the State Opera on the other.

(See WEST GERMANY in this section.)

GOERING, HERMANN WILHELM (1893–1946). One of Hitler's earliest associates and his designated successor, this obese, drug-addicted specimen of the "master race" was described at the Nuremberg Trials as "half-militarist, half-gangster." His crude bluster and obsession with gaudy uniforms and facial cosmetics masked an indolent, amoral personality that Hitler could always count upon to toady if not to do a job. Goering's failure to provide effective command leadership of the German Luftwaffe decided the final outcome of the European war fairly early in the conflict. By 1941 he had all but ceased to function in his numerous official positions and his presence was largely decorative and ceremonial.

In **West Berlin** a childhood home (1896–1901) stood at an unknown address in the Fregestrasse. Much later, as a Reichstag deputy, he lived with his first wife, Karin von Kantzow, in flats at Berchtesgadenerstrasse 16 (1927–28) and at Badenschestrasse 7 (1928–31). As president of the Reichstag, Goering occupied the Reichstag Presidential Palace from 1932 until the 1933 Reichstag

fire, which not only gutted the Reichstag but gave Hitler a pretext for suspending all civil liberties. Evidence exists that the Nazis themselves, with Goering strongly implicated, set the fire. The Reichstag, built in the late 19th century, was restored after World War II and now displays exhibits on German history since 1800. It stands on the Platz der Republik.

The aforementioned Presidential Palace, where many a political maneuver was plotted in those early days when the Nazis still had to abide by a semblance of parliamentary democracy, stood across the street at the rear of the Reichstag building in **East Berlin**. The street today (formerly Friedrich-Ebert-Strasse) is now split by the Berlin Wall, and the Presidential Palace is gone. Nazi arsonists in 1933 apparently entered the Reichstag through underground heating pipes that connected the two buildings beneath the street.

Also in East Berlin, Goering resided in the Kaiserhof Hotel, Hitler's early headquarters, in 1931 and 1932 (see the entry on Adolf Hitler later in this section). In 1934 he cleared a site on the corner of Stresemannstrasse and Niederkirchnerstrasse south of the Leipzigerplatz and built himself a luxurious town house at German taxpayer expense; he also changed the name of Stresemannstrasse to Hermann-Goering-Strasse. The German populace generally viewed Goering's opulent lifestyle with amused tolerance and tacit approval, almost as if he supplied a yearned-for element of royal pomp in Hitler's ascetic circle. Today Hermann-Goering-Strasse is again Stresemannstrasse, Niederkirchnerstrasse is a section of the Berlin Wall, and Goering's mansion, his Berlin home until 1945, is gone.

"He who tortures an animal hurts the feelings of the German people," said Goering, the creator of Nazi concentration camps. In 1933 he took over a 100,000-acre state land preserve northeast of Berlin as his private hunting reserve. There he planned, designed, and built Karinhall, a massive steep-roofed stone and timber structure named for his deceased first wife. One biographer described it as "a monumental curiosity, a kind of ancient German baronial hall equipped with every luxury and combining a massive simplicity with showmanship of wealth and power." It had a central Gothic facade and white-pebbled outside walls. Rooms included a marble banquet hall, art gallery, council, guest and reception chambers, a basement gymnasium, and an attic with a huge model train layout. For Goering, the entire complex was a stage for acting out his medieval (and railroading) fantasies. He draped himself in opulent sashes and robes, flashed expensive rings, bracelets and brooches, even powdered and rouged his complexion. Huge mastiffs and at least one adult lion stalked the halls. Deer, elk, bison, and wild horses were protected for Goering's own elaborate hunting parties in the surrounding forests and plains of the Schorfheide. He spend much time there during World War II; on D-Day in 1944 he was shooting, not Allied planes in Normandy, but gamebirds at Karinhall. As Russian armies approached in 1945, Goering packed up his treasures—several boxcar loads—and assigned a Luftwaffe paratroop division to mine the house. Nothing remains of Karinhall, which stood on the shore of Lake Wuckersee in the **Schorfheide** region.

In **Lichterfelde**, a West Berlin suburb, Goering studied and resided from 1909 to 1912 in the old military training college now known as the Steu-

benhaus, located since 1873 in the Finckensteinallee. It later housed American troops stationed in Berlin.

(See WEST GERMANY in this chapter; also Chapter 1, AUSTRIA.)

GOETHE, JOHANN WOLFGANG VON (1749–1832). More museums and memorials in both East and West Germany are devoted to Goethe than to any other German. A poet, novelist, scientist, and philosopher who took all knowledge for his province, Goethe also held important public office in the ducal court at Weimar. His work remains Germany's foremost contribution to world literature.

Goethe attended the University of **Leipzig** from 1765 to 1768 and roomed at Neumarkt 3.

Goethe made his permanent home in **Weimar** from 1775 until his death. From 1776 to 1782 he resided in what is now known as Goethe's Garden House in the Corona-Schröter-Strasse. The two-story white barnlike structure, given to him by his

THE NATIONAL GOETHE MUSEUM. In **Weimar**, Goethe's home from 1775 until his death in 1832, the poet's large house at Frauenplan 1 survives just as he left it.

Visitors cannot obtain a better picture of the man and his times than by viewing these rooms.

beloved palace employer, Duke Karl August, displays original furnishings and memorabilia including some of Goethe's sketches. (Open Wednesday—Monday 9:00—12:00, 1:00—5:00; 2945; admission.) The National Goethe Museum at Frauenplan 1, which was restored in 1908, stands adjacent to the two-story yellow-stucco house he occupied from 1782 to 1789 and from 1792 to his death. The house dates from 1709. In the museum, chronological exhibits relate to his life and work, and his art collection is also displayed; the Marxist treatment of *Faust* is intriguing. Rear rooms of the house are arranged as Goethe prescribed in his will and represent how he wished posterity to view him. The six front rooms reveal Goethe as his contemporaries actually saw him, and this contrast as well as the rooms themselves reveal much about this complex figure. (Museum and house open Tuesday—Sunday 9:00—1:00, 2:00—5:00; 2472; admission.)

In **Ilmenau**, Goethe's summer home from 1776 to 1831 now houses the Museum of Local Life in the Amtshaus at Markt 7. Displayed along with material on local history is a Goethe Room containing his geological collection. (Open January 10—March 15, daily 10:00—11:00, 1:00—3:00; May 15—October 15, Monday—Saturday 9:00—11:30, 1:00—4:30; 2222; admission.) He also used the two-story 1783 Gabelbach Hunting Lodge, a timber structure at Waldstrasse 24. Restored in 1970, the house displays memorabilia. (Open April—October, Tuesday—Sunday 9:00—12:00, 1:00—5:00, except closed Tuesday in April, September, October; 2626; admission.)

The Goethe Memorial Museum, housed in the Botanical Institute at Goethe-Allee 26 in **Jena**, was his residence during visits to this town from 1817 to 1822. Souvenirs of those visits and of his friends are on display. (Open April 15—October 15, daily 9:00—1:00; 8222312/11; admission.)

Among the other houses which display memorabilia of brief stays by the poet is the Goethe Memorial Museum in the old four-story white-stucco castle of **Grosskochberg**, which exhibits material on Goethe and Charlotte von Stein, his highly influential and mostly platonic companion of the 1770s and 1780s, and probably the most important woman in his life. (Open Tuesday—Sunday 9:00—12:00, 1:00—5:00, except closed Tuesday, September—April; Teichel 428; admission.)

At **Stützerbach** the Goethe House and Glass Museum at Sebastian-Kneipp-Strasse 18 also

shows mementos of his visits there. (Open May—August, Tuesday—Sunday 9:00—12:00, 1:00—5:00; September—April, Wednesday—Sunday 9:00—12:00, 1:00—4:00; 277; admission.)

The 16th-century Dornburg Castle at **Dornburg** exhibits a Goethe Memorial Room commemorating his stay in the summer of 1828. (Inquire locally for admission information.)

Goethe tomb: Goethe and Schiller Mausoleum, **Weimar**.

(See WEST GERMANY in this chapter; also Chapter 1, AUSTRIA, SWITZERLAND; also Chapter 2, FRANCE; also Chapter 8, ITALY.)

GRIMM, JAKOB LUDWIG (1785–1863). GRIMM, WILHELM KARL (1786–1859). The Grimm brothers, though scholarly philologists, remain best known for their collection, *Grimm's Fairy Tales* (1812–15), based on numerous interviews with German peasants.

As distinguished professors in **West Berlin**, they resided in a now long-gone house at Lennestrasse 8 on the southeast edge of the Tiergarten from 1841 until their deaths. Some sources, however, give their address as Linkstrasse 7 along the Berlin Wall in **East Berlin**.

Grimm brothers tombs: St. Matthew's Church Cemetery, **West Berlin**.

(See WEST GERMANY in this chapter.)

HANDEL, GEORG FREDERICK (1685–1759). The building identified as the composer's birthplace in **Halle** stands at Grosse Nikolaistrasse 5. Actually he was born in an adjoining house known as "Zum Gelben Hirsch" ("The Yellow Stag"), which stood at the corner of Grosse Nikolaistrasse and Kleine Ubrichstrasse. The present building, which displays Handel memorabilia and a collection of musical instruments, dates only from 1800. Handel probably used its courtyard for a boyhood play area. Son of a barber-surgeon, the composer lived at his birthplace until 1703. (Inquire locally for admission information.) Halle hosts a Handel Festival each year in late May and early June with orchestras and opera companies from all over Europe.

(See Chapter 5, ENGLAND; also Chapter 6, LONDON; also Chapter 7, IRELAND.)

HEGEL, GEORG WILHELM FRIEDRICH (1770–1831). In **East Berlin**, the influential philosopher's last home from 1818 stands at Am

Kupfergraben 5 off the Hegelplatz. It was partially destroyed during World War II.

Hegel tomb: Dorotheenstadt and Friedrichswerder Cemetery, **East Berlin**.

(See WEST GERMANY in this chapter.)

HIMMLER, HEINRICH (1900–1945). Almost alone in the cynical top circle of Nazis surrounding Hitler, the Gestapo chief actually believed that "the Final Solution" he so rigorously implemented was a noble cause. Without such a "true believer" orchestrating it, the Holocaust could probably never have occurred despite Germany's anti-Semitic activity. The precise location of Himmler's **West Berlin** home has never been revealed. It was a small unpretentious villa surrounded by a high stucco wall in the Grunewald section, an area bristling for blocks around with security guards and guns during World War II. The house probably survives there somewhere.

Exhibits: Himmler's Gestapo headquarters stood next door to Hermann Goering's mansion at Niederkirchnerstrasse 8, **East Berlin**. Theologian Dietrich Bonhoeffer was one noted prisoner there (see the entries on Bonhoeffer and Goering earlier in this section). The 1886 building was, ironically, the former Berlin Ethnographical Museum and was destroyed in the war. The Berlin Wall has inherited both the infamy and the site.

In **West Berlin** a marker identifies the "Final Solution House" at 56-58 Am Grossen Wannsee. It was here that Himmler met with his subordinates Reinhard Heydrich and Adolf Eichmann on January 20, 1942, to discuss the demographics of the extermination of European Jewry as ordered by Hitler.

(See WEST GERMANY in this chapter.)

HITLER, ADOLF (1889–1945). The Nazi fuehrer's early residence in **East Berlin** from about 1930 to 1933, when he became chancellor, was the Kaiserhof Hotel, Berlin headquarters of the National Socialist Party. After their election to power, Nazis memorialized the old hotel as the seat of their final struggle for control of the nation's destiny. It was destroyed during World War II. Occupying part of its site on the corner of Kaiserhofstrasse and Mauerstrasse is the Thälmannplatz U-Bahn (subway) station, faced with red marble from the demolished Reich Chancellery that stood nearby.

The "old" Reich Chancellery, into which Hitler moved in 1933, stood at Wilhelmstrasse (now Otto-Grotewohl-Strasse) 78, with Hitler's private apartments at number 77. Purchased by the Prussian government in 1830, the stuccoed palace became Otto von Bismarck's official residence as Prussian and German chancellor in 1862 (see the entry on Bismarck earlier in this section), and all subsequent chancellors up to Hitler's regime lived there. In 1938 the "new" Reich Chancellery was built adjacent to the old with its long frontage on Vossstrasse to the south. Designed according to Hitler's specifications by his architect, Albert Speer, the immense building was constructed to last for centuries—though Hitler regarded it as only a temporary official residence until he could rebuild Berlin on a far grander scale. Hitler liked to escort visiting diplomats through his lavish, oversized office with its marble-topped table, gigantic tapestry-hung halls and corridors with their plush carpets and furnishings. One of its last visitors was British Prime Minister Winston Churchill in 1945, when it looked considerably different. Until the final month of the war, when he moved underground, Hitler continued to use his office despite heavy bomb damage to parts of the building.

In March 1945 he moved permanently to the large concrete bunker beneath the chancellery rear garden, connected to the chancellery buildings by a system of tunnels. Roofed with 16 feet of concrete and 6 feet of earth above that, it was "undoubtedly the safest place in Berlin," wrote Speer. Hitler had slept there since February, and from there, a trembling, hysterical wreck of a man, he conducted the last phases of the war, shouting irrational orders to nonexistent armies as the Third Reich crumbled around him. Nobody could quite summon the courage, even then, to shoot him and spare Germany its final death agonies, so his contempt for the German people and nation ran its full course. There Hitler married his long-time mistress Eva Braun, a dim-witted young woman whose presence had always been carefully concealed from the German people. He also wrote his last testament, in which he disclaimed all responsibility for the war and charged the German people to continue "merciless opposition to international Jewry." Finally, as Russian troops approached central Berlin, he killed himself in the last act of a life devoted to murder. He had not underestimated German willingness, even in the end, to follow his own course to its suicidal end in this dismal cave. The bodies of Adolf and Eva Hitler were burned by makeshift cremation in the chancellery garden as Russian artillery shells crescendoed the event; Soviet troops recovered the bodies there a few days later.

Today most of the western length of Otto-Grotewohl-Strasse, where stood the official buildings of Hitler's 12-year Reich, is a level grassy area adjacent to the Berlin Wall with no structural remnant surviving. Both old and new chancelleries were demolished after the war; their stone materials were used for the construction of the Thälmannplatz U-Bahn station (page 109) and for the Soviet War Memorial in the Tiergarten, **West Berlin**. Hitler's bunker was blown up after the war, and a mound covers the concrete rubble. Today, of course, the scene in no way resembles the chaotic littered and cratered battleground of May 1945.

(See WEST GERMANY, BELGIUM in this chapter; also Chapter 1, AUSTRIA; also Chapter 5, ENGLAND.)

KAFKA, FRANZ (1883–1924). The Bohemian writer, a major influence on 20th-century literature, lived in **West Berlin** at Grunewaldstrasse 13 for four months in 1923 and 1924 just before his final physical collapse. A tablet marks this house where he occupied two rooms with his last lover, Dora Dymant.

(See Chapter 1, AUSTRIA.)

LENIN, VLADIMIR (1870–1924). In **Leipzig**, the Russian revolutionary lived in 1914 at Bernhard-Göring-Strasse 45, the former publishing house of the *Leipziger Volkeszeitung*.

Exhibit: The Lenin Memorial at Rosa-Luxemburg-Strasse 19-21, headquarters of the *Leipziger Volkeszeitung* since 1900, displays a collection relating to Lenin's political achievements as well as furniture from his **Leipzig** residence (see above; inquire locally for admission information.) The *Iskra* Memorial at Russenstrasse 48 marks the reconstructed building in which Lenin published the first issues of his Bolshevik newspaper *Iskra*.

(See WEST GERMANY, FINLAND, in this chapter; also Chapter 1, SWITZERLAND; also Chapter 3, PARIS; also Chapter 6, LONDON.)

LISZT, FRANZ (1811–1886). The virtuoso pianist and composer lived in **Weimar** for two lengthy periods. From 1848 to 1861 he served as court music director for the grand duke, and it was his most fertile period as a composer. In 1870 he returned as the Abbé Liszt after taking minor orders

THE ALTENBURG, HOME OF FRANZ LISZT. Now a museum at Marienstrasse 17, the **Weimar** residence of the composer and piano virtuoso was his final home.

in the Roman Catholic church and spent the rest of his life teaching, composing and traveling. His home, Altenburg, survives as the Liszt Museum at Marienstrasse 17; portraits, musical manuscripts, first editions, and memorabilia are on display. (Open Tuesday—Sunday 9:00—5:00; admission.)

(See WEST GERMANY in this chapter; also Chapter 1, AUSTRIA, SWITZERLAND; also Chapter 3, PARIS; also Chapter 8, ITALY.)

LUTHER, MARTIN (1483–1546). He has been called "the last medieval man and the first modern one, a political conservative and a spiritual revolutionary." In 1983, the year of his 500th birthday, there were some 350 million Protestants in the world but Luther's Christian doctrine was no more acceptable to the East German government than to the official authorities of his homeland during his own lifetime, though in both cases it was tolerated. Nevertheless, in 1983 the government widely publicized the Luther anniversary, emphasizing his "positive social message," and even organized packaged tours to his homes and scenes of prominent activity. For a nation whose surly treatment of tourists has become a cliché of travel reportage, this occasion marked a hopeful break. The Augustinian monk who became a religious reformer and changed the course of European history could, after all, hardly be ignored. What's done is done, and East German officialdom tries to make the best of it. No saintly celibate, Luther enjoyed an ample table, good beer, coarse jests, and deeply opinionated notions—he was, for instance, one of the most vicious anti-Semites in history. This earthy monk's defiance of established church doctrine not only reformulated theology in a Protestant mold but also resulted in a period of intense reform in the Roman Catholic church that had excommunicated him. Yet, with an arrogance that was probably at least as offensive to the archbishops as his heresy, Luther never considered himself a "Protestant," but a reformer "more catholic than the Pope," and he called his Roman opponents "heretics."

His birthplace in **Lutherstadt Eisleben**, a two-story house, stands at Lutherstrasse 15-16. It was his home for only his first few months. Displayed in the house in an exhibit on his life and work plus a collection of Luther Bibles. (Open Tuesday—Friday 9:00—12:00, 2:00—4:00, Saturday 9:00—12:00, Sunday 10:00—12:00; 2903; admission.) Luther never lived in the town again but, ironically, he died there in the house of the town clerk during a visit in 1546. This latter house ("Sterbehaus") is located at Andreaskirchplatz 7. A two-story stucco dwelling, it displays Luther memorabilia, portraits, letters, and other documents. (Open same hours as birthplace; admission.)

The son of an ambitious copper miner who became a successful mining entrepreneur, Luther grew up and attended school at nearby **Mansfeld** (1484–96), where his father bought a stone house that survives at Lutherstrasse 26. It is one of the few Luther dwellings that is not a museum. The old school stands at Lutherstrasse 8.

At **Eisenach** Luther resided in the "Cotta House" with his maternal relatives while attending St. George's Parish School from 1497 to 1501. The house stands at Georgenstrasse 50.

Luther entered the Augustinian monastery at **Erfurt** in 1506, subjecting himself to strenuous fasts, austerities, and soul-searchings. "If ever a monk got to heaven by his monkery," he later said, "I was that monk." He was ordained a priest in 1507 and taught there until 1510. The monastery at Komturgasse 8, containing Luther's dormered cell, was mostly destroyed by fire in 1872. It was undergoing reconstruction in 1983.

Lutherstadt Wittenberg became his permanent home in 1511. He had taught theology and lived in the 1502 monastery of Augustinian Eremites from 1508, except for a year's interval in 1509–10.* There, angered at the peddling of in-

dulgences by corrupt clergy, Luther formulated his 95 theses of 1517; they exploded across Europe in waves of popular indignation and support, profoundly shifting the political as well as religious currents of the continent. His refusal to recant led to his 1521 excommunication, which has never been lifted despite a large current body of Catholic opinion that considers him an important reformer. It was only owing to the protection of Frederick the Wise, Elector of Saxony, that Luther was not burned at the stake, as were many church reformers before him. There, too, he laid aside his priestly cowl in 1524 and the following year brought Katherine von Bora, a former nun, as his wife. The couple had six children. By this time Luther's supporters were many, and he was given the monastery as his permanent residence and teaching hall in 1525; it has been known as the Luther House from that year. Luther hosted numerous sick and indigent people there during the plague year of 1527. The place was normally crowded with family, friends, students, and exiled clerics, and he preached sermons to them in the Lutherhalle, today an archive of Lutheriana. He wrote extensively—torrents of tracts, sermons, manifestos, and hymns, including "A Mighty Fortress" and "Away in a Manger." He also completed, in 1534, his translation of the Old Testament. Visitors may see his large oak-paneled study in its original condition, the scene of his famed table talk and writings. This large white-stuccoed building containing Luther's rooms and a Reformation museum is located at Collegienstrasse 54. (Open Tuesday—Sunday 9:00—5:00; 2671; admission.)

Following his defiance of papal authority before Emperor Charles V at Worms in 1521, Luther was declared an outlaw. For his own safety he agreed to a mock abduction that removed him from the tense scene in Wittenberg for 10 months. His place of exile (1521–22) was Wartburg Castle, towering over the village of **Wartburg**, which was placed at his disposal by the Saxon elector. As "Junker Georg," Luther grew a beard and wrote 14 works at a feverish pace. There, in 11 weeks, he also accomplished his famous translation of the New Testament from Greek to vernacular German. Wartburg was also the place, according to Lutherian legend, where he threw an inkwell at the devil during a period when he felt himself troubled by "evil spirits." The castle, originally built in 1070 and restored in the 19th century, displays Luther's room. (Inquire locally for admis-

---

*In the still-surviving tower of the cloister, it is said, Luther experienced a sudden breakthrough of insight into Scripture, sometimes called his "tower experience." Some Luther scholars claim that he found this spiritual release (along with a physical one) not in the tower study but in the latrine, where he often suffered from chronic constipation.

sion information.)

Luther tomb: Castle Church, **Lutherstadt Wittenberg**.

Exhibits: In **Eisenach** the so-called "Luther House" at Lutherplatz 8 displays material on the Reformation. (Open daily, 9:00—1:00, 2:00—5:00; 4983; admission.)

On October 31, 1517, Luther posted his 95 theses challenging the doctrine of indulgence on the door of the Castle Church in **Lutherstadt Wittenberg** (at least, that's the traditional story), and Protestants still keep October 31 as Reformation Day in memory of the event that marked a watershed in Christendom. Posting notices of various sorts on this particular church door was common practice, since it served as the university "bulletin board." The original wooden door was destroyed by fire in 1760; the present bronze door, installed in 1838, is engraved with the text of the theses and is hinged to the original door frame.

A cast of Luther's hands, taken from his deathbed, may be seen in the Market Church of Our Dear Lady at **Halle**.

(See WEST GERMANY in this chapter.)

MAHLER, GUSTAV (1860–1911). The Austrian composer lived in **Leipzig** from 1886 to 1888 as conductor of the Leipzig Symphony Orchestra. He resided in a second-floor apartment at Gottschedstrasse 4.

(See WEST GERMANY in this chapter; also Chapter 1, AUSTRIA.)

MARX, KARL (1818–1883). The Socialist philosopher attended the University of Berlin from 1836 to 1841 and occupied some eight lodgings. Only one of the houses survives: Luisenstrasse 60, now part of the Chamber of Deputies building in **East Berlin**. Marx roomed there in 1838 and 1839.

In the East Berlin suburb of **Stralau**, Marx sought country air at Alt-Stralau 4 in the autumn of 1837. The cottage lodging displays a Marx memorial in the gardens.

Exhibit: The 1814 birthplace of Jenny von Westphalen, who married Karl Marx in 1843 after a seven-year engagement, is now a museum devoted to the Marx family at Jenny-Marx-Strasse 20 in **Salzwedel**. She lived there until 1816. (Inquire locally for admission information.)

(See WEST GERMANY, BELGIUM in this chapter; also Chapter 2, FRANCE; also Chapter 3, PARIS; also Chapter 6, LONDON.)

MENDELSSOHN-BARTHOLDY, FELIX (1809–1847). Son of a banker and a resident of Berlin from 1811 to 1829, the Romantic composer resided with his parents until 1825 at a house in the Neue Promenade, **West Berlin**.

In **East Berlin** the family occupied a seven-acre estate at Leipzigerstrasse 3, including a palatial mansion, garden house, and numerous outbuildings. According to biographer Schima Kaufman, the estate "was like a tree with many branches. It did not so much house the Mendelssohns as become a living member of the family," and they considered it the shrine and center of their existence. Formerly a part of Frederick the Great's hunting preserve bordering on the Tiergarten, the property was inherited by Mendelssohn in 1843; he turned it over to his sisters, who continued to live there. In 1901, having been sold to the Prussian government, the mansion was vastly modified and enlarged to house the upper chamber of the Prussian Diet. Reconstructed after World War II, it now holds government offices.

In **Leipzig** Mendelssohn conducted the famed Gewandhaus Orchestra from 1835 to 1846. His last home, at which he died of a cerebral hemorrhage (strokes were endemic to the family), stood in the Königstrasse.

Mendelssohn tomb: Berlin Burial Grounds, **West Berlin**.

Exhibits: The Museum of the History of **Leipzig** in the Old Town Hall has a Mendelssohn Memorial Room which contains autographs, a piano, and other memorabilia. (Inquire locally for admission information.)

In **West Berlin** the Music Department of the State Library contains the Mendelssohn Archive, which displays some of the composer's manuscripts, and many items of personal memorabilia. It is located at Archivstrasse 11 in the suburb of Dahlem. (Open Monday—Friday 10:00—4:00; 832-70-91; admission.)

(See WEST GERMANY in this chapter.)

NAPOLEON I (1769–1821). During the French emperor's invasion of Prussia in 1806, following the Battle of Jena, he triumphantly entered Berlin and established himself at Charlottenburg Palace in **West Berlin**. There, wrote Emil Ludwig, Napoleon dictated "the greatest, most unbloody, and most dangerous of all his declarations of war": the closing of European harbors to English ships, thus severing all commerce between England and the continent. Also at this time, he occupied the palace of Sans-Souci in **Potsdam**. Though a worshipful admirer of Frederick the Great, who had resided in both palaces, Napoleon despised Frederick's Hohenzollern descendants and quickly asserted control over them (see the entry on Frederick II earlier in this section).

(See BELGIUM in this chapter; also Chapter 1, AUSTRIA, SWITZERLAND; also Chapter 2, FRANCE; also Chapter 3, PARIS; also Chapter 8, ITALY, SPAIN.)

NIETZSCHE, FRIEDRICH WILHELM (1844–1900). A native of the village of **Röcken** near Lützen, the philosopher-poet whose idea of the "will to power" profoundly influenced 20th-century thought was born in the village rectory next to the church pastored by his father.

He spent six of his most formative years (1858–64) in the royal boarding school at **Schulpforta** near Naumburg. Once a Cistercian abbey, the grounds covered 73 walled acres beside the Saale River. Its present status is uncertain.

Naumburg was Nietzsche's family home with his sister and widowed mother from 1858. Until his mental breakdown in 1889, the bachelor philosopher often resided with them at Weingarten 18 and did much of his early writing there. Nietzsche's devoted sister, Elizabeth Förster-Nietzsche, cared for him there from 1889 to 1897.

In 1897 she and her now completely debilitated brother moved to **Weimar**, where she established Nietzsche's last home and the Nietzsche Archive in the three-story Villa Silberblick at Luisenstrasse 36. The philosopher died there, but Elizabeth, who lived until 1935, continued to guard and supervise the ongoing archive. Many scholars accuse her of distorting the philosopher's views to make him appear racist, a charge given weight by Adolf Hitler's enthusiastic visit there in 1934 and his donation of an adjacent memorial building. Soviet authorities, who considered Nietzsche's writings little more than Fascist propaganda, locked and sealed the Nietzsche Archive in 1945 and the building has never been reopened.

Earlier as a student at **Leipzig** Nietzsche lodged at Lessingstrasse 22 (1868–69).

Nietzsche tomb: Village cemetery, **Röcken**.

(See WEST GERMANY in this chapter; also Chapter 1, SWITZERLAND.)

PIUS XII (1876–1958). Before his 1939 election as pope, Eugenio Cardinal Pacelli served as apostolic nuncio from the Vatican to Germany. His address from 1925 to 1929 was Rauchstrasse 21, **West Berlin**. Pius's steady refusal, as pope, to condemn Hitler's aggressive policies against other nations and against the Jews drew much postwar criticism and remains a highly controversial subject.

(See Chapter 8, ITALY.)

RICHTHOFEN, MANFRED, BARON VON (1892–1918). The dashing "Red Baron," flying ace of World War I and a legendary figure of aviation history, was a native of Breslau (now Wroclaw, Poland). His permanent family home from 1900 was Schweidnitz (now Swidnica, Poland) on a street later named Richthofenstrasse. In 1945 Soviet troops seized the house, which had been converted to a Richthofen museum, and dispersed its contents.

In 1909 and 1910 Richthofen attended the military training college in the West Berlin suburb of **Lichterfelde**. A fellow student there was Hermann Goering, who succeeded the baron as last commander of the deadly Richthofen Fighting Squadron (see the entry on Goering earlier in this section).

Richthofen tomb: Invaliden Cemetery, **East Berlin**.

SCHILLER, FRIEDRICH VON (1759–1805). Dramatist, lyric poet, and historian, Schiller ranks with Goethe in the number of German museums and memorials devoted to him. (Since up-to-date admission information is not readily gained from centralized East German services, information should be locally sought for the relevant houses noted below.) Having offended the Duke of Württemberg in Mannheim with his play *The Robbers* (1782), and deserted the army, Schiller escaped as a fugitive from Mannheim in 1783 and resided for eight months under the name of Doctor Ritter at the rural estate of friends in **Bauerbach**. There he wrote the play *Love and Intrigue* (1784) and began his influential drama *Don Carlos* (1787). The Schiller House Museum in the village displays memorabilia of his stay.

In 1785 Schiller moved to **Leipzig**, where he resided for several months at the summer cottage of his publisher Göschen, now known as Schiller's Cottage at Menkestrasse 42. There he wrote his "Ode to Joy," best known for its use by Beethoven in his Ninth Symphony. Exhibits relate to the writer's brief residence in the house.

Another Göschen residence where Schiller often visited stands at what is now Schillerstrasse

25 in **Grimma**. It also has a display of memorabilia.

At **Dresden** where Schiller resided from 1785 to 1789 at what is known today as Schiller's Cottage, Schillerstrasse 19, he completed *Don Carlos* and wrote several long, didactic poems.

At Goethe's suggestion Schiller was appointed professor of history at the University of **Jena** in 1789 and remained there for a decade, devoting himself to historical treatises and his dramatic trilogy *Wallenstein* (1798–99). His home in what is now the Schiller Gässen is today the Schiller Memorial Museum; it contains original furnishings and personal items.

Schiller's last home from 1799 stands at what is today Schillerstrasse 12 in **Weimar**. There he produced the great mass of writing—plays, poems, history—of his last decade, including his most popular work, *William Tell* (1804). Displayed there is an exhibit on his life and works plus part of his library.

Schiller tomb: Goethe and Schiller Mausoleum, **Weimar**.
(See WEST GERMANY in this chapter.)

SCHÖNBERG, ARNOLD (1874–1951). The Austrian composer resided for several lengthy intervals in Berlin, where he taught, experimented with atonality, and originated the 12-tone technique to provide a coherent basis for atonal composition. His first **West Berlin** home, from 1901 to 1903, was Lettestrasse 9. From 1911 to 1913 he lived at the Villa Lepcke, Machnowerstrasse and Dietloffstrasse in the southwestern suburb of Zehlendorf. This two-story house, where he wrote *Pierrot Lunaire* (1912), was destroyed in 1945. From 1913 to 1915, also in Zehlendorf, he resided on the second floor of Berlinerstrasse 17a and there developed the 12-tone technique. Composer Alban Berg was a frequent visitor.

Schönberg's final period in West Berlin (1924–33) was marked by frequent moves. His various addresses included the Pension Bavaria at Steinplatz 2 (1926); Kantstrasse 4 and Nussbaumallee 17 (1927–28); and Nürnbergerplatz 3 (1930).
(See Chapter 1, AUSTRIA.)

SCHUMANN, ROBERT (1810–1856). The Romantic composer's birthplace, which was his home until 1817, stands at Hauptmarkt 4 in **Zwickau**. Visitors may see original furnishings, portraits, manuscripts, and the program collection

BIRTHPLACE OF ROBERT SCHUMANN. In **Zwickau** this house survives as a memorial dedicated to the Romantic composer.

of Schumann and his wife, pianist Clara Wieck Schumann. (Inquire locally for admission information.)

In **Leipzig**, where Schumann studied law in 1828 and 1829 and resided until 1844, the composer moved some six times between 1830 and 1836. "He had no more business trying to plow through the sand dunes of Saxon law," wrote Richard Anthony Leonard, "than John Keats had trying to be a surgeon." Until 1830 he spent much time and briefly resided at the Wieck home, where he began lessons under renowned piano teacher Friedrich Wieck and met his nine-year-old daughter, Clara. This house stood in the center of old Leipzig at Grimmaische Gasse 36. After a long, harrowing courtship over Wieck's furious opposition, the couple finally married in 1840 and settled in a first-floor apartment at Inselstrasse 15, where they lived until 1844. There Schumann wrote most of his best-known *lieder*, his First and Second symphonies, chamber music, and his cantata *Paradise and the Peri* (1843). In 1844 the composer suffered an alarming, incapacitating depression; it was an ominous sign of the suffering that was to cripple and finally end his career.

A change seemed advisable and the couple moved to **Dresden** in 1844. Until 1846 they resided at Waisenhausstrasse 35 in the "Altstadt" section; the whole street, since rebuilt, was wiped out during the Dresden bombing holocaust of 1945. The Schumanns' last Dresden home, until

1849, was a first-floor apartment at nearby Reit-bahnstrasse 20, now also gone.

(See WEST GERMANY in this chapter.)

STRAUSS, RICHARD (1864–1949). A resident of Berlin from 1898 to about 1917, the composer led the Berlin Philharmonic Orchestra during this period. Most of his addresses were in **West Berlin**. These included Knesebeckstrasse 30 (1898–1903), Joachimsthalerstrasse 17 (1903–10), Hohenzollerndamm 7 (1910–13), and Heerstrasse 2 (1913–17). During these years Strauss composed his operas *Salome* (1905), *Elektra* (1909) and *Der Rosenkavalier* (1911).

(See WEST GERMANY in this chapter; also Chapter 1, AUSTRIA.)

VOLTAIRE, FRANÇOIS-MARIE AROUET (1694–1778). The French philosopher began cor-responding with Prince Frederick of Prussia (later Frederick the Great) in 1736. Not until 1750, however, was the Francophile king able to per-suade Voltaire to accept royal hospitality at **Pots-dam**. Voltaire's period of residence at Sans-Souci Palace lasted two years. At first the comradeship between the philospher and the intellectual king was convivial and mutually stimulating: "I find a port after fifty years of storm," wrote Voltaire. But trifles of disagreement mounted in time to antipa-thy. As much as any outright causes of conflict, the pair seem to have simply become bored with each other; mutual deference for two such high-powered personalities became tiring. Voltaire's re-turn from Germany actually amounted to flight from another suddenly stormy "port." At Sans-Souci Palace his rooms may be viewed along with some memorabilia of his stay. (See the entry on Frederick II earlier in this section.)

(See Chapter 1, SWITZERLAND; also Chapter 2, FRANCE; also Chapter 3, PARIS.)

WAGNER, RICHARD (1813–1883). The com-poser of Romantic, monumental operas was a na-tive of **Leipzig**, where his reconstructed birthplace stands at Am Brühl 3. Demolished in 1886, the original three-story structure was known as the "Red and White Lion."

Wagner grew up in **Dresden**, his home from 1814 to 1827, but none of his residences survive. The family house of actor Ludwig Geyer whom Wagner's widowed mother married in 1814 (and whom the composer believed to be his actual fa-ther), stood at Waisenhausgasse 12. Much later, as *Kapellmeister* of the Dresden Opera (1843–49), Wagner lived with his first wife, Minna Planer, at Ostra-Ufer 6. His operas *Tannhäuser* (1845) and *Lohengrin* (1850) were products of this period. Wagner fled from Dresden to Switzerland when his active participation in the revolution of 1848 resulted in a warrant for his arrest.

Exhibits: Wagner found inspiration for the third act of *Tannhäuser* when he passed through the town of **Eisenach** with Minna in 1842. The Reuter-Wagner Museum at Reuterweg 2 displays material on Wagner's career, as well as that of the poet Fritz Reuter (1810–1874) who later lived and died in this house. (Open Tuesday-Sunday 10:00—12:30, 2:30—5:00; 3971; admission.)

In Graupa, a **Dresden** suburb, the Wagner Mu-seum at Richard-Wagner-Strasse 9 displays memorabilia and pictures of the composer. Wag-ner composed part of *Lohengrin* there. (Inquire lo-cally for admission information.)

(See WEST GERMANY in this chapter; also Chapter 1, AUSTRIA, SWITZERLAND; also Chapter 2, FRANCE; also Chapter 3, PARIS; also Chapter 8, ITALY.)

WILHELM II (1859–1941). The last kaiser, who ruled Germany during World War I, was forced to abdicate in 1918 as part of the price of Allied peace terms. A son of Wilhelm I, a grandson of British Queen Victoria, and a collateral descen-dant of Frederick the Great, Wilhelm received more blame than he personally deserved for that conflict; few biographers have accused him of pos-sessing outstanding qualities of any sort. His **East Berlin** birthplace was probably the former palace of Kaiser Wilhelm I, located on the south side of the Unter den Linden across from Humboldt Uni-versity. Built in 1834, this palace was the main city residence of Wilhelm I from that date until his death in 1888. Bombs gutted it during World War II. Since restored, it now serves as one of the Hum-boldt University buildings. Wilhelm II's own city residence from 1888 was usually the Stadtschloss of Frederick the Great, a site now occupied by the Marx-Engels-Platz (see the entry on Frederick II earlier in this section).

The kaiser's favorite home was probably the rococco New Palace in **Potsdam**, one of the four palaces in Sanssouci Park near the summer resi-dence of Frederick the Great. Reminders of Kaiser Wilhelm, however, have been carefully purged from the scene. (Open summer, daily 9:00—5:00; admission.)

(See WEST GERMANY, THE NETHERLANDS in this chapter.)

WEST GERMANY

Most British and American travel guidebooks labeled "Germany" actually concern themselves only with the Federal Republic of Germany. Baedeker, Michelin, and the rest apparently consider this western nation of the country sufficiently representative of the whole, which of course it is not. It is, however, the largest German nation, extending from the North Sea to the Bavarian Alps, politically composed of 11 *Länder* (regional provinces). The *Land* of West Berlin, islanded in East Germany, occupies a special, anomalous status under the federal system.

During the postwar four-power conferences, it was Soviet intransigence over German reparations, not excesses of charity, that led the Western Allies to reverse their policy of long-term military occupation of West Germany and to compete for autonomous German support in the Cold War. To structure this new policy, they set about creating a German state from the shambles of Nazi dictatorship. Construction of this state began with German elections of *Länder* parliaments, which in turn elected a federal constitutional assembly in 1948. The machinery of a parliamentary democracy gradually arose under the watchful eye of occupation authorities. In 1949 the Federal Republic came into existence, led by Chancellor Konrad Adenauer, with an elected president and with the seat of government located in Bonn. (Berlin is still the official capital.) For a politically naive, Nazi-corrupted people whose entire democratic experience consisted of hardly more than the post-World War I decade, the new constitution and federal system worked supremely well. Adenauer's earnest pursuit of a German state integrated within the European context led to national sovereignty in 1955. Since then the Federal Republic has come a bulwark of Western European economic and defense interests, allying itself strongly with the United States. Rearmed by the U.S., an ingratiating West Germany has become the ominous "front line" for American missile installations.

While U.S. Marshall Plan aid was vital in Germany's early years of recovery, the "economic miracle" guided by Finance Minister Ludwig Erhard during the 1950s owed much to currency reform, to the Common Market, and most of all to the legendary industriousness of the German people. German factories, formerly heavily dependent on coal, have diversified to other energy sources. The Ruhr, one of the world's busiest industrial regions, makes West Germany the world's fourth largest steel producer. Today, indeed, the nation ranks as the world's fourth largest economic power. Labor remains in short supply with about 40 percent of the work force being women, the highest of any Common Market country. Most agricultural income derives from livestock farming. A postwar population increase of 8.7 million represented not a higher birth rate but a massive influx of East German refugees, who have now been successfully assimilated. Hamburg is the nation's largest city, followed by Munich and Cologne.

West Germany displays one of Europe's most scenically varied landscapes, rising from plains in the north to the ancient, worn-down mountain ranges of central Germany and the rugged Alps of the south. The Rhine, not only a vital commercial channel and wine-producing region, has etched a cherished place in German national consciousness because of the romantic legends associated with its hero mythology. Yet this "spiritual" aspect of the Rhine has certainly been overemphasized; the river has degenerated into one of the world's filthiest and is often called "Europe's longest sewer."

As in East Germany, World War II destruction eliminated many dwellings of notable historic Germans. A number of them, such as Goethe's birthplace in Frankfurt, have been rebuilt from the ground up, however, maintaining rigorous fidelity to their original construction. Germans are a culture-loving people, despite (and perhaps, to some degree, because of) their profound lapse in the matter during World War II. At bottom, indeed, most Germans believe that their country is still *"Deutschland über alles"* in music and the arts. But Germany's substantive creative vigor is mainly a matter of history and probably will remain so for decades to come.

The choice of available West German travel guidebooks is, on the whole, poor but improving. Almost alone among German cities, Nuremberg has made some attempt to confront the reality of its Nazi past through a small 1977 brochure describing its National Socialist sites (*Nürnberg: 1933–1945*). *The Music Guide to Austria and Germany* (1975) by Elaine Brody and Claire Brook is a good specialized guide in English; and an excellent German-language guidebook to literary sites is *Literarischer Führer durch Deutschland* (1983) by Fred and Gabriele Oberhauser. (Neither of these books actually concern Germany, of course, only *West* Germany.)

ADENAUER, KONRAD (1876–1967). Chancellor of the Federal Republic from 1949 to 1963 and the custodian of West Germany's postwar recovery, Dr. Adenauer was a native of **Cologne** and resided there for most of his life. All of his city homes, including his birthplace in Balduinstrasse,

were destroyed during World War II. The house he built in 1911 at Max-Bruch-Strasse 6 was his residence throughout his long tenure (1917–33) as chief mayor of Cologne. At war's end in 1945 he returned to find a goat nibbling grass in the heaps of shattered masonry that had been his home. After Adenauer's 1944 arrest by the Gestapo, he

KONRAD ADENAUER HOUSE. Overlooking the Rhine River at **Bad Honnef-Rhöndorf**, the postwar German chancellor's house was designed, and much of it constructed by, Adenauer himself. There he "sat out" most of World War II, though British and American artillery shelling in 1945 made it a perilous place indeed. Adenauer retired there again, and permanently, in 1963. His study exhibits personal furnishings and memorabilia.

was confined for some weeks in a detention camp at Cologne's trade fairgrounds, located at Kennedy-Ufer near the Hohenzollern Bridge on the Rhine's east bank.

Deposed as mayor and harassed by Nazi officialdom who feared his quiet authority and prestige, Adenauer fled in 1933 to the Abbey of **Maria-Laach**, an 11th-century Benedictine monastery located on the west shore of the Laacher See. He remained sheltered there for a year, safe from the Nazis but isolated from his family and suffering from inactivity. Today a center of liturgical activity, the abbey is one of the most architecturally impressive monasteries north of the Alps. Visitors may tour the 12th-century Abbey Church (apply at the porter's lodge) and hear High Mass sung on Sundays and Vespers during the week.

During the years 1935 to 1944 Adenauer was left alone by the Nazis. From the enforced sale of his Cologne property, he obtained enough money to buy a plot of land in the Rhine Valley at **Bad Honnef-Rhöndorf**. He built a house on the hillslope above the river, installed his family there, and devoted most of the next decade to cultivating an elaborate rose garden. The long terrace walls that bank his estate were his own handiwork; he also carried up most of the terrace stones by hand from the Rhine shore below. Though Adenauer had refused involvement in the plot, after the assassination attempt on Hitler in 1944 he was arrested and imprisoned by the Gestapo. Released shortly before the end of the war, he returned to Rhöndorf. Then, as Allied forces approached the Rhine in 1945, Adenauer's property suddenly became a no-man's land. From a hilltop vantage point, he witnessed bombardment from both sides. British artillery aiming at this assumed enemy lookout point forced Adenauer, his family, and several escaped French war prisoners he was hiding, into the cellar of the house, where they waited out the battle. "Twelve American shells landed in my garden," Adenauer wrote. "Three of them hit my house from the front, while the back of the house was under German mortar fire from the right bank of the Rhine." He completed repairs after the war, and this house remained his home for the rest of his life. Retiring there permanently in 1963, he received many notable visitors. When he died there, he had become a world statesman who, more than anyone, had renewed hope in the idea of a Germany that could again achieve a civilized respectability among nations.

During 1944, as an escaped fugitive calling himself Dr. Weber, Adenauer hid out in the quaint mill village of **Nister Mühle**, some 64 kilometers southeast of Cologne. Discovered there by the Gestapo, he was taken to Brauweiler Prison in **Brauweiler**, a town west of Cologne. Both he and his wife, Gussi, were confined there in separate quarters and celebrated their silver wedding anniversary in different parts of the same building. They were released in 1945 shortly before the end of the war.

Adenauer's official residence as federal chancellor was the Schaumburg Palace, the white-walled structure at Adenauer-Allee 139 in **Bonn**. Succeeding chancellors who have occupied the palace include Ludwig Erhard, Kurt Kiesinger, Willy Brandt, Helmut Schmidt, and Helmut Kohl.

Adenauer tomb: Waldfriedhof, **Rhöndorf**. Chancellor Adenauer's House at Konrad-Adenauer-Strasse 8a displays original furnishings, memorabilia, and exhibits illustrating his life and work. (Open Tuesday—Sunday 10:00—4:30; free.)

AQUINAS, ST. THOMAS (1225–1274). The Italian scholastic theologian and philosopher lived in **Cologne** from 1248 to 1252, studying under St. Albertus Magnus. He probably resided during most of this period in the 1226 Dominican convent that stood in the Stolkgasse on the site of the present main post office, directly opposite the entrance of the Enggasse.

(See Chapter 3, PARIS; also Chapter 8, ITALY.)

BEETHOVEN, LUDWIG VAN (1770–1827). A native of **Bonn**, the composer lived there until 1792, when he moved permanently to Vienna. His birthplace at Bonngasse 20, where he resided until 1774, stands in the old district of the city and is now a museum. Beethoven's parents occupied the second story of this house in impoverished circumstances. His father, a minor court musician and alcoholic tyrant, drove the youngster unmercifully, hoping to exhibit him as a Mozart-like prodigy on the clavier. This scheme fell flat, but by age 13 Beethoven had published several piano sonatas and variations. Among the items displayed in Beethoven's Birthplace are a number of ear trumpets he used during the time he became increasingly deaf, a life mask, original scores, portraits, and the small organ he played at age 10 in the Minorite Church. There is also a wooden stick

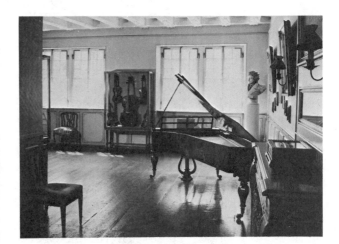

BEETHOVEN'S BIRTHPLACE. The aspect of the composer's **Bonn** neighborhood has changed considerably since the old engraving was made, but the house itself survives in recognizable shape at Bonngasse 20, both in front and garden views, and displays a wealth of Beethoven memorabilia.

that he may have used when he had become completely deaf; held between the teeth, its other end was touched on the piano strings in an attempt to "hear" vibrations from the instrument. Occasional lectures and concerts are given in the house; Pablo Casals performed there in a concert of *The Archduke* trio in 1958. The house narrowly escaped destruction during World War II because its caretaker bravely knocked off incendiary bombs that had fallen on the roof. (Open April 1—September 30, Monday—Saturday 9:00—1:00, 3:00—6:00, Sunday 9:30—1:00; October 1—March 31, Monday—Saturday 9:30—1:00, 3:00—5:00, Sunday 10:00—1:00; 63-51-88; admission.)

Beethoven's later Bonn addresses included Rheingasse 7 (1774-85), where his father was raised, and Wenzelgasse 462 (1785-92), where his parents died. Neither house has survived.

Exhibits: Next door to Beethoven's Birthplace in **Bonn**, the Beethoven Archive, Bonngasse 18, contains what is probably the world's finest resource collection on the composer. Entry to the archive, which is mainly for the use of scholars and researchers, is by permission, and a letter of recommendation is advisable for those who wish to study or investigate the material. (Open Monday—Friday 9:00—1:00, 3:00—5:00; closed August; 63-51-88; admission.) The International Beethoven Festival is a biennial September event that draws famed musicians and orchestras to Bonn from all over the world. Performances occur in the modernistic Beethovenhalle in the Theaterstrasse. (For information, contact Kulturamt der Stadt Bonn, Kurfürstenstrasse 2-3, 52 Bonn-Bad Godesberg; 8-60-06-45.)

At **Koblenz** the 1746 birthplace of Maria Keverich Beethoven, the composer's mother, stands near the Ehrenbreitstein Citadel (her father was a chef in the castle) and displays Beethoven memorabilia. (Inquire locally for admission information.)

(See Chapter 1, AUSTRIA.)

BISMARCK, OTTO VON (1815-1898). "Bismarck's unique creation is the Germany we have known in our time," wrote William L. Shirer, "a problem child of Europe and the world for nearly a century." In 1871, four years after becoming Prussian chancellor and the same year he became first chancellor of the united German Empire, the apostle of "blood and iron" diplomacy was given an estate at Friedrichsruh by Kaiser Wilhelm I. The

BISMARCK WELCOMES THE KAISER TO HIS ESTATE. Aged and infirm, the retired first chancellor of the German Empire greets the recently crowned Wilhelm II at Bismarck's **Friedrichsruh** home. The picture dates from 1896, two years before the death of the "Iron Chancellor." His mausoleum is located on the property.

house was a former hotel, and it is said that the "Iron Chancellor" didn't bother to remove the room numbers over the doors when he moved in. He gradually extended the property by purchase until his estate became one of Germany's largest landholdings. Most of his land was timbered—his affection for his trees achieved somewhat eccentric if not bizarre proportions at times. Bismarck moved to this estate permanently in 1894, received visits from Kaiser Wilhelm II, and finally died there at an infirm 83. The estate is located in the Saxon Forest at **Aumühle-Friedrichsruh**, 29 kilometers east of Hamburg. During the centennial of the founding of the Second Reich in 1971, news accounts reported a clash between 300 demonstrators trying to lay a wreath at the house and 500 counterdemonstrators trying to prevent it. The Bismarck Museum, housed in the chancellor's final home, displays original furnishings, memorabilia, manuscripts, and exhibits relating to Bismarck's life and career. (Open April 1—September 30, Tuesday—Saturday 9:00—6:00; October 1—March 31, Tuesday—Saturday 9:00—10:00 a.m., Sunday 9:00—4:00; admission.)

As a student at the University of **Göttingen**, where he fought his first duel, Bismarck lodged in a house in the Bürgerstrasse near the Leine Canal (1832-33), which is now marked.

The village of **Hausen**, north of Bad Kissingen, was Bismarck's vacation residence at the time of an 1874 assassination attempt. The house displays original furnishings and memorabilia in the study, drawing room, and bedroom he used. A marker on the 18th-century house details the story of this episode. (Inquire locally for admission information.)

In **Frankfurt am Main**, Bismarck's residence during his tenure as Prussian envoy to the Bundestag (1851–58) stood at Grosse Gallusstrasse 19.

Bismarck tomb: Bismarck Mausoleum, **Aumühle-Friedrichsruh**.

(See EAST GERMANY in this chapter).

BONHOEFFER, DIETRICH (1906–1945). An anti-Nazi activist, the influential theologian attended the University of **Tübingen** from 1923 to 1925 and during part of this period resided at the Igel fraternity house on the campus, located west of the Wilhelmstrasse. He resigned from the fraternity when it restricted membership to "Aryans."

Bonhoeffer was hanged at Flossenbürg concentration camp during the final phase of World War II. There is a memorial chapel on the site at **Flossenbürg**.

Bonhoeffer tomb (unmarked): Concentration camp site, **Flossenbürg**.

(See EAST GERMANY in this chapter; also Chapter 6, LONDON.)

BRAHMS, JOHANNES (1833–1897). A native of **Hamburg**, the composer was born in a five-story wooden tenement called "Schluter's Hof" at Speckstrasse 60, which was his home to about 1837. This structure was destroyed during World War II. The site is marked, and two rooms have been reconstructed at the Brahms Memorial (see *Exhibit* below).

In **Düsseldorf**, where Brahms lived in 1856 and 1857, his residence is marked at Haroldstrasse 14. Here began his long attachment to pianist Clara Schumann, wife of composer Robert Schumann. Brahms became a protégé of the Schumanns, took his meals at their house, and studied counterpoint there (see the entry on Robert Schumann later in this section).

At **Detmold** Brahms served as music director of the Lippe court in 1857. He found life in the 16th-century castle dominating the town (also the ancestral seat of Prince Bernhard, consort of former Queen Juliana of the Netherlands) extremely dull and undemanding, but he earned enough money to carry him awhile, and he composed two

notable serenades there. Royal souvenirs and tapestries are displayed. (Open for guided tours April 1—October 31, daily 9:30—12:00, 2:00—5:00; November 1—March 31, daily 10:00—11:00, 3:00—4:00; admission.)

During summers from 1865 to 1875 Brahms lived at Maximilianstrasse 85 in **Baden-Baden**, today the Brahms Museum. He wrote his Second Symphony and *Alto Rhapsody* (1870) in these rooms. "Invariably the central event of every summer," wrote Richard Anthony Leonard, "was Brahms's visit to Baden, where Clara Schumann maintained her home. He gave music lessons to the children, and he played for Clara the new works that he was preparing for the coming winter season." (Open Monday, Wednesday, Friday 10:00—12:00, 3:00—5:00, Sunday 10:00—1:00; 70172; admission.)

Exhibit: The Brahms Memorial Rooms at Peterstrasse 39 in **Hamburg** consist of two rooms reconstructed from Brahms's tenement birthplace; they display photographs, letters, manuscripts, musical instruments, and the composer's death mask. Kenneth Bernstein, writing in 1983, reported that "one eerie overtone is provided by the next-door neighbor, who happens to be a piano teacher; the sound effects are unnerving." (Open Tuesday, Friday 12:00—1:00, Thursday 4:00—6:00; 34-42-18; admission.)

For further information, contact the Brahms Society at Bahnhofstrasse 35, Hamburg (phone 86-02-64).

(See Chapter 1, AUSTRIA.)

BRECHT, BERTOLT (1898–1956). The highly influential Marxist playwright was born in **Augsburg** at Auf dem Rain 7, but his parents soon moved to Bei den Sieben Kindeln 1. It was his home until 1900. The house often pointed out by Augsburgers as "Brecht's birthplace," however (the playwright has only recently achieved grudging acceptance as a native son), is Bleichstrasse 2, which was his home from 1900 to the 1920s. He did much of his early writing in his attic room there.

Brecht wrote his first plays while studying medicine in **Munich** in 1917 and 1918, and occupying a succession of cheap rooms at Maximilianstrasse 43, Adalbertstrasse 12, and Kaulbachstrasse 63.

(See EAST GERMANY, DENMARK, FINLAND, SWEDEN in this chapter; also Chapter 1, SWITZERLAND.)

CHAPLIN, SIR CHARLES SPENCER "CHARLIE" (1889–1977).

Exhibit: The William Staudinger Chaplin Archive at Bingerstrasse 5 in **Darmstadt** displays pictures, posters, and memorabilia of the English film comedian who fiercely satirized Hitler in *The Great Dictator* (1940). (Inquire locally for admission information.)

(See Chapter 1, SWITZERLAND; also Chapter 6, LONDON.)

CHARLEMAGNE (742–814). The Frankish king, and later Holy Roman emperor, established his permanent capital at **Aachen** in 794 and made the city a primary center of European culture and civilization. By inheritance and conquest, he gained rule over the immense territories that now include France and Germany, unifying them for the first time into one European empire. Nothing survives of this two-story wood and marble palace except two stone towers, the Granusturm and Marktturm. Until a 13th-century fire destroyed it, the palace stood on the site of the present 14th-century Town Hall, which was built on the old foundations in the city center. Nineteenth-century frescoes in a second-floor chamber illustrate the life of Charlemagne. Interesting descriptions of the royal city include *Aix-la-Chapelle in the Age of Charlemagne* (1963) by Richard E. Sullivan, and *Daily Life in the World of Charlemagne* (1978) by Pierre Riché. (Open Monday—Friday 8:00—1:00, 2:00—5:00; Saturday—Sunday 10:00—1:00; admission.)

Earlier, from about 768 to 784, a favorite residence of Charlemagne was his palace at **Ingelheim**, which he filled with art treasures, mosaics, and statuary sent from Italy. Burned down in 1274, it was restored in the next century but fell permanently in 1689. Ruins of the palace chapel were incorporated into the transept and choir of the Church of St. Remigius.

Charlemagne tomb: Cathedral, **Aachen**.

Exhibit: **Aachen** Cathedral, which Charlemagne began building in about 800, displays notable treasures of the emperor's reign. Charlemagne's marble throne, where he sat during ceremonial occasions, is located in the upper section of the cathedral. (Open for guided tours; apply to the keeper of the Treasury; admission.) The cathedral's Treasury displays a reliquary bust of Charlemagne containing part of his cranium, the crown that reputedly once sat on it, and Charlemagne's Bible, dating from about 800. (Open Monday—Saturday 9:00—1:00, 2:00—6:00, Sunday 10:30—1:00, 2:00—5:00; admission.)

(See THE NETHERLANDS in this chapter; also Chapter 2, FRANCE.)

COLERIDGE, SAMUEL TAYLOR (1772–1834). The English poet studied philosophy at **Göttingen** University in 1799. A plaque marks his residence at Weenderstrasse 64.

(See Chapter 5, ENGLAND; also Chapter 6, LONDON.)

CONSTANTINE I, THE GREAT (272–337). The first Christian Roman emperor had not yet converted when he made his imperial residence at **Trier**, the Roman capital of Gaul, from 306 to 315. Archaeology since World War II has revealed what appear to be remnants of his imperial palace beneath the Trier Cathedral, the oldest central part of which dates from the fourth century. Medieval tradition ascribed the construction of this earliest church on the site to St. Helena, mother of Constantine. The cathedral is approached via its forecourt, the Domfreihof. (Open daily, 7:00—12:00, 2:00—6:00; donation.)

Part of the imperial palace erected by Constantine was the imposing Roman basilica, which stands nearby in the Konstantinplatz. Originally it probably served as Constantine's massive reception chamber, and later as a royal hall for Carolingian and Frankish princes and archbishops. South and east walls were demolished in the 17th century to permit expansion of the adjacent Elector's Palace. In the 19th century the basilica became an evangelical church. Air raids in 1944 resulted in heavy damage, but the building was restored after the war. Most of the western wall and apse consist of the original Roman construction, albeit with considerable patchwork. The interior measures 67 meters in length, 27.5 meters in width and 30 meters in height. This building is probably the only existing structure in the world that housed the Roman emperor who made Christianity "legal"— and thus, more than any religious saint, spread its dominion over the Western world. A fascinating archaeological account is Edith Mary Wightman's *Roman Trier and the Treveri* (1970). (Basilica open summer, Monday—Saturday 9:00—1:00, 2:00—6:00, Sunday from 11:00; free.)

Exhibit: Today people keep photographs of their loved ones beside them. The Romans, from the same impulse, also liked pictures or busts of their families near at hand. Some remarkable fourth-century paintings excavated after World War II from the imperial chamber ceiling beneath **Trier** Cathedral are displayed in the Episcopal Museum, Banthusstrasse 6. Figures in the frescoes are said to represent St. Helena and the emperor's wife, Fausta. (Open Monday—Friday 10:00—12:00, 3:00—5:00; Saturday—Sunday 10:00—1:00; admission.)

(See Chapter 5, ENGLAND; also Chapter 8, ITALY.)

DOSTOEVSKI, FEODOR MIKHAILOVICH (1821–1881). At the famous **Bad Ems** spa, the Russian novelist "took the waters" several times between the years 1874 and 1879. He usually stayed at what is now the Russicher Hof at Römerstrasse 23. The last Russian czar, Nicholas II, was also an important guest there.

(See EAST GERMANY in this chapter; also Chapter 1, SWITZERLAND; also Chapter 8, ITALY.)

TWO VIEWS OF CONSTANTINE'S BASILICA. The Roman emperor made **Trier** the headquarters of the Western empire in A.D. 306 and lived there until 315. Today a Protestant church, the Basilica was probably part of Constantine's imperial palace, possibly his audience or reception hall. The massive structure as it looked in 1600, as painted by Alexander Wiltheim, is compared with its much-restored appearance in a recent photograph.

DÜRER, ALBRECHT (1471–1528). A native of **Nuremberg**, the Renaissance painter resided there most of his life, though he traveled widely. His birthplace, which he later bought from his brother, is long gone from its site at Burgstrasse 27 (some sources give the address as Winklerstrasse 20). It remained his family home until 1509.

Dürer was an apprentice to a Nuremberg painter, Michael Wohlgemut, from 1486 to 1490 and during this period probably resided at Wohlgemut's home, which stood at Burgstrasse 21.

In 1509 Dürer bought the 15th-century gabled dwelling now known as the Dürer House at Albrecht-Dürerstrasse 39 and occupied it until his death. "Hiding from his shrewish wife Agnes, who always wondered why he did not make more money," according to Phyllis Méras in *The Mermaids of Chenonceaux* (1983), "the artist would climb to the second floor of his house and quietly draw. When she got to be entirely too much for him, he would flee to a neighboring sausage shop to eat and drink with his friend the poet, cobbler and *Meistersinger*, Hans Sachs." Original interiors and personal memorabilia, as well as original drawings, engravings, and copies of paintings Dürer

ALBRECHT DÜRER HOUSE. The Renaissance painter occupied this 15th-century house, still a famous **Nuremberg** landmark, during his last two decades. A number of his art works are displayed there.

executed in this house are on display (Open summer, Tuesday—Sunday 10:00—5:00; winter, Tuesday—Friday 1:00—5:00, Saturday 10:00—9:00, Sunday 10:00—5:00; admission.)

Dürer tomb: Johannes Cemetery, **Nuremberg**.

Exhibits: The most important displays of Dürer paintings and graphic works in Germany may be viewed at the German National Museum, Kornmarkt 1, **Nuremberg** (open Tuesday—Sunday 9:00—4:00; admission); and at the Old Pinakothek, Barerstrasse 27, **Munich**, where his *Self-Portrait* (1500) and *The Four Apostles* (1526)—two of his best-known canvases—are exhibited (open Tuesday—Sunday 9:00—4:30, also Tuesday, Thursday 7:00—9:00 p.m.; admission; Sunday, holidays free).

(See Chapter 1, AUSTRIA.)

EINSTEIN, ALBERT (1879–1955). Probably no person has so embodied the popular idea of genius as this mathematician-physicist. He formulated the theory of relativity, which underlies the entire structure of modern physics, and in the company of the "immortals" of human history can only be ranked with such minds as those of Socrates, Michelangelo, Shakespeare, and Newton. Einstein lived and worked in Germany for most of his life and only left in 1933 because, as a Jew, he was appalled at the increasing levels of terrorism waged by Hitler's "master race." The Nazis were outraged at his 1933 renouncement of German citizenship, but had he stayed, he would probably have died in a concentration camp. German physicists became the laughing stock of the scientific world when they denounced his immense achievements as part of a "Jewish plot" to pollute science.

Einstein was a native of **Ulm**. His birthplace at Bahnhofstrasse 20, destroyed during World War II, remained the family home until 1880. In 1946, when asked whether the street formerly named for him in his native town had again become Einsteinstrasse, he said, "Whether anything has been changed since then I do not know, and I know even less when the next change will take place; but I do know how to restrain my curiosity." During the Einstein centennial in 1979, West German President Walter Scheel questioned the legitimacy of Germany's participation: "We cannot overlook the fact that Einstein would have objected to his name being connected with this ceremony if he lived." Ulm today does have its Einsteinstrasse again, for whatever it's worth.

Munich, where he grew up (1880–95), was stony ground indeed for a mathematical prodigy. "Your presence in the class destroys the respect of the students," he was told by one teacher at the Luitpold Gymnasium (high school), which stood until World War II at Müllerstrasse 33. The family home with its large garden stood in the suburb of Sendling at an unidentified address in the Adelreiterstrasse.

(See EAST GERMANY in this chapter; also Chapter 1, SWITZERLAND.)

ERASMUS, DESIDERIUS (1466?–1536). Finding the repressive atmosphere too uncomfortable in his longtime adopted home at Basel, Switzerland, the Dutch humanist resided during most of his later years (1529–35) in **Freiburg im Breisgau**. In 1531, after having been the guest of Emperor Maximilian, Erasmus bought a house of his own but found little satisfaction in it. "This house I have bought," he wrote, "makes me no end of trouble. . . there is not a place in the whole of it suited to my body." Built about 1516 and called "The Child Jesus,"the building later became known as the "Haus zum Walfisch" ("Whale House") and was occupied by a wholesale wine merchant. Only remnants of the original structure survive—among them an oriel window over a Gothic doorway—in the present building at Franziskanerstrasse 3.

(See BELGIUM, THE NETHERLANDS in this chapter; also Chapter 1, SWITZERLAND; also Chapter 3, PARIS; also Chapter 5, ENGLAND.)

FAUST, JOHANN (?–1538?). Goethe based his poetic drama *Faust* on this legendary necromancer, charlatan, and adventurer who wandered Europe and created sufficient stir to arouse an entire body of lore and apocrypha—with which numerous folktales, plays, and operas have taken ample liberties (see the entry on Johann Wolfgang von Goethe later in this section). His real name was probably Georg Faust, but facts about his life are sparse. Many sources give his birthplace as Knittlingen, but primary documents indicate that Helmstadt near Heidelberg may have been his native village. He apparently studied at Heidelberg University during the 1480s, then spent the rest of his life traveling as a kind of free-lance philosopher, healer, and con artist. Faust earned his living mainly as an astrologer, and his fortunes veered wildly between positions of power and influence at royal courts and gutters of disgrace. Presumably

he talked a lot and, not infrequently, too much. At least one city, **Ingolstadt**, ejected him (ca. 1528); his reputed dwelling bears a marker at Harderstrasse 7. But he always seemed able to drum up another scheme, miracle, and audience—no wonder writers and musicians have found him so irresistible.

A small house at Magister-Faust-Gasse 47 in **Bad Kreuznach** is also said to have hosted the itinerant doctor when he taught school in the town in 1507.

Exhibit: Whether or not he ever lived in **Knittlingen**, the Faust Memorial Museum at Kirchplatz 2 displays material on his life and legend as well as its many literary outgrowths. (Open Tuesday—Friday 9:30—12:00, 1:30—5:00; 07043–31212; admission.)

FRANK, ANNE (1929–1945). Probably Germany's most significant writer of the 20th century and possibly for years to come, Annelies Marie Frank wrote *The Diary of a Young Girl* (1952) while hiding from the Gestapo in the Netherlands. Her birthplace in **Frankfurt am Main** stands at Marbachweg 307. A two-story yellow-stucco house, it was her home for only her first year. Her next home, from 1930 to 1933, when the family moved to Amsterdam, has been marked (by city youth organizations) at Ganghoferstrasse 24.

Following the 1944 capture of her family in Amsterdam, her last home was the notorious Bergen-Belsen concentration camp, where 30,000 Jews died. Anne Frank died there of typhus—and all of her family except her father likewise lost their lives there— about a month before the end of World War II. Now the site of a memorial operated by the Federal State of Lower Saxony and sponsored by the Association for Christian-Jewish Cooperation, Bergen-Belsen is as green and tasteful a murder site as one could want to see—including the common-grave mounds, in one of which lies the writer. An Anne Frank Room in the entrance House of Documents is a memorial to her.* The camp site is located via signs seven kilometers southwest of **Bergen**.

(See THE NETHERLANDS in this chapter.)

---

*Because Germany viciously abandoned any possible right to claim her, something about the presence of Anne Frank memorials anywhere in the country strikes many people as odious in the extreme. Perhaps it is best to consider such memorials expressive of the world community, as indeed they are. Anne Frank belongs to people who cherish those values that Germany once represented in the world.

FREDERICK II, THE GREAT (1712–1786).

Exhibit: Memorabilia of the Prussian king who was not only a soldier but a scholar is displayed in Hohenzollern Castle, cradle of the Swabian Zollern family who ruled Prussia and the German empire from 1701 to 1918. The present castle on the site dates only from 1867, however. Displayed in the castle treasury are uniforms, decorations, flutes, and tobacco jars that belonged to the monarch. The castle is located off Road 27 about five kilometers south of **Hechingen**. (Guided tours daily, summer 8:00—5:30, winter 8:00—4:30; admission.)

Frederick II tomb: Protestant Chapel, Hohenzollern Castle, **Hechingen**.

(See EAST GERMANY in this chapter.)

GOEBBELS, JOSEPH (1897–1945). Unlike many of Hitler's minions, the "little doctor" never believed in the Nazi mystique he so expertly concocted for the masses. For him, the entire era of the Third Reich was a long episode of showmanship and cynical manipulation of minds. As Hitler's propaganda minister, the frail rat-faced Goebbels controlled all communications media during the Nazi regime, determining the content of German newspapers, books, radio programs, and films.

Goebbels was a native of **Rheydt**. From infancy, when he suffered a deformity that crippled his right foot, until 1917 he lived with his lower middle-class Catholic family at Dahlenerstrasse 156. A solid two-story structure, the house survived World War II. The town welcomed him hysterically during his wartime visits, decking the house with swastika banners, but enraged him in 1945 when Rheydt replaced those banners with white flags as American troops approached. He swore terrible vengeance on his townsfolk, a threat he was long past being able to carry out. In 1942, the people had placed Rheydt Castle, the moated, 16th-century chateau overlooking the town, at his disposal; Goebbels resided there during his infrequent visits thereafter. Today a museum, the castle exhibits collections on regional history and the local weaving industry. (Open March 1—October 31, Tuesday—Sunday 10:00—6:00; November 1—February 28, Wednesday, Saturday 11:00—5:00; admission.)

The only Nazi bigwig in Hitler's inner circle who could claim much of an education, Goebbels attended five universities from 1917 and finally took a doctoral degree in literature from Heidel-berg University in 1921; thenceforth he was known as "Doktor Goebbels" in his thuggish milieu. Some of his student rooms included Portstrasse 18 at **Bonn** (1917–18); Breisacherstrasse 2 and Goethestrasse 8 at **Freiburg im Breisgau** (1918); and Blumenstrasse 8 in **Würzburg** (1918–19). He roomed in the Romanstrasse, **Munich**, in 1919 and 1920.

At Hitler's mountain retreat in **Berchtesgaden**, Goebbels maintained chalet quarters near those of his master. American demolition wiped out this entire lavish complex in the final days of World War II (see the entry on Adolf Hitler later in this section).

(See EAST GERMANY in this chapter.)

GOERING, HERMANN WILHELM (1893–1946). While Hitler's henchman and creator of the Luftwaffe liked to think of himself as a medieval paladin, he was in reality a fawning sybarite. Once a skillful pilot who shot down 22 Allied planes during World War I, Goering served as Hitler's toughest, most efficient crony during the early years of National Socialism, but by 1940 had become a ludicrous caricature of himself—a gross, indolent, drug-addicted creature whom not even the Nazis could take seriously. Hitler apparently tolerated him simply for old times' sake. Goering, lest anyone forgets, created the Gestapo and the Nazi concentration camps.

The son of a minor diplomat posted to Haiti, Goering was born in Marienbad Sanatorium at **Rosenheim**. His mother, rejoining her husband in Haiti, left him in **Fürth**, where he lived with a foster family until 1896 and later attended school.

From 1901 to 1913 Goering lived with his parents at Veldenstein Castle, an 18th-century construction built atop the ruins of an 11th-century Franconian fortress. The castle was owned by Ritter Hermann von Epstein, Goering's Jewish godfather and his mother's 15-year lover (Goering's father also continued to live there). "The rich world of his godfather represented medieval Germany," wrote biographers Roger Manvell and Heinrich Fraenkel, "and excited in him a desire for feudal power that he was never to lose." A daredevil lad, Goering liked to scale the sheer walls of the castle. In 1939, with the death of Frau von Epstein, Goering inherited what he always called his "family castle" and spent frequent intervals there, hunting in his 4,000-acre private hunting preserve. The castle stands between **Velden** and Neuhaus about 25 kilometers northeast of Nuremberg. Only private roads approach the castle, though the Nuremberg-Bayreuth railroad line passes it.

During the 1930s Goering built a chalet near Hitler's Berghof at **Berchtesgaden**, the scenic Alpine setting for a Nazi conclave of villas and guest hotels (see the entry on Adolf Hitler later in this section). There, during the last days of World War II, he stored his immense collection of art and antiquities in some 50 nearby rooms; Goering had commandeered a special train to move the loot from his abandoned East German home, Karinhall, while war materiel sat on sidings throughout Germany for lack of locomotives. On April 23, 1945, he was arrested at his Berchtesgaden house by the German SS on the order of a beleaguered Hitler, who accused Goering of treason and ordered him shot. Only the rapidly disintegrating military situation saved him, and Goering turned himself over to American troops a few days later with utmost relief. His chalet was heavily damaged by the Allied bombing raid on April 26, and nothing remains of it today.

Goering's last residence was the Palace of Justice Prison in **Nuremberg**, where he was confined as a war prisoner from August 1945 to October 1946. Imprisonment did wonders for him physically; it weaned him of his drug habit and trimmed his excess weight. Once again he was the vigorous man who had committed himself to Hitler in 1922. Goering occupied a 9-x-13-foot-cell (number 5) and he died there on the eve of his execution, October 15, 1946. Despite their constant surveillance of prisoners and much-touted security precautions, American and British jailers lost several of their top-ranking Nazi prisoners by suicide. For months Goering had had a cyanide pill hidden in his cell, right under his captors' noses, and he finally used it in a last successful bid to outwit them. Some of the nine-month sessions of the International Military Tribunal (Nuremberg trials), where Goering sat in the dock with 20 other top Nazis, were held in the adjacent courtroom 600 of the Palace of Justice. Some 200 other Germans were also tried there for war crimes between 1945 and 1949. The Palace of Justice at Karlstrasse and Augustinerstrasse dates from 1877; previously it was the site of an Augustinian monastery.

(See EAST GERMANY in this chapter; also Chapter 1, AUSTRIA.)

GOETHE, JOHANN WOLFGANG VON (1749–1832). Germany's greatest writer, whose

influence on the national character has been profound, was a native of **Frankfurt am Main**. Goethe's birthplace at Grosser Hirschgraben 23, built about 1590, was originally two Gothic houses; they were purchased by his grandmother in 1733 and joined together by his father in 1755. Acquired in 1863 by the Freies Deutsches Hochstift, which still owns and maintains it, the yellow-stucco house was reduced to ashes by a bombing raid on March 22, 1944, but by 1951 had been fully reconstructed using many of the original materials. Today the three-story dwelling where Goethe lived with his patrician family until 1775 appears exactly as he knew it and contains numerous items and utensils familiar to the family. The ground floor remains almost entirely original with its stone flooring and walls. The "Peking room" on the first floor, the best in the house, was used for family gatherings and celebrations. Also on this floor are the music room, where Goethe played the cello and his musical family practiced on the piano and lute, and Goethe's small office, in which he

GOETHE'S BIRTHPLACE. Meticulously reconstructed after a 1944 bomb demolished it, Grosser Hirschgraben 23 in **Frankfurt** is Germany's foremost Goethe museum. The poet, born in 1749, lived here with his prosperous family until 1755. This cultivated household provided a notable intellectual background for the "last Renaissance man" of Europe.

began his legal practice. Goethe's birth room is on the second floor. On the third floor, the poet's study contains his bureau-desk and furniture items owned by Lotte Buff, his model for the character "Lotte" in his novel *The Sorrows of Young Werther* (1774). In the adjacent room stands the high desk where he wrote *Werther* and the first version of *Faust* (1808), and the toy puppet theater he received as a Christmas gift from his grandmother. Three museum rooms, probably servants' quarters, trace the development of the Faust legend and contain drawings by Goethe plus numerous paintings and engravings. In the garden below, a lime tree planted on Goethe's birthday in 1825 survives. Annexed to the house on the north, the Goethe Museum contains an archive of 16,000 manuscripts as well as a wealth of pictorial matter and books relating to the poet and his times. More than 100,000 tourists visit annually. (House and museum open April 1–September 30, Monday—Saturday 9:00—6:00, Sunday 10:00—1:00; October 1—March 31, Monday—Saturday 9:00—4:00, Sunday 10:00—1:00; 28-28-24; admission.)

Exhibits: During World War II many German soldiers carried copies of Goethe's *Faust* in their knapsacks. "The Faust legend," wrote Terence Prittie, "is almost certainly a part of the German enigma, whereby a single nation has produced artists, composers, philosophers, thinkers and poets in profusion—as well as Hitler, the most terrible mass murderer in human history." Kenneth Rexroth, who called Goethe "the only major poet produced by the business ethic," said that "*Faust*, as a

moral tract, is as dangerous as the hydrogen bomb." The Goethe Museum at Jägerhofstrasse 1 in **Düsseldorf** displays a special room devoted to the Faust legend and to Goethe's adaptation of it (see the entry on Johann Faust earlier in this section). The 30,000 or so exhibits in the museum include many of his manuscripts, sketches, portraits, and first editions. The building itself is a copy of a house that Goethe had admired (Open Tuesday—Sunday 10:00—5:00; 44–69–35; admission.)

Goethe memorabilia is also displayed in the Museum of Local Life at Kirchstrasse 7 in **Emmendingen** (inquire locally for admission information).

Places associated with Goethe's literary characters include the Rossmarkt in **Frankfurt am Main**, the former town execution site where Margarete Brandt, prototype for Faust's Margaret, died in 1772 for killing her own child.

In **Wetzlar**, "Lotte's House," the home of Lotte Buff, the fiancée of "Young Werther" and Goethe's own hopeless love, stands at what is now Lottestrasse 8-10; it exhibits material on Goethe, and first editions of *Werther*. (Open Tuesday—Saturday 9:00—12:00, 2:00—5:00, Sunday 9:00—12:00; admission.) The "Jerusalem House," home of the tragic K. W. Jerusalem who shot himself in 1772 and provided Goethe's prototype for Werther, stands in the Schillerplatz. The book provoked a wave of suicides among young German romantics. Memorabilia of Jerusalem are exhibited. (Inquire locally for admission information.)

(See EAST GERMANY in this chapter; also Chapter 1, AUSTRIA, SWITZERLAND; also Chapter 2, FRANCE; also Chapter 8, ITALY.)

GRIMM, JAKOB LUDWIG (1785–1863).
GRIMM, WILHELM KARL (1786–1859).

Two of nine children, these scholars, librarians, philologists, folklorists, and collectors of the German oral traditions eventually published as *Grimm's Fairy Tales* (1812–15) were also inseparable lifelong companions. Their birthplace and home in **Hanau** until 1791 is now long gone.

Their childhood home in **Steinau** (1791–96) stands at Brüder-Grimm-Strasse 80. Called the "Tribunal" ("Amtshaus") because of their father's position as justice of the peace, the large house faces an attractive courtyard. The father died there in 1796. (Inquire locally for admission information.)

A PARLOR ROOM IN GOETHE'S BIRTHPLACE. Original furnishings of the house had been safely removed before its 1944 destruction, so this reconstructed parlor containing the family's "Sunday best" would look quite familiar to the poet today.

From 1805 to 1830 and again from 1838 to 1841, the brothers resided in **Kassel**, where they worked as court librarians to King Jérôme Bonaparte of Westphalia and to the Hessian elector. They probably resided during most of these periods in Wilhelmshohe Castle, the 18th-century palace surmounting the city some 14 kilometers west of central Kassel. There Napoleon's brother, King Jérôme Bonaparte, held a brilliant court from 1807 to 1813; most of the palace furnishings reflect his era and occupancy. Much later (1870), Napoleon III was confined there after his defeat at Sedan. Galleries in the castle also display art of the classical period, plus Dutch and Flemish masters. Kaiser Wilhelm II used the palace as his frequent summer residence (see entry on Wilhelm II later in this section.) From 1822 to 1824 the Grimms lived in one of the gate watchtowers. A massive forested park caps the entire top of the hill, providing a scenic view of the city and setting for the castle. Palace and park are approached via the Wilhelmshöher Allee. (Open Tuesday—Sunday, 10:00—5:00; admission.)

At **Göttingen** the brothers taught in the famed Göttingen University from 1830 to 1838. The house where they resided and also lectured is marked at Goetheallee 6. Expelled from Göttingen for leading a political protest against the ruling king of Hanover, they were welcomed in Berlin, where they spent the rest of their lives.

Exhibits: At **Steinau** the Palace Museum displays a memorial collection to the brothers. (Guided tours Tuesday—Sunday 10:00—12:00, 1:00—4:00; admission.)

The Brothers Grimm Museum at Schöne Aussicht 2 in **Kassel** displays many relics including manuscripts, portraits, letters, and drawings. (Open Tuesday—Friday 10:00—6:00, Saturday—Sunday 10:00—1:00; admission.)

Nearby, in the village of **Niederzwehren**, stands the dwelling of the real "author" of the tales, if folk stories can ever be said to issue from a single source. Katharina Viehmann, the "fairy-tale woman" from whom the brothers derived most of the stories they later compiled into their classic collection, lived at what is now (the somewhat cavalierly named) Brüder-Grimm-Strasse 46. The brothers made copious notes during their frequent visits there. The house is not open to the public.

The Bergwinkel Museum in the 1440 castle at **Schlüchtern** also exhibits Grimm memorabilia. (Inquire locally for admission information.)
(See EAST GERMANY in this chapter.)

GUTENBERG, JOHANNES (1398–1468). A native of **Mainz**, the printer and goldsmith whose original name was Gensfleisch, and who became famous for his invention of movable type, resided there for most of his life. Gutenberg's patrician birthplace and virtually lifelong home was a three-story house at the intersection of Christofsstrasse and Schusterstrasse. It is long gone.

Exhibit: The first Bible ever printed came from Gutenberg's press at **Mainz** in 1454. Today 48 complete or partial Gutenberg Bibles still exist. For this accomplishment the printer paid a heavy price: the entire project was done on credit, and when Gutenberg could not pay, he was forced to abandon his shop, tools, and Bibles to his partner-creditor. It is said that he died destitute. The Gutenberg Museum at Liebfrauenplatz 5 is a reconstruction of the printing shop where for two years he laboriously hand-fashioned some 46,000 pieces of type while fending off lawsuits and loan collectors. A hand press like the one he used, a Gutenberg Bible, and other early examples of printing are on display. A film and exhibits on bookbinding are also shown. (Open Tuesday—Saturday 10:00—6:00, Sunday 10:00—1:00; closed January; free.)
(See Chapter 2, FRANCE.)

HEGEL, GEORG WILHELM FRIEDRICH (1770–1831). The idealist philosopher, whose dialectics profoundly influenced the study of history, was a native of **Stuttgart**, born at Eberhardstrasse 53. The house where he spent most of his childhood until 1788 stood at Langessstrasse 7; it was destroyed in an air raid during World War II.

In **Bamberg** Hegel lived at Pfahlplätzchen 1 from 1806 to 1808 and there wrote *The Phenomenology of the Spirit* (1807). The house is marked with a tablet.
(See EAST GERMANY in this chapter.)

HEINE, HEINRICH (1797–1856). This lyric poet, probably Germany's most popular writer next to Goethe, caused the Nazis much embarrassment because he was Jewish. Though they struck his name from his works, they never even tried to prohibit the quoting of them, so deeply embedded were they in German culture. Heine was born in **Düsseldorf**, the son of a merchant, at Bolkerstrasse 53, a small one-story house where he lived until 1809. The front of the house was entirely rebuilt in 1821, and the dwelling itself was demolished in 1890; the present house is a "reconstructed reconstruction" and was completed after bomb damage during World War II. From 1809 to 1819 Heine lived with his family across the street at Bolkerstrasse 44, which survives as the inn "Zum Goldenen Kessel." In this street the poet watched Napoleon I parade through the town he had just occupied. From then on, Heine was a lifelong Francophile, and he eventually moved permanently to Paris.

In **Göttingen**, where Heine attended the university in 1820–21 and 1824–25, graduating as Doctor of Laws, he lodged at Weenderstrasse 50. The house is marked.

Heine lived in **Munich** in 1827 and 1828; the house is marked at Hackenstrasse 7.

Exhibits: In **Düsseldorf** the Heine Archive at Bilkestrasse 14 holds the largest collection of his manuscripts, including his best-known poem "Die Lorelei" (1827), which Goebbels's propaganda ludicrously ascribed to "an unknown author." Also displayed are Heine letters, his personal library, death mask, and books by and about him. (Open Monday—Friday 9:00—4:00; 42–24–25; admission.)

Hamburg, where he resided briefly at various times during the 1820s, displays Heine autographs and portraits at the State and University Library, Moorweidenstrasse 40 (inquire locally for admission information); and at the Historical Museum, Holstenwall 24 (open Tuesday—Sunday 10:00—5:00; admission). The building occupied by Heine's publishers, Hoffmann und Campe, also bears a marker at Harvestehuder Weg 41.

(See Chapter 3, PARIS; also Chapter 6, LONDON.)

HESSE, HERMANN (1877–1962). The novelist and 1946 Nobel Prize winner, whose works explored the "physical versus spiritual" theme in human nature, did most of his major writing in Switzerland, his home after 1912. A native of the Black Forest region, his four-story birthplace stands at Marktplatz 6 in **Calw**. The family moved in 1881 to Switzerland, then returned to Calw in 1886, residing at Bischofstrasse 48. This was Hesse's home until 1889 and again at intervals from 1893 to 1902. Today it is the Calw Regional

Museum and Hesse Memorial. Memorabilia of the writer are displayed. (Open Monday—Friday 2:00—4:00, Saturday 2:00—5:00, Sunday 10:00—12:00; 07051–1951; free.)

At **Tübingen**, where Hesse worked in a bookshop from 1895 to 1899, he lodged in a desolate ground-floor room at Herrenbergerstrasse 28; there he read widely and began a lifelong habit of self-education.

From 1904 to 1912 he lived with his first wife, Maria Bernoulli, in the village of **Gaienhofen**, at first renting a two-story 17th-century house on the village square opposite the church. In 1907 he built a two-story brick house, the area's first villa, on a hill overlooking the village and this remained his home until 1912. Both houses remain privately occupied.

(See Chapter 1, SWITZERLAND.)

HIMMLER, HEINRICH (1900–1945). "Had he stayed in his rightful place in society," wrote one biographer, "he could have been an overefficient and priggish executive, a small-time official or minor educationalist." Instead he became the architect of the Holocaust, chief of the Gestapo, and the most feared man in Nazi Germany, even among his nefarious colleagues. Like all the top Nazis, he was good to his wife, dog, and children; the atrocities he unleashed on others, however, will probably never be fully gauged. Unlike the more intelligent and cynical Goering and Goebbels, who adjusted their bigotries to fit policy, Himmler was anti-Semitic from rabid conviction. His mild, bespectacled appearance masked a rigid mind of appalling density which was coupled with a bureaucratic talent for organization and intrigue.

The son of a schoolmaster, Himmler was born in a second-floor flat at Hildegardstrasse 2 in **Munich**, which was his home during his first year. His childhood home of longest duration (1904–13) was a third-floor apartment at Amalienstrasse 86. As a student at the Technical High School, he occupied a room at Amalienstrasse 28 (1919–20), and took his meals in a boardinghouse at Jägerstrasse 8.

Other early homes included Theresienstrasse 39 in **Passau** (1902–04); Altstadt 1-1/2 in **Landshut** (1913–19); and an unidentified parental home in **Ingolstadt** (1919–22).

Precise locations of Himmler's later addresses are difficult to document. His first married home with Margarete Concercowo in 1928 was a small farm she bought at Waltrudering, a **Munich** suburb, where they raised produce and poultry.

With his rise in the Nazi hierarchy during the 1930s, he bought a villa called "Lindenfycht" near **Gmund** at the head of Lake Tegernsee. There he installed his wife and daughter more or less permanently but rarely stayed for lengthy intervals himself.

He also kept mistress Hedwig Potthast, by whom he had two children, in his villa near Berchtesgaden at **Schönau**.

Exhibits: Himmler's memorials are the World War II concentration camp sites where his SS apparatus murdered millions of Germans and other Europeans with terrible efficiency. No visitor who wants to "know Germany" can afford to bypass these graveyards which represent a 12-year period of barbarism unequaled in history. Prominent evidence of Himmler's works exists at **Bergen**-Belsen (see the entry on Anne Frank earlier in this section), **Dachau, Flossenbürg**, and other places. Access to the camp sites, with their mounds and monuments, is well marked by directional signs. (See EAST GERMANY in this chapter.)

HITLER, ADOLF (1889–1945). It was hard to believe that anyone could take him seriously, this uncouth, compulsively talkative, Chaplinesque ex-corporal with his plastered cowlick and scowling features. It wasn't as if he concealed his intentions—his *Mein Kampf* (1924) laid it all out rather plainly. Unfortunately, few people read the book, and those who did couldn't or wouldn't believe he was serious—thus few did take him seriously until it was far too late.

A native of Austria, Hitler made his permanent home in **Munich** from 1913, entering Germany to avoid military service for the Austrian monarchy he despised. His first lodging in the city was a dismal rented room at Schleissheimerstrasse 34. In 1920, following his six-year term in the German army, he occupied two rooms on the first floor of a house at Thierchstrasse 41, where he began his political activism and where he returned after his Landsberg imprisonment in 1924.

By 1929 he had transformed the tiny German Workers' Party, which he had joined as its seventh member, into the National Socialist German Workers' Party—a violent, brawling organization that attracted numerous disillusioned World War I veterans—and had become its *Fuehrer* (leader). Also in 1929, describing himself in the city directory as a "painter and writer," he moved

into quarters that would remain his private residence for the rest of his life, a nine-room flat on the second story of Prinzregentenplatz 16. Hitler resided with his niece, Angela "Geli" Raubal, until the latter's suicide there in 1931. (Precise circumstances of their relationship and her death have never been satisfactorily explained. For weeks afterward, Hitler was inconsolable and talked of suicide himself. According to his own statement, she was the only woman he ever loved.) Heavy security was maintained at Hitler's flat from 1933 on, and a large staff was kept on hand for his occasional visits thereafter from Berlin. This building remained almost untouched by bombing in World War II.

Hitler's official residence in Munich from 1937 was the "Fuehrerbau," which stood at Arcisstrasse 12 near the Königsplatz. Though he seldom actually resided there, he often used it for conferences and party occasions. There on September 29–30, 1938, the Munich Pact, which sacrificed Czechoslovakia to Hitler's takeover and has become a synonym for appeasement, was signed by Hitler, Italian dictator Benito Mussolini, French premier Edouard Daladier, and British prime minister Neville Chamberlain. It was a last, desperate and ultimately futile attempt to avoid war by giving Hitler what he wanted. The site of the Fuehrerbau is now occupied by the 1957 Amerika-Haus, a conference center for the purpose of furthering German-American relations.

Hitler's Munich *Putsch* of 1923, in which he attempted to seize control of the Bavarian government, resulted in his imprisonment for high treason at Landsberg Prison, located 80 kilometers west of Munich at **Landsberg am Lech**. There, along with some 40 other Nazis, Hitler spent slightly over a year (though he had been sentenced to five years) in rather comfortable circumstances; he ate well and received many gifts and visitors. It was there, too, that Hitler began dictating *Mein Kampf* to his secretary, Rudolf Hess, who voluntarily shared his imprisonment for this purpose. Hitler occupied room seven, a large, sunny chamber on the first floor. "Without my imprisonment," he said long afterward, "*Mein Kampf* would never have been written. That period gave me the chance of deepening various notions for which I then had only an instinctive feeling." Loaded with pretention and tiresome repetition, "*Mein Kampf* is a remarkably interesting book for anyone trying to understand Hitler's mind," wrote biographer

Alan Bullock, "but as a party tract or a political best-seller it was a failure, which few, even among the party members, had the patience to read."

Soon after his release on parole in 1925, Hitler rented Haus Wachenfeld, a modest villa built by a Hamburg merchant about 1910 and located on the Obersalzberg above **Berchtesgaden** in the Bavarian Alps. There he brought his widowed half-sister, Angela Raubal, and her 17-year-old daughter, "Geli," to keep house for him, and finished dictating *Mein Kampf*. He bought the chalet a few years later, and enlarged and remodeled it in 1935; it then became known as the Berghof. It was dominated by a stone porch and huge picture window with a grand view of the Untersberg, the mountain where in German mythology Charlemagne sleeps and will one day arise to restore the German empire: "It is no accident that I have my residence opposite it," said Hitler. According

AERIAL VIEW OF HITLER'S BERGHOF. Taken September 1, 1936, this photograph reveals the extensive Nazi conclave that had grown around the fuehrer's alpine retreat near **Berchtesgaden**, most of it built with little regard for the landscape's matchless scenic values. The area bristled with security emplacements of various kinds. A prominent feature of Hitler's chalet was the large stone terrace fronting the slope below. American bombers leveled almost every visible structure shown here just before the war's end in 1945.

to his favorite architect Albert Speer, Hitler's self-designed ground plan for the Berghof, "would have been graded D by any professor at an institute of technology." Hitler probably spent more time there than at any of his other residences. Eva Braun supplanted Angela Raubal as Hausfrau in 1936, and Hitler entertained many statesmen, including Chamberlain and Austrian chancellor Kurt von Schuschnigg, whom he mercilessly browbeat. A large complex of security buildings, SS barracks, guest hotels, and housing areas soon grew around the Berghof nucleus. All of the top Nazis and their entourages swarmed to the area, building their own Alpine chalets and setting up office quarters. Hitler's private henchman, Martin Bormann, bought up acres of the surrounding countryside, forcing owners of centuries-old farmsteads to sell. Bormann also had a huge network of underground tunnels and bunkers constructed—some 79 of them, with machine-gun emplacements at their entrances—and succeeded in despoiling the matchless Alpine scenery with his roads and construction sites. Even Hitler spoke wistfully of looking for a quieter mountain retreat after the war. Most subsurface construction occurred in 1943, with imported Czech and Italian labor. Despite Albert Speer's pleas for the release of these men and their supplies for urgent wartime tasks, Bormann kept the crews at work until the final weeks of the war. Eventually the restricted security area covered some seven square kilometers; it was surrounded by chain-link fences, barbed wire, and patrol outposts. Hitler's last lengthy stay there was from February to July 1944, the period when the Allies invaded Normandy. A heavy bombing raid on April 26, 1945, left the entire complex in ruins—ruins which were soon pilfered by the local population and American troops. Every vestige of the complex was soon razed; only a few basement walls mark the Berghof site, and the tunnel network is blocked with rubble. The Bavarian government, embarrassed by the huge number of tourists eager to see the Berghof site and the underground complex, banned the publicizing of the area in 1978 but thousands of visitors still come each year. The Obersalzburg is approached via Road 319 up a very steep gradient that climbs about four kilometers east from Berchtesgaden.

Several kilometers above the Berghof site survives the only remnant of Hitler's works in the area: the "Tea House," a one-story stone lodge on the summit of Mount Kehlstein, presented to him

"NOW THAT I KNOW MEN, I PREFER DOGS." So said Adolf Hitler, but even dogs and children shied away from the leader of the "master race." On the terrace of the Berghof about 1938, he poses with "Blondi," the shepherd dog he poisoned before his own suicide in 1945, and with his longtime secret mistress Eva Braun, who died with him in Berlin. Today hardly a trace remains of this mountainside villa where so many plans for war were hatched.

as a 50th birthday gift in 1939 by Bormann. The latter employed 3,000 workers for three years to blast a one-lane road into the mountainside for access. The last 400 feet was by vertical tunnel and a large brass-lined elevator, which still functions. The engineering feat was impressive. Hitler himself only ascended to the lodge five times. American troops christened it the "Eagle's Nest" in 1945; it was narrowly saved from demolition after the war. Owned today by the Bavarian government, it is operated by the Berchtesgaden Alpine Association. Thousands of tourists ascend here each year by postal bus (the only vehicle authorized) and elevator. The lodge itself is now an inn called the Kehlsteinhaus, with a panoramic Alpine view that is spectacular. (Bus-shuttle service from the Obersalzberg, mid-May—mid-October, every half hour 8:30—6:00; fare.)

Bad Godesberg, one of Germany's oldest spas and now a residential suburb of Bonn and center of the international diplomatic community, was a favorite Hitler retreat from the 1920s. He usually resided at the Rheinhotel Dreesen, Rheinaustrasse 1, which was operated by an early Nazi crony. "The Nazi leader had often sought out the hotel," wrote Wiliam L. Shirer, "as a place of refuge where he could collect his thoughts and resolve his hesitations." There, in 1934, he set into motion the "blood purge" of the SA organization and its leader, Ernst Roehm. In 1938 he conferred at the hotel with British prime minister Neville Chamberlain during the days preceding the disastrous Munich Pact, a meeting vividly described by Shirer in his *Berlin Diary* (1941).

In **Nuremberg**, scene of the annual Nazi party congresses (see *Exhibits* below), Hitler and his deputy, Rudolf Hess, always stayed at the Deutscher Hof, still a functioning hotel at Frauentorgraben 29.

Exhibits: Though negative monuments to the

Hitler regime abound in Germany if one knows where to look for them (e.g., building ruins, concentration camp sites, war cemeteries), important auxiliary sites associated with the fuehrer himself remain, of course, unmarked, and most Germans crave poor memories in the matter. Nevertheless it is not a bad thing to remember Hitler—for both historical and moral reasons. Thus, despite understandable German preferences for showing us their wine festivals, Rhine cruises, and Black Forest clocks, there is at least equal relevance in viewing reminders of a Germany that has had somewhat more influence, in one way or another, on most of us.

In **Munich**, birthplace of the Nazi movement, the scene of Hitler's audacious *Putsch* in November 1923 was the 19th-century Bürgerbräukeller, a large yellow-brown beer hall at Kellerstrasse 4 near the Rosenheimerplatz. From 1933 to 1939 annual celebrations were held there on November 8 to commemorate the failed coup, and Hitler always addressed these meetings. A cleverly planted time bomb wrecked the hall in 1939 just 12 minutes after Hitler's departure from the podium, killing seven people (including Eva Braun's father) and wounding 63 others. After the war it was learned that the bombing was apparently instigated by the Gestapo and sanctioned by Hitler as a means of increasing his popularity in the country after the beginning of the war. The restored beer hall became a Nazi shrine; it was sheltered by a thick reinforced concrete pad, giving it the aspect, said one observer, of a "huge trolley barn." After 1939 the anniversaries were held in another hall, the Löwenbräukeller. Hitler last addressed his cronies there in 1942 during the German defeat at Stalingrad. Allied bombing destroyed part of the Bürgerbräukeller, but a portion of the building survived the war and served as an American military club until the mid-1950s, when it reopened to ordinary customers. It was finally razed entirely in 1979 for an urban renewal project, and no evidence remains today of where it stood. The Löwenbräukeller survives in the Stiglmaierplatz.

The site of the shooting confrontation between the 2,000-strong Nazis and the Munich police on the morning of November 9, 1923, was at the end of the narrow Residenzstrasse near the Odeonsplatz. Hitler fled the scene as 16 of his compatriots and three policemen died, and Hermann Goering was badly wounded (see the entry on Goering earlier in this section). Ten years would elapse before Hitler achieved what he started out to do on this street.

The Brown House, which Hitler bought in 1930 to house the party central offices, was the former Barlow Palais, an 1828 structure located at Briennerstrass 45. Bombs destroyed it during the war.

In **Nuremberg**, the site of the Nazi party congresses staged each September from 1933 through 1939 was the Reichsparteitagsgelande, a complex of buildings and grounds that Hitler intended to make the party capital because he considered Nuremberg, with its medieval aspect, the "most German" of any city in the nation. Director Leni Riefenstahl filmed *Triumph of the Will*, technically the best propaganda film ever made, during the 1934 party rally. From the 1935 congress at Nuremberg came the notorious Nuremberg Laws, which deprived German Jews of citizenship and civil rights and instituted a series of pogroms. Several of the massive concrete and granite structures of Luitpold Arena, too costly to dismantle, survive near Zeppelin Field, which is now used as the city fairgrounds parking lot. Flower beds and race tracks now cover most of this area where thousands of uniformed Nazis annually massed to renew their fanaticism. It is located in the southeastern suburb of Dutzendteich.

(See EAST GERMANY, BELGIUM in this chapter; also Chapter 1, AUSTRIA; also Chapter 5, ENGLAND.)

IBSEN, HENRIK (1828–1906). The Norwegian playwright resided in **Munich** for two productive periods. From 1875 to 1878 he lived in a ground-floor apartment of a house that stood at Schönfeldstrasse 17; there he wrote *Pillars of Society* (1877). He occupied a large apartment at Amalienstrasse 50 in 1879 and 1880. His later residence (1885–91), an elegant apartment, survives at Maximilianstrasse 32. Ibsen wrote *Rosmersholm* (1886), *The Lady from the Sea* (1888), and *Hedda Gabler* (1890) there.

(See NORWAY in this chapter; also Chapter 8, ITALY.)

KEPLER, JOHANNES (1571–1630). The birthplace of the man who "explored" the solar system and formulated the laws of planetary motion stood in **Weil der Stadt**. It was his home until 1576. Kepler's grandparents owned the house, which eventually burned down in a fire that destroyed much of the town in 1648. The present house on the site of what is now Keplergasse 2 dates from around that time and was probably built to a similar design. Now the Kepler Museum, the house displays collections on the astronomer's life and work. (Open Monday—Friday 9:00—12:00, 2:00—4:00, Saturday 10:00—12:00, 2:00—5:00, Sunday 11:00—12:00, 2:00—5:00; 07033-6011; admission.)

In **Maulbronn** Kepler attended the old Protestant (formerly Cistercian) seminary, founded in 1147, from 1586 to 1589. The abbey buildings where Kepler resided are surrounded by a long perimeter wall. (Open Tuesday—Sunday 8:00—12:00, 2:00—6:00; admission.)

Kepler's last lodging, the 16th-century home of a friend, stands at what is now Keplerstrasse 5 in **Regensburg** and is also a Kepler Museum with exhibits on the astronomer's contributions to science. Kepler died in the house after a brief illness. (Inquire locally for admission information.) (See Chapter 1, AUSTRIA.)

LENIN, VLADIMIR (1870–1924). As an exile from the czarist regime in Russia, Lenin roomed in **Munich** during 1900 and 1901 at Kaiserstrasse 53. He published the revolutionary paper *Iskra* during this residence.

(See EAST GERMANY, FINLAND in this chapter; also Chapter 1, SWITZERLAND; also Chapter 3, PARIS; also Chapter 6, LONDON.)

LISZT, FRANZ (1811–1886). The last lodging of the pianist-composer, whose daughter Cosima married composer Richard Wagner in 1870, was in **Bayreuth** where he came in July 1886 to attend the Wagner Festival. Suffering from pneumonia, Liszt lay alone and neglected while the busy festival activities went on around his lodging house at Siegfriedstrasse 1. He died there about a week after his arrival.

Liszt tomb: Municipal Cemetery, **Bayreuth**.

(See EAST GERMANY in this chapter; also Chapter 1, AUSTRIA, SWITZERLAND; also Chapter 3, PARIS; also Chapter 8, ITALY.)

LUTHER, MARTIN (1483–1546). In **Augsburg** the beleaguered monk attended a hearing in 1518, the year after he had dared to question the Roman Catholic doctrine of indulgences and been accused of heresy. The result of the hearing was Luther's excommunication. His residence during those anxious weeks was the Carmelite monastery, of which St. Anne's Church in the Annastrasse is the only surviving portion.

During the Imperial Diet session at Augsburg in 1530, the Protestants formulated the Augsburg Confession—which has since become the classic statement of Lutheran doctrine—and Luther himself watched events from a six-month haven at **Coburg**. Veste Coburg, the 16th-century fortress of the Saxe-Coburgs, one of the largest bastions in Germany, was his residence. For much of his stay, Luther suffered ill-health. Located two kilometers east of town via the Festungstrasse, the Prince's Palace in the fortress grounds displays Luther's room together with a collection of autographs, memorabilia, and portraits. (Open April 1—October 31, Tuesday—Sunday 9:00—12:00, 2:00—4:00; November 1—March 31, Tuesday—Sunday 2:00—3:30; admission.)

Nothing remains of Luther's 1521 residence in **Worms**, where he appeared before Emperor Charles V and refused to revoke his heresy. A shopping mall now occupies the site. The bishop's residence, where the hearings were held and where Luther supposedly uttered those ringing Protestant words "Here I stand. I can do no other," stood in what is now a garden alongside the 12th-century St. Peter's Cathedral. "Here before Kaiser and Reich stood Martin Luther," says the memorial tablet.

(See EAST GERMANY in this chapter.)

MAHLER, GUSTAV (1860–1911). The Austrian composer and conductor occupied a second-floor apartment at Obere Karlsstrasse 17 in **Kassel** for a year while directing the local orchestra (1883–84).

In **Hamburg**, where he conducted the State Opera from 1891 to 1897, he resided at several apartment addresses including Bundesstrasse 10, Parkallee 12, and Bismarckstrasse 86.

(See EAST GERMANY in this chapter; also Chapter 1, AUSTRIA.)

MANN, THOMAS (1875–1955). Novelist and 1929 Nobel Prize winner, Mann resided during his early years in **Lübeck**. The patrician "Buddenbrookhaus" at Mengstrasse 4, his ancestral home, was owned by his paternal grandparents and dates from 1758. Mann and his elder brother, novelist Heinrich Mann, spent much time there until 1891, but it was neither his birthplace, as is often claimed, nor the main residence of his parental family. An Allied air raid in 1942 gutted most of the baroque building, but the facade survived and the rest was later rebuilt. Though Volksbank offices now occupy the house, a mezzanine room has been restored to the period style of Mann's first novel, *Buddenbrooks* (1901), which used the house and city for its setting. From 1875 to 1881 Mann lived with his parents at Breitestrasse 36; the house was demolished after severe bomb damage in World War II and another building now occupies the site. Mann's father built a town house in 1881 at Beckergrube 52, where the family resided until the father's death in 1891. Roeckstrasse 9 was Mann's last home in Lübeck (1891–92); he lived there with his widowed mother and sisters.

From 1894 to 1933 the novelist resided at a number of addresses in **Munich**. His earlier lodgings included an eight-room, ground-floor apartment at Rambergstrasse 2 from 1894 to 1896, again with his mother and sisters; Feilitzschstrasse 32 (1899–1900), where he completed *Buddenbrooks;* Konradstrasse 11, another ground-floor flat where he lived from 1902 to 1905 and wrote *Tonio Kröger* (1903); Franz-Josephstrasse 2, his first married home with Katia Pringsheim (1905–10), a furnished apartment given to the couple by his father-in-law; and Mauerkircherstrasse 13, from 1910 to 1914. By 1914 Mann had become prosperous from his writing and built a three-story stone house at Poschingerstrasse 1 (now Thomas-Mann-Allee 10) in the suburb of Bogenhausen. There he wrote many of his best-known works, including *The Magic Mountain* (1924). Because of Nazi harassment and the threat of arrest, Mann left the country in 1933 and never returned to live in Germany. Nazi authorities confiscated the property, which suffered severe damage during the war.

The novelist's favorite country retreat was the Landhaus Thomas Mann, a two-story Bavarian villa he built in 1908 at **Bad Tölz** and continued to use during summers from 1908 to 1917. It stands at Heissstrasse 25. Mann wrote *Death in Venice* (1913) there.

Exhibits: In **Lübeck** the Schabbelhaus Restaurant at Mengstrasse 48-50 displays a Thomas Mann Room and has books, autographs, and Mann relics on view.

The Thomas Mann Collection of the University Library at **Düsseldorf**, Konigsallee 22, may be seen only by appointment with the secretary of the collection. First editions, photographs, letters, and other documents are displayed. (Phone 32-78-17.)

(See Chapter 1, SWITZERLAND; also Chapter 8, ITALY.)

MARX, KARL (1818–1883). A native of **Trier**, the Socialist philosopher lived in his birthplace at Brückenstrasse 10 until 1819. Nazis used this 1727 structure from 1933 to 1945 as the publication center for the newspaper *Nationalblatt*. It was returned to the German Social Democratic Party after the war and now displays an impressive permanent exhibit on Marx's life and works, including letters and memorabilia. Established by an international committee of Social Democrats, the birthplace museum has become a virtual shrine for Marxists from all over the world. (Open daily, 10:00—1:00, 3:00—6:00, except closed Monday morning; admission.) A much more important Marx dwelling in Trier, from the standpoint of his growth and scholarly development, is Simeonstrasse 8. His father bought this 1760-built house near the Porta Nigra in 1819. Marx lived there until 1835 and again in 1841 and 1842, just before he left Germany permanently. An optical shop now occupies the ground floor.

At **Bonn**, Marx attended the university in 1835 and 1836, residing in rooms at Josephstrasse 764.

Exhibit: Marx's collaborator on the *Communist Manifesto* (1848) and *Das Kapital* (1894) and his fre-

KARL MARX BIRTHPLACE. In West Germany's oldest city of **Trier**, this dwelling became the Socialist philosopher's first home in 1818. The present building, as seen in this 1983 view during the Marx death centennial, is a postwar restoration after Nazis used the house for publishing a party newspaper. It has become a world Marxist shrine.

quent benefactor, Friedrich Engels (1820–1895), is memorialized at **Wuppertal** with a collection on his life and work. (Inquire at Town Hall.)

(See EAST GERMANY, BELGIUM in this chapter; also Chapter 2, FRANCE; also Chapter 3, PARIS; also Chapter 6, LONDON.)

MENDELSSOHN-BARTHOLDY, FELIX (1809–1847).

A native of **Hamburg**, his home until 1811, the Romantic composer lived in a three-story house, now long gone, called "Marten's Mill" on the Elbe River. An anti-Semitic pogrom instituted by the French occupiers of the city caused his family's flight to Berlin.

In **Düsseldorf,** where he served as director of music from 1833 to 1835, Mendelssohn lived at Jan-Wellem-Platz 1 and there composed his oratorio *St. Paul* (1836). This house was destroyed during World War II; the present house on the site is marked with a plaque. Düsseldorf Nazis, ashamed of this resident, melted down Mendelssohn's statue in the Stadttheater. After the war, when Mendelssohn was back in favor, a new bust was unveiled inside the opera house. International musicians reserve a special cynical smile for Düsseldorf.

(See EAST GERMANY in this chapter.)

MOZART, WOLFGANG AMADEUS (1756–1791).

Exhibit: In **Augsburg**, at Frauentorstrasse 30, stands the Mozart Memorial Museum. It occupies the 1719 birthplace of Leopold Mozart, musician-impresario father of the Austrian musical genius. Leopold Mozart lived there until 1737, when he moved to Salzburg. In 1777 Wolfgang Mozart visited his father's Augsburg home and performed a concert in the city; he was treated with considerably more respect than in his native Salzburg. An Augsburg newspaper announced that "Mr. Mozart will do his best to entertain his fellow-citizens for a few hours." From Augsburg, in a typically colloquial letter to his father, Mozart described how he improvised on a theme given to him: "I took the theme for a walk and in the middle I began in the major with something very playful . . . then returned to the theme again, ass-backwards this time." Today the house displays documentation on the Mozart family and memorabilia of both father and son. Concerts of 18th-century music are periodically presented for small audiences by the German Mozart Society. (Open Monday, Wednesday—Friday, 10:00—12:00,

2:00—5:00; Saturday—Sunday 10:00—12:00; admission.) The annual Augsburg Mozart Festival usually occurs in May. For information, write Deutsches Mozartfest, Bahnhofstrasse 11, 8900 Augsburg; or call 0821–25588.

(See Chapter 1, AUSTRIA; also Chapter 3, PARIS; also Chapter 6, LONDON.)

MÜNCHHAUSEN, HIERONYMUS, BARON VON (1720–1797).

How could truth be told if there were no liars? One of the most cheerfully outrageous yarn spinners of all time, Baron Munchhausen is the patron saint of tall-tale artists and tavern heroes everywhere. A soldier by profession, he wrote nothing so far as is known, but his oral tales were widely repeated, compiled, elaborated on, and "improved" by others. His birthplace at **Bodenwerder** (the village was his lifelong home) is now the Town Hall, and there the Baron Münchhausen Museum displays items relating to this refreshing character. (Inquire locally for admission information.)

Münchhausen tomb: Village cemetery, **Bodenwerder**.

NIETZSCHE, FRIEDRICH WILHELM (1844–1900).

In **Bonn**, where he attended the university in 1864 and 1865, the philosopher came under the profound influence of Schopenhauer's work, *World as Will and Idea* (see the entry on Arthur Schopenhauer later in this section). As Will Durant related, "He took the book to his lodgings and read every word of it hungrily. . . The dark color of Schopenhauer's philosophy impressed itself permanently upon his thought." Nietzsche's lodging survives at the corner of the Gudenauergasse and Bonngasse and is marked with a tablet.

(See EAST GERMANY in this chapter; also Chapter 1, SWITZERLAND.)

RICHARD I, COEUR DE LION (1157–1199).

Captured during his return from the Third Crusade, the English king was held for ransom in 1193 by Emperor Heinrich VI. He was not freed until a year later when an enormous sum was transferred from England's coffers. The king's place of confinement was Trifels Castle on a scenic height about seven kilometers southeast of **Annweiler**. An old imperial residence, Trifels once held the royal treasure and is said to have housed the Holy Grail of Arthurian romance. Reconstructed during 1937 in a Romanesque style, it now displays copies of the German imperial crown jewels—plus a magnificent panoramic view of the Wasgau region. (Open February 1—November 30, Tuesday—Sunday 9:00—1:00, 2:00—6:00; admission.)

(See Chapter 1, AUSTRIA; also Chapter 2, FRANCE; also Chapter 5, ENGLAND; also Chapter 6, LONDON.)

RILKE, RAINER MARIA (1875–1926). W. H. Auden called Rilke "the Santa Claus of loneliness," and the novelist and poet's works have drawn increasing interest since his death. Born in Prague, Rilke lodged in **Munich** furnished rooms during World War I. His addresses included the Pension Pfanner at Finkenstrasse 2 (1914); the Villa Alberti at Keferstrasse 2 (1915–17); and Ainmillerstrasse 34 (1918–19).

Earlier (1898), at **Worpswede**, he joined the small artists' colony established there, and he returned at intervals throughout the early 1900s. His first dwelling was the Barkenhof, a frequent meeting place of painters and writers. Later he and his wife, sculptor Clara Westhof, lived in a farmhouse; it has since burned down.

(See Chapter 1, SWITZERLAND; also Chapter 2, FRANCE; also Chapter 3, PARIS.)

ROMMEL, ERWIN (1891–1944). This career soldier and charismatic World War II field marshal—Hitler's favorite general until he was implicated in the 1944 plot to depose the fuehrer—has achieved an almost legendary status for his military prowess as "the Desert Fox." That reputation is largely undeserved, say leading generals of the postwar German Bundeswehr; his strategic understanding was "slight," and he "panicked when faced with great tasks."

A native of **Heidenheim**, where his father taught school, Rommel built his career during World War I as a tank commander, and at various military posts in Germany. His family home with his wife, Lucie Mollin, and their young son, Manfred (who became the Christian Democratic mayor of Stuttgart in 1974), was **Herrlingen**. It was there that he returned in August 1944 to recover after being critically injured in a dive bomber attack. Watched by the Gestapo after the abortive bomb plot against Hitler, Rommel received a sinister visitor in October of that year. General Wilhelm Burgdorf presented him with the fuehrer's ultimatum: stand court martial and be executed, or swallow a cyanide pill and die a hero. To protect his wife and son, Rommel chose

the latter. His death occurred in Burgdorf's staff car parked a few hundred yards from Rommel's home on the Blabeuren road. The official story given to the press was that Rommel had died of a brain hemorrhage.

Four days later at **Ulm**, the 16th-century Town Hall in the Marktplatz was the scene of one of the most lavish state funerals of the Hitler regime—and surely the most disgraceful moment in its own history—as Nazi top brass gathered around Rommel's swastika-bannered coffin and Field Marshal von Rundstedt crowed, "His heart belonged to the fuehrer." Only after the war ended was the true story revealed. Just as sordid, from a military aspect, was how an army once famed for the integrity of its officer corps so abjectly submitted to an obsessed leader whose basic contempt for the German people was boundless.

Rommel tomb: Village cemetery, **Herrlingen**.

RUBENS, SIR PETER PAUL (1577–1640). The Flemish painter, noted for his buxom nudes, was probably a native of Siegen though biographers cannot be certain about this. He lived with his family in **Cologne**, however, from 1578 to 1587 in a now long-gone house that stood at Sternengasse 10. Today it is the site of a telecommunications center.

(See BELGIUM in this chapter; also Chapter 8, SPAIN.)

SCHILLER, FRIEDRICH VON (1759–1805). Schiller was one of Germany's foremost men of letters, and several residences and museums memorialize him. His birthplace and home until 1765 stands at Nikolastorstrasse 31 in **Marbach am Neckar**. The modest half-timbered house displays the single bedsittingroom and tiny kitchen on the ground floor where his mother and army-surgeon father lived. On the floor above, where the artisan owner of the house resided, is a collection of family memorabilia, manuscripts, and portraits. (Open daily 9:00—12:00, 1:00—5:00; admission.)

Schiller attended the Latin school in **Ludwigsburg** from 1766 to 1770. His residences, both now gone, included Mömpelsgardstrasse 26 and Stuttgarterstrasse 26.

Ten kilometers west of **Stuttgart** via the Solitude road stands the 18th-century Solitude Castle, the forest manor where Schiller's father served as an overseer from 1770 and laid out a model tree nursery. It was also the site of the Karlsschule, where Schiller studied law from 1773

BIRTHPLACE OF FRIEDRICH VON SCHILLER. Born in 1759, the man who would become Germany's foremost writer next to Goethe resided in this modest house at **Marbach** until 1765. This old photograph probably dates from around 1900. The house is now a Schiller museum.

to 1775. Exhibits there relate mainly to Württemberg royalty, and to the palace's rococo interior. (Inquire locally for admission information.)

In 1775 the Karlsschule or Akademie transferred to **Stuttgart**; and Schiller, residing there, switched from law to medicine, completing his studies in 1780. The site, just east of the baroque New Castle, which faces the Schlossplatz, is now occupied by the Academy Garden, a pleasant park. Schiller began his first notable play, *The Robbers* (1782), in this military school as an 18-year-old student. Following his graduation he served as a regimental surgeon until he deserted in 1783. He lived at Eberhardstrasse 63; the site is marked.

In 1783 and 1784 Schiller saw his first plays performed at the National Theater in Mannheim. During his period there he fled capture as an army deserter but soon learned that he would not be arrested and returned to Mannheim, residing across the Rhine in Mannheim's twin city of **Ludwigshafen** at what is now Schillerstrasse 6. Portraits, letters, first editions, and Schiller memorabilia are displayed at the house. (Inquire locally for admission information.)

Exhibits: The huge National Schiller Museum surmounts the town of **Marbach am Neckar** on the Schillerhöhe and is the main depository of Schiller documents and relics, as well as those of many other Swabian writers. (Open daily, 9:00—5:00; 07144–6060; admission.)

At **Lorsch**, Schiller's family home from 1765 to 1768, the Museum of Local Life in the restored 12th-century monastery surmounting the village displays memorabilia of the writer's stay. (Inquire locally for admission information.)

(See EAST GERMANY in this chapter.)

SCHOPENHAUER, ARTHUR (1788–1860). The profoundly influential "philosopher of pessimism" resided from 1831 in **Frankfurt am Main**. His home from 1843 stood at Schöne-Aussicht 17. Schopenhauer habitually dined in the Hotel d'Angleterre, which stood at Kaiserstrasse and Bahnhofsplatz.

Earlier, from 1809 to 1811, Schopenhauer taught at the University of **Göttingen**, where he lived at Geismartstrasse 64.

Schopenhauer tomb: New Cemetery, **Frankfurt am Main**.

Exhibit: The Schopenhauer Museum and Archive at Bokkenheimer-Landstrasse 134-8 in **Frankfurt am Main** displays memorabilia of the philosopher plus collections on his life and works. (Inquire locally for admission information.)

SCHUMANN, ROBERT (1810–1856). In 1850 the composer and his wife, piano virtuoso Clara Wieck Schumann, moved to **Düsseldorf**, the final scene of Schumann's creative life. Schumann's mental health was precarious but before it broke completely (in 1854) he attempted to fulfill his duties as conductor of an orchestral and choral society. The Schumanns' first lodging (1850–51) was a now long-gone apartment at the corner of the Grabenstrasse and Alleestrasse, and there the composer produced his last symphony (the *Rhenish*). In 1852 the family of eight moved into a three-story house at Bilkerstrasse 15, which survives and is marked. There Schumann's behavior became increasingly erratic, and he complained of single musical notes sounding continuously in his ears. Young composer Johannes Brahms, a protégé of the couple, spent several weeks with them in 1853 (see the entry on Brahms earlier in this section). On Febuary 27, 1854, clothed only in dressing gown and slippers, the tortured composer flung himself into the Rhine from a bridge. Though rescued, he was no longer able to function, and Clara Schumann was forced to seek institutional care for him.

Schumann's last residence, thus, was an asylum at Endenich, now a part of **Bonn**. There, for his remaining two years, the schizophrenic composer remained isolated from his family at the insistence of the chief physician, and his lucid intervals alternated with frequent relapses. Finally, as he lay dying, Clara and Brahms were allowed to come. "With a great effort he put his arm around me," wrote Clara. "Not for all earthly treasure would I exchange that embrace." Located at Sebastianstrasse 182, the former asylum, now called the Schumannhaus, was partially rebuilt after World War II damage and contains the Bonn municipal library. The Schumann Memorial Room displays letters and documents relating to the composer and his circle. (Open Wednesday—Monday 10:00—12:00, Monday, Friday 4:00—7:00, Wednesday-Thursday 3:00—6:00, Sunday 11:00—1:00; 77–656; free.)

Schumann tomb: Old Cemetery, **Bonn**.

(See EAST GERMANY in this chapter.)

SCHWEITZER, ALBERT (1875–1965).

Exhibit: At Saalgasse 15 in **Frankfurt am Main**, the Schweitzer Memorial Museum and Archive displays collections on the life and work of the scholar, physician, and humanitarian. (Open Monday, Wednesday—Thursday 8:00—4:30, Tuesday 8:00—7:00, Friday 8:00—4:00; 2–04–51; admission.)

(See THE NETHERLANDS in this chapter; also Chapter 2, FRANCE; also Chapter 3, PARIS.)

STRAUSS, RICHARD (1864–1949).
The composer's **Munich** birthplace, which was destroyed during World War II, stood at Altheimereck 2. The site is marked on the brewery building which replaced it. As court conductor for the Bavarian Regent Luitpold, Strauss resided from 1894 to 1898 at two addresses: Hildegardstrasse 2 and Herzog-Rudolfstrasse 2. His major works *Till Eulenspiegel, Thus Spake Zarathustra, Don Quixote* and *Ein Heldenleben* all date from this period.

A favorite vacation resort during this period was the home of his in-laws, the Villa de Ahna at **Marquardstein**.

Strauss built his permanent home overlooking the Krammer River at **Garmisch-Partenkirchen** in 1908. He used it only during summers until about 1930 but finally retired and died there. Erected from the proceeds of his opera *Salome* (1905), the 19-room structure at Zoeppritzstrasse 42 was the place where he composed most of his later orchestral works. Today, as the Strauss Museum, it displays exhibits on his life and works plus original furnishings and memorabilia. (Inquire locally for admission information.)

Strauss tomb: Strauss Museum, **Garmisch-Partenkirchen**.

(See EAST GERMANY in this chapter; also Chapter 1, AUSTRIA.)

WAGNER, RICHARD (1813–1883).
Wagner's towering operas represented the height of Romantic musical development and, to many Germans, the mountainous peak of all music. Whatever his faults of character (and they were many and profound), musically Wagner expressed the German "soul" to a degree that no other composer has remotely equaled. Probably his rabid anti-Semitism, as much as his ponderous, nationalistic themes of German mythology, also made him the Nazis' favorite composer.

Though he endured numerous privations and critical neglect for much of his life, Wagner's final decades were cushioned by the patronage of Bavarian king Ludwig II, the so-called "mad king." Mad or not, Ludwig nevertheless recognized Wagner's genius at a time when hardly anyone else did, idolized him, and brought him to wide recognition. In 1864, when Ludwig ascended the throne, he installed the composer in a palatial mansion at Briennerstrasse 21 in **Munich**, and it become Wagner's residence for the next year. Cosima von Bülow, Wagner's mistress and the wife of conductor Hans von Bülow, came to supervise his household, and Wagner outfitted it lavishly. The premiere of his opera *Tristan und Isolde* was the first fruit of Ludwig's patronage. Wagner's extravagant lifestyle became a national scandal in 1865, however, and forced Ludwig to withdraw support. The mansion itself was a victim of World War II bombing.

In 1872, now married to Cosima, Wagner moved to **Bayreuth**, chose a dramatic hilltop site for his Festspielhaus, and supervised every detail of its construction. In the composer's mind the immediate purpose of the building was to serve as an

THREE VIEWS OF HAUS WAHNFRIED. Richard Wagner designed his final home in **Bayreuth** and made it his permanent residence from 1874. The close frontal view shows the bust of his patron, Bavarian King Ludwig II. Wagner's workroom, where he composed *Parsifal*, now hosts visitors to the house, which is today a memorial dedicated to the composer.

ideal theater for presentations of his *Ring* tetralogy. He laid the foundation stone in 1872, and the first operatic performance was *Das Rheingold* in 1876. Haus Wahnfried, also designed by Wagner and made possible by another substantial gift from Ludwig II, was the composer's permanent home from 1874. There he finished composing the final opera of the *Ring* cycle, *Götterdämmerung*, and wrote *Parsifal* (1882). Wahnfried remained Cosima Wagner's home until her death in 1930. Then it became the home of Wagner's son, Siegfried, and daughter-in-law, Winifred, who welcomed Adolf Hitler there during the 1930s. Bombed in 1945, the stone house has since been restored. Today Wahnfried at Richard-Wagner-Strasse 48 is the Wagner Museum, and displays original furnishings, letters, photographs, and much memorabilia of the composer and his works. It is also the setting of the annual musical festival Wagner originated. Since 1976 it has been the central Wagner Archive for materials by and about the composer. (Open daily, 9:00—5:00; admission.)

Wagner tomb: Haus Wahnfried grounds, **Bayreuth**.

Exhibits: Of Wagner, Richard Anthony Leonard wrote, "there are no longer any legends about him

as a man; his works need none." Stripped of their pretentions—the esoteric philosophizing, mystical allegory, and high-flown poetry—Wagner's works survive because of the music alone. In **Bayreuth** the annual Wagner festivals continue each August, as they have since 1876; they have been directed since 1966 by the composer's grandson, Wolfgang Wagner.

The wood and brick Festspielhaus (see above) at Luitpoldplatz 9 still hosts the *Ring* performances; "the wooden seats are unmercifully uncomfortable," reports Kenneth Bernstein, "but they add to the excellence of the acoustics." (Guided tours April 1—September 30, Tuesday—Sunday 10:00—11:30, 1:30—3:00; 0921–5722; admission.) The Richard Wagner Society at Elsastrasse 5, which maintains most of the Wagner sites in Bayreuth, may be contacted for further information (phone 23713). For information on the annual Wagner festival, write Bayreuther Festspiele, Postfach 2320, 8580 Bayreuth 2; or call Bayreuth 5722.

In **Nuremberg** the Library of the German National Museum at Kornmarkt 1 displays the manuscript of Wagner's *Die Meistersinger von Nürnberg* (1868). (Open Tuesday, Thursday 9:00—5:00, Wednesday 1:00—9:00, Friday 9:00—4:00, Saturday 9:00—1:00; 20–39–71; admission.)

(See EAST GERMANY in this chapter; also Chapter 1, AUSTRIA, SWITZERLAND; also Chapter 2, FRANCE; also Chapter 3, PARIS; also Chapter 8, ITALY.)

WILHELM II (1859–1941). At **Kassel**, where the future World War I kaiser attended school from 1874 to 1877, he occupied quarters in the Prince's Court, Königstrasse. Also near Kassel, the hilltop palace of Wilhelmshohe became his favorite summer residence after he inherited the crown in 1888 (see the entry on the brothers Grimm earlier in this section.)

The Villa Frank in the Koblenzerstrasse at **Bonn** was the crown prince's villa during his attendance at the university there in 1877 and 1878.

(See EAST GERMANY, THE NETHERLANDS in this chapter.)

THE LOW COUNTRIES: BELGIUM, LUXEMBOURG, THE NETHERLANDS

This bell-shaped region shows much less variation in its flat, near-sea-level topography than in the peoples who inhabit the three small nations that occupy it. Containing the densest population in Europe for its size, the Low Country region is also one of the most highly industrialized in the world. In government, its nations cherish democracy with a passion equal only to that of Britain and the Scandinavian countries. One of the most war-torn areas of Europe, it has seen armies of almost every European power come and go, despoiling its landscape, ruining its cities, ravaging its populace. Rarely has it invited or participated in such geopolitical spasms. Again and again, it has raised itself from the infamy of war and claim of the sea. And through centuries of experience it has become a world teacher, not only of patience and survival but of humane prosperity.

An excellent regional guidebook for literary homes and sites in the Low Countries—available, unfortunately, only in French—is the *Guide Littéraire de la Belgique de la Hollande et du Luxembourg* (1972) by Bodart et al.

BELGIUM

A bilingual, bicultural society, Belgium exemplifies a nation with built-in hostilities and conflicts that are nevertheless subordinated to the larger goal of unity. Hearing the hot, sometimes taunting dialogue that occurs between the Dutch-speaking Flemings in the north and the French-speaking Walloons in the south, one might expect the imminent outbreak of civil war on any given day. (Only 15 percent of Belgians speak both languages.) But it has been like that in Belgium since 1830 when the country achieved independence

from the Netherlands. In the final analysis, while tempers occasionally erupt into fisticuffs and street protests, Belgians are Belgians before they are Flemings and Walloons—a fact that less politically sophisticated European nationals find hard to digest. For people or nations unable to get beyond conventional "either-or" types of thinking, Belgian politics tempt disbelief. Still, don't speak French in the north or Dutch in the south if you can avoid it; even "family" tolerance has its limits.

Minus natural geographical frontiers of its own, Belgium has probably been the most walked-upon nation of Europe—a veritable carpet for every power-mad prince and fuehrer who wanted to wipe his feet. Through 20 centuries, from Caesar's legions to Hitler's panzers, every major European power has occupied the country at least once. Waterloo, Ypres, the Bulge were only the most recent battles waged on Belgian soil for European control, warfare that has left Belgium a nation of military cemeteries loaded with non-Belgian graves. "The Belgians don't go to war," as one observer wrote, "the wars come to them." As the northern gateway to France and Germany, through the continental rivers that empty on its North Sea coast, Belgium's location is ideal for commerce but perilous for its national safety, and has always been so.

Antwerp, the world's third largest seaport, is Belgium's largest city. Brussels, the capital, ranks fourth below Ghent and Liege. If Europe can be said to have a capital—or if it ever needs one—that capital may well be Brussels, seat of the multinational European Economic Community—the Common Market which has transformed European economics since World War II. Brussels itself, ironically, is a Flemish island uneasily surrounded by Walloon Belgium.

Belgium's total population numbers about 10 million. The country has had a constitutional monarchy since 1830, with kings from the German Saxe-Coburg family serving as chiefs of state. Belgians clearly know what they want and don't want in a king. The failure of Leopold III to act as they thought proper when Hitler smashed through the country forced the king's postwar abdication in favor of his son, Baudouin I, who still rules. Suffrage is universal in Belgium; in fact, failure to vote results in a fine. According to Dennis Briskin, "The Belgians are Europe's worst drivers. Even the French say so" (new drivers have been licensed only since 1968).

Belgium's most famous progeny have been artists, including the Flemish master Bruegel and Peter Paul Rubens; the last homes of both stand proudly open to the public.

Many of the country's other notable residents have been non-Belgians who found Brussels, especially, a civilized refuge in time of trouble.

BAUDELAIRE, CHARLES PIERRE (1821–1867). The French poet resided from 1864 to 1866 in **Brussels**, where he was stricken with the fatal syphilitic complication that paralyzed him and ravaged his mind before it killed him. His main residence was the unpretentious Hôtel du Grand Miroir, where he suffered extreme privation and became a recluse, refusing to walk out on his indebtedness to his landlady and ashamed to venture outside because of the condition of his clothes and shoes. This hotel stood near the Grand Place on an old street that ran west from there toward the Bourse.

(See Chapter 3, PARIS.)

BRONTË, CHARLOTTE (1816–1855).
BRONTË, EMILY (1818–1848).
The English novelist sisters attended and taught in the boarding school of Constantin Héger in **Brussels** for several months in 1842. Charlotte returned alone in 1843 and fell in love with M. Héger; her autobiographical novel *Villette* (1853) strongly reflects this place and period of her life. The Pensionnat Héger stood in a street called the Rue d'Isabelle, today the Rue Ravenstein, corner of Rue Baron Horta. The main room of the Palace of Beaux Arts, which is used for various cultural events, supposedly occupies the actual school site.

(See Chapter 5, ENGLAND.)

BRUEGEL, PIETER (1525–1569). Perhaps the greatest Flemish painter of all, "Peasant" Bruegel has long eluded biographical chroniclers. Records are few, and many details of his life can only be surmised. His birthplace may have been the village of **Groote-Brögel** about five kilometers west of Bree on route 21. Oral tradition asserts that a 19th-century farmhouse on a 13th-century foundation, a place called "Ooievaarsnest" ("Stork's Nest"), is the birthplace site. Another site in the Netherlands, with apparently as good a claim, also contends for the honor.

Bruegel's last residence from 1563 is now the Bruegel Museum at 132 Rue Haute in **Brussels**, and displays paintings, documents, and memorabilia relating to his life. The painter pro-

PIETER BRUEGEL HOUSE. With its entrance below the modern street level, this restored house where the Flemish master painted the teeming, vibrant canvases for which he remains best known stands in **Brussels** and is now a Bruegel museum. The painter resided there from 1563 until his death six years later.

duced most of his best-known works there, including *Massacre of the Innocents* (ca. 1564) and *Peasant Wedding Dance* (ca. 1566). (Open May—October, Tuesday, Thursday, Saturday 2:00—6:00; admission.)

Bruegel tomb: Church of Notre Dame de la Chapelle, **Brussels**.

Exhibit: Bruegel's canvases teem with humanity—people celebrating, working, dying. Only 48 of them survive. Several may be seen in the Royal Museum of Beaux Arts (Gallery of Old Masters) in a section devoted to Bruegel. The museum at Rue de la Régence 3 stands on a corner of the Place Royale, **Brussels**. (Open Tuesday—Sunday 10:00—5:00; 513–96–30; admission.)

(See Chapter 1, AUSTRIA.)

BYRON, GEORGE GORDON, LORD (1788–1824). The English poet and leading Romantic figure resided briefly in **Brussels**, in 1816, after his final departure from England, at 51 Rue Decale; there he composed the Waterloo stanzas of his epic poem, *Childe Harold's Pilgrimage*

(1812–18). Byron's companion was his personal physician, Dr. John Polidori, and the two were on their way to Italy. The address was a fashionable hotel at the time. Later it was converted to a private residence for lawyer-writer Edmond Picard, who until 1920 kept open house for hundreds of Europe's most distinguished poets, artists, composers, and musicians.

(See Chapter 1, SWITZERLAND; also Chapter 5, ENGLAND; also Chapter 6, LONDON; also Chapter 7, SCOTLAND; also Chapter 8, GREECE, ITALY.)

ERASMUS, DESIDERIUS (1466?–1536). In Anderlecht, a suburb of **Brussels**, the Dutch scholar, monk, and reformer stayed at the guest house of a religious order in 1521 and there wrote some 22 of the letters for which he probably remains best known, documents that provide a matchless picture of his times. The German painter Albrecht Dürer visited him there and painted his portrait; it now hangs in the Louvre. Erasmus was always too liberal (some say Christlike) a Christian for church authorities to tolerate, however, and he soon fled to Switzerland. The Gothic-Renaissance dwelling, built in 1515, is now known as the Erasmus House and displays material on his life and works, including a Latin first edition of his satire *In Praise of Folly* (1509). Period furnishings and Flemish paintings are also exhibited. Located at 31 Rue du Chapitre, the house is operated by the International Center of Humanism. (Open Sunday—Monday, Wednesday—Thursday, Saturday 10:00—12:00, 2:00—5:00; 521–13–83; admission.)

(See WEST GERMANY, THE NETHERLANDS in this chapter; also Chapter 1, SWITZERLAND; also Chapter 3, PARIS; also Chapter 5, ENGLAND.)

HITLER, ADOLF (1889–1945). During the June 1940 German invasion of France, the Nazi dictator resided at Wolfschlucht ("Wolf's Gorge"), his field headquarters. From there he left on June 21 in a state of euphoric joy to humble the surrendering French generals in the historic railroad car at Compiègne and returned the same night. The entire village of **Brûly-de-Pesche**, where the headquarters occupied several buildings, had been evacuated and was guarded by heavy German security forces. Hitler's bunker was a modest underground chamber, but he preferred to watch the occasional air attacks from the ground and usually stayed in a simple hutment. (Bunker open Easter—September, daily 9:00—12:00, 1:00—7:00; admission.)

(See EAST GERMANY, WEST GERMANY in this chapter; also Chapter 1, AUSTRIA; also Chapter 5, ENGLAND.)

HUGO, VICTOR (1802–1885). In 1861 the French Romantic novelist penned the Waterloo chapter of *Les Misérables* (1862) at the Hôtel des Colonnes in **Mont St. Jean**, a short distance south of Waterloo. The building is marked.

(See LUXEMBOURG in this chapter; also Chapter 2, FRANCE; also Chapter 3, PARIS; also Chapter 5, ENGLAND.)

MARX, KARL (1818–1883). Expelled from France for his political activities, the Socialist philosopher resided at several addresses in **Brussels** from 1845 to 1848. They included 24 Place du Petit-Sablon (1846), and 19 Place Ste-Gudule and 42 Rue d'Orléans (1847). Friedrich Engels, Marx's collaborator, lodged with Marx and his family in a shabby apartment at 5-6 Rue de l'Alliance on occasion.

(See EAST GERMANY, WEST GERMANY in this chapter; also Chapter 2, FRANCE; also Chapter 3, PARIS; also Chapter 6, LONDON.)

MORE, SIR THOMAS (1478–1535). In 1515 the English lawyer and humanist, future lord chancellor for Henry VIII and Roman Catholic martyr, sketched out his best-known work, the "political romance" *Utopia* (1516), at **Antwerp**. His lodging was a turreted house called "De Spieghel"; it is now the rear portion of a modern building at the west end of the street called Oude Beurs. Erasmus may have visited More there (see the entry on Erasmus earlier in this section).

(See Chapter 6, LONDON.)

NAPOLEON I (1769–1821). The French emperor suffered final crushing defeat in 1815 at Waterloo. During this last battle of his career he made his headquarters at the Caillou farm (now a museum) located several kilometers north of **Genappe** on route N5. He breakfasted there before the battle, confidently predicting rapid defeat of Wellington's English troops (see the entry on the Duke of Wellington later in this section). The museum displays original furnishings, and memorabilia of Napoleon. (Inquire locally for admission information.)

Exhibits: The battlefield of **Waterloo**, where some 140,000 men contested for the future of Europe and 39,000 of them died, is located three kilometers south of the town via route N5. The Waterloo-Gordon crossroads mark the front line of Wellington's outnumbered forces. Numerous markers and memorials identify various points on the rolling farmland where the eight-hour battle raged. Battle panoramas, a wax museum, and a copy of Napoleon's death mask may be seen at the Museum of the Emperor, located near the Lion Monument west of the above-mentioned intersection. (Open April—September, daily 9:00—6:00; October—March, daily 10:15—4:45; admission.)

(See EAST GERMANY in this chapter; also Chapter 1, AUSTRIA, SWITZERLAND; also Chapter 2, FRANCE; also Chapter 3, PARIS; also Chapter 8, ITALY, SPAIN.)

RODIN, AUGUSTE (1840–1917). In **Brussels**, the French sculptor resided at a number of ad-dresses from 1871 to 1877. Two of them were 15 Rue du Bourgmestre, and 36 Rue du Pont-Neuf.

(See Chapter 2, FRANCE; also Chapter 3, PARIS.)

RUBENS, SIR PETER PAUL (1577–1640). The Flemish painter, probably best known today for his voluptuous nudes, was also a hugely versatile, prolific creator of portraits, altarpieces, church and palace interiors, historical scenes, and panoramic landscapes. **Antwerp** was his lifelong home, though not constant residence, from 1587. He lived with his mother in the Kloosterstraat until 1609, then in the same street lodged with the Brant family until 1617; Isabella Brant became his first wife. Neither house survives.

In 1610 Rubens bought land along the Wapper Canal and built a luxurious mansion, his "dream house," for which he drew the plans and super-vised construction. Finished in 1616, the house and studio—separated by a courtyard—became a noted meeting place for Flemish artists and nobles.

VIEWS OF THE RUBENS HOUSE. In **Antwerp** the Flem-ish painter designed and built this palatial estate from 1610 to 1616, and the restored mansion functions today as a Rubens museum. These various exterior and in-terior views are from an old engraving by Jacobus Har-rewyn.

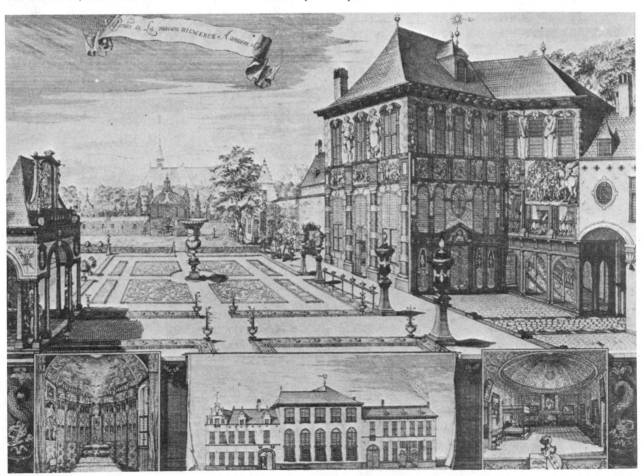

Rubens lavishly decorated the interior with his own collections though did not adorn the exterior of the house. Inside, wrote one biographer, "sculpture reached from the ground to the cornice; bas-reliefs, high reliefs, carving in the round, festoons and garlands." His Italianate baroque studio building and the portico between courtyard and gardens were also elaborately ornamented. As his fame and number of commissions increased, Rubens established a virtual art factory, drawing up sketches for his assistants to render into final works of art. Isabella Brant Rubens died in the mansion in 1626, and the artist brought his second wife, Hélène Fourment, there in 1630. Ten years later, Rubens himself died there. Over the next three centuries the property declined and fell into disrepair; when it was purchased by the city of Antwerp in 1937 little remained of the original structures except the house framework, the baroque portico, and the small garden house. A skillful restoration followed, however, using Rubens's plans and paintings to recreate rooms and gardens. Furnished with period items, the house was opened as a memorial to the painter in 1946. Today visitors may tour the rooms, viewing numerous Rubens sketches and canvases as well as works of his contemporaries and items from his own large art collection. A few pieces of personal memorabilia may also be seen. Sunday afternoon chamber music concerts are frequently presented. The Rubens House is located at 9-11 Rubenstraat. (Open daily, 10:00—5:00; 32–47–51; admission.)

From 1635 the artist often resided at his huge country estate, Het Steen, often called Rubenssteen. This 12th-century château remained occupied by his widow until her own death in 1681 and was much modified and restored in 1875 and 1918. Its exterior may be viewed from route A1, two kilometers west of **Elewijt**, northeast of Brussels.

Rubens tomb: Church of St. Jacques, **Antwerp**.

Exhibits: In **Antwerp** there are some outstanding Rubens collections. Several of his most notable works may be seen in the 14th-century Antwerp Cathedral (now undergoing long-term restoration) at the Handschoenmarkt. Rubens's triptych *Raising of the Cross* (1610) plus an *Assumption* (1626) and *Resurrection* rank among his finest church art. (Open April—October, Monday—Friday 12:00—5:00, Saturday 12:00—3:00, Sunday 1:00—4:00; October—March, Monday—Friday 2:00—5:00, Saturday—Sunday, same as above; donation.) The Plantin-Moretus Museum at Vrij-

dagmarkt 22 displays 18 Rubens paintings as well as sketches and engravings. (Open daily, 10:00—5:00; admission.) In the Royal Gallery of Fine Arts, Leopold de Waelplaats, there are two Rubens rooms; the exhibits are mostly altarpieces which were commissioned for various Antwerp churches. (Open Tuesday—Sunday 10:00—5:00; admission.) The Antwerp house occupied by the artist's parents before his birth is marked in the Meir and now contains a ground-floor shop.

In **Brussels** a renowned Rubens collection of both large canvases and smaller works is housed in the Museum of Ancient Art (see the entry on Pieter Bruegel, *Exhibit*, earlier in this section).

(See WEST GERMANY in this chapter; also Chapter 8, SPAIN.)

VAN GOGH, VINCENT (1853–1890). In 1879 and 1880 the Dutch pastor's son who believed his life's work lay in evangelism ministered to the coal miners of **Cuesmes**, a village about two kilometers southwest of Mons. His practice of Christianity, which included giving away all his possessions and living in poverty, was considered "overzealous" by local authorities and mine owners, and his neurotic "Christ complex" accomplished little. This period marked van Gogh's decision to give up preaching and begin painting. Entirely self-taught, he began drawing and practicing the basic principles of art at the hovel he shared with a miner's family at 8 Rue du Pavillon. The small house has been restored and displays period items and van Gogh memorabilia. (Open Tuesday—Sunday 10:00—12:00, 2:00—6:00; admission.)

(See THE NETHERLANDS in this chapter; also Chapter 2, FRANCE; also Chapter 3, PARIS.)

WELLINGTON, ARTHUR WELLESLEY, DUKE OF (1769–1852). The British soldier and statesman defeated Napoleon I, the one-time master of Europe, on the battlefield at **Waterloo** in 1815 (see the entry on Napoleon I, *Exhibits*, earlier in this section). Wellington's residence, both before and immediately after the battle, may be viewed at 147 Chausée de Bruxelles. An inn at the time and now the Wellington Museum, it displays his field maps and a collection of personal effects. (Open Tuesday—Sunday 9:00—12:00, 1:00—6:00; admission.)

An earlier 1815 residence, during the "100 days" of Napoleon's restoration before his final defeat, is now the Museum of the Treaty of **Ghent** (commemorating the treaty which ended the An-glo-American War of 1812). Souvenirs of Wel-lington's stay are also exhibited. The building is the former Hôtel d'Hane-Steenhuyse, an 18th-century mansion where Wellington shared quar-ters with the soon-to-be restored Louis XVIII of France. It stands in the Veldstraat. (Inquire locally for admission information.)

(See Chapter 3, PARIS; also Chapter 5, ENG-LAND; also Chapter 6, LONDON; also Chapter 7, IRELAND; also Chapter 8, SPAIN.)

LUXEMBOURG

Luxembourg is both the name of the country and of its largest city; the latter numbers about 80,000 people, less than one-quarter of the nation's population. Ethnically the people of Luxembourg are a French-German mixture but consider them-selves culturally distinct. While French is the offi-cial language, the normal spoken language is a German dialect called Letzeburgesch; newspapers are mostly in German, too. Both languages are taught in school, however. The country is about 80 kilometers long from north to south, and 55 kilometers wide at its broadest central part. Rugged scenery and the Ardennes Forest mark the northern area, while the Moselle valley is a prime wine producing region. Luxembourg produces more steel per capita than any other country—1 percent of the world's total.

Luxembourg has existed as a distinct political entity since the year 963, when it became a fief of the Holy Roman Empire. Since 1815 it has been ruled by the House of Nassau, and the govern-ment is headed by a prime minister. Separation of church and state is unthinkable here: the state pays the salaries of all priests, rabbis, and Protes-tant pastors.

Though the country was often visited by major historic figures, only one notable figure included in this book resided in Luxembourg for any length of time: novelist Victor Hugo, a frequent refugee from France.

HUGO, VICTOR (1802–1885). The French nov-elist stayed in **Vianden** for extensive intervals in 1862, 1863, 1865, 1870 and 1871. His "house at the corner of the Our River bridge" was destroyed during World War II, but an adjacent 1948 recon-struction of the house is now the Victor Hugo Museum. Fronted by a Rodin bust of the writer, it displays manuscripts, other documents, and

memorabilia. (Open April—October, daily 9:30—12:00, 2:00—6:00; admission.)

(See BELGIUM in this chapter; also Chapter 2, FRANCE; also Chapter 3, PARIS; also Chapter 5, ENGLAND.)

THE NETHERLANDS

As presently constituted, the kingdom of the Netherlands dates from 1813.* (Originally it in-cluded Belgium, but that country seceded in 1830.) Before that time there existed a United Dutch Republic, a confederation of northern European provinces that rose to naval, commer-cial, and artistic eminence in the 17th century and became a major colonial power. By 1650 the Dutch navy was twice as large as English and French fleets combined.

The country has a long tradition of liberalism and religious tolerance. It not only "tolerated" but welcomed minorities as diverse as Jews from Spain and Portugal (of whom Spinoza was a de-scendant), Huguenots from France, Pilgrims from England, and Roman Catholics who chose to re-main after the country revolted from Spanish con-trol because of the Inquisition. Even Germany's discredited kaiser was allowed to settle after World War I. Many German Jews found refuge in the Netherlands during the 1930s (Anne Frank, for instance) until the Nazi invasion, and many Dutch risked and lost their own lives to protect them. Today the country is about evenly divided between Protestants and Catholics, with the bare majority of Protestants somewhat resentful of the strong Catholic political cohesion. When they need services performed or want to buy some-thing, many Dutch first want to know the reli-gious affiliation of doctor or butcher.

Yet despite this religious conservatism, border-ing on chauvinism, the Dutch in other ways rank among Europe's more liberal, "laid-back" peoples. Outside Scandinavia most European and Ameri-can communities, even those originally populated by Dutch emigrants, are far more rigid and con-servative than the typical Dutch village. One rea-son may be that the Dutch can't afford to be obsessively private in their affairs (of any sort). In a country of 14 million people, the world's most densely populated nation, they have necessarily

---

*The country is also known as Holland, though not by the Dutch themselves. Holland is actually two provinces—North and South Holland—of the country's western coastal area. They contain about half of the total Netherlands population.

learned to live with each other. Yet the Dutch have not only survived but have mightily prospered under such crowding, giving the lie to that civic planning gospel which blames "crowded conditions" for most of the world's urban woes. Instead of seeking territory from neighboring nations, the Dutch "lift" new land from the sea and are masters of marine hydraulics (they sneer at the American fiction of the boy who stopped up the dike with his finger, and Dutch schoolchildren remain ignorant of the tale). In this way the Dutch have literally earned almost half their land area—much of it still below sea level—over the past thousand years. Networks of dikes, dams, sluices, canals, and pumps have created this area, and maintenance against the sea requires constant vigilance. Land reclamation projects are increasing, with an average addition of 26 square kilometers of land per year expected throughout the 20th century. Efforts focus on the IJsselmeer (Zuiderzee), a pocket of the North Sea that cuts deeply into the country.

One of the best-functioning democracies in the world, the Netherlands is governed by a bicameral parliament under a constitutional monarchy; the latter has been headed by the House of Orange-Nassau since 1813. Amsterdam, the official capital, is also the largest city, followed by Rotterdam (the world's busiest seaport) and The Hague, which is the seat of government.

Two great scholars and philosophers, good men of profound significance—Spinoza and Erasmus—were Dutchmen. The Dutch are proud that Anne Frank, though German-born, lived most of her brief, shining life in the Netherlands, if only because Germany didn't want her. The country's most renowned historical figures, however, were artists: Bosch, van Gogh, and, of course, Rembrandt, to name only those three who appear in these pages. Many homes or museums devoted to noted Dutch historical figures may be seen and visited in the Netherlands, one of Europe's most comfortably civilized nations.

BOSCH, HIERONYMUS (ca. 1450–1516). The painter whose allegorical fantasies still puzzle and involve viewers with their intricate, grotesque visions was born Hieronymus van Aken but took his surname from his native town of 's-Hertogenbosch. There is no evidence that he ever lived anywhere other than this immediate area. His adult home was said to be a half-timbered house that stood beside the central marketplace, one of the dwellings pictured in his painting *Cloth Market at 's-Hertogenbosch*.

About 32 kilometers south of 's-Hertogenbosch, the country village of **Oirschot** provided settings for his series *The Seven Deadly Sins*. Bosch's wife, Aleid van de Meervenne, had inherited a house and land there, and Bosch probably painted his earliest works in the village (ca. 1470s).

(See Chapter 8, SPAIN.)

BRADFORD, WILLIAM (1590–1657). The Pilgrim governor of America's Plymouth Colony lived with a group of other English separatists for about 12 years before their *Mayflower* voyage to the New World. In 1608 and 1609 they lived in **Amsterdam**. The tiny alley where they resided, now called the Engelse Pelgrimsteeg and extending from the north end of the Rembrandtsplein, is the last vestige of their Amsterdam stay.

In **Leyden**, one of the most religiously tolerant cities in Europe where the separatists resided from 1609 to 1620, their spiritual center was the house of their pastor John Robinson, which stood in the Kloksteeg, a small, cobblestone street that hasn't changed much. A stone tablet on the restored 1683 Jan Pesijnshofje almshouse, a brick house, marks the site.

Exhibits: The Pilgrim Fathers' Documents Center at 2a Boisotkade in **Leyden** displays archive photographs relating to the Pilgrims, and maps of the city as it existed when they lived there. (Open Monday—Friday 9:00—12:00, 2:00—4:30; free.)

In the Delfshaven quarter of **Rotterdam**, the Pilgrim Fathers' Church at 20 Voorhaven dates originally from 1417. In 1620 the youngest and strongest members of the Leyden separatist community (including Bradford) met there the night before they sailed on the *Speedwell* to England, thence on the *Mayflower* to America. (Open Monday—Friday; donation.) Nearby, the 1650 Guildhouse of the Grain Sack Carriers at 13–15 Voorstraat displays an exhibit on the Pilgrim Fathers. (Open Tuesday—Saturday 10:00—5:00, Sunday 11:00—5:00; admission.) A tablet on the quay (Pelgrimstraat) marks the spot where the Pilgrims boarded their vessel and left continental Europe.

(See Chapter 5, ENGLAND.)

CHARLEMAGNE (742–814). In 777 the Frankish king and Emperor of the West established a castle residence at **Nijmegan**. Built on the Roman foundations of a previous palace, it was rebuilt by Emperor Frederick Barbarossa in 1155, and his son, Emperor Henry VI, was born there in 1165. The present scanty ruins in the Valkhof garden at the end of the Burchtstraat date from the 11th and 12th centuries. Barbarossa's palace was demolished in 1769. (Gardens open; free.)

Exhibit: In **Nijmegan** a room of the Stedelijk Museum in the Nonnenstraat is devoted to the Volkhof site with pictures and models. (Open Monday—Saturday 10:00—5:00, Sunday 1:00—5:00; admission.)

(See WEST GERMANY in this chapter; also Chapter 2, FRANCE.)

DESCARTES, RENÉ (1596–1650). The French philosopher resided in the Netherlands for two decades (1629-49) and wrote his most important works there, "frequently changing his residence that he might continue his work without interruption," according to one account. In **Amsterdam** he lived at 6 Westermarkt from about 1630 to 1634; now restored, the gabled house is marked by a tablet. Descartes approvingly noted that "everyone is so engrossed in furthering their own interests that I could spend the whole of my life there without being noticed by a soul."

(See SWEDEN in this chapter; also Chapter 2, FRANCE; also Chapter 3, PARIS.)

FRANK, ANNE (1929–1945). Businessman Otto Frank's family, including his bright, talented daughter Anne, found civilized refuge in **Amsterdam** in 1933 after their homeland Germany elected barbarism. Until 1942, when the Gestapo

A SHRINE OF WORLD WAR II. In this unpretentious building at 263 Prinsengracht in **Amsterdam**, Anne Frank resided during most of her final two years. Along with her family, she lived a whispered existence in the top-floor apartment as they hid from the Gestapo and Anne wrote her famous *Diary*. Today thousands of people come here each year to honor the memory of this young author whose unquenchable spirit made final mockery of Hitler's *Mein Kampf*. The first view shows the house as it looked in 1940. Most of the front brickwork has been refaced since the war.

began rounding up Dutch Jews, the family lived in an unidentified house near the Merwedeplein area. Then, as the net closed, the Franks secreted themselves and four others in the attic apartment of an obscure, 17th-century row house alongside a canal at 263 Prinsengracht. There they lived for 25 months; there Anne Frank wrote the famous diary she called "Kitty" (The Diary of a Young Girl), probably the major piece of literature to emerge from World War II; and there on August 4, 1944, betrayed by an informer, they were arrested by the Gestapo and sent to concentration camps. Only Otto Frank survived the war. He devoted the rest of his life (he died in 1980) to preserving his daughter's memory through the Anne Frank Foundation, which restored the house in 1960 and opened it to the public. "In spite of everything," Anne Frank wrote, "I still believe that people are really good at heart . . . I can feel the suffering of millions and yet, if I look up into the heavens, I think that it will all come right, that this cruelty too will end, and that peace and tranquility will return again." In The Diary of a Young Girl lies the final stunning defeat of the pathetic "super race." The Nazis were rightly terrified of people like Anne Frank and her family, for at 263 Prinsengracht civilization held; and the address marks the death site, if any, of Hitler's dreams.

More than 300,000 people per year—many of them young Germans with anguished, pointed questions for their parents—step into Anne Frank's world behind the bookcase concealing the stairway at 263 Prinsengracht. It is a wrenching experience, and many visitors will echo the words of veteran travel writer Arthur Frommer: "The effect is searing, heartbreaking, infuriating beyond belief." Magazine pictures of Hollywood movie stars remain on the walls where Anne pasted them, and the contrast between these remnants of a teenager's fantasy life and the reality of her caged isolation give the cheap pictures a priceless, almost transcendental value. Enough tears have been shed here to wash away Buchenwald, were it possible. The only consolation is, of course, the mightiness of her faith, the precision of her prophecy, the immortality of her words. The original diary written here is on display, together with some household effects. Two adjoining houses form the International Youth Center of the Anne Frank Foundation, which is maintained by royalties from the play adapted from the Diary and by contributions. Other exhibits show documents

and photographs relating to the Frank family and to World War II. (Open Monday—Saturday 9:00—5:00, Sunday 10:00—5:00; 242837; admission.)

(See WEST GERMANY in this chapter.)

LINNAEUS, CAROLUS (1707–1778). From 1735 to 1737 the Swedish botanist, who founded the modern science of taxonomy, served as overseer of the private zoo and arboretum of English banker George Clifford at Clifford's estate, Hartekamp. Now called Linnaeushof, the estate is a large recreational area located at 4 Rijksstraatweg in **Bennebroek**. The park includes gardens, woodland, picnic facilities, and play areas for children. Linnaeus had just completed his Systema Naturae (1735) when he came to live here. (House and estate open April 1–September 30, daily 9:00—6:00; admission.)

(See SWEDEN in this chapter; also Chapter 5, LONDON.)

REMBRANDT VAN RIJN (1606–1669). Renowned for his portaits but also famed for his etchings and drawings, Rembrandt was a native of **Leyden**. His birthplace stood in the Weddesteeg, and it remained his home until 1631.

In **Amsterdam**, his lifelong home after 1631, Rembrandt's first residence and studio (1631–36) was the home of art dealer Hendrik van Ulenborch, whose cousin Saskia became Rembrandt's wife in 1633. This home remains privately owned at 2 Jodenbreestraat. With his wife's money and his own credit, Rembrandt bought the three-story dwelling next door at 4 Jodenbreestraat in 1639. At this house, now known as the Rembrandt House, the painter resided until bankruptcy forced him to sell it in 1658 (though he was allowed to stay there until 1660). Saskia, who often modeled for him, died there in 1642. During the early, extravagant years of their marriage, Rembrandt filled the house with collectibles of every sort—art, weapons, rich fabrics to ornament his models—but after Saskia's death he could never again make ends meet. From 1649 he lived at the house with his son's former nurse, Hendrikje Stoffels, who became his mistress, model, and companion. Many of his famed self-portraits and The Night Watch (1642), which some acclaim as the greatest painting of all time, were done here. The family resided on the lower floor, while Rembrandt used the second floor for his studio. The third story was added shortly after Rembrandt left

REMBRANDT'S HOUSE. From 1639 to 1660 the painter enjoyed his most affluent period and created some of his best-known works in this **Amsterdam** dwelling. It is now a museum primarily devoted to the display of Rembrandt's etchings.

the house. Today the red-shuttered dwelling, which was narrowly saved from destruction in 1906 when it was purchased by the city, exhibits numerous sketches of the master as well as more than 250 of his etchings. It is one of the largest Rembrandt collections in the world. Also on view are his etching press and several of his copperplates. Seeing works of art in the same rooms where they were created is not a common experience and it is especially poignant in Rembrandt's house with its restored 17th-century interior. *Rembrandt's House* (1978) by Anthony Bailey gives a detailed account of the painter's years here. (Open Monday—Saturday 10:00—5:00, Sunday 1:00—5:00; 249486; admission.)

Rembrandt's last home, from 1660, is 184 Rozengracht. Hounded by creditors, the painter spent his final years as an employee of an art firm established by Stoffels and his son, and finally died there.

Rembrandt tomb: Westerkerk, **Amsterdam**.

Exhibits: Rembrandt painted another of his best-known works, *The Anatomy Lesson* (1632), at the 15th-century Waag (weighing house), 4 Nieuwmarkt, **Amsterdam**. Upper chambers there were used as guild rooms for the city's surgeons, and the painter recorded the famous scene of Dr. Tulp dissecting a corpse very soon after his own arrival in Amsterdam. Today this structure houses the Amsterdam Historical Museum and Jewish Historical Museum. (Open Monday—Saturday 9:30—5:00, Sunday 1:00—5:00; 242209; admission.) *The Night Watch* and 18 other Rembrandt oil paintings are displayed in one of the world's great art museums, the Rijksmuseum at 42 Stadhouderskade. (Open Monday—Saturday 10:00—5:00, Sunday 1:00—5:00; 732121; admission.)

The *Anatomy Lesson* hangs in the Mauritshuis Museum, 8 Korte Vijverberg, **The Hague**. (Open Monday—Saturday 10:00—5:00, Sunday 11:00—5:00; admission.)

SCHWEITZER, ALBERT (1875–1964).

Exhibit: The Alsatian missionary, physician, and philosopher has a museum and archive devoted to him in **Deventer**. Exhibits relating to his life and work may be seen at the Schweitzer Museum, 89 Brink. (Inquire locally for admission information.)

(See Chapter 2, FRANCE; also Chapter 3, PARIS.)

SPINOZA, BENEDICT (1632–1677). In 1954 Israeli prime minister David Ben Gurion proposed that Spinoza's 1656 excommunication from the Portuguese Synagogue in **Amsterdam** for heresy be revoked. His suggestion was rejected. Thus the great pantheistic scholar and philosopher, one of the few truly great religious men of his age, remains an outcast from his own cultural heritage. Those who love learning, however, are richer for the life of this gentle man, a lens grinder by trade, whose lifelong quest was a search for intellectual truth. The site of his birthplace at 41 Waterlooplein recently held a gas station; Spinoza lived in his parents' home there until his expulsion from the Jewish community.

From 1660 to 1665, his most creative years, Spinoza lived at **Rijnsburg**, working at his trade and writing his *Improvement of the Intellect* and *Ethics* (1677). His reconstructed house, now a museum operated by the Spinoza Society of the Hague, stands at what is now 29 Spinozalaan and displays personal memorabilia, his grinding tools, desk,

SPINOZA'S LAST HOME. From 1671 to his death in 1677, the great philosopher who supported himself as a lens grinder occupied rooms and work space in this house, shown in a 1932 view, at **The Hague**. A small museum reveals details of the scholar's humble life there.

period furnishings, and recreated library. (Inquire locally for admission information.)

The philosopher spent his last years, from 1670, in **The Hague**, gently refusing the honors and offers that began to accumulate despite the controversies that continued to rage around him. He first resided at 32 Stille Veerkade. The 1646 Lutheran household where he lodged from 1671 also survives at 72-74 Paviljoensgracht. Dust from Spinoza's years of lens grinding had affected his lungs, and he died there at age 44. The two-story brick house contains a small museum and exhibits a few of the scholar's personal effects. Its neighborhood remains very "old-world" and is still occupied mainly by Spaniards and Portuguese, like Spinoza's ancestors, and he would probably still feel quite comfortable there. (Inquire locally for admission information.)

Spinoza tomb (site): Churchyard, New Church, **The Hague**.

VAN GOGH, VINCENT (1853–1890). A native of **Zundert**, which was his home until 1864, the painter noted for his shimmering, powerful landscapes, still lifes, and portraits was the son of the local pastor. His rectory birthplace survives at 26 Markt.

Another rectory home survives in the village of **Nuenen**; van Gogh lived there with his parents from 1883 to 1885, following his failure as a missionary-evangelist in Belgium. It was while residing there that he decided to become a landscape painter.

Exhibit: The world's foremost exhibit of van Gogh art and documents—some 200 oils and 500 drawings, plus numerous letters and manuscripts—is the National Vincent van Gogh Museum at 7 Paulus Potterstraat in **Amsterdam**. (Open Monday—Saturday 10:00—5:00, Sunday 1:00—5:00; admission.)

The Rijksmuseum Kroller-Muller in the Hoge Veluwe National Park at **Otterlo** also has an outstanding van Gogh collection. (Open April—October, Monday—Saturday 10:00—5:00, Sunday 11:00—5:00; November—March, daily 1:00—5:00; admission.)

(See BELGIUM in this chapter; also Chapter 2, FRANCE; also Chapter 3, PARIS.)

WILHELM II (1859–1941). After his 1918 forced abdication, the last German kaiser spent his final two decades at an 18th-century country mansion which the Dutch government set aside for him at 10 Langbroeckerweg, a short distance west of **Doorn**. Once a summer palace of the bishops of Utrecht, the spacious estate with its large gardens and park provided a quiet permanent retreat for Germany's World War I leader, whom nobody—least of all the Germans—wanted anything more to do with. The aged kaiser spent most of his time caring for his gardens and arboretum. Still, despite the fact that he obsequiously praised Hitler, the Nazis worried about the (unlikely) possibility of interference from him, and during the early years of World War II the Gestapo guarded the estate to make sure he didn't leave. He didn't, and died there. Today at Doorn House may be seen original furnishings, possessions, and paintings collected by the last of the Hohenzollern rulers. (Open

DOORN HOUSE. LAST HOME OF THE KAISER. This 1921 view shows the mansion as it looked when Wilhelm II retired there after his forced abdication at the end of World War I. Located near **Doorn**, it displays numerous possessions and relics of the last monarch of Germany. Wilhelm is buried on the estate.

March 15—October 31, Monday—Saturday 9:00—12:30, 1:30—5:00, Sunday 1:00—5:00; admission.)

Before the Dutch government settled him on his final estate, the kaiser's residence was Amerongen Castle (1918–20), the 1676 château at **Amerongen**. It displays fine porcelain, tapestries, and French furniture. (Open April 1—October 31, Tuesday—Saturday 10:00—5:00, Sunday 2:00—5:00; November 1—March 31, by appointment; admission.)

Wilhelm II tomb: Doorn House, **Doorn**.

(See EAST GERMANY, WEST GERMANY in this chapter.)

SCANDINAVIA: DENMARK, FINLAND, NORWAY, SWEDEN

Scandinavia, Europe's northernmost region, consists essentially of two peninsulas—the drooping, 1,930-kilometer tongue of land comprising Norway and Sweden, and the smaller peninsula of Denmark, which juts up from continental Europe. While not technically a part of Scandinavia, Finland, which rims the land mass of the Soviet Union, is usually grouped with the three Scandinavian kingdoms. Iceland, which is not treated in this book, is also often considered part of Scandinavia.

Denmark, Norway, and Sweden share many common roots in their history, languages, and political traditions. Probably their foremost characteristic is their mutual dependence and cultural focus on the sea. All three nations have long, incredibly complex coastlines, and all of their major cities are also major world seaports. Another common denominator is their heritage of constitutional monarchies and long traditions of democratic government. Politically, they insist on enlightened, skillful leadership and have seldom lacked it. The present borders were generally affixed by 1659, when Sweden won a sharp conflict with Denmark. Today these countries make up the world's prime example of supremely functional democratic socialism. "The welfare policy of all three nations," writes Hammond Innes, "differs from that of other countries in its emphasis on the prevention of distress rather than on its cure." Social aid does not await trouble or indigency here but forestalls them, and no official attention dwells on who does or does not "deserve" such aid.

All of the Scandinavian countries are healthy, prosperous nations with standards of living that rank among the world's highest. Their reluctance to join in the enthusiastic ideological controversies of world politics that consume so much energy and so many resources of larger countries, coupled with their outstanding success in providing for their own peoples and their basic disinterest in converting anyone else to their sensible ways, evoke little emulation but frequent criticism of the carping kind from both Eastern and Western ideologues. In the meantime, Scandinavians go on about their extremely gainful pursuits.

Finland's racial heritage is altogether different, but its regional concerns and geographical aspects are similar to those of the three kingdoms. From 1397 to 1523 the three kingdoms were united in the Kalmar Union. Norway belonged, at various times, to Denmark and Sweden, and Finland was also a part of Sweden from the 13th century until 1809.

Out of three main Scandinavian centers poured the "Viking hordes" that raided, pillaged, and settled throughout much of Europe from the eighth through eleventh centuries. These centers were Skiringssal in Norway, Birka in Sweden, and Hedeby in Denmark. Pushed by a population explosion that seems odd today in view of the present modest Scandinavian numbers, the Norsemen in their longboats and "dragon ships" spread terror along coastlines from the North Sea to the

Mediterranean. Unencumbered by Christian notions of warfare, they most often stormed ashore in fierce, brief forays of killing and looting, and compelled tribute known as Danegeld to hold off devastation. In some places, however—most notably in Ireland, eastern England, Frisian Holland, Normandy in France, and Novgorod and Kiev in Russia—they found new homes and merged into the native populations. The Norman Conquest of England in 1066 was essentially a long-deferred victory of the Vikings who had overrun Normandy two centuries before. Today the few remnants of that age in Scandinavia itself are best seen in the Hall of the Viking Ships at Oslo, where Norse vessels excavated from burial mounds are displayed, though even these are only small examples of the much larger warship longboats that ravaged European coasts.

The seagoing tradition, if not the warlike proclivities of Scandinavians, has continued into the modern age. Polar and arctic exploration in the early 20th century was mainly a Norwegian sea initiative; and England and America built much of their Polar accomplishments on the initiatives of Nansen and Amundsen. Thor Heyerdahl's *Kon Tiki* and *Ra* voyages provide more recent examples of Norwegian sea mastery.

Between latitudes 64 and 66 N., Finland, Norway, Sweden, and the western Soviet Union are inhabited by the Lapps, a people closely related to the Finns. Traditionally nomadic, the Lapps, like birds, pay no great attention to national borders and depend heavily on semidomesticated reindeer herds, and on farming and fishing. As a race, they are Europe's shortest people—four or five feet in height. More than half of all Lapps, who number about 34,000, live in Norway.

All the Scandinavian nations except Sweden suffered heavily in World War II. Denmark and Norway fell to the Nazi invaders; Finland allied with Germany in response to invading Soviet troops (who paid dearly for their effort); while Sweden maintained a precarious neutrality.

Today the Scandinavian nations are more closely linked than ever before. The Nordic Council, established in 1952, has abolished passport and work permit requirements between the countries, thus creating a common labor market and mutual social welfare benefits. Despite their many links and similarities, however, Scandinavian nations and peoples display profound differences in character and temperament. Such differences are perhaps best seen in the lives of some of the notable Danes, Finns, Norwegians, and Swedes of the following pages.

DENMARK

"Melancholy Danes" are about as uncommon as Danes named Hamlet. A lighthearted people, Danes are probably the most carefree, readiest-to-smile national group in Europe—at least so they seem. Not for Danes the heavy romanticism, ponderous self-analysis, or religio-patriotic fervors that so preoccupy other peoples East and West. They have inhabited their jutting corner of Europe for millenia; there isn't much they haven't seen and not a great deal they revere. If you must bring "serious concerns" to Denmark—including an interest in historical homes—prepare to endure some goodnatured chaffing. Danes somehow give the impression that they have forgotten more about human nature than most of us will ever know. Among European peoples, they seem more "grown-up," less rigid and volatile in day-to-day matters than most. Few Danes are ever too busy to enjoy life or share a laugh at their own (or even your) expense.

This smallest Scandinavian country, about half the size of Scotland, has nevertheless exerted the largest influence in the region. While it controlled all of the Scandinavian nations under its crown from the 14th to 16th centuries (and Norway until 1814), it has never given up its own crown to a Swede, Norwegian, or Finn. One of the oldest continuous monarchies in history, its unbroken line of Oldenburg rulers extends back to 1448, while the Danish flag has remained unchanged since 1219. Copenhagen, Denmark's largest city and capital, is also Scandinavia's largest, outranking Stockholm by a few million; about one-quarter of the country's five million population lives there.

Three-quarters of the country consists of Jutland, the peninsula that extends north from Germany between the North and Baltic seas. The large eastern islands of Zealand and Fyn, plus some 500 smaller islands, account for the rest of Denmark. Unlike the rugged, frigid mountainscapes of its northern neighbors, Denmark's topography lies flat or gently rolling; its climate is mild. Denmark's economy relies mainly on the export of industrial goods and agricultural products.

The latter come principally from small, mixed-plot farms.

A major European sea power until the 17th century, Denmark today is one of the world's model progressive democracies, with the oft-stated goal of providing "the greatest possible happiness for the greatest number of people." It probably achieves the ideal classless society to a much greater degree than any other nation in the world, for Danes do take some things seriously—they genuinely believe in individual equality, perversely refusing to judge a person's worth by economic criteria.

ANDERSEN, HANS CHRISTIAN (1805–1875). In Denmark you must call him "Ho Tsay (H. C.) Andersen" if you wish to be understood. "Today," wrote biographer Monica Stirling, "his stories are never out of print, his house in Odense is never without visitors. . . and there is never a moment when there is not somewhere in the world a child who is reading Hans Christian Andersen for the first time." The popular children's writer (who himself probably suffered from the reading disability known as dyslexia) was born at **Odense** in the tiny, red-tiled, one-story house at Hans Jensensstraede 39–43; or so it is generally believed (though nobody is quite certain) since the house had earlier belonged to his grandmother, at least from 1802 to 1804. The magic of Andersen's name has transformed this once dismal, back-street neighborhood into an expensive, prestigious section of the city. Andersen was born on a bed constructed from a funeral bier. In the words of Phyllis Méras, "his father was a shoemaker, his mother an alcoholic washerwoman. His paternal grandfather was the village madman who sported chicken feathers and flowers in his hair and was always followed about by a troupe of jeering children." Today the little house, acquired by the city in 1905, displays a wealth of Andersen memorabilia, including portraits, letters, awards,

THE BIRTHPLACE OF HANS CHRISTIAN ANDERSEN. Memorabilia of the beloved children's author crowd this small house, where Andersen probably spent his first two years, in **Odense**. A slum section of the city at the time, the neighborhood has been transformed because of its associations (Andersen's name is magic in Denmark) and is now a distinctly upper-class district.

manuscripts, drawings, and first editions of his *Fairy Tales* (1835). Also exhibited here and in adjoining buildings acquired in 1930 are original furnishings, Andersen's famed top hat and umbrella, and miscellaneous personal items. The luggage he carted to hotels all over Europe included a coil of rope in case fire broke out in any place he happened to lodge. (Open April 1—May 31, September daily 10:00—5:00; June 1—August 31, daily 9:00—7:00; October 1—March 31, daily 10:00—3:00; 13-13-72; free.)

Andersen's boyhood home (1807–19), a one-room flat at Munkemöllestraede 3, now contains a museum of local life. "On the roof," he wrote, "there stood a great chest filled with soil, my mother's sole garden. In my story of the 'Snow Queen' that garden still blooms." It was from this home that the youth decided in 1819 to seek his fortune in Copenhagen. "First you go through terrible suffering," he told his worried mother, "and then you become famous." (Open April 1—September 30, daily 10:00—5:00; October 1—March 31, daily 12:00—3:00; admission.)

A prolific writer of "serious" works, Andersen considered his best-known tales "trifles" long after they had made his name beloved throughout Europe. He made his permanent home in **Copenhagen** from 1819, and as a lifelong, unwilling bachelor suffered much from loneliness and hypochondria. Being everybody's favorite "uncle storyteller" became at times a severe trial to the shy, ungainly Andersen, but he did his best to fulfill the role in public at least. His later homes were furnished apartment dwellings, at least two of which survive in Copenhagen's waterfront area. He resided at Nyhavn 67 at intervals from 1848 to 1865; his last city home was Nyhavn 20. Andersen visited and dined frequently at the home of his friend and patron, Jonas Collin, director of the Royal Theater; the house survives at Store Strandstraede 3. Andersen called this place his "Home of Homes," though his heavy emotional dependence on Collin made the place a scene of frequent turmoil for him.

Andersen died at Rolighed, the estate of friends, the Melchior family, where he spent his final month afflicted with cancer. The manor, an 18th-century miniature of Copenhagen's Rosenborg Palace, is located in the Rosenvaenget in the eastern part of the city.

At Glorup Manor, a 15th-century baroque house located one kilometer north of **Länga**, where Andersen stayed on some 30 occasions, his rooms are preserved as they were during his visits. (Open Sunday—Thursday 9:00—6:00; admission.)

Andersen tomb: Assistens Cemetery, **Copenhagen**.

Exhibits: The Royal Library at Christians Brugge 8 in **Copenhagen** displays a collection of Andersen drawings, paper collages, diaries, letters, and manuscripts. (Open Monday—Saturday 9:00—7:00; free.) At the Bakke House Literary Museum, the 18th-century former manor home of philosopher K. L. Rahbek whom Andersen frequently visited, there is a display of material about the writer. The museum is located at Rahbeks Allé 23. (Open Wednesday—Thursday, Saturday—Sunday 11:00—3:00; admission.)

BRECHT, BERTOLT (1898–1956). In 1933 the German playwright had to flee his Nazi homeland. He bought a house in **Skovbostrand**, and wrote *Private Life of the Master Race* (1938) and *Life of Galileo* (1938–39) there. The house, where he lived until 1939, remains privately owned at an undisclosed address.

(See EAST GERMANY, WEST GERMANY, FINLAND, SWEDEN in this chapter; also Chapter 1, SWITZERLAND.)

GAUGUIN, PAUL (1848–1903). The French painter and ex-stockbroker, destitute and desperate in 1885, came to **Copenhagen** and resided briefly with his estranged Danish wife and her family at Gammell Kongevej 105. Mette-Sophie Gad and her parents could not understand why he had thrown away a moderately successful business career to indulge his "whim for painting," as they called it. The family eventually drove him out of the flat. He returned in sad shape to Paris, and later fled to Tahiti where he painted the colorful impressions of native life for which, after his death, he became best known.

(See Chapter 2, FRANCE; also Chapter 3, PARIS.)

HAMLET (2nd century B.C.?). The character of the "Prince of Denmark," tragic protagonist of Shakespeare's 1601 play, was apparently based on one Prince Amleth as recorded by Danish chronicler Saxo Grammaticus in the 12th century. Nobody can now say whether such a figure actually existed. If he did, though, one place he quite certainly never appeared was at Elsinore where Shakespeare set his play. The area inhabited by the "real" Prince Amleth is said to be near **Slyng-**

borg on Jutland, where a memorial stone marks his supposed grave in the Ammel Hede south of the village.

Exhibits: Like Wilhelm Tell in Switzerland and Robin Hood in England, the literary character of Hamlet has earned a quasi-biographical status despite a fair likelihood that he never lived at all. Such a status has been partially achieved by the careful marking of "sites," of course; at Kronborg Castle in **Elsinore**, for instance, one may see the flag battery where Hamlet saw his father's ghost and set in motion the events of crime and passion that form the basis of the play. The square Renaissance palace, dominating the town from its headland on the narrow sound facing the Swedish city of Hälsingborg, dates orginally from the early 15th century and became a favorite royal residence, but most of the present structure is 17th century and later. Performances of *Hamlet* by various touring companies are presented in the large courtyard during June. (Open April, October, daily 11:00—4:00; May—September, daily 9:30—5:00; November—March, daily 11:00—3:00; admission.) At the Elsinore City Museum, located in the 16th-century Marienlyst Castle approached via the St. Annagade, is a Hamlet collection that any lover of the play will want to see. (Open May—September, daily 1:00—4:00; October—April, Wednesday, Friday 1:00—3:00; free.)

KIERKEGAARD, SÖREN (1813–1855). Philosopher and rebel theologian whose works became a source for 20th-century existentialist philosophy, Kierkegaard dwelled in **Copenhagen** for his entire life and for well over half of that time on at his childhood home, which stood at Nytorv 2. Then from 1837 on he resided at a number of addresses, including Lövstraede 128 (1837–38); Nörregade 230A (1840–44); Nörregade 43 (1850–51); and Österbrogade 108A (1851–52). He sold the family home at Nytorv 2 in 1847, after having returned there to live in 1844. His last home from 1852, a cramped, two-room flat, was in the house located at Bredgade 70.

Kierkegaard tomb: Assistens Cemetery, **Copenhagen**.

Exhibits: The Museum of the City of **Copenhagen** at Vesterbrogade 59 displays a collection relating to Kierkegaard's life and work. (Open April—October, daily 10:00—4:00, Tuesday 7:00 p.m.—9:00 p.m.; November—March, Tuesday—Sunday 1:00—4:00, Tuesday 7:00 p.m.—9:00

p.m.; admission.) Kierkegaard manuscripts are displayed at the Royal Library, and additional material may be seen at the Bakke House Literary Museum (see the entry on Hans Christian Andersen, *Exhibits*, earlier in this section.)

FINLAND

In contrast to its other Scandinavian neighbors, Finland—called *Suomi* by the Finns themselves—lies low, mountainless, and full of lakes. Contrasts are, in fact, numerous. It is the most "arctic" of Scandinavian nations, one-third of it lying above the Arctic Circle. Its language, which is related to Estonian and Hungarian, is entirely unlike the mutually similar Danish, Norwegian and Swedish. And politically the country is a relatively new nation, having only achieved independence from Russia, which had conquered the country in 1809, in 1917. From the 13th century the country had been part of Sweden.

Finland is also the only Scandinavian country without a constitutional monarchy, being a multiparty Socialist republic guided by a strong president. World War II confronted the nation with unpleasant options. Because of Soviet invasion in 1939, Finland turned to the Axis for support and fiercely resisted the Russian onslaught. Some 7 percent of the population died or became casualties in that war. Harsh postwar terms forced it to cede large amounts of territory to the Soviet Union.

Despite their long history of subjugation by Sweden and Russia, the Finns—some five million in number—are and always have been fiercely nationalistic. Though culturally it is Western oriented, Finland in its uneasy position on the edge of the Soviet sphere maintains strong economic and security ties to Russia. Helsinki is the capital and largest city.

International attention has focused on the Finns' diverse skills in architecture, forestry, and Olympic sports. Finland was Lenin's springboard for revolution in Russia; his 1917 arrival at the "Finland station" in Moscow signaled the uprising that led to the Communist regime. As for notable Finns, Jean Sibelius, whose *Finlandia* is probably his best-known work, not only represented musical genius but came to symbolize the country's nationalistic aspirations. He, above all Finns, is revered and memorialized.

BRECHT, BERTOLT (1898–1956). As World War II engulfed his native Germany, the playwright sought refuge in **Helsinki** during 1940 and 1941, then emigrated to the United States for the duration of the war. He lodged first in a small unfurnished apartment at Linnankoskenkatu 20, and there finished his play *The Good Woman of Sezuan* (1940). With his family he then occupied a larger apartment at Koeydenpunojankata 13; it was his last home in Europe for six years.

(See EAST GERMANY, WEST GERMANY, DENMARK, SWEDEN in this chapter; also Chapter 1, SWITZERLAND.)

LENIN, VLADIMIR (1870–1924).

Exhibit: The Russian revolutionary leader took refuge in Finland often during the years immediately prior to the 1917 Bolshevik coup that established the Soviet government. At **Tampere**, the Lenin Museum, Hallituskatu 19, displays a collection relating to his life and work. (Inquire locally for admission information.)

(See EAST GERMANY, WEST GERMANY in this chapter; also Chapter 1, SWITZERLAND; also Chapter 3, PARIS; also Chapter 6, LONDON.)

SIBELIUS, JEAN (1865–1957). Finland's great composer, a master symphonist of the 20th century, published virtually nothing after 1926 despite many promises and the public's high expectations. His birthplace at Hallituskatu 11 in **Hämeenlinna**, a wooden house dating from 1834, was his home until 1868. Today it displays his piano, harmonium, and many manuscripts. Concerts of his music are presented in the summer. (Open daily; concerts July—August, Wednesday, 3:00; admission.)

The composer's boyhood summer home, a one-story wooden structure on a stone foundation, also survives in the village of **Loviisa**. There in 1891 Sibelius returned to work on his *Kullervo* (First) Symphony.

In 1904 the composer built his permanent home at **Järvenpää**, a two-story, white-timbered house he called the Villa Ainola after his wife, Aino Jarnefelt. There, beginning with his Third Symphony, he wrote all of his later works and welcomed many notable visitors. "The Americans are accustomed to the idea that famous men live like lords," he said. "They expect to find a castle here and are very disappointed when they see our little house." Yet the comfortable simplicity of the beamed ceilings and hardwood walls (extended on the upper floor in 1911) continue to attract nu-

VILLA AINOLA, HOME OF SIBELIUS. The composer built this residence at **Järvenpää**, a rambling structure of rustic interiors in the Finnish forest he loved, and lived there from 1904 to the end of his long life. Though Sibelius composed nothing for publication during his final three decades, the house is probably Finland's most popular museum, and displays numerous exhibits on the composer's life and works.

merous admirers of his music. Original furnishings and memorabilia evoke details of his five decades there. "A big black Steinway, a gift from friends on his fiftieth birthday," wrote Kenneth Bernstein, "stands just where he ignored it; he was a violinist, not a pianist, and in any case worked only in his head." Bernstein also noted the numerous empty cigar boxes stacked in odd places. "For all the tobacco he obviously consumed, he lived to be ninety-two. But he quit composing at sixty." Not only Sibelius but the nation was outraged when his home was burglarized in 1952. Before this episode, he had never locked his doors. (Inquire locally for admission information.)

Sibelius tomb: Villa Ainola, **Järvenpää.**

Exhibit: In **Turku** the Sibelius Museum at Piispankatu 17 displays a collection relating to the composer and to the history of Finnish music, which includes manuscripts and relics. (Inquire locally for admission information.)

(See Chapter 1, AUSTRIA; also Chapter 2, FRANCE; also Chapter 3, PARIS.)

NORWAY

Norway is the smallest of the Scandinavian nations in terms of population with barely four million residents. Stretching further north, it is also the most rugged and mountainous of them. About 70 percent of the land is naked rock. Norway's 1,770-kilometer length is greater than any other

European nation's except the Soviet Union, yet at its far-north narrowest point, it measures only five kilometers in width.

Of Teutonic origin, Norwegians are typically tall and fair. With the possible exception of the Danes, whom they resemble temperamentally, Norwegians are probably Europe's most friendly, relaxed people. The hard physical struggle with their landscape gives them little time or energy for neuroses (despite Ibsen's dramas), and the suicide rate ranks extremely low. Though more conservative and less urbane than Danes, their open, almost childlike (though not childish) qualities make meeting them an experience as rare and bracing as their own mountain air.

Norway was governed by the Danish crown from 1397 to 1814, when it was ceded to Sweden. Not much older than Finland as a nation, it achieved independence only in 1905. A Danish prince, Haakon VII, became constitutional monarch by election, and his house continues to rule. Norway's monarch has much more power than most monarchs possess nowadays: the king may veto legislation, though his veto, in turn, may be overridden by the Storting (parliament). No European monarchy is as democratically accessible to the people. On designated days, virtually anyone may enter the palace and consult with the king. The aim of Norway's socialistic system is to guarantee personal "security regardless of individual success," an aim it fulfills with model efficiency. Oslo, Norway's capital and largest city, resumed that medieval name in 1925 after being known from 1624 as Christiania after its Danish king, Christian IV. Overrun by the Nazis despite tough resistance in 1940, postwar Norway quit its formerly neutral stance and allied its political interests with the West. Fishing, timber, petroleum and hydroelectric power industries, together with a large international shipping fleet, govern Norway's economy.

Seamen and explorers rank among Norway's foremost historic notables. Ibsen in literature and Grieg in music gave the country international status in the arts. Most of these eminent Norwegians are well represented by house-museums that welcome visitors to the unique heritage of Europe's topmost nation.

AMUNDSEN, ROALD (1872–1928). The polar explorer, first man to reach the South Pole, was a native of **Borge**. His birthplace and childhood home, Tomta, was restored in 1972; it is now the

Amundsen Memorial and displays memorabilia. This one-story house was the family home only during Amundsen's infancy, but the family continued to reside there during summers for many years. It stands on Highway 111. (Apply to caretaker.)

In **Oslo**, Little Uranienborg was Amundsen's boyhood home from 1872 to about 1890. A two-story villa on the crest of a knoll that was, at the time, little more than a fenced forest clearing at the edge of the city, it remains unmarked at Uranienborgveien 9.

Bundefjord, a two-story, Swiss-chalet-style house Amundsen bought in 1908, remained his lifelong home. He furnished the rooms to resemble shipboard cabins and there planned his 1910–11 expedition to Antarctica. Accessible during his lifetime only by foot or water, the house may now be reached by road; it displays possessions and furnishings of the explorer at Roald Amundsensveien 192 in **Svartskog**. (Open May 15—September 15, daily 11:00—5:00; admission.)

Exhibits: In **Oslo** the Fram Museum in the Bygdöynes displays the three-masted, 800-ton vessel that in 1911 carried Amundsen to Antarctica, where he raced the Englishman Robert Falcon Scott to the South Pole (Scott never came back). The *Fram* was built for Fridtjof Nansen's 1893–96 expedition to the North Pole, and Otto Sverdrup also used it for his 1898–1902 polar voyage (see

HOME OF A POLAR EXPLORER. The seamed Viking face of Roald Amundsen had yet to face Antarctic blizzards when he bought Bundefjord, his permanent home at **Svartskog**, in 1908. Its Swiss-chalet exterior contrasts vividly with interior rooms that the bachelor mariner decorated to resemble the sparse accomodations of shipboard quarters.

the entries on Nansen and Scott later in this section). This ship, it is said, has penetrated further both north and south than any other vessel in the world. Also on display is the 40-ton *Gjöa*, the sloop which Amundsen steered through the Northwest Passage between 1903 and 1906. A tourist attraction in San Francisco for many years, the vessel "came home" in 1972 in time for Amundsen's birth centennial. (Open April—October, daily 12:00—3:00; also May 1—14, September, daily 11:00—5:00; May 15—August 31, daily 10:00—6:00; November, Sunday 12:00—3:00; November—March, by appointment; 558090; admission.) The Ski Museum at the Holmenkollen, top of the Olympic ski jump just behind the city, displays equipment used by Amundsen at the South Pole as well as equipment used by Nansen and Scott. (Open March—May 14, October—November, Saturday—Sunday 10:00—4:00; May 15—August 15, daily 10:00—9:00; August 16—31, to 8:00; September, to 6:00; 02-142019; admission.) The Ethnographical Museum of the University of Oslo at Frederiksgaten 2 exhibits a collection of Eskimo artifacts assembled by Amundsen. (Open summer,

Tuesday—Sunday 11:00—3:00; rest of year, Tuesday—Sunday 12:00—3:00; 02-330070; free.)

The Sandefjord Maritime Museum at Prinsensgate 18 in **Sandefjord** displays a collection relating to Amundsen's career which was assembled by Helmer Hanssen, his mate on several expeditions. (Open May—September, Monday—Saturday 12:00—5:00, Sunday 12:00—6:00; October—April, Sunday 12:00—4:00; 033-65211; free.)

GRIEG, EDVARD (1843–1907). The composer's birthplace at Strandgaten 152 in **Bergen** disappeared during World War II.

On the grounds of the Hotel Ullensvang on Road 47 at **Lofthus** stands the small wooden work cottage Grieg used from 1877 to 1880, when he spent summers in Lofthus. Called "The Compost" by local farmers because of its earthy appearance, it was first moved to the Ullensvang rectory in 1880 for a children's playhouse but was ultimately placed here. The cottage contains a piano used by Grieg. (Call Lofthus 61–100 for information.)

In 1884 the composer built his permanent home, Troldhaugen ("Troll Hill"), on a promontory overlooking Lake Nordasvann at **Hop**, eight kilometers south of Bergen. The two-story Victorian house with balcony is now a Grieg museum and displays original furnishings, awards, photographs, and manuscripts. His Steinway grand

TWO VIEWS OF TROLDHAUGEN. High on a bluff overlooking Lake Nordasvann at **Hop**, the composer Edvard Grieg built this Victorian balconied house in 1884 and resided there for the rest of his life. The lake view of the house also shows his solitary work hut at the base of the bluff. Both buildings, now Grieg museums, are viewed by many visitors annually.

piano, an 1892 gift from the city of Bergen, is still played during summer concerts presented in the house. Grieg, who had a profound feeling for nature, refused to trim the trees or shrubs on his property, preferring to let them grow wild. Below the house on the lakeshore stands the one-room cottage he built for a work hut. The battered upright piano there was too high for the diminutive composer, and visitors may observe what he used to lift himself to the required height—the collected works of Beethoven stacked on the piano stool. (Open May 2—October 1, daily 11:00—2:00, 3:00—6:00; 05-272261; admission.)

Grieg tomb: Troldhaugen, **Hop**.

IBSEN, HENRIK (1828–1906). The birthplace of the great naturalistic dramatist, the Stockmann House, burned down in the great fire that destroyed much of **Skien** in 1886. It stood opposite the church in the main square. From 1831 to 1835 the family resided in the Altenburggaarden, located in what is now Henrik Ibsens Gate.

The later family home in the Snipetorpgaten, a two-story wooden dwelling, also survives under private ownership and is marked. Though Ibsen

BIRTHPLACE OF IBSEN. This old engraving shows the public square in **Skien**, with the playwright's first home on the left. Fire destroyed the dwelling in 1886.

himself only resided there in 1843 and 1844, it remained the parental home to which he returned at intervals until 1865. Paintings and caricatures he drew on the door panels may be seen in the Folk Museum at Skien (see *Exhibits* below).

At **Venstöp**, house and outbuildings of the small farm occupied by the family from 1835 to 1843 still survive. There the youngster began reading voraciously from a trove of books left in the attic by a previous owner and constructed a puppet theater, which may still be seen. Venstöp Farm, operated by the Skien Folk Museum, is located three kilometers north of Skien via the Maelagaten. (Open daily, 12:00—6:00; 035-25749; admission.)

Ibsen lived in **Grimstad** from 1844 to 1850, and was employed as an apothecary's apprentice. From 1846 he resided in the apothecary shop, now the Ibsen House and Grimstad Museum at Henrik Ibsens Gate 13. It was there that he wrote his first play, *Catalina* (1850). Ibsen memorabilia, manuscripts, letters, and the pharmacy equipment he used are displayed in this 1839 structure. (Open June—August, daily 10:00—3:00; September—May, apply to caretaker; 041-40545; admission.)

In **Bergen** Ibsen learned theater from the ground up when he worked as stage manager and somewhat hesitant director at the Bergen Theater (1851–57). From 1853 he occupied a rear apartment in the theater itself. This building, now the Theatrical Museum, was reconstructed after World War II damage; it stands in the Manufakturhuset and displays exhibits relating to the city's long history of staging drama. (Apply to caretaker.)

During Ibsen's first period in **Oslo** (1857–64), where he worked at the Norwegian Theater and married Suzannah Thoresen, he resided in lodgings at the corner of the Akersgaden and Carl Johansgade. After his return from Germany in 1891 he leased an apartment at Viktoria Terasse 13b, where he wrote *The Master Builder* (1892) and *Little Eyolf* (1894). Ibsen's last home from 1895, and the place he died, was a first-floor apartment in the Arbinsgade (corner of Drammersveien). There he wrote his last two plays, *John Gabriel Borkman* (1896) and *When We Dead Awaken* (1900). Rooms from this apartment may be seen at the Skien museum (see *Exhibits* below).

Ibsen tomb: Our Savior's Cemetery, **Oslo**.

Exhibits: At **Skien** the Telemark and Grenland

Folk Museum in the Brekkeparken shows memorabilia of Ibsen's homes at Skien and Oslo. His reading room, blue drawing room, and bedroom from his last home are recreated with the original furnishings. (Open May 15—September 15, Monday—Saturday 10:00—7:00, Sunday 12:00—6:00; 035-23594; admission.)

In **Oslo** the Norwegian Folk Museum at Museumsveien 10 displays Ibsen's study from his last home. (Open summer, daily 10:00—6:00; rest of year, Monday—Saturday 11:00—4:00, Sunday 12:00—4:00; 02-558090; admission.)

(See *WEST GERMANY* in this chapter; also Chapter 8, ITALY.)

NANSEN, FRIDTJOF (1861–1930). Arctic explorer, scientist, humanitarian, world statesman, and 1922 Nobel Peace Prize winner, Dr. Nansen paved the way for the more spectacular polar exploits of such men as Amundsen, Peary, and Byrd. He made **Oslo** his home for almost his entire life. His birthplace, Store Fröen, was his mother's estate, a two-story farmhouse with a large courtyard that stood beside the Frogner River; it was his family home to about 1877. The area has been engulfed by the city's expanding suburbs.

In 1900 Nansen designed and built his final home, Polhögda, a large brick house secluded by red pines at Fridtjof Nansensvei 17. From his tower study there in 1910 Nansen watched his protégé, Roald Amundsen, set off in the *Fram* for the Antarctic. Nansen wrote many of his books there and died on the verandah, exhausted from years of overwork. He bequeathed the house to the University of Oslo, stipulating that it not be turned into a museum but be used as a functional research center for polar and oceanographic studies and related political aspects. Since 1958 it has been owned and occupied by the Nansen Foundation, a research institute concerned with the law of the sea, seabed resources, and similar subjects.

Exhibit: Built to Nansen's specifications, the ship *Fram* spent three years (1893–96) frozen in the polar ice of the far North, demonstrating his theory that the ice cap was far from stationary. The *Fram* was designed to surmount the heavy pressure ridges of ice that had smashed lesser ships to kindling. The iced-in ship didn't quite carry Nansen over the Pole, but it got him to within five degrees, closer than anybody else had approached at the time. Probably the strongest-hulled ship ever built, the *Fram* rests in long-honored retirement at

the Fram Museum in **Oslo**, not far from where it first set out (see the entry on Roald Amundsen, *Exhibits*, earlier in this section).

(See Chapter 6, LONDON.)

SCOTT, ROBERT FALCON (1868–1912).
Exhibits: Intending to become the first man to reach the South Pole, the English explorer ran a futile race with Roald Amundsen in 1912 and died on the return journey. Equipment he used on this expedition is displayed at the Ski Museum in **Oslo** (see the entry on Amundsen, *Exhibits*, earlier in this section).

In the mountain village of **Vinstra**, the 1902 Fefor Höifjellshotell displays mementos of Scott's stay there while training for his South Pole expedition.

(See Chapter 5, ENGLAND; also Chapter 6, LONDON.)

SWEDEN

By far the largest, most populous, and most industrialized of the Scandinavian nations, Sweden shares the long Scandivanian peninsula with Norway, separated from that country by a rugged mountain spine. In contrast to Norway in the west, most of Sweden has flat or rolling terrain. Iron ore and timber provide the basis of its prosperous economy.

Swedes have occupied their land for at least 5,000 years, longer than almost any other Europeans can claim. Sweden held Finland for some 600 years and also Norway for almost a century (1814–1905). Earlier, Sweden was a Danish subject in the Kalmar Union (1397–1523); in the latter year, Gustavus Vasa created an independent Swedish kingdom. Sweden's Baltic empire in the 17th century included parts of Poland and Prussia, but its aggressive policies under Charles XII, leading to the Swedish invasion of Russia, met ultimate defeat. In 1818 the Bernadotte dynasty was installed; it still rules Sweden's constitutional monarchy. Like the other Scandinavian nations, Sweden has been and remains a world leader in advanced social policies and legislation (in 1977 the parliament even banned official use of the titles "Miss," "Mrs." and "Mr.") The people are highly taxed to support the country's socialistic system, but most of them view the returns as well worth the individual expense.

During World War II Sweden drew considerable resentment from its Nazi-invaded neighbors for its policy of armed neutrality, a policy that was both determined and frequently compromised by Swedish notions of expediency and self-interest. Sweden's liberal postwar assistance to the war-impoverished nations helped erase some of this ill feeling, but the fact cannot be glossed over that World War II was economically prosperous for Sweden—a vastly different experience from the ordeals suffered by its neighbors east, west, and south. Sweden today maintains its heavily armed neutrality, refusing to attach itself politically to any superpower alliance, watching the rest of the world choose up sides but opting to remain free of such global games itself. The firmness of this Swedish resolve causes occasional apoplectic reactions from both superpowers, but Swedes characteristically let them fume and go on about their own considerable business. From such a neutral vantage point issue the world-renowned Nobel Prizes for honoring achievement in various areas of human endeavor.

Those who like to compare Scandinavian temperaments say that Swedes are less open and friendly, much more reserved, formal, industrious, and work-oriented than Danes, Finns and Norwegians. Swedes agonize more over daily life and public policy, and believe in a "right way" of doing things; the "melancholy Danes," it is said, all live in Sweden. The least and last Christianized of Western European countries, Sweden is officially Lutheran but displays no large interest in religion; church attendance is extremely low. Stockholm is the capital, chief seaport, and largest city.

Notable Swedes who have reflected combinations of the national character include scientist Carolus Linnaeus, tortured dramatist August Strindberg, philosopher Emanuel Swedenborg (whose astounding mysticism was as curiously dry and formal as his scientific treatises), and Dag Hammarskjöld, whose introverted private journal contrasted sharply with his assertive diplomatic skills in the world arena. All of them are represented by surviving dwellings in Sweden today.

BRAHE, TYCHO (1546–1601). He was known as a Dane because his homes stood on what, until 1658, was Danish territory. The home sites of the great astronomer and mathematician, however, have long been Swedish territory.

The island of **Ven**, located in Öre Sound off Landskrona, occupies only seven and a half square kilometers. It was granted to the astronomer by

King Frederick II of Denmark in 1576 and became Brahe's intensely active observatory and home for 21 years. On the high center of the island he built his dwelling, Uraniborg ("Castle of the Heavens," named in honor of Urania, the muse of astronomy), on a perfectly symmetrical scale. The house stood at the center of a square, walled enclosure whose four corners were aligned to the four compass points. An arbor projected from the center of each 18-foot-high wall. Actually a palatial structure, the house front extended about 100 feet with Gothic Renaissance towers and an octagonal pavilion in the middle. A short distance south of the house, Brahe erected another observatory, which he called Stjerneborg, in 1584. There he perfected the art of astronomical observation before the invention of telescopes, designing and building mathematical instruments of great precision, his remarkably accurate calculations laying the basis for our modern Gregorian calendar. The Earth, in Brahe's universe, centered the solar system, with sun and planets revolving around it. "He built his universe," wrote one biographer, "as he built Uraniborg and Stjerneborg—a world of perfect symmetry." After the king's death, Brahe's royal support vanished and he was forced to leave, ultimately becoming a court astronomer in Prague. Brahe's island buildings had all disappeared by the early 1600s; by 1646 the site was an open field, which it has essentially remained. Brahe's old well survives, however, and the central part of the site where his elaborate manor stood is now a sunken garden. Excavations in 1824, 1901, and 1924 recovered many small items and fragments, some of which are exhibited in the small museum adjacent to the site. Also displayed are Brahe's death mask and various documents relating to the scientist's work here. The island is accessible via boat service from Landskrona. (Inquire locally for admission information.)

Exhibit: More excavated items from Uraniborg may be seen in the Museum of Cultural History at the Kuturen in **Lund**. (Inquire locally for admission information.)

(See EAST GERMANY in this chapter.)

BRECHT, BERTOLT (1898–1956). On the island of **Lidingö**, off the coast of Stockholm, the refugee German playwright occupied the former studio of a sculptor in 1939 and 1940. There, surrounded by pine forest, he wrote two of his best-known stage works, *Mother Courage and Her Children* (1939)

and *The Good Woman of Sezuan* (1940). The house stood at Lövstigen 1.

(See EAST GERMANY, WEST GERMANY, DENMARK, FINLAND in this chapter; also Chapter 1, SWITZERLAND.)

DESCARTES, RENÉ (1596–1650). In 1650 the French philosopher and mathematician came to **Stockholm** to tutor young Queen Christina in philosophy. Unaccustomed to both the severe northern winter and the early hour set by the queen for her lesson (5 a.m.), Descartes took ill almost immediately and died of pneumonia shortly thereafter. The present 550-room Royal Palace on the northern edge of the city island of Gamla Stan (Stockholm's Old Town) replaced the one in which Descartes died after the first palace burned down in 1697, so there is little associated with the philosopher to be seen. The state apartments, art collections, antiques, statuary, the royal crown jewels, and numerous other items associated with the Swedish monarchy are on view. (Hours vary for each collection; admissions.)

(See THE NETHERLANDS earlier in this chapter; also Chapter 2, FRANCE; also Chapter 3, PARIS.)

HAMMARSKJÖLD, DAG (1905–1961). Noted for his diplomatic skill and immense personal integrity, the second secretary-general of the United Nations was a native of **Jönköping**. His birthplace, built in 1888, stands at Ostra Storgatan 91.

As the son of a provincial governor, the bache-

DAG HAMMERSKJÖLD'S STUDY. The recreated room at the world diplomat's home in **Backäkra** reproduces his office in New York, where he served as United Nations secretary-general for eight crucial years. Furnishings and mementos are original.

lor Hammarskjöld lived from 1917 to 1930 with his parents in Uppsala Castle, the 1540 governor's residence and former royal palace overlooking **Uppsala** where Queen Christina had abdicated in 1654 because of her conversion to Catholicism. "The whole of that ancient castle of the Vasas," wrote Hammarskjöld biographer Sven Stolpe, "was a storybook world. What is now the hall of state was then a wonderful playroom," and the youth delighted in leading exploring expeditions through passages of the ancient fortress.

Hammarskjöld willed his summer home at the Baltic village of **Backäkra** to the Swedish Tourist Association with the proviso that the six-room, one-story farmhouse be made available to host international conferences and vacationing members of the Swedish Royal Academy. (Inquire locally for admission information.)

Hammarskjöld tomb: Municipal Cemetery, **Uppsala**.

Exhibit: A Hammarskjöld Memorial Room in the municipal museum at **Jönköping** commemorates the diplomat. (Inquire locally for admission information.)

LINNAEUS, CAROLUS (1707–1778). Born Carl von Linné in the Lutheran parsonage at **Räshult**, the botanist who created the binomial taxonomic system for classifying organisms was a latter-day Adam, giving plants and animals Latin designations for genus and species. His birthplace, a simple turf-roofed homestead built by his father, stands in the Linnégärden, Highway 23. (Open April 15—June 14, August 16—October 15, Tuesday—Sunday 9:00—6:00; June 15—August 15, daily 9:00—6:00; admission.)

In 1741, as professor of medicine at **Uppsala** University, Linnaeus occupied the house reserved for him, a two-story, orange-stucco dwelling that "looked more like an owl's nest or a den of thieves," he said, "than a professor's residence." He built an orangery (hothouse) and established a large garden in which he cultivated seeds and plants brought to him from all over the world. This property became his permanent home, and he died there. Eight years later the garden was transferred to another location, but the Swedish Linné Society, which now owns and maintains house and gardens, restored it on the original site at Svartbacksgaten 27 during the early 1900s. The orangery, which was rebuilt in 1955 in modified form, now provides lecture rooms and offices. Today the "Linneanum," as the house is known, hardly resembles either nest or den. "To visit the house or walk around the garden today is to come very close to Linnaeus," states biographer Wilfrid Blunt. Personal relics and exhibits on the botanist's life and career, including his scientific instruments, may be seen. (Open Tuesday—Sunday 9:00—5:00; free.)

In 1758 Linnaeus purchased an estate at **Hammarby** which became his favorite summer retreat. He enlarged the modest quarters and in 1766 built himself a tiny stucco hut on a knoll above the timber manor ("my little back-room") as a private museum to house his natural history collections. Purchased by the nation in 1879 and since restored, the Linnaeus Museum displays many original furnishings as well as the 16-foot-square "hut." Though the same kinds of flowers Linnaeus knew still grow in the garden, one change he would immediately notice is the much more luxuriant vegetation surrounding the buildings. The Linnaeus Museum is signposted in the village. (Inquire locally for admission information.)

Linnaeus tomb: Cathedral, **Uppsala**.

(See THE NETHERLANDS in this chapter; also Chapter 6, LONDON.)

STRINDBERG, AUGUST (1849–1912). Obsessed with the "war between the sexes," reflecting the frequent domestic crises of his own three marriages, the antifeminist playwright was also an important forerunner of modern expressionism in his surrealistic "dream plays." A native of **Stockholm**, Strindberg resided there for much of his life. None of his earliest homes survive. From 1899 to 1901 he lived at Banergaten 31. An apartment at Karlavagen 80, which he occupied from 1901 to 1908, was the site of his brief third marriage to actress Harriet Bosse, who was 30 years younger. There he also wrote most of his mystical, less bitter "dream plays" and Swedish historical dramas. Strindberg's final home, from 1908, was the "Blue Tower" at Drottninggaten 85, so named from its spiral outside staircase paved in blue stone. He resided on the top floor alone, attempting his last love affair with his landlord's daughter, 20-year-old Fanny Falkner (whose parents summarily ended the romance), and finally died there. Today visitors may see Strindberg's furniture, manuscripts, and other memorabilia in these rooms. (Open Tuesday—Saturday 10:00—4:00,

also Tuesday 7:00p.m.—9:00p.m., Sunday 12:00—5:00; admission.)

Strindberg tomb: New Church Cemetery, **Stockholm**.

Exhibits: Strindberg's recreated study from his last home may be seen in the Nordic Museum on the Djurgarden, **Stockholm**. (Open June—August, Monday—Friday 10:00—4:00, Saturday—Sunday 12:00—5:00; September—May, closed Monday; admission.) The Royal Library in the Sturegatan displays Strindberg manuscripts. (Open daily, 10:00—4:00; free.)

(See Chapter 3, PARIS.)

SWEDENBORG, EMANUEL (1688–1772). The teachings of this versatile scientist, philosopher, and religious mystic inspired the founding of the Swedenborgian sect and New Jerusalem Church, which became especially popular during the 19th century. **Stockholm**, where he was born Emanuel Swedberg, remained his most frequent home despite numerous travels and occasional residences elsewhere. His exact birthplace site remains unknown. Swedenborg bought a large rectangular lot in 1743, enlarged the modest country house on the property, and surrounded the whole with a high wooden fence. This remained his permanent home until his 1771 departure for England, and it was there that he wrote such mind-boggling esoterica as the *Arcana Coelestia* (1749–56), *Divine Love and Wisdom* (1763), and *The True Christian Religion* (1771). Nothing of Swedenborg's house and large garden survives at Hornsgatan 43, but one outbuilding from his back garden—the one-room cottage where he did much of his writing during summers—may be seen in Skansen Park's Open-Air Museum on the Djurgärden. (Park open daily; admission.)

Earlier, from 1692 to about 1702, he lived with his family in a large stone house that stood on the cathedral square in **Uppsala**; his Lutheran bishop father was rector and dean of Uppsala Cathedral.

Swedenborg tomb: Cathedral, **Uppsala**.

(See Chapter 6, LONDON.)

Chapter 5
GREAT BRITAIN: ENGLAND

Great Britain, Europe's largest island, consists of England, Scotland and Wales.* Because of Britain's profusion of notable historical figures, various parts of the country are treated separately here. The great historical and cultural nucleus of England's 46 counties is, naturally enough, London. Chapter 6 focuses exclusively on that city, while Chapter 7 deals with Scotland, Wales, and both the Irish Republic and Northern Ireland. Great Britain and the United Kingdom are not synonymous, of course, since the United Kingdom includes Northern Ireland.

England, the largest portion of Great Britain, lies south of Scotland and east of Wales. Except for these borders, its sea boundaries span an 1,800–mile coastline. No part of England lies more than 70 miles from the North or Irish seas or the English Channel coast. From the Scottish border to the English Channel, England stretches about 365 miles. Its land surface, a sag-and-swell glacial topography, contains relatively few rivers and no startling extremes of elevation. Though the entire country lies well north of Winnipeg's latitude, the arching Gulf Stream provides a mild, damp climate that gives rise to the visitor's favorite complaint but which the English consider a civilized norm.

England's population of about 44 million constitutes about four-fifths of the island's total. This long-mixed melting pot of peoples makes such ethnic stews as the United States look "uncooked" in comparison. During its long, painful evolution—culminating in the distinctive if not easily defined "British character" known today—England's ethnic panorama has reflected the historical population shifts and power movements on the continent.

What we know as England today is a fusion of peoples, cultures and languages that invaded its shores in wave upon wave. Evidences of the earliest known settlers, collectively labeled Iberians, remain in earthworks and in the enigma of Stonehenge. The fair-haired Celts, who invaded about 600 B.C. from northern Germany and Holland, left the ancient surviving languages of Wales, Scotland and Ireland. These were tribal cultures, intensely warlike but finally no match for the strictly disciplined Roman legions, led first by Julius Caesar in 55 B.C. The Roman conquest of Britain was completed under Claudius almost a century later. Hadrian's Wall, erected in A.D. 123 and remnants of which still exist, crossed northern England from the rivers Solway to the Tyne, marking the northern limit of this conquest.

Rome ruled England for three and a half centuries, far longer than most present nations have existed. Yet, because of England's isolation and distance from the Mediterranean power center, the country was never permanently "Latinized" as

*Geographically, the "island" of Great Britain actually includes numerous offshore islands as well, such as the Isle of Wight, Isle of Man and the Channel Islands.

was France. The Romans left plenty of ruins and roads, which still carry traffic, and they established several important city sites. But, like 19th-century British colonialists in Africa and Asia (and probably with the same type of chauvinism), they held but did not settle; it was not "home" to them.

The most important invasions as far as the later ethnic character of the country was concerned were those of the Germanic Angles, Saxons and Jutes, beginning about A.D. 450. In less than two centuries, these agrarian peoples had established seven kingdoms—Kent and Wessex in the south, and Mercia and Northumbria further north were the most important—and had evolved a recognizably "English" language from their dialects. It remained only a spoken language, however, until the Saxon scholar-king, Alfred the Great, sponsored translations of works from Latin into "the language we all know." During this period, the country was regularly besieged by the Danes (Vikings), who by 1020 completed their conquest of England under Canute. English Christianity, meanwhile, had been incorporated with European Catholicism by the Synod of Whitby in 664, and England remained Catholic for eight centuries. As the remote "backstairs" of the continent, however, the country carried no important weight in European affairs for more than a thousand years. Instead, it served as a kind of convenient way station for whoever happened to be raiding and plundering—a doormat for free-floating hostility, as it were. For a longer time than Great Britain has existed, England remained supremely invadable.

England's historic watershed was, of course, the last invasion in its history: the Norman Conquest in 1066, led by a French warrior who held an outdated claim to the English throne. William the Conqueror, crowned William I, violently dispersed the Anglo-Saxon nobility, and French became England's official language, remaining so until the 14th century. William ruthlessly unified and strengthened the former Saxon kingdoms under a central government and established a rigorous feudal system on the Norman model.

England achieved cultural independence and national feeling as a result of the Hundred Years War (1337–1453), an ultimately futile and absurd attempt to conquer France. Conflict between state and church was savagely ended by Henry VIII, and the long reign of his daughter, Elizabeth I, heralded the golden age of English history. The country's sense of national patriotism was still new and shining when Shakespeare wrote of "this blessed plot, this earth, this realm, this England." From the 16th century, as the world's most powerful nation, England was the center of an empire larger than any before or since, ultimately controlling more territory than its Saxon-Norman forebears ever knew existed—about one-fifth of the earth's surface and one-fourth of its population. Not until World War I did the long decline of the British empire begin. Its last years came in 1947 and 1948, when India and several other Asian countries were granted self-determination; and the British Commonwealth of Nations, a loose association of mostly independent countries that had replaced the old colonial structures, was established.

Since the Norman Conquest, Britain has had 40 monarchs of nine royal houses, all directly descended from William the Conqueror—and, by collateral ancestry, from Alfred the Great. George III was the last sovereign who actually ruled Great Britain in any absolutist sense. His rule, if not his reign, was quickly truncated after the loss of the American colonies, an event that firmly established the dominant roles of prime minister and House of Commons in the British government. British monarchs have been safer ever since; previously, the English had killed five of their kings.

Increasingly, the monarchy became a symbolic institution whose main participation in government was—and is—"to be consulted, to encourage and to warn." The kings and queens that followed George III on the throne have existed mainly to be seen, not heard, for it is the royal presence that counts, "happy and glorious," reminding Britons everywhere that as long as a sovereign exists for God to save, their world is not without order and meaning. Thus, on a practical level, the British monarchy has a strong ceremonial function, which serves the nation's sense of self-identity, continuity and purpose. Within its restrictive setting, however, it may exert an informal influence in the chambers of state.

Perhaps England's greatest gift to civilization has been the common law, that body of unwritten opinion based on general observance that has formed the basis of most Western democratic systems. In a country whose economy has been predominantly socialist since World War II, it remains a profound paradox—just one of many in this enchanting land—that the hierarchical class system not only survives but prospers. This fact, like England's sturdy adherence to a largely unwritten constitution, is another of those characteristic anomalies that seem inherently irrational and unworkable, yet in English hands turn out "right as rain."

England manages nicely without guns for its populace; it also manages without the incessant propaganda that less confident nations push. In contrast to both totalitarian and technocratic societies, its people are treated as neither social nor economic "cogs," and the difference shows in the country's low crime rate and high levels of health care and education. Drug addiction, to give one example, is not a matter for Scotland Yard but for physicians and rational medical programs. Individual eccentricity, far from being merely tolerated, is expected and valued as the normal prerogative of any Englander. Above all, the English value their self-respect. In short, the country probably embodies more of the civilized social ideal than any other world nation today.

This condition did not come about quickly or easily. Through its long history, England has experienced most of the social spasms and conflicts that still afflict many other nations. It has arrived, via a difficult history and well-learned lessons from that history, at a point where it views anything less than concern for the individual welfare as unpatriotic—a view that leaves most other nations of the world still fumbling in the dust politically. Though pressing economic and social problems do exist, approaches to their solution typically center on the English regard for individual justice. In this important respect, it must be said, England still sets the standard and remains the mightiest world power.

England's historical figures are known for some of the world's greatest achievements, especially in the fields of literature and statecraft. An obscure tradesman's son of modest schooling and faint ambition named William Shakespeare became the supreme English poet and master psychologist of the ages. With his often comic but always sharply-observed novels, Charles Dickens brought about large social and educational reforms. Kipling spoke for Victorian imperialism by making it seem high-minded and altruistic. Shelley, Keats, Byron, and Wordsworth implanted literary ideals that still affect how poets think and are thought of. And writers such as D. H. Lawrence, Virginia Woolf, and George Orwell helped revolutionize 20th-century literature.

England's notable "men for all seasons" encompassed not only men—either in the past or today. Its greatest, most accomplished monarch was probably Elizabeth I. With glowing language and firm rule, she presided over the country's richest golden age—an age of creativity, of diplomacy and growing sea power. Sir Francis Bacon, Sir Thomas More, Benjamin Disraeli and, in our own times, Sir Winston Churchill, were not only activists of vast political skills but scholars who mixed thinking and doing to a degree seldom seen in other countries. Their lives illustrate that in England, if hardly anywhere else, statecraft exists as one of the humanities.

The homes of such eminent men and women survive in quite impressive numbers throughout English cities and villages. For all of its rainwashed climate, neither England's land nor buildings appear to erode very swiftly. Much of that appearance is owed to the constant care of a people to whom the past is a vital ingredient of today. The English, in the words of one observer, "would never think of leveling an ancient monastery or tearing up an early Roman roadway simply because it now serves no useful purpose." To the English, such actions are a species of vulgarity; it just isn't done. Destruction of ancient buildings has resulted mostly from the ravages of time (though ruins are often carefully preserved) or from the bombs and rockets of World War II.

Most houses that are open to the public are operated by or affiliated with one of three major organizations. The Department of the Environment is the government agency responsible for most royal buildings and many ancient monuments such as castle ruins or sites. The National Trust, founded in 1894, is Britain's largest private landowner and preservation society, maintaining ownership of more than 200 historic buildings. Many private owners of historic properties belong to the Historic Houses Association, which promotes their common interests as well as public access to the properties themselves. Twelve regional offices of the English Tourist Board, each encompassing areas made up of several counties, also welcome queries on houses within their respective areas. Neil Burton's *British Historic Houses Handbook* (1982) details the homes of most notable Englanders, as well as many others, that are open to the public.

No country is so richly self-endowed in excellent guidebooks to its history. The two outstanding literary guides, indispensable for any actual or armchair pilgrim, are *A Literary Gazetteer of England* (1980) by Lois H. Fisher; and *The Oxford Illustrated Literary Guide to Great Britain and Ireland* (1981) by Dorothy Eagle and Hilary Carnell. Also interesting is the narrative atlas *Literary Landscapes of the British Isles* (1979) by David Daiches and John Flower. Jane Murray's *The Kings and Queens of England* (1974) and *Royal Palaces* (1972) by Olwen Hedley are also useful. Probably the best all-around historical guidebook is Philip A. Crowl's *The Intelligent Traveller's Guide to Historic Britain* (1982).

Since English community names are often duplicated in the various counties, the appropriate county name is parenthesized after the city or village entry in the following pages.

ARNOLD, MATTHEW (1822–1888). The birthplace of the influential poet and critic is long gone from its site on Ashford Road at **Laleham** (Surrey), his home until 1828.

Arnold's father, Dr. Thomas Arnold, became headmaster of Rugby School in **Rugby** (Warwickshire) in 1828. The Headmaster's House, the turreted, ivy-covered building that was Matthew Arnold's home until his father's death there in 1842, still stands on the southeast corner of School House, Old Quad, Lawrence Sheriff Street, and Rugby's headmasters still live there.

In 1833 Thomas Arnold built Fox How, a large stone family house about three-quarters of a mile northwest of **Ambleside** (Westmorland). This area was beloved by poet William Wordsworth, who negotiated Arnold's purchase of the estate below Loughrigg Fell and helped with building plans (see the entry on Wordsworth later in this chapter). Fox How became Matthew Arnold's holiday retreat from 1834 to the end of his life. Among the eminent guest he entertained there were Thomas Carlyle and Ralph Waldo Emerson. The house remains privately owned.

Arnold's last home, in which he lived from 1873, was Pain's Hill Cottage, which he described as "a nutshell of a house." It fronted open fields at **Cobham** (Surrey). This house is gone from the site now known as Matthew Arnold Close, located west of a small 18th-century bridge over the River Mole.

Arnold tomb: Parish churchyard, **Laleham**.
(See Chapter 6, LONDON.)

ARTHUR (470s?–537?). The legendary "king of the Britons" reigned supreme for centuries as the unifying symbol of English independence. In the long, violent history of the British monarchy, numerous kings invoked Arthur's charismatic image to help legitimize or empower their own rule, much as American politicians invoke the image of Abraham Lincoln today. The Tudors, especially, took great pains to claim direct descent from Arthur. Whether or not he ever actually existed, until the 18th century at least, the English universally believed that he did. Over the course of ten centuries he became a virtual god-king, a messianic embodiment of history who would return, it was said, in a moment of paralyzing crisis to vanquish the foe and unite England under one triumphant banner.

The Arthur we know today is the literary creation of Sir Thomas Malory. His *Le Morte D'Arthur* (1485) is an embellished collection of Arthurian tales which had circulated throughout the Middle Ages. The first written allusions to Arthur were those of Gildas (sixth century) and Nennius (ninth century). Geoffrey of Monmouth treated him as a historical personage in his *History of the Kings of Britain* (1136).

Did Arthur exist? Modern scholars hedge. The consensus, in the words of Geoffrey Ashe, is that "the Arthurian Legend, however wide-ranging its vagaries, is rooted in an Arthurian Fact." But "historically speaking, the Arthurian Fact is far clearer than Arthur himself." His period was the chaotic epoch between Roman and Anglo-Saxon England. What meager evidence there is suggests that he was not a king in any proclaimed sense but a Romanized Celtic soldier, a "rustic noble" who led a vagabond army of "knights" against sixth-century Saxon invaders.

Most Arthurian literature gives his birthplace as Tintagel Castle, located on a rocky headland near the coastal village of **Trevena** (Cornwall). Since ruins of the present castle date from the 12th to 14th centuries, they hardly represent "King Arthur's Castle," as the tourist brochures would have us believe. Excavations have disclosed that a Celtic monastery, established by St. Juliot, stood there from about 500 to 850. An earlier castle might have occupied the site, but excavations thus far have not confirmed this. The site on Tintagel Head off route 3263 is slowly crumbling into the sea; the headland itself has become a virtual island

LEGENDARY BIRTHPLACE OF A LEGENDARY FIG-URE. Ruins of Tintagel Castle near **Trevena** surmount a rocky Cornwall headland, the reputed site of King Arthur's birth. Except for a long literary tradition, no evidence exists that Arthur (if he lived at all) ever lived there. King Arthur's castle, if it ever stood, must have predated the present castle by at least seven centuries. Yet the rugged setting is certainly conducive to Arthurian romance, and the place remains an important literary if not biographical site.

connected by a narrow, railed causeway to the mainland. (Open March 15—October 15, Monday—Saturday 9:30—6:30, Sunday 2:00—6:30 and from 9:30 between April and September; October 16—March 14, Monday—Saturday 9:30—4:00; Sunday 2:00—4:00; admission.)

The site of Camelot, Arthur's capital, has intrigued generations of poets, pilgrims and historians. There are four possible sites, all derived from literature written long after Camelot's supposed existence: Caerleon in Wales; Camelford (Cornwall); Winchester (Hampshire); and **South Cadbury** (Somerset). The latter, specifically the ruins of the sixth-century Cadbury Castle, an 18-acre hill fort, is currently the preferred possibility among Arthurian scholars and archaeologists. During the 1960s, extensive excavations (the most thorough of any site in England) revealed Cadbury Castle as "a major defensive work" with a 60- by 30-foot banquet hall that *could* have been Arthur's. Treasures of artifacts also revealed Cadbury as an important Neolithic site. While Leslie Alcock reported that "we did not find the fabulous Camelot, nor add anything directly to historical knowledge about Arthur as a person," the scientific team concluded that Cadbury was certainly "a military site in use at the time when Arthur was a warrior." The only visible remains are a low cir-

cle of turf-covered ramparts, approached via a steep footpath from the village post office.

Glastonbury is also in Somerset. Its 12th-century abbey ruins, said to be Arthur's "Isle of Avalon," are also traditionally identified as his grave site, according to a discovery by abbey monks in 1191. Archaeology has established that a grave did exist on this spot. Also found was the base of an abbey shrine where Arthur and Queen Guinevere were supposedly interred in 1278; their tomb is said to have remained there until dissolution of the monastery in 1539. Visitors may see the latter grave site, now marked on a green lawn that was once the center of the abbey choir. (Ruins open June—August, daily 9:00—7:30; September—May, daily 9:30—sunset; 0458–32267; admission.)

Exhibits: Both western and northern England boast numerous sites claiming Arthurian significance, including places where various tales say he fought, died and now sleeps until some wanderer shall arouse him by cutting the garter and sounding the magic horn.

Today in the village of **Tintagel**, the Hall of Chivalry and King Arthur's Hall have stained glass windows and paintings depicting the legends; there is also a library of Arthurian literature. These halls are operated by the Fellowship of the Round Table. (Open daily, 10:00—5:30; admission.)

The 18-foot-diameter oak table displayed in the great hall of Winchester Castle at **Winchester** (Hampshire) is an impressive 14th-century antique, but obviously it is not Arthur's "round table," as once claimed. Only about 25 people could have squeezed around this colorful board, while the "true" round table could accommodate 150 knights. Researchers in 1976 concluded that the Winchester table was probably built for Edward III in 1336 for his Order of the Garter, fulfilling his vow to restore Arthur's circle of knighthood. The table paintings, however, do not predate 1510. Winchester Castle was a frequent residence of William the Conqueror and the place where Sir Walter Raleigh was condemned to death in 1603 (see the entries on Raleigh and William the Conqueror later in this chapter). The Norman castle stands on Castle Avenue off High Street. (Open Monday—Friday 10:00—5:00; also April—September, Saturday 10:00—6:00, Sunday 2:00—6:00; and October—March, Saturday—Sunday 2:00—5:00; 0962–4411; donation.)

AUDEN, WYSTAN HUGH (1907–1973). The porticoed Georgian house where the poet was born and lived for his first year remains at 54 Bootham Street in **York** (North Yorkshire).

In **Solihull** (Warwickshire), a suburb of Birmingham, an Auden boyhood home survives at 13 Homer Road (1913–15). His home from 1918 to 1920 is located at 42 Lordswood Road in **Harborne**, another Birmingham suburb.

One of Auden's last residences was a 16th-century stone cottage, a former brewhouse on the grounds of Christ Church College in **Oxford** (Oxfordshire), where he conducted poetry seminars in 1972 and 1973. The house remains in the service of the college.

(See Chapter 1, AUSTRIA; also Chapter 8, ITALY.)

AUSTEN, JANE (1775–1817). The birthplace of the novelist who chronicled genteel country life with subtle irony and wit was the village rectory in **Steventon** (Hampshire), her home until 1801. Nothing remains of the house, demolished more than a century ago; its site, marked by a metal pump on the same spot as the Austen family well, is located in a field alongside the lane leading to the 13th-century church where her father pastored for four decades. Austen wrote all of her best-known novels there, including *Sense and Sensibility* (1811), *Pride and Prejudice* (1813) and *Northanger Abbey* (1818), though none were published during her Steventon residence.

In **Bath** (Avon), she occupied several residences with her family from 1801 to 1806. They lived from 1801 to 1804 at 4 Sydney Place off Pulteney Street, where she revised *Northanger Abbey*; this dwelling remains privately owned. At 27 Green Park Buildings, their next lodging, Rev. George Austen died in 1805. Only a portion of this building survives; its eastern side was demolished during World War II. Bath was a frequent setting for episodes in Austen's novels, and several buildings used in her scenes still exist.

The Jane Austen Memorial Trust maintains the novelist's home in **Chawton** (Hampshire). Chawton Cottage, now known as "Jane Austen's House," is a brick, two-story house built as an alehouse-inn about 1700. With her mother and sister, Austen lived, wrote and gardened there from 1809 to 1817, the period when she wrote *Mansfield Park* (1814), *Emma* (1816) and *Persuasion* (1818). Her desk, books, pictures, handiwork items, numerous family possessions and period furnishings bring Jane Austen's world to life. Divided into three tenements following the Austen residency, the interior of the house has been beautifully restored. (Open April 1—October 31, daily 11:00—4:30; November 1—March, Wednesday—Sunday 11:00—4:30; Alton 0420–83262; admission.)

Austen's residence during her final two months of life, a three-story brick structure then operated by one Mrs. David, still stands at 8 College Street in **Winchester** (Hampshire). The author had come to Winchester seeking medical treatment for an illness that was probably Addison's disease. Cared for by her sister Cassandra ("I live chiefly on the sofa," she wrote), she continued to work on her novel *Persuasion* almost until the very last. Jane Austen died at this address.

Austen tomb: Winchester Cathedral, **Winchester**.

Exhibit: A few of the novelist's personal belongings are displayed at the City Museum near the cathedral in **Winchester**. (Open Monday—Saturday 10:00—5:00, Sunday 2:00—4:00; free.)

BACON, SIR FRANCIS (1561–1626). Scientist, philosopher, prominent lawyer, and first notable English essayist, Bacon occupied his family's country estate near **St. Albans** (Hertfordshire) from about 1568. In 1563 Elizabeth I had commanded his father, Sir Nicholas Bacon, to build an estate as a reward for his services as lord keeper of the seal. Using materials from the demolished 11th-century St. Albans Abbey, Sir Nicholas completed the Tudor house with its 70-foot-square courtyard in 1568, named it Gorhambury House, and acted as host to his queen several times. The son, educated there by his mother, inherited Gorhambury in 1601. He enlarged the house and lavishly revamped its interior and grounds. Both house and grounds are said to have utilized the symbols of Freemasonry in pattern and arrangement of features. After his banishment from public life in 1621, Bacon retired to Gorhambury and pursued full-time research and writing, of which *The Advancement of Learning* (1605) was one result. Bacon often employed musical ensembles to play in adjoining chambers while he worked, as a kind of pre-piped music system. Today only the ruins of Bacon's house remain in Gorhambury Park adjacent to the present Gorhambury House (see below), though the porch he designed is relatively intact. Bacon usually resided there only during winters. His elaborately landscaped summer residence was Verulam House, which he built near several ponds on the estate about one mile away; this house was demolished in the late 1600s. Between the summer and winter houses, Bacon built three parallel roads to enable his guests' coaches to drive abreast. Often, he dictated his thoughts to a secretary while walking on the estates, later incorporating the notes into essays and treatises.

Bacon tomb: St. Michael's Church, **St. Albans**.

Exhibit: The present Gorhambury House, built in 1784 and the home of Bacon's collateral descendant, the Earl of Verulam, displays furnishings from the old Bacon manor house plus portraits and books. Gorhambury stands two-and-one-half miles northwest of **St. Albans**, near the junction of routes A14 and A5. (Open May—September, Thursday 2:00—5:00; St. Albans 54051; admission.)

(See Chapter 6, LONDON.)

BECKET, ST. THOMAS À (1118?–1170). As Roman Catholic archbishop of Canterbury, England's highest religious prelate, Becket opposed the secular authority of his friend and king Henry II over the church, a conflict that first drove him into exile, then—upon his return—brought him to violent martyrdom in Canterbury Cathedral. (See *Exhibits* below). From 1162 until his exile two years later, and again in 1170, Becket's official residence was the archbishop's palace in **Canterbury** (Kent). This manor, in which Becket first confronted his assassins, stood until about 1635 in the cathedral precincts on Palace Street. Traces of the old house are visible in Walpole House on the site.

But Canterbury was a relatively infrequent residence for the contentious archbishop. A favorite retreat was the archbishop's palace at **Otford** (Kent), of which a tower ruin and St. Thomas' well, an oblong basin, remain. A row of cottages occupies the site of the long gallery. Elizabeth I sold this property, which the Danish king Offa had acquired in 790, in 1601.

In **Charing** (Kent), only ruins remain of the archbishop's palace, another of Becket's favorite residences during journeys to and from London.

Similarly, only small fragments remain of the Norman Berkhamsted Castle in **Berkhamsted** (Hertfordshire), Becket's residence in earlier days when he was chancellor for Henry II. An extensive

lawn now covers the 15,000-square-yard outer court. Also on this site William the Conqueror accepted the surrender of London from Edgar Atheling in 1066; and Geoffrey Chaucer may have resided there as clerk of works in about 1388 (see the entries on Chaucer and William the Conqueror later in this chapter).

Exhibits: Inside **Canterbury** Cathedral, visitors may see the marked spot, on the floor of the northwest transept, where four of Henry's knights hacked the archbishop to death when he refused to leave the cathedral precincts. The murder occurred at the foot of some steps (no longer in existence) which led to the choir. Years of penance, both by the king who in an exasperated moment had cried "Are there none to free me of this low-born priest?" and by the assassins, who had taken the king at his impulsive word, followed the act. Becket was canonized in 1172, and his ornate tomb above the high altar in Trinity Chapel attracted thousands of pilgrims annually until Henry VIII destroyed the martyr's shrine in 1538. The present cathedral, now the official seat of the Church of England, has been much modified since Becket's time. Founded in 597, it was sacked by Danish invaders in 1011, completely rebuilt in 1067, and heavily damaged by fire in 1174. The present nave dates from 1374, the central bell tower from the late 15th century. Much of the huge Norman crypt, however, the site of Becket's first tomb under the Trinity Chapel and Corona, is original. (Open daily; free.)

A few relics of the churchman were rescued at great peril from the anticlerical destruction of 1538. Two reliquaries in the Church of St. Thomas, Burgate Street, **Canterbury**, contain some of those accusatory finger bones and a piece of vestment worn by the archbishop. The church is open daily.

(See Chapter 2, FRANCE; also Chapter 6, LONDON.)

BENTHAM, JEREMY (1748–1832). From 1814 to 1818 the utilitarian philosopher rented Forde Abbey, located four miles southeast of **Chard** (Dorset) via signposts. This abbey had functioned as one of England's important Cistercian monasteries for 400 years before Henry VIII ordered it closed around 1540. Abbey buildings were converted into a lavish private palace shortly afterward, and substantial alterations were completed by 1660. Little has changed since, and the rooms where

Bentham acted as host to his protégé, young John Stuart Mill, and his family for prolonged periods contain period furnishings and decorations. Visitors are shown the great hall, the saloon, a conservatory and smaller rooms that are remnants of the original abbey structure. Forde Abbey is owned and operated by Mr. M. Roper. (Open May—September, Wednesday, Sunday 2:00—6:00; garden only, March—April, October, Sunday 2:00—4:30; South Chard 0460–20231; admission.)

(See Chapter 6, LONDON.)

BLAIR, ERIC ARTHUR. ("GEORGE ORWELL") (1903–1950). The first English home of the novelist-essayist was the town of **Henley-on-Thames** (Oxfordshire), to which the family came from India, where Blair's father had served in the English diplomatic corps, in 1907. They resided at Nutshell, their small house on Western Road until 1912. In 1915 they returned to the town and lived at 36 St. Mark's Road until 1917. Between these two stays (1912–15), they resided at Roselawn, a country house on Station Road at Shiplake.

Southwold (Suffolk) became the family home in 1921, though Blair himself spent the years from 1922 to 1927 in Burma. On his return he lived with his parents, first in a house in Queen Street, then in 1932 and 1933 at Montague House, a two-story brick house at 36 High Street.

From 1936 to 1940, Blair (now known as Orwell) lived with his first wife, Eileen O'Shaughnessy, in an ancient cottage, formerly a general store, in **Wallington** (Hertfordshire). He raised chickens, geese and goats on his patch of ground— the rambler roses he planted in the front garden still flourish as a large hedge on the private property—and opened a small grocery in the cottage to supply the village.

Blair tomb: Parish churchyard, **Sutton Courtenay** (Oxfordshire).

(See Chapter 3, PARIS; also chapter 6, LONDON; also Chapter 7, SCOTLAND.)

BLAKE, WILLIAM (1757–1827). "Felpham is a sweet place for Study, because it is more Spiritual than London," wrote the poet, painter and mystic to a friend. "Now Begins a New Life.... I am more famed in Heaven for my works than I could well conceive." William and Catherine Blake took a two-story thatched cottage with six rooms in 1800 at **Felpham** (West Sussex) and lived there

until 1803. Blake experienced "voices of celestial inhabitants" and the vision of a ladder of angels winding through the village and ending at his cottage. But his increasing disaffection with the area culminated in an unpleasant episode in which he was brought to trial for sedition after throwing a drunken soldier out of his garden. The white-walled house remains privately owned behind the Thatch Inn.

(See Chapter 6, LONDON.)

BRADFORD, WILLIAM (1590–1657). The ancestral home of the Pilgrim colonist and 31-year governor of America's Plymouth colony is Austerfield Manor, a two-story farmhouse located near **Austerfield** (South Yorkshire) on route 18.

(See Chapter 4, THE NETHERLANDS.)

BRITTEN, BENJAMIN (1913–1976). All of the composer's homes outside London were in the county of Suffolk. His seashore birthplace and home until 1930, a three-story mansion where his father practiced dentistry, stands at 21 Kirkley Cliff Road in **Lowestoft**.

At **Snape**, he purchased a converted windmill and used it for a residence studio from 1938 to 1940 and at intervals thereafter. There he composed his opera *Peter Grimes* (1945).

Crag House in **Aldeburgh**, his seafront home at 4 Crabbe Street, was his residence for the decade 1947–57. Britten lived there with tenor Peter Pears, whom he often accompanied on piano at vocal recitals. It was there that he composed his opera *Billy Budd* (1951). The Red House, a two-story brick dwelling also in Aldeburgh, was Britten's last home, from 1957, and the place where he died. Today this dwelling holds the Britten-Pears Library, established by the two musicians in a wing of the house in 1973. It is the main Britten archive. Scholars and research students may visit by written appointment.

In 1970, Britten bought Chapel House at **Horham**. He used this two-story dwelling overlooking fields as a refuge from the noise of aircraft which could be heard at his Aldeburgh home.

Britten tomb: Parish churchyard, **Aldeburgh**.

(See Chapter 6, LONDON.)

BRONTË, ANNE (1820–1849).
BRONTË, CHARLOTTE (1816–1855).
BRONTË, EMILY (1818–1848).

The novelist sisters, who spent most of their lives at a bleak Yorkshire parsonage, have become one of literature's legends. Anne recorded her unhappy experiences as a governess in *Agnes Grey* (1847). Charlotte wrote *Jane Eyre* (1847), the classic novel of romantic love. Emily produced one of the 19th century's most powerful novels, *Wuthering Heights* (1847), chilling as a shriek of moorland wind in its portrait of relentless human passion. "Read at the right time," wrote Judith Chernaik, "*Wuthering Heights* is a book that changes one's life permanently."

The Brontë's parsonage birthplace in **Thornton** (West Yorkshire), a small, terraced house at 74 Market Street, is marked by a plaque. Villages named Thornton are common in Yorkshire; this one is a western suburb of the town of Bradford. The privately owned dwelling was the Brontë home until 1820.

In that year, the family moved to the parsonage at **Haworth** (West Yorkshire) which became their home for the rest of their lives. This rugged moorland village has since been engulfed by the "Brontë cult," and hosts some 200,000 visitors annually. Visitors will note the Heathcliff Cafe, Brontë shops and tour buses, as well as the original Black Bull Inn, a favorite haunt of the Brontë's painter brother, Branwell.

BRONTË PARSONAGE. Anne, Charlotte and Emily Brontë spent most of their short lives in this bleak moorland rectory at **Haworth**, where their father, Rev. Patrick Brontë, served as minister, and there wrote most of the novels for which they became famous. A line of trees now screens the foreground churchyard from the house as seen in this old photograph.

St. Michael's parish church, on the site adjacent to the parsonage, where the authors' father Rev.

Patrick Brontë preached, and where Charlotte married curate Arthur Nicholls in 1854, was rebuilt in 1881. Only a fragment of the original tower remains. But the Brontë parsonage, a 1799 stone house, still overlooks the churchyard. Acquired as a public memorial in 1928, the downstairs rooms have been meticulously restored in accordance with descriptions given by Charlotte's first biographer, Elizabeth Gaskell, who visited the house in 1853. The only real differences today are a line of fir trees between parsonage and churchyard, which serve to block the front-window view of what amounts to a forest of headstones; and north and west wings which were added to the parsonage in 1872. The Brontë Society now operates the parsonage as a museum, displaying Rev. Brontë's study, the parlor where Emily wrote *Wuthering Heights* and where the sisters read their manuscripts to each other, and the dining room containing the couch on which Emily died. (All of the Brontë siblings except Anne died in the parsonage.) There are several pews from the original parish church, plus letters and manuscript excerpts. By far the greatest number of relics on display belonged to Charlotte—including shawls, dresses, bonnets, embroideries, and even her spectacles. "Best time to come," advises Patricia Ledward in *A Guide to Literary Europe*, "is at the end of summer, when the huge moors—the only place Emily could find release of spirit—blaze with colour." A more typical Brontë scene, however, is "in bad weather, when the trees drip, when the gleaming grave-stones crowd ominously about the house, [when] you can almost hear Emily coughing on her hard sofa and see dear, gentle Anne wanly sewing in badly-lit rooms."

Author Judith Chernaik expresses another view: "One can only imagine how the Brontës would have hated it, how appalled Charlotte would have been by the display of her faded pink nightgown and nail brush, how Mr. Brontë would have blanched at the sight of his nightcap perched on the mantelpiece." Chernaik thinks that the Brontë novels are important precisely because they "express a vision of life stripped of the genteel trivia the Brontë Society offers admirers, all those paraphernalia of women's lives that serve so well to hide, if not to suffocate, the spirit within." (Open April—September, Monday—Saturday 11:00—5:30, Sunday 2:00—5:30; October—March, Monday—Saturday 11:00—4:30, Sunday 2:00—4:30; 0535–42323; admission.)

Thorpe Green Hall, the Rev. Edmund Robinson mansion in **Little Ouseburn** (North Yorkshire), is where Anne Brontë served as governess to the Robinson daughters from 1841 to 1845. Her brother Branwell joined her as a tutor to the son in 1843 but was dismissed for drunkenness in 1845. Anne's novel *Agnes Grey* derives from her experiences there. The house remains privately owned.

Anne Brontë died at 2 The Cliff in **Scarborough** (North Yorkshire), where she had come to view scenes from her novel. The site of her last residence, razed about 1870, is the present location of the Grand Hotel.

A house associated with Charlotte Brontë stands on Oxford Road in **Gomersal** (West Yorkshire), home of her friends Mary and Martha Taylor. The 18th-century brick house appears in her novel *Shirley* (1849) as "Briarmains." Charlotte often stayed there during the period 1831–40, and a room in the house displays a Brontë exhibit. Known as "The Red House," the dwelling also exhibits period furnishings similar to those familiar to the novelist. It is owned and operated by the Kirklees Metropolitan Council. (Open April—October, Tuesday—Saturday 10:00—6:00, Sunday 1:00—5:00; November—March, Tuesday—Saturday 10:00—5:00; Cleckheaton 0274–872165; free.)

Anne Brontë tomb: St. Mary's Cemetery, **Scarborough**.

Charlotte and Emily Brontë tombs: St. Michael's Church, **Haworth**.

Exhibits: The scene most evocative of the Brontë art and reality is, of course, the moorland at **Haworth**. Just minutes away from the parsonage museum (see above) are the miles of rolling, windswept, bracken highlands and marshes especially beloved by Emily. Deserted stone farmhouses huddle in the sags of this wild landscape, among them the possible models for the manors in *Wuthering Heights*: "Wuthering Heights" itself (the bleak, deserted High Withins or Top Withins, located about three miles southwest across the moors from Haworth via Pennine Way Path); and "Thrushcross Grange" (probably Ponden Hall, perhaps also a model for Wuthering Heights, located across the bridge in the Sladen Valley north of High Withins). Walking directions and maps to these houses and other local spots associated with the family, may be obtained at the parsonage museum.

(See Chapter 4, BELGIUM.)

BROWNING, ELIZABETH BARRETT (1806–1861). The poet's birthplace was **Kelloe** (Durham), where her parents occupied the 18th-century Coxhoe Hall until 1809. Now gone, it stood in a conifer grove east of the Kelloe-Coxhoe Road near its junction with route B6291. Elizabeth was christened in the small parish church located on a now private dirt road.

Just south of **Colwall** (Herefordshire), off route A4154, is the site of Hope End, the estate purchased by her father and Elizabeth Barrett's childhood home. She remembered the large mansion as a "Turkish house . . . crowded with minarets and domes, and crowned with metal spires and crescents." There the precocious youngster was educated and by the age of eight was reading Homer in the original Greek. In 1820, while saddling her pony, she suffered the spinal injury that made her a lifelong, drug-dependent invalid. Some of her early poems, "The Lost Bower" and "Aurora Leigh," for instance, describe scenes of Hope End. The house was rebuilt after the family left in 1832, but the stables with minarets and quarter-moons remain on the 40-acre property and have been converted to a small hotel.

From 1832 to 1835 the Barretts lived at **Sidmouth** (Devon), first at 7-8 Fortfield Terrace (1832–33), then in a large Georgian house called Belle Vue in All Saints Road, now the Cedar Shade Hotel. During her residence here she published her first poetry as well as *Prometheus Bound* (1833), which inspired her first correspondence with Robert Browning.

In seaside **Torquay** (Devon), she lived at Bath House (now Hotel Regina), 1 Beacon Terrace, from 1838 to 1841. Instead of improving her health, though, her stay was calamitous; the death of her favorite brother Edward in an 1840 sailing accident prostrated her so that her return to London was delayed for a year. The hotel looks much the same as it did in 1840.

(See Chapter 6, LONDON; also Chapter 8, ITALY.)

BUNYAN, JOHN (1628–1688). The Nonconformist preacher, tinker and author of *Pilgrims Progress* (1678) resided in Bedfordshire throughout his life. His birthplace cottage site in **Harrowden** is marked by a granite block in the fields, approached via Old Harrowden Lane. "Except in dry weather," report the authors of *The Oxford Literary Guide*, "the going is heavy and the mud can be a chastening reminder of the Slough of Despond." Bunyan lived there until 1644.

During the 1640s and 1650s he lived in the nearby village of **Elstow**, where he played on the village green—the spot where he said he experienced his conversion in 1653. The site of his house is marked on Bedford Road.

In 1655 Bunyan and his family moved to **Bedford**. The present Bunyan Cottage at 17 St. Cuthbert's Street, while probably not the original house, is of similar construction. Imprisoned in 1660, for preaching without a license, Bunyan was held for 12 years in the now long-gone county gaol at High and Silver streets and began writing *Pilgrim's Progress* there in 1666. He spent a further year in the prison in 1676–77.

Exhibits: The medieval Moot Hall on the village green in **Elstow** displays a collection of furniture, books and documents relating to Bunyan and his period. (Open Tuesday—Saturday 11:00—5:00, Sunday 2:00—5:30; Bedford 0234–66889; admission.)

Adjacent to the Bunyan Meeting House on Mill Street in **Bedford**, the Bunyan Museum, built in 1850, houses the main collection of Bunyan relics and materials. It stands on the site of the barn where Bunyan preached (legally) from 1672. Visitors may see the barred, grated doors that held Bunyan in the county gaol, his chair from the original vestry, the pulpit from which he preached at Zoar Church in London, a tin fiddle and wooden flute he made and many other items of personal memorabilia. (Open Tuesday—Saturday 10:00—12:00, 2:30—4:30, or by appointment; 0234–58627; admission.) Bedford Public Library in Harpur Street also displays Bunyan relics and numerous editions of his works in its Frank Mott Harrison Collection. (Open Monday—Saturday 10:00—6:00; free.)

(See Chapter 6, LONDON.)

BURKE, EDMUND (1729–1797). In 1768 the statesman-orator borrowed money to buy a large estate called The Gregories in **Beaconsfield** (Buckinghamshire), where he entertained many well-known guests, including Dr. Samuel Johnson (see the entry on Johnson later in this chapter) and the painter Sir Joshua Reynolds. Burke died there, and the house, which he had renamed Butler's Court, burned down in 1813. The present structure was rebuilt on the site, and houses cover part of the original 400-acre estate.

At **Bath** (Avon), Burke sought to regain his health in 1796 and 1797. His lodging is marked at 11 North Parade, which was also the 1771 residence of poet-novelist Oliver Goldsmith.

Burke tomb: Parish church, **Beaconsfield**.

(See Chapter 6, LONDON; also Chapter 7, IRELAND.)

BYRON, GEORGE GORDON, LORD (1788–1824). In 1798 the young future poet and romantic literary idol of his generation inherited the family estate at Newstead (see below), but he and his family could not afford to live there. Byron and his mother took temporary lodgings in **Nottingham** (Nottinghamshire); their residence on St. James Street is owned by the Nottingham Corporation but does not presently admit visitors.

Though Byron occasionally visited his ancestral estate of Newstead Priory, he did not occupy it until 1808. The Byron family had acquired the confiscated priory in 1540 and converted its buildings into a mansion surrounding the original cloister. By the time the poet (sixth Lord Byron) inherited it, Newstead was described as "a heap of rubbish." Though determined to settle and renovate, Byron lived there intermittently for only a decade before debts forced him to sell the estate. Its wealthier succeeding owner proceeded to restore the mansion and most of the present exterior dates from this restoration, completed in 1860. Today, the Nottingham City Council displays Byron's chambers; his ornate bedstead, the circular desk on which he wrote a portion of *Childe Harold's Pilgrimage* (1812), his boxing gloves, and some oak chairs covered with embroidery done by his half-sister and sometime lover Augusta Leigh, are among the articles on view. Other notable items include the shoe lasts Byron used to try to correct his congenital club foot, and a goblet made from a human skull that was excavated on the property and used by the poet and his carousing friends during his housewarming. (Another calculated act was his burial of Boatswain, his dog, on the site of the former church's high altar.) Galleries linking the main apartments also exhibit Byron mementos. The Charles II Room, where that monarch once bunked, has some of Byron's letters on display; and the Roe-Byron collection of manuscripts may be viewed in the salon.

Byron used much of the Newstead atmosphere and environs in his *Don Juan* (1819–24). Later

NEWSTEAD ABBEY, LORD BYRON'S FAMILY ES-
TATE. Byron himself resided in the former priory ac-
quired in 1540 by an ancestor for only about a decade.
Maintenance costs finally forced him to sell it. Located at **Linby**, the house is now a Byron museum displaying many personal items of the prototypical "romantic poet."

guests who stayed in the house and wrote about it included American authors Washington Irving (1835) and Joaquin Miller. Scottish missionary David Livingstone also lived briefly in the mansion. Newstead Abbey stands at **Linby** (Nottinghamshire), 11 miles north of Nottingham. (Gardens open January—November, daily 10:00—dusk; house open Good Friday—September 30, daily 2:00—5:15; Bidworth 06234–2822; admission.)

Byron married Isabella Milbanke at her home Seaham Hall in **Seaham** (Durham) on January 2, 1815. It was an ill-fated pairing. The couple lived at the house briefly after their honeymoon. Now a county hospital, Seaham Hall admits only the sick—an irony that Byron would vastly appreciate. "Any former elegance," wrote literary historian Lois H. Fisher, "has been eradicated by clinical linoleum floors, waiting rooms and aspidistras. All that remains of its association with Byron is the fireplace in the drawing room."

Byron tomb: Hucknall Torkard church, **Hucknall** (Nottinghamshire).

Exhibits: Byron relics are displayed at the 17th-century privately owned Thrumpton Hall in **Nottingham**. (Open by appointment for parties of 20 or more; 0602–830333.)

In **Bath** (Avon), the Museum of Costume displays the poet's Albanian outfit, worn by him in 1809. The museum is located in the Assembly Rooms on Bennett Street. (Open April—October, Monday—Saturday 9:30—6:00, Sunday 10:00—6:00; November—March, Monday—Saturday 10:00—5:00, Sunday 11:00—5:00; 0225–61111; admission.)

The home of Augusta Leigh, Byron's half-sister and reputed mistress, is today a country hotel, Swynford Paddocks, located at **Six Mile Bottom** (Suffolk).

(See Chapter 1, SWITZERLAND; also Chapter 4, BELGIUM; also Chapter 6, LONDON; also Chapter 7, SCOTLAND; also Chapter 8, GREECE, ITALY.)

CARROLL, LEWIS. See CHARLES LUTWIDGE DODGSON.

CHAUCER, GEOFFREY (1345?–1400). England's first major poet wrote *The Canterbury Tales* (ca. 1387–1400), probably while living at his estate somewhere near **Gadshill** in Kent, but the precise spot remains unknown.

At **Woodstock** (Oxfordshire), the privately owned Chaucer House on Park Street is said to stand on the site of a Gothic dwelling owned by Thomas Chaucer, the poet's son. According to tradition, the poet stayed there at intervals during his later years.

Chaucer may have occupied the Winchester Tower at Windsor Castle, **Windsor**, while employed as master of the works in 1390 (see the entries on Victoria and William the Conqueror later in this chapter; also see the entry on St. Thomas à Becket earlier in this chapter).
(See Chapter 6, LONDON.)

CHURCHILL, SIR WINSTON (1874–1965). According to journalist and travel writer R. W. Apple, Jr., "a kind of Churchill industry has sprung up in Britain, devoted to keeping his memory alive." But the patient, as Churchill might have phrased it, is not likely to depart soon in any case. The birthplace of the great wartime prime minister and English historian was the ancestral Churchill estate, Blenheim Palace, located south of **Woodstock** (Oxfordshire) on route A34. "At Blenheim," he said, "I took two very important decisions: to be born and to marry." The massive estate was never his permanent home, but he visited the house of his forebears frequently, both in childhood and later life.

Queen Anne gave the estate, formerly the site of Woodstock Manor (see the entry on Elizabeth I later in this chapter), to John Churchill, First Duke of Marlborough, in 1704 as a reward for defeating the French at the Battle of Blenheim in Bavaria. Sir John Vanbrugh designed the seven-acre English baroque palace, a masterpiece of the style, and building lasted from 1705 to 1725. Lancelot "Capability" Brown landscaped its 2,000-acre parkland. Today, the property is owned by the present Duke of Marlborough. Visitors may tour palace and grounds and view the room where Lady Jennie Jerome Churchill delivered Winston prematurely. Among the memorabilia on display are paintings, documents, photographs, baby clothes, and a lock of the five-year-old Winston's hair. (Palace open mid-March—October 31, daily

BLENHEIM PALACE. The ancestral estate and birthplace of Sir Winston Churchill near **Woodstock** was built in the 18th century for soldier John Churchill, first Duke of Marlborough, and named for a crucial battle he won against French forces in Bavaria. Sir Winston's premature birth in the palace was unexpected—his mother was visiting relatives there at the time. Exhibits show relics of his infancy ("All babies look like me") and other Churchillian memorabilia.

11:30—5:00; grounds open daily 9:00—5:00; 0993–811325; admission.)

At the four-story Lansworth House, 29-30 Brunswick Road in **Hove**, a Brighton (Sussex) suburb, the young Churchill attended a private boarding school from 1884 to 1888.

In 1922 Churchill purchased Chartwell, the country manor where he usually lived when not in London for the next 37 years. This Elizabethan structure, originally a farmhouse, was much altered and enlarged by Churchill. Neil Burton's *British Historic Houses Handbook* describes the building as "a formless red brick pile whose only redeeming feature is a very pretty 18th-century wooden doorway." The ponds on the 79-acre property were strewn with brush during World War II to help camouflage the estate from the air. Today the house, operated by The National Trust, is a museum and shrine to the statesman. Drawing room, dining room, library and Churchill's study, where he wrote and dictated most of his books, are kept as they were during his lifetime. An upstairs museum includes exhibits of photographs, numerous awards received by Churchill, and a uniform room displaying one of his famous denim "siren suits" plus cases of ceremonial garb, military uniforms and samples from his enormous collection of hats. Outside, a brick wall for which he did much of the masonry himself from 1925 to 1932 is marked by a plaque. Churchill's studio, where many of his paintings are displayed, is located in the garden. An excellent book to read before visiting Chartwell is Robin Fedden's *Churchill at Chartwell* (1969). Chartwell is located two miles south of **Westerham** (Kent) off route B2026 via signs. (House open March—November, Tuesday—Thursday 2:00—6:00, Saturday—Sunday 11:00—6:00; also Wednesday—Thursday in July and August from 11:00; studio and garden open, April-mid-October, same hours as above; Crockham Hill 073–278–368; admission.)

CHARTWELL. Sir Winston Churchill acquired his permanent estate near **Westerham** in 1922, massively restoring and enlarging the original Elizabethan farmhouse, and made it his frequent haven throughout his life. A 1939 photograph shows the statesman-historian in his study, where he wrote most of his books. He also spent much time painting in his garden pavilion, where a frieze records the Battle of Blenheim. Today Chartwell is England's primary museum and shrine to its wartime prime minister.

Though he never felt much at home there, Churchill resided frequently at Chequers, the official country residence of British prime ministers, especially on weekends during World War II. Chequers is located near **Aylesbury** (Buckinghamshire) on route 413. Lord Lee of Fareham gave this Tudor mansion on its 1,500-acre farm-and-woodland estate to the government in 1921 for use by prime ministers, a purpose it still serves. David Lloyd George was its first official occupant (see the entry on Lloyd George later in this chapter). Admission is restricted to those with government permission—perhaps most easily obtained through a member of Parliament.

Another of Churchill's wartime weekend headquarters was Ditchley Park at **Enstone** (Oxfordshire). Built about 1725, this mansion was the ancestral estate of the forebears of American Gen. Robert E. Lee, and the Lee family owned it for 350 years. Ditchley Park is now an Anglo-American conference center. (Open briefly in summer; 060–872–346; admission.)

Churchill tomb: St. Martin's parish churchyard, **Bladon** (Oxfordshire).

(See Chapter 6, LONDON; also Chapter 7, IRELAND.)

COLERIDGE, SAMUEL TAYLOR (1772–1834). The philosopher, poet and critic was born in the now long-gone rectory at **Ottery St. Mary** (Devon), a town that he cherished. The feeling was far from mutual when he returned for a visit as a man of controversial views. This was Coleridge's home until age 9. A small plaque on the churchyard wall is his only commemoration.

Coleridge and his wife, Sarah Fricker, spent their six-month honeymoon in 1795 and 1796 in **Clevedon** (Avon). The privately owned two-story stone cottage marked with a plaque on Old Church Road, though identified as his residence, may not actually be the one the couple stayed in—Coleridge remembered the cottage as a one-story dwelling.

The happiest period of the poet's life was spent with his wife and child at **Nether Stowey** (Somerset), where they lived from 1796 to 1798 at what is now called Coleridge's Cottage in Lime Street. It was also a productive period, during which he produced his best-known works *The Rime of the Ancient Mariner* (1798) and *Kubla Khan* (1816). Then a low, thatched structure of four rooms, it had a large garden where the poet and his friends William Wordsworth, Charles Lamb and William Hazlitt often walked and talked (see the entry on Wordsworth later in this chapter). He was not a careful gardener, believing it "unfair to prejudice the soil towards roses and strawberries." During the 19th century, the house was much enlarged and became an inn. Its original parlor, however, displays various documents relating to the poet's stay. The house is operated by The National Trust. (Open April—September, Sunday—Thursday 2:00—5:00; winter by written appointment to Coleridge's Cottage, Nether Stowey, Somerset; 0278–732662; admission.)

According to tradition, Coleridge composed *Kubla Khan* in 1797 after an opium-induced dream at Ash Farm, located off route A39 from Porlock Hill near **Culbone** (Somerset). A knock at the front door interrupted his reverie, and he was never able to recall the completion of the poem envisioned in his dream. Broomstreet Farm also claims to be the site. It, too, is off route A39.

In 1800, Coleridge moved with his family to a hillside house at **Keswick** (Somerset) known as Greta Hall, a two-family dwelling. It was here that his marital problems and drug addiction increased, and in 1803 he abandoned his family. In that year, the house became the last home of poet Robert Southey, who renovated it in 1809. Today the structure serves as a boardinghouse for the girls' school at Keswick. It is located a short distance west of the town above the River Greta.

(See Chapter 4, WEST GERMANY; also Chapter 6, LONDON.)

CONRAD, JOSEPH (1857–1924). The Polish-born author whose sea novels combined adventure with close analysis of human psychology, Conrad and his wife inhabited what he called "a damned jerry-built rabbit hutch" in **Stanford-le-Hope** (Essex) in 1896. There he finished *The Nigger of the Narcissus* (1897) and, in 1897, moved to Ivy Walls, an Elizabethan farmhouse on the edge of the village. Neither house survives; a more recent dwelling occupies the site of Ivy Walls.

All of Conrad's later dwellings were in Kent. In 1898 he moved to **Postling**, where he rented a farm from author Ford Madox Ford for the next decade. Pent Farm remains visible from route B2068 just outside the tiny village. Conrad wrote *Lord Jim* (1900), *Nostromo* (1904) and *The Mirror of the Sea* (1906) there. Author H. G. Wells and playwright George Bernard Shaw were among his visitors (see the entries on Shaw and Wells later in this chapter).

The author suffered a "nervous breakdown" from overwork at his next home (1909–10) in **Aldington**. Aldington Knoll, the small farmhouse that Conrad took over from Ford, overlooks Romney Marsh. Conrad wrote his story "The Secret Sharer" there and completed *Under Western Eyes* (1909).

Chance (1913) and *Victory* (1915) were written at Capel House, Conrad's farmhouse dwelling at **Orlestone**, where he lived from 1910 to 1919. It remains privately owned.

Bishopsbourne was the author's final home and he lived there from 1919. At Oswalds, now the village rectory, he suffered severe health and financial problems and died of a heart attack. A later resident (early 1930s) in this privately occupied dwelling was author Alec Waugh.

Conrad tomb: St. Thomas Church Cemetery, **Canterbury** (Kent).

(See Chapter 1, SWITZERLAND; also Chapter 6, LONDON.)

CONSTANTINE I, THE GREAT (272–337). Constantine, who made Christianity the official religion of the Roman Empire in A.D. 323, was proclaimed Roman emperor (i.e., Augustus of the West) in 306 at **York** (North Yorkshire). Known as Eburacum, the fortress on the River Ouse was a major Roman colonial outpost when Constantius I, his father, named Constantine his successor and died there after the two had successively countered a Pict invasion. Thus from York, it might be said, began the events that were to culminate in a Christian Europe. Nobody can be certain of the imperial palace site in York, but results of various archeological excavations suggest that it stood in the vicinity of the Old Station Yard in Railway Street. Across the river, on the east bank, stood the Roman fortress, of which the Multiangular Tower survives as a ruin at the old west-angle wall.

(See Chapter 4, WEST GERMANY; also Chapter 8, ITALY.)

COWARD, SIR NOËL PEIRCE (1899–1973). The versatile playwright, composer and actor purchased Goldenhurst, a 149-acre farm estate, near **Aldington** (Kent) about 1927. He linked together the 16th-century farmhouse and large barn and rented out 100 acres to a tenant farmer. In this house he wrote many of his plays and entertained celebrities from all over the world. "The drive ran

from the house through the wood to the main entrance," wrote his longtime companion Cole Lesley, "and was the ritual walk for Noël and his guests on Sunday afternoons." Financial problems compelled Coward, sorrowfully, to give up the estate in 1956. It remains privately owned on route 2.

(See Chapter 1, SWITZERLAND; also Chapter 6, LONDON.)

CROMWELL, OLIVER (1599–1658). The Puritan soldier who became dictator of the Commonwealth after the execution of Charles I was born at **Huntingdon** (Cambridgeshire). His birthplace, now known as Cromwell House, was built on the site of a 13th-century Augustinian monastery, and the dwelling's construction used many of the ruin's old stones and foundations. The house, now incorporated in a later structure, is operated as a library by the Huntingdon Research Centre in High Street. Cromwell lived there until 1631.

From 1631 to 1636 he tenant-farmed in **St. Ives** (Cambridgeshire), working land southeast of the town. A 14th-century structure called Cromwell's Barn, north of the village, is traditionally associated with his residence there. His mother's birthplace is now the privately occupied vicarage of St. Mary's Church.

Cromwell tomb (head only, unmarked): Sidney Sussex College, **Cambridge** (Cambridgeshire).

Exhibits: In **Huntingdon**, the Cromwell Museum is located in the former grammar school where Cromwell received his early education. The two-story building with its original Norman front had been a medieval hospital before Cromwell's day. Samuel Pepys also attended school there from 1642 to 1645 (see the entry on Pepys later in this chapter). Today the museum in High Street displays numerous relics and memorabilia relating to Cromwell. (Open Tuesday—Saturday 11:00—1:00, 2:00—5:00, Sunday 2:00—4:00; 0480–52181; free.)

Chequers, the prime minister's official residence near **Aylesbury** (Buckinghamshire), has a famous collection of Cromwell portraits and relics, but admission there is restricted to those with government permission—perhaps most easily obtained through a member of Parliament. (See the entry on Sir Winston Churchill earlier in this chapter.)

(See Chapter 6, LONDON.)

DARWIN, CHARLES ROBERT (1809–1882). The birthplace of the naturalist and main proponent of the theory of biological evolution through natural selection was The Mount, a three-story brick house on the River Severn in **Shrewsbury** (Shropshire). Darwin lived there until 1825 but often returned for visits until the house was sold in 1842. It remains privately owned in Mount Street.

At **Cambridge** (Cambridgeshire), where Darwin attended Christ's College from 1828 to 1831, he roomed in chambers just above the doorway of G Staircase, Front Court, St. Andrew's Street. The building remains functional in the college complex.

Down House, **Downe** (Kent), Darwin's last home from 1842, is now a museum dedicated to his memory and operated by the Royal College of Surgeons. There Darwin conducted garden experiments and wrote *The Origin of Species* (1859) and *The Descent of Man* (1871), his two epochal scientific treatises. The main portion of the three-story Down House was built on its 18-acre estate by Darwin's father about 1800. Charles Darwin made various additions and further alterations were carried out by his family after his death. Visitors may leisurely inspect all the rooms on the ground floor, which include Darwin's study and drawing room with original furnishings; and museum rooms with numerous family items and exhibits relating to the theory of evolution. An interesting object in the garden is Darwin's "worm stone," which he used for measuring silt increments resulting from earthworm activity. Darwin's granddaughter, writer and engraver Gwen Raverat, wrote an interesting account of growing up at Down House in *Period Piece* (1952). The house became a private boarding school before its acquisition as a museum; Irish novelist Elizabeth Bowen studied there in 1911. Down House is located in Luxted Road off route A233. (Open except February and late December, Tuesday—Thursday, Saturday—Sunday 1:00—6:00; Farnborough 0689–59119; admission.)

(See Chapter 6, LONDON; also Chapter 7, SCOTLAND.)

CHARLES DARWIN'S STUDY AT DOWN HOUSE. The great biologist's home, which he occupied permanently from 1842 and where he wrote the works that revolutionized scientific thought regarding the origin and development of species, stands in the London suburb of **Downe**. Original furnishings and possessions reveal numerous intriguing details of his quiet domestic life. Note the portable desk, for example, on his wheeled armchair.

DEBUSSY, CLAUDE-ACHILLE (1862–1918). The French composer completed one of his most popular works, *La Mer*, in the seaside Grand Hotel at **Eastbourne** (East Sussex) while vacationing there in 1905. The 170-room hotel still welcomes guests.

(See Chapter 2, FRANCE; also Chapter 3, PARIS; also Chapter 8, ITALY.)

DEFOE, DANIEL (1660?–1731). At **Chadwell St. Mary** (Essex), the novelist resided intermittently from 1694 to 1703 while managing a tile works in nearby West Tilbury. His residence was the thatched daub-and-wattle cottage across from the church. Called the Sleepers because of its lodging function for medieval pilgrims while waiting to cross the Thames, the house remains privately owned and preserved. Local tradition asserts that Defoe hid out there in 1718 to avoid arrest on a charge of libel and that he wrote part of *Robinson Crusoe* (1719) there.

(See Chapter 6, LONDON.)

DICKENS, CHARLES (1812–1870). The popular novelist's birthplace is now the Dickens Birthplace Museum, operated by Portsmouth City Museums at 393 Old Commercial Road in **Portsmouth** (Hampshire). The two-story brick building, dating from about 1800, stood in a comparatively rural area at the time of his birth. Though the family moved when Dickens was only four months old, the fact that he remembered nothing of it distressed him during an 1866 visit to the house. Period and original furnishings—including the couch on which Dickens died at his last home in Gadshill (see below)—are displayed. The only item from his infancy is a built-in kitchen dresser. (Open daily 10:30—5:30; 0705–827261; admission.) The family's home from 1812 to 1814 was a three-story house at 16 Hawke Street which was destroyed during World War II.

Chatham (Kent) was the place of the author's happiest memories and, according to biographer John Forster, "the birthplace of his fancy." The family occupied 11 Ordnance Terrace from 1817 to 1821, a three-story brick dwelling that survives.

Gadshill Place in **Gadshill** (Kent) was Dickens's last home. Dickens had first seen the 18th-century two-story brick house as a boy when his father had told him that if he grew up to be a clever man he might someday own this house or one like it.

FIRST HOME OF DICKENS. The novelist remembered nothing of his first four months at his **Portsmouth** birthplace, a fact that bothered him when he returned for a visit in 1866. A few Dickens items are on display. The photograph probably dates from about Dickens's centennial year of 1912.

Dickens bought the 14-room house as a summer residence in 1856, then four years later decided to make it his permanent home. He did little writing in the house, preferring to work in a small Swiss chalet erected on the estate across route A226; a tunnel beneath the roadway connected Dickens's front lawn with the chalet. In the two-story chalet, which was an 1865 gift from French actor Charles-Albert Fechter, Dickens worked on *A Tale of Two Cities* (1859), *Great Expectations* (1860–61), *Our Mutual Friend* (1864) and *Edwin Drood* (1870). The chalet was moved to Rochester in 1961 (see below). Dickens died at Gadshill Place, which remains privately owned.

On England's south coast, **Brighton** (Sussex) became a frequent working retreat for the novelist. In 1837 he worked on *Oliver Twist* (1837–39) at the Old Ship Hotel, 38 Kings Road, which was again his lodging in 1841 while writing *Barnaby*

Rudge (1841). His other Brighton residences included 148 Kings Road (1847), where he worked on *Dombey and Son* (1847–48), the still functional Bedford Hotel. In 1852, while writing *Bleak House* (1852), he lodged in rooms at 1 Junction Parade.

Dickens occupied several summer residences in **Broadstairs** (Kent), his favorite holiday resort from 1838 until 1851. He spent most of the latter year at Bleak House, a castellated Victorian mansion atop the cliffs on Victoria Parade. Dickens leased this residence—then known as "The Fort"—in 1850 (a subsequent owner named it Bleak House) and there finished *David Copperfield* (1849–50). But "vagrant music" often interrupted his concentration; the street musicians of small talent and large sound who played to tourists finally drove Dickens out. His study—"about the size of a warm bathroom"—bedroom and dining room are furnished with the novelist's possessions and memorabilia. (Open Easter—June, October—November, daily 10:00—6:00; July—September, daily 10:00—9:00; Thanet 0843–62224; admission.)

Previous dwellings in Broadstairs include 40 Albion Street, where Dickens finished *Nicholas Nickleby* (1838–39) in 1839, now part of the Royal Albion Hotel; and Lawn House where he lived in 1840 while writing *The Old Curiosity Shop* (1840). It became part of the Archway House Hotel in 1859.

Exhibits: In **Wisbech** (Cambridgeshire), the Wisbech and Fenland Museum, which includes the town library, displays the manuscript of *Great Expectations* and autographed first editions of Dickens's books. (Open Tuesday—Saturday 10:00—1:00, 2:00—5:00; free.)

The Dickens House Museum in **Broadstairs** is located in the house he described as Betsy Trotwood's in *David Copperfield*, with its parlor refurbished according to his description. Letters and other memorabilia are on view. (Open April—October, daily 2:30—5:30; June—September, Tuesday—Thursday 7:00p.m.—9:00p.m. also; Thanet 0843–62853; admission.)

The author's writing chalet that he used extensively at Gadshill (see above) was moved to the grounds of Eastgate House, the **Rochester** (Kent) Museum in High Street, in 1961. There is also a room devoted to Dickens in the museum. (Open daily 10:00—12:30, 2:00—5:30; Medway 0634–44176; admission.) Restoration House, a 1587 manor on Maidstone Road, was Dickens's model for "the Satis House" in *Great Expectations*.

(Open April—September, first Thursday of each month, 10:00—2:00; admission.)

Dickens's England (1970), by Michael and Mollie Hardwick, is an interesting survey of places associated with the novelist.

(See Chapter 6, LONDON.)

DISRAELI, BENJAMIN (1804–1881). An early home of the prime minister and novelist, a 17th-century manor, remains at **Bradenham** (Buckinghamshire). Owned by his father Isaac D'Israeli from 1826, the house and gardens held great nostalgia for the son, who tried to purchase the property without success about 1845. Bradenham Manor gardens, which Disraeli described in *Endymion* (1880), are occasionally open to the public (inquire locally).

Hughenden Manor was a late 18th-century house when Disraeli and his wife bought it in 1847, and it remained his frequently used country estate until his death. In 1862 the couple modernized the house, installing terraces, fronting it with a Victorian brick exterior and renovating rooms in a Gothic style. Created Earl of Beaconsfield in 1876, Disraeli wrote his novels *Lothair* (1870) and *Endymion* there, and his study remains just as it was when he died. The National Trust operates the house; Disraeli's books, manuscripts of his novels, letters, locks of hair and various other items are displayed. Hughenden Manor stands in **Hughenden** (Buckinghamshire) on route A4128. (Open April—October 31, Wednesday—Saturday 2:00—6:00, Sunday 12:30—6:00; March and November, Saturday—Sunday 2:00—5:00; High Wycombe 0494–32580; admission.)

Disraeli tomb: Hughenden Manor Church, **Hughenden**.

(See Chapter 6, LONDON.)

DODGSON, CHARLES LUTWIDGE. ("LEWIS CARROLL") (1832–1898). The mathematical scholar best known for his classic children's story *Alice's Adventures in Wonderland* (1865) was born in a parsonage near **Daresbury** (Cheshire), his home until age 11. Only the gateposts remain on the marked site in Morphany Lane today, one and one-half miles south of the village. Fire destroyed the house in 1883. Lois H. Fisher recounts that the lad of precocious imagination "was on speaking terms with every conceivable form of lower life he could find. One of his more interesting experiments supposedly was encouraging combat among earthworms; he even supplied them with arms (small lengths of pipe) to use."

From 1843 to 1850 the Dodgson family resided in the Old Rectory opposite St. Peter's Church at **Croft** (route 167, North Yorkshire.) Part of the boy's improvised railroad line survives on the extensive privately owned grounds.

Dodgson spent almost 47 years at **Oxford** (Oxfordshire), where he lectured in mathematics at Christ Church College from 1856. His early rooms were located in Peckwater Quadrangle. His model for the character of Alice was Alice Liddell, daughter of the college dean. A shy, stammering man, Dodgson became an Anglican deacon and never married, but he always enjoyed a great affinity with children. His last Oxford residence (1868–97) was a 10-room suite on the first floor of northwest Tom Quadrangle, where he experimented with photography and frequently entertained guests in his rooms. The Oxford lodgings remain private college property.

Chestnuts on Castle Hill, **Guildford** (Surrey), belonged to Dodgson's sisters and he was a frequent guest at this three-story house from 1868. In 1897 he moved there permanently and died there the following year. The house remains in Quarry Street.

During the decade 1877–87 Dodgson also often vacationed at **Eastbourne** (East Sussex). A plaque marks his lodgings at 7 Lushington Road.

Dodgson tomb: Guildford Cemetery, **Guildford**.

Exhibit: The Guildford Museum and Muniment Room adjoining Castle Arch in Quarry Street, **Guildford**, displays Dodgson letters and memorabilia. (Open Monday—Saturday, 11:00—5:00; 0483–505050; free.)

Christ Church Library in **Oxford** also displays exhibits relating to its longtime faculty member (see the entry on Thomas, Cardinal Wolsey later in this chapter).

DONNE, JOHN (1572–1631). Pyrford Place in Warren Lane at **Pyrford** (Surrey) occupies the site of the Francis Wolley house, where the future cleric and poet and his 16-year-old bride took refuge from her outraged father. They lived there from their 1601 marriage until 1605.

(See Chapter 6, LONDON.)

DOYLE, SIR ARTHUR CONAN (1859–1930). The author set up his medical practice in 1882 at 1 Bush Villas, Elm Grove, in the Portsea section of **Portsmouth** (Hampshire). At the site of this house, which bombs destroyed during World War II, Doyle wrote his first Sherlock Holmes tale, *A Study in Scarlet*, in 1887. He also produced his novels *Micah Clarke* (1888) and *The White Company* (1891) there. Doyle lived there until 1889.

Most of the Holmes stories, however, were written in Doyle's ground-floor study at 12 Tennison Road, **South Norwood** (Surrey), where he lived during the 1890s. This house is gone.

In 1896 the author built Undershaw at **Hindhead** (Surrey). Sheltered by large trees, it was his home until 1907 and remains privately owned.

His last home from 1907 was Windlesham Manor, a five-gabled shingled structure in Sheep Plain, **Crowborough** (East Sussex). Badly cheated on the price, Doyle often referred to the property as "Swindlesham." There, in a study in the gables, he did most of his later writing, pursued his interest in spiritualism, and often acted as host to Rudyard Kipling (see the entry on Kipling later in this chapter). Doyle died there. The house, which the Conan Doyle family owned until 1955, is now a private nursing home.

Bignell House at Bignell Wood near **Minstead** (Hampshire) was Doyle's second home from the mid-1920s. A brick house, which he built and linked with a Saxon barn on the property, Bignell provided seclusion for Doyle's seances and meditations. After fire damaged the house in 1929, he rebuilt and repaired it. The property remains privately owned at Wittensford Bridge.

Conan Doyle tomb: Parish churchyard, **Minstead**.

(See Chapter 1, SWITZERLAND; also Chapter 6, LONDON; also Chapter 7, SCOTLAND.)

DRAKE, SIR FRANCIS (1540?–1596). "No other single captain," wrote Alan Villiers, "did more to humble the Spanish Empire and lay the foundation for England's mastery of the high seas." This little red-bearded, chubby-faced sailor whom Villiers called "Queen Elizabeth's favorite sea dog" was born at Crowndale Farm about one mile south of **Tavistock** (Devon) on the River Tavy. A tablet on a nearby farmhouse in the Yelverton road indicates the site.

At **Plymouth**, a major Elizabethan seaport, Drake purchased a house located at the top of Looe Street, opposite the Guildhall in the oldest part of the city, about 1573. It is said that Drake was playing bowls on Plymouth Hoe, a promontory jutting into Plymouth Sound (and still a bowling green), when the Spanish Armada appeared in 1588. Sailing from Plymouth against the wind and with just 54 ships, Drake attacked the massed 130-ship armada with fire ships off the coast of Calais, France, shattering the formation and completely disorganizing the Spanish fleet. Drake's Plymouth home, from which he had earlier set out on his round-the-world voyage in the *Golden Hind* (1577–80), is long gone.

Three miles west of **Yelverton** between route A386 and the River Tavy stands the stone Buckland Abbey, which Drake bought in 1581 with his share of booty pirated from Spanish ships during his global circumnavigation. Originally a 13th-century Benedictine monastery church, it was converted by Sir Richard Grenville into the present three-story mansion during the 1570s. Several rooms were renovated 200 years later, and others were rebuilt after a 1937 fire. The great hall occupies the original church's nave. Drake relics include a stout wooden chair made from a *Golden Hind* timber, a gilded cup given him by Elizabeth I, and "Drake's drum," which, says patriotic legend, will sound by itself to warn England of danger. There is also memorabilia of Sir Richard Grenville. The house is operated by The National Trust and Plymouth Corporation. (Open Good Friday—late September, Monday—Saturday 11:00—6:00, Sunday 2:00—6:00; October to Wednesday before Easter, Wednesday, Saturday—Sunday 2:00—5:00; 082-285-3607; admission.)

Exhibit: On route B4509 at the south end of **Berkeley** (Gloucestershire), the 14th-century Berkeley Castle—site of the murder of Edward II in 1327—displays Drake's oak sea chest, which he used aboard the *Golden Hind*. Mr. and Mrs. R. J. Berkeley own and operate the property which has belonged to the Berkeley family for more than six centuries. (Open April, September, Tuesday—Sunday 2:00—5:00; May—August, Tuesday—Saturday 11:00—5:00, Sunday 2:00—5:00; October, Sunday 2:00—4:30; 0453-810-332; admission.)

(See Chapter 6, LONDON.)

DRYDEN, JOHN (1631–1700). Called the "literary dictator of his age," the playwright, essayist and poet was born in the Old Rectory, now called Dryden House, opposite the church of Aldwinkle All Saints in **Aldwinkle** (Northamptonshire). The vine-covered house with thatched gables was occupied by his maternal grandfather, the rector, and remains private. Dryden visited there often during his childhood. The long-gone manor in **Titchmarsh**, where Dryden spent his childhood and which remained his family home probably until 1676, is marked by an elm tree near Dryden's Close.

At **Charlton** (Wiltshire), a reconstructed Elizabethan mansion—home of his father-in-law, the first Earl of Berkshire—became the author's refuge from the London plague in 1665 and 1666. The original house in Charlton Park burned down in 1962. Dryden composed his *Annus Mirabilis* (1667) there.

Dryden spent the summers of 1698 and 1699 at Cotterstock Hall in **Cotterstock** (Northamptonshire), the 17th-century, E-shaped stone manor owned by his cousin, Elizabeth Steward. He occupied an attic room in a western gable and there wrote *Fables Ancient and Modern* (1700). (Open by written appointment, Cotterstock Hall, Cotterstock, Northamptonshire.)

(See Chapter 6, LONDON.)

EDWARD VIII (1894–1972). Sandringham House at **Sandringham** (Norfolk), one of the royal family's country estates, is described by writer Neil Burton as "an unwieldy and sprawling house." Queen Victoria bought the estate in 1861 for her eldest son, later Edward VII, but the present Jacobean brick house dates from 1870. A ballroom was added in 1883 and a top floor was rebuilt after a fire in 1891. Edward's son, George V, considered Sandringham "better than anywhere in the world" and died there in 1936. His son, Edward VIII—uncrowned king during 1936 before he abdicated to marry Wallis Warfield Simpson—also spent frequent periods there. George VI, who succeeded Edward to the throne after his abdication, was born there in 1895, visited frequently throughout his life, and died there in 1952.

Visitors may view four lavishly furnished main rooms and several corridors. A museum occupying the old stables displays royal trophies, gifts and antique automobiles. Elaborate gardens and grounds include two small lakes. Guided tours occur every one and one-half hours. Sandringham is located via signs off routes A149 and A148. (Open [except when the royal family is in residence, which is usually December–January] from Easter Sunday—July 18, August 8—September 30, Monday—Thursday 10:30—4:45, Sunday 11:30—4:45; King's Lynn 0553-2675; admission [goes to charity].)

Windsor Castle in **Windsor** (Berkshire) has been one of the royal family's principal residences since Victoria made it her main refuge from London; it had been only occasionally used by royalty after George III (see the entries on George III and Victoria later in this chapter). From a suite in the Augusta Tower, where he had played as a child, Edward VIII broadcast his abdication speech on December 11, 1936, and spent his remaining 36 years as the duke of Windsor, an international, largely indolent celebrity. When his father was Prince of Wales, Edward spent much of his childhood at nearby Frogmore House, described as "more of a family necropolis than a house." This mansion adjoins the mausoleum of Victoria and Prince Albert and remains royal property.

Edward's private—and favorite—residence when he was Prince of Wales was Fort Belvedere near **Sunningdale** (Surrey), formerly known as Shrub Hill Tower. Built in 1757 for a son of George II, and enlarged about 1830, it was given to Edward by his father in 1930. The prince renovated the run-down fortress, courted Wallis Simpson there, and continued to use it as his personal retreat throughout his 326-day reign as king. It remains a private residence and is located off route A30.

Edward VIII tomb: Palace garden, Frogmore, **Windsor**.

Exhibit: Two miles northeast of **Grantham** (Lincolnshire) on route A607, Belton House displays an exhibit on Edward, who frequently visited there both as Prince of Wales and king. Built between 1685 and 1688 for Sir John Brownlow, the H-shaped stone house remains owned by the current Lord Brownlow. The only known portrait of Edward as king is displayed, as well as other memorabilia. (Open April 9—October 3, Tuesday—Sunday 2:00—5:00; 0476–66116; admission.)

(See Chapter 2, FRANCE; also Chapter 3, PARIS; also Chapter 6, LONDON; also Chapter 7, SCOTLAND.)

ELIOT, GEORGE. See MARY ANN EVANS.

ELIOT, THOMAS STEARNS (1888–1965). The American-born poet, a revolutionary in literature but a staunch traditionalist in religion and politics, resided for a brief period at Pikes Farm near **Crowhurst** (Surrey). The 17th-century brick farmhouse, home of his publishing colleague Frank Morley, was Eliot's refuge in 1933 and 1934, the period immediately following his sepa-

ration from his first wife. Eliot dined in the farmhouse with the Morleys but otherwise occupied two rooms of a cottage, which came to be called "Uncle Tom's Cabin," on the property. Pikes Farm remains privately owned and sequestered off route A22.

Eliot tomb: Parish church, **East Coker** (Somerset).

(See Chapter 6, LONDON.)

ELIZABETH I (1533–1603). "Though God hath raised me high," she said in 1601, "yet I count this the glory of my crown, that I have reigned with your loves." The 45-year reign of Elizabeth I, one of England's greatest and best-loved monarchs, encompassed an unprecedented period of national achievement in diplomacy, exploration, culture and economic prosperity.

As the daughter of the uxoricidal Henry VIII and ill-fated Anne Boleyn, and the half-sister of paranoid Queen Mary, Elizabeth endured an anxious childhood, then—during "Bloody Mary's" reign—house arrest and outright imprisonment. She never lost her well-learned suspicion of men as husbands (though liked them well enough otherwise) and so never married.

Elizabeth was residing at Ashridge Palace, three miles north of **Berkhamsted** (Hertfordshire), when Mary I ordered her arrested for conspiracy to seize the throne in 1554—a charge of which the young princess was probably wholly innocent. The present mansion at Ashridge Park dates from 1808 and stands on the site of the former monastery/palace. Much of the 3,800-acre deer park is now National Trust property, while the house itself is a management training center. (Open certain summer weekends; Little Gaddesden 044–284–3491.)

Following her 1554 imprisonment at the Tower of London, Princess Elizabeth was confined to the royal manor at **Woodstock** (Oxfordshire), her home for a year. This 12th-century mansion built by Henry I was replaced in 1705 by Blenheim Palace, later the birthplace of Sir Winston Churchill (see the entry on Churchill earlier in this chapter). As queen, Elizabeth gave the estate to Sir Edward Dyer, and she visited there in 1600. The exact site of the old manor, also frequented by Henry I, Henry II, and Edward II, is marked by a stone cairn near Vanbrugh's bridge across the River Glyme.

In 1555 Elizabeth was allowed to move to Hatfield House, a favorite place of her girlhood and the residence most associated with her precoronation period. There, in November 1558, her status changed overnight—from virtual prisoner to queen of England. Robert Dudley, a lifelong friend whom she later created Earl of Leicester, was among the first to arrive with the news of Mary's death and shout "long live the Queen." It is said that Elizabeth received the news while seated beneath an oak at Hatfield. The seven-foot hollow stump of that oak was recently lifted from its original site and placed under cover in the Old Palace yard. On November 20 Elizabeth assembled her first council in the palace before proceeding to London. Henry VIII had taken over the Old Palace in 1538 but seldom stayed there. The original 1497 structure was razed in 1607 by Robert Cecil, First Earl of Salisbury, but he used many of its bricks to build the present Hatfield House on the site. He also retained a wing and banqueting hall of the original palace. Today this magnificent estate is owned by the Marquess of Salisbury, a direct descendant of Robert Cecil. On display in the fine rooms are portraits and memorabilia of Elizabeth, including her garden gloves, silk stockings and embroidered lace hat. Hatfield House is located in **Hatfield** (Hertfordshire) opposite the railway station. (Open March 25—October 10, Tuesday—Saturday 12:00—5:00; Sunday 2:00—5:30; gardens also open Monday 2:00—5:00; Hatfield 62823; admission.) Medieval banquets are still held in the Old Palace (phone Hatfield 62055 for details).

Before she became queen, Elizabeth also occasionally resided at Windsor Castle, **Windsor** (Berkshire), where she was tutored in languages by Roger Ascham. As queen, she especially enjoyed the castle during summers but, as with all her residences, seldom prolonged her stay—the unsanitary odors in castles that were too long occupied offended her. During the 1570s she added the fine stone terrace that stands beneath her apartments on the north side of the castle's eastern (upper) ward. "Here in the evenings she liked to walk, moving very fast," wrote Christopher Hibbert, "as though she were hurrying away from a ghost or trying to keep warm in ice-cold air, but never losing her dignity or appearing to bustle as her sister Mary had done." Queen Elizabeth's Gallery, which she added in 1583, now houses much of the extensive royal library, a favorite haunt of her collateral descendant Prince Charles, the current Prince of Wales.

(See the entries on George III, Henry VIII and Victoria later in this chapter.)

Exhibits: The 12th-century Sudeley Castle in **Winchcombe** (Gloucestershire) displays Elizabeth's christening robe. This was the home of her stepmother, Catherine Parr, who died as the wife of Sir Thomas Seymour in 1548. Elizabeth visited there in 1547 and 1548 (see the entry on Richard III later in this chapter).

England's oldest museum (1677), the Ashmolean in Beaumont Street in **Oxford** (Oxfordshire), displays Elizabeth's riding boots and embroidered gloves. (Open Tuesday—Saturday 10:00—4:00, Sunday 2:00—4:00; 0865—512651; free.)

(See Chapter 6, LONDON.)

ERASMUS, DESIDERIUS (1466?–1536). The Dutch theologian and scholar lived in **Cambridge** (Cambridgeshire), where he taught Greek at Queens' College from 1511 to 1514. Erasmus Tower in the southwest corner of the first court yard is said to be his lodging. Though they were supposedly the best rooms in the college, he complained about them constantly. He also deplored the wines—"I am being killed with thirst"—and criticized his students. Erasmus introduced the study of Greek to the university and worked on his New Testament Latin translation while living there. Queens' College, on Queens' Lane off Silver Street, boasts the most complete group of medieval college buildings (15th century) in the university.

(See Chapter 1, SWITZERLAND; also Chapter 3, PARIS; also Chapter 4, WEST GERMANY, BELGIUM, THE NETHERLANDS.)

EVANS, MARY ANN. ("GEORGE ELIOT") (1819–1880). The novelist, who adopted a male pseudonym in order to bypass sexist prejudice, was born at South Farm, **Arbury** (Warwickshire). Located two miles southwest of Nuneaton, it is still privately owned. Her girlhood home from 1820 to 1841 was Griff House, a two-story house that now operates as a hotel on route A444. Most of her novels draw on people and places she knew in this area. The large garden behind Griff House was the model for the "Hall Farm" garden in *Adam Bede* (1859). The "Round Pond" of *The Mill on the Floss* (1860), however, barely survives in a field adjacent to the house.

At **Coventry**, she attended school from 1832 to 1835 at 48 Little Park Street. From 1841 to 1849, she lived with her widowed father at Bird Grove, which remains privately owned on George Eliot

Road, and was raised as a strict evangelical. As a result of long visits with manufacturer Charles Bray and such guests as Robert Owen, Herbert Spencer, Thackeray and Emerson, Eliot abandoned Christianity and became a freethinker. Rosehill, Bray's home, remains privately owned on St. Nicholas Street. Coventry inspired the town of *Middlemarch* depicted in her 1871 novel.

During the spring and summer of 1871, George Eliot worked on this book at **Shottermill** (Surrey) southwest of Haslemere. She and her longtime companion, George Henry Lewes, whom she considered her husband, rented Brookbank, which has since been divided into two private houses; one is still called Brookbank, the other Middlemarch. The yew tree in back which shaded her as she wrote is still visible. Tennyson first met the novelist at Brookbank and read his poems to her there.

In 1876 George Eliot and Lewes bought a country house called The Heights in **Wormley** (Surrey). It is now known as "Rosalyn Court." Tennyson and Henry James visited the couple there (see the entries on Alfred, Lord Tennyson and Henry James later in this chapter). After Lewes's death in 1878, Eliot married John W. Cross, a close friend of hers and Lewes, in 1880. They returned to the house in the autumn of that year, just before her death.

Exhibits: The **Nuneaton** Museum and Art Gallery at Riversley Park displays possessions and memorabilia in its George Eliot Collection. (Open summer, Monday—Friday 12:00—7:00, Saturday—Sunday 10:00—7:00; winter, Monday—Friday 12:00—5:00, Saturday—Sunday 10:00—5:00; 0682-326211; free.) Annual summer ceremonies are held in the George Eliot Memorial Garden on Church Street in commemoration of her.

(See Chapter 1, SWITZERLAND; also Chapter 6, LONDON; also Chapter 8, ITALY.)

FIELDING, HENRY (1707–1754). Sharpham Park, the birthplace of the author whose *Joseph Andrews* (1742) and *Tom Jones* (1749) are major landmarks in the history of the English novel, remains privately owned at **Sharpham** (Somerset). A 16th-century manor owned by his maternal grandparents, it is now a farmhouse. Fielding was born in a room called the harlequin chamber, and the manor was his home until 1710. Fielding modeled Squire Allworthy's house in *Tom Jones* after his birthplace.

East Stour, a Dorset village, was Fielding's boyhood home (1710–19) and first married home (1734–36). The original manor house that belonged to his paternal grandfather and which Fielding inherited stood on the site of the present 19th-century stone house just west of the parish church, a place now known as "Church Farm." Financial problems followed the couple's quick spending of Fielding's inheritance and caused their return to London in 1736.

At **Widcombe** (Avon), a suburb of Bath, Fielding was the frequent guest of Ralph Allen at Widcombe Lodge, an 18th-century manor. While living there in 1748, Fielding probably worked on his novel *Tom Jones*. A later novelist, Horace Annesley Vachell, lived there from 1927 to 1952. The house remains privately owned.

(See Chapter 6, LONDON; also Chapter 8, PORTUGAL.)

FRANKLIN, BENJAMIN (1706–1790). In 1771 the American statesman and scientist, then serving a diplomatic tenure in London, came to Twyford House, a manor located at the top of the hill in **Twyford** (Hampshire). The house, owned by Jonathan Shipley, Bishop of St. Asaph, became Franklin's haven while writing the first part of his notable *Autobiography* (1868). The garden study he used still remains on this estate.

(See Chapter 3, PARIS; also Chapter 6, LONDON.)

GEORGE III (1738–1820). During George's long and eventful reign, the American and French revolutions exploded, though mental illness (which severely handicapped his later years) meant the monarch was not always fully aware of their impact. Britain's king for 59 years and the last monarch allowed to exert any real control over Parliament, George came from German rather than English stock but unlike the two Georges who preceded him, he made serious efforts to anglicize both himself and the monarchy. One of his frequent boyhood homes was Cliveden, the estate owned by the Duke of Buckingham, built in the 1660s. That mansion burned down in 1795 (only the original terrace remains), as did its successor on this magnificent site in 1849. The present Cliveden House, operated by The National Trust, dates from 1850. Acquired by American millionaire William Waldorf Astor in 1893, the palatial manor, formal gardens and large park also became the home (1919–64) of controversial member of parliament Lady Nancy Astor, whose husband, Lord Waldorf Astor, inherited the estate. Cliveden, now a study center operated by California's Stanford University, is located two miles north of **Taplow** (Buckinghamshire) on route B476. Four rooms are open to the public and display Astor furnishings and treasures. (House open April—October, Saturday—Sunday 2:30—5:00; grounds open daily 11:00—6:30; Burnham 062-86-5069; admission.)

The favorite residence of the king after 1778 was Windsor Castle at **Windsor** (Berkshire), where he spent long periods of his reign. On Castle Hill he built a new mansion on the site of the one formerly occupied by Queen Anne, and it became known as the "Upper Lodge." "For the first time in his life," wrote Christopher Hibbert, "he seemed to be happy." But royal domestic etiquette and routine were so rigid and uneventful that life at Windsor became deadly monotonous for the king's retinue. After 1811, when the future George IV became prince regent, George III existed there in a "daze of unknowing." "Until nearly the end," wrote biographer J. C. Long, "he was ambulatory and in a white tunic haunted the corridors of Windsor at all hours." He died there (see the entry on Victoria later in this chapter).

George III tomb: St. George's Chapel, Windsor Castle, **Windsor**.

Exhibit: At **Maidstone** (Kent), the king's "traveling chariot" may be seen at the Tyrwhitt Drake Museum of Carriages in Mill Street. (Open April, September, Monday—Saturday 9:00—1:00, 2:00—5:00, Sunday 2:00—5:00; 0622-54497; admission.)

(See Chapter 6, LONDON.)

HANDEL, GEORG FREDERICK (1685–1759).

Exhibits: A large collection of musical scores, manuscripts and memorabilia relating to the German-born composer is owned by Gerald Coke at Jenkyn Place, **Bentley** (Hampshire). Admission to view the Coke Collection must be prearranged (04204-3118).

Chillington Manor House in St. Faith's Street, **Maidstone** (Kent), displays a portable harpsichord used by the composer. (Open March—October, Monday—Saturday 10:00—6:00; October—March, Monday—Saturday 10:00—5:00; 0622-54497; free.)

A Handel manuscript collection and another portable harpsichord are exhibited at the Henry Watson Music Library of the Manchester Public Libraries, St. Peter's Square in **Manchester** (Greater Manchester). (Open Monday—Saturday 9:00—9:00; free.)

(See Chapter 4, EAST GERMANY; also Chapter 6, LONDON; also Chapter 7, IRELAND.)

HARDY, THOMAS (1840–1928). One of England's major regional novelists, Hardy occupied several houses in his native Dorset, most of which remain. He was born in **Higher Bockhampton**, his home for most of his first 30 years. The thatched cottage secluded in beech and chestnut forest is accessible off Cuckoo Lane via a ten-minute walk from the Thorncombe Wood parking lot. Hardy details his birthplace as "Tranter Dewey's house" in *Under the Greenwood Tree* (1872). He wrote this novel as well as *Far From the Madding Crowd* (1874) in the window seat of his bedroom which overlooks "Egdon heath," now modified by forestry plantations. A small collection of Hardy memorabilia is displayed in the house. Though owned by The National Trust, Hardy's Cottage is still used by private tenants, from whom permission to visit must be secured in writing (Hardy's Cottage, Higher Bockhampton, Dorset; Dorchester 2366.) The one-acre garden is always open.

At **Sturminster Newton**, Hardy rented Riverside Villa, a gray stone mansion on Rickett's Lane overlooking the River Stour, from 1876 to 1878 while writing *The Return of the Native* (1878). It was, he recalled, "our happiest time." This town became "Stourcastle" in *Tess of the D'Urbervilles* (1891).

In 1885 Hardy retired permanently to **Dorchester**, where he had resided at intervals from 1849. He designed and built a Victorian brick villa, Max Gate, on the Wareham Road (route 35) and resided there for the rest of his life, enlarging the house in 1898 and 1908. There he wrote *The Mayor of Casterbridge* (1886—Dorchester figures as "Casterbridge" in many of his novels), *Tess of the D'Urbervilles* and *Jude the Obscure* (1895). Hardy's first wife Emma died at Max Gate in 1912 (Hardy himself was to die there later, too). Emma's death ended a long, unhappy marriage; the novelist remarried in 1914. Some of his noted guests at the house included A. E. Housman, John Galsworthy and Hilaire Belloc. The current private owners have transformed what was a rather gloomy edifice with its attics and false turrets into a house much less reminiscent of a Hardy novel.

Exhibits: The Dorset County Museum in High West Street at **Dorchester** displays a reconstruction of Hardy's study at Max Gate together with manuscripts and other memorabilia. (Open Monday—Friday 10:00—5:00, Saturday 10:00—1:00, 2:00—5:00; 0305–62735; admission.)

For Hardy devotees who wish to familiarize themselves with his Wessex and Casterbridge settings, a detailed tour guide may be obtained from the Secretary, Thomas Hardy Society Ltd., The Vicarage, Haselbury Plucknett, Crewkerne, Somerset.

(See Chapter 6, LONDON.)

HARVEY, WILLIAM (1578–1657). The physician who first mapped the circulatory system and demonstrated how the heart works was born in **Folkestone** (Kent). His birthplace, now long-gone, later became a post house. It probably stood at the junction of Church and Rendezvous streets. Harvey lived there until age 10.

From 1593 to 1599 Harvey studied at Gonville and Caius College, **Cambridge** (Cambridgeshire). The medieval but still functional buildings in Trinity Street may well be the only Harvey lodgings that survive anywhere.

Harvey tomb: Parish church, **Hempstead** (Essex).

(See Chapter 6, LONDON.)

HENRY VIII (1491–1547). England's greatest Tudor king resided at Windsor Castle, **Windsor** (Berkshire), quite often as a young man. His father, Henry VII, built the Albert Memorial Chapel in the castle. As king, Henry spent intervals there with his wives Catherine of Aragon and Anne Boleyn. And it was to Windsor that he fled grieving in 1537 when his third wife, Jane Seymour, died; and there, as he aged and increased 17 inches in girth in five years, that pulleys and ropes were installed to help him cope with staircases. A suit of his colossal armor is displayed in the state apartments at the top of the grand staircase. Another splendid sight is the king's 16th-century shield, possibly a gift from Francis I of France in 1520. (See the entries on Elizabeth I, George III and Victoria in this chapter.)

The Oatlands Park Hotel at 146 Oatlands Drive, **Weybridge** (Surrey), marks the site of Oatlands, a palace destroyed during the Civil War. Henry VIII acquired it in 1529 along with Whitehall in London and secretly married Catherine

Howard there in 1540. Poet-novelist Maurice Hewlett was born there in 1861.

Henry VIII tomb: St. George's Chapel, Windsor Castle, **Windsor**.

(See Chapter 6, LONDON.)

HITLER, ADOLF (1889–1945). Biographer Robert Payne (*The Life and Death of Adolf Hitler*, 1973) found compelling documentary evidence—the unpublished memoirs of Hitler's English sister-in-law, Bridget Hitler—that Germany's future dictator spent about five months (of profound dissatisfaction) during 1912 and 1913 at **Liverpool** (Merseyside) as the ungracious guest of his half-brother Alois and Alois's wife Bridget. Their three-room apartment remains privately owned at 102 Upper Stanhope Street.

Exhibit: The Dorset Military Museum at **Dorchester** (Dorset) displays the fuehrer's desk, obtained after the war from the Reich Chancellery in Berlin. The museum is located at The Keep, Bridgport Road. (Open Monday—Saturday 9:00—5:00, except Saturday 9:00—12:00 October—June; 0305–64066; admission.)

(See Chapter 1, AUSTRIA; also Chapter 4, EAST GERMANY, WEST GERMANY, BELGIUM.)

HUGO, VICTOR (1802–1885). The French Romantic novelist and libertarian lived in exile during the regime of Napoleon III, whom he had fiercely opposed as "Napoleon the Small," from 1852 to 1870. His first home, as close to France as he could manage, was at **St. Luke's** on the English Channel Island of Jersey. His seaside residence from 1852 to 1855 is now the Maison Victor Hugo hotel. Jersey expelled him when he defended a newspaper's right to print a derogatory reference to Queen Victoria.

In 1855 Hugo moved with both his wife Adèle and mistress Juliette Drouet to **St. Peter Port**, capital of Guernsey, another Channel Island, and lodged at 20 Hauteville. The next year he moved to Hauteville House, 38 Hauteville, which became his ornate home until Napoleon's overthrow in 1870. He returned for occasional visits, however, the last time in 1878. Hugo wrote some of his best-known works there, including *Les Misérables* (1862) and *Toilers of the Sea* (1866), the latter set in Guernsey. The granite house, built about 1800 and now owned by the City of Paris, surmounts the harbor and has a particularly splendid view from the plate-glass eyrie that Hugo built and used as his studio. The novelist's initials are adorned everywhere in egomaniacal splendor. Memorabilia are displayed. (Open April—September, daily 10:00—11:30, 2:00—4:30; October—March, daily 10:30 or by appointment; Guernsey 0481–21911; admission.)

Both islands are accessible by plane or ferry from Southampton (Hampshire).

(See Chapter 2, FRANCE; also Chapter 3, PARIS; also Chapter 4, BELGIUM, LUXEMBOURG.)

JAMES, HENRY (1843–1916). The American-born novelist, a major influence on 20th-century literature, bought Lamb House at **Rye** (East Sussex) in 1898 and lived there until 1912, though he held the house until his death. This Georgian two-story brick dwelling, built for Rye mayor James Lamb in 1721, remains one of the most attractive of its type in England, keenly reflective of the fastidious author. The National Trust displays James's morning room, dining room and study; among the memorabilia on view are his desk, portraits and several items of original furniture. James installed the French windows leading to the garden. The small garden house, where he dictated *The Wings of the Dove* (1902), *The Ambassadors* (1903) and *The Golden Bowl* (1904), was destroyed by a bomb in 1940. Some of James's guests included Joseph Conrad, G. K. Chesterton, Stephen Crane, his psychologist brother William James, Hugh Walpole, and H. G. Wells (see the entries on Conrad and Wells in this chapter). Novelist E. F. Benson later occupied the house until his death in 1940. Lamb House is located in West Street near Church Square. (Open April—October, Wednesday, Saturday 2:00—5:30; admission.)

(See Chapter 3, PARIS; also Chapter 6, LONDON; also Chapter 8, ITALY.)

JOAN OF ARC (1412–1431).

Exhibit: Tiverton Castle, originally a Norman stronghold with 15th-, 16th- and 18th-century additions, displays a Joan of Arc gallery in its medieval gatehouse. Art exhibits illustrate various theories about her life. Located alongside St. Peter's Church on the outskirts of **Tiverton** (Devon), the castle is owned by Mr. and Mrs. Ivar Campbell. (Open Easter holiday, May 17—September 24, Sunday—Thursday 2:30—5:30; 0884–253200; admission.)

(See Chapter 2, FRANCE.)

JOHNSON, SAMUEL (1709–1784). Though probably more read about than read today, the ungainly Dr. Johnson has, nevertheless, through his wit, massive presence and the biographical labors of James Boswell, come to represent an entire period of English literary life and culture. Johnson was born in a house which still stands in **Lichfield** (Staffordshire). In the words of Neil Burton, though, visitors need a "fairly strong imagination to bring the place to life." His father, a bookseller, built the three-story dwelling about 1707 and used part of the ground floor as his shop. Johnson spent most of his first 28 years there. A precocious child, he almost didn't survive boyhood. Scrofula and smallpox scarred him for life, and harsh schoolroom discipline gave him morbid phobias. As headquarters of the Johnson Society, this house on Breadmarket Street in the center of Lichfield is now a museum operated by the Lichfield Council. It displays various Johnsonian relics and portraits plus a notable Johnson library. (Open May—September, Monday—Saturday 2:00—5:00, Sunday 2:30—5:00; October—April, Monday—Saturday 10:00—4:00; 05432–24972; admission.) School and inn sites relating to Johnson's life in the town are also marked. Edial Hall, an 18th-century manor where Johnson taught a private school for only three pupils (including future actor David Garrick) from 1735 to 1737, remains privately owned southwest of Lichfield.

In 1731 and 1732 Johnson served as usher in the grammar school at **Market Bosworth** (Leicestershire) and lodged at Bosworth Hall, where his autocratic patron, Sir Wolstan Dixie, treated him harshly. This manor also remains privately owned.

Exhibit: Johnson attended Pembroke College at **Oxford** (Oxfordshire) in 1728 and 1729 until he ran out of money and had to withdraw. He occupied tower rooms over the former gateway. The college library displays some of Johnson's letters and manuscripts, his college desk, some of his books and his large, much-used china teapot. Pembroke College, dating from 1624, is located off St. Aldate's; the library is housed in the original medieval Broadgates Hall refectory. (Open daily; check locally for hours and admission.)

(See Chapter 6, LONDON.)

KEYNES, JOHN MAYNARD, LORD (1883–1946). Keynes, diplomat and philosophical father of the "planned economy," was born in a "solid, roomy Victorian house" at 6 Harvey Road, **Cambridge** (Cambridgeshire). His parents, who survived him, resided there throughout their lives, and he often returned for visits.

During World War I and for some years after, Keynes occupied a country refuge—Charleston Manor just north of **Westdean** (East Sussex). Originally Norman, the house had Tudor and Georgian portions added to it. Keynes's Bloomsbury friends, Leonard and Virginia Woolf, were frequent visitors (see the entry on Virginia Woolf later in this chapter); and Lytton Strachey worked on his biographical *Eminent Victorians* (1918) there. (House open Wednesday by appointment; write Mrs. David Garnett, Charleston Farm, Lewes, Sussex; gardens open April—October, daily 11:00—6:00; admission.) A few hundred yards away stands Tilton, an estate which had once belonged to his family ancestors and which Keynes rented in 1937. He farmed 300 acres there, eventually increased to 570, and while he seldom spent more than weekends and vacations on the farm until his last years, he considered it his permanent home and did, in fact, die there.

(See Chapter 6, LONDON.)

KIPLING, RUDYARD (1865–1936). Apologist of British imperialism in his novels, verse and stories (as perhaps only an India-born Englishman could be), Kipling was nevertheless influential from a purely literary standpoint. And his reputation has grown especially in recent years. All of his surviving homes except the last remain privately owned.

Sent to England to be educated in 1871, Kipling first boarded with a family named Holloway at 4 Campbell Road, **Southsea** (Hampshire). Theirs was a fanatically religious household that taught him, he said, how to lie; he lived in what he called this "house of desolation" until 1877.

From 1878 to 1882 he attended the United Services College at **Westward Ho!** (Devon), a much more pleasant residence. He later described his chums and schooldays there in *Stalky & Co.* (1899). The "twelve bleak houses by the shore" that constituted the college are now privately owned dwellings on Kipling Terrace. Eighteen acres on the hill behind the school, the scene of Kipling's outdoor play and boyhood walks, are now owned by The National Trust and named Kipling Tors as a public memorial.

Following the novelist's sudden, angry return from a four-year residence in the United States, Kipling and his wife, Caroline, lived for almost a year (1896–97) at Rock House in Rock House Lane, **Maidencombe** (Devon). Life there grew increasingly depressing, a feeling that Kipling attributed to the *feng-shui*, or "spirit," of the house it-

self. It was there, nevertheless, that he worked on the engaging tales that became *Stalky & Co.*

In 1897 the Kiplings lived with his uncle, the painter Sir Edward Burne-Jones, at North End House in **Rottingdean** (East Sussex) and there he wrote his rousing poem "Recessional" (1897). Later that year they moved to The Elms on the village green, where they lived year-round until 1899 and during summers until 1902. Kipling finished *Stalky & Co.* and also wrote *Kim* (1901) and the *Just So Stories* (1902) at this house.

BATEMANS, HOME OF RUDYARD KIPLING. From 1902 until his death in 1936, this 1634 stone house near **Burwash** remained the writer's beloved home. England's literary spokesman for imperialism did much of his notable work there. He and Caroline Kipling also designed the garden aspect seen in this 1969 view.

Kipling's last permanent home, from 1902, was Bateman's, a large 17th-century manor near **Burwash** (East Sussex). He was immediately fond of the "grey stone lichened house—A.D. 1634 over the door—beamed, panelled, with old oak staircase, and all untouched and unflaked." *Puck of Pook's Hill* (1906) and *Rewards and Fairies* (1910) were among the books written in his large, comfortable study. In this room visitors may see the raised chair he used to compensate for his short stature, and the table he described as "ten feet long from north to south and badly congested." Kipling furnishings and mementos, including his 1907 Nobel Prize, are displayed by The National Trust and reveal much about the writer's life and activities. He and his wife designed the present garden and planted yew hedges. He also adapted an old gristmill on the property to generate electricity; today the original machinery grinds flour for tourists. "Pook's Hill" is visible from the lawn. Bateman's is located one-half mile south of route A265 from the west end of Burwash via signs. (Open March—May, October, Saturday—Thursday 2:00—6:00; June—September, Monday—Thursday 11:00—6:00, Saturday—Sunday 2:00—6:00; 0435-882302; admission.)

Exhibit: In **Rottingdean**, the Grange Museum, a former vicarage adjacent to Kipling's 1897 residence, is now the town library and museum. Its Kipling Room displays relics, letters, portraits and early editions of the author's books. (Open Monday—Tuesday, Thursday—Saturday 10:00—5:00, Sunday 2:00—5:00; Brighton 0273-31004; free.)

(See Chapter 6, LONDON.)

LAWRENCE, DAVID HERBERT (1885–1930). As a social rebel, whose novels broke many conventional barriers in their treatment of sex and the subconscious, D. H. Lawrence was never less than controversial. England, as events proved, greatly feared his presence. He was a native of the coalmining town of **Eastwood** (Nottinghamshire), "the hard pith of England" he called it, and his two-story brick birthplace—his home until age two—survives at 8a Victoria Street. His mother, whose neurotic influence affected him throughout his life, sold lacework and aprons there on the ground floor—and Lawrence never quite escaped those apron strings. From 1887 to 1891 the family resided at 26 Garden Road, a two-story brick house described in *Sons and Lovers* (1913) as "the Bottoms." It was restored in 1973 by the Association of Young Writers. (Open July—August, daily 10:00—6:00; admission.) The family's next home (1891–1902), which Lawrence called "Bleak House" because of its exposure to the wind and its dismal view of miners' tenements, was 8 Walker Street on the town edge. In 1902 the family moved to 97 Lynn Croft Road, which masquerades under many names in Lawrence's novels: "Bestwood" in *Sons and Lovers*, "Woodhouse" in *The*

Lost Girl (1920) and "Beldover" in *Women in Love* (1921). He last returned to visit the house in 1926.

After fleeing London to escape official harassment, Lawrence and his wife, Frieda, leased Higher Tregerthen, a farm cottage located one and one-half miles northeast of **Zennor** (Cornwall), where he worked on *Women in Love* in 1916 and 1917. Local villagers, suspicious of the bearded antiwar intellectual and his German wife, suspected the pair of spying and signaling German submarines off the nearby seacoast. A police raid on the cottage found nothing incriminating, but the Lawrences were told to move on. They did, and England soon lost one of its major writers.

Mountain Cottage, rented for Lawrence by his sister Ada, was the novelist's home for a year (1918–19); near **Middleton-by-Wirksworth** (Derbyshire), this hillside bungalow remains privately owned.

(See Chapter 2, FRANCE; also Chapter 6, LONDON; also Chapter 8, ITALY.)

LAWRENCE, THOMAS EDWARD (1888–1935). "Lawrence of Arabia," the Welshborn soldier, writer and eccentric loner, lived from 1894 to 1896 at Langley Lodge, a brick villa at **Langley** (Hampshire). The precocious youngster early discovered that his parents were not married (they never did marry), though parents and children always maintained a family facade.

Lawrence's home from 1896 to 1910—and again in 1919 after his years as a guerrilla in the Middle East desert—was the three-story, brick Victorian house at 2 Polstead Road in **Oxford** (Oxfordshire). His father built him a small studybungalow in the back garden there when Lawrence entered Jesus College in 1906. Lawrence also occupied rooms in All Souls College, High Street, as a Fellow from 1919 to 1921. There he began writing the manuscript which, after several years and various versions, resulted in *The Seven Pillars of Wisdom* (1926).

A plaque marks Lawrence's lodgings at 13 Birmingham Street in **Southampton** (Hampshire), where he lived as an enlisted member of the Royal Air Force in 1933 and 1934.

The Hotel Ozone at **Bridlington** (Humberside) was Lawrence's last military lodging in 1934 and 1935. He occupied a tower room overlooking the harbor.

Lawrence's last home and favorite refuge from 1923 was Clouds Hill, a former gamekeeper's cottage, located two miles northeast of **Moreton**

(Dorset), which he occupied at intervals until his death. Craving anonymity, he had changed his name first to John Ross, then to T. E. Shaw. He rented the rundown brick cottage, then bought it in 1925 as a holiday retreat, set about repairing it and worked on *The Seven Pillars of Wisdom* there. The Greek lettering he inscribed over the door means "Does Not Care," which he loosely translated as "Don't Worry" (he fretted constantly). After he left the RAF in 1935, he intended to make Clouds Hill his permanent home but had lived there only two months when he died in a motorcycle accident. As one observer noted, "There was never a better candidate for the accident syndrome."

"At present I am sitting in my cottage and getting used to an empty life," Lawrence wrote the day before his death. Yet "to think of Clouds Hill as T. E.'s home is to get the wrong idea of it," said novelist E. M. Forster, Lawrence's frequent guest. "It wasn't his home, it was rather his pied-à-terre, the place where his feet touched the earth for a moment, and found rest." The cottage, now owned by The National Trust, displays his furnishings as he left them: "its contents are as enigmatic as its owner," noted Patricia Ledward. The two ground floor rooms, which held a large woodpile during Lawrence's occupancy, now display editions of his writings, while the upper room, where he wrote and listened to his gramophone, is now called the "music room." Lawrence's desert sleeping bag, labeled "Meum," is among the items displayed. The house remains without electricity, as he preferred. Clouds Hill stands on the Puddletown road north of Bovington Camp, then a headquarters of the Royal Tank Corps in which Lawrence had perversely enlisted as a private in 1922. (Open April—September, Wednesday—Friday, Sunday 2:00—5:00; October—March, Sunday 1:00—4:00; admission.)

Lawrence tomb: Moreton Cemetery, **Moreton**.

Exhibit: The third and final draft of Lawrence's book, *The Seven Pillars of Wisdom*, is displayed in the Bodleian Library at **Oxford** (see the entry on Percy Bysshe Shelley, *Exhibit*, later in this chapter).

(See Chapter 6, LONDON; also Chapter 7, WALES.)

LLOYD GEORGE, DAVID (1863–1945). Though Welsh by ancestry, the Liberal member of Parliament for 55 years and prime minister from 1916 to 1922, was born in **Charlton-up-Medlock** (Greater Manchester). His small, brick two-story birthplace at 5 New York Place remains privately owned.

An avid golfer, Lloyd George built a house adjoining the golf course at **Walton Heath** (Surrey) in 1912. Suffragettes blew up the unfinished structure in protest against his policies in 1913, but it was soon rebuilt. Lloyd George spent every available moment away from his duties there until he sold the house in 1919. Often he was accompanied by his mistress of many years, Frances Stevenson, who much later became his second wife.

On behalf of himself and future prime ministers, Lloyd George accepted an official country residence called Chequers near **Aylesbury** (Buckinghamshire) from Lord Lee of Fareham in 1921 (see the entry on Sir Winston Churchill earlier in this chapter). Lloyd George often stayed there on weekends throughout his remaining time in office.

In 1921 Lloyd George bought a 100-acre hilly tract at **Churt** (Hampshire) and built a manor that "satisfied him on two counts," wrote biographer Peter Rowland. "It was near to London and far away from his wife and other unwelcome visitors." He called the estate "Bron-y-de"—Welsh for "breast of the south"—wrote his *War Memoirs* (1933–36) there, and engaged in extensive farming operations, raising poultry and pigs and growing fruit. By 1944, when he departed for his last home in Wales, he had increased his holdings to 700 acres and employed 80 men.

(See Chapter 6, LONDON; also Chapter 7, WALES.)

MALTHUS, THOMAS ROBERT (1766–1834). The Rookery, birthplace of the economist and demographer, stands about one mile west of **Dorking** (Surrey) on route A25. Precocious though he was, Malthus probably remembered little of this estate with its numerous outbuildings. His father, a prosperous but restless farmer and an admirer of French social theorist Jean-Jacques Rousseau (who once stopped there for a visit), sold the property in 1768.

From 1773 to 1782 Malthus (who was born with a hare lip) was privately educated by Rev. Richard Graves at Claverton House near Bath (Avon). The three-story manor built about 1610 had been the former home of Ralph Allen, on whom Henry Fielding based his character "Squire Allworthy" in *Tom Jones* (1749). Demolished in 1819, the house was soon rebuilt as the present Claverton Manor. Now a museum, operated by the American Museum in Britain, it displays various period exhibits of American history up to 1860. Visitors will find no reminders of Malthus, however. The manor is located two-and-one-half miles east of Bath at **Claverton** via route A36. (Open March 27—October 31, Tuesday—Sunday 2:00—5:00; other times by arrangement; Bath 0225–60503; admission.)

At **Hertford Heath** (Hertfordshire), Malthus taught political economy from 1805 at East India College. A four-story Tudor mansion, the east side of which Malthus and his family inhabited from 1809 until his death, it is privately occupied on the campus of what is now the amalgamated Haileybury and Imperial Service colleges. Malthus bought this house in 1815 and built a wooden summerhouse in the garden. He wrote five revised editions of his influential *Essay on the Principle of Population* (1798) at the house and endured waves of bitterly emotional criticism against his treatise.

Malthus tomb: Bath Abbey, **Bath**.

(See Chapter 6, LONDON.)

MARCONI, GUGLIELMO (1874–1937). The Italian electronic wizard, who developed wireless telegraphy, did most of his important work in sea-coast England—Italy wasn't interested in his work—where he set up transmitters for transatlantic demonstrations of his device.

In about 1910 Marconi established his family home at Eaglehurst, in **Fawley** (Hampshire), a sprawling manor on one floor with two-story wings and an 18th-century tower. This remained his home until 1916. He was not much of a family man, however, and only spent relatively brief periods away from his coastal laboratories and transmission towers.

Exhibit: The Borough Museum at the Old Butter Market, **Helston** (Cornwall), displays an early wireless exhibit. (Open Monday—Saturday 10:30—12:30, 2:00—4:30, except closes at 12:00 Wednesday; 03265–61672; free.)

Also in Cornwall at Poldhu Point near **Poldhu Cove**, a monument marks the site of the first wireless transmission across the Atlantic, sent by Marconi at this place in 1901. The station was demolished in 1933.

(See Chapter 6, LONDON; also Chapter 8, ITALY.)

MARLOWE, CHRISTOPHER (1564–1593). The birthplace of this violent poet, playwright and probable spy for Elizabeth I stood at 57 St. George's Street in **Canterbury** (Kent) until 1942, when German bombs destroyed it.

From 1580 to about 1587 Marlowe studied at Corpus Christi College, Cambridge (Cambridge-shire). He is believed to have occupied a converted storeroom on the ground floor to the right of the Old Court staircase and a tablet at the building on Trumpington Street indicates the possible spot. Though the precise location of this room is more traditional than evidential, there is no question that his room did face the Old Court on the north side in the same general area. While the exteriors of the 14th-century Old Court buildings remain unchanged, the rooms themselves have been considerably remodeled. Marlowe probably wrote his play *Tamburlaine the Great* (1590) at the college.

(See Chapter 6, LONDON.)

MARY, QUEEN OF SCOTS (1542–1587). Britain's present queen, Elizabeth II, is a direct 13th generation descendant of Mary, Queen of Scots. Ruler of Scotland (1542–67) and one-year queen of France (1559–60), this enigmatic cousin of Elizabeth I—a Catholic and a Stuart—was both the victim and apparent instigator of numerous religious and palace intrigues in her devious quest to gain the throne of England. It was not she who succeeded Elizabeth I, however, but her son, as James I. Imprisoned for 18 years before Elizabeth executed her for conspiracy of treason, Mary lived unwillingly in England from 1568.

Her first lodging, for two months, was Carlisle Castle. Her apartments in the 14th-century Queen Mary's Tower, where she was confined, have been restored. Located in central **Carlisle** (Cumbria), the castle founded in 1092 by William II was one of the strongest in northern England. Most of the original buildings have disappeared but the massive Norman keep, dating from 1160, survives. Classified as an Ancient Monument, the castle is operated by the Department of the Environment on Castle Street. (Open March 15—October 15, Monday—Saturday 9:30—6:30, Sunday 2:00—6:30; October 16—March 14, Monday—Saturday 9:30—4:00, Sunday 2:00—4:00; admission.)

For six months of 1568–69 Mary was held at Bolton Castle, a late 14th-century privately owned structure that today is half ruins, half restaurant. "The two ranges containing the great hall and the main gate are both ruined," reports Neil Burton, "and charmingly overgrown with wild flowers and bushes, in a way which the Department of the Environment would never allow." Visitors have access to the old courtyard, ruins and empty chambers. Bolton Castle is located one and one-half miles north of **Leyburn** (North Yorkshire) on route 6108. (Open April—October,

Tuesday—Sunday 10:00—6:00; November—March, Tuesday—Sunday 10:00—4:00; Wenleysdale 0969–23408; admission.)

At intervals from 1569 to 1585 Mary was lodged in Tutbury Castle. Now a peaceful ruin whose extant portions date mostly from the 17th and 18th centuries, Tutbury was originally built in 1070. John of Gaunt constructed the 14th-century mansion and both it and two 15th-century towers survive. Of all her many prisons, Tutbury was the one most loathed by the unfortunate queen. The buildings were in a state of decay when she lived there: dampness and bad odors permeated the wood and plaster chambers, and cold drafts made her miserable. It was at this castle, she felt, that her imprisonment truly began. Located at **Tutbury** (Staffordshire) on route A50, the castle ruins are operated by the Duchy of Lancaster. (Open April—September, daily 10:00—6:00; October—March, daily 10:00—4:00; Burton-on-Trent 0283–812129; admission.)

From 1570 to 1584 Mary spent most of her captivity in the custody of the Earl of Shrewsbury at **Sheffield** (South Yorkshire), but neither of her two lodgings have survived. The Norman castle, destroyed in 1644, stood at the present vicinity of Castle Green and Castle Street. Ruins of Manor Lodge, a 16th-century mansion, stand east of Norfolk Park on Norfolk Road. Chartley Hall, where she stayed eight months (1585–86) before her final weeks at Fotheringhay, occupies the site of the original moated mansion that held her. It stands about halfway between **Stafford** and **Uttoxeter** on route 518.

There is almost no trace of Fotheringhay Castle—only the grassy mound of the great keep—where Mary underwent her long-delayed trial, spent her last bitter days in 1586 and 1587 and where, in hideous ceremonies, her head was literally hacked from her body by a fumbling executioner. While Elizabeth I piously disclaimed (after the fact) that she intended her cousin's execution, the circumstances that led to Mary's death were palpably acts of the queen. Following the execution, the castle rapidly deteriorated—nobody wanted to live there anymore. Most of its walls and materials were quarried for buildings in the nearby villages of Oundle, Benefield, Hemington and Tansor. Richard III had been born in this castle in 1452 (see the entry on Richard III later in this chapter). There is no admission to the castle

ruins, but they may be viewed from a footpath that leads two miles northwest of **Warmington** (Northamptonshire).

Exhibits: Arundel Castle in High Street, **Arundel** (West Sussex), owned by the Duke of Norfolk, displays the rosary, crucifix and prayer book that Mary carried to her execution. (Open April—October, Sunday—Friday 1:00—5:00; 0903–883136; admission.)

The City of Peterborough Museum in Priestgate at **Peterborough** (Cambridgeshire) also displays personal relics of the queen. (Open June—August, Tuesday—Saturday 10:00—5:00, Monday 2:00—5:00; September—May, Tuesday—Saturday 12:00—5:00; 0733–43329; admission.)

Needlework panels and embroidery crafted by Mary, an accomplished seamstress, may be viewed at Oxburgh Hall, maintained by The National Trust on Stoke Ferry Road at **Oxborough** (Norfolk). (Open April 1—October 10, Saturday—Wednesday 2:00—5:30; Gooderstone 03621–258; admission.)

Exhibits and memorabilia pertaining to the royal house of Stuart are displayed in the 17th-century Chiddingstone Castle, located five miles east of **Edenbridge** (Kent) off route B2027. Included are letters and a lock of Mary's hair. (Open March 28—October 31, Tuesday—Friday 2:00—5:30, Saturday—Sunday 11:30—5:30; Penshurst 0892–870347; admission.)

(See Chapter 2, FRANCE; also Chapter 3, PARIS; also Chapter 7, SCOTLAND.)

MAUGHAM, WILLIAM SOMERSET (1874–1965). The popular novelist, orphaned at age 10, endured a severe childhood at **Whitstable** (Kent), where he lived with his uncle, a vicar, and aunt from 1884 to the 1890s. *Of Human Bondage* (1915), Maugham's best-known novel, concerns this period—he called the town "Blackstable" in the book. The old vicarage, which he revisited in 1948 and 1951, remains on Canterbury Road.

Maugham tomb: King's School, **Canterbury** (Kent).

(See Chapter 2, FRANCE; also Chapter 3, PARIS; also Chapter 6, LONDON.)

MILL, JOHN STUART (1806–1873). The economist and philosopher spent long intervals during four of his childhood years—though his eager-to-educate father never really permitted him a childhood—at Forde Abbey near **Chard** (Dorset), where his family were guests of philosopher

Jeremy Bentham from 1814 to 1818. There the precocious youngster came under the powerful daily influence and instruction of Bentham, who occupied the converted monastery (see the entry on Bentham earlier in this chapter).

(See Chapter 2, FRANCE; also Chapter 6, LONDON.)

MILTON, JOHN (1608–1674). Educated at Christ's College, **Cambridge** (Cambridgeshire), from 1625–32, this major poet did much of his early writing there, including "On the Morning of Christ's Nativity" (1629). The first-floor rooms, on the north side of the First Court, that he is said to have occupied (possibly from 1626), were visited in 1787 by an awed William Wordsworth who recorded the experience in *The Prelude* (1850; see the entry on Wordsworth later in this chapter). The Fellows' Garden off St. Andrew's Street displays a gnarled mulberry tree which, though impressively aged, probably has no direct associations with Milton despite claims that he planted it; it is apparently the last survivor from a large planting in 1609. (Gardens open Monday—Saturday 10:30—12:30, 2:00—4:00; free.)

The traditional site of the Milton home at **Horton** (Buckinghamshire), where the poet lived with his parents from 1632 to 1640, is Berkin Manor near the village church. The original house on the site was demolished in 1795. Milton probably wrote the poems *L'Allegro* (1632), *Il Penseroso* (1632), *Comus* (1634) and *Lycidas* (1637) there.

Milton's only surviving home is the two-story timber and brick cottage in **Chalfont St. Giles** (Buckinghamshire), where he sought refuge with his family for eight months (1665–66) during the London plague. The 16th-century cottage, which was loaned to him, was the place he finished his epic poem *Paradise Lost* (1667). The house was purchased by public subscription in 1887 and dedicated as a museum to the poet who set out "to justify the ways of God to man." Two ground floor rooms display Milton relics, including a lock of his hair, plus rare editions of *Paradise Lost*, portraits and books. Now called "Milton's Cottage," it stands on the hillside above the church. (Open February—October, Tuesday—Saturday 10:00—1:00, 2:00—6:00, Sunday 2:00—6:00; November, Saturday—Sunday only; 024-07-2313; admission.)

(See Chapter 6, LONDON.)

NELSON, HORATIO, LORD (1758–1805). The birthplace of England's greatest naval hero, who lost his life at the Battle of Trafalgar, was the rectory at **Burnham Thorpe**. It is located one mile south of Overy Staithe (Norfolk) off route 149. The two-story, L-shaped house on 30 acres occupied by his clergyman father—and where his mother died in 1767—was Nelson's home until about 1770. He lived there again, with his wife, Frances Nisbet Nelson, from about 1786 to 1793. This house was demolished in 1802, though a portion of one wall was incorporated into a later coach house on the property. Remnants of the Nelson gardens survive near the present rectory dwelling.

At **Bath** (Avon), Nelson occupied the marked lodging at 2 Pierrepont Street during intervals between commissions during the 1780s.

Exhibits: Collections of Nelsonian relics and papers are numerous in England. At **Buckler's Hard** (Hampshire), the Maritime Museum on the shipyard site where several of Nelson's vessels were built displays models of *HMS Victory* and the admiral's baby clothes. (Open April—October, daily 10:00—6:00; November—March, daily 10:00—4:30; 059063-203; admission.)

The Royal Naval Museum at the Royal Dockyard, Portsea Hard in **Portsmouth** (Hampshire), exhibits a fine Nelsonian collection that depicts his career; furniture, ship models, paintings, and a Trafalgar panorama are among the items on view. Adjacent is Nelson's much-restored, drydocked flagship *Victory*, outfitted in yellow-and-black as it was at Trafalgar. Visitors may tour the ship, see Nelson's cabin and the spot where he fell when a bullet lodged in his spine. (Ship open March—October, Monday—Saturday 10:30—5:30, Sunday 1:00—5:00; November—February, Monday—Saturday 10:30—4:30, Sunday 1:00—4:30; 0705-822351, ext. 23111; free. Museum open Monday—Saturday 10:30—5:00, Sunday 1:00—5:00; 0705-822351, ext. 23868; admission.)

(See Chapter 6, LONDON; also Chapter 7, WALES.)

NEWTON, SIR ISAAC (1642–1727). Woolsthorpe Manor at **Colsterworth** (Lincolnshire) was the mathematician-physicist's birthplace and family home. The two midwives at his delivery predicted that the frail, premature infant who lived to age 84 would not survive the day. Regarded as a "woolgatherer" during his boyhood, Newton was to show what one biographer called "an almost terrifying power of concentration" as well as a profound intuitiveness. During an

18-month return stay at the manor to avoid the plague in 1665 and 1666, Newton discovered the principles of differential calculus, of the light spectrum and of gravitation. The small limestone house, built about 1620, has period furnishings on display plus some kitchen graffiti thought to have been inscribed by Newton. An apple orchard in front is said to be the place where, according to Voltaire, a falling apple inspired Newton's theory of gravitation. Visitors may see a descendant of the legendary tree (but are not allowed to pick apple souvenirs!). The property, located in Newton Way, is operated by The National Trust. (Open April—October, Monday, Wednesday, Friday—Saturday 11:00—12:30, 2:00—6:00; Grantham 0476-860338; admission.)

WOOLSTHORPE MANOR, BIRTHPLACE OF SIR ISAAC NEWTON. The stone house shown in this old engraving was also the great scientist's refuge in 1665 and 1666, when he formulated several important principles of physics. Today it exhibits Newton relics and period furnishings.

In nearby **Brantham**, Newton boarded at the residence of an apothecary at the north end of High Street while attending King's School (1650s) in the town; this lodging is now the north wing of the George Hotel.

Newton's home from 1667 to 1701 was **Cambridge** (Cambridgeshire). As a fellow of Trinity College, the bachelor scholar roomed on the first floor, north side, of the Great Gateway off Trinity Street. In these rooms, Newton worked out the calculations of his *Principia Mathematica* (1687), one of the monumental achievements of the human mind. Lord Bertrand Russell, a worthy mathematical successor, occupied these same rooms in 1944 (see the entry on Russell later in this chap-

ter). College courts and precincts are usually open to visitors during daytime.

Exhibits: In **Grantham** (Lincolnshire), the Grantham Library and Museum on St. Peter's Hill displays Newton memorabilia. Open Monday—Friday 9:30—5:00, Saturday 9:30—12:30; 0476-3926; free.)

The College Library on the west side of the Great Court at Trinity College, **Cambridge** (see above), also displays Newton relics, including his private book collection.

(See Chapter 6, LONDON.)

NIGHTINGALE, FLORENCE (1820–1910). The founder of professional nursing and pioneer of hospital reform fought not only the entrenched sexism of her day but also the opposition of her own wealthy family in order to enter medical service. Ultimately she transformed nursing from a squalid low-level job performed by scullery maids to a highly trained profession, formulating standards that no physician had dared attempt. Born in Italy, Nightingale resided until 1825 at Lea Hurst, the large mansion built by her father on the River Derwent near **Crich** (Derbyshire). The house, now a private retirement home, stands on the east side of route 6. Her family used the house only as a summer residence after 1825.

The family winter home after 1825, and Nightingale's home base until 1896, was Embley House near **Wellow** (Hampshire) off route 31. It remains privately owned.

A favorite residence during her years of struggle and success was Claydon House, the home of her sister, Lady Parthenope Verney. Nightingale's bedroom and various mementos of her career are displayed by The National Trust. Built in 1754, this manor seat of the Verney family (which still occupies part of the house) retains only the west end of the original mansion, with 19th-century additions including the south front. Its interior rococo ornamentation creates some of the most lavish and extravagant room decoration in England. Chamber concerts are presented in the house from June to October. Claydon House, reached via signposts, stands near **Middle Claydon** (Buckinghamshire). (Open April—October, Monday 12:30—5:30, Tuesday—Wednesday, Saturday—Sunday 2:00—5:30; Steeple Claydon 029-673-349; admission.)

Nightingale tomb: Parish churchyard, **East Wellow** (Hampshire).

Exhibit: The Royal Army Medical Corps Historical Museum at **Aldershot** (Hampshire) displays Nightingale relics and memorabilia. (Inquire locally for admission information.)

(See Chapter 6, LONDON; also Chapter 8, ITALY.)

ORWELL, GEORGE. See ERIC ARTHUR BLAIR.

PENN, WILLIAM (1644–1718). The prominent Quaker preacher and colonial founder of Pennsylvania spent four years (1672–76) at Basing House, a large two-story manor on the north side of the High Street in **Rickmansworth** (Hertfordshire). This was Penn's first married home; a more recent building now occupies the site.

Penn bought a house in **Warminghurst** (West Sussex) in 1676 and lived there until 1699. Once owned by a Benedictine priory, then by the ancestral family of Percy Bysshe Shelley (see the entry on Shelley later in this chapter), the two-story slate-roofed house was occupied by his son after 1699. Penn made occasional visits until debts forced him to sell the property in 1708. Later, the estate became a deer park. The Duke of Norfolk, a later owner, demolished the house, it is said, because of persistent rumors that it was haunted.

From 1710, Penn's last home was at **Ruscombe** (Buckinghamshire), where he died. Located on the south side of the railroad near an estate called Southbury Farm, Penn's house was destroyed in 1830.

Penn tomb: Jordan's Graveyard, Jordan's Quaker Meeting House, **Chalfont St. Giles** (Buckinghamshire).

(See Chapter 6, LONDON; also Chapter 7, IRELAND.)

PEPYS, SAMUEL (1633–1703). Near **Brampton** (Cambridgeshire), the lad who would pen one of the world's best-known diaries resided from 1642 to 1646 in the household of Sir Edward Montagu, his great-uncle. Pepys had been sent there in order to escape Civil War violence in London. Hinchingbrooke House, which remained in the Montagu family until 1962, stands one-half mile west of town on route A604. The manor was originally converted from the ruins of a Benedictine convent in 1538, and ancestors of Oliver Cromwell owned it until 1627. Restored after a damaging fire in 1830, the house now forms part of Hinchingbrooke Comprehensive School. There are few original furnishings. (Open March—July, Sunday 2:00—5:00; Huntingdon 0480–51121;

admission.) Pepys's own family home, a 16th-century timber-framed farmhouse to which later brick extensions were added, stands privately owned near Bell End. Pepys returned there frequently during the 1660s. On one occasion, when Dutch invasion threatened, he is said to have sent his wife and father there from London to bury his money in the garden. But to Pepys's vast annoyance the two simply weren't cut out to be conspirators—they buried the money in broad daylight and promptly forgot where. (Open March—July, Sunday 2:00—5:00; other times by appointment, Monday—Saturday; Huntingdon 0480–53431; admission.)

Exhibit: The diarist willed his books and papers to Magdalene College, **Cambridge** (Cambridgeshire), from which he had graduated in 1654. The Pepysian Library, located at the east end of the second court in a building that dates from about 1680, displays his books (arranged by his own hand on his own shelves), plus the six famous manuscript volumes of his *Diary* in his personal shorthand (not deciphered until 1825) and other papers and relics. (Open during college terms and July—September, Monday—Saturday 11:30—12:30, 2:30—3:30; 0223–61543; free.)

(See Chapter 6, LONDON.)

POPE, ALEXANDER (1688–1744). At **Binfield** (Berkshire), the house called "Pope's Manor" is probably an extension of Whitehill House, the 17th-century brick dwelling bought by the poet's father in 1698. The row of Scotch firs on the family's original 14-acre property still exists. Pope lived there from 1700 until the house was sold in 1717 and did his first writing there, including *An Essay on Criticism* (1711). He also began his translation of Homer's *Iliad* (1715–20) at the house. Deformed and stunted by a congenital bone disease, Pope described the dwelling as: "A little house with trees a-row/And like its master very low." Later additions and alterations increased the size of Pope's Manor, which remains privately owned.

In **West Grinstead** (West Sussex), John Caryll's house, which the poet often visited and where in 1712 he wrote his mock-heroic poem *The Rape of the Lock* (1714), is gone. "Pope's Oak," however, the tree under which he is said to have penned the lines, may be viewed from a footpath in West Grinstead Park, site of the manor.

In 1718 Pope spent much of the summer at **Stanton Harcourt** (Oxfordshire), where he finished his work on the *Iliad*. The 15th-century Harcourt manor had already fallen to ruins when Lord Harcourt offered use of the family chapel tower to the poet. "Pope's Tower," where he sequestered himself in a fourth-floor chamber, survives in the village, and "few places that the poet inhabited are more suggestive of his memory," according to biographer Peter Quennell. The tower was said to be haunted by two female ghosts—one an adulteress who had sinned in the tower, the other a murder victim—and the nearby pool was actually exorcized by a bishop in 1865. Pope apparently had no problems with prior residents, however.

Exhibits: At Rousham House off route A423 at **Steeple Aston** (Oxfordshire), Pope guested along with John Gay and Horace Walpole and enjoyed the large gardens. Still the private 25-acre estate of the Cottrell-Dormer family, the 1635 manor displays portraits, autographed letters of Pope, and an inscribed 1735 edition of his *Works*. (House open April—September, Wednesday, Sunday 2:00—5:30; gardens open daily 10:30—5:30; 0869–47110; admission.)

Hartlebury Castle at **Hartlebury** (Hereford and Worcester) has been the seat of the bishops of Worcester for more than 1,000 years, though the present sandstone castle dates mainly from the 17th-century. The Bishop Richard Hurd library in the castle contains a number of books that belonged to Pope, including a copy of Chaucer given to him in 1700. (Contact Bishop's Secretary for appointment; Hartlebury 029–96–410.)

(See Chapter 6, LONDON.)

RALEIGH, SIR WALTER (1554?–1618). Hayes Barton, the farmhouse birthplace of the Elizabethan courtier, poet and colonial adventurer, stands one mile west of **East Budleigh** (Devon) via Hayes Lane. Raleigh was born in the upper west room of the Tudor manor and lived there until about 1569. His smoking room is over the porch. In 1584, when Raleigh wanted to buy back the house, the new owner refused to sell. According to Lois H. Fisher, "an attempt by an American to remove the entire house to Virginia in 1884 failed because a single 80-foot main beam ran the entire length of the house," thus preventing sectional movement for transportation. The house, privately operated, is obviously meant to belong where it is. (Open June—September, Monday—Friday 2:15—5:00; admission.)

Elizabeth I granted Raleigh lease of Sherborne Old Castle at **Sherborne** (Dorset) in 1591. Originally the property belonged to the 12th-century Sherborne Abbey; the bishop of Salisbury, whose seat was there, laid a curse on the castle to prevent its transfer from the bishopric. Raleigh, however, began to repair the old building, but quickly gave it up to erect "The Lodge" in 1594, today known as Sherborne Castle. In 1599 he was given the property; but by 1603, when he stood condemned by Elizabeth's successor, James I, the castle was confiscated and given to Robert Carr, a court favorite. At the time of Raleigh's death, Sir John Digby was the owner and he added two wings on each side, converting the property into a castle-size structure. Thus, the house built by Raleigh is the central portion of today's structure. The house is still owned by the Digby family. Visitors may see Raleigh's will plus other documents, period furnishings and portraits. Sherborne Castle, stands just south of town off route A30 (open Easter Saturday—May 31, Thursday, Saturday—Sunday 2:00—5:30; June 1—September 30, daily 2:00—5:30; 093–581–3182; admission.)

(See Chapter 6, LONDON; also Chapter 7, IRELAND.)

RICHARD I, COEUR DE LION (1157–1199). "More than any other King of England," wrote biographer John Gillingham, "Richard the Lionheart belongs, not to the sober world of history, but to the magic realm of legend and romance." More French than English by ancestry, language and inclination, and an avowed homosexual, this handsome warrior king spent only 10 months of his 10-year reign (1189–99) in England. He preferred to defend his Normandy and Anjou possessions and to lead the Third Crusade, for which he almost auctioned his kingdom. Troubadours and later writers, among them Sir Walter Scott, greatly romanticized his exploits and courage—as often happens to the safely dead extremists of history.

As the son of Henry II and Eleanor of Aquitaine, Richard Plantagenet was born at Beaumont Palace in **Oxford** (Oxfordshire). Nothing remains of this castle (also the probable birthplace of his brother, King John), which stood at the western end of Beaumont Street until 1595. In that year, St. John's College bought the palace remnants for materials—about 1,000 wagonloads of stone and timber—and used it for construction of the college library, which still stands on the south side of Canterbury quadrangle off St. Giles Street. An ivy-covered masonry arch, enclosed by a fence at 302 Woodstock Road on school property, is the only ruin of the original palace that survives.

At **Winchester** (Hampshire), Richard underwent a second coronation in 1194 and during that time lived at Winchester Castle (see the entry on Arthur, *Exhibits*, earlier in this chapter).

(See Chapter 1, AUSTRIA; also Chapter 2, FRANCE; also Chapter 4, WEST GERMANY; also Chapter 6, LONDON.)

RICHARD III (1452–1485). The only English king since the Norman Conquest to fall upon a battlefield—and the only one without a splendid ornate tomb—Richard III still evokes controversy among historians. Was he the child-murderer depicted by Shakespeare? Or did Tudor propaganda cast an able if ruthless king into a falsely malicious role? The facts remain elusive; suffice it to say that this monarch, who reigned only two years (1483–85), still has staunch scholarly defenders.

His birthplace was the now long-gone Fotheringhay Castle near **Warmington** (Northamptonshire), his home to age five with his parents Richard, Duke of York, and Cicely Neville (see the entry on Mary, Queen of Scots earlier in this chapter).

A Neville family property, where Richard lived from age nine to 13 and at frequent intervals after his marriage to Anne Neville (1472–82), was Middleham Castle at **Middleham** (North Yorkshire). It became his principal residence as lieutenant-general in the north and was given to him by his brother, Edward IV. Richard's son, Edward, died there in 1484. Today the castle lacks roofs and floors, but many of the walls enclosing the square keep, built in 1170, survive. Living quarters were mainly in that keep, surrounded by a 13th-century wall plus outbuildings added in the 14th and 15th centuries. Private houses now cover most of the former outer ward. Classified as an Ancient Monument, the impressive ruins are maintained by the Department of the Environment. (Open March 15—October 15, Monday—Saturday 9:30—6:30, Sunday 2:00—6:30; October 16—March 14, Monday—Saturday 9:30—4:00, Sunday 2:00—4:00; admission.)

Warwick Castle on the River Avon at **Warwick** (Warwickshire) was Richard's home, probably from 1465 to 1468, where he lived under the custody of his cousin and future father-in-law, Richard Neville, Earl of Warwick ("the Kingmaker"). Nothing remains of the original wooden castle built in 1068 except an earth mound. While many of the present walls date from the 14th century and would be recognized by Richard III today, the state rooms underwent extensive additions and alterations from the 17th through 19th centuries. Historical displays, including armor, paintings, tapestries and furnishings relate mainly to medieval Earls of Warwick. Warwick Castle is owned and operated by Madame Tussauds Ltd. (Open March 1—October 31, daily 10:00—5:30; November 1—February 29, daily 10:00—4:30; 0926-49421; admission.)

Another residence used by Richard as lieutenant-general and as Duke of Gloucester was Barnard Castle, also an Ancient Monument, located on the northwest side of **Barnard** (Durham) on a cliff above the River Tees. An important medieval military center, it was built about 1250 by the Balliol family, of whom John Balliol became king of Scotland in 1292. Later owned by the Neville family, it passed to Anne Neville from her father. Richard enlarged the castle and built Brackenbury Tower. Most of the ruins date from the 13th and 14th centuries. (Open same hours as Middleham Castle; also April—September, Sunday 9:30—4:30; admission.)

One of Richard's favorite residences was another Neville estate, the 14th-century Sheriff Hutton Castle, a small part of which stands deserted in a private farmyard at **Sheriff Hutton** (North Yorkshire). Two footpaths give access to the ruins; the castle served as headquarters of Edward IV's Council of the North. (Open by permission of owners; donation.)

Pomfret Castle, scene of the starvation murder of Richard II in 1400, was built in 1080. It was the official seat of the Duchy of Lancaster, which Richard of Gloucester used as chief steward of the duchy during the 1470s. "Bloody Pomfret," as Shakespeare called it, was a frequent place of execution during the Wars of the Roses. Also called and spelled "**Pontefract**" (West Yorkshire), the castle stood just above the present All Saints Church; a few ruins of the keep and a tower survive there in a public park.

As Duke of Gloucester, Richard was granted Sudeley Castle in **Winchcombe** (Gloucestershire) in 1469 and rebuilt its east side inner court. He occupied his splendid state apartment there at intervals until 1478. Built in 1398, the castle became the later home of Catherine Parr, widow of Henry VIII and wife of Admiral Sir Thomas Seymour, the uncle of Edward VI. She died in childbirth at Sudeley in 1548. The inner courtyard was demolished during the 17th century, and the castle lay a neglected ruin for almost 200 years. New owners began restoration in the 19th century, and most of the interior decoration and furnishings date from that period (an exception is Marie Antoinette's bedhangings). The site of the original great hall, where Richard held forth, is now a Victorian corridor housing an autograph collection. The dungeon tower, which survives from the original castle, displays various exhibits and a large collection of toys and dolls. Sudeley Castle, located one-half mile southwest of town off route A46, is owned and maintained by the Dent-Brocklehurst family. (Open March 11—October 31, Tuesday—Sunday 12:00—5:30; 0242–602308; admission.)

The last residence of Richard III was **Nottingham** Castle (Nottinghamshire), the king's headquarters preceding the fateful 1485 Battle of Bosworth Field, which ended the Wars of the Roses. He called Nottingham his "castle of care," for there in 1484 he received the crushing news of his young son's death and, it was reported, went "nigh mad" with grief. He completed new state apartments there at about the same time. This castle has also had traditional associations from an earlier period with Robin Hood (see the entry below). Only a much-restored gatehouse built in 1252, a piece of wall and a stone bridge remain of the medieval castle, which stood on a sandstone bluff. Honeycombed with underground passages, the castle was demolished in 1651. The present manor on the site of the old upper ward off Castle Road dates from the late 17th century and functions as Nottingham Castle Museum, operated by Nottingham City Council as a local exhibit center and art gallery. (Open April—September, daily 10:00—5:45; October—March, daily 10:00—4:45; 0602–411881; admission.)

Richard III tomb (site): Bow Bridge, **Leicester** (Leicestershire).

Exhibit: The Bosworth Battlefield Centre, two miles south of route B585 from **Market Bosworth** (Leicestershire), introduces visitors to the ground where Richard III was slain by the forces of Henry Tudor (later Henry VII), thus ending the Wars of the Roses and the House of York monarchy. Battlefield markers, an exhibition and a diorama describe the epochal battle. "Unfortunately," as Philip A. Crowl warns, "historians disagree as to what actually happened so the explanations may not be as accurate as might be wished." (Open daily; check locally for admission information.)

(See Chapter 6, LONDON.)

ROBIN HOOD (ca. 1290?–1346?). Not much doubt exists that one or more actual people inspired the lively cycle of medieval ballads about the legendary outlaw archer of Nottinghamshire. But, as Lois H. Fisher remarks, "historians have had as much difficulty in tracing Robin as the sheriff of Nottingham had." The difficulty lies in deciding which of several possible individuals he may have been—some seven likely names and locales have been traced. J. W. Walker in *The True History of Robin Hood* (1973) makes a plausible (though not undisputed) case for one Robert Hood, basing his theory on documents from the Wakefield Manor court rolls and the household expense account of Edward II; while J. C. Holt discredits Walker's research in his *Robin Hood* (1982), a useful survey. An earlier Robert Hood, identified as a fugitive in 1230, is favored by Maurice Keen in *The Outlaws of Medieval England* (1961). And there have been other Hoods, Hods, and Robynhods suggested among "merrie old England" surnames. Attempts have also been made to identify him as Robert FitzOoth, Earl of Huntington; but scholarly consensus has now largely abandoned the idea, favored by some upper-class antiquarians, that Robin was actually a nobleman in disguise. Most researchers believe that the evidence so far cannot justify a positive identification; on several counts, however, Walker's evidence seems internally consistent. Proceeding on the basis of Walker's Robert Hood as a plausible Robin Hood—and suspending final judgment on whether he was *the* Robin Hood—we can trace his movements fairly closely.

Hood was the son of Adam Hood, a forester employed by the lord of Wakefield Manor in **Wakefield** (West Yorkshire). This estate covered a large part of the area from Normanton on the east to the borders of Lancashire on the west. Robert Hood was supposedly born somewhere in the present city that grew around the manor house.

We next see Robert Hood in 1316, when he bought a 30- by 16-foot piece of land at "Bickhill" or "Bitchhill" on the Wakefield Manor estate—the later Wakefield market place. According to Walker, documents reveal that he built a five-room house and lived there until 1323 with his wife Matilda. As a "contrarient" who supposedly participated in the battle of Boroughbridge under the Earl of Lancaster against soldiers of Edward II, Hood forfeited his property and escaped to the forest of Barnesdale with his wife. At this time, it is said, he changed his name to Robin and that of his wife to Marian.

Barnesdale Forest, a wild, almost inaccessible refuge for outlaw types, occupied about 30 square miles in South Yorkshire, about five miles from **Askern** (on route 19) west to **Badsworth**, and about six miles south from the River Went—an area traversed by route A1 today. Only remnants of the forest survive.

Contiguous with Barnesdale Forest on the south was Sherwood Forest, an immense woodland that covered most of western Nottinghamshire—some 16,000 acres, about 30 miles long by eight miles wide—an area that became another refuge for Hood and his associates. He supposedly met Edward II himself at Nottingham Castle in 1324 (see the entry on Richard III above); was won over by the king and went to London with him; but returned that same year and spent the rest of his life in Sherwood and Barnesdale forests. Sherwood Forest exists today only in isolated tracts in the northern part of the county. It includes the parks of Welbeck, Clumber, Worksop and Thoresby, collectively known as the Dukeries. The "Major Oak" near Edwinstowe, a tree that probably dates only from the 16th century despite claims that it is 1,400 years old, was a reputed meeting place for Robin and his men. The Sherwood Forest Visitors' Centre, located one-half mile north of **Edwinstowe** on route B6034, lies within about 150 acres of the surviving medieval forest. The centre provides maps and guides to this scenic area and to nearby sites traditionally identified with Robin and his motley crew. (Open daily; check locally for hours; 0623–823202; admission.) As J. C. Holt cautions, however, "the Robin Hood place names illustrate the spread of the legend, not the doings of the outlaw"—a distinct difference to be remembered or not, as one chooses, in "Robin Hood country."

Robin Hood's last lodging, Walker believes, was Kirklees Priory, a Cistercian nunnery of bad repute, at **Kirklees** (West Yorkshire). Ill and "desiring there to be let blood," says the *Harleian Miscellany* (1744–46), "[Robin] was betrayed and made bleed to death." Only ruins of the 12th-century buildings remain. According to Walker, the surviving 15th-century gatehouse, widely advertised as the place where Robin Hood bled to death, has no connection with the outlaw.

Robin Hood tomb (reputed): Kirklees Priory, **Kirklees**.

(See Chapter 6, LONDON.)

ROUSSEAU, JEAN-JACQUES (1712–1778). The French writer and philosopher, banished from France because of his *Émile* (1762), came to England in 1765 and stayed until 1767. In 1766 and 1767, he wrote the major part of probably his best-known work, the *Confessions* (1781–88), at Wootton Hall in **Wootton** (Staffordshire), loaned to him by the owner. Rousseau lived there with his mistress, Thérèse Levasseur, and spent much time roaming and botanizing in the surrounding hills. The mystified local people called him "Roos Hall." His increasing paranoia, a fear that he was about to be poisoned, caused the couple's departure. Only the entrance gates of Wootton Hall survive in the village.

(See Chapter 1, SWITZERLAND; also Chapter 2, FRANCE; also Chapter 3, PARIS; also Chapter 8, ITALY.)

RUSKIN, JOHN (1819–1900). As a writer and scholar of immensely varied knowledge and interests, Ruskin deeply influenced British arts and architecture and helped shape the socialist movement. In 1871, as Slade Professor of Art at Christ Church College, **Oxford** (Oxfordshire), from which he had graduated in 1843, the author and art critic was also made an honorary fellow of Corpus Christi College. At intervals from 1879 he occupied rooms on the first floor of staircase 2 in the Fellows' building, where he also exhibited some of his choicest art treasures.

Also in 1871, Ruskin bought his last home, Brantwood, at **Coniston** (Cumbria) in what is now Lake District National Park. He bought the property without seeing it but knowing that the scenery was superb. After finding the 1797 country cottage in a state of damp decay, he immediately set about repairing and enlarging it, adding a dining room, studio, tower and gateway, landscaping his 200-acre grounds and building a harbor on Coniston Water. Until 1879, and again in 1883 and 1884, Ruskin commuted from there to his duties at Oxford. At the end of this period he retired in seclusion to his cottage and did his last writing there (his autobiography *Praeterita*, 1885–89) as his physical and mental health declined. Nature trails on the grounds pass the stone seat he fashioned as a slate "throne" and where, in his later years, he sat for hours in "silent unknowing." Brantwood, operated by the Ruskin Museum, displays Ruskin's original furnishings plus part of his library and many of his watercolors. Visitors may also see his boat harbor and, in the driveway coach house, his boat, carriage and traveling bath. Brantwood is located in East Lakeside Road off route B5285. (Open Good Friday—October 31, Sunday—Friday 11:00—5:30; November 1—Good Friday, by appointment; 09664–396; admission.)

Ruskin tomb: Parish churchyard, **Coniston**.

Exhibit: The John Ruskin Museum in Yewdale Road, **Coniston** village, displays an abundance of Ruskin memorabilia, including early drawings, manuscripts, notebooks, his walking stick, painting equipment, mineral collection and other personal relics. (Open Easter—October 31, daily 10:00—dusk; 09664–359; admission.)

(See Chapter 6, LONDON; also Chapter 7, SCOTLAND.)

RUSSELL, BERTRAND, LORD (1872–1970). The Welsh-born philosopher and mathematician, one of the towering intellects of the 20th century, was best-known for his pacifism and iconoclastic writings on politics and morals. All of his extant homes remain privately owned or occupied.

In **Cambridge** (Cambridgeshire), Russell occupied rooms at various intervals throughout his life. As a student in 1890, he lodged in Whewell's Court, Trinity College; again at Trinity as a mathematics lecturer (1910–11), in I Building, Nevile's Court; and finally in 1944, as a lecturer, in the old Trinity rooms of Sir Isaac Newton (see the entry on Newton earlier in this chapter).

At **Fernhurst** (West Sussex), the ornate two-story manor called Friday's Hill was his frequent residence during the early 1890s. This was the estate of Logan Pearsall Smith, prominent American Quaker and socialist, whose daughter Alys became Russell's first wife in 1894. From 1896 to 1902 the couple lived in a nearby 16th-century cottage called "the Millhanger," to which they added several rooms. There Russell began his collaboration with Alfred North Whitehead, producing the scholarly landmark *Principia Mathematica* (1910–13). "In this cottage many of the happiest times of my life were passed," he recalled.

"The most unhappy moments of my life," conversely, were spent at the 17th-century Mill House at **Grantchester** (Cambridgeshire), where he, Prof. Whitehead and their wives resided in 1902 while the two scholars finished the *Principia*. This was Whitehead's home from 1898 to 1906.

Russell underwent a self-described emotional "awakening" there that miserably affected his marriage, though it lasted nine more years. This house, which stood adjacent to Byron's Pool on the Trumpington Road and was also the site of "The Reeve's Tale" in Chaucer's *Canterbury Tales*, burned down in 1928.

In 1905 Russell and his wife built a house at Bagley Wood, Lower Copse, on the southern outskirts of **Oxford** (Oxfordshire), their home until 1910.

From 1924 until about 1927 Russell's summer home with his second wife, Dora Black, was Carn Voel, a seaside cottage at **Porthcurno** (Cornwall).

Telegraph House, a building used for a semaphore station between Portsmouth and London during the reign of George III, became the experimental Beacon Hill School, which the Russells established in 1927 in order to test their unconventional theories on childhood education. "The house was ugly and rather absurd," he wrote, "but the situation was perfect." Some 230 acres of isolated downland forest surrounded the house; a one-mile road was built from North Marden. **South Harting** (West Sussex), five miles away, was the nearest larger village. Russell wrote *Marriage and Morals* (1929) and *The Conquest of Happiness* (1930) there. Dora Russell continued to manage the school after their 1935 separation and divorce.

(See Chapter 3, PARIS; also Chapter 6, LONDON; also Chapter 7, WALES.)

SCOTT, ROBERT FALCON (1868–1912). The birthplace of the Antarctic explorer, who perished in a race with Roald Amundsen to discover the South Pole, was **Devonport** (Devon), his home to about 1880. The small farm called Outlands, inherited by his father, stood near Stoke Damerel.

Exhibits: Scott Polar Research Institute, operated by the University of Cambridge in Lensfield Road, **Cambridge** (Cambridgeshire), displays numerous relics of Scott's first Antarctic expedition (1900–04), plus some of his watercolors and sketches. (Open Monday—Saturday 2:30—4:00; 0223–66499; free.)

(See Chapter 4, NORWAY; also Chapter 6, LONDON.)

SCOTT, SIR WALTER (1771–1832). The Scottish novelist wrote most of *Kenilworth* (1821) during an 1815 stay in the King's Arms Hotel at **Kenilworth**

(Warwickshire). His room still contains the original furnishings.

(See Chapter 7, SCOTLAND.)

SHAKESPEARE, WILLIAM (1564–1616). The birthplace of the greatest dramatist in the English language was probably **Stratford-upon-Avon** (Warwickshire), where his half-timbered parental home survives on Henley Street. It is known that John Shakespeare, his tradesman father, bought this house in 1575. Since most biographers presume the house is the same one that he had rented from 1552, it is assumed that William Shakespeare was born there, but there is no solid documentary evidence of this. There is no question, however, that he did live there, probably until his marriage to Anne Hathaway in 1582. The birthplace actually consists of two modest two-story houses, once part of a longer row. In the eastern house, it is said, John Shakespeare carried on business as a glover and wool merchant, while the western house served as the family dwelling. According to tradition, the playwright was born in the upper chamber identified as his birth room.

SHAKESPEARE'S BIRTHPLACE. A native of **Stratford**, England's foremost dramatist and poet probably resided in this parental home until his 1582 marriage. These 1847 engravings by E. Duncan show views of the

Again, there is no evidence that the eastern house had been built by 1564; today, however, it serves as a museum displaying books, manuscripts, period relics, pictures and the desk that Shakespeare is said to have used at the Stratford Free School. The combined houses remained owned by collateral descendants until 1806. In 1847 they were obtained by the Shakespeare Birthplace Trust. The building was carefully restored in 1858 to its supposed 16th-century appearance, using as much of the original timber and materials as possible. No original furnishings remain, but period items are authentic and resemble those that the family knew and used. Signatures of literary greats who have made the pilgrimage there, including those of Thomas Carlyle and Sir Walter Scott, are scratched in a window pane of the birth room. A small garden is planted with flowers and herbs mentioned in Shakespeare's works. Entrance is via the large Shakespeare Centre. (Open April—October, Monday—Friday 9:00—6:00, Sunday 10:00—6:00; November—March, Monday—Friday 9:00—4:30; Sunday 1:30—4:30; 0789–4016; admission.)

house as it existed then, but not much has changed today. It remains one of the world's best-known literary shrines.

Some biographers believe that when Shakespeare and Anne Hathaway were first married they resided with his family until he went to London in 1585. Because of John Shakespeare's large household and William's invisible means of support, however, the couple may have lived with Anne's widowed mother at Shottery, a village to the west but now basically part of Stratford. "Anne Hathaway's Cottage," also owned by the Shakespeare Birthplace Trust, is actually a 12-room, timber-framed farmhouse with thatched roof. Again, its authenticity as her home is based on plausible tradition rather than on clear proof, though Hathaways did live there from 1470 until 1911. The house is smaller than it was in the 16th century. Its hall and east wing are original, with the western portion added about 1600 and other portions removed. There are many Hathaway furnishings, some of them quite possibly known to Shakespeare himself, "but the thousands of people trudging through the building each day," reports Neil Burton, "can make it difficult to appreciate the items of interest." Anne Hathaway's Cottage stands one mile northwest of central Stratford between routes A422 and A439. One may enjoy a pleasant walk through fields from Stratford to the cottage—a route probably trudged many times by Shakespeare during his courtship. (Open same hours as for Shakespeare's Birthplace; 0789–292100; admission.)

In 1597 Shakespeare bought New Place in Stratford, one of the largest houses in the town. Standing on almost an acre of land in the town center, the 15th-century house was shabby and rundown, and the playwright—obviously a wealthy man by then—spent much energy and money restoring the house and increasing the size of his estate. He did not settle there permanently, however, until 1611. It was his last home. A later owner, Rev. Francis Gastrell, outraged the town as well as the literary world by wantonly destroying the house in 1759 because he was bothered by the influx of pilgrims wanting to see Shakespeare's home. (Not only was the fellow a sorehead, he had no business sense; Stratfordians have never since permitted anyone of the surname Gastrell to dwell in the town.) The foundation of New Place may be seen in the garden adjacent to Nash's House in Chapel Street. This three-story brick and timber manor belonged to Thomas Nash, the first husband of Shakespeare's granddaughter, Elizabeth

Hall. Period furnishings and local historical exhibits are displayed by the Shakespeare Birthplace Trust. (Nash House and New Place garden open April—October, Monday—Friday 9:00—6:00, Sunday 2:00—6:00; November—March, Monday—Friday 9:00—12:45, 2:00—4:00; 0789–292325; admission.)

A persistent village tradition in **Clifford Chambers**, two miles south of Stratford, maintains that Shakespeare's actual birthplace was the rectory next to the parish church there. His mother, it is said, came to reside there with relatives in 1564 because of an outbreak of plague in Stratford. All that is known for certain is that other Shakespeares did reside in this village during his lifetime.

Some scholars believe a local tradition that Shakespeare wrote most of his sonnets plus the play *Love's Labour's Lost* (1595) at Titchfield Abbey, **Titchfield** (Hampshire). The 13th-century abbey, dissolved by Henry VIII in 1537, was rebuilt as a mansion called Palace House in 1542; and lexicographer-translator John Florio, a friend of Shakespeare, tutored the Earl of Southampton, Shakespeare's patron, there in 1590. Most of the house was destroyed in 1781, leaving only a gatehouse and wall fragments. The ruins, classified an Ancient Monument by the Department of the Environment, show outlines of the abbey buildings plus unearthed medieval floor tiles. It has been claimed that the aforementioned play plus *Romeo and Juliet* (1595), *A Midsummer Night's Dream* (ca. 1595) and *Twelfth Night* (ca. 1600) were first performed for the Earl in the great hall which adjoined the ruined abbey cloister. The ruins stand one-half mile north of the village off route A27. (Open March 15—October 15, Monday—Saturday 9:30—6:30, Sunday 2:00—6:30; October 16—March 14, Monday—Saturday 9:30—4:00, Sunday 2:00—4:00; admission.)

Shakespeare tomb: Holy Trinity Church, **Stratford-upon-Avon**.

Exhibits: **Stratford-upon-Avon**, center of the Shakespeare "industry," is full of monuments and dedications to the dramatist who put this old market town on the world map and brings thousands of people each year to pay tribute to his genius. Tourists will have no trouble locating the major sights and activities plus plenty of minor ones. The plays, of course, are regularly performed at the Royal Shakespeare Theatre. Much of the town has been restored to a 16th-century style that is best seen on foot. Finally, advises Patricia Ledward, "to do Stratford properly you will need an official guide book and several days. And if an overdose of sights nauseates you, a visit to his tomb in Holy Trinity Church will restore sanity and a sense of proportion."

(See Chapter 6, LONDON.)

SHAW, GEORGE BERNARD (1856–1950). Shaw's Corner at the southwestern end of **Ayot St. Lawrence** (Hertfordshire) is the small brick house where the playwright, wit, and professional enemy of conventional opinion made his home from 1906 to the end of his life. Until his wife's death in 1943, the house served only as his country refuge from London; he retired there permanently, however, during World War II. Built in 1902, the house and its interior remain as he left it when he died—though his living rooms, remarks Neil Burton, "are now a little dried-up." His study displays his desk, filing cabinet, books and photographs. His hat collection and 1925 Nobel Prize may also be seen, as well as other memorabilia. The summerhouse, where he worked, stands at the bottom of the large sloping garden. Among the plays he wrote there, in whole or part, were *The Doctor's Dilemma* (1906), *Pygmalion* (1913) and *Saint Joan* (1923). Shaw enjoyed pruning the trees in his garden and fell while doing so at age 94—an accident that led eventually to what seemed to many of his admirers an untimely death. His cremated ashes, mingled with those of his wife, were scattered without ceremony in the garden. Shaw's Corner is operated by The National Trust. (Open March, November, Saturday—Sunday 11:00—1:00, 2:00—6:00; April—October, Wednesday—Sunday, same hours; Stevenage 0438–820307; admission.)

(See Chapter 6, LONDON; also Chapter 7, IRELAND.)

SHELLEY, PERCY BYSSHE (1792–1822). The Romantic poet's birthplace was a first-floor room in Field Place, an enlarged 13th-century house that remains privately owned in **Warnham** (West Sussex). This was Shelley's home until 1802, but he returned for brief intervals. On one evening in 1815 his father refused him admission because of his flaunted "atheism," "immoral conduct" and

rebellious lifestyle. Shelley sat on the doorstep that night, it is said, reading Milton's *Comus*, until a servant let him in for breakfast. Financial considerations of the estate finally brought Sir Timothy Shelley to a grudging reconciliation with his brilliant, perverse son. Shelley wrote part of *Queen Mab* (1813) in the house. Field Place stands near the 14th-century church about one and one-half miles southwest of the village. Under the auspices of the National Gardens Scheme, the estate gardens are occasionally open to the public (for information, contact the NGS, 57 Lower Belgrave Street, London SW1; 01–730–0355.)

Shelley's first-floor rooms at University College, **Oxford** (Oxfordshire), where he lived in 1810 and 1811, are now used as a junior common room, located at the stair to the right of the hall in the corner of the quadrangle. There he penned his audacious *The Necessity of Atheism* (1811), a pamphlet that got him quickly expelled. Today the college memorializes him with a special domed chamber that houses a recumbent marble statue of the poet. The memorial is located in the northwest corner of the main quadrangle, staircase 3. (Memorial open in term, daily 2:00—4:00; vacations, daily 10:00—6:00; free.)

Several scattered cottages and lodgings were briefly occupied by the wandering poet and his wife, Harriet Westbrook, between 1811, the year of their marriage, and her 1816 suicide. Most of these still exist in private ownership, including 20 Coney Street in **York** (North Yorkshire), 1811; the rebuilt "Shelley's Cottage" (now Shelley's Cottage Hotel) in **Lynmouth** (Devon), 1812; Shelley's Cottage in Chestnut Hill, **Keswick** (Cumbria), 1813; and Reeds Hill Farm near Church Hill House Hospital, **Easthampstead** (Berkshire), 1814. With Mary Godwin, he lodged at 4 Roman Pavement and 6 Queen Square in **Bath** (Avon), 1816.

After Shelley's marriage to Mary Godwin in 1817, the couple leased Albion House in West Street, **Great Marlow** (Buckinghamshire). Poet-novelist Thomas Love Peacock had secured the house for the couple, who stayed until early 1818. This was Shelley's final home in England. There he wrote *The Revolt of Islam* (1818); and Mary Shelley, pregnant with their daughter, finished her horror classic *Frankenstein* (1818). The two-story Albion House, much altered inside, remains privately owned.

Exhibits: The Bodleian Library at **Oxford** displays, among its literary treasures in the old Divinity School, Shelley's notebook containing his "Ode to the West Wind" (1820) and the volume of Sophocles he was carrying when he drowned in Italy. The Bodleian Library is housed in four buildings at Parks Road and Broad Street. (Open Monday—Friday during term 9:00a.m.—10:00p.m., Saturday 9:00—1:00; 0865—44675; free.)

Boscombe Manor in Beechwood Avenue, **Bournemouth** (Dorset), now containing the Casa Magni Shelley Museum, was the home of Shelley's only son, Sir Percy F. Shelley. The collection of Shelley memorabilia displayed by the Bournemouth Borough Council was removed from the poet's last home at Lerici, Italy. (Open June—September, Monday—Saturday 10:30—5:00; October—May, Thursday—Saturday 10:30—5:00; 0202—21009; admission.)

(See Chapter 1, SWITZERLAND; also Chapter 6, LONDON; also Chapter 8, ITALY.)

SMITH, JOHN (1580—1631). The soldier, New World explorer and colonist of Virginia was born at **Willoughby** (Lincolnshire), where his father owned a small farm of seven acres, including three orchards. None of the buildings survive.

Exhibit: In **Alford** (Lincolnshire), the Alford Manor House Folk Museum in West Street, operated by the Lincolnshire and South Humberside Trust for Nature Conservation, has a display relating to Smith's life and adventurous career. (Open May—September, Monday—Wednesday, Friday 10:30—1:00, 2:00—4:30; 05212—2278; admission.)

(See Chapter 6, LONDON.)

STEVENSON, ROBERT LOUIS (1850—1894). The Scottish poet, essayist and novelist spent three enormously productive years (1884—87) in **Bournemouth** (Dorset). They were his last years in Britain. In 1885 he bought Sea View, a villa perched on the cliff overlooking the English Channel; he renamed it "Skerryvore" (after the lighthouse built by his family in Argyll), sequestered himself "like a weevil in a biscuit" and placed a model lighthouse at the street entrance. There Stevenson wrote part of *A Child's Garden of Verses* (1885), *The Strange Case of Dr. Jekyll and Mr. Hyde* (1886) and *Kidnapped* (1886). Among Steven-

son's visitors at the house were poet William Ernest Henley and novelist Henry James (see the entry on James earlier in this chapter). Located on Alum Chine Road, the house was destroyed during a 1940 air raid; its site is now a Stevenson memorial garden. The model Skerryvore lighthouse is still there.

(See Chapter 1, SWITZERLAND; also Chapter 2, FRANCE; also Chapter 7, SCOTLAND.)

SWIFT, JONATHAN (1667—1745). In 1689, as secretary to statesman Sir William Temple, the Irish-born author who would become one of Britain's foremost literary masters lived at Temple's estate, Moor Park, located one and one-half miles southeast of **Farnham** (Surrey) on Moor Park Lane. Swift again served Temple there in 1691—94 and in 1696—99. In the garden there, it is said, William III showed Swift how to cut asparagus in the Dutch manner so as to use both stalk and tip. Somewhat more significantly, Swift wrote the satires *A Tale of a Tub* (1704) and *The Battle of the Books* (1704) there; and also met his beloved "Stella" (Esther Johnson), a ten-year-old girl who also lived on the estate, to whom he wrote his *Journal to Stella* (1948). The 17th-century manor has been extensively altered and is now Moor Park College for Adult Christian Education. "Stella's Cottage" stands privately owned a short distance north.

(See Chapter 6, LONDON; also Chapter 7, IRELAND.)

TENNYSON, ALFRED, LORD (1809—1892). The birthplace of the Victorian poet was Somersby House, the two-story rectory of his stern, sometimes abusive father, Rev. George Tennyson, in **Somersby** (Lincolnshire). Rev. Tennyson, who designed the house's east wing extension, educated his son at home. There, in his attic study, Tennyson wrote his first poetry and later recalled the house in his long poem *In Memoriam* (1850). Tennyson lived there until 1837. Adjacent to Somersby Grange, the house remains privately owned in the village.

Beech Hill House, in the tiny village of **High Beech** (Essex), was his home with his mother from 1837 to 1840. The poet deplored "a want of men and birds" but enjoyed skating on the pond there. The house was rebuilt in 1850.

Much of *In Memoriam* was written at the Old Rectory in **Shawell** (Leicestershire), the home of his father's ward, Sophy Elmhirst, and a frequent lodging of the poet at intervals for almost 50 years. Tennyson wrote in the garden summerhouse because he was not permitted to smoke his pipe in the house.

In 1853 Tennyson leased Farringford House at **Freshwater** (Isle of Wight). Three years later he bought the then-secluded yellow-brick and stucco building with the proceeds of his dramatic monologue *Maud* (1855). In his top-floor study and his garden summerhouse or later west-wing study, he composed *The Charge of the Light Brigade* (1854), *Enoch Arden* (1864), and parts of *Idylls of the King* (1859–85). Tennyson's numerous guests, whom he liked to conduct on walking tours of the scenic downland (now known as Tennyson Down), included most of the best-known writers of his time. After 1868, he spent only winters there. Farringford House is now a hotel, located off Bedbury Lane.

Two miles south of **Haslemere** (Surrey) but actually in the county of West Sussex, Tennyson built his last home, Aldworth, on a hillside ledge in the forested Black Down country in 1868. Originally planning a small house, he kept expanding the project until the result was a large stone manor with mullioned windows, pinnacled dormers and a large hall. There he wrote many of his Arthurian poems and his collection, *Ballads* (1880). Aldworth, where Tennyson died, remains privately owned.

Exhibit: The Usher Art Gallery in Lindum Road, **Lincoln** (Lincolnshire), displays numerous relics, manuscripts, portraits and editions of Tennyson's works. (Open Monday—Saturday 10:00—5:30, Sunday 2:00—5:00; 0522–27980; admission.)

(See Chapter 6, LONDON.)

THACKERAY, WILLIAM MAKEPEACE

(1811–1863). The novelist and satirist of Victorian manners lived briefly in **Tunbridge Wells** (Kent) on two occasions. As a boy in 1825, he resided at a house called Bellevue on the common; and in 1860 he lived in another house facing the green, now known as "Thackeray House."

Clevedon Court, operated by The National Trust on route B3130 at **Clevedon** (Avon), is a 14th-century manor that displays a typical medieval design in its central great hall and end rooms. Thackeray wrote part of *Vanity Fair* (1848) there

during frequent visits, and portrayed the house as "Castlewood" in *Henry Esmond* (1852). Parts of the house are remnants of an earlier 13th-century manor. Portraits, furnishings and exhibits relate to the Elton family, who have lived there since 1709. (Open April—September 30, Wednesday—Thursday, Sunday 2:30—5:30; 0272–872768; admission.)

(See Chapter 6, LONDON.)

THOMAS, DYLAN

(1914–1953). In 1945 and 1946 the Welsh poet and his family resided with historian A. J. P. Taylor at Taylor's home in **Oxford** (Oxfordshire), occupying a summerhouse in Taylor's garden. Thomas wrote many scripts for the BBC there that soon brought him wider attention than he had known. This property, called Holywell Ford Cottage, remains privately owned off St. Cross Road.

Thomas is still the talk of quiet **South Leigh** (Oxfordshire), where he rented the Manor House, a large whitewashed cottage in a field at the edge of the village (1947–49). "Village life was never the same," reported one observer, after Thomas's frequent drunken escapades and consequent "misunderstandings" with Caitlin, his not-to-be-outdone wife: once she tried to tip over his caravan studio—with Thomas inside.

(See Chapter 6, LONDON; also Chapter 7, WALES.)

TOLKIEN, JOHN RONALD REUEL

(1892–1973). Master of fantasies based on old English chronicles, the novelist was a linguistics scholar at Oxford for most of his life. In **North Oxford** (Oxfordshire) at 20 Northmoor Road, his home from 1929 to 1947, he produced *The Hobbitt* (1937) and much of his trilogy, *The Lord of the Rings* (1954–56). Tolkien sold this two-story slate-roofed house after his children had grown and left.

As an English professor at Merton College, Tolkien next resided in **Oxford** at 3 Manor Road, a small brick house (1947–50); then, from 1950 to 1953, at 99 Holywell. During the years 1953 to 1968, his home was 76 Sandfield Road in **Headington**, an Oxford suburb. His last Oxford home, from 1972, was a Merton College flat at 21 Merton Street.

In his retirement interval from 1968 to 1972, Tolkien and his wife, Edith Bratt, lived in a modern bungalow at 19 Lakeside Road in **Poole** (Dorset), their last home together before her death in 1971.

Tolkien tomb: Wolvercote Cemetery, **Oxford**.

VICTORIA (1819–1901). The fiercely conventional, muffin-shaped little queen, who reigned longer than any other British monarch before or since, gave her name to a historical era and her progeny to the thrones of Europe (along with the hemophilia that afflicted a fair number of them). An intensely shy, private person, she became even more so after the death of her consort, Prince Albert, in 1861; she never stopped grieving for him and wore black from the day of his death to her own.

As an infant she often resided (1819–20) with her parents at Woolbrook Cottage, now the Royal Glen Hotel, in **Sidmouth** (Devon). Her father, Prince Edward, Duke of Kent and Strathearn, died there in 1820.

Some of her happiest childhood days were spent at Claremont House near **Esher** (Surrey). Architect Sir John Vanbrugh built the first small house on the property for himself. Soldier-imperialist Robert Clive purchased it in 1768 and built the present yellow-brick house, with its Corinthian portico designed by Lancelot "Capability" Brown and Henry Holland. During Victoria's childhood, it was the home of her cousin, Prince Leopold, who became Leopold I of Belgium. Victoria and Albert used the house as their earliest summer retreat during the first years of their marriage. After they bought Osborne House (see opposite), Victoria gave Claremont to the deposed Louis-Philippe, the "citizen king" of France, who stayed from 1848 until his death there in 1850. Claremont, now a girls' school operated by the Claremont Fan Court Foundation Ltd., displays few original furnishings but provides a good idea of 18th-century interior decoration. The landscaped garden, one of the earliest that survives in England, is operated by The National Trust; a separate entrance gains access from route A307. Claremont House itself stands one-half mile southeast of Esher on route A244 opposite Milbourne Lane. (House open February—November, first full weekend of each month, 2:00—5:00; garden open April 1—October 31, daily 9:00—7:00; November 1—March 31, daily 9:00—4:00; Esher 67841; admission.)

At **Brighton** (East Sussex), the Royal Pavilion is the lavish fantasy castle built by George IV, Victoria's uncle, as Prince of Wales. Originally a farmhouse leased by the prince in 1786 for his secret wife, Maria Fitzherbert, the structure was enlarged; then, between 1815 and 1822, architect John Nash converted it into an Indian-Chinese-Moorish palace of onion domes, minarets, and spires. A belief prevailed at the time that it was modeled after the Kremlin in Moscow. Though Victoria occupied it during her early years as queen, she disliked its ostentation and lack of privacy, and she closed it as a royal residence in 1845. The gilt and glitter are indeed "a bit much" in the main rooms; devotees of historical "romance novels" can see what a true regency interior looked like. Since World War II, the Royal Pavilion has been brilliantly restored with most of its original furnishings and portraits. It is operated by the borough of Brighton and located in the center of the city fronting the Old Steine. (Open July—September 30, daily 10:00—6:30; October 1—June, daily 10:00—5:00; 0273–603005; admission.)

Victoria's favorite official residence was Windsor Castle at **Windsor** (Berkshire), a residence of English monarchs since the time of William the Conqueror (see the entry on William the Conqueror later in this chapter). The castle had been relatively little used as a royal residence, however, after the reign of George III (see the entry on George III earlier in this chapter). Prince Albert, whom Victoria first met at Windsor, brought about its renewed use; the castle became a refuge from the London they both detested. In 1861, Albert died in a chamber called the Blue Room, now Prince Philip's study in the private apartments of the Upper Ward; Victoria's uncles, George IV and William IV, had also died there. Until her own death, Victoria ordered that the room remain precisely as it was when her "angel" died. Fresh clothing was laid out on Albert's bed every evening and hot water poured into his basin. Her son, Edward VII, an elderly man by the time he succeeded her and annoyed at his mother's 40-year attempts to make time stand still, totally refurbished these apartments, even installing bathrooms. During most of her reign, Victoria occupied a four-room suite in the Victoria Tower. Only parts of Windsor's 13-acre complex of buildings and grounds are open to the public and even these are subject to closure at short notice, whenever the royal family is in residence. St. George's Chapel, the burial place of eight British monarchs, and the 800-year-old state apartments (main ceremonial rooms) are usually open to visitors. The central medieval Round Tower built by Henry II and the private apartments of the royal family on the south and east sides of the upper ward are never open to the public. (Precincts open mid-March—April 30, September 1—late October, daily 10:00—5:15; late October—mid-March, daily 10:00—7:15; buildings open mid-March—late October, Monday—Saturday 10:30—5:00, Sunday 1:30—5:00; late October—mid-March, Monday—Saturday 1:30—3:00; state apartments closed mid-March—June, December; 075-35-68286; precincts free, admission to buildings.)

WINDSOR CASTLE, ROYAL DOMICILE OF NINE CENTURIES. Almost the entire history of British royalty is enshrined within these walls. This aerial view shows only the eastern, upper-ward portion of the castle; private royal apartments occupy the corner building at the extreme right. In 1066 William the Conqueror erected the first timber stockade at **Windsor** on the hilltop site of the 1170 Round Tower, which centers and surmounts the castle (at left in picture). George III undertook massive reconstruction of this residential ward during his reign, and the castle became Queen Victoria's favorite refuge from London. The royal family resides at Windsor during certain annual events and sometimes on weekends.

Victoria's frequent seaside home, probably her favorite residence of all, was Osborne House at **East Cowes** on the Isle of Wight. She purchased the 1,000-acre estate in 1845. Over the next few years arose the present Italianate dwelling with its view that reminded Prince Albert of the Bay of Naples. The large wing built for the royal household is now a convalescent home for civil servants. Rooms and corridors of the house dis-

play trophies, colonial gifts presented to the queen at her two jubilees, and lavish "Victorian" decoration. Victoria and Albert's private suite, by contrast, is simply furnished; its original contents remain untouched from the day of Albert's death by command of his widow. Victoria herself chose to die there in the most private family home she had ever known. Osborne House, located on route A3021 one mile southeast of East Cowes, is operated by the Department of the Environment. (Open Easter Monday—June, September—early October, Monday—Saturday 11:00—5:00; July—August, Monday—Saturday 10:00—5:00; 0984-393622; admission.)

Victoria tomb: Frogmore Mausoleum, **Windsor**.

Exhibit: Railroad coaches used by the queen are displayed at the National Railway Museum in Leeman Road, **York** (North Yorkshire). Victoria made rail travel respectable; her first journey by train was in 1842. She never allowed a speed of more than 40 mph, however. (Open Monday—Saturday 10:00—6:00, Sunday 2:30—6:00; 0904-21261; free.)

(See Chapter 6, LONDON; also Chapter 7, SCOTLAND.)

WAUGH, EVELYN (1903–1966). The novelist and satirist of the English upper classes bought his first country estate, Piers Court, in 1937. An 18th-century manor house on 41 acres, it is located at **Stinchcombe** (Gloucestershire) near Stroud. Waugh lived there until 1939, then leased it out as a small school for London evacuees during World War II. He called the estate "Stinkers," designed the gardens, and resided there again from 1945 until he sold it in 1956. There he wrote his novels *The Loved One* (1948), *Men at Arms* (1952) and *Officers and Gentlemen* (1954).

The author's last home, a hilltop manor at **Combe Florey** (Somerset), rebuilt on the site of an Elizabethan house in the village park, was his last home from 1956. His wife, Laura Herbert Waugh, raised a Jersey herd on the rolling farmland acres. Waugh died there.

Waugh tomb: Parish Churchyard, **Combe Florey**.

(See Chapter 6, LONDON.)

WELLINGTON, ARTHUR WELLESLEY, DUKE OF (1769–1852). The Irish-born soldier who sent Napoleon to final defeat in the 1815 Battle of Waterloo spent the rest of his life as a revered if sometimes unpopular politician, serving as prime minister from 1828 to 1830. In 1817, Wellington's grateful nation gave him Stratfield Saye House, located off route A33 north of **Basingstoke** (Hampshire). This house, the culmination of a long search for an estate that would appropriately reward the hero, dates from about 1630. Alterations were made by Wellington himself from 1830 to 1840, but little has been changed since his time. Rooms, furnishings, paintings collected by Wellington and mementos are displayed by the current Duke of Wellington, descendant of Arthur Wellesley. The grave of Copenhagen, the "iron duke's" charger, is marked on the grounds, and Wellington's six-wheeled funeral carriage, designed by Prince Albert, is displayed. His own private chambers in the house occupied the southwest corner of the ground floor; the Duke spent intervals there for the rest of his life. It was the favorite home of his wife and she died there in 1831. (Open Sunday before Easter to last Sunday in September, Saturday—Thursday 11:30—5:00; 0256–882882; admission.)

Wellington's favorite home was Walmer Castle, in which he died. Now operated by the Department of the Environment on the seafront at **Walmer** (Kent), it was constructed as a coastal defense in 1540 near the site of Julius Caesar's first British landing (55 B.C.) Walmer Castle has been the official residence of the Lord Wardens of the Cinque Ports since the early 18th century. This appointed position, largely honorary, was occupied by Wellington from 1829 to his death. His rooms have been restored to their original appearance, and an exhibit displays memorabilia of England's most notable soldier. (Open April—September, Tuesday—Saturday 9:30—1:00, 2:00—7:00, Sunday 2:00—7:00; October—March, Tuesday—Saturday 9:30—1:00, 2:00—4:00, Sunday 2:00—4:00; admission.)

(See Chapter 3, PARIS; also Chapter 4, BELGIUM; also Chapter 6, LONDON; also Chapter 7, IRELAND; also Chapter 8, SPAIN.)

WELLS, HERBERT GEORGE (1866–1946). Wells "projected the phases of his life into the places where he lived," wrote biographers Norman and Jeanne MacKenzie, "and when he was done with one, he was ready to be done with the other." The immensely prolific novelist, historian and social commentator spent long intervals of his boyhood at Uppark, a late 17th-century manor located one

mile south of **South Harting** (West Sussex) on route B2146. Sarah Wells, his mother, was a housekeeper there from 1880 to 1893, and they occupied rooms "below stairs," as befitted the help. Wells read voraciously from the manor library and described this place and its surroundings as "Bladesover" in his novel *Tono-Bungay* (1909). An earlier brief resident was Emma Hart, who came as the 15-year-old mistress of Sir Harry Featherstonhaugh, son of the owner; she later married Sir William Hamilton and became the celebrated mistress of Lord Horatio Nelson (see the entry on Nelson earlier in this chapter). She is said to have once danced on the dining room table. Now operated by The National Trust, Uppark displays 18th- and 19th-century furnishings and paintings. (Open April—September 30, Wednesday—Thursday, Sunday 2:00—6:00; Harting 073–085–317; admission.)

With his second wife, Amy "Jane" Robbins, Wells rented a home called Lynton in Maybury Road, **Woking** (Surrey), in 1893 and resided there until 1897, the period of his first important writing. There he wrote *The Invisible Man* (1897) and began *The War of the Worlds* (1898), bicycling the neighborhood in malicious glee to collect details of the village he would "completely wreck and sack" in the latter novel.

In the summer of 1894 he wrote *The Time Machine* (1895) at Tusculum Villa, 23 Eardley Road in **Sevenoaks** (Kent).

Wells resided at **Sandgate** (Kent) from 1898 to 1909, a period of great literary productivity and domestic turbulence. His first home there consisted of two beach cottages. In 1899 he moved to Arnold House at 20 Castle Road while awaiting completion of nearby Spade House, which Wells himself designed. From late 1900 until he gave it up in 1909, Wells lived in the house in what has been called "a basically polygamous relationship" with "Jane" Wells and his mistress, Amber Reeves. From his garden study flowed novels that included *The Food of the Gods* (1904), *Kipps* (1905), *Ann Veronica* (1909) and *Tono-Bungay*. Among his guests were George Bernard Shaw, Joseph Conrad, Henry James and Arnold Bennett (see the entries on Conrad, James and Shaw earlier in this chapter). Now a privately owned vegetarian guest house, the home is open to visitors only by appointment (inquire locally).

At **Little Easton** (Essex), Easton Glebe was the writer's home for long intervals between 1912 and

1930. The two-story, ivy-covered brick dwelling remains privately owned.

(See Chapter 6, LONDON.)

WESLEY, CHARLES (1707–1788).
WESLEY, JOHN (1703–1791).

John Wesley, the evangelist founder of Methodism, and his hymn-writer brother, Charles, were born at the Old Rectory in **Epworth** (Humberside). The present brown-brick house, operated by the World Methodist Council, was rebuilt in 1709 on the ashes of the brothers' birthplace which was burned down by a mob opposed to the political views of Rev. Samuel Wesley, their father, earlier that year. John Wesley recorded that the family experienced some strange "poltergeist" phenomena in the rebuilt house in 1716. Restored in 1957, the house displays period furnishings plus items associated with the enormous Wesley family (John Wesley was the 15th of 19 children). Epworth Old Rectory stands at the edge of the village on the road toward Owston Ferry. (Open March—October, Monday—Saturday 10:00—12:00, 2:00—4:00, Sunday 2:00—4:00; November—February, by appointment; 0427–268; donation.)

A SHRINE OF WORLD METHODISM. The birthplace of John and Charles Wesley, the "Old Rectory" stands in **Epworth**. Rebuilt after a fire in 1709 and restored in 1957, it exhibits Wesley furnishings and memorabilia.

As a Fellow of Lincoln College, **Oxford** (Oxfordshire), John Wesley had rooms over the passageway between the two quadrangles. Restored by American Methodists in 1928, they may be viewed today. Wesley occupied them at intervals from 1726 to 1735 and founded a society of Methodists there (though Wesley himself was not a denominationalist and never gave up his priesthood in the Church of England). A pulpit used by Wesley during his student days at Christ Church College (1720–26) is displayed in the Lincoln College chapel off Turl Street. (Lincoln College open Monday—Saturday 2:00—5:00, Sunday 11:00—5:00; free.)

John Wesley built the first Methodist chapel in the world at **Bristol** (Avon) in 1739 and rebuilt it in 1748. Called the "New Room," it displays the original communion table, pulpit and benches, and Wesley's upstairs living quarters. He used this building mainly as a training center for ministers, observing their pulpit performance from a window of his upper apartment. Restored in 1930, the New Room is located in Broadmead. (Open Monday—Tuesday, Thursday—Saturday 10:00—4:00; 0272–24740; free.) Charles Wesley lived at 4 Charles Street in Bristol from 1749 to 1771.

Wesley's Cottage, near Alturnum at **Trewint** (Cornwall), is the small 18th-century cottage where John Wesley resided six times between 1744 and 1762 when he came to preach. Restored in 1950, this Wesley shrine hosts Sunday services in summer and displays testaments and period furnishings. (Open daily, 9:00—dusk; Pipers Pool 056686–572; free.)

Exhibits: The Borough Museum and Art Gallery in the Vicarage Gardens at **Scunthorpe** (Humberside) displays a fine collection of John Wesley memorabilia. (Open Monday—Saturday 10:00—5:00, Sunday 2:00—5:00; 0724–843533; Monday—Friday free, Saturday—Sunday admission.)

(See Chapter 6, LONDON.)

WILDE, OSCAR (1854–1900).
WILDE, OSCAR (1854–1900). The poet, playwright and eccentric leader of the "art for art's sake" aesthetic movement claimed two major turning points in his life: "when my father sent me to Oxford, and when society sent me to prison."

At Magdalen College in High Street, **Oxford** (Oxfordshire), Wilde occupied three fine paneled rooms overlooking the River Charwell on the "kitchen staircase" from 1874 to 1878. (College open during term, Monday—Saturday 2:00—5:00, Sunday 10:00—5:00; summer, daily 10:00—7:00; free.)

In **Reading** (Berkshire), Wilde occupied cell C 3.3 of Reading Gaol from 1895 to 1897, the low point of his life. Convicted of homosexual practices with Lord Alfred Douglas, Wilde used a plank for a table and wrote *De Profundis* (1905), a moving account of his conduct. *The Ballad of Reading Gaol* (1898) was probably written after his release. The jail, since rebuilt, adjoins the ruins of a Benedictine abbey in Forbury Road.

(See Chapter 3, PARIS; also Chapter 6, LONDON; also Chapter 7, IRELAND.)

WILLIAM THE CONQUEROR (WILLIAM I) (1027–1087). The Norman duke, who defeated Harold II at the Battle of Hastings in 1066 and thereby replaced Anglo-Saxon supremacy in England, feudalized the country through four years of bloody conquest but spent only brief, occasional periods in England. He resided long enough to found eight castles himself, however, and to delegate the establishment of many other bastions for holding and centralizing the government of his new kingdom. Not a gentle ruler, he nevertheless forced political stability; he also brought with him a rich Norman-French culture in language, architecture and social life that planted the seeds of modern England. The castles constructed by William were characteristic Norman fortifications—stockaded wooden structures built atop a ditched motte (mound) and encircled or winged by a bailey (court) containing open space and outbuildings. Some years after the Conquest, most of the castles were rebuilt on the same pattern in stone for permanence. Thus Windsor Castle (**Windsor**, Berkshire), which first arose about 1070, still reflects (though on a much modified and enlarged scale) its original wooden outline. To the Normans, such strategically placed castles were islands of military strength in the sea of hostility that was invaded England; they were not only centers of local rule but important symbols of the "united kingdom" that was William's goal. As such, they were not originally intended as royal residences but as permanent control points for imposing a new style of government on the country.

William attended councils at Winchester Castle, **Winchester** (Hampshire), in 1070, 1072 and 1076, residing in this ancient seat of Saxon kings during these periods (see the entry on Arthur, *Exhibits*, earlier in this chapter).

Exhibits: Near Hastings, the town of **Battle** (East Sussex) grew around Battle Abbey which William founded in 1066 to mark and commemorate the site of his epochal victory over the Saxons. Nothing remains of the church. A school and ruins of later buildings now occupy this site where King Harold fell mortally wounded. Further southeast near the railroad tracks on route B2204, a garage stands on the site of William's command post. The Battle and District Historical Society Museum in Langton House facing the 14th-century Abbey Gateway displays a diorama of the Battle of Hastings and a reproduction of the Bayeaux Tapestry. (Open Easter—October, Monday—Saturday 10:00—1:00, 2:00—5:00; 04246–2722; admission.)

(See Chapter 2, FRANCE; also Chapter 6, LONDON.)

WINTHROP, JOHN (1588–1649). The Puritan lawyer, first governor of Massachusetts Bay Colony, and founder of Boston was a Suffolk native, born in **Edwardstone** of a prosperous family. Groton Manor, his ancestral homestead in the tiny hillside village of **Groton**, is long gone. New England historian Samuel Eliot Morison, who found an ancient mulberry tree on the site some years ago, likened this area of Suffolk to New England in its rolling countryside, style of farmhouses and village greens. Winthrop, besides practicing law, became squire of the Groton estate, overseeing its lands and governing its population of farmers and tradesmen, until his departure for the New World in 1630.

WOLSEY, THOMAS, CARDINAL (1473?–1530). "There's scarcely any indication," wrote biographer Charles W. Ferguson, "that Wolsey had any personal religious conviction or that he felt himself a priest. He was an official in shepherd's clothing." One of England's most powerful and ambitious politicians, this lord chancellor to Henry VIII aspired to the papacy—but his failure to secure an annulment of the king's marriage to Catharine of Aragon led to his dismissal. Wolsey "died on his own" before the bloodthirsty king could arrange to collect his clever head on a charge of treason.

Born in Silent Street next to 3 The College Gateway in **Ipswich** (Suffolk), Wolsey was the son either of a wool merchant or butcher (sources disagree). The shop—now long gone—was his home until 1479, when the family moved to the vicinity of Rosemary Lane and Dog's Head Street. In Ipswich today may be seen a brick ruin in College Street called "Wolsey's Gate," the only remnant of the college he founded there in 1527.

Wolsey also founded Christ Church College in **Oxford** (Oxfordshire) in 1525. It was built on the site of a former priory in Cornmarket Street and became the university's largest college. The prelate "spent money like a drunken prince," wrote Lois H. Fisher, in his efforts to create a learning institution unrivaled in grandeur and prestige. (Christ Church remains, in fact, one of the most socially eminent and traditional of Oxford's colleges.) At Christ Church Library, on the south side of Peckwater Quadrangle, the cardinal's hat and chair are on display. (Open July, September, Monday—Friday 2:00—4:30, by appointment; 0865–43957; admission.) Also at Christ Church (known locally as "The House") resided, at various times, Sir Thomas More, Sir Philip Sidney, Richard Hakluyt, Robert Burton, John Ruskin, Charles Lutwidge Dodgson and W. H. Auden (see the entries on Auden, Dodgson and Ruskin earlier in this chapter.)

On the way to his London trial for treason, Wolsey's illness and mental distress led to a stopover at **Leicester** (Leicestershire). He lodged at the 12th-century Abbey of St. Mary of the Meadows—and there, clothed in a hair shirt, died. Among his reputed last words were "if I had served God as diligently as I have done my king, He would not have given me over in my grey hairs." The site of the abbey, utterly destroyed by Henry VIII along with Wolsey's tomb, is located at Abbey Park in the northern area of Leicester.

(See Chapter 6, LONDON.)

WOOLF, VIRGINIA (1882–1941). As a child, the novelist and essayist spent many holidays in **St. Ives** (Cornwall). The family of editor Sir Leslie Stephen, her father, resided in summer from 1882 to 1895 at Talland House, Talland Road, a large private house since converted to flats. One of her playmates there was Rupert Brooke, who would later become one of the best-known poets of World War I. Virginia Woolf used this Cornish coastal area as background in many of her works, most notably in *To the Lighthouse* (1927).

From 1912 to 1919 Virginia and her husband, publisher and writer Leonard Woolf, leased Asham House near Lewes (East Sussex). Said to be haunted, this house was the subject of her posthumous collection *A Haunted House* (1943). It remains privately owned in the tiny village of **Asheham**, located four miles southeast of Lewes on route B2109.

Virginia Woolf did most of her important writing at Monk's House in nearby **Rodmell**. An 18th-century two-story brick and stone house, it was the Woolfs' country home from 1919 until her death and they spent considerable periods there. Following their evacuation from London and Virginia's increasing mental instability in 1940, they returned to Monk's House. The next year she drowned herself in the River Ouse that flows nearby, and Leonard Woolf buried her ashes in the garden. There are current plans to open this house to the public (inquire locally).

Exhibit: The author was a frequent guest during the 1920s at Knole, the lifelong home and ancestral estate of poet-novelist Victoria Sackville-West, located one mile southeast of **Sevenoaks** (Kent) off route A225. Henry VIII, who acquired the 15th-century manor in the 1540s, vastly enlarged it to palace size. The National Trust, which now owns the huge estate, displays lavish 17th-century interiors and furnishings of the Sackville family. Among the items preserved are Virginia Woolf's manuscript of her novel *Orlando* (1928), for which Knole provided the setting. (Park open daily to pedestrians; house open April—September 30, Wednesday—Saturday 11:00—5:00, Sunday 2:00—5:00; October—November, Wednesday—Saturday 11:00—4:00, Sunday 2:00—4:00; 0732–453006; admission.)

(See Chapter 6, LONDON.)

WORDSWORTH, WILLIAM (1770–1850). The handsome two-story stone house that was the poet's birthplace stands at the west end of High Street in **Cockermouth** (Cumbria). Built in 1745, the house with its back garden sloping down to the River Derwent was also the birthplace of the poet's lifelong companion, his diarist sister Dorothy, born in 1771. Inside, the elegant rooms reflect the comfortable status of their father, an estate agent to Sir James Lowther. Period furnishings, the original staircase and fireplace, and Wordsworth memorabilia are displayed by The National Trust. In this house, Wordsworth learned his love of poetry and both it and the town recur in his poems, notably *The Prelude* (1850). Wordsworth lived there until his mother's death in 1778. (Open April—October 31, Monday—Wednesday, Friday—Saturday 11:00—5:00, Sunday 2:00—5:00; 0900–824805; admission.)

For the next eight years (1779–87), Wordsworth attended the Free Grammar School in

Hawkshead (Cumbria). The two-story school building is now a village museum, displaying among its old schoolroom items the oak desk on which the lad carved his name. (Open May— September, Tuesday—Wednesday, Friday— Sunday 2:00—5:00; admission.)

It is believed that Wordsworth lodged as a boarding student during this period at Green End Cottage (private) in the village of **Colthouse**, one-half mile east of Hawkshead.

Penrith, the Cumbrian birthplace of Wordsworth's mother, became the family home following his father's death in 1783. There he lived with his stern grandparents and uncle during school holidays. The house, called "Burrowgate," is not the same one that now occupies the site.

Racedown Lodge, a three-story farmhouse where William and Dorothy Wordsworth lived from 1795 to 1797, stands on Lewesdon Hill near the village of **Bettiscombe** (Dorset), visible from route B3165. Discouraged when he first moved there, Wordsworth found his poetic voice and began to write steadily. Samuel Taylor Coleridge visited in 1797, and the two poets took long walks over the scenic downland (see the entry on Coleridge earlier in this chapter).

Near **Holford** (Somerset), the brother and sister resided near Coleridge at Alfoxton House (1797–98), accessible from a lane beside the village church. Their night walks, armed with telescopes and notebooks, and their north country accents aroused local suspicions that they were spies for French revolutionaries. Wordsworth's favorite walk to the summit of the Quantock hills can be followed. The house is now a hotel.

In 1799, returning with Coleridge from Germany, they stayed in the 18th-century brick house owned by Thomas Hutchinson at **Sockburn** (Durham). Sockburn Farm, located on a peninsula extending into the River Tees, remains privately owned and difficult of access. There, Wordsworth fell in love with his future wife, Mary Hutchinson, and worked on *The Prelude*. On a later visit he wrote *The White Doe of Rylstone* (1815).

Wordsworth's remaining homes were all located in the Lake District of Cumbria, a 900-square-mile area of the scenic Cumbrian Mountains. Though many writers visited and several lived in this area of misty valleys and pure lakes, Wordsworth's presence as the foremost "lake poet" formed the main magnet, then and now, for literary pilgrims. Today much of this spectacular scenery has become National Trust property for the continued enjoyment of climbers, walkers and naturalists, who can still find many of the poet's favorite places as he knew them.

William and Dorothy Wordsworth settled at Dove Cottage, then known as the Dove and Olive Branch Inn, at **Grasmere** in late 1799. There he also brought his wife Mary in 1802, and three of their children were born in the cottage. The poet wrote much of his best work in this crowded household. Among his noted visitors were Coleridge, Thomas De Quincey, Charles and Mary Lamb and Sir Walter Scott. The two-story, seven-room Dove Cottage, located in Town End one-half mile southeast of the village center, is owned by the Dove Cottage Trust which has maintained it as a public memorial since 1890. Most of the furnishings are original. The poet also devoted much time to his hillside garden and orchard behind the house. After the Wordsworths' departure, De Quincey occupied Dove Cottage at intervals from 1809 until 1834. (Open March, October, Monday—Saturday 10:00—1:00, 2:00—4:30; April—September, Monday—Saturday 9:30—1:00, 2:00—5:00; 09665–464; admission.)

In 1808 the Wordsworths sought more spacious housing northwest of Grasmere. Allen Bank at the foot of Easedale became their home until 1811. In that year they moved to the Grasmere vicarage, which stood beside the bridge opposite the church. But the poet's youngest two children died there in 1812 and, pained by the proximity of the churchyard, the family made its final move in 1813.

From that year until his death, Wordsworth lived at Rydal Mount, an unpretentious whitewashed stone house dating from 1550, with 18th- and 19th-century additions. There he wrote almost half of his poetic works, became England's poet laureate in 1843 and welcomed scores of noted literary guests. The poet designed the four acres of hillside garden there and planted the daffodils that still bloom on the slope called "Dora's Field," now owned by The National Trust. "The grounds at Rydal Mount," as Lois H. Fisher points out, "are inseparably associated with many poems." Beloved by all, Wordsworth aged gracefully and died there as one of history's few poets who lived a long, happy life. Today Rydal Mount, owned by Wordsworth descendant Mary Henderson, displays many original furnishings, his study, first editions, portraits and memorabilia. It is located on route A591 at **Rydal**, three miles north of Ambleside. (Open March—October, daily 10:00—5:30; November-mid-January, daily 10:00—12:30, 2:00—4:00; Ambleside 09663-3002; admission.)

Exhibit: The Wordsworth Museum near Dove Cottage in **Grasmere** displays the poet's manuscripts, notebooks, first editions and personal relics. (Open same times as Dove Cottage; admission.)

WREN, SIR CHRISTOPHER (1632–1723). England's most famous architect, and a noted astronomer, Wren was a native of **East Knoyle** (Wiltshire), where his father was rector. Most of the rectory, which was Wren's home to about age two, was demolished in 1799, but 15th-century portions of it were incorporated into the west side of the later rectory, now called Knoyle Place.

Wren lived in **Oxford** (Oxfordshire) from 1649 to 1657 and for periods thereafter. Educated at Wadham College (1649–53), and a Fellow of All Souls College (1653–57), he achieved a brilliant reputation as one of England's finest scientific minds.

Exhibit: In the library of All Souls College, **Oxford**, are displayed Wren's designs for St. Paul's Cathedral in London, his best-known work. (Inquire locally for admission information.)

(See Chapter 6, LONDON.)

YEATS, WILLIAM BUTLER (1865–1939). One of Britain's most notable poets, the Irish-born Yeats lived in **Oxford** (Oxfordshire) at 4 Broad Street (gone) from 1919 to 1921. At **Thame**, 16 miles east, Yeats and his wife then occupied what is now the Red House Children's Book Shop at 42 High Street. It has a Yeats Room with exhibits on the poet.

One of Yeats' favorite residences was Chantry House in Church Street, **Steyning** (West Sussex), where he was often a guest during the 1930s. He began his verse play *Purgatory* (1939) there and wrote much of his last poetry in the house. It remains privately owned.

(See Chapter 2, FRANCE; also Chapter 6, LONDON; also Chapter 7, IRELAND.)

Chapter 6
GREAT BRITAIN: LONDON

Because the vast majority of British notables lived in London at some time during their careers, this city warrants a chapter to itself.

"If the entire world's surface were suddenly covered by ice or engulfed by the oceans, and only one scrap of South Kensington were spared," wrote Charlotte and Denis Plimmer, "travelers from another planet could still form a pretty shrewd notion of what human civilization had been all about." That "scrap" of London contains the royal colleges of Art and of Music, the Royal Geographical Society, the Imperial College of Science and Technology, the Science Museum and the massive Victoria and Albert Museum. The Natural History Museum there would also place "human civilization" in its rightful context for these space travelers.

To most outsiders, however, London is Big Ben, Westminster Abbey and Trafalgar Square. The borough of Westminster originated as the minster (cathedral) in the west. It was founded in 1065 by Edward the Confessor on the site of a sixth-century abbey. William the Conqueror built his palace on the site of today's Parliament buildings; this complex and the area of Whitehall to the north have held the seat of British government ever since.

St. Paul's Cathedral was the eastern minster in the adjoining City of London. The oldest part of London, the City—as it is known—encompasses one square mile and maintains its old Roman-wall boundaries under a cheerfully undemocratic sys-

tem of Lord Mayor and council. The City today (also called the Square Mile) is the financial center of London—the Bank of England, the Royal Exchange, Lloyd's, the City markets—and also home of the medieval trade guilds, which continue their traditional and spectacular banquets and ceremonials. Not including St. Paul's Cathedral, which soars on Ludgate Hill, the City contains 39 churches—11 of them survivors of the Great Fire of 1666 and 23 of them designed by Sir Christopher Wren. Today's resident City population numbers less than 5,000, but a working force of nearly four million crowds its narrow streets during weekdays. Through England's centuries of bloody political strife, the City has often financed exploring expeditions and military ventures but has always guarded its own neutrality and independence, even from royalty. Downriver, the venerable Tower of London survives as a rather more sinister symbol of British power and majesty. Though long a palace, it is chiefly remembered as a prison for some of England's most notable historical figures who came into conflict with royalty.

So the heart of London is actually twin-centered; the two cities are not visibly distinct from each other on the ground, but they remain quite apart in terms of history, traditions and self-perception.

London has existed for some 40 years less than the present year on our calendars, so it is about as old as Christianity. It owes its location to the occupation troops of the Roman Emperor Claudius, who found the Celtic fishing village to be the first fordable spot above the river's North Sea mouth, about 50 miles away. (Julius Caesar had probably crossed the Thames there in 54 B.C.) Londinium, the walled north-bank settlement built by the troops, became the hub for the Roman conquest of England. The road system they radiated from London to all parts of the country still underlies numerous modern highways. London's first bridge across the Thames probably crossed a few feet east of the present London Bridge; massive timbers laid by Roman engineers to support the span were recently unearthed in the Billingsgate market area. London soon became a thriving Roman center, one of the largest north of the Alps, and remnants of Roman London are constantly being recovered in the City as street or building excavation occurs. Ironically, the craters made by World War II bombs and the pits of new construction on their sites provided a convenient impetus for exploring Roman London, which in most places lies about 20 feet below the present pavements. Much of this historical treasure finds a permanent home in the Museum of London, which is located in the street called London Wall where stood a portion of the three-mile wall that rimmed the landward side of Londinium. Surviving sections of the wall may be seen in the Tower of London and the Noble Street-Cripplegate area.

With the decline of their empire, the Romans vacated Londinium. By the year 410 the city had languished, though was probably never wholly abandoned. Under the Anglo-Saxon invaders, however, it gradually recovered its importance as a port and commercial center. The Saxon scholar-king, Alfred the Great, rebuilt London as a walled, garrisoned town designed to fortify southern England against Danish invasion—a function it fulfilled. Its increasing commercial power and wealth gave the city on the Thames a marked degree of political independence; English monarchs down to the Stuart age had to woo London to their schemes, could never afford to take it for granted. Gradually, the center of government was drawn from the old Wessex capital of Winchester to Westminster which, by the time of the Norman Conquest (1066), was the official as well as actual capital of the country. Along with the City it had a combined population of perhaps 30,000. London remains the capital, of course, not only of England but of the entire United Kingdom of Great Britain and Northern Ireland.

London's population grew rapidly, especially from the 16th century. At its first census in 1801, it numbered over one million souls, about one-ninth of the total population of England and Wales. By 1850, with numbers approaching three million, it was the world's largest city and remained so until topped by New York City in 1910. Today it is third largest, after Tokyo and New York. London reached its largest population number in 1939—about eight and one-half million; by 1975 it had declined to seven million, representing about one-seventh of the England and Wales population.

Today's London has, of course, far outgrown its two original cities on the Thames. In 1965, the regional authority of Greater London was established with 12 inner boroughs (not including the City) and 20 outer boroughs, a total of 610 square miles. Numerous communities in the counties of Surrey, Kent, Essex, Middlesex and Hertfordshire now fall within the Greater London area; and such communities, where relevant, are included in this chapter under their own names as parts of London.

The River Thames itself, London's main highway of transportation until the 17th century, is vastly less busy than it was just two decades ago, as major seaport facilities have transferred 26 miles downstream to Tilbury. For 150 years this mighty river was also London's disgrace, breeding typhoid and cholera epidemics, foul odors and unsightly filth. During the past 30 years, however, London has shown what can be done with a supposedly "dead" river, one of the world's worst polluted channels. The Thames Water Authority's strict standards have reduced pollution by 90 percent; salmon and water birds are again establishing themselves; and the Thames now provides most of the water needed by the basin's 12 million population.

Thus, the London of Chaucer and Shakespeare is hardly the London of Samuel Johnson or Charles Dickens; nor is today's London the bomb-smashed city of Winston Churchill. Yet elements of all these periods remain. The Great Fire of 1666, which started in Pudding Lane, wiped out four-fifths of the City just one year after at least 75,000 inhabitants had perished from bubonic plague. During the London Blitz of 1940 some 3,000 people died and certain areas suffered tremendous damage from German air attacks. But along with the modern steel and glass towers that arose from the bomb craters of World War II and now dominate the skyline, remnants of Roman, medieval and Elizabethan London still coexist with much more numerous Georgian and Victorian structures.

Probably no city in the world has been so conscientiously well-served by literary and historical guidebooks. Among the standards, Stuart Rossiter's *Blue Guide to London* (1983) is by far the best for the historically minded. The less comprehensive Michelin *Green Guide*, updated in regular editions, is also excellent. The *Guide to Literary London* (1973), by George G. Williams, provides interesting and (what is rarer) thorough coverage of sites and buildings associated with London writers and their works. Less ambitious though with in-depth surveys of notable homes are *Where They Lived in London* (1972), by Maurice Rickards, and Katy Carter's *London & the Famous* (1982). The guidebooks mentioned in the introduction to Chapter 5 are also superb for London.

The Greater London Council has erected blue plaques on some 400 surviving residences of historic notables, many of them included in the following pages. Though one observer has noted that the council's selection tends more toward respectable than eminent names, no other major world city has undertaken such a systematic, large-scale program marking its past. The *Blue Plaque Guide to London* (1982), by Caroline Dakers, lists these markers and their texts and locations. It is characteristic of Londoners not only to inform themselves on the 2,000-year history of their city but to do it in a way that makes that heritage easily accessible (other cities might well emulate). The love of learning and historical panoply, unique among world capitals, and the effort to bring the past into visible relationship with the present permeate the streets and daily life of London.

In the following pages, inner London boroughs are given in parentheses after the addresses in order to facilitate the finding of houses and sites. Outlying areas are printed in bold type and, again, the borough is given in parenthesis. Unless otherwise indicated, a boldfaced or parenthesized designation applies to all addresses within the paragraph in which it appears.

ARNOLD, MATTHEW (1822–1888). One of Victorian England's finest minds, the poet, critic and educator lived for a decade (1858–68) in a rented house that still stands at 2 Chester Square (Westminster).

At the foot of Byron Hill in **Harrow on the Hill,** (Harrow), Arnold occupied Byron House, a large brick dwelling, from 1868 to 1873. On his plot of more than an acre, Arnold cultivated a large garden and orchard trees. Though the land has now been subdivided for housing, his favorite grapevine still flourishes in one of the smaller gardens. (See Chapter 5, ENGLAND.)

BACON, SIR FRANCIS (1561–1626). "I have taken all knowledge to be my province," announced Bacon in an age when that could still be said without undue arrogance by a man of genius. The birthplace of the lawyer, philosopher and scientist was York House on the Strand (Westminster).* Once the residence of the archbishops of York, this mansion had become the official house of the lord keeper of the seal, a position held by Bacon's father, Sir Nicholas Bacon, who died there in 1579. There the elder Bacon conducted the 1570 inquest on the involvement of Mary, Queen of Scots in the murder of her husband, Lord Darnley. Francis Bacon lived there until 1579; he also lived there from 1618 to 1621 when he was lord chancellor. His bribery conviction and traumatic removal from public office in 1622 forced him to sell the lease of this house "where my father died, and where I first breathed; and there will I yield my last breath, if so please God and the King." But it was not to be. Located just southeast of the Strand-Villiers Street intersection, its site adjoining the present York Buildings in the Victoria Embankment gardens, the house was demolished, ironically enough, the same year that Bacon died. During his later residence there, he had produced at least 12 drafts of his *Novum Organum* (1620). Poet John Donne lived there between Bacon's two occupancies (see the entry on Donne later in this chapter), and Restoration dramatist George Farquhar resided there later.

Bacon's longest period of residence was at a building he leased at 1 Gray's Inn Square (Camden), his London home and official chamber from 1577 to 1622, when he retired in anguish to St. Albans (though he kept the residence until his death). The Verulam Buildings at the northeast

---

*Not to be confused with York House built by Thomas, Cardinal Wolsey at Whitehall (see the entry on Wolsey later in this chapter).

corner of the square (a centuries-later residence of Sir William Schwenck Gilbert) now occupy this site. In the adjacent Gray's Inn Gardens, which remain as pleasant as Bacon knew them (some authorities say he designed them), he frequently strolled with Sir Walter Raleigh and other notables (see the entry on Raleigh later in this chapter). Until recently, catalpa trees brought from America and planted there by Bacon still survived. (Gardens open May—July, daily 12:00—2:00; August—September, daily 9:30—5:00; free.)

Twickenham Park, a long-gone estate covered today by the area known as St. Margaret's in **Twickenham** (Richmond upon Thames), was Bacon's part-time residence from 1592 to about 1605. His stone-faced brick dwelling with portico and wings stood near a small lake. Apparently given him by the Earl of Essex, the estate—called "Twitnam" by Bacon—was tree-bordered and spacious. Elizabeth I visited him there (see the entry on Elizabeth later in this chapter), and Bacon wrote some of his earlier essays on the estate. "Whenever he could steal a day from his labours in Gray's Inn," wrote biographer Bryan Bevan, "he liked to ride there, making it his house of philosophy and letters, as his lodging in Gray's Inn was his house of politics and law."

"Death comes to young men and old men go to death," Bacon wrote. His last lodging was the house of the Earl of Arundel, where he was taken after suffering exposure during an outdoor experiment in food preservation; he had stuffed a hen with snow to determine how well the cold would preserve meat. Arundel House stood until 1825 on the present site of St. Michael's Church in South Grove Street, **Highgate** (Haringey). Parts of the house cellar remain in the church's undercroft. This church also houses the tomb of Samuel Taylor Coleridge (see the entry on Coleridge later in this chapter).

(See Chapter 5, ENGLAND.)

BECKET, ST. THOMAS À (1118?–1170). The birthplace of the martyred archbishop of Canterbury stood at 86 Cheapside (the City) between Ironmonger Lane and Old Jewry. It was his home to about age 10. Becket's sister built a hospital memorializing him on this spot 20 years after his assassination. This is the present site of Mercers' Hall, Ironmonger Lane.

(See Chapter 2, FRANCE; also Chapter 5, ENGLAND.)

BENTHAM, JEREMY (1748–1832). The greatest happiness for the greatest number was the central tenet of Utilitarianism, espoused by this philosopher and economic theorist. His birthplace stood at the northeast corner of Creechurch Lane and Duke's Place, a place called Red Lion Yard (the City).

From 1766 to the 1780s Bentham resided in Lincoln's Inn (Camden), the complex of law buildings between Chancery Lane and Lincoln's Inn Fields. Most of the original communal structures dating from the 16th to 18th centuries survive. Bentham lived first at 1 Elm Court, then at 6 Old Buildings in the gabled brick structures rebuilt in 1609. Lincoln's Inn is entered through the massive 1518 gatehouse in Chancery Lane. (Gardens open daily, 12:00—2:30; free.)

According to biographer M. P. Mack, Bentham's last home from 1792, a small brick house surrounded by a large walled garden, stood "at the midpoint of a triangle made by Buckingham Palace, Whitehall, and Parliament" in Queen Anne's Gate, off Birdcage Walk bordering St. James's Park (Westminster). On Bentham's property to the south (now the northeast corner of Petty France and Tothill Street) stood the small house occupied by John Milton from 1652 to 1660. Bentham revered the historical association and, when he felt that visitors weren't properly impressed, tapped them smartly with his cane. ("On your marrow bones, sir!") Essayist-critic William Hazlitt rented the Milton house from Bentham during the years 1812 to 1819. Demolished in 1877, it is the present site of Queen Anne's Mansions, which house the Home Office.

Exhibit: A most unusual Bentham exhibit is— well, the man himself. At University College, Bentham's padded skeleton clothed in his own garments and capped by a wax, lifelike head cast from his features sits in a glass display case with his cane. Bentham had willed his entire estate to the London Hospital (now University College Hospital) provided that he could be present at board meetings as a preserved "auto-icon"; his actual head, mummified, is kept in the college safe. For 92 years, his presence was duly recorded, though marked "not voting," at the meetings. He no longer attends but stares back at visitors from his seat in the cloisters of University College, Gower Street (Camden). (Open by application to the Secretary, University College; 01–387–7050.)

(See Chapter 5, ENGLAND.)

BERLIOZ, HECTOR (1803–1869). The French composer visited London five times between 1847 and 1855, usually to conduct concerts. His only London dwelling still in existence—he lived there for about two months in 1851 while judging musical instruments for the Great Exhibition—stands at 58 Queen Anne Street (Westminster). The four-story Georgian brick building also hosted Beethoven Quartet Society concerts at the time; and Berlioz, rooming upstairs, said he "could easily hear the whole performance by simply opening my door. . . Come in, come in, welcome proud melody!"

(See Chapter 2, FRANCE; also Chapter 3, PARIS; also Chapter 8, ITALY.)

BLAIR, ERIC ARTHUR. ("GEORGE ORWELL") (1903–1950). Few later acquaintances knew his real name, so closely identified did this political novelist and critic become with his pseudonym. In 1917 the family came to London and resided for a year in Kensington at 23 Cromwell Crescent; then moved to 23 Mall Chambers in Notting Hill Gate, their home until 1921. Returning from Burma in 1927, Orwell stayed briefly at 10 Portobello Road in "cheap, small, and austere" rooms.

Blair taught and roomed at The Hawthorns, a boys' school located in Church Road, **Hayes** (Hillingdon) in 1932 and 1933. The locale is a corner house that remains privately owned. There he wrote much of *Down and Out in Paris and London* (1933).

In late 1934 and early 1935 he lodged and worked in a book shop at Warwick Mansions in Pond Street, South End Green, Hampstead (Camden); now a chess players' cafe, a marker identifies the site. Blair moved into a first-floor flat at 77 Parliament Road in 1935; then, later that year, shared a three-room flat in a yellow-brick house at 50 Lawford Road until 1936. At these places he worked on his comic novel *Keep the Aspidistra Flying* (1936).

In 1940 Blair and his wife moved into a two-room, fourth-floor flat at 18 Dorset Chambers, Chagford Street (Westminster). The next year they occupied a fifth-floor apartment at 111 Langford Court, Abbey Road, where visitors and bombed-out friends slept on camp beds in the living room.

Bombs struck his lodgings in 1944 at 101a Mortimer Crescent, Hampstead (Camden), just after he had completed one of his best-known novels,

Animal Farm (1945), a corrosive satire on Soviet-style revolution. Blair had lived there from 1942, occupying a ground floor and basement.

Later in 1944, the family rented third-floor rooms at 27b Canonbury Square (Islington), and this remained Blair's home until 1946, the year after his wife's death. The house was so cold and Blair was so poor during his last winter there that he had to chop up some of his small son's toys for firewood.

His last, three-month address (1949–50) was University College Hospital in Gower Street (Camden). There, shortly after marrying Sonia Brownell, he expired from tuberculosis.

(See Chapter 3, PARIS; also Chapter 5, ENGLAND; also Chapter 7, SCOTLAND.)

BLAKE, WILLIAM (1757–1827). "It is amusing," wrote Kenneth Rexroth, "that the Age of Reason thought Blake mad, for he is distinguished by an extraordinary sanity in a world in which men like him were being driven to the wall. . . As the cash nexus spread over humane culture like a net, strangling all other values but profit, the poets and novelists reacted to it—Blake understood it." Painter, engraver, mystic and poet, Blake lived in London for all but three years of his life. His birthplace, a four-story building where his draper father operated a shop on the ground floor (and where Blake, at age 10, saw his first vision—a tree filled with angels) stood until 1963 at 74 Broadwick Street (plaque on 8 Marshall Street, corner of Broadwick, Westminster). This was Blake's family home until 1782. He operated a printing-engraving shop next door in 1784 and 1785.

The home site of his master, James Basire, where Blake apprenticed as an engraver, is now occupied by the Royal Masonic Institution for Girls at 31 Great Queen Street (Camden). Blake resided there from 1771 to 1778.

Back in Westminster, Blake and his wife, Catherine Boucher, inhabited a narrow house at 28 Poland Street from 1785 until 1793. He wrote *Songs of Innocence* (1789) and *The Marriage of Heaven and Hell* (1790) in this house, now long gone.

Blake Buildings now occupy the site of 13 Hercules Buildings (Lambeth), a series of brick tenements which were torn down about 1930. The Blakes resided there from 1793 to 1800 and besides surprising their guests—who sometimes found the couple reading aloud in the nude—

Blake wrote his *Songs of Experience* (1794) in the lodgings.

WILLIAM BLAKE'S HOME. The poet's only surviving London dwelling, where he lived on the ground floor from 1803 to 1821, stands at 17 South Molton Street. His rooms have been long occupied by shops, but the upper housefront retains its original appearance.

From 1803 to 1821 the couple occupied rooms on the ground floor of 17 South Molton Street (Westminster). This four-story brick building is Blake's only surviving London residence; a street-front shop now occupies the rooms where he wrote *Jerusalem* (1804) and assembled his last art exhibits. Blake's final home, from 1821, was two ground-floor rooms at 3 Fountain Court, a three-story brick house in an alley that once ran between 103 and 104 The Strand. He completed *Illustrations of the Book of Job* (1826) and died there.

Blake tomb: Bunhill Fields (Islington).

Exhibit: Some of Blake's most impressive works may be viewed in gallery 7 of the Tate Gallery, Millbank (Westminster); the entire room is devoted to his powerful linear images and apocalyp-tic visions, including his illustrations for Dante's *Divine Comedy.* (Open Monday—Saturday 10:00—6:00, Sunday 2:00—6:00; 01–821–1313; free.)

(See Chapter 5, ENGLAND.)

BONHOEFFER, DIETRICH (1906–1945). The German Lutheran theologian whom his country-men put to death during the very last days of World War II pastored in England for two years before the war. From 1933 to 1935 he resided in Manor Mount, the two-story brick parsonage of the Reformed Church of St. Paul at **Sydenham** (Southwark).

(See Chapter 4, EAST GERMANY, WEST GERMANY.)

BOSWELL, JAMES (1740–1795). "I wish," wrote Samuel Johnson to Boswell in 1778, "that you would a little correct or restrain your imagination, and imagine that happiness... may be had at other places as well as London." From 1762, the Scottish lawyer and biographer of Johnson visited and lodged often in London, mostly to be near his mentor. His first lodging, where he wrote most of his *London Journal* (1750), stood almost across from 10 Downing Street (Westminster), the prime minister's residence. He first met Dr. Johnson in Thomas Davies' bookshop at 8 Russell Street in 1763, and thereafter spent almost every spring in London, "the best place." In 1786, after Johnson's death, Boswell and his family finally moved to London permanently, taking a house in Great Queen Street, the present site of Freemasons Hall. He wrote much of *The Life of Samuel Johnson* (1791) there. In 1791, widowed, chronically depressed, and drinking heavily, Boswell moved to 122 Great Portland Street where he completed the *Life* and died. The site of his house is marked on the present building. (See the entry on Samuel Johnson later in this chapter.)

(See Chapter 7, SCOTLAND.)

BRITTEN, BENJAMIN (1913–1976). While the composer's London apartments were numerous, he mainly used them as pieds-à-terre for his urban musical activities; for composition he preferred his quieter village home in Suffolk. From 1935 to 1937 he lived with his sister at 559 Finchley Road (Camden), a four-story apartment building; and from 1943 to 1946 at 45A St. John's Wood High Street (Westminster). Succeeding addresses included 22 Melbury Road (Kensington), 1948–53; 5 Chester Gate (1953–58) and 59 Marlborough Place (Westminster), 1958–65; and 99 Offord Road (1965–70) and 8 Halliford Street (Islington), 1970–76. All of these brick apartment structures remain privately occupied.

(See Chapter 5, ENGLAND.)

BROWNING, ELIZABETH BARRETT (1806–1861). The Victorian poet hated London when, in 1836, her father moved the family from Sidmouth to 99 Gloucester Place (Westminster), a four-story building faced with yellow brick where Elizabeth lived an indoor existence. The house is marked by tablet.

At 50 Wimpole Street (Westminster), the Barrett family home from 1838, Elizabeth lived as a virtual prisoner in her bedroom, allowed few visitors by her tyrannical father. One he did allow—perhaps because he thought Elizabeth was now too old and unattractive to consider romance—was poet Robert Browning, six years younger than she (see the entry on Browning below). When Mr. Barrett refused to permit Browning to take her to Italy for her health, however, the pair eloped. Elizabeth took her dog and her maid with her and never returned. The four-story brick house fell in 1936, and the street that Elizabeth remembered as gloomy has been much altered by rebuilding since 1900. The present building on the site displays a marker.

Her last residence in England, where the couple stayed during an 1855 visit, stood at 13 Dorset Street (Westminster). There she worked on *Aurora Leigh* (1857) and received such visitors as Alfred, Lord Tennyson and Dante Gabriel Rossetti (see the entry on Tennyson later in this chapter). The present house on this site dates from a later time.

(See Chapter 5, ENGLAND; also Chapter 8, ITALY.)

BROWNING, ROBERT (1812–1889). A London native, the poet was born in Southampton Street (gone), Camberwell (Southwark). His nearby boyhood home, where he lived until 1846, stood adjacent to the present marker at 179 Southampton Way. Browning's London visits were only occasional during his marriage to Elizabeth Barrett (see the entry on Elizabeth Barrett Browning above), but after her death he settled at 19 Warwick Crescent (Westminster) where he lived from 1861 to 1887. People wondered how Browning, who had an active social life as a widower, could find time to write but he produced *The Ring and the Book* there in 1868–69. The site is now occupied by more recent flats. Browning's last London home, from 1888, was 29 De Vere Gardens (Kensington).

Browning tomb: Westminster Abbey (Westminster).

Exhibit: A Browning Room in St. Marylebone Church in Marylebone Road (Westminster) displays relics of the poet. He and Elizabeth Barrett were married in this church in 1846. (Call 01–935–7315 for admission information.)

The Browning Society of London may be contacted at 01–385–5361 for further information.

(See Chapter 8, ITALY.)

BUNYAN, JOHN (1628–1688). The dissenting evangelist and author often preached in London, but records of his residences are almost nonexistent. His final lodging, the home of a grocer friend, John Strudwick, stood at the present intersection of Snow Hill and Holborn Viaduct (the City). Bunyan died there only a few days after his arrival.

Bunyan tomb: Bunhill Fields (Islington).

(See Chapter 5, ENGLAND.)

BURKE, EDMUND (1729–1797). The Irish-born statesman and orator resided at several London addresses from 1750. He first lodged in a room over the gateway of Inner Temple Lane off Fleet Street (the City). (Also see the entry on Henry Fielding later in this chapter.)

In Westminster, Burke dwelled in Tothill Street; at 72 Brook Street; and at 37 Gerrard Street (1787–93). One of Burke's neighbors at the latter address, now a restaurant, often spied "that great orator during many a night after he had left the House of Commons, seated at a table covered with paper, attended by an amanuensis who sat opposite to him." Burke's last permanent residence in London (1793–94) was 67 Duke Street.

(See Chapter 5, ENGLAND; also Chapter 7, IRELAND.)

BYRON, GEORGE GORDON, LORD (1788–1824). A London native, the poet was born at what is now 24 Holles Street (Westminster). Then a cheap lodging house, and now the site of a department store, the building has a sculpture by

Barbara Hepworth on the southwest wall. Byron lived with his mother at 16 Piccadilly in 1801.

Byron held frequent, brief Westminster residences from 1805 until he left England in 1816. Byron House, privately owned at 8 St. James's Street, occupies the site of the house where he lived in 1812. It was there, after the publication of the first two cantos of *Childe Harold's Pilgrimage*, that he "awoke one morning and found myself famous." Byron lived at 4 Bennet Street in 1813–14; then married Isabella Milbanke and settled into 139 Piccadilly Terrace in 1815. Soon convinced that he was deranged, Isabella left him permanently in 1816 and took their infant daughter with her. One of Byron's frequent out-of-house lodgings from about 1808 to 1816 was Long's Hotel at the east corner of Clifford and New Bond streets; he last visited with Sir Walter Scott there in 1815. None of Byron's London dwellings have survived.

Exhibit: Byron's publisher was John Murray, now at 50 Albemarle Street (Westminster); the offices display many Byron relics, including manuscripts and locks of his hair. (Call 01–493–4361 for admission information.)

(See Chapter 1, SWITZERLAND; also Chapter 4, BELGIUM; also Chapter 5, ENGLAND; also Chapter 7, SCOTLAND; also Chapter 8, GREECE, ITALY.)

CARLYLE, THOMAS (1795–1881). The Scottish historian and essayist spent the last 47 years of his life in a house that still stands at 24 Cheyne Row (Chelsea). Carlyle wrote his two most famous works there: *The French Revolution* (1837), which he entirely rewrote after John Stuart Mill accidentally burned the manuscript (see the entry on Mill later in this chapter), and *Frederick the Great* (1857–65). Carlyle and his wife, Jane Welsh, moved into the brick three-story row house in 1834 after a long search for a suitable dwelling; "and here," he wrote, "we spent our two and thirty years of hard battle against Fate." In 1853 Carlyle built a "silent room," with double walls and skylight window, at the top of the house to eliminate distraction from the street noises that always bothered him. But the soundproofing for his attic study was a failure—its acoustics somehow amplified sounds from the nearby Thames so that it actually became the noisiest room in the house. Carlyle nevertheless used it for his study until 1865, then resignedly withdrew to the ground

floor. Carlyle rented the house on long lease for £35 per year. Most of the eminent literary people of his time visited him there at one time or another. He outlived his wife by 15 years and died there. Today this 1708 house remains essentially as the Carlyles knew it, and many of their furnishings, clothing items, letters, manuscripts, and a wealth of other personal memorabilia are displayed. The house has been a Carlyle memorial since 1896. Carlyle House is now operated by The National Trust as one of England's most eloquent, well-preserved literary shrines. (Open April—late October, Wednesday—Saturday 11:00—5:00, Sunday 2:00—5:00; 01–352–7087; admission.)

The first London residence of the Carlyles (from intervals between 1831 and 1834) was 33 Ampton Street (Camden).

(See Chapter 7, SCOTLAND.)

CARROLL, LEWIS. See CHARLES LUTWIDGE DODGSON.

CHAPLIN, SIR CHARLES SPENCER ("CHARLIE") (1889–1977). Biographer John McCabe found some interesting parallels between Chaplin, the great film comic, and novelist Charles Dickens (see the entry on Dickens later in this chapter): "Both deprived and insecure as children, both raised in a cruel London slum, temperamentally both Chaplin and Dickens were a curious mix of the recluse and the exhibitionist, and they found life essentially comic with deeply pathetic overtones." Chaplin was born in a flat in East Street (Southwark).

Until the early 1900s he and his half-brother, Sydney, lived with one or another parent in a succession of dismal tenements in Lambeth. Sometimes, with no place to call home, they scrounged food like the street urchins who appear in some of Chaplin's earliest films. Shortly after his birth, he lived with his mother and brother in "three tastefully furnished rooms" at West Square and St. George's Road. In 1896, with their mother in a lunatic asylum, the boys went to live with their genial alcoholic father and his unpleasant mistress at 287 Kennington Road, a three-story brick structure that remains privately owned. The family occupied two first-floor rooms for about a year and Charlie never forgot how "sad" everything looked—the wallpaper, horsehair furniture, even the light filtering in "as if from under water." Later rooms with his temporarily recovered mother (ca. 1900–01) stood at 261 Kennington Road and 3 Pownall Terrace, both destroyed during the Blitz. In later life Chaplin revisited his childhood scenes on several occasions, seemingly drawn by a complex mixture of emotions. While this background probably deepened his artistry, as with Dickens it also produced psychological scars that had profound effects on his life and work.

(See Chapter 1, SWITZERLAND; also Chapter 4, WEST GERMANY.)

CHAUCER, GEOFFREY (1345?–1400). Few specific addresses of the "father of English poetry" are known and the London that Chaucer knew no longer exists. His tenement birthplace site, however, has been narrowed to the area of Whittington Gardens in Upper Thames Street (the City). From 1374 to 1386 Chaucer lived at 2 Aldgate High Street, where the medieval Aldgate entrance to the City stood until 1760. While occupying these rooms over the gate itself, located about 25 feet from the Jewry Street corner in front of the present post office, Chaucer wrote *Troilus and Criseyde* (ca. 1385).

In 1399 he took a 53-year lease on a house in the gardens of Westminster Abbey (Westminster), a site now covered by the 16th-century Henry VII Chapel. Chaucer died in this tenement dwelling and lies in Poets' Corner, Westminster Abbey, not far from his last home site. G. G. Coulton's *Chaucer and His England* (1957) is one of several interesting volumes concerning the surroundings, far different from today, that Chaucer knew.

Exhibit: The Tabard Inn, from which Chaucer's 29 pilgrims set out for Canterbury and told their *Canterbury Tales* (ca. 1387–1400), stood on the present site of Talbot Yard, an alley off Borough High Street (Southwark). The present "Old Tabard Inn" stands at the alley entrance; Chaucer's original, however, was demolished in 1629 at a site further down the alley.* "Beware of other innkeepers who claim the site," warns Patricia Ledward. "Even in Chaucerian England, accuracy was never their strong suit." Lois H. Fisher in her massive *Literary Gazetteer of England* (1980) gives the medieval pilgrim route from the inn as east on Tabard Street to Old Kent Road, thence to the old Roman road of Watling Street (route A2) all the way to Canterbury.

---

* David Daiches in *Literary Landscapes of the British Isles* (1979) claims that the inn lasted until 1875.

(See Chapter 5, ENGLAND.)

CHURCHILL, SIR WINSTON (1874–1965). Prime minister during Britain's "finest hour" (the 1940 Battle of Britain), historian, and orator, Churchill made London his political base from 1900. Many of his numerous homes and lodgings remain. His parents, Lord Randolph and American-born Jennie Jerome Churchill, brought him to their new house at 48 Berkeley Square (Westminster) in 1875. They lived there until 1877. From 1880 to 1882 the Churchills resided at 29 St. James's Place; and from 1882 to 1892 at 2 Connaught Place. From 1900 to 1906 Winston lived in a flat at 105 Mount Street. His first married home with Clementine Hozier in 1908 was 12 Bolton Street. From 1909 to 1911 and again in 1917 and 1918, the couple leased 34 Eccleston Square, and Churchill rose to parliamentary prominence while living there.

As first lord of the admiralty from 1911 to 1915 and in 1939 and 1940, Churchill occupied Admiralty House, the official naval residence dating from 1786. Located in the complex of government buildings in Whitehall (Westminster), Admiralty House stands just south of Trafalgar Square and Admiralty Arch. Today government offices occupy the former residence, previous inhabitants of which included William IV as duke of Clarence and statesmen Arthur Balfour and Sir Austen Chamberlain.

The Churchills resided in the large home of Winston's brother, Jack, at 41 Cromwell Road (Kensington), from 1915 to 1917.

They lived at 2 Sussex Square (Westminster), from 1920 to 1924. This house has been demolished. Churchill became chancellor of the exchequer in 1924 and lived in the chancellor's official residence at 11 Downing Street, next door to the prime minister's residence, until 1929. For the next decade the Churchills lived in a flat in Morpeth Mansions on Morpeth Terrace.

Churchill became prime minister in 1940 and occupied the official residence at 10 Downing Street (Westminster) until 1945, and again from 1951 to 1955 (see the entry on Benjamin Disraeli later in this chapter). When the London Blitz began, however, the Churchills moved into "the Annexe," first floor rooms in Storey's Gate, directly over the underground War Rooms. The War Rooms, converted from a maze of storage areas and tunnels that probably dated back hundreds of years, served as the government's secret command post throughout World War II. The key office in this narrow warren of chambers was the map room, where Churchill traced the daily progress of the war. He also spent many working days and evenings in his bedroom there—"always reluctantly," wrote Graham Cawthorne, "for he hated being driven underground by German bombs and was usually very short-tempered when he emerged in the morning"—and from it broadcast many of his wartime speeches. "Churchill's lavatory," resembling a pay toilet with a lock, was actually a top-secret room designed to provide complete security for his transatlantic phone calls to American President Franklin D. Roosevelt. Overhead timber beams, steel girders, and a three-foot concrete cap protected the chambers, which never took a direct hit from bombs or rockets. The rooms, though preserved with their contents intact, were rarely opened after the war; then, in 1982, the Imperial War Museum began restoring 19 rooms of the complex and it was officially opened to the public as a memorial in 1984. Rooms have been sealed with glass to prevent deterioration and, in the words of one project historian, look "like everyone just went out at lunchtime for a beer." Churchill's broadcast desk and private quarters are prominent features. The entry is from Great George Street. Because of the narrow space limits and great popularity of this museum, visitors are advised to make reservations at least two months in advance. (Curator, Churchill War Rooms, c/o 41 sub-E, Treasury Chamber, Parliament Street, London SW1P 3AG; or call 233–8904 before 9:30 a.m.; admission.)

Churchill's last home, a two-story brick town house, stands at 28 Hyde Park Gate (Kensington). Suddenly deposed as prime minister after the war, he bought the house as a London base in 1945 and resided there and at his Kent country house until his death—except for the period 1951 to 1955, when he again served as prime minister. Churchill later purchased number 27 next door and joined the two houses to provide space for his large staff and for entertainment functions. After turning out volumes of history and remaining active in the House of Commons until 1964, he celebrated his 90th birthday at Hyde Park Gate as hosts of well-wishers gathered outside. A short time later, Churchill died at the house.

(See Chapter 5, ENGLAND; also Chapter 7, IRELAND.)

COLERIDGE, SAMUEL TAYLOR (1772–1834). The Romantic poet, critic and philosopher lived at several London addresses. From 1781 to 1790 he studied and lodged at Christ's Hospital school, part of the Grey Friars Monastery which stood in Newgate Street (the City). Charles Lamb was a fellow student. Coleridge began writing verse at the school. The structure was later demolished.

Two houses, marked with plaques, commemorate his residency in other areas. He lived at 7 Addison Bridge Place (Kensington), formerly 7 Portland Place during 1811–12; and at 71 Berners Street (Westminster) during 1812–13—the original house was demolished in 1907.

Opium-addicted, Coleridge sought help from surgeon James Gillman in 1816 and resided at Gillman's home for the rest of his life. This house stands marked but privately owned at 3 The Grove, **Highgate** (Haringey). Coleridge did his last writing there and died at the house.

Coleridge tomb: St. Michael's Church, **Highgate**.

(See Chapter 4, WEST GERMANY; also Chapter 5, ENGLAND.)

CONRAD, JOSEPH (1857–1924). A resident of London at intervals from 1878, the Polish-born author settled at 17 Gillingham Street (Westminster) in 1894, a house which had been his occasional residence since 1891. He completed *Almayer's Folly* (1895) there and began *An Outcast of the Islands* (1896).

In 1904 Conrad lived at 17 Gordon Place (Kensington). He and his family often "house-sat" for his friend John Galsworthy, the novelist, at 14 Addison Road. Conrad's second son was born there in 1906.

His last London residence (1905) was 32 St. Agnes Place (Lambeth).

(See Chapter 1, SWITZERLAND; also Chapter 5, ENGLAND.)

COWARD, SIR NOËL PEIRCE (1899–1973). The versatile playwright, lyricist, composer and actor was a London native, born in "genteel poverty" at **Teddington** (Richmond upon Thames). Helmsdale, the "unpretentious abode" of the family, stood on Waldegrave Road and was his home to age five.

Coward achieved his first renown as a playwright while living at 111 Ebury Street (Westminster), a boardinghouse operated by his mother from 1917. He first occupied a tiny attic room there but as his fortunes rose he moved to successively lower quarters, eventually taking over the first floor and decorating his bedroom with murals and scarlet walls. The house was sold in 1928 but Coward rented his old suite there until 1930.

His new home at 17 Gerald Road (Westminster) remained his studio and base until 1955, when high taxes forced him to let it go. Coward occupied the upper part of the large house, which is set far back from the road. He spent his last years in Switzerland and Jamaica.

Exhibit: The visitor's book from Coward's estate in Kent—a virtual autograph roster of 20th-century notables—is displayed at the Garrick Club, 15 Garrick Street (Westminster). (Call 01–836–3846 for information.)

(See Chapter 1, SWITZERLAND; also Chapter 5, ENGLAND.)

CROMWELL, OLIVER (1599–1658). As England's lord protector and ruler during the commonwealth period from 1649, when the monarchy was temporarily deposed, Cromwell the man and his methods have never ceased to evoke controversy among historians and the English. From 1637 to 1647 he occupied two City residences: a house on the south side of Long Acre (1637–43), and a house in Drury Lane (1646–47). The site of his residence in King Street (Westminster) where he lived in 1647 is now occupied by the widened Parliament Street and government offices north of Parliament Square.

Cromwell took over the two royal palaces of the executed Charles I in 1650 and occupied them until his death. Hampton Court in **Hampton** (Richmond upon Thames) was his favorite. At Westminster, Cromwell ruled at Whitehall Palace and died there (see the entry on Henry VIII later in this chapter).

(See Chapter 5, ENGLAND.)

DARWIN, CHARLES ROBERT (1809–1882). The first London home of the great naturalist who formulated the theory of evolution through natural selection was a house located at 41 Great Marlborough Street (Westminster). He lived there from 1836 to 1838. He then occupied a dwelling he called "Macaw Cottage" (for its drawing-room color scheme), located at 110 Gower Street (Camden) from 1839 to 1842. The house was demolished during World War II. A plaque marks the

site on the present building, which is, appropriately, the biology department of London University.

Darwin tomb: Westminster Abbey (Westminster).

(See Chapter 5, ENGLAND; also Chapter 7, SCOTLAND.)

DEFOE, DANIEL (1660?–1731). Born Daniel Foe, the journalist and novelist spent most of his life in London but few of his addresses are precisely known. His birthplace was somewhere in the parish of St. Giles Cripplegate (the City). He operated as a business agent on the north side of Cornhill from 1683 to 1692, when he went bankrupt. A religious dissenter, he wrote a satirical pamphlet that resulted in his 1703 imprisonment at Newgate. London's chief prison from 1782 until it was demolished in 1902, it stood on the site now held by the Central Criminal Court at Newgate Street and Old Bailey. Other famous prisoners included Sir Thomas Malory, who may have written *Le Morte D'Arthur* (1485) there, and William Penn (see the entry on Penn later in this chapter). Defoe was pilloried for his offense but his *Hymn to the Pillory* (1704), composed at Newgate, evoked so much popular sympathy that he was pelted with flowers instead of garbage (August 1, 1703). The site of this occurrence is near the Temple Bar in Fleet Street.

In **Stoke Newington** (Hackney), Defoe and his family lived on the north side of Stoke Newington Church Street in 1708. Then (ca. 1714) he built a house on the present site of No. 95 (marked with a plaque) which was his home until 1730. The original brick house was demolished in 1859 and Defoe Road now extends across the actual site. Defoe did most of his major writing there, including *Robinson Crusoe* (1719) and *Moll Flanders* (1722).

Defoe died a fugitive from an unnamed "wicked, perjur'd and contemptible enemy" at his last lodgings in Ropemaker Street (the City).

Defoe tomb: Bunhill Fields (Islington).

(See Chapter 5, ENGLAND.)

DE GAULLE, CHARLES (1890–1970). The autocratic French soldier and later president fled France as Nazi troops pushed back the French army in 1940. As biographer Pierre Galante wrote, "Free France was born in London and... started its official life as a poor lodger in a small furnished flat at No. 6 Seamore Place in Mayfair." Seamore

Place is now Curzon Place (Westminster), and the three-room apartment where de Gaulle lodged as a refugee without an army remains privately owned. Another frequent residence after 1940 was the Connaught Hotel at Mount Street and Carlos Place. De Gaulle's headquarters as leader of Free French forces from 1940 to 1945 was 4 Carlton Gardens (inscribed with a tablet).

De Gaulle's wartime "domestic" lodging, shared with his wife, Yvonne, on weekends from 1941 to 1944, was Frognal House, which remains privately owned in Frognal, a street in Hampstead (Camden).

(See Chapter 2, FRANCE; also Chapter 3, PARIS.)

DICKENS, CHARLES (1812–1870). England's most popular novelist spent most of the years between 1822 and 1860 in London, whose underside he vividly depicted in such novels as *Oliver Twist* (1838) and *David Copperfield* (1850). "Dickens did not love London as Dr. Johnson had loved it," wrote David Daiches. Yet, both fascinated and repelled by what he saw and experienced there, he came to know it thoroughly. Volumes have been written on associations relating to Dickens in London, both to his actual life and his fiction. Among the best of these is *In the Steps of Charles Dickens* (1955) by William Addison; and *The London Dickens Knew* (1970) by Geoffrey Fletcher. All of the author's London residences are gone except the one noted below.

As a child, Dickens was living with his impoverished family at 147 Gower Street (Camden) when his father, John Dickens, was arrested and placed in debtors' prison (Marshalsea Prison, one high wall of which remains at 163 Queen's Head Yard, Southwark). Dickens spent Sundays at the prison with his family in 1824. During the week, he worked at a blacking factory on the present site of Charing Cross Station, and at its later site on the southwest corner of Chandos Place and Bedford Street (Westminster).

Dickens's first married home (1836–37) was 15 Furnival's Inn, which stood until 1897 on the site of the Prudential Assurance Company Building on the north side of Holborn between Brooke Street and Leather Lane (the City). There he worked on *The Pickwick Papers* (1836–37) and *Oliver Twist*.

His next home, the only surviving Dickens dwelling in London, is now the Dickens House Museum, operated by Dickens House Trustees at 48 Doughty Street (Camden). In this three-story, 12-room house where Dickens lived from 1837 to 1839, the author completed the two novels mentioned above and began *Nicholas Nickleby* (1839) and *Barnaby Rudge* (1841). His two eldest daughters were born there, and there his beloved sister-in-law, Mary Hogarth, died at age 17, a loss that Dickens never fully overcame. Today this house where Dickens achieved his first fame displays a wealth of memorabilia, documents, manuscript pages and portraits, as well as a reference library. Many of the furnishings, not present in the house when Dickens lived there, were brought from his last residence in Rochester (see Chapter 5). These include the lectern from which he gave public readings and his last writing table. His study, bedroom, and Mary Hogarth's room exhibit various aspects of the writer's career and family life. The house came very near demolition in 1922 and was rescued by the Dickens Fellowship, which shares ownership with the City and County of London. (Open Monday—Saturday 10:00—5:00; 01-405-2127; admission.)

CHARLES DICKENS'S HOME. Just before the popular novelist achieved the height of his fame (1837–39), he and his large family inhabited this dwelling at 48 Doughty Street, today the Dickens House Museum. It remains the only survivor of the author's several London dwellings.

Reflecting his sudden upward mobility from 1839 to 1851, Dickens lived in what he called "a house of great promise (and great premium), undeniable situation, and excessive splendour" located at 1 Devonshire Terrace (Westminster), where he enjoyed a walled garden and wrote *A Christmas Carol* (1843) and *David Copperfield*, among other works. Demolished in 1958, the mansion stood on the present site of Ferguson House, the porch of which displays bas-relief sculptures of Dickens and the fictional characters he created there. Ferguson House, a commercial building, overlaps the site at Marylebone Road and Marylebone High Street near York Gate.

The author leased Tavistock House, at the northeast corner of Tavistock Square (Camden), in 1851 and lived there until 1860, writing *Bleak House* (1852), *A Tale of Two Cities* (1859) and the beginning of *Great Expectations* (1860–61). There he endured the final dissolution of his unhappy though exceedingly prolific marriage (10 children) and began his affair with actress Ellen Ternan. Dickens, who became increasingly interested in the theater at Tavistock House, built a small garden stage there, produced juvenile dramas and even acted in them. A later resident was French composer Charles Gounod. B.M.A. House (British Medical Association) now occupies this site.

After 1860 Dickens usually spent a few months of each year in furnished quarters in London (see Name Index and Gazetteer) but never again occupied a home of his own in the city.

Dickens tomb: Westminster Abbey (Westminster).

(See Chapter 5, ENGLAND.)

DISRAELI, BENJAMIN (1804–1881). Twice prime minister, a favorite of Queen Victoria, and the author of several romantic novels, Disraeli was a London native (he called it "a nation, not a city"). He was born at 22 Theobalds Road (Camden), a four-story brick house where Disraeli lived with his family until 1818. His father, novelist Isaac D'Israeli, wrote several books there. Had his father not decided to have his children baptized Christians, Disraeli would not have had a political career, since Jews were excluded from Parliament at the time. From 1818 to 1829, the family lived at 6 Bloomsbury Square.

After his 1839 marriage to the widowed Mrs. Wyndham Lewis, Disraeli resided at her home—

except when serving as prime minister—until her death in 1872. This house is located at 93 Park Lane (Westminster). It was there that Disraeli produced most of his novels, including *Coningsby* (1844) and *Sybil* (1845).

THE PRIME MINISTER'S RESIDENCE. One of London's most famous addresses is 10 Downing Street in the heart of Westminster, official residence of British prime ministers since 1735. Despite its deceptively modest front facing the narrow street, the house is actually a 60-room mansion. Among its notable residents have been Benjamin Disraeli, The Duke of Wellington, David Lloyd George, and Sir Winston Churchill.

As prime minister, Disraeli occupied 10 Downing Street (Westminster) in 1868 and from 1874 to 1880. Built in 1721, this simple Georgian brick house—a much larger place than it looks, it contains 60 rooms—has served as the official prime minister's residence since 1735, when Sir Robert Walpole became the first to use it as such. Earlier the site was the home of George Villiers, second duke of Buckingham. Eminent prime ministers who have lived there include Sir Winston Churchill, the Duke of Wellington, William E.

Gladstone, David Lloyd George, Neville Chamberlain and Sir Anthony Eden (see the entries on Churchill, Lloyd George and the duke of Wellington in this chapter). The residence is not open to the public. R. J. Minney's *No. 10 Downing Street: A House in History* (1963) details the persons and events that have made this dwelling one of the most significant in England.

After his wife's death, Disraeli occupied 2 Whitehall Gardens as his private London residence (1875–80). It is now a parking lot opposite Whitehall Court where that street enters Horseguards Avenue (Westminster). Upon his 1880 retirement from politics, Disraeli, now Lord Beaconsfield, took a nine-year lease on 19 Curzon Street with the proceeds of his novel *Endymion* (1880). "I always wanted to die in London," he wrote. "It gives one six more months of life." The new lease, he believed, "will see me out." While bedridden there during his last illness, he was told that Queen Victoria would visit him if desired. "No," he said, "she would only ask me to take a message to Albert," referring to her constant widow's weeds (see the entry on Victoria later in this chapter). This four-story brick house indeed "saw him out" less than a year after he moved in. (See Chapter 5, ENGLAND.)

DONNE, JOHN (1572–1631). A London native, the poet and prelate was born in a now long-gone house in Bread Street (the City), his home until about 1576.

He lived and studied law at Lincoln's Inn in Chancery Lane (Camden) from 1592 to 1594 (see the entry on Jeremy Bentham earlier in this chapter), but maintained chambers there until 1624.

From 1596 to 1601, Donne served as secretary to Sir Thomas Egerton, lord keeper of the seal, at York House (Westminster; see the entry on Sir Francis Bacon earlier in this chapter).

"It was the scene for centuries of so much inhuman cruelty, vicious greed, and unspeakable suffering that the heart quails to think of it." Thus did one London antiquary describe Fleet Prison, where Donne was held for a brief period in 1601 after being arrested for secretly marrying Ann More, a minor and his cousin. Located on Farringdon Street near Fleet Lane (the City), the site had held a prison since Norman times. Twice burned and rebuilt—in 1666 and 1780—it incarcerated important state prisoners and later debtors before

being finally demolished because of its disgraceful conditions in 1846. Other noted prisoners there included John Cleland, who wrote *Fanny Hill* (1748–49) at the prison, and William Penn (see the entry on Penn later in this chapter). Congregational Memorial Hall now occupies this site.

At **Mitcham** (Merton), the two-story house occupied by Donne's growing family from 1606 to 1611 stood in Whitford Lane, the site of modern housing today.

Installed as dean of St. Paul's Cathedral on Ludgate Hill (the City) in 1621, Donne moved into the deanery, which stood on the southwest side of the cathedral, and this was his last home. The present deanery, rebuilt by Sir Christopher Wren on the site in 1670, occupies the lane south of St. Paul's Churchyard near the City Information Centre (see the entry on Wren later in this chapter).

Exhibit: The present St. Paul's Cathedral, where Donne preached so many of his famous sermons, is not the same building he knew. That Gothic cathedral, either third or fourth on the Ludgate Hill site since A.D. 604, was destroyed in the London fire of 1666. Architect Sir Christopher Wren promptly began a new baroque cathedral on the ruins and the final stone was set in 1708. World War II inflicted minor bomb damage on this largest cathedral in Britain, and subsequent repairs followed Wren's scheme. Only Donne's tomb monument, a statue showing him standing in his shroud, survived the 1666 fire. Today it occupies its almost exact original position on the east side of the south choir aisle. Donne had posed for the painting from which this statue was carved in the study of his house during his last illness; the epitaph is also his own composition. (Open daily 8:00—7:00, Sunday 8:00—6:00, except limited access during services; free.) (See Chapter 5, ENGLAND.)

DOYLE, SIR ARTHUR CONAN (1859–1930). The Scottish physician and author, best known for his Sherlock Holmes stories, resided in London at intervals from 1890. From about 1900 Doyle occupied a flat at 15 Buckingham Mansions, Victoria Street (Westminster). The building is long gone.

Exhibits: The Sherlock Holmes Pub at 10 Northumberland Avenue (Westminster) displays a museum relating to Doyle's famous detective. Included is the reconstructed sitting room of the chambers of Holmes and Dr. Watson at 221b Baker Street, first exhibited at the 1951 Festival of Britain. (Open Monday—Saturday, 12:00—2:00, 6:00—8:45; 01–930–2644.)

The fictional site of Holmes's Baker Street lodgings in Westminster is actually occupied by the Abbey National Building Society, but until 1930 the highest address number in Baker Street was 85, so there never was a 221B at the time Holmes "lived" there. The house facade at 109 Baker Street, however, resembles the Holmes-Watson residence as described by Doyle. The Sherlock Holmes Society of London may be contacted for further information (Upper Warlingham 3172).

(See Chapter 1, SWITZERLAND; also Chapter 5, ENGLAND; also Chapter 7, SCOTLAND.)

DRAKE, SIR FRANCIS (1540?–1596). The explorer, privateer and favorite naval captain of Elizabeth I made his home in London from 1588, though seafaring kept him absent for long periods. His large mansion, The Herbery, for which he obtained a 71-year lease, stood until the 17th century at the present site of Cannon Street Station, Upper Thames Street (the City), fronting the river.

Exhibits: The *Golden Hind*, Drake's 102-foot-long wooden galleon, which became the first English sailing vessel to circumnavigate the globe (1577–80), was drydocked in 1581 by order of Queen Elizabeth to serve as a memorial to Drake's accomplishment. Displayed in a dammed-up pool beside the Thames at **Deptford** (Lewisham), the ship was the site of the 1581 ceremony in which Elizabeth knighted Drake for his spectacular piracy of Spanish vessels and the treasure (loot estimated at over $30 million) he brought back to England. Only 37 years later, royal neglect had sadly affected the memorial. The ship lay bleached and rotting, scavenged for wood and littered with garbage and trash, and the remaining skeleton sank and was gradually buried in Thames flood silt. In 1975, almost 400 years after Elizabeth legitimized Drake's exploits, an attempt was made to locate and excavate remnants of the vessel at Deptford. Working from old maps and much guesswork, Museum of London diggers probed a site described as "about the size of a foundation for a three-bedroom ranch house" near the point known as Queen Elizabeth's Stairs, but they failed to discover the ship. Further work, however, may yet yield results in or near this area.

The National Maritime Museum in **Greenwich** (Greenwich) displays an astrolabe and lodestone (magnet) used by Drake (see the entry for Lord Nelson later in this chapter).

(See Chapter 5, ENGLAND.)

DRYDEN, JOHN (1631–1700). Poet Robert Graves said that Dryden "found English poetry brick and left it marble—native brick, imported marble." This foremost author and poet of his time was a London dweller from the 1650s. None of his several residences survive (see Name Index and Gazetteer). He did some of his most important writing, including *All for Love* (1678) and *Absalom and Achitophel* (1681), at his home in Salisbury Court, a now long-gone street slightly west of the present Dorset Rise off Tudor Street (Westminster); Dryden lived there from 1673 to 1682. His last home from 1686 stood at 44 Gerrard Street (tablet on Number 43). There he wrote *The Hind and the Panther* (1687); one of his best-known poems, it reflects his Catholic conversion. The private house on this site dates from a later period.

Dryden tomb: Westminster Abbey (Westminster).

(See Chapter 5, ENGLAND.)

EDWARD VIII (1894–1972). A popular king for almost a year, Edward abdicated in 1936 in order to marry "the woman I love"—American Wallis Warfield Simpson—thereby incurring much public disfavor and virtual exclusion from Britain's royal family. After his marriage, he led a rather pointless existence as the duke of Windsor, an "international celebrity." He was born Edward Albert Christian George Andrew Patrick David Saxe-Coburg-Gotha (though he was known to his family and closest intimates simply as "David") at White Lodge, the mansion in Richmond Park, **Richmond** (Richmond upon Thames), given to his parents, the future George V and Queen Mary, by Queen Victoria. Built as a hunting lodge for George II in 1727, the house was enlarged during the 1750s; its flanking pavilions were linked and the entrance portico was added in the early 19th century. The house served as lodgings for various members of the royal family, including George VI when he was duke of York, but since 1955 the Royal Ballet School has occupied the building. While no exhibits relate specifically to Edward VIII, who lived there only during infancy, three ground-floor rooms display some of the original royal furnishings. White Lodge, operated by the Governors of the Royal Ballet School, mainly functions as a museum of ballet and training center for young dancers. (Open August, daily 2:00—6:00; 01–748–1236; admission.)

One of Edward's boyhood homes (1903–10) was the red-brick Marlborough House, built for the duke of Marlborough by Sir Christopher Wren in 1709 and subsequently altered and enlarged. Later occupants included the future Belgian king Leopold I, and the future Edward VII and George V (the latter was born there in 1865). Queen Alexandra and Queen Mary, wives and later widows, of Edward VII and George V respectively, spent their last years at Marlborough House. Located at the western end of Pall Mall (Westminster), it now houses the Commonwealth Information Centre and Reading Room. When not in use for conferences, state apartments with many original furnishings may be viewed by prearranged tour. (Open Easter—September, Saturday—Sunday, public holidays, by appointment; 01–930–8071; admission.)

Edward's own official establishment after World War I until he became king was York House, the northside portion of St. James's Palace. World War I general Lord Kitchener of Khartoum lived there in 1915 and 1916. It is now a private royal residence (see the entry on Henry VIII later in this chapter). Edward also resided at Buckingham Palace, both as Prince of Wales and king (see the entry on George III later in this chapter).

(See Chapter 2, FRANCE; also Chapter 3, PARIS; also Chapter 5, ENGLAND; also Chapter 7, SCOTLAND.)

ELIOT, GEORGE. See MARY ANN EVANS.

ELIOT, THOMAS STEARNS (1888–1965). American by birth and English by choice, the poet and critic lived in London from 1914. In 1915 he and his first wife, Vivienne, occupied 18 Crawford Mansions in Crawford Street (Westminster). According to biographer Robert Sencourt, this was "a vulgar quarter where their rough, crude charwoman talked boldly of abortions, and so went down into literary history as Lou in *The Waste Land*." In 1915 and 1916 the Eliots shared the flat of Bertrand Russell in Bury Street (see the entry on Russell later in this chapter).

During the early 1920s, Eliot lived at 5 Chester Row (also numbered 57 Chester Terrace, West-

minster). About 1922 he moved to 68 Glentworth Street, a house made affordable by a $2,000 literary prize for *The Waste Land* (1922). Around 1929 he moved to No. 98 in the same street and Vivienne Eliot continued to reside there after their 1933 separation.

Eliot's London lodging during 1933 and 1934 was the Victorian mansion at 33 Courtfield Road (Kensington). During the years 1934 to 1939 he resided with Rev. Eric Cheetham, vicar of St. Stephen's Church, in the clergy house at Gloucester Road and Southwell Gardens, where he wrote his verse plays *Murder in the Cathedral* (1935) and *The Family Reunion* (1939). Eliot was churchwarden at St. Stephen's for 25 years.

The poet resided during World War II (1939–45) at Shamly Green, a house overlooking **Richmond** (Richmond upon Thames).

After World War II Eliot shared bachelor apartment quarters (1942–57) with editor-critic John Hayward at Carlyle Mansions, corner of Cheyne Walk and Lawrence Street (Chelsea). This building had been the last home of novelist Henry James, another American expatriate (see the entry on James later in this chapter).

Eliot's last home, and by all accounts his happiest, was with his second wife, Valerie Fletcher, at Kensington Court Gardens in Kensington Court (Kensington).

From 1925 Eliot worked for the publishing company of Faber & Faber at 24 Russell Square (Westminster), where he maintained a director's office from 1929 until his death.

(See Chapter 5, ENGLAND.)

ELIZABETH I (1533–1603). Last of the Tudor monarchs, daughter of Henry VIII and Anne Boleyn, and one of England's most intelligent and popular rulers, Elizabeth was born at Placentia Palace in **Greenwich** (Greenwich), a residence she used throughout her life. At the two-story gatehouse there in 1581, according to legend, Sir Walter Raleigh swept off his cloak and laid it in the mud to keep his queen's feet dry (see the entry on Raleigh later in this chapter). Her first stay there as queen was in 1559.

Between her mother's execution in 1536 and her father's death in 1547, Elizabeth moved constantly between several royal palaces. "There were sound practical reasons for this restless existence," wrote biographer Alison Plowden. "In such large establishments, crowded with hangers-on and with only the most primitive sanitary arrangements, it was obviously a sensible precaution to vacate the premises at regular intervals to allow for a general 'sweetening' and cleaning up." A frequent residence during this period was Chelsea Palace. Elizabeth was also often taken to Eltham Palace during her infancy "on account of the salubrity of the air." Hampton Court was a common childhood residence and also, briefly, her prison in 1555. As queen, Elizabeth suffered two bouts of smallpox there, in 1562 and 1572. (For these and palaces mentioned in the following text, see the entry on Henry VIII later in this chapter.)

Ruins of Elsynge Hall remain on the grounds of Forty Hall near **Enfield** (Enfield). This Tudor manor was Elizabeth's residence in 1547; there she and her younger brother received the news of his accession to the throne as Edward VI. Forty Hall, built in 1629, is operated by the London borough of Enfield as an art gallery and furniture museum. It stands one mile north of Enfield. (Open Easter—September, Tuesday—Friday 10:00—6:00, Saturday—Sunday 10:00—8:00; October—Easter, Tuesday—Sunday 10:00—5:00; 01–363–8196; free.)

In 1554, as the unwitting victim of Sir Thomas Wyatt's conspiracy to depose her half-sister, Mary Tudor, from the throne, Princess Elizabeth was arrested at Whitehall Palace and imprisoned for two months in the formidable Tower of London. Brought by barge, she entered this bastion via the riverside Traitor's Gate, the Tower's main entrance in a century when the Thames was London's main thoroughfare. Her cell in the upper story of the 13th-century Bell Tower was—and is—a grim circular chamber lighted only by arrow slots cut into eight-foot thick walls. Twenty years earlier Sir Thomas More had been confined in the chamber below this one. Located in the southwest corner of Tower Green, the adjacent timber-framed Queen's House, dating from 1530, was known as the Lieutenant's Lodgings until 1880. Elizabeth dined there during her incarceration. Later it served as an interrogation chamber for conspirator Guy Fawkes (1605); subsequent prisoners there included William Penn and Nazi leader Rudolf Hess. In a small upper room of the north wing, Elizabeth's mother, Anne Boleyn, awaited execution in 1536. Presently the official residence of the Tower governor, Elizabeth's lodgings are not open to the public. Princess Elizabeth's Walk is the top of the western rampart that

extends from Bell to Beauchamp towers, where she took exercise. Her brief confinement gave her a lifelong horror of the Tower; though still an official royal palace at the time of her reign, she never visited it as queen. (See the entries on More, Penn and the Tower of London later in this chapter).

Upon her release, Elizabeth spent the four years until her own accession to the throne under virtual house arrest at several lodgings. As queen, Hampton Court and Whitehall Palace became her main London residences. She also frequently spent winters and held spring court at Richmond Palace where she died.

Queen Elizabeth's Hunting Lodge in Ranger's Road near **Chingford** (Waltham Forest) in Epping Forest, now houses the Epping Forest Museum which displays forestry exhibits. The timber-framed building, built about 1543, served as a base for royal hunts into Waltham Forest, of which Epping Forest is a relic. After the English defeat of the Spanish Armada in 1588, Elizabeth is said to have ridden her white palfrey up the staircase of the lodge from sheer exuberance. This museum is operated by the Corporation of London and Conservators of Epping Forest. (Open Wednesday—Sunday, 2:00—6:00; 01–529–6681; admission.)

Elizabeth lived at Somerset House during part of her sister Mary's reign; during her own, however, she resided there only at brief intervals. She used it mainly as council and ceremonial chambers and a "grace and favor" residence for court favorites and numerous foreign diplomats and suitors, willing objects of the "virgin queen's" masterful teasing. The present Somerset House, a structure dating from 1776 to 1790 with 19th-century wings, occupies the 1547 site of Lord Protector Edward Somerset's palace on the Strand at Waterloo Bridge (Westminster). It houses the Board of Inland Revenue and the Probate Registry.

Elizabeth occasionally used Nonsuch Palace near **Malden** (Kingston upon Thames) during her last years. There the impulsive, ill-fated Robert Devereaux, Earl of Essex, burst into her chambers in 1599 and set in motion the events that led to his execution for treason.

Palaces and Progresses of Elizabeth I (1962), by Ian Dunlop, describes Elizabeth's most important residences in detail.

Elizabeth I tomb: Westminster Abbey (Westminster).

Exhibits: The Norman Undercroft Museum, entered from the Dark Cloister at Westminster Abbey (Westminster), displays Elizabeth's wax funeral effigy, remade in 1760, along with those of other notable monarchs. These representations of the royal corpses, usually extremely accurate likenesses, were used for display purposes in place of the body itself which hardly outlasted the lengthy funeral ceremonies. Also displayed is the illuminated service book used by Elizabeth during her 1559 coronation in the Abbey; and the ring she gave one of her favorites, the hot-headed Earl of Essex—he returned it to the queen in hopes of a pardon just before his 1601 execution for a witless act of treason. (Open April—October, daily 9:15—5:00; November—March, Monday—Friday, 9:30—5:00; admission.)

One of Elizabeth's many skills was playing a keyboard instrument called virginals that resembles the harpsichord. Elizabeth's preserved virginals may be seen in Room 52 of the massive Victoria and Albert Museum in Cromwell Road (Kensington). (Open Monday—Thursday, Saturday 10:00—6:00, Sunday 2:30—6:00; 01–589–6371; free.)

(See Chapter 5, ENGLAND.)

EVANS, MARY ANN. ("GEORGE ELIOT") (1819–1880). The novelist chose her pseudonym because she wanted to be judged as a writer, not as a "woman writer." George was the Christian name of her married lover, George H. Lewes, with whom she lived for 24 years; and Eliot, she said, was simply "a good mouthful." Her first London address, as "Marian Evans," was the lodging of publisher John Chapman at 142 The Strand (Westminster), where she shared quarters at intervals from 1851 to 1853 with both Chapman's wife and mistress. In 1853 she moved to 21 Cambridge Street and lived there until she met Lewes. Neither of these houses survive.

From 1855 to 1859 the couple lived in **Richmond** (Richmond upon Thames) at 8 Parkshot, present site of the Richmond Court House, where she wrote *Adam Bede* (1859) and first used her pseudonym. The pair next lived in **Wimbledon** (Merton) (1859–60) at 31 Wimbledon Park Road, a house she described as "a tall cake, with a low garnish of holly and laurel." She wrote *The Mill on the Floss* (1860) in this residence, which is now divided into two privately owned flats. Prying eyes and neighborhood gossip about the couple's un-

married bliss, however, made them eager to "transfer our present house to someone who likes houses full of eyes all round him."

From 1860 to 1863 they lived at the site of 16 Blandford Square (Westminster); there she wrote *Silas Marner* (1861) and began *Romola* (1863). The Priory at 21 North Bank, a long-gone road formerly curving south off Lodge Road (site of the Great Central Railway track where it crosses Grand Union Canal), was the couple's last home together from 1863. "This house," wrote Katy Carter, "became a focal point for literary London, where admirers came to pay court to the famous authoress, regarded, as her literary reputation increased, by all but prudes as one of the foremost moralists of the day." She wrote *Felix Holt* (1866) and *Middlemarch* (1871–72) there. George Lewes died there in 1878, and the grieving author went into weeks of seclusion.

Following her 1880 marriage to American banker John Walter Cross and a trip to Venice, the couple moved to Evans's last home at 4 Cheyne Walk (Chelsea). Built in 1717, this brick-faced, two-story dwelling was the scene of shortlived happiness, for the author died there only three weeks later.

Evans tomb: Highgate Cemetery, **Highgate** (Haringey).

(See Chapter 1, SWITZERLAND; also Chapter 5, ENGLAND; also Chapter 8, ITALY.)

FARADAY, MICHAEL (1791–1867). The physicist whose discoveries formed the basis of all subsequent work in electromagnetism (he designed the first primitive motor and dynamo and developed the laws of electrolysis) was a London native and lifelong dweller. His boyhood home from 1796 to 1804 stood in Charles Street near Manchester Square (Westminster). In 1804 Faraday was apprenticed to a bookbinder at 48 Blandford Street, a four-story brick building, and lived there until 1812. A ground-floor shop still occupies the old bindery where Faraday began copying and binding his own notes from scientific lectures he attended.

Faraday occupied two rooms as an assistant to Sir Humphry Davy at 21 Albemarle Street (Westminster), now restored to its 1845 appearance and displayed by the Royal Institution as Faraday's Laboratory and Museum. As Faraday's lodging from 1813 to 1858, it was the scene of his most important discoveries. Visitors may see some of his original equipment plus exhibits tracing the significance of his work. (Open Tuesday, Thursday 1:00—4:00; other times by arrangement; 01-409-2992; admission.)

On Hampton Court Green stands the bow-windowed cottage given to Faraday in 1858 by Queen Victoria, his permanent home after 1862. Faraday died there. Not open to the public, it may be externally viewed off Hampton Court Road in **Hampton** (see the entries on Henry VIII and Victoria later in this chapter).

Faraday tomb: Highgate Cemetery, **Highgate** (Haringey).

Exhibit: The Cuming Museum at 155 Walworth Road (Southwark) displays memorials and exhibits pertaining to Faraday. (Open Monday—Friday 10:00—5:30, Thursday to 7:00, Saturday 10:00—5:00; 01-703-3324; free.)

FIELDING, HENRY (1707–1754). Fielding, a magistrate and the author who established the literary form of the novel in *Tom Jones* (1749) and other works, resided in London at intervals from 1728. In 1736 he and his wife, Charlotte, lived with her relatives at 16 Buckingham Street while he wrote plays and managed the Haymarket Theatre. Both house and theater are long gone; the present Haymarket Theatre, also called the Theatre Royal, was designed by John Nash in 1821 at Haymarket and Charles II Street (Westminster), near the original theater site, and still presents dramatic productions.

Fielding soon entered the Middle Temple to study law. From 1740 he held assigned, third-floor chambers at 4 Pump Court, east of Middle Temple Lane (the City), his official barrister's residence for the rest of his life. Fielding wrote his novel *Joseph Andrews* (1742) there. Buildings in this area suffered heavily from World War II bombing, but careful restoration has preserved much of their 16th- and 17th-century appearance. Middle Temple Hall, which Elizabeth I opened in 1576 and where in 1601 she witnessed Shakespeare acting in *Twelfth Night*, would have been familiar to Fielding as the communal center of student life— as it was to Edmund Burke (1750s), Sir Walter Raleigh (1576–77) and William Makepeace Thackeray (1831–32). (Hall open Monday—Saturday 10:00—12:00, 3:00—4:30; 01-353-4355; free; see the entries on Burke, Elizabeth I, Raleigh, Shakespeare, and Thackeray in this chapter).

After his wife's death in 1744, Fielding resided with his daughter, his sister, and Mary Daniel (his wife's maid, whom he married amid a chorus of derisive comment in 1747) in Beaufort Buildings, which stood in The Strand opposite Exeter Street (Westminster).

In 1747 and 1748 Fielding lived in Holly Lane, **Twickenham** (Richmond upon Thames) and probably wrote part of *Tom Jones* there. The wooden cottage site is now occupied by a more recent row of houses.

In 1749, as an unpaid justice of the peace for Westminster, Fielding next occupied Magistrate's House, long gone from 19-20 Bow Street (Westminster). In the lower front room there he officiated until 1754 as one of London's most efficient and incorruptible police magistrates: reducing the office's income from fees and bribes ("about £500 a year of the dirtiest money upon earth," he said); reforming court practices; and founding the "Bow Street Runners," the first nucleus of London's Metropolitan Police. He also found time to complete *Tom Jones*, his best-known novel.

Milbourne House in Station Road at High Street, **Barnes** (Richmond upon Thames), a much-altered privately owned structure, was his part-time home from 1748 to 1753.

Fielding's last London residence (1754) stood in Fordhook Avenue, **Acton** (Ealing).

(See Chapter 5, ENGLAND; also Chapter 8, PORTUGAL.)

FRANKLIN, BENJAMIN (1706–1790). The American statesman, journalist and scientist spent some 17 years in London and, until the American Revolution at least, he regarded England (as did many Americans) as "home." "I am a Briton," he proudly boasted. Franklin spent three periods in London: from 1724 to 1726, 1758 to 1762 and 1764 to 1775.

As an apprentice printer in 1724, he first lodged with James Ralph in Little Britain Street (the City), south of the Church of St. Bartholomew the Great. He worked for almost a year in Palmer's Printing House, Bartholomew Close, a small side street off Little Britain. The shop occupied the third floor of a building connected with the 14th-century Lady Chapel (rebuilt in 1896) of St. Bartholomew the Great, London's oldest parish church. "Why Lady Chapel was given over to 'trade' in the 18th century remains uncertain," wrote Nicholas Lynn, "but it was in these rather somber surroundings that young Franklin set up such books as William Wollaston's *The Religion of Nature Delineated* (a best-seller in 1725) and produced his own first literary opus, *A Dissertation on Liberty and Necessity, Pleasure and Pain.*" This chapel, which later became a public house, dance hall and fringe factory, has been restored to its original appearance and now serves as Chapel of the Imperial Society of Knights Bachelor.

After a falling-out with Ralph in 1725 (Franklin had pursued his friend's mistress), he moved to lodgings on the west side of Sardinia Street near the southwest corner of Lincoln's Inn Fields (Camden) and remained there until he returned to America the next year. His workplace was Watts' Printing House, which stood on the south side of Wild Court between Wild Street and Kingsway (Westminster). Franklin revisited the Watts shop in 1768, spotted his old screw-type press, and had a nostalgic drink of porter with the workmen.

No longer a somewhat "pushy" youth but a shrewd man of public affairs whose brilliant scientific reputation preceded him, Dr. Franklin next came "home to England" in 1757 as a diplomat representing the Pennsylvania Assembly. His residence until 1762—and from 1764 to 1775—survives at 36 Craven Street (Westminster). This four-story house with a brick facade and original iron railings and balconies remains much as it was when he lived there, despite damage from World War II bombs. Franklin resided in four furnished rooms there along with his son William and a slave. He fitted one of the hearths with his own "Pennsylvania fireplace" invention. Franklin cavorted in typical flirtatious style with Polly Stevenson, his landlady's daughter, at this address. His later years there, as American rebellion loomed, were full of anxiety. As official harassment increased and charges of treason became imminent, he left England forever in 1775, the year the American Revolution began. This building, Franklin's only surviving home in the world, now houses offices of the British Society for International Understanding—a memorial that he could not have better prescribed for himself.

(See Chapter 3, PARIS; also Chapter 5, ENGLAND.)

FREUD, SIGMUND (1856–1939). Like so many of the best minds of his time, the Austrian psychiatrist and founder of psychoanalysis spent his final years in London as a refugee from Nazism. His first residence, in 1938, was 39 Elsworthy Road (Camden), where he wrote *An Outline of Psycho-Analysis* (1940). Then, after an operation for recurrent mouth cancer, he settled at 20 Maresfield Gardens, Hampstead, his last home. In this ivy-covered mansion, Freud's daughter, Anna, recreated his Vienna study in a back room; it had French windows that opened onto a garden. There he wrote his last book, *Moses and Monotheism* (1939). Nursed by Anna, Freud spent his last weeks in the room and died there. Anna Freud, herself a prominent psychoanalyst, continued to occupy the house for many years. (Inquire locally for admission information.)

Freud tomb: Golders Green Cemetery (Barnet). (See Chapter 1, AUSTRIA.)

GANDHI, MOHANDAS KARAMCHAND (1869–1948). The Indian revolutionary and exponent of passive resistance as a political tactic came to London as a student in 1888 and resided at various lodgings in West Kensington, Holborn and Bayswater until 1891. At 20 Baron's Court Road (Kensington), he lived with an Anglo-Indian family while studying law at the Inner Temple (the City). A plaque marks Kingsley Hall, a three-story house in Powis Road (Tower Hamlets), where Gandhi lived for three months in 1931 while representing the Indian Congress in London.

GEORGE III (1738–1820). George's reign of 59 years (1760–1820) was exceeded only by that of his granddaughter Queen Victoria. A grandson of George II, he was the first king of the ruling House of Hanover to consider himself more English than German. He was also the last British monarch to exert control over Parliament. Though not a very bright man at his best, he remained fairly popular despite the disastrous loss of the American colonies during his reign. As he aged, the king became increasingly handicapped by long spells of what he called "nervousness"—irrationality, compulsive talking, and violent behavior requiring his occasional confinement in a straitjacket. Modern physicians have diagnosed his illness as hepatic porphyria, a malady of the metabolic system. He was seldom lucid after 1811. The disease finally left him deaf, blind and completely witless.* His birthplace was Norfolk House at 31 St. James's

Square (Westminster), a house owned by the dukes of Norfolk from 1722 to 1937. He lived there until 1741. George's father, the crown prince Frederick Louis, had leased the brick mansion in 1737 after he had been banished from court by *his* father, George II. The present Norfolk House is a 1939 reconstruction on the site and as such served Gen. Dwight D. Eisenhower as World War II allied headquarters from 1942 to 1945.

George spent part of his boyhood years at a country estate near London. The site of Kew House (also called the "White House") at **Kew** (Richmond upon Thames), is located east of Holly Walk along Kew Road in the 288-acre Kew Gardens, still officially called the Royal Botanic Gardens. As king, he and Queen Charlotte later used Kew House from 1772 until its destruction in 1802; the site of its east wing is marked by a sundial in front of the present Kew Palace.

Their earlier married home, Richmond Lodge (1760s–72), stood west of Holly Walk fronting the Thames. This had been the home of George II and Queen Caroline, who first acquired the Kew estate in 1721; but George III found it too small for his 15 children.

Kew Palace, also known as the "Dutch House," which they occupied at intervals from 1802, became one of the king's favorite lodgings (though intended as only temporary while he awaited completion of the riverbank Castellated Palace, which was never finished). Built in 1631, the heavily ornamented and gabled red-brick structure is extremely small for a palace. George IV later occupied it as Prince of Wales, and Queen Charlotte died there in 1818. Another well-known resident was novelist Fanny Burney, who served the queen as keeper of the robes and tried to avoid encounters with the unpredictable king. Period furnishings in the king's dining room, queen's drawing room and other chambers—plus memorabilia of George III and his family—give a

fairly accurate picture of the royal life at Kew, though little of the original interior decoration survives. The formal queen's garden at the rear is designed as a mid-17th-century bower. Kew Palace is operated by Kew Gardens, Department of the Environment. (Gardens open daily, summer 10:00—8:00, winter 10:00—4:00; palace open April—mid-October, Monday—Saturday 11:00—5:30, Sunday 2:00—6:00; 01–940–1171; admission.) About one mile south of Kew Palace, via Holly Walk or the Lion Gate from Kew Road, stands Queen's Cottage; a two-story thatched house built for Queen Charlotte in 1772 and used by the royal family for summer picnics, it is now furnished as though prepared for one. (Open April—September, Saturday—Sunday 11:00—5:30; admission.)

Of the London royal palaces, Hampton Court was anathema to George III, for there the irascible George II had once physically and verbally cuffed him. St. James's Palace was more of a ceremonial than residential palace, though George IV, eldest son of George III, was born there in 1762 (see the entry on Henry VIII later in this chapter for information about these palaces).

BUCKINGHAM PALACE. George III purchased the original mansion in St. James's Park in 1762, and later additions vastly expanded its size. The palace has been the sovereign's official London residence since Queen Victoria ascended the throne in 1837 and is never open to the public.

George III's main London residence was Buckingham Palace, which he bought in 1762. The original structure was known as "Buckingham House"; it had been built on the site of James I's mulberry orchard in 1703 by the Duke of Buckingham. After George's death, architect John Nash

---

*In terms of conventional historical thought, of course, the diagnosis is irrelevant. As Jane Murray points out in her excellent *The Kings and Queens of England* (1974), ". . . we are always being told not to make our historical judgments out of context. We are not supposed to apply twentieth-century standards to the Duke of Marlborough's taking money from his mistress to get started in life (this was perfectly all right in the seventeenth century) or to Richard Coeur-de-Lion's killing women, children, and 'babies at the breast' (this was perfectly all right in the twelfth). We would certainly be judging George III and his circle in terms of our century, not his, if we thought of him as the victim of a physical disease. In context, George III was a madman. This is what he thought he was, this is what his doctors and family and court and country thought. History developed on the basis of this premise."

was commissioned to build additions to the original mansion in 1825, and it was enlarged again for Queen Victoria. The palace has been the sovereign's official London residence since Victoria's accession in 1837. Its western Bath-stone facade facing the 40-acre palace gardens and lake remains essentially as Nash designed it, while the east wing dates from 1847. The entire eastern facade was refaced with Portland stone in 1913. The palace interior and state apartments, never open to the public, are richly decorated with splendid colored marbles, and bronze, ivory and gold attachments plus fine staircases, chandeliers, pilasters, and paneling. The ballroom, site of George III's octagon library until 1854 (see *Exhibits* below), hosts state banquets and investitures. Edward VII was born in the palace in 1841 and died there in 1910. Present royal apartments are located in the north wing; the royal standard flies when the sovereign is in residence. (On the countless rooms in Buckingham Palace, Prince Charles remarked in 1983: "I haven't counted them. There are some we haven't been in, but quite a few people might have been living in them for several years unbeknownst.") Buckingham Palace is located at the western end of St. James's Park in Buckingham Palace Road (Westminster).

Exhibits: At the Royal Mews in Buckingham Palace Road (Westminster), visitors may see a panoply of vehicles used by royalty for state occasions. The gold state coach was first used by George III when he opened Parliament in 1762 and has carried every monarch to his or her coronation since George IV's in 1820. (Open Wednesday—Thursday 2:00—4:00; 01–930–4832; admission.)

The King's Library, occupying the east-side, ground-floor hall of the British Museum, entered from Great Russell Street or from Montague Place (Camden), preserves the magnificent Buckingham Palace library of George III. Donated to the nation by George IV, it contains many early editions, fine bindings and ancient manuscripts. (Open Monday—Saturday 10:00—5:00, Sunday 2:30—6:00; 01–636–1555; free.)

(See Chapter 5, ENGLAND.)

GILBERT, SIR WILLIAM SCHWENCK (1836–1911). The librettist of comic operas in collaboration with composer Sir Arthur Sullivan (see the entry on Sullivan later in this chapter), Gilbert was born at 17 Southampton Street (Westminster), home of his maternal grandfather. His main

childhood home (1837–57), however, was 4 Portland Place.

Educated in the law and also a professional home-guard soldier until 1883, Gilbert occupied chambers briefly at 1 Verulam Buildings, Gray's Inn (Camden; see the entry on Sir Francis Bacon earlier in this chapter).

From 1868 until 1876 he resided at 8 Essex Villas (Kensington); there Gibert began his long, occasionally stormy collaboration with Sullivan. Their first major effort, *Trial by Jury* (1875), opened at the Royalty Theatre, which stood at 73 Dean Street (Westminster).

From 1878 to 1883 Gilbert lived at 24 The Boltons (extension of Gilston Road, Chelsea). In 1883 he moved to 39 Harrington Gardens (Kensington), his home until 1890. Gilbert designed and built this house, which combines medieval Dutch and Victorian styles, and there he wrote such operas as *The Mikado* (1885), *The Yeomen of the Guard* (1888) and *The Gondoliers* (1889). The east wing of the house was restored in 1972; the Society of Genealogists now occupies the west wing. Nonmembers may use the library on payment of a daily fee. (Open Tuesday—Sunday; call 01–373–7054 for information.)

Breakspears, Gilbert's rented summer home from 1883 to 1890, remains privately owned at **Harefield** (Hillingdon) north of Uxbridge. A tennis enthusiast, he spent many hours on his large court there.

In 1890 he bought Grimsdyke House, located in Grimsdyke Park on the edge of **Harrow Weald** (Harrow) common, and occupied it frequently until his death, which occurred there after he rescued a girl from drowning in his pool. He converted his 110 acres into a virtual nature refuge. According to Lois H. Fisher, "his passionate fondness for wildlife made him issue orders to his gamekeeper and staff that nothing was to be caught or trapped; indeed, even birds and deer entered the library without fear." His annual Christmas parties for village children continued there long after his death. Today Grimsdyke House, dating from 1872, is known as Grimsdyke Country Hotel. Location scenes for the film *The Crimson Cult* were shot there in 1970. Standing on Old Redding Road, it hosts Sunday musical evenings; dinner is served and Gilbert and Sullivan selections are played (call 01–954–4227 for information).

Gilbert's urban London addresses from 1894 included 36 Prince's Gardens (Kensington) where he lived until 1898; and a town house at 90 Eaton Square (Westminster) where he lived from 1907–11.

Gilbert tomb: Parish churchyard, **Great Stanmore** (Harrow).

Exhibits: The Gilbert and Sullivan Pub at 23 Wellington Street (Westminster) displays relics of the collaborators (01–836–6930).

Richard D'Oyly Carte built the Savoy Theatre at Savoy Court (Westminster) for Gilbert and Sullivan performances in 1881; an argument between the collaborators, ostensibly over carpeting for the theater, led to a three-year hiatus (1890–93) in their partnership. This was the first public building in the world to be lighted by electricity. The Savoy still presents stage performances (call 01–836–8888 for information).

HANDEL, GEORG FREDERICK (1685–1759). The German-born oratorio composer resided in London for 47 years. He composed most of his best-known works in the three-story brick house he bought at 25 Brook Street (Westminster) in 1723. Though his English never became more than barely adequate, he enjoyed rich patronage and hosted numerous elegant banquets. In 1740 Handel composed the *Messiah* in 24 days, during which time he never left the house. After he had completed part II of the work, a servant found him in tears at his worktable in the ground-floor music room. "I did think I did see all heaven before me and the great God himself," he wept. Handel died in the house only a few days after attending a *Messiah* performance. An extra floor was added to the house in the late 19th century, and Handel's ground-floor living rooms were converted to a shop in 1906.

Handel's first London lodging in 1712 was Old Burlington House, now occupied by the Royal Academy of Arts in Piccadilly (Westminster). He lived there under the patronage of the Earl of Burlington until 1718 and possibly later as well. Originally built in 1665, this manor underwent three major remodelings and refacings from 1715 to 1873 and little resembles the house in which Handel rubbed shoulders with some of the foremost English artists and writers of his time. Only the ground floor of the right wing remains from the original structure. (See the entry on Carolus Linnaeus later in this chapter.)

At Canons, the **Edgware** (Barnet) estate of Handel's chief patron, the Duke of Chandos, the

BIRTHPLACE OF HANDEL'S *MESSIAH*. The German-born composer spent most of his life in London and from 1723 occupied this house at 25 Brook Street. There in 1740 he composed his oratorio *Messiah* in 24 days of intense labor. The ground-floor rooms occupied by Handel have held shops since 1906.

composer created his first oratorio, *Esther* (1720). Handel served as the duke's resident composer and private choirmaster from 1718 to 1720, and the little organ he used may be seen in the parish church of St. Lawrence, built by the duke in Whitchurch Lane. Canons Park, now mostly subdivided, was originally the Chandos estate. The North London Collegiate School for Girls, dating from 1850, now occupies the site of the mansion which was demolished in 1747.

Handel tomb: Westminster Abbey (Westminster).

Exhibits: The Thomas Coram Foundation for Children, formerly the Foundling Hospital to which Handel donated both money and personal memorabilia, is located at 40 Brunswick Square (Camden). Displayed there are Handel's manuscript score of the *Messiah*, the organ keyboard he used when performing the oratorio, and other relics. All performances of the *Messiah* were given for charity during the composer's lifetime. (Open Monday—Friday 10:00—4:00; 01–278–2424; admission.)

The Museum of Instruments at the Royal College of Music, Prince Consort Road (Kensington), includes a spinet used by Handel in its Donaldson Collection of 300 instruments. (Open by appointment; 01–589–3643; admission.)

(See Chapter 4, EAST GERMANY; also Chapter 5, ENGLAND; also Chapter 7, IRELAND.)

HARDY, THOMAS (1840–1928). The novelist and poet resided in London at frequent intervals from 1862. His first lodgings (1862–67) were 16 Westbourne Park Villas (Westminster). He worked as an architectural draftsman for a firm at 8 St. Martin's Place, which moved to 8 Adelphi Terrace in 1867.

From 1874 to 1876 Hardy and his wife, Emma, resided at a house called St. David's, Hood Road, in **Surbiton** (Kingston upon Thames), where he worked on *The Return of the Native* (1878).

In 1878 they moved to The Larches at 1 Arundel Terrace, 172 Trinity Road, in **Upper Tooting** (Wandsworth). Owing to Hardy's eye for young, attractive women, his marriage turned sour there; though as Katy Carter points out, "their troubles were partly caused by the house itself. On the northernmost corner of the terrace . . . it was always cold and exposed to the vagaries of the weather." Snow drifted through doors and windows during the harsh winter of 1880–81. Hardy became severely ill, suffering from a lung hemorrhage, and returned to his native Dorset in 1881. This three-story, yellow-brick villa remains privately owned.

(See Chapter 5, ENGLAND.)

HARVEY, WILLIAM (1578–1657). The physician and anatomist, who discovered how the human circulatory system works, lived in London during his most important work. His home stood at an unknown site in the near vicinity of St. Martin Ludgate Church on Ludgate Hill (the City). He was chief physician from 1609 to 1643 at St. Bartholomew's Hospital, largely rebuilt on its original site in Giltspur Street.

Exhibit: The Royal College of Physicians, to which Harvey donated most of his property and personal memorabilia, preserves his surgical instruments, lecture wand and annotated books and papers. The building is located at 11 St. Andrew's Place (Camden). (Inquire at 01–935–1174 for admission information.)

(See Chapter 5, ENGLAND.)

HAYDN, FRANZ JOSEPH (1732–1809). The Austrian "father of the symphony," who composed 104 symphonies plus string quartets, oratorios and the tune that later became "Deutschland über Alles," visited London twice on concert tours, producing major works each time. "The most astonishing thing about Haydn's two London visits," wrote musicologist Richard Anthony Leonard, "is the fact that, in spite of the quantity of music he had to produce and the strenuous conditions under which he had to produce it, his work during this period is the finest of his entire career." The 12 symphonies he wrote in London for impresario Johann Peter Salomon continue to be his most frequently performed works.

In 1791 and 1792 Haydn lodged at 18 Great Pultney Street (Westminster), completing Symphony No. 94 ("Surprise") among others for the occasion of his visit. He resided at 1 Bury Street during 1794 and 1795; among the works he introduced and conducted on this tour was his Symphony No. 103 ("Drum-roll").

Exhibit: The Museum of Instruments at the Royal College of Music displays a clavichord that Haydn used during his English concert tours (see the entry on Georg Frederick Handel earlier in this chapter).

(See Chapter 1, AUSTRIA.)

HEINE, HEINRICH (1797–1856). The German lyric poet and satirist spent only a brief time in London in 1827 and thoroughly hated it. "Never send a poet to London," he afterward advised, despising in equal measure the climate, cooking, flagrant materialism and class distinctions he observed. One large reason for his discomfort was that he never bothered to learn the language, discovering to his profound disgust that "no one understands German." His three-month lodgings remain privately owned at 32 Craven Street (Westminster).

(See Chapter 3, PARIS; also Chapter 4, WEST GERMANY.)

HENRY VIII (1491–1547). An innovative, powerful and quite unscrupulous (some say psychotic)
monarch who beheaded two of his six wives and
severed the Church of England from Rome, thus
beginning the English Reformation, Henry Tudor
ruled for 38 years. The son of Henry VII and Elizabeth of York, he was born in Greenwich Palace,
also called Placentia. His own daughters, Mary I
and Elizabeth I (see the entry on Elizabeth I earlier
in this chapter), were also born at the palace and
his son, Edward VI, died there in 1553. Built during the period 1426–34, "Bella Court" was embellished and renamed Placentia Palace by Margaret of Anjou, queen of Henry VI. Henry VIII
transformed Placentia into a vast royal estate,
adding towers and halls, a jousting yard and a
large armory. He used the palace throughout his
life, and so did his heirs. There he hosted Holy
Roman Emperor Charles V in 1522 and there he
courted Anne Boleyn, his ill-fated second wife
and mother of Elizabeth I. Used as a barracks and
prison during the dictatorship of Oliver Cromwell, the derelict palace was demolished
(1662–69) by Charles II, who commissioned a
new, never completed mansion. During the late
1600s, the Royal Hospital for Seamen incorporated this so-called King Charles block and,
through the next century, added three others. The
northeastern Queen Anne block (completed 1814)
occupies the site of Placentia Palace. In 1873 the
entire complex became the Royal Naval College
and thus it remains. A vaulted crypt below Queen
Anne Block, not open to the public, is the only
visible remnant of Placentia though excavations in
1970 and 1971 revealed many traces of the old
buildings. The college, which teaches modern
military courses, displays many historic sights in
its court, painted hall and chapel, but few of them
have any association with Henry VIII. Greenwich
Park, a 180-acre complex that includes the college,
National Maritime Museum and Queen's House
(completed for Henrietta Marie, consort of
Charles I, in 1635), fronts the Thames along Romney Road in **Greenwich** (Greenwich). (College
open Friday—Wednesday, 2:30—5:00;
01-858-2154; free.)

The several palaces in the London area used by
Henry VIII included two that he seized from his
chief minister, Thomas, Cardinal Wolsey (see the
entry on Wolsey later in this chapter). Hampton
Court Palace, taken over by the king in 1525, was
begun nine years earlier by Wolsey and many of

HAMPTON COURT, PRIDE OF HENRY VIII. Begun in
1514 by Thomas, Cardinal Wolsey, Hampton Court Palace near suburban **Hampton** was seized by the king in
1525 and vastly enlarged. The present palace, no
longer used by royalty, reflects Sir Christopher Wren's
renovations during the reign of William and Mary,
though original chambers of Wolsey, Henry VIII, and five
of the king's six wives may still be seen.

his original designs and chambers survive. The
palace, a series of two-story structures, covered
about eight acres and contained about one thousand rooms of unparalleled opulence. Henry made
vast additions and alterations, including gateway
wings, moat, drawbridge, a great hall, a fountain
court, a jousting yard, tennis court, gardens and
orchards. He embellished Anne Boleyn's Gateway
during her brief reign as his queen (1533–36).
Though the Tudor state rooms were destroyed,
their elaborate entrance—the Great Watching
Chamber, built by Henry in 1536—survives. The
Haunted Gallery, according to an old tale, supposedly resounds to the ghostly screams of
Henry's fifth wife, Catherine Howard, vainly beg-
ging mercy from the scaffold. She was indeed residing there when arrested; the king, meanwhile,
was saying prayers in the Chapel Royal, which he
had lavishly transformed to its present appearance. Henry lived at Hampton with each of his
wives except the first, Catherine of Aragon. His
son, Edward VI, was born there in 1537, and his
third wife, Jane Seymour (who is also said to
haunt the corridors), died there the same year.
Later Elizabeth I suffered smallpox in the palace,
and Oliver Cromwell was stricken with his final
illness there (see the entry on Cromwell earlier in
this chapter). Charles II later designed the modern
garden layout but following his reign Hampton

Court remained virtually neglected until the accession of William and Mary. They set out to renovate the palace, employing Sir Christopher Wren for the purpose. Wren swept away most of Henry's turrets, towers and crenellations (see the entry on Wren later in this chapter). The present east front, state apartments and Banqueting House date from this period (1689–1702). George II was the last monarch to use Hampton Court as a residence; he opened the palace to public view. Some 25 royal grace-and-favor apartments are still occupied by distinguished pensioners. Hampton Court, located on Hampton Court Road one mile east of **Hampton** (Richmond upon Thames), is operated by the Department of the Environment. (Open March, April, October, Monday—Saturday 9:30—5:00, Sunday 2:00—5:00; May—September, Monday—Saturday 9:30—6:00, Sunday 11:00—6:00; November—February, Monday—Saturday 9:30—4:00, Sunday 2:00—4:00; 01-977-8441; courtyards free, state apartments admission.)

In 1529, Whitehall Palace, Wolsey's second London residence, was also confiscated by Henry VIII for his own use. Originally a mansion for the archbishop of York in 1240, "York Place" passed by bequest to the see of York. Wolsey, as archbishop and cardinal, acquired it in 1514 and enlarged the estate to 23 acres in London's present Whitehall district (Westminster). The king renamed it "Whitehall" and continued to build, embellish and expand the palace on a lavish scale. During his reign, Whitehall extended from modern Trafalgar Square south to Westminster Hall, and from the Thames west to St. James's Park—an area that still holds the seat of British government and numerous official buildings. Whitehall Palace, however, was not a discrete structure but an intricate conglomeration of manor houses, offices and courtyards that grew with no apparent planning or direction. Henry brought Anne Boleyn there in 1533, and he married Jane Seymour there three years later. Henry VIII died at Whitehall, a savage, swollen creature with festering sores who bore no resemblance to the handsome, idealistic king of 1510. Fire devastated the original 1581 Banqueting House, familiar to Elizabeth I, in 1619. Rebuilt by James I in 1622, this is the only building that survives from the later Whitehall complex. Charles I stepped from a window of this structure to his execution in 1649; and his successor, Lord Protector Oliver Cromwell, died there in 1658.

William of Orange accepted the crown of England there in 1689 and was the last monarch to reside at Whitehall. Fire swept and leveled Whitehall Palace, except for the Banqueting House, in 1698. Today the Banqueting House, splendidly designed by Inigo Jones, stands empty between Horseguards Avenue and Richmond Terrace after almost 400 years of hosting lavish ceremonials, then serving as a royal chapel and museum. When the English killed their king Charles I, "this event changed the character of the building," wrote Jane Murray. "It has never been simply a banqueting house since; and there has been some uncertainty about what to use it for." (Open Tuesday—Saturday 10:00—5:00, Sunday 2:00—5:00; 01-212-4785; admission.) The only Tudor remnants of Whitehall Palace that remain are a few walls and windows in a small quadrangle behind the Old Treasury building off Downing Street.

The last royal residence built in London was St. James's Palace, corner of St. James's Street and Pall Mall (Westminster). Henry VIII chose the site especially for Anne Boleyn and demolished a leper hospital dedicated to St. James the Less to accommodate the building. According to antiquary John Stow, he "built there a goodly manor, annexing thereunto a park, closed about with a wall of brick now called St. James's Park, serving indifferently to the said manor and to the manor or palace of White Hall." Henry built his red-brick, turreted palace around four courts in 1532. Fire destroyed the east wing in 1809. The only surviving parts of the palace that remain unchanged are the gate house at the bottom of St. James's Street and the Chapel Royal with its Holbein ceiling. Until Whitehall Palace burned, St. James's served as a relatively small and simple pied-à-terre for the monarchs, but from 1698 to 1861 it functioned as the sovereign's official London residence. Henry's daughter, Mary I, died there in 1558, and James III ("the Old Pretender") and Charles II were born there. Charles I spent his last night before execution there in 1649; and William III and Mary, Victoria and Prince Albert, and George V and Mary of Teck were all married in the Chapel Royal. The first three Georges and their mistresses lived there, but Victoria abandoned it as a royal residence in 1837, the year she became queen. Edward VIII, however, occupied York House, part of the complex, and Mary, the widow of George V, lived at Clarence House, another portion, until her death in 1953. Today, Elizabeth, the queen mother, lives at Clarence House. While foreign ambassadors are still formally accredited to the Court of St. James, they have no actual duties there. Houses and apartments therein remain largely occupied by members of the royal household staff. State rooms, though rarely used, remain closed to the public. Visitors may view the buildings via the inner courtyards, however, and attend Sunday service in the Chapel Royal. Henry VIII drained St. James's Park from a virtual swamp and stocked deer there. James I and Charles II introduced exotic animals and birds, and the long lake with its island remains a refuge for pelicans and waterfowl. (Park always open.)

Henry and his first wife, Catherine of Aragon, frequented Richmond Palace, **Richmond** (Richmond upon Thames), royal residence through six reigns, during the 1520s. The first palace overlooking the Tudor jousting ground that is now Richmond Green was a 12th-century manor which was enlarged by Edward III. He died there in 1377 and the manor was demolished in 1394. A second palace called "Shene," begun by Henry V, was completed by Edward IV and confiscated from his queen, Elizabeth Woodville, by Henry VII. In 1499 it too burned. Henry VIII's father rebuilt it on a lavish scale, naming it Richmond after one of his lordly titles. Domed towers and turrets crowned the ten-acre edifice which was by far the most splendid in England. Henry VIII died there; Elizabeth I often resided there and also died at the palace; and the future Charles I stayed there during the London plague of 1625. The palace was stripped after his execution, and by the 18th century little remained of it. Today only the outer gateway of Henry VII's palace survives. The present Old Palace, Wardrobe, and Trumpeters' House (which exiled Austrian statesman Klemens von Metternich occupied in 1849) are 18th-century structures incorporating materials salvaged from the Richmond Palace ruins. Though the buildings are not open, the Old Palace courtyards are plainly marked and visitors are free to wander. Manors in nearby Richmond Park, a longtime royal hunting preserve and now a wildlife refuge, were later occupied by George II as king and Georges V and VI and Edward VIII as princes (see the entry on Edward VIII earlier in this chapter).

Chelsea Palace, built by Henry VIII in 1537 for his third bride, Jane Seymour, stood on the site of the 1765 houses at 19-26 Cheyne Walk (Chelsea) until about 1755. The two-story brick mansion of some 30 rooms was also a childhood residence of Edward VI and Elizabeth I. After Henry's death, his widow, Catherine Parr, occupied it until her death in 1548; then Anne of Cleves, Henry's divorced fourth wife, lived there until her 1557 death. The garden extended over what is now 1-18 Cheyne Walk.

Bridewell Palace, a Norman structure restored by Henry VIII in 1522, stood on New Bridge Street near Blackfriars Bridge (the City). The king lived there with Catherine of Aragon and received Emperor Charles V there. The entire third act of Shakespeare's last play, *Henry VIII* (1614), is set at Bridewell. In 1553 Edward VI gave Bridewell to the City, which converted it to an orphanage. Rebuilt after the London fire of 1666—and again in 1829—it functioned as a prison for vagrants and prostitutes until its bad reputation finally resulted in its 1864 demolition. The 1931 Unilever House (an office building) now occupies part of this site.

Until Henry VIII took over Whitehall, the main London residence of English monarchs was Westminster Palace. Edward the Confessor built the first palace on today's Parliament Square (Westminster), just south of Westminster Bridge. William the Conqueror greatly enlarged it. In 1097 his son, William II, added Westminster Hall which is the only surviving remnant of the palace. The superb oak hammerbeam roof, commissioned by Richard II, dates from 1394. "William's palace continued for centuries," in the words of one London guidebook, "never actually being demolished but gradually disappearing beneath frequent rebuildings caused by fires of which the most devastating were those of 1298, 1512 and finally 1834." Henry VIII abandoned the palace as a royal residence after the 1512 fire. The present Palace of Westminster, seat of Parliament, dates from the years 1840–60. Bombs destroyed the House of Commons portion in 1941, but it was rebuilt by 1950. The 240 x 70-foot Westminster Hall was the scene of royal feasts and ceremonies throughout the Middle Ages. Until 1882 it served as England's chief law court. Inside this venerable structure, some of England's most eminent men—including Sir Thomas More and Charles I—stood trial for their lives (see the entry on More later in this chapter). Oliver Cromwell was inaugurated as lord protector there; and George V, George VI and Sir Winston Churchill laid in state there after their deaths. Tours throughout the palace begin at the

Norman Porch beside Victoria Tower. (Palace open Saturday, holiday Monday and following Tuesday 10:00—5:00; in August, Monday—Tuesday, Thursday 10:00—5:00; in September, Thursday 10:00—5:00; Hall open during Parliamentary recess, Monday—Friday 10:00—4:00, Saturday 10:00—5:00; during Parliamentary session when neither House is sitting, Monday—Thursday 10:00—1:30, Saturday 10:00—5:00; 01-219-3090; free.)

The foundations of moated Eltham Palace, a favorite royal resort from the time of Edward II to Elizabeth I, were recently excavated. The only part of the original palace still standing is the 100-foot-long great hall, built by Edward IV in 1480 and repaired in 1931 by the property lessee, Stephan Courtald, who also built a house within the moat. Some of the royal apartment ruins may be explored but most are inaccessible to the public. The palace was neglected by Elizabeth I, and she was the last monarch to live there. Operated by the Department of the Environment, Eltham Palace is located off Court Road in an approach road called Tilt-Yard in **Eltham** (Greenwich). (Open April—October, Thursday, Sunday 10:30—12:15, 2:15—6:00; November—March, same hours except 2:15—4:00; 01-859-2112; free.)

Until excavations began in the summer of 1959, Henry's castle of Nonsuch near **Malden** (Kingston upon Thames) was more myth than actual site. Henry built his "last and most remarkable palace" in 1538, constantly enlarging and developing the massive estate until his death. But by 1688 the palace had been demolished. Excavations in 1959 and thereafter, at the southwest end of the present Nonsuch Park in Malden Road, revealed the dimensions of the palace. The park represents only a small portion of the former grounds.

Exhibit: The increasing physical girth of the king as he aged may be traced in the remarkable collection of armor housed in the Greenwich Royal Armour gallery on the third floor of the White Tower in the Tower of London (the City). Originally a council chamber, erected by William the Conqueror and completed by William II in 1100, this room displays several of Henry's metal suits constructed at his Placentia Palace armory; they include a tournament armor of 1514 for himself and his horse, a 94-lb. suit dating from 1520, and a bright steel armor of greater girth made in 1540. A breech-loading weapon used by this sports-loving

king, one of the earliest made, is also exhibited. (See the entry on the Tower of London later in this chapter; also see the entries for Oliver Cromwell and Elizabeth I earlier in this chapter.)

(See Chapter 5, ENGLAND.)

JAMES, HENRY (1843–1916). The American-born author, a naturalized British citizen, loved London ("the most complete compendium of the world") and even enjoyed its fogs and drizzle. He made England his permanent home in 1876, settling that year in first-floor lodgings at 3 Bolton Street (Westminster), which remained his home until 1885. There he wrote *Daisy Miller* (1879), *Washington Square* (1881) and *The Portrait of a Lady* (1881), among other highly influential novels.

In 1886 he moved to a large recently built fourth-floor apartment at 34 De Vere Gardens (Kensington) which was his home until 1898. Among the works James produced there were *The Tragic Muse* (1890), *What Maisie Knew* (1897) and *The Spoils of Poynton* (1897). The building is now called "Hale House."

During his 14-year residence in the town of Rye in East Sussex, James kept winter rooms in London at the Reform Club, 104 Pall Mall (Westminster).

Because women were barred from the Reform Club, James sought other lodgings where his female secretary, Theodora Bosanquet, could help him. In 1913 he made his last permanent home at 21 Carlyle Mansions in Cheyne Walk (Chelsea), where he delighted in his two front rooms overlooking the Thames. A later occupant of this building was T. S. Eliot (see the entry on Eliot earlier in this chapter). James died in his flat there just after being awarded the Order of Merit for his support of the British cause in World War I.

(See Chapter 3, PARIS; also Chapter 5, ENGLAND; also Chapter 8, ITALY.)

JOHNSON, SAMUEL (1709–1784). An ugly, lumpy man of slovenly dress, with bad skin and atrocious table manners, Johnson never won accolades for his appearance, but his powerful, eccentric personality drew many friends, and his razor wit and intelligence made him England's foremost literary and cultural arbiter in the century following Shakespeare. Though he did not settle finally in London until 1737, his associations with the city thereafter were so minutely detailed by his disciple and biographer, James Boswell, that our historical views of 18th-century London are often framed in terms of Dr. Johnson's life and activities (see the entry on Boswell earlier in this chapter). "Johnsonian London," as Neville Braybrooke remarks, "is a phrase as vivid as Tudor or Elizabethan London." Said Johnson himself, "When a man is tired of London, he is tired of life."

His first visit, at age two and suffering from scrofula, was for the curative purpose of "the Queen's touch." Queen Anne did touch him—but, according to Boswell, "without an effect." Lodgings of the boy and his mother in 1712 were with bookseller John Nicholson at his shop, the "King's Arms," which stood at an unknown spot in Little Britain Street (the City).

Johnson occupied numerous lodgings in London from 1737 but only one survives; even many of the streets familiar to him have disappeared. The intersection of Wellington Street and The Strand now covers the site of his first room in a stay-maker's house in the now long-gone Exeter Street (Westminster). From 1738 to 1741 Johnson and his wife, Elizabeth "Tetty" Porter, lived in Boswell Court, also gone; court buildings cover this site in Carey Street opposite Serle Street.

Extreme poverty marked Johnson's next few years. In 1749 he moved to 17 Gough Square (the City), his only definitely identified surviving London residence. This four-story brick house, Johnson's home for a decade, dates from the late 17th century. It was the scene of eight years of labor compiling 41,000 entries for A Dictionary of the English Language (1755); in it he defined lexicographer as "a harmless drudge." Johnson probably chose the house for the well-lighted garret which occupied the entire fourth floor; he used it as a work chamber and six copyists worked hard to keep up with him. Living rooms and bedrooms occupied the three lower floors. Johnson relics there include his work table and other furniture, paintings, prints, letters, and a first edition of the dictionary. A massive chain, mute testimony to his phobias, still guards the front door. Sir Joshua Reynolds, the painter, was a frequent guest after Tetty Johnson's death in 1752. The dwelling, which afterward suffered long periods of neglect, was restored in 1911 and is now operated by Dr. Johnson's House Trust. Bomb damage during World War II was repaired, and today the house presents a clear picture of Johnson's domestic environment. (Open May—September, Monday—Saturday 11:00—5:30; October—April, Monday—Saturday 11:00—5:00; 01–353–3745; admission.)

Johnson's beloved wife, Tetty, 21 years his senior, suffered from increasing ill health as well as probable alcoholism and drug addiction. For several years before her death she lived apart from Johnson at Priory House in Hampstead (Camden), where he frequently visited her. He wrote The Vanity of Human Wishes (1749) there. Located opposite Frognal Lane, the house was demolished in 1925.

Also in Camden, Johnson lodged during 1759 and 1760 in attic chambers at 2 Staple Inn, which stood in the first court of the former Inn of Chancery. He is believed to have written his novel Rasselas (1759) there in a single week in order to pay his mother's funeral expenses—though he may have completed the book at Gough Square before he moved. The area, now restored, suffered heavy bomb damage during World War II.

From 1760 to 1765, Johnson resided at 1 Inner Temple Lane, the gated street opposite Chancery Lane, a site on the corner of Fleet Street (the City) now occupied by Johnson's Buildings.

Johnson frequently visited and stayed at the town house of his friends Henry and Hester Thrale in Southwark from the mid–1760s to 1782. This dwelling, which Johnson considered his second home and where he worked on his Lives of the English Poets (1779–81), stood near Bankend in Park Street.

With an assorted group of eccentrics and dependents that he had collected as housemates, Johnson moved in 1765 to "a good house" at 7 Johnson's Court, off Fleet Street (the City), his home until 1776. The present house on the site dates from a later period. Johnson wrote A Journey to the Western Islands of Scotland (1775) there. In 1776 he moved to his last address at 8 Bolt Court off Gough Square, where he finished Lives of the English Poets and enjoyed a garden and the nursing attentions of novelist Fanny Burney. Johnson died in this house, now long gone.

From 1766 until his death, he often journeyed to the Thrales' large country house, Streatham Park in **Streatham** (Lambeth). Sites of the kitchen garden, where Johnson built an oven and conducted chemistry experiments, and the house itself have been built over on Thrale Road. The guest cottage that Johnson occupied, however, was rescued and re-erected in 1968 on the grounds of Kenwood House (The Iveagh Bequest), an art museum operated by the Greater London Council. The cottage may be viewed from the outside. Kenwood House is located off Hampstead Lane on the north edge of Hampstead Heath, Hampstead (Camden; grounds open daily; 01–348–1286; free).

Johnson tomb: Westminster Abbey (Westminster).

Exhibits: Most of what we know about Johnson comes from his table talk via James Boswell. A great lover of informal gatherings or "clubs"—we would call them literary "bull sessions"—Johnson organized selected groups of men at various times throughout his London years and presided at numerous favorite pubs and taverns, providing Boswell with reams of reportage. Probably nobody's conversation has been so assiduously recorded before or since. Most of the Johnsonian meeting places have long since disappeared. Two that survive include Ye Olde Cheshire Cheese in Wine Office Court off 145 Fleet Street (the City) and Ye Olde Cocke Tavern at 22 Fleet Street (rebuilt 1887). Though Boswell never mentioned the former, which was built in 1667, it is reasonable to assume Johnson's patronage during his Gough Square years, and his supposed seat is marked with a plaque. The chair from which he held forth at Ye Olde Cocke Tavern is now displayed in his Gough Square house (see above).

(See Chapter 5, ENGLAND.)

JONSON, BENJAMIN ("BEN") (1572–1637). The prominent Elizabethan playwright, a London native, left few identifiable sites for historians to mark and none of his homes or lodgings survive. A house in Northumberland Avenue (Westminster) was his probable birth site.

In 1597 he was imprisoned for almost three months at the Old Marshalsea Prison (Southwark; see the entry on Charles Dickens earlier in this chapter) for collaborating on *The Isle of Dogs* (1597), "a lewd plaie . . . contaynge very seditious and sclandrous matter." He again went to prison—this time Newgate (see the entry on Daniel Defoe earlier in this chapter)—in 1598 for killing a fellow actor in a duel but narrowly escaped execution and was freed after forfeiting his property.

He apparently lived in the Blackfriars area of the City from 1607 to 1616, probably in the vicinity of the 1596 Blackfriars Theatre, which stood at the present site of Playhouse Yard and Blackfriars Lane.

By the late 1620s he was living in his last home, a small cottage located between St. Margaret's Church and Westminster Abbey in St. Margaret Street (Westminster), where he died. Tradition says he was buried upright in Poets' Corner, Westminster Abbey, so as to gain a head start on resurrection day.

KEATS, JOHN (1795–1821). The Romantic poet, a London native educated as a physician, was born at 85 Moorgate (the City). Site of the Swan and Hoop Livery Stables owned by his maternal grandfather, it was Keats's home until about 1800.

In 1815 and 1816, while studying medicine at Guy's Hospital in Borough High Street (Southwark), Keats lodged alone at 8 Dean Street, only a remnant of which remains as Stainer Street. He moved to St. Thomas Street over a candlemaker's shop in 1816.

Later the same year he resided with his brothers at 76-78 Cheapside (the City), a house that arched over a passage leading to Bird-in-Hand Court. There he wrote most of his first collection of *Poems* (1817). During this period he visited a display of the recently imported Elgin marbles at 137-138 Piccadilly (Westminster), which inspired his notable "Ode on a Grecian Urn" (1819).

Keats gave up medicine and in 1817 and 1818 occupied a tall, narrow house at 1 Well Walk, Hampstead (Camden) with his brothers. There his older brother, Tom, died and Keats wrote part of *Endymion* (1818). The site is adjacent to the present Wall's Pub.

Later in 1818 he moved to one of the two Keats residences that survive in London, the two-story white stucco dwelling called Wentworth Place, now known as "Keats House" in Keats Grove, Hampstead (Camden). Built in 1815 as two cottages (combined in 1838), the houses were owned by Keats's friend Charles Armitage Brown. Keats and Brown occupied half of the present house, while Keats's fiancée Fanny Brawne and her mother rented the other half. Keats pined for love and wrote most of his best-known poems there, including "Ode on a Grecian Urn," "Ode to a Nightingale" (1819)—the stump of the plum tree under which he wrote this poem remains in the garden—and "The Eve of St. Agnes" (1819). He left the house during the summer of 1819 but returned in the fall. In early 1820 came the first signs of tuberculosis—the rampant wasting disease that afflicted so many Romantic poets—but, again, Keats left for the summer. By August he was back and in bad physical shape. The Brawnes nursed him for a month before the poet, on medical advice, left England for Rome and his last lodgings. The Chester Room annex on the east side of the house, added in 1838 when the Keats and Brawne cottages were joined, is now a Keats museum operated by Camden Borough Council. Restored to their 1820 appearance, the rooms contain numerous literary and personal relics of both Keats and Fanny Brawne, including letters, lecture notes, annotated books and other items. (Open Monday—Saturday 10:00—1:00, 2:00—6:00, Sunday 2:00—5:00; 01–435–2062; admission.)

Keats's 1819 lodging away from Wentworth Place was 25 Great College Street (Westminster), present site of the 1940 Church House in Dean's Yard close to Westminster Abbey.

In 1820 his summer residence was 2 Wesleyan Place (privately owned) in Kentish Town (Camden) south of Hampstead.

(See Chapter 8, ITALY.)

KEYNES, JOHN MAYNARD, LORD (1883–1946). The economist, whose revolutionary monetary philosophy and theory of government regulation has largely ruled the postwar economic policies of Western nations, occupied several London addresses in the Bloomsbury area (Camden) from the early 1900s until his death. These included flats at 38 Brunswick Square (ca. 1911) and at 3 Gower Street (ca. 1915–16). From 1916, he resided with his wife, ballet dancer Lydia Lopokova, at 46 Gordon Square. Together with No. 47, the house next door, where he used only the first-floor drawing room and rented out the rest, it remained his London home until his death.

(See Chapter 5, ENGLAND.)

KIPLING, RUDYARD (1865–1936). The versatile author of stories, ballads and novels (and Britain's primary literary apologist for imperialism) was born in India, background for much of his best-known work.

A six-story building now called "Kipling House" at 43 Villiers Street (Westminster) was the author's residence from 1889 to 1891; in the latter year his health broke and "all my Indian microbes joined hands and sang for a month in the darkness of Villiers Street." Noise, smoke and grime characterized this busy commercial area. Kipling kept mostly to his three dingy, fifth-floor rooms, distrusting London literary society and writing tirelessly until two or three in the morning. "Never was life so utterly isolated," he reported. "I must confess I enjoy it, though there are times when I feel utterly lonely. But then I can watch the fire, and weave tales, and dream dreams." In these rooms (numbers 16, 17, and 18) Kipling wrote *The Light that Failed* (1890) and *Barrack Room Ballads* (1892).

From 1892 until his death, Kipling's chief London residence was Brown's Hotel at 17-24 Dover Street (Westminster). The hotel's Kipling Room commemorates his many visits. The Kipling Society at 18 Northumberland Avenue may be contacted for further information (01–930–6733).

(See Chapter 5, ENGLAND.)

LAWRENCE, DAVID HERBERT (1885–1930). The novelist resided at 12 Colworth Road, **East Croydon** (Croydon), from 1908 to 1911 while teaching at what is now the Davidson Road Secondary Modern School. At night, he wrote verse and his first novel, *The White Peacock* (1911). In 1911, he moved to 16 Colworth Road and lodged with the John W. Jones family, where they all shared a small, bare kitchen without electricity. These identical brick and concrete houses remain privately owned.

The writer's later London addresses included 9 Selwood Terrace (Kensington) in 1914–15 and 1 Byron Villas, a two-story brick house in the Vale of Health, Hampstead (Camden). The latter was his first married home with his German-born wife, Frieda von Richthofen. They lived in ground-floor rooms there for five months (1915), enduring official harassment for their resistance to World War I and prosecution for Lawrence's novel *The Rainbow* (1915), suppressed as obscene. "It is the end of my writing for England," he finally declared. Subsequent lodgings in 1917 were 138 Earl's Court Square (Kensington); and 44 Mecklenburgh Square (Camden), a flat loaned to the couple by American poet Hilda Doolittle ("H.D.") and their residence until 1918. This was their last London home.

(See Chapter 2, FRANCE; also Chapter 5, ENGLAND; also Chapter 8, ITALY.)

LAWRENCE, THOMAS EDWARD (1888–1935). Soldier, adventurer and author, "Lawrence of Arabia" was a complex, high-strung man of enormous paradoxes and eccentric behaviors. "I think I had a mental breakdown," he reflected about his stay at 14 Barton Street (Westminster) in 1920. In this three-story brick house, dating from 1722, Lawrence worked on a third version of *The Seven Pillars of Wisdom* (1926); he had lost the first draft while changing trains and burned the second. He led a characteristically solitary existence, shunning publicity, sleeping days and writing at night; deeply depressed, he was haunted with a sense of failure that never entirely lifted. Lawrence kept this attic apartment until 1928 as his occasional London residence.

(See Chapter 5, ENGLAND; also Chapter 7, WALES.)

LENIN, VLADIMIR (1870–1924). The Russian Bolshevik leader resided in London during 1902 and 1903 during his exile from czarist Russia. His apartment site, where he and his wife Nadezhda Krupskaya lodged as Mr. and Mrs. Jacob Richter, is now part of the Royal Scot Hotel, 100 King's Cross Road (Islington), and is marked with a plaque.

(See Chapter 1, SWITZERLAND; also Chapter 3, PARIS; also Chapter 4, EAST GERMANY, WEST GERMANY, BELGIUM, FINLAND.)

LINNAEUS, CAROLUS (1707–1778).

Exhibit: Carl von Linné (Linnaeus was the Latinized name he preferred), the Swedish botanist who founded the system of binomial nomenclature, the basis of modern taxonomic classification in biology, left huge collections of preserved plants, dried fishes, insects and shells. Most of this material plus manuscripts, letters and books was bought from his estate in 1784 and remains intact in the Linnean Society of London. It is said that a photographer making a photo record of the collection in 1940 was stung on the arm by a nettle dried and mounted almost 200 years earlier. The Linnean Society, located in the west wing of Burlington House and part of the Royal Academy of Arts, displays part of the botanic collection (some 19,000 sheets of pressed plants) assembled by the scientist in formulating his *Systema Naturae* (1735). Burlington House is located in Piccadilly (Westminster; see the entry on Georg Frederick Handel earlier in this chapter). (Open daily 10:00—6:00; 01–734–1040; admission.)

(See Chapter 4, THE NETHERLANDS, SWEDEN.)

LIVINGSTONE, DAVID (1813–1873).

Livingstone tomb: Westminster Abbey (Westminster).

Exhibit: Relics of the Scottish-born missionary and explorer are held at the Royal Geographical Society, Exhibition and Kensington roads (Kensington). Admission is by permission of the director (01–589–0648).

(See Chapter 7, SCOTLAND; also Chapter 8, PORTUGAL.)

LLOYD GEORGE, DAVID (1863–1945). British prime minister during and after World War I, the "Welsh wizard" resided at many London addresses throughout his almost six decades of public life. From 1893 to 1899 he lodged and occasionally sublet a flat at 30 Palace Mansions, Addison Road (Kensington).

His next home, from 1899 to 1903, was 179 Trinity Road (Wandsworth); he then moved to 3 Routh Road. It was here that his eldest daughter died in 1907, plunging him into such grief that he could not bring himself to enter the house again.

In 1907 and 1908 he lived at 5 Cheyne Place (Chelsea).

As chancellor of the exchequer from 1908 to 1915, he lived in the official treasury residence at 11 Downing Street (Westminster), where visitors noted that he spoke Welsh among his family and domestic help. As prime minister from 1916 to 1922, Lloyd George resided in the next-door house, 10 Downing Street; Sir Winston Churchill eventually succeeded him at both Downing Street houses (see the entries on Churchill and Benjamin Disraeli earlier in this chapter).

From about 1923 Lloyd George lived at 10 Cheyne Walk (Chelsea); and finally, from the later 1920s until his death, made his London home at 2 Addison Road (Kensington).

(See Chapter 5, ENGLAND; also Chapter 7, WALES.)

MALTHUS, THOMAS ROBERT (1766–1834). Trained as a cleric, the economist and teacher addressed the social problems of poverty through his widely influential *Essay on the Principle of Population* (1798). Though he apparently wrote the work in London, precisely where remains unknown. He is known to have resided in a series of garrets during the late 1700s and early 1800s, and apparently made 57 Great Russell Street (Camden)—the office and residence of his friend, solicitor William

Bray—his London base and occasional lodging about 1800. He never lived in London after 1805, though he often visited the city.

(See Chapter 5, ENGLAND.)

MARCONI, GUGLIELMO (1874–1937). In order to find anyone interested in his epochal development of long-distance wireless telegraphy, the Italian inventor had to go to London. With his mother he lodged at 71 Hereford Road (Kensington) in 1896 and 1897. There he gathered his equipment for demonstration to British authorities, conducted last-minute experiments in two top-floor rooms, and applied for his first patent. This three-story house remains privately owned, as does 67 Talbot Road, where he moved in 1897.

(See Chapter 5, ENGLAND; also Chapter 8, IT-ALY.)

MARLOWE, CHRISTOPHER (1564–1593). The Elizabethan playwright, second only to Shakespeare in the estimation of many drama critics, spent much of his short, violent lifetime in London—and in trouble with various authorities—but his addresses remain mostly unknown. In 1589, he lodged in Norton Folgate (the City) with poet Thomas Watson. Later that year he and Watson were arrested for suspected complicity in a murder and spent a brief period behind bars at Newgate Prison (see the entry on Daniel Defoe earlier in this chapter).

Taking refuge from the London plague in 1593, Marlowe resided with his shadowy patron, Thomas Walsingham, at Scadbury Manor, the latter's 14th-century moated mansion and 1,000-acre estate near **Chislehurst** (Bromley). Marlowe also stayed there at various intervals from 1583 and composed his unfinished poem *Hero and Leander* (1598) there. Demolished in the early 18th century, the manor house provided timbers for a large farmhouse built two miles away. When that house, in turn, was demolished, the owner of the Scadbury ruins retrieved the gigantic beams and reconstructed part of the manor's great hall with them in 1921. Today this reconstructed hall is itself deteriorating. Some of the overgrown brick walls of the original manor survive, as does the wide, picturesque moat.

The site of Eleanor Bull's tavern at **Deptford** (Lewisham), where Marlowe was murdered in a brawl (possibly set up for the purpose) remains unidentified.

Marlowe tomb: St. Nicholas Churchyard, **Deptford**.

(See Chapter 5, ENGLAND.)

MARX, KARL (1818–1883). The German economic philosopher, whose socialist theories were corrupted to form the basis of totalitarian Communism, made London his permanent home from 1849. In 1850 he and his family lived at 64 Dean Street (Westminster); the house has since been demolished. From 1851 to 1856 they resided at 28 Dean Street in a four-story building that dates from 1734. This period, according to Katy Carter, "marked the nadir of his life, both privately and publicly." Three of his six children died in the family's first-floor, two-room flat, and their poverty was so extreme that Marx sometimes had to pawn his clothes. "In the apartment," wrote one visitor at the time, "there is not one clean and good piece of furniture to be found: all is broken, tattered, and torn, everywhere clings thick dust, everywhere is in the greatest disorder." Marx was spending most of his time during these years at the British Museum (seat G7, Reading Room), researching the first volume of *Das Kapital* (1859). Only the charity of Marx's collaborator, Friedrich Engels, prevented the family's utter starvation. The building now holds a restaurant on its ground floor.[*]

In 1856, armed with a small inheritance, Marx moved his family to 46 Grafton Terrace, Kentish Town (Camden); and in 1863 to 1 Maitland Park Road, which was their home until 1875. Their impoverishment continued until 1869, when Engels was able to provide Marx with a permanent income. Marx's last home from 1875 was 41 Maitland Park Road, destroyed during the London Blitz in 1940. His long-suffering wife, Jenny, died in the house in 1881, as did Marx two years later.

Marx tomb: Highgate Cemetery (Haringey).

(See Chapter 2, FRANCE; also Chapter 3, PARIS; also Chapter 4, EAST GERMANY, WEST GERMANY, BELGIUM.)

MASARYK, JAN (1886–1948). The Czech statesman and diplomat, son of Czechoslovakia's first

---

[*] There is double irony in the present situation. Not only do food aromas mock the scene of the Marx family's dire malnutrition, but when the plaque commemorating Marx was erected in 1967, the restaurant owner complained that "my clientele is the very best. . . rich people. . . nobility and royalty—and Marx was the person who wanted to get rid of them all!"

president, was apparently murdered by Communist thugs who greatly feared his civilizing influence (still too threatening for his Soviet satellite country to accept). Masaryk resided for 20 years in London as the official representative of his nation. The Czech legation, where he served as ambassador from 1925 to 1938, was located at 8-9 Grosvenor Place (Westminster). From 1939 until his death, Masaryk occupied a flat at Westminster Gardens, Marsham Street; he resided there only intermittently after the end of World War II in 1945.

MAUGHAM, WILLIAM SOMERSET (1874–1965). Sardonic tale spinner, antiromantic but enormously popular and prolific, the novelist was trained as a physician during the years 1892–97 at St. Thomas's Hospital, fronting the Thames (Lambeth). He lodged during this period at 11 Vincent Square (Westminster), a house now occupied by the Church Commission. His first novel, *Liza of Lambeth* (1897), was written during this time.

Though amply qualified to do so, Maugham never practiced medicine after he graduated. Until his later years he wandered the world but usually retained lodgings in London for stays of greater or lesser durations. His addresses included 27 Carlisle Mansions (Westminster) during the years 1900–05; and 23 Mount Street during the years 1908–11. In 1911 Maugham bought the 1734 Georgian mansion at 6 Chesterfield Street, a place which, according to biographer Ted Morgan, "established him as a member of a privileged minority." Maugham married Syrie Barnardo while living there, and it became their home until 1919. He worked in a small ground-floor study and there produced his best-known novel, *Of Human Bondage* (1915).

From 1919 to 1923 the couple lived at 2 Wyndham Place (Westminster), a four-story Georgian house; then from 1923 to 1925 in a five-story house with slate mansard roof at 43 Bryanston Square.

Maugham's last London home (1925–27) was 213 King's Road, with an annex at 72 Glebe Place (Chelsea). By this time his marriage was all but ended, and he occupied only the top floor of the house bought for his wife.

During Maugham's later visits to London—and especially in 1940 while awaiting government journalistic assignments—a favorite residence was the Dorchester Hotel in Park Lane (Westminster).

(See Chapter 2, FRANCE; also Chapter 3, PARIS; also Chapter 5, ENGLAND.)

MILL, JOHN STUART (1806–1873). A London native who resided there for most of his life, the philosopher and economist was born at 12 Rodney Terrace, now Rodney Road (Camden), his home until 1810. His father, James Mill, began educating the lad in Greek there at age three. The house was later demolished.

From 1814 until 1831 Mill lived with his parents at what is now 40 Queen Anne's Gate (Westminster), a house provided by Jeremy Bentham, Mill's mentor and chief philosophical influence, who lived next door (see the entry on Bentham earlier in this chapter). Earlier, in 1810, the Mills had briefly occupied the garden cottage on this property; poet John Milton had lived there from 1651 to 1660 (see the entry on Milton below).

From 1831 to 1836 the Mill family resided in a large villa in what is now Vicarage Gate off Church Street (Kensington); the redoubtable James Mill died there in 1836. Mill lived from 1836 through the 1840s at 18 Kensington Square, supporting his mother and two sisters by working as a clerk for the East India Company (site located at Fenchurch and Leadenhall streets, the City). There he wrote his best-known treatise, *Principles of Political Economy* (1848).

In 1851 Mill married Harriet Taylor, his intimate friend of 20 years, after she became a widow. He bought a square brick house at Blackheath Park in **Greenwich** (Greenwich) and made it his home for two decades. His last London home, where he lived as a widower (1871–73), was 10 Albert Mansions, Victoria Street (Westminster). Neither of these later dwellings survive.

(See Chapter 2, FRANCE; also Chapter 5, ENGLAND.)

MILTON, JOHN (1608–1674). As both a Renaissance humanist and a Puritan, the poet's life exemplified immense contrasts and paradoxes. Milton was a London native, yet as Neville Braybrooke observed, "like Bacon [he] is more admired than loved; his mark on English poetry is immortal, but his mark in the capital is limited to a bust in (new) Bread Street." None of his many lodgings (see Name Index and Gazetteer) have survived; the London Milton knew was mostly destroyed by the Great Fire of 1666. His birth-place in a tenement called the "Spread Eagle" stood on the east side of Bread Street (the City) south of Cheapside, "where a small court opened up just beyond the present third doorway," according to Lois H. Fisher. This was his home until about 1632. The long-gone house became a tourist mecca during Milton's lifetime.

Milton's home from 1645 to 1647 stood on the site of 17 the Barbican (the City). His father died there. Milton tutored students at the house.

Almost totally blind by 1651, Milton moved into a "pretty garden house" in Petty France (Westminster), where his wife, Mary Powell, died the next year. Supporting four small children, the poet stayed there throughout his second marriage to Katherine Woodcock (1656–58). As a strong supporter of Oliver Cromwell, Milton fled this house in 1660 when the protectorate failed. The house, demolished in 1877, later belonged to Jeremy Bentham and was occupied briefly by John Stuart Mill and William Hazlitt (see the entries on Bentham, Cromwell and Mill earlier in this chapter).

Milton hid out in Bartholomew Close (the City) for three months in 1660 before his arrest and pardon. From 1660 to 1663 he resided in a house at the end of Jewin Street, where he began his epic poem *Paradise Lost* (1667); this no longer extant street was located off Aldergate Street. It is said that he began work at 4:00 a.m. and, if kept waiting by his scribe, would roar "I want to be milked!" At a house in the present Bunhill Row, he finished *Paradise Lost* and also wrote *Paradise Regained* (1671) and *Samson Agonistes* (1671). Except for two brief periods, Milton resided there from 1663 until he died. The house stood somewhere between the present Dufferin and Chiswell streets.

(See Chapter 5, ENGLAND.)

MORE, SIR THOMAS (1478–1535). One of the numerous victims of Tudor royalty who placed allegiance to the king second to the pope, this remarkable scholar and statesman—a "man for all seasons"—was canonized as a saint in 1935. He dwelled in London almost all his life, but none of his early family homes remain. He was born in Milk Street (the City).

From about 1490 to 1492 he was lodged for religious training in the household of John Morton, archbishop of Canterbury, at Lambeth. Much later (1534), More's reappearance at Lambeth Palace, where he refused to swear the required oath to Henry VIII, resulted in his imprisonment (see the entry on Henry VIII earlier in this chapter). The present Lambeth Palace, residence of archbishops of Canterbury since 1262, still displays its medieval appearance despite 19th-century additions and alterations to its ancient brick walls. The gatehouse and Lollards' Tower date from the 15th century. Located in Lambeth Palace Road at the south end of Archbishop's Park, the palace admits occasional groups by appointment. (Call 01–928–8282 for information.)

After a short period in 1496 at Lincoln's Inn (Camden; see the entry on Jeremy Bentham earlier in this chapter), More lodged at the Charterhouse in Clerkenwell (Islington) while lecturing in law. The Charterhouse, a Carthusian monastery when More resided there, later became a Tudor mansion, hospital, boys' school, and finally a retirement home for friars. Henry VIII removed many of the original materials when he dissolved the monastery in 1536; the present building is thus a conglomerate of styles and time periods. More probably lived there until his 1505 marriage. The building is located north of Charterhouse Square. (Open April—July, Wednesday 2:45—5:00; admission.)

From 1505 until 1518 More resided in Bucklersbury Street (the City). Then he moved to Crosby Hall, the 15th-century mansion built by Sir John Crosby that originally stood on Crosby Square, and lived there until 1523. The relocated portion of Crosby Hall in Chelsea is the only domestic structure of More's that survives (see the entry on Richard III later in this chapter). There he wrote his best-known work, *Utopia* (1516).

More's last property was a large elaborate estate where he built a two-story brick house with inner courtyard, large gardens, orchards and a zoo. His house stood astride the present Beaufort Street on the present site of Covent Chapel (Chelsea). Noted visitors he welcomed there included Henry VIII, whose genial informality hardly deceived More. "If my head could win him a castle in France, it would not fail to go," he told his son-in-law at the time. More retired to the estate after his 1532 resignation as lord chancellor and stayed, amid increasing pressure to renounce the pope, until his 1534 arrest. More saw his home confiscated by the king before his death. Known later as Beaufort House, it resided numerous later noted occupants including the Elizabethan statesmen Sir William Cecil (Lord Burghley) and his son, Sir Robert Cecil, Earl of Salisbury. The property became dilapidated and was eventually acquired by British Museum founder Sir Hans Sloane; in a widely criticized action, he demolished the house in 1740. Blocks of flats known as Beaufort Mansions now occupy much of the original estate site.

Scholars still disagree on whether More's defiance of the king was an act of piety or more a matter of ego. Confined to the Tower of London in 1534, he spent his last 14 months there writing religious treatises and resisting desperate, solicitous attempts by his family and friends to make him bend his attitude and thus save his own life. Though the confinement broke his health, he preferred what he viewed as martyrdom. A ground-floor chamber in Bell Tower is identified as More's cell, though traditional sources insist that his actual lodging was Beauchamp Tower. More was condemned to be hanged, drawn and quartered at the infamous Tyburn gibbet, but Henry VIII exercised "Tudor leniency" and permitted a more merciful beheading, which was accomplished on Tower Hill (see the entry on the Tower of London later in this chapter).

More Tomb: St. Peter ad Vincula Church, Tower of London (the City).

(See Chapter 4, BELGIUM.)

MOZART, WOLFGANG AMADEUS (1756–1791). The Austrian composer was an eight-year-old concert pianist prodigy when he visited London with his impresario father, Leopold, and his sister in 1764. The children performed for George III and gave numerous public concerts, most notably in Ranelagh Gardens alongside the Thames at Chelsea Embankment (Chelsea).

Their first lodgings were in Cecil Court (Westminster), a street now lined with book shops. They next lodged over a shop at 20 Frith Street. Both of these buildings are gone, but Mozart's next London residence at 180 Ebury Street (Chelsea) survives. The family stayed there for just seven weeks while Leopold Mozart recovered from an illness. Because complete rest and quiet were prescribed for the father, the children spent the time composing; and there Wolfgang wrote his first symphonies (K. 16, K. 19) plus six sonatas for harpsichord, which he later played for Queen Charlotte.

(See Chapter 1, AUSTRIA; also Chapter 3, PARIS; also Chapter 4, WEST GERMANY.)

NANSEN, FRIDTJOF (1861–1930). Norwegian polar explorer and international statesman, Nansen served as his country's ambassador to Britain from 1906 to 1908. During this period he resided in the Norwegian Embassy at 25 Belgrave Square (Westminster).

(See Chapter 4, NORWAY.)

NELSON, HORATIO, LORD (1758–1805). One of England's greatest military heroes, whose victory in the 1805 Battle of Trafalgar broke Franco-Spanish control of the seas during the Napoleonic wars, the admiral resided in almost a dozen London dwellings at intervals from 1783. In 1787 he lived at 5 Cavendish Square (Westminster). Probably his only other residence which still survives is 103 New Bond Street, where he convalesced in great pain from the amputation of his right arm during the winter of 1797–98. Nelson's arm had been shattered in the Battle of Tenerife, but he made a complete recovery at this address and soon rejoined his Mediterranean fleet. The four-story building is now occupied by a shop on the ground floor. From 1799 Nelson's London addresses were determined by proximity to those of Lady Emma Hamilton, his mistress, and her befuddled husband, Sir William Hamilton. One such lodging was 147 New Bond Street—the Hamiltons lived at 150. Both houses are now gone.

Nothing remains of Nelson's farm on the River Wandle near **Wimbledon** (Merton). Merton Place, as it was known, was acquired by Lady Hamilton in 1801 for the *menage à trois*; after Sir William's death in 1803, the couple made it their permanent home. Nelson kept a large menagerie and made enthusiastic plans for developing the estate, while Lady Hamilton entertained lavishly during his frequent absences. There, he said, stood "all which I hold dear in this world." The Battle of Trafalgar aborted his retirement schemes, however, and Lady Hamilton, left with virtually nothing after his death, sold the estate in 1808. The house stood near the west end of Reform Place toward Nelson Grove Road at the present site of Merton Place apartments. Boundaries of the estate are marked by the present Quicks, Merton, Morden, Haydons and Abbey roads, with the old well located in a back yard at 61 High Street. The house was destroyed about 1840.

Nelson's London residence during his last year was Gordon's Hotel at 44 Albemarle Street (Westminster). He spent his last night in England, however, at Walker's Hotel, 33 Dean Street, just before the Battle of Trafalgar which cost his life. Both buildings are gone.

Nelson tomb: St. Paul's Cathedral (the City).

Exhibits: The Public Record Office Museum in Chancery Lane (Westminster) displays the Trafalgar log of Nelson's flagship *HMS Victory*. (Open Monday—Friday 1:00—4:00; 01–405–0741; free.) Two more *Victory* logbooks and a Nelson letter may be seen in the manuscript saloon in the Granville Library, ground floor east, at the British Library, Great Russell Street (Camden). (Open Monday—Saturday 10:00—5:00, Sunday 2:30—6:00; 01–636–1544; free.)

Madame Tussaud's famous waxworks museum in Marylebone Road (Westminster) presents a realistic "you are there" exhibit of the Battle of Trafalgar, leaving little of the smoke and sound effects to one's imagination. (Open daily, 10:00—6:00; 01–935–6861; admission.)

The Nelson Galleries of the National Maritime Museum in **Greenwich** (Greenwich) exhibit a variety of relics including Nelson's uniform worn at Trafalgar, his eyeshield and left-hand gloves. (See the entry on Sir Francis Drake earlier in this chapter).

(See Chapter 5, ENGLAND; also Chapter 7, WALES.)

NEWTON, SIR ISAAC (1642–1727). The great mathematician's major discoveries were behind him in 1689 when he first resided at intervals in London. Appointed Master of the Mint in 1693, he moved permanently from Cambridge and occupied quarters on the west side of Bell Tower in the Tower of London (see the entry on the Tower of London later in this chapter).

In 1697 Newton moved to 88 Jermyn Street (Westminster), his home until 1700; from that year until 1709, the period when he served as president of the Royal Society, he resided next door at 87 Jermyn Street, now with an altered front. His niece, Catherine Barton, who kept house for him, recalled his characteristic absent-mindedness: "his gruel, or milk and eggs that was carried to him warm for supper, wd eat cold for breakfast."

From 1710 to 1724, now a scholar of formidable reputation, Newton lived at 35 St. Martin's Street

(Westminster), where he used a rooftop garret for a private observatory. Novelist Fanny Burney later wrote *Evelina* (1778) there. The building is now occupied by the Westminster Reference Library (open Monday—Saturday, free).

WHERE NEWTON VIEWED THE STARS. Tucked between taller buildings, 35 St. Martin's Street, where Sir Isaac Newton resided from 1710 to 1724, was probably the highest structure in the neighborhood at the time. He used a rooftop garret for his observatory. A library now occupies the scientist's former home.

Suffering from several ailments, Newton resided during his last three years in Kensington Church Street (Kensington). Bellingham Mansions occupy the site of the then rural house where Newton died.

Newton tomb: Westminster Abbey (Westminster).

Exhibit: Impatient with the politics and fragile egos he encountered at the Royal Society, Newton withdrew from this company of scientists early in his career; later, however, he not only led the organization but rescued it from bankruptcy and established its procedures on a sound practical and systematic basis. From 1710 to 1780, the Society was located in a house at the far end of Crane

Court (the City), where Newton presided over meetings from 1703 until his death. Today the Royal Society's address is 6-9 Carlton House Terrace (Westminster). Newton's reflecting telescope, which he made in 1671, his watch, a sundial he made as a boy at Woolsthorpe, a lock of his white hair, and his *Principia Mathematica* (1687) manuscript are displayed. (Inquire at Royal Society for admission information.)

(See Chapter 5, ENGLAND.)

NIGHTINGALE, FLORENCE (1820–1910). Almost singlehandedly, Nightingale raised nursing from a squalid, undesirable job to a skilled profession. Her only surviving London home stands privately owned at 47 Harley Street (Westminster), her quarters in 1853–54 when she managed the Institution for the Care of Sick Gentlewomen.

After the end of the Crimean War in 1856—the war that amply demonstrated the value of scientific nursing and transformed "the lady with the lamp" into a world humanitarian—she resided mainly in London. At first she made her quarters (1856–61) in the Burlington Hotel, which stood in Old Burlington Street (Westminster). She was living there when she established the first school of nursing at St. Thomas's Hospital (Lambeth).

Her last home, from 1865, was a four-story brick house bought for her by her father at 10 South Street (Westminster). With her retinue of cats she lived quietly, serving as a government consultant and advisor on various topics. She died there after several years of infirm senility. The house has since been demolished.

(See Chapter 5, ENGLAND; also Chapter 8, ITALY.)

PENN, WILLIAM (1644–1718). The Quaker writer, preacher, colonist and founder of the American state of Pennsylvania was a London native born in the shadow of the Tower of London. On Tower Hill (the City), scene of numerous executions in the century preceding his birth and the site of a permanent gallows throughout his life, the son of Admiral Sir William Penn came into the world in a house located in tiny George Court. It ran adjacent to the old London wall on the east side of Tower Hill, somewhere in the vicinity of today's Cooper's Row. By 1655 the family was living in Tower Hill Road just north of the Tower moat. From 1660 to 1670, Penn's family residence was the Navy Office Gardens, his father's place of employment, on the east side of Seething Lane northwest of the Tower. From there, Penn was disowned by his irate father in 1663 for religious nonconformance, though later the two were reconciled. The building burned down in 1673.

Unfortunately, Penn's associations with the Tower were hardly finished. For nine months in 1668 and 1669 he was confined in the west wing of the Lieutenant's Lodgings for religious "blasphemy." "The Tower is to me the worst possible argument in the world," he said, yet it was there that he composed his best-known work, *No Cross, No Crown* (1668). (See the entry on the Tower of London later in this chapter).

Penn was twice more imprisoned in London: at Newgate for six months in 1671; and in debtors' prison at Fleet in 1708 (see the entries on Daniel Defoe and John Donne earlier in this chapter).

Dates are uncertain, but he lived for a time (probably 1701 to 1706) in a house on the southwest corner of Norfolk Street and The Strand (Westminster). Harassed by creditors and Christians of less peaceful persuasions than his own, according to one London antiquarian, "he chose the house as one he might, upon occasion, slip out by water." There too, it was said, he spied out his waiting visitors from a peephole in his door. When creditors asked to see him, his servant replied, "He has already seen thee, but does not like thee."

Exhibit: Friends' House, headquarters of the Society of Friends in Euston Road (Camden), displays documents relating to Penn and the founding of Pennsylvania. (Call 01-388-1977 for admission information.)

(See Chapter 5, ENGLAND; also Chapter 7, IRELAND.)

PEPYS, SAMUEL (1633–1703). The naval bureaucrat, famous for the uninhibited *Diary* (1825) he kept between the years 1660 and 1669 which provides a vivid picture of Restoration London, was a native of London and lived there for most of his life. His birthplace stood in Salisbury Court off Fleet Street (the City); a plaque marks the site.

Pepys began writing his noted *Diary* while living in a garret with his wife, Elizabeth, and servant, Jane, in Axe Yard (1658 to 1660). Gone since 1767, Axe Yard was located at about the present intersection of King Charles and Parliament streets (Westminster).

As a member of the Navy Board, Pepys resided on the east side of Seething Lane just north of Pepys Street (the City) from 1660 to 1679. There he recorded his observations of the London plague in 1665 and the Great Fire of 1666. He regretfully ended his *Diary* in 1669 because of failing eyesight. Intended strictly for his own use and written in his own shorthand code, it was not deciphered until almost 200 years after his death. In that same year, his wife Elizabeth died. Nothing remains of the Pepys house.

Now secretary of the admiralty and a member of Parliament, Pepys fell under suspicion of treason during the "popish plot" of 1679. He was committed to the Tower of London, where he spent three months, and narrowly escaped the type of execution he had witnessed so often on Tower Hill (see the entry on the Tower of London later in this chapter).

From about 1680 to 1687 Pepys lived at 12 Buckingham Street (Westminster). There he set about clearing his name and was reinstated to the admiralty in 1683. He moved the admiralty offices there the next year. The neighboring buildings of 13 and 14 Buckingham Street were blown up to prevent the spread of a fire in 1684. When they were rebuilt in 1687, Pepys moved his quarters to 14 Buckingham Street, and the entire row became known as York Buildings. He lived there until 1700. After his 1689 retirement, Pepys concentrated on building his 3,000-volume library and opened his rooms as an informal literary salon, hosting Fellows of the Royal Society. Today 12 Buckingham Street, a privately owned three-story building, is the only Pepys residence that survives in London though it is much altered. Demolished and rebuilt again in 1791, 14 Buckingham Street became the later residence of chemist Sir Humphry Davy.

In failing health by 1700, Pepys gave up his Westminster lodgings and moved to the house of his former servant, William Hewer, at Clapham (Lambeth). A mansion built by the architect of the Houses of Parliament, Sir Charles Barry, the Elms now occupies the site of Hewer's "wonderfully well-furnished house" where Pepys died. It faces the common at 29 North Side and is now part of a residential center called the Hostel of God.

Pepys tomb: St. Olave's Church (the City).

Exhibits: Two pubs display Pepys memorabilia. Prince Henry's Room at 17 Fleet Street (the City) is an upstairs, Tudor-paneled tavern filled with reminders of the convivial diarist. (Open Monday—Friday 1:45—5:00, Saturday 1:45—4:30; 01-353-7323.) The Samuel Pepys on Brooks Wharf, 48 Upper Thames Street, occupies a former warehouse. (Open same hours as above; 01-248-3514.)

(See Chapter 5, ENGLAND.)

POPE, ALEXANDER (1688–1744). A London native, the poet included numerous references to London locations and street names in his works. Stunted and crippled by Pott's disease though he was, Pope became the virtual literary dictator of his neoclassical age. He was born in a house in Plough Court off Lombard Street (the City); a plaque identifies the site.

Pope occupied many London lodgings throughout his life. From 1716 to 1718 he lived with his parents at what is now the Fox and Hounds & Mawson Arms inn at 110 Chiswick Lane South in **Chiswick** (Hounslow), where he worked on his translation of Homer's *Iliad* (1715–20). His father died there in 1717.

In 1718 Pope leased a two-story villa with five adjacent acres at **Twickenham** (Richmond upon Thames) and made this house, located in Crossdeep, his lifelong home. A passionate landscape gardener, he spent much time embellishing his grounds, which extended across the present route 310. It is said that he planted the first weeping willow tree in England on his frequently flooded lawn alongside the Thames. To link his road-divided gardens, Pope built a connecting tunnel beneath the road, a grotto of rock slabs and crystals, and the idea soon became fashionable. Pope wrote his most important works at this estate, including *The Dunciad* (1728), *Moral Essays* (1731–35) and *An Essay on Man* (1733–34). Known as "the wasp of Twickenham" for his literary attacks on friends, he still entertained numerous famed guests, conducting them proudly over his grounds. Pope died at the house. In the early 19th century, the owner of his original house demolished it because of her annoyance at the crowds of literary pilgrims who came. Today the Victorian house identified as "Pope's Villa" occupies the same site (the third successive house to do so). St. Catherine's Convent for Girls now occupies this house and property, including the still extant grotto. (Grotto open Saturday, by permission; 01-892-1201; donation.)

Pope's part-time inner London residence from about 1718 was a house he bought at 9 Berkeley Square (Westminster), now long gone. There, just before moving to Twickenham, he penned his "Farewell to London" ("Dear, damn'd distracting town, farewell!")

Pope tomb: Parish Church, **Twickenham**. (See Chapter 5, ENGLAND.)

PURCELL, HENRY (1657?–1695). Probably England's foremost native composer and an influential force on 20th-century music, Purcell was born in London and apparently lived in Westminster throughout his short life. None of his homes have survived. His birthplace was probably a house located on the south side of Great Almonry—a long-gone residential area that stood just south of today's Tothill Street—around the site of a large parking area near the Tothill and Victoria Street intersections. From about 1680 to 1684, Purcell resided in St. Ann's Street near Old Pye Street. He occupied a house in Bowling Street (formerly Bowling Alley) from 1684 to 1692. Purcell's last home, from 1692, stood in Marsham Street.

Purcell tomb: Westminster Abbey (Westminster).

Exhibit: Purcell was chief organist at the church of St. Clement Eastcheap in King William Street (the City). This brick church, designed in 1683 by Sir Christopher Wren, claims to be the source of the "oranges and lemons" nursery rhyme about the bells of "St. Clemens," a reminder of the Spanish tradesmen who hawked citrus fruit from nearby London Bridge. The finely carved organ played by Purcell is still in the church. (Usually open weekdays from 10:00; free.)

RALEIGH, SIR WALTER (1554?–1618). The adventurer, colonizer, courtier, historian and poet—a favorite of Elizabeth I until displaced in her affections—first came to London in 1576, when he resided in the Middle Temple precincts (see the entry on Elizabeth I and Henry Fielding earlier in this chapter).

In 1583 Elizabeth granted Raleigh a large 14th-century manor called Durham House. It occupied the area from Adelphi Terrace to The Strand, and from Robert Street east to Adam Street—a site that now includes the massive Adelphi block south of John Adams Street (Westminster). Once the official residence of the bishops of Durham, the mansion was also a childhood home of soldier-poet Sir Philip Sidney. Raleigh's turret study overlooked the Thames, a prospect John Aubrey called "as pleasant perhaps as any in the world." This was Raleigh's London home until James I compelled him to relinquish it and committed him to the Tower in 1603. The house was destroyed in the late 1700s.

Though personable and able, Raleigh was also a tireless political manipulator—and a not very skillful one at times. His testing of royal tolerance landed him in the Tower of London on three separate occasions. In 1592 an enraged Elizabeth sent him there for five weeks after she discovered his secret marriage to one of her maids of honor, Elizabeth Throckmorton. Raleigh occupied a chamber in St. Thomas's Tower over Traitor's Gate, a tower built by Henry III and restored in 1866. James I imprisoned Raleigh in the Tower for plotting against him and ever afterward bore him a grudge despite Raleigh's wide popularity. Raleigh was condemned to death in 1603 on this charge, but his sentence was reprieved and he spent the next 12 years in the Bloody Tower, where he maintained upper-story apartments along with his wife and two black servants. His laboratory hut, a former hen house in the Tower garden where he experimented with chemicals and compounded drugs, became a meeting place for eminent guests including Ben Jonson (see the entry on Jonson earlier in this chapter) and even members of the royal family, despite the king's rage. Crowds gathered below the outside walls to catch a glimpse of Raleigh during his daily walk on the parapet between the Bloody Tower and the Lieutenant's Lodging—a route that his previous monarch, Elizabeth, had come to know well before she became queen. In his Tower apartments, Raleigh wrote poetry and began his *History of the World* (1614), of which he completed one volume. In 1604, the king, angered at Raleigh's popular following, ordered him to be treated like the prisoner he was supposed to be. Raleigh's privileges were withdrawn, and a warden with an old grudge against him replaced the former sympathetic lieutenant. The prisoner began a drastic physical decline. Today Raleigh's chambers in the Bloody Tower, the upper part of which has been rebuilt after severe deterioration, display his pocket watch plus a copy of the *History* he wrote there.

Apparently, Raleigh suffered a stroke in 1606 and was allowed to recuperate in a room built for him adjacent to his garden laboratory. Among his noted visitors was Capt. John Smith (see the entry on Smith later in this chapter). Later he was moved to lodgings in the Brick Tower on the northeast wall, which he occupied until he was released in 1616 in order to lead an expedition to Guiana. This tower was completely destroyed in an 1841 fire but was soon rebuilt.

On his return from what turned out to be a disastrous expedition in 1618, Raleigh tried to bluff his way out of trouble before a commission of inquiry headed by Sir Francis Bacon (see the entry on Bacon earlier in this chapter); in consequence his death sentence of 1603 was revived. He was again committed to the Tower—first to the Queen's House, then to the Wardrobe Tower, which faced the east window of the Chapel of St. John in the inner ward along the old Roman city wall. Thus King James had his vengeance at last. Raleigh met his death gallantly in Old Palace Yard (Westminster) at what is now the north end of Abingdon Street, an area consisting mostly of a parking lot. Raleigh spent his last night at the gatehouse of Dean's Yard, Westminster Abbey. This structure, demolished in 1776, stood at the present site of the red granite column memorializing Crimean War casualties. (See the entry on the Tower of London in this chapter).

Raleigh tomb: St. Margaret's Church (Westminster).

(See Chapter 5, ENGLAND; also Chapter 7, IRELAND.)

RICHARD I, COEUR DE LION (1157–1199). "One should not judge Richard as a King," wrote William Seymour, "for he was scarcely more than a chivalrous knight with a touch of the troubadour, called by birth to rule and by inclination to fight." He spoke no English, spent as little time as possible in England, and devoted most of his short life to plundering England's treasury in order to protect his French dominions. His defenders have been mainly literary romantics, to whom he has always cut an imposing (if bloodthirsty) figure.

A son in the rebellious flock of Henry II and Eleanor of Aquitaine, Richard spent only weeks in London during his 10-year reign (1189–99). His brief residence after his coronation was Westminster Palace (see the entry on Henry VIII earlier in this chapter).

(See Chapter 1, AUSTRIA; also Chapter 2, FRANCE; also chapter 4, WEST GERMANY; also Chapter 5, ENGLAND.)

RICHARD III (1452–1485). England's last Yorkist monarch reigned only 25 months (1483–85). The brother of Edward IV, he served briefly as regent for his young nephew, Edward V, before seizing the throne, imprisoning the king and his brother in the Tower of London and probably ordering the youngsters' murder there in 1483. (Historians still debate Richard's responsibility for the deaths, though circumstantial evidence—especially after discovery of two boys' skeletons beneath a White Tower stair in 1674—indicates that he may well have resembled the ambitious villain portrayed by Shakespeare and Tudor propaganda. Sir Winston Churchill, for one, believed him guilty. Richard still has his stout defenders, however; there is no solid proof either way.)

About 1475 Richard, then duke of Gloucester, either bought or rented Crosby's Palace, a manor built by Sir John Crosby in 1466 as his London residence. This structure with its great hall stood at the present site of Crosby Square off Bishopsgate (the City). Richard may have been offered the crown there in 1483. Sir Thomas More was a later resident of the house (see the entry on More earlier in this chapter). While most of the palace had disappeared by 1672, Crosby Hall survives today on a different site. Dismantled in 1908, it was re-erected at its present location in Cheyne Walk (Chelsea). During World War I, it hosted war refugees and now serves as a college hall for the British Federation of University Women. (Open Sunday—Monday, Wednesday—Friday 10:00—12:00, 2:00—5:00; Tuesday 10:00—12:00; 01–352–5354; free.)

Baynard Castle, built about 1100 by one "Baynard that came with the Conqueror" and rebuilt in 1428, became one of Richard's chief London residences as king. His predecessor, Edward IV, had also lived there. Henry VII reconstructed it, and Lady Jane Grey occupied it before her nine-day reign as queen in 1553. It was destroyed in the Great Fire of 1666. Today the Mermaid Theatre in Puddle Dock off Upper Thames Street (the City) occupies this site.

Westminster Palace (Westminster) was Richard's primary London residence (see the entry on Henry VIII earlier in this chapter).

Contact the Richard III Society, 41 Woodsford Square, Kensington (01–435–2391), for further information.

(See Chapter 5, ENGLAND.)

ROBIN HOOD (ca. 1290?–1346?). The outlaw yeoman of Nottinghamshire, subject of numerous medieval tales and ballads, probably did actually exist, though which of several possible persons he may have been remains elusive. A documentary case was made by J. W. Walker for one Robert Hood, to whom the heading dates apply. A man of that name was employed for nine months by Edward II in 1324 as a *valet de chambre* at Westminster Palace (Westminster). Edward brought others of the Sherwood Forest band there to serve him too, claims Walker. The men bedded, according to palace records, on the floor of the great hall but returned to their forest haunts the same year. Few historians would state that this Robert Hood and *the* Robin Hood were positively the same man, but it is intriguing to speculate that among the robes of state that have graced this ancient hall through the ages, a few crude ghosts in Lincoln green may stride (see the entry on Henry VIII earlier in this chapter).

(See Chapter 5, ENGLAND.)

ROSSINI, GIOACCHINO ANTONIO (1782–1868). For about eight months in 1823 and 1824, the Italian operatic composer lived at 90 Regent Street (Westminster). During this period he gave several concerts and enjoyed being lionized by London music lovers. The house is long gone.

(See Chapter 2, FRANCE; also Chapter 3, PARIS; also Chapter 8, ITALY.)

RUSKIN, JOHN (1819–1900). The influential Victorian author, art critic and historian was a London native, born at 54 East Hunter Street (Camden), which was his home to age four. This house was demolished in 1969. A marker on the present house indicates the site.

From 1823 to 1843 the family lived at 28 Herne Hill (Lambeth), a large villa where Ruskin wrote the first volume of *Modern Painters* (1843). Then, between 1843 and 1848, the year of his marriage, Ruskin lived with his parents at 163 Denmark Hill (Southwark). This large house with a verandah and portico stood on seven acres that included a stable and farmyard. There Ruskin wrote later volumes of *Modern Painters* (1846–60) and *The Stones of Venice* (1851–53). He and his wife, Euphemia Gray, also lived there until 1852, then moved to 30 Herne Hill, bought by Ruskin's father for the couple, and resided there until 1854. Even though married and living at Herne Hill, he continued to work in his parents' home during the day, expecting his wife to drive there for dinner each day. An only child and emotionally crippled by a strongly possessive mother, Ruskin could not make the marriage work. "Effie" Ruskin escaped from the unconsummated union in 1854 and received an annulment. After she fled this kind of life, Ruskin himself returned "home" and lived at Denmark Hill until 1872, after both his parents had died there. The house became a hotel called Ruskin Manor before its demolition in 1947. Ruskin Park, a 36-acre preserve commemorating the author, lies almost directly opposite this home site. Both Herne Hill dwellings were demolished in 1906.

(See Chapter 5, ENGLAND; also Chapter 7, SCOTLAND.)

RUSSELL, BERTRAND, LORD (1872–1970). Mathematician, philosopher, professional gadfly and social reformer, Russell quarreled with most of the conventional thought he encountered on three continents during his long lifetime yet somehow managed to remain the "laughing philosopher" of his generation. His contributions to humanistic thought and his stern, six-decade opposition to "studying war" have yet to be fully evaluated. Though a Nobel literary prizewinner, few recent British literary guidebooks list him. He remained much ahead of his time when he died at 97.

Though not born in London, Russell spent his boyhood there and resided there at intervals until his later years. From 1876 to 1894 and for occasional periods thereafter, Russell's home was Pembroke Lodge, **Richmond** (Richmond upon Thames). Now a cafeteria, this rambling manor, built about 1800, was granted to Lord John Russell, Bertrand's grandfather and a British prime minister, by Queen Victoria during the 1840s. After Lord Russell's death in 1878, Bertrand's grandmother continued to live there and raise her orphaned grandsons. Bertrand was a solitary, sensitive youth. In later life he detested seeing how the former 11-acre garden had been broken up and subdivided ("this garden played a very large part in my life up to the age of eighteen," he said) but he eventually opined that the changes were not so bad. There, he wrote, "I grew accustomed to wide horizons and to an unimpeded view of the sunset. And I have never since been able to live happily without both." Pembroke Lodge stands on the west side of Richmond Park. (Open January—October daily; November—December, Saturday—Sunday; 01-940-5676.)

From 1902 to 1904 Russell and Alys Pearsall Smith, his first wife, lived at 14 Cheyne Walk (Chelsea). Later addresses included 34 Russell Chambers, Bury Street (Westminster), in 1915–16, which his mistress, Lady Ottoline Morrell, helped furnish and where he lodged poet T. S. Eliot (see the entry on Eliot earlier in this chapter); 57 Gordon Square (Camden) where he shared quarters with his brother, Lord Frank Russell, from 1916 to 1918; and 36 Sydney Street (Chelsea) in 1921–27, where he lived with his second wife, Dora Black, and where two of their children were born. As an outspoken pacifist during World War I, he was jailed as a security risk and, as prisoner 2917, sat out much of 1918 in Brixton Prison, an 1820 structure at the end of Jebb Avenue on Brixton Hill (Lambeth).

Russell's last London home, a large mansion at 41 Queens Road, **Richmond** (Richmond upon Thames), was his residence from 1950 to 1955. He occupied the upper two floors, while his son's family lived in the lower two.

(See Chapter 3, PARIS; also Chapter 5, ENGLAND; also Chapter 7, WALES.)

SCOTT, ROBERT FALCON (1868–1912). After his first Antarctic expedition (1900-04), the naval officer and ill-fated explorer returned to London and fame. As a bachelor, he lived with his mother and sisters at 56 Oakley Street (Chelsea), a house built in the 1850s that remains privately owned. There he prepared public lectures and worked on his book *The Voyage of the Discovery* (1905). Scott also worked on his book at 22 Eccleston Square (Westminster), the home of his mentor, the explorer Sir Clements Markham. Scott lived in Chelsea until 1908 when he married sculptor Kathleen Bruce.

The couple made their home at 174 Buckingham Palace Road (Westminster), which has since been demolished. There Scott planned his last Antarctic expedition and, in 1910, set out on his tragic race against Roald Amundsen to the South Pole.

Exhibits: *HMS Discovery*, the research ship used by Scott in his first expedition, displays relics of the explorer and his polar quest. Now part of the historic ship collection maintained by the Maritime Trust and currently undergoing restoration, it remains open to the public. The ship is permanently berthed at St. Katharine's Dock, just east of Waterloo Bridge off Victoria Embankment (Westminster). (Open daily 1:00—5:00; 01-481-0043; admission.)

In the manuscript saloon of the British Library may be seen Scott's last diary, written during the final days of his disastrous return journey from the South Pole in 1912. "For God's sake look after our people" was his last entry. The diary was discovered along with the bodies of Scott and three of his associates seven months later. (See the entry on Lord Nelson, *Exhibits*, earlier in this chapter.)

(See Chapter 4, NORWAY; also Chapter 5, ENGLAND.)

SHAKESPEARE, WILLIAM (1564–1616). While giving the world one of its greatest literary treasuries, the dramatist and poet left few personal tracks—a fact which has encouraged various attempts to descredit his authorship and to discover the "real" Shakespeare.* Though apparently a resident of London as early as 1585, little trace of Shakespeare emerges there until about 1592—and locations of his lodging sites until about 1611, when he retired to Stratford-upon-Avon, are in most cases tentative and imprecise. No structure that housed him in London is known to exist today. After 1597 he is believed to have resided in the vicinity of the Globe Theatre, in which he was a stockholder and member of the actors' company. Fifteen of his plays were performed in this small circular wooden building, erected in 1599 and destroyed by fire in 1613. The second Globe Theatre on the site was demolished by Puritans in 1644. Its location is marked in Park Street (Southwark), an area now dominated by warehouses. A third reconstruction of the Globe, begun in 1983, is scheduled for completion by 1989. Shakespeare probably lodged in the immediate vicinity of Clink Street and Bankside just north of Park Street.

Other possible addresses, based on assessment records, may have included lodgings in Worship Street "six doors from Norton Folgate" (Tower

---

* For a discussion of various claimants by the present author, see "Who Really Wrote Shakespeare's Plays?" in *The People's Almanac #2* (1978), by David Wallechinsky and Irving Wallace, pp. 384–90.

Hamlets); and Silver and Monkwell streets, possibly from 1598 to 1604. At the latter address, it is believed, Shakespeare wrote *The Merry Wives of Windsor*, *As You Like It*, *Julius Caesar*, *Hamlet*, *Othello*, *Macbeth*, and *King Lear*, among others. Both streets, now gone, were located west of the present Wood Street between London Wall and Love Lane (the City).

Shakespeare bought a house in 1613 at what is now Ireland Yard and St. Andrew's Hill (the City), possibly the old gatehouse of a Dominican monastery that stood there. He apparently used this house during his visits from Stratford and bequeathed it to his daughter, Susanna Hall.

Exhibits: Shakespeare's will with his signature (one of only six signatures that exist) is displayed at the Public Record Office Museum (see the entry on Lord Nelson, *Exhibits*, earlier in this chapter).

The Bear Gardens Museum in Bear Garden Alley (Southwark), close to the site of the Globe, shows exhibits relating to Elizabethan playhouses. (Open Wednesday—Sunday 10:30—5:30, Wednesday—Thursday by appointment; 01–928–6342; admission.)

(See Chapter 5, ENGLAND.)

SHAW, GEORGE BERNARD (1856–1950). The acerbic, Irish-born playwright, journalist and socialist orator made his home in London from 1876 to 1906 and lived there part-time until 1943. Of his six addresses during this lengthy period only one dwelling survives, at 29 Fitzroy Square (Camden). Shaw was writing unsalable novels when he and his mother moved there in 1887. He remembered pounding his way through the great keyboard classics there while employed as a newspaper music critic, causing anguish to his neighbors and especially to his mother, who gave piano lessons. She never complained, he reported, but sometimes went away to cry. "When I look back on all the banging, roaring, and growling inflicted," he said, "I am consumed with useless remorse." There he also became politically active and wrote his first plays of social philosophy and protest, including *Mrs. Warren's Profession* (1893), *Arms and the Man* (1894), *Candida* (1894) and *The Devil's Disciple* (1897). Shaw lived in the house until his marriage in 1898. The four-story building remains part of a stuccoed terrace dating from about 1835 and is little altered. Virginia Woolf was a later resident of the house (see the entry on Woolf later in this chapter).

With his wife, Charlotte, Shaw made his London home from 1899 to 1927 at 10 Adelphi Terrace (Westminster). The flat had previously been owned by Charlotte. There Shaw wrote *Man and Superman* (1905), *Major Barbara* (1905), *Androcles and the Lion* (1912), and *Pygmalion* (1913), among others. Shaw liked the fact that the Adelphi lurked secretly behind the busy Strand. "I live in the heart of London, miles from anywhere," he said. The site is marked on the present building at the corner of Robert Street.

The couple's last London address, until Charlotte Shaw's death in 1943, was 4 Whitehall Court (Westminster), now the site of an office building.

(See Chapter 5, ENGLAND; also Chapter 7, IRELAND.)

SHELLEY, PERCY BYSSHE (1792–1822). The brilliant, erratic poet's many London stops were always brief and usually only one step ahead of outraged fathers, creditors, bailiffs or other authority figures whom Shelley was exceedingly skillful at dodging (see Name Index and Gazetteer). One house that survives, his refuge in 1811 after being suspended from Oxford University for rampant atheism, stands at 15 Poland Street (Westminster), on the corner of Great Marlborough Street.

(See Chapter 1, SWITZERLAND; also Chapter 5, ENGLAND; also Chapter 8, ITALY.)

SMITH, JOHN (1580–1631). From 1616 the adventurer and colonist kept four "modest rooms" at an unidentified site in The Strand (Westminster). There he also kept a succession of mistresses and wrote the books that made him famous—if not wealthy—most notably the *Generall Historie of Virginia, New-England, and the Summer Isles* (1624). Smith died there, not old in years but physically infirm from 10 lifetimes crowded into one.

In 1623 he lived with his platonic friend Frances Stuart, Duchess of Richmond, at Richmond Palace, **Richmond** (Richmond upon Thames), and completed the aforementioned book (see the entry on Henry VIII earlier in this chapter).

Smith tomb: Church of the Holy Sepulchre (the City).

(See Chapter 5, ENGLAND.)

SULLIVAN, SIR ARTHUR SEYMOUR (1842–1900). The composer, and collaborator with Sir William Schwenk Gilbert on numerous comic operas, Sullivan was a London native and virtual lifelong dweller. His birthplace remains at 8 Bolwell Street (Lambeth), former site of the 18th-century Vauxhall Gardens. He lived there until 1845.

His later Westminster addresses included 3 Ponsonby Place (1850s–61); 139 Westbourne Terrace (ca. 1863); 47 Claverton Terrace (ca. 1864); and 9 Albert Mansions (ca. 1877). His last home from 1881, 1 Queen Anne's Mansions, 60 Victoria Street, had a lush interior decor described by a friend as "an Arabian nightmare." The latter house is the only one of his Westminster residences known definitely to survive. (See the entry on Sir William Schwenk Gilbert earlier in this chapter.)

Sullivan tomb: St. Paul's Cathedral (the City).

SWEDENBORG, EMANUEL (1688–1772). The Swedish scientist, philosopher and mystic visited London several times and spent his last year there. In 1744 he lodged at 26 Warner Street (Islington), which still stands, one of the few remaining structures known to have housed him. Swedenborg's last lodging was the home of a wigmaker at 26 Great Bath Street, where he had also resided for seven months in 1769. The long-gone house stood in the vicinity of the present Rosebery Avenue near his former lodging, and Swedenborg died there.

(See Chapter 4, SWEDEN.)

SWIFT, JONATHAN (1667–1745). The Irish-born satirist, novelist and poet—probably the most powerful English prose writer of the 18th century—occupied many brief London lodgings during his frequent stays, but none of them survive and their sites are not precisely known. In 1710, and again in 1713 and 1722, he lodged on the west side of Bury Street (Westminster), about halfway between Jermyn and King streets. Swift's last London dwelling, in 1727, stood in New Bond Street.

(See Chapter 5, ENGLAND; also Chapter 7, IRELAND.)

TENNYSON, ALFRED, LORD (1809–1892). Poet Laureate of England, immensely popular in his own day and still widely admired by those who like their poetry elegiac or inspirational, Tennyson resided in London frequently for brief periods. The only exception was the period 1850 to 1852, when he lived at Chapel House (private) in Montpelier Row, **Twickenham** (Richmond upon Thames).

Tennyson tomb: Westminster Abbey (Westminster).

(See Chapter 5, ENGLAND.)

THACKERAY, WILLIAM MAKEPEACE (1811–1863). From 1837 to 1844 the Victorian novelist and his bride, Isabella Shawe, lived at 13 Coram Street (Camden). By 1840 they had three children, and Isabella suffered a mental breakdown from which she never recovered.

At 88 St. James's Street (Westminster), during the early 1840s, the novelist wrote *The Memoirs of Barry Lyndon, Esq.* (1844).

Thackeray's last homes remain privately owned in Kensington. From 1846 to 1853 he lived with his two daughters at what is now 16 Young Street, a double-fronted Georgian house. There, in his back study, he wrote most of his best-known works. "Down on your knees, you rogue," he once exclaimed to a friend, "for here *Vanity Fair* was penned. I will go down with you, for I have a high opinion of that little production myself." There he also wrote *Pendennis* (1848–50) and *Henry Esmond* (1852).

Thackeray wrote his last novels at 36 Onslow Square (1853–60). His last home, from 1862, remains at 2 Palace Green. Thackeray designed and built this brick house after demolishing an old house on the property; he died there. (Also see the entry on Henry Fielding earlier in this chapter.)

Thackeray tomb: Kensal Green Cemetery, **Kensal Green** (Brent).

(See Chapter 5, ENGLAND.)

THOMAS, DYLAN (1914–1953). The Welsh poet lived intermittently in London from 1933, occupying numerous brief lodgings. Probably his residence of longest duration was 9 Wentworth Studios on the east side of Manressa Road (Chelsea); he lived in this single-story house (now gone) during 1942–44.

In 1951, just before his first American tour, he occupied a basement flat at 54 Delancey Street (Camden), where an old house trailer in the rear garden served as his study.

(See Chapter 5, ENGLAND; also Chapter 7, WALES.)

TOWER OF LONDON. The royal seat of medieval London and of England itself, the Tower is not just one structure but an entire complex of walls, turrets and towers built on 18 acres in the southeast corner of the City. In 1067 William the Conqueror chose the site of what was to be his London stronghold on a rise of ground beside the Thames at the southeastern angle of the old Roman wall. His aim was to protect his conquest not only from Norse invaders via the Thames but from angry Londoners who had resisted his siege of their walled city for several weeks. The site of a previous Roman fortress burned by the Celtic Queen Boudicca in A.D. 61, the small hill overlooking the river seemed the ideal spot, and the first wooden tower and palisade were completed in three months.

In 1078 William commissioned Gundulf, a Norman monk and architect, to replace this garrison fort with a large permanent structure. Though somewhat modified in succeeding centuries, this four-story 90-foot-tall White Tower (so-called from its exterior whitewash, long since worn away) was intended as the keep and is essentially the same Norman structure that centers the Tower complex today. "Though it is the oldest structure of all," wrote Charlotte and Denis Plimmer, "it looks almost new, so firm are its lines, so clean and straight its walls. Strangely, the White Tower also appears somehow less military, less truculent, than the bastions which encircle it—almost a fantasy conceived by Tolkien and designed by Disney." Its Caen limestone and Kent ragstone walls vary from 11 to 15 feet in thickness. Measuring 118 x 107 feet and cornered by turrets, the building looks, and very nearly is, square. William's son, William II, strengthened and repaired the Tower. Then, during the reigns of Henry III (the monarch most responsible for the Tower's present appearance) and Edward I, massive additions—bastions, gateways, towers, moat and protective walls—were built to surround the keep, making the Tower of London one of the most invulnerable fortresses in medieval Europe. By 1500 there were

THE TOWER OF LONDON. Sited by William the Conqueror along the River Thames in 1067, this grim medieval complex represents the conversion of England to a feudal domain. Not only an important military fortress, state prison, and execution block for some of Britain's most notable names, the Tower served as a royal residence until the reign of Charles II. The massive White Tower with its corner bastions rises in the center of the 18-acre complex, and numerous smaller towers protect the outer walls.

19 tower bastions along the inner and outer walls; Henry VIII added the last two during his reign.

The Tower has served many purposes, both practical and symbolic, throughout its 900-year history. Beyond its military importance (it is the oldest continuously occupied fortress in the Western world and was fully garrisoned until the 1960s), it was intended as a royal palace, and most English monarchs from William I to Charles II—over 20 in all—resided there for greater or lesser periods. The White Tower itself held the earliest royal apartments; they occupied the top two floors. By the 13th century the royal household and private gardens occupied a row of buildings along the Roman wall line between the White Tower and Lanthorn Tower on the south. Oliver Cromwell destroyed these quarters but left the rest of the structures intact. From Tudor times up to the present, the Tower of London has served as the ceremonial royal residence from which coronation processions to Westminster Abbey begin.

Many notable episodes in English history have occurred within the Tower walls. Mobs stormed the walls during the Peasants' Revolt of 1381; Richard II signed over his crown to Henry IV there in 1399; Henry VI was murdered there in 1471; the young York princes were murdered in 1483, probably by order of Richard III, in the Bloody Tower. (See the entries on Henry VIII, Richard III and William the Conqueror in this chapter.)

The Tower's most notorious use, however, was as a prison and place of execution. Some of the best-known figures in English history were confined there for greater or lesser offenses and periods. They included Elizabeth I, Sir Thomas More, William Penn, Samuel Pepys and Sir Walter Raleigh (see entries on each of these people earlier in this chapter). Other prisoners were Queen Anne Boleyn, Queen Catherine Howard, Lady Jane Grey, the Earl of Essex, the Earl of Leicester, Archbishop Thomas Cranmer, Bishops Hugh Latimer and Nicholas Ridley, Guy Fawkes and—in this century—Roger Casement (1916) and German Deputy Fuehrer Rudolf Hess (1941). There were two main places of execution: the northern end of Tower Green, a space south of the Chapel Royal of St. Peter ad Vincula, where Boleyn, Howard, and Robert Devereaux, Earl of Essex, died; and Tower Hill, just northwest of the walls at a marked site in Trinity Square Gardens. More, Thomas Cromwell and Archbishop William Laud were among those who met death at this site.

Many changes, resulting from new construc-tion, demolitions, disastrous fire, World War II bombings, and the simple ravages of time have affected these acres since the 11th century. All of the existing older walls and structures have undergone restoration, designed to preserve their medieval appearance, at various times. Today the chief function of the White Tower is to house the Royal Armouries, one of the world's most notable collections of antique armor and weapons. An entire panoply of medieval offensive, defensive and ceremonial weapons—German and Italian as well as English—is displayed, including the custom-made metal suits of Henry VIII (which became ever larger in girth as he aged) and of Charles I. The Royal Armour gallery is housed in the original Council Chamber, where Richard II gave up his throne and where an enraged Richard III (then lord protector) ordered Lord Hastings, one of his chief obstacles to the throne, to summary execution outside.

The Jewel House, located at one end of the 1845 Waterloo Barracks, houses one of the most spectacular displays in London. Exhibited there are all the potent symbols of English rule—the coronation regalia and crown jewels, including the historic ceremonial crowns worn by the monarch on state occasions, as well as royal orbs, sceptres and swords of state.

The Tower of London on Tower Hill (the City) is operated and maintained by the Department of the Environment. Visitors may take conducted tours or wander at will. Main attractions include the colorful Elizabethan uniforms of the Yeomen warders ("Beefeaters"), the nightly Ceremony of the Keys, and royal salutes on ceremonial occasions. Excellent guidebooks are available on the premises; but R. J. Minney's *The Tower of London* (1970) provides a fine preparation. There is a small extra charge for admission to the Jewel House. (Open March—October, Monday—Saturday 9:30—5:00, Sunday 2:00—5:00; November—February, Monday—Saturday 9:30—4:00; 01-709-0765; admission.)

VAN GOGH, VINCENT (1853–1890). In 1873 and 1874 the Dutch painter boarded at 87 Hackford Road (Lambeth). The house, which was run by the widow of a French curate, is marked with a plaque. Pining for home—and his landlady's engaged daughter, Ursula Loyer—van Gogh was working as an apprentice art dealer at this time.

Returning in 1876 to work as a curate himself—in a London school—he resided at 160 Twickenham Road, **Richmond** (Richmond upon Thames). This house is also marked.

(See Chapter 2, FRANCE; also Chapter 3, PARIS; also Chapter 4, BELGIUM, THE NETHERLANDS.)

VICTORIA (1819–1901). At her death she was the only sovereign that most of her subjects had ever known. Britain's longest reigning monarch (63 years), Victoria gave her name to the era—to the imperialism and the art and culture of 19th-century Britain. Neither a remarkably bright or personable lady, she yet embodied the British empire with such solid rectitude that her entirely predictable habits and opinions, along with her dowdy appearance and humorless conservatism, won massive respect for the monarchy—a feeling that had been in decline during the reigns of her Georgian predecessors. Probably the last British monarch to attempt to wield any political influence beyond her constitutional role, she relied heavily upon her consort, the German-born Prince Albert, for guidance in state affairs. Following his death in 1861, she withdrew into almost constant seclusion for her remaining 40 years as queen. Her typical garb was black mourning dress. The children and grandchildren of Victoria and Albert occupied many of the thrones of pre-World War I Europe. To her, Europe was a complex of family estates, and war with the Germany ruled by her grandson, Kaiser Wilhelm II, would have been unthinkable.

Princess Victoria, daughter of the fourth son of George III, was born at Kensington Palace. It was her main residence until 1837 when she learned that she would succeed her uncle, William IV, to the throne. The palace's first royal occupant had been William III. He purchased the rebuilt 1661 brick mansion called "Nottingham House" in 1689 and hired Sir Christopher Wren to make additions (see the entry on Wren later in this chapter). Kensington became the main London residence of William and Mary and their next three successors (Queen Anne, George I and George II). Further enlargements were made for George I in 1720, but no reigning monarch after George II lived there. The two-and-one-half-story mansion rambles around three inner courts. Only Victoria's affection for her childhood home prevented its demolition a century ago. Today much of the palace is still lived in by various peripheral members of the royal family, but the state apartments have been open to the public since 1899. Among the

rooms on view is the one where Victoria was born. Some of her toys, dolls, and clothing, plus numerous portraits, ornaments, royal knickknacks, and other memorabilia are on view in the adjacent suite. Queen Mary, the consort of George V, grandmother of Elizabeth II and herself a cousin of Victoria, was born in this same room in 1867. The Victorian rooms were redecorated to their present appearance under her direction. Kensington Palace, operated by the Department of the Environment, is located on the west side of Kensington Gardens (Kensington). (Open Monday—Saturday 9:00—5:00, Sunday 1:00—5:00; 01–937–9561; admission.)

Victoria's London residence throughout her reign was Buckingham Palace (Westminster), which she made the most important and private palace of the royal domain—though, for her, it was not private enough; she escaped from it as often as she could, especially after Albert's death (see the entry on George III earlier in this chapter).

Until 1861, St. James's Palace (Westminster) was Victoria's official London residence, used mostly for ceremonial occasions. She and Albert, her first cousin, were married in the Chapel Royal there in 1840 (see the entry on Henry VIII earlier in this chapter).

Exhibits: The Royal Mews at Buckingham Palace displays several items used to transport the queen, including the gold state coach she used at her coronation and her state sledge for jaunts in the snow (see the entry on George III, *Exhibits*, earlier in this chapter).

The London Museum adjacent to Kensington Palace (see above) exhibits Victoria's 1837 coronation robe along with much other royal ceremonial regalia. (Open same hours as Kensington Palace; 01–937–9816; admission.)

(See Chapter 5, ENGLAND; also Chapter 7, SCOTLAND.)

WAGNER, RICHARD (1813–1883). The German Romantic composer spent four unpleasant months in London ("the hardest money I have ever earned") as conductor of the London Philharmonic in 1855. To Franz Liszt he wrote that "I live here like a damned soul in hell. How wretched I am in these surroundings, that are utterly repugnant to me, is indescribable." Wagner worked on *Die Walküre* (1856) in his lodgings, which stood at 22 Portland Place (Westminster).

(See Chapter 1, AUSTRIA, SWITZERLAND; also Chapter 3, PARIS; also Chapter 4, EAST

GERMANY, WEST GERMANY; also Chapter 8, ITALY.)

WAUGH, EVELYN (1903–1966). The satiric novelist's birthplace remains privately owned at 11 Hillfield Road, West Hampstead (Camden). It was his home until 1907. Waugh's elder brother, Alec, a novelist whose fame preceded Evelyn's but who was eventually far outshone by the younger's works, was also born there in 1898.

The youngsters grew up at Underhill, the three-story house built by their publisher father at 145 North End Road, **Golders Green** (Barnet), which was their home until 1917. "No one passing Underhill today would be able to guess at the kind of family life that we enjoyed there," wrote Alec Waugh in 1962. "There is a perpetual roar of traffic; there is no sense of privacy. It was a very different place in 1910 with its lawns and greenhouses and rosebeds behind the shelter of high hedges." He reported that a gas station had been installed in the former garden.

Waugh and his first wife, Evelyn Gardner, made their first home (1928–29) in a tiny flat at 17A Canonbury Square (Islington). His first novel, *Decline and Fall* (1928), was published during their residence.

His first married home with his second wife, Laura Herbert, was 21 Mulberry Walk (Chelsea). The couple lived there in 1937, just before acquiring their Gloucestershire estate.

(See Chapter 5, ENGLAND.)

WELLINGTON, ARTHUR WELLESLEY, DUKE OF (1769–1852). Britain's most notable 19th-century soldier, who ended Napoleon's career at Waterloo, bought Apsley House in 1817 as his permanent London residence. Built in 1768, the original small brick mansion was enlarged and refaced in stone by Wellington in 1828. He added the portico and a western extension containing the Waterloo Gallery; the latter was the scene of various annual banquets and ceremonies he hosted which commemorated the famous battle. Located at 149 Piccadilly, Hyde Park Corner (Westminster), at the southeast corner of Hyde Park, the house was known as No. 1, London, during the 19th century. Apsley House remained in the Wellington family until 1947 when the seventh duke presented it to the nation as a memorial to his noted ancestor. Operated today by the Victoria and Albert Museum, Apsley House Museum displays an abundance of Wellington memorabilia,

lavish furnishings and decor, plus the trophies, paintings, and awards that were showered on the duke throughout his long public career. The main rooms have been restored to their 19th-century appearance and one gets the impression that this public idol lived out his last years in what was—even then—a virtual museum. (Open Tuesday—Thursday, Saturday 10:00—6:00, Sunday 2:30—6:00; 01-499-5676; admission.)

While serving as prime minister (1828–30), Wellington occupied the official residence at 10 Downing Street (Westminster) for 18 months while Apsley House was undergoing extensive renovation (see the entry on Benjamin Disraeli earlier in this chapter).

Wellington tomb: St. Paul's Cathedral (the City).

(See Chapter 3, PARIS; also Chapter 4, BELGIUM; also Chapter 5, ENGLAND; also Chapter 7, IRELAND; also Chapter 8, SPAIN.)

WELLS, HERBERT GEORGE (1866–1946). The first important writer of science fiction, as well as the author of numerous other novels, social tracts, polemics, and history, Wells spent much of his lifetime at various London addresses. Atlas House, a small three-story row dwelling at 170 High Street in **Bromley** (Bromley), was his birthplace and home until 1880. In this impoverished house, now long gone, his father maintained a china shop.

Later, Wells roomed with aunts in Camden at 181 Euston Road during 1884–87, and at 46 Fitzroy Road during 1889–91. His first married home was 28 Maldon Road (Wandsworth), from which he fled in 1893 with Amy Robbins, one of his students at University Tutorial College. She became his second wife in 1895, and they lived at 12 Mornington Terrace (Camden) for a year. During the late 1920s Wells occupied a succession of flats. Then, from 1928 to 1936, he settled at 47 Chiltern Court Mansions, Marylebone Road and Baker Street (Westminster).

Wells's last home stands at 13 Hanover Terrace (Camden), one in a row of privately owned mansions dating from 1822. There he wrote his last, increasingly pessimistic, works; painted murals in a garage room; and stubbornly refused to leave during the London Blitz though his front door was blown in more than once, it is said. An internationalist, he had predicted the development of the atomic bomb in 1914 and lived long enough to bear bitter witness to the fulfillment of his prophecy. Wells died at this house, convinced that his own literary influence had perished along with the world's chances for peace.

(See Chapter 5, ENGLAND.)

WESLEY, CHARLES (1707–1788).
WESLEY, JOHN (1703–1791).

Charles, who wrote some 6,500 hymns, and his brother John, the evangelist founder of Methodism, resided in London during most of their later years. Charles's house stood on the presently marked site at 1 Wheatley Street (Westminster). It was his home from 1771 until his death.

From 1739 until 1779 John Wesley's chapel, school, and lodgings were located in the Foundry, an old government arsenal that Wesley repaired and used as his headquarters and the first Methodist bookroom; he preached there to massive open-air congregations. The Foundry stood near the present site of 19A Tabernacle Street (Islington). Susanna Wesley, the brothers' mother, died there in 1742.

John Wesley's last home was the City Road Chapel, which he built in 1778. His own four-story house is part of the chapel enclave located at 47 City Road (Islington). His first-floor study, bedroom, and prayer room display numerous furnishings, books, articles of clothing, and memorabilia concerning both brothers. Charles, a frequent visitor, stayed on the second floor; some of his hymn manuscripts are exhibited there. The house, narrowly rescued from flames during the Blitz in 1940, was completely restored in 1978. An adjacent chapel, site of John Wesley's sermons, is a 1978 reconstruction of the original structure which burned down in 1899. His mahogany pulpit may be seen there. Wesley's Chapel and house are operated by private trustees. (House open summer, Monday—Saturday 10:00—4:00, and by arrangement; admission; Chapel open daily, 8:30—6:00; Sunday services 11:00; 01–253–2262; free.)

Charles Wesley tomb: Marylebone Parish Churchyard (Westminster).

John Wesley tomb: Wesley Chapel Cemetery (Islington).

Exhibits: The 1669 birthplace of Susanna Annesley Wesley, mother of 19 Wesleys including John and Charles, is now Annesley House, owned by the Methodist Women's Fellowship and located at 7 Spital Yard, a cul-de-sac off Bishopsgate (the City).

John Wesley organized his first society of Methodists at 28 Aldersgate Street (the City) in 1738, shortly before he claimed his own conversion there. The site is marked.

At 10-11 West Street (Westminster) stands an arched doorway, a remnant of the chapel of La Tremblade, one of London's original Huguenot churches. John Wesley, Charles Wesley and George Whitefield often preached there from 1742. The upper part of the pulpit they used may be seen in the south aisle of St. Giles-in-the-Fields Church, St. Giles High Street (open daily; free).

(See Chapter 5, ENGLAND.)

WILDE, OSCAR (1854–1900). The Irish-born poet, playwright, and wit made London his permanent base from 1876 until his imprisonment for "homosexual practices" in 1895. During the years 1876 to 1878, he occupied rooms at 13 Salisbury Street (Westminster), where he acted as host to actresses Lillie Langtry and Ellen Terry.

He moved to 1 Tite Street (Chelsea) in 1878 and there became known in London artistic and literary circles for his wit and extravagant dress. Wilde lived there until 1881. Following his marriage to Constance Lloyd in 1884, the couple settled at 34 Tite Street, a three-story brick house that remains privately owned. Wilde had the interior decorated in shades of white and employed painter James Whistler to design the upstairs drawing room. The house was frequently featured in fashion magazines of the day and became a popular literary and artistic salon—until, that is, 1895, when Wilde's world fell apart. There he was confronted by the Marquis of Queensberry, outraged father of his lover, Lord Alfred Douglas, in 1894 and thus began the incredible chain of events that led to Wilde's arrest, spectacular trial and imprisonment. The house (now known as "Oscar House") was put up for auction and many of its contents were pillaged or lost during Wilde's transformation from society darling to scapegoat.

Wilde lodged at the Cadogan Hotel, still at 75 Sloane Street (Westminster), during his trial in 1895. Despite a brilliant defense, he was convicted of sodomy. He was then imprisoned for three months in a 13 x 7-foot cell at Pentonville Prison, Caledonian Road (Islington); for five months at Wandsworth Prison, Heathfield Road (Wandsworth); then, until 1897, at Reading Gaol in Reading. He never resided in London again.

(See Chapter 3, PARIS; also Chapter 5, ENGLAND; also Chapter 7, IRELAND.)

WILLIAM THE CONQUEROR (WILLIAM I) (1027–1087).

See the entry on the Tower of London earlier in this chapter.

(See Chapter 2, FRANCE; also Chapter 5, ENGLAND.)

WOLSEY, THOMAS, CARDINAL (1473?–1530).

The powerful lord chancellor, chief minister of Henry VIII and virtual dictator of England during Henry's reign until his abrupt disgrace and fall from power, lived opulently in London from about 1510 to 1529.

In 1514 as archbishop of York—just before becoming lord chancellor—Wolsey acquired York House, later known as Whitehall Palace (Westminster). He enlarged the buildings and grounds to 23 acres and used it as his chief London residence until Henry VIII confiscated the property in 1529 and made it his own domicile (see the entry on Henry VIII earlier in this chapter).

Wolsey had to give up Hampton Court Palace at **Hampton** (Richmond upon Thames) in the same way. Wolsey built this eight-acre, lavish country manor on a 2,000-acre site purchased from the Knights of St. John of Jerusalem in 1514. Its one thousand or so rooms, including 280 guest rooms, were richly paneled, furnished, and maintained by almost a thousand servants. The scale of ornate luxury can scarcely be imagined, even in well-preserved Hampton Court today, and revealed Wolsey as a true "prince" of the church. Here he and his mistress lived in opulent splendor and produced two children. His personal wealth and palaces far outshone the king's own, a fact that did not escape Henry's notice. When Henry asked the cardinal why Hampton Court had been built on such a lavish scale, Wolsey must have swallowed at least once before replying, "To show how noble a palace a subject may offer his sovereign." Thus did Wolsey thoughtfully "present" Hampton Court to his monarch in 1525—an offer which was immediately accepted. Henry further altered and enlarged the palace and it served as one of England's main royal residences until the reign of George II. Today many of Wolsey's original chambers, furnishings, and tapestries may still be seen at Hampton Court. Wolsey's Closet, Wolsey's Rooms (actually guest chambers), and the Chapel Royal are among the surviving portions of the palace as he knew it and display priceless remnants of his clerical lifestyle. Clock Court was Wolsey's main courtyard. (For admission information, see the entry on Henry VIII earlier in this chapter.)

Following his "gift" to the king, Wolsey occupied Richmond Palace, **Richmond** (Richmond upon Thames), briefly in 1530 (see the entry on Elizabeth I earlier in this chapter).

(See Chapter 5, ENGLAND.)

WOOLF, VIRGINIA (1882–1941).

The five-story birthplace of the novelist and essayist, daughter of biographer Sir Leslie Stephan, stands at 22 Hyde Park Gate (Kensington). It was her home until her father's death in 1904. American poet and diplomat James Russell Lowell, her godfather, was a frequent visitor at the house. The children's nursery was on the topmost floor. Following the deaths of her mother and a sister, Virginia suffered the first of her recurrent mental breakdowns there.

In 1905 she joined her remaining family at 46 Gordon Square (Camden), her home until 1907. This house was the later long-time residence of economist John Maynard Keynes. Woolf's next home, which she occupied with her brother Adrian from 1907 to 1911, was 29 Fitzroy Square, the earlier home of George Bernard Shaw (see the entries on Keynes and Shaw earlier in this chapter). There they continued their custom hosting weekly social gatherings which formed the genesis of the literary movement known as the Bloomsbury Group. At 38 Brunswick Square, her home in 1911 and 1912, she shared quarters with Leonard Woolf and other friends; this house is gone.

Following her marriage to Woolf in 1912 and a serious breakdown in 1913, the couple moved to Hogarth House in **Richmond** (Richmond upon Thames) and decided to buy a printing press, partly to aid Virginia's recovery. The hobby soon turned into a profitable business; their Hogarth Press published T. S. Eliot's *The Waste Land* (1922) in addition to their own works. Hogarth House in Paradise Road was the eastern portion of a large brick semidetached house built about 1748. Since its 1972 restoration, however, the entire building (now converted to private offices) has been known as Hogarth House. The Woolfs lived and worked there from 1915 to 1924.

Back in Bloomsbury at 52 Tavistock Square (Camden), they operated the Hogarth Press in the basement, lived on the top two floors, and rented out the lower floors. There Virginia Woolf worked on her novels *Mrs. Dalloway* (1925) and *To the Lighthouse* (1927). This house remained their home until 1939. It was bombed out during World War II and the Tavistock Hotel presently occupies the site. The Woolfs' last London home from 1939 until bombing forced their evacuation in 1940 was 37 Mecklenburgh Square (now gone).

(See Chapter 5, ENGLAND.)

WREN, SIR CHRISTOPHER (1632–1723). The brilliant architect who designed some of England's finest public buildings and private palaces, did not become a regular London resident until 1657. In that year he became professor of astronomy at Gresham College, which stood until 1768 in Old Broad Street (the City) ans was formerly the Elizabethan residence of the college founder Sir Thomas Gresham. Wren resided there until 1661. The building was also the first headquarters of the Royal Society, founded in 1645 as the Philosophical Society, with Wren among its earliest members.

During his three-decades of work on St. Paul's Cathedral (see *Exhibits* below), Wren is said to have lodged at several addresses, including Cardinal's Wharf, 49 Bankside (Southwark); 5 Walbrook Street (the City); Carter Lane (the City); and in a mansion in Great Russell Street (Camden) which was demolished in 1823. But dates and precise sites are far from certain.

Wren's only existing residence stands at Hampton Court, **Hampton** (Richmond upon Thames; see the entry on Henry VIII earlier in this chapter). Located on Hampton Court Green west of the palace approach, the old Court House was Wren's permanent home from 1706 and he died there. Visitors are not admitted to the building. Wren designed and rebuilt the entire east front (plus several other portions) of Hampton Court Palace in the late 17th-century.

Wren tomb: St. Paul's Cathedral (the City).

Exhibits: Wren built 53 churches in London following the Great Fire of 1666; of these, 23 remain. He is most noted, of course, for his reconstruction of St. Paul's Cathedral atop Ludgate Hill (the City). Wren labored for 33 years (1675–1708) on Britain's largest cathedral. An accomplished mathematician and astronomer but untried as an architect when he began, he submitted numerous designs to the church authorities. They were all rejected but finally, in his position as surveyor general, Wren commenced the job on the king's authority. A church has occupied this site since the year 604; Wren's cathedral is probably fourth or fifth. During the disastrous bombing raid of December 29, 1940, Wren's could be seen above the smoke and flames of burning London and became a symbol for Londoners of British resolve during the Blitz. Though the cathedral itself suffered only minor damage, there were suggestions that it be demolished and rebuilt. Prime Minister Churchill, however, insisted on its repair. Wren's Latin epitaph is in the crypt: "If you seek his monument, look around you." In the trophy room off the north trifolium Wren's models and drawings are displayed as well as relics pertaining to the history of the cathedral. (Open Monday—Saturday, 8:00—7:00, Sunday 8:00—6:00; free.)

(See Chapter 5, ENGLAND.)

YEATS, WILLIAM BUTLER (1865–1939). The Irish-born poet, whom T. S. Eliot called "the greatest of our time," resided in London at intervals from the age of two. From 1867 to 1874, the family lived at 23 Fitzroy Road, Chalk Farm (Camden). The privately owned house is marked with a plaque.

Yeats' lawyer father, John Butler Yeats (who later became a noted painter), moved the family to 14 Edith Road (Kensington) in 1874. It was their home until 1876.

At 5 Woburn Walk, Woburn Place (Camden), Yeats lived on the second floor—and later occupied most of the house—with his mistress, novelist Olivia Shakespear, at intervals from 1895 to 1917. In 1917 he married Georgie Hyde-Lees. Irish patriot, diplomat and actress Maud Gonne, Yeats's friend and almost lifelong mystical obsession, lived there for a period after he left. The house is marked with a plaque.

After 1917, Yeats's London stays were brief and infrequent.

(See Chapter 2, FRANCE; also Chapter 5, ENGLAND; also Chapter 7, IRELAND.)

ZOLA, ÉMILE (1840–1902). In 1898 and 1899, the French novelist found himself blacklisted and harassed as a result of his involvement in the notorious Dreyfus Affair. He chose exile in London until an official amnesty enabled his return to Paris. During that tense year he lodged at the Queen's Hotel, still located at 122 Church Road, **Croydon** (Croydon).

(See Chapter 2, FRANCE; also Chapter 3, PARIS.)

CHAPTER 7
IRELAND, SCOTLAND, WALES

IRELAND

Roman soldiers never set foot on this island (the only European land except Scandinavia they never touched) but Roman Catholicism came, saw and conquered more thoroughly than Julius Caesar ever tried anywhere. Therein, say some observers, lies the root of the "Irish problem." Never subjected to the so-called civilizing influence of Roman administration, Ireland nevertheless applied the Roman Christian doctrine so rigorously that even a recent Italian pope spoke of Irish Catholicism as "a terrifying thing."

Ireland is as universally Christian a country as exists—there is no true separation of church and state in either north or south. While the power of the church is not quite so all-pervasive as it was even a generation ago, the parish priest or Protestant clergyman remains, in most Irish towns today, the ultimate authority not only in religious life but in education and government. Ireland is the only European country "where Christ and Caesar," as James Joyce wrote, "are hand in glove," at least to such an uninhibited extent. Religion and politics are still so closely entwined that attempting to view them separately is futile.

When has there not been an "Irish problem"? The only Irish who have never resented and fought English control over the island are the northern Protestant Anglo-Irish and Scotch-Irish descended from 17th-century colonials, but even

they have fought, and fight, with other Irish over the issue. Until the 20th century Irish nationalism was mostly a matter of cultivating anarchy against the intransigent English. Historical English efforts to "de-Catholicize" Ireland, despite a 19th-century genocidal and Gestapo-like strategy designed to starve and terrorize the Irish into submission, met with spectacular failure. Indeed, the record of England's attempts to subjugate this people by law, force, and finally bribery planted a dismal blot on that kingdom. Even when attempts to rectify previous errors were finally undertaken, English efforts often seemed bumbling and half-hearted. Today a more humane England continues to pay a large price for those misguided efforts. As a result of such past policies, the Irish learned how to wage underground war. They became expert guerrillas, masters of strike-and-fade tactics, the bomb in the public square, the booby trap, assassination in the night. And old habits die hard. Since the 1922 partition of Ireland into two separate states, disaffected Irish have preyed mostly upon other Irish in this manner.

Gaelic Celts overpowered a Bronze Age people on this island in about 350 B.C., and from these invaders the majority of Irish are descended. St. Patrick, no Irishman himself, began converting the island from its Druidic religions in the year 432, and Viking invaders began building the first towns 400 years later. The English first established control in 1172 under Henry II. From then until the Irish partition, Irish history was a succession of bloody rebellions, English reprisals, land confiscations, population displacements, penal laws against Catholics, and terrible famine. Potato blight, virtually wiping out the staple item of the Irish diet, not only killed some 1.5 million people between 1846 and 1851 but forced another million to emigrate, depleting the population to 6.5 million.

Dublin's Easter Week rebellion of 1916 began the series of events that led to Irish independence. Formation of the guerrilla Irish Republican Army (IRA) plus hunger strikes and relentless underground warfare finally wore down British resolve. At the direct plea of George V for a peaceful settlement, the treaty of 1922 created the Irish Free State as a member of the British Commonwealth, while six Ulster counties in the north remained a province of the United Kingdom. The Free State (Éire) remained neutral during World War II. In 1949, however, the Free State suddenly removed itself from the Commonwealth and proclaimed itself the Republic of Ireland. This was not a decision based on long-term self-interest, and many Irish today profoundly deplore the move as a hasty, unwise action, while Northern Ireland's official attitude has been, "you made your bed, now lie in it."

Thus a strong antipartition movement arose after the division in the dominantly Catholic Republic of Ireland. Coupled with discrimination against minority Catholics in Protestant Ulster, this movement has been the source of most Irish conflict since World War II. At bottom, of course, lie the Catholic-Protestant differences that make this island the only place in the world where Christians, as a measure of patriotism, still maim and kill each other. The long-outlawed IRA has continued its armed raids into Northern Ireland, where these actions have often backlashed violently on the local Catholic population. Despite the imposing walls of hate built by such violence, however (and not least of the hate peddlers are certain members of the ubiquitous clergy), people of good will on both sides attempt to seek and find ways of reconciliation.

A major factor in the conflict is the industrial dominance and prosperity of Northern Ireland as contrasted to the Republic's much less developed economy; the southern Irish claim British favoritism for Northern Ireland because of its Protestantism, while Ulster insists that its own economic prosperity is more a matter of racial character, and

that the "Celtic Irish" are just not as ambitious. The northerners worry that a "papist" takeover would not only threaten their rights to divorce and contraception but undermine Protestant education. Britain is, of course, committed to the continued existence of Northern Ireland as part of the United Kingdom and has ruled it directly from London since 1978. Thus England continues to be a target for antipartitionist terrorism. And thus the "Irish problem" continues as fanatics go on waging vicious if undeclared war over matters that most of the Christian world resolved centuries ago.

Rimmed with steep mountain ranges, the island extends about 150 miles wide and 275 miles long, and contains a variety of terrain. Ireland's climate is cool and moist with no extremes of temperature. The southern four-fifths that comprise the Republic contain about 3.5 million people; Dublin, the capital, is also the largest city. Today the ancient Irish language, Gaelic, is spoken only in the extreme south and west, despite repeated Republican attempts to make it the national language. Northern Ireland's population approaches two million with the capital in Belfast. Thus the total Irish population remains considerably below its numbers at the height of the potato famine.

Most of the notable Irish figures included in the following pages resided in what is today the Republic. (Only St. Patrick dwelled much in Ulster; both Catholics and Protestants consider him the patron saint of Ireland.) The Irish are, of course, noted for their glowing language and the art of lyrical declamation (the label of "blarney" is a typical Irish discounting of the gift). Even the humblest waitress or street peddler often displays that remarkable "way with words," a gift embellished with great skill in another Irish institution—the pub. From this tradition have emerged some of literature's most expert and entertaining "talkers"—Joyce, Shaw, Wilde, Yeats, to name but a few. Even some of the transplanted English, as Dean Swift essentially was, seem to have found the Irish atmosphere superbly conducive to their art. Ireland reveres its talkers and doers both (especially after their deaths); and visitors who enter this volatile, most Christian country on earth will find ample memorials to them.* An in-

---

*Since many important Irish heroes—Brian Boru, Wolfe Tone, Daniel O'Connell, Charles Parnell, Eamon de Valera, among others—played no very significant roles beyond domestic political ones, they are not included in these pages.

teresting guidebook to sites concerning Irish writers is *A Literary Guide to Ireland* (1973) by Susan and Thomas Cahill.

BURKE, EDMUND (1729–1797). The **Dublin** birthplace of the great Whig politician and political theorist was 12 Arran Quay, now long gone, which was his home until 1736.

(See Chapter 5, ENGLAND; also Chapter 6, LONDON.)

CHURCHILL, SIR WINSTON (1874–1965). As a child, the World War II English prime minister lived with his parents in the Viceregal Lodge, now the residence of the Irish president, located in Phoenix Park north of the Main Road in **Dublin**. This manor dates from 1751.

(See Chapter 5, ENGLAND; also Chapter 6, LONDON.)

HANDEL, GEORG FREDERICK (1685–1759).

Exhibit: Handel's oratorio *The Messiah* was first performed on April 13, 1742, at a now long-gone **Dublin** music hall in Fishamble Street, with the composer conducting from the harpsichord. The manuscript score used that epochal night may be seen in Marsh's Library (see the entry on Jonathan Swift, *Exhibits*, later in this section.)

(See Chapter 4, EAST GERMANY; also Chapter 5, ENGLAND; also Chapter 6, LONDON.)

JOYCE, JAMES (1882–1941). A native and life-long lover of **Dublin**, though he spent most of his life in self-imposed exile from Ireland, the author was born at 41 Brighton Square, a two-story red-brick house marked with a plaque. It was his home until 1885. Joyce's subsequent family homes in Dublin were numerous as his restless father seemingly moved the family whenever the lease came due. Several of these houses survive. From 1885 to 1888 the family lived at 23 Castlewood Avenue. Then, after an absence of five years, they returned to Dublin and occupied a four-story house at 14 Fitzgibbon Street, now a vacant lot (1893–94). While attending Belvedere College (1893–98), Joyce lived for part of that period with his parents at 17 North Richmond Street; "a quiet street," he wrote, the houses showing "brown imperturbable faces." (This house has since been painted bright red.) The family lived at 8 Inverness Terrace, Fairview (Royal Terrace at the time, or "Royal Terrors, Fearview," as he called it in *Finnegans Wake*) in 1902.

In **Bray**, where the family resided from 1888 to 1891—in hopes, said Joyce's father, that the train fare from Dublin would keep his wife's relatives away—their home at 1 Martello Terrace, a three-story balconied house, was the setting for early scenes in Joyce's *A Portrait of the Artist as a Young Man* (1916). "The place may have a tired look to today's visitor," wrote Susan and Thomas Cahill, "but in 1891 it figured in a psychic explosion within a little boy that ultimately contributed to his breaking up the establishment of modern English prose."

For most of this period, however, Joyce himself resided at Clongoweswood College, a Jesuit boarding school located about a mile and a half north of **Clane** on route L25. Owned by the Jesuits since 1813, the original medieval castle on the site had been destroyed by British soldiers in 1641 and restored in the 18th century. Until 1891 the sensitive lad endured an inmate-like existence heightened by the drill-sergeant discipline of the priests. The third-floor dormitory where he huddled amid the institutional bed rows survives, as does the college chapel and infirmary, but most of the classrooms he knew have been replaced. The Jesuit fathers welcome visitors today and are glad to point out scenes mentioned in *A Portrait*, but it is wise to call beforehand (phone CW6422).

John Joyce withdrew his son from the school in 1891 and moved the family to Leoville, a house at 23 Carysfort Avenue in **Blackrock** near Dublin, their home until 1893.

In suburban **Sandycove**, the Martello Tower in Sandycove Avenue East is Dublin's only official monument to the writer. Joyce lodged in the tower, along with fellow writer Oliver St. John Gogarty, for a week in September 1904 just before his permanent departure from Ireland; the opening scene of his book *Ulysses* (1922) is set here. The 1804 tower was one of a series constructed as coastal defenses against the threat of Napoleonic invasion and now houses the James Joyce Museum. Joyce mementos, first editions, photographs, manuscripts, and his death mask are displayed. (Open May—September, Monday—Saturday 10:00—1:00, 2:00—5:15, Sunday 2:30—6:00; other times by arrangement with the Regional Tourist Office in Dun Laoghaire; admission.)

MARTELLO TOWER. Author James Joyce resided in this old coastal defense bastion at **Sandycove** for a brief period in 1904 just before he left Ireland. It figures prominently in his novel *Ulysses*. Today it holds Ireland's only museum to the writer whose love-hate affair with his homeland marked some of the most significant literature of the 20th century.

Exhibits: In 1893 Joyce began a five-year term in Belvedere College at 6 Great Denmark Street, the Jesuit dayschool in **Dublin** that profoundly influenced his development as a man and writer, unforgettable scenes of which he etched in *A Portrait*. Tales of the pre-Jesuit history of this 1775 mansion fed the sexual imagination of the precocious student (a former countess owner had supposedly committed adultery there) despite the priests' covering of the painted Venus on the ceiling of the Venus Room. Still a Jesuit domain with "one of the finest interiors of all the Georgian houses left in Dublin," report the Cahills, Belvedere College remains essentially the same. The classrooms where Joyce first encountered Charles Lamb's *Adventures of Ulysses* are now staff rooms, however, and the chapel where the violent hell-fire sermons recorded in *A Portrait* left him shaking is now part of the science department. The gymnasium-theater where Joyce acted in a Whitsuntide play was demolished in 1971. (Open school holidays and after-school hours.)

Joyce maintained that if Dublin were destroyed, it could be precisely rebuilt from his works. As Anthony Burgess wrote on the occasion of Joyce's birth centennial in 1982, "Joyce has created Dublin. He has turned it into a place as mythical as Dante's Inferno, Paradiso, and Purgatorio all in one.... Joyce couldn't live in Dublin, but he couldn't leave it alone." In Dublin, June 16 is celebrated as "Bloomsday," the 1904 day in the life of the city wanderer in *Ulysses*, Leopold Bloom. The facade of Leopold and Mary Bloom's house stands marked at 7 Eccles Street, actually the home of Joyce's friend J. F. Byrne, where Joyce himself "went to pieces" one day when he thought his wife, Nora Barnacle, had deceived him. Joyce still evokes a measure of passionate hostility in Dublin, but at least the city no longer ignores him. On Bloomsday, Dubliners turn out in force to follow Bloom's meticulously detailed trail around a city that, despite vast changes since 1904, remains very recognizable as Joyce country. City maps showing the settings of *Ulysses* are easily available in Dublin, and a number of "literary pilgrimage" books provide excellent preparation for the Dublin Joyce seeker. Among these are *James Joyce's Dublin* (1950) by Patricia Hutchins and *The Joyce Country* (1960) by William York Tindall.

The National Library in Kildare Street displays the manuscript of *A Portrait* as well as Joyce first editions. (Open Monday—Friday 10:00—9:45, Saturday 10:00—12:45; free.)

(See Chapter 1, SWITZERLAND; also Chapter 2, FRANCE; also Chapter 3, PARIS; also Chapter 8, ITALY.)

PATRICK, ST. (ca.389–ca.461). The patron saint of Ireland may not have driven out the frogs and snakes from Ireland as his legend attests, but he did expel (and assimilate part of) the ancient Druid religion, which was often associated with "reptiles, demons and magicians." Not Irish by birth, he was probably a Romano-English farm boy of prosperous family who first came to Ireland as a captured slave in about 405. His real name was Succat, but he was also called Cothrigge, later Latinized as "Patricius." Most of the sites associated with him are located in Northern Ireland and in northern parts of the Republic, though few are well authenticated.

About five miles east of **Broughshane** rises "Slemish," a 1,500-foot-high "mountain" long assumed to be the spot where Patrick solitarily tended his master's sheep for six years, the place where he experienced his conversion, and the region from whence he fled his servitude to the European continent.

About the year 432 he returned as a Christian missionary and bishop to Ireland, traveling widely, evangelizing, baptizing and founding churches. "His course," wrote Charles Francis Potter, "seems to have been from County Down, where he began his work, through County Meath into Ulster, and then into Connaught." Patrick established his central church and monastery at **Armagh** in about 444. Excavations in the garden of 36 Scotch Street, a Georgian town house, indicate this as the possible site of his church.

In his later years Patrick probably retired to the monastery he had founded in **Saul** near the point where he had landed in 432. There he probably wrote his *Confession* and died. Remnants of the 12th-century Saul Abbey on the site may be viewed on route 25 east of Downpatrick. St. Patrick's Memorial Church, built at the village outskirts in 1932 to mark the 1,500th anniversary of the apostle's arrival, also marks the traditional site of the barn given to Patrick by Dichu, a local chieftain convert. There, it is said, Patrick began the conversion of Ireland.

St. Patrick tomb (reputed): St. Patrick's Cathedral churchyard, **Downpatrick**.

(See Chapter 2, FRANCE.)

PENN, WILLIAM (1644–1718). The English Quaker and colonist-founder of Pennsylvania resided at his ancestral estate in **Macroom** from 1656 to 1658. This 13th-century castle was the 1621 birthplace of his father, Admiral Sir William Penn. The later Penn mansion, however, burned down in 1921.

Another family castle, now in ruins, stood in **Shanagarry**. The younger Penn lived there in 1666 and 1667, returning for a visit in 1698.

(See Chapter 5, ENGLAND; also Chapter 6, LONDON.)

RALEIGH, SIR WALTER (1554?–1618). The Elizabethan English adventurer, courtier, poet and colonizer came to Ireland in 1587 as a soldier in the Irish Wars. In 1588, as the warden (mayor) of **Youghal**, he bought and briefly occupied Myrtle Grove, an Elizabethan gabled house. There is apparently no justification for frequent claims that Raleigh reviewed the manuscript of Edmund Spenser's *Faerie Queene* with its author beneath the old front-yard yew tree, that he astounded the natives by smoking Virginia tobacco in his brass pipe, or that he planted the first potato in Ireland on the site. Raleigh sold the house along with his grant of 42,000 acres in 1602, long after his departure. The house stands northeast of the parish church.

(See Chapter 5, ENGLAND; also Chapter 6, LONDON.)

MYRTLE GROVE, HOME OF SIR WALTER RALEIGH. He probably didn't introduce his neighbors to tobacco or plant the first Irish potato there, as popular accounts proclaim, but the Elizabethan adventurer and poet lived there for about a year (1588–89) while serving as warden of **Youghal**. The manor centered a huge land grant owned by Raleigh and remains privately owned.

SHAW, GEORGE BERNARD (1856–1950). The acerbic playwright's birthplace stands in **Dublin** at 33 Synge Street. It was his home until 1866. The family's later Dublin address was 1 Hatch Street. Shaw attended the now-defunct Wesleyan School at 79 Stephen's Green during the 1860s (a "damnable prison," he called it) from which he was expelled in 1868. A six-month attendance at the Central Model Boys School, still a fortresslike institution in Marlborough Street, left him with a lifelong repugnance for formal education. From 1871 until his 1876 escape to London, he worked as a solicitor's clerk at 15 Molesworth Street; "of

GEORGE BERNARD SHAW BIRTHPLACE. The center house, 33 Synge Street, was the playwright's **Dublin** home for his first 10 years. Unlike James Joyce, Shaw bore little nostalgia for his early Dublin years and seldom returned to Ireland after his "escape" at age 20.

all the damnable waste of human life that ever was invented," he said, "clerking is the very worst."

At **Dalkey**, a coastal suburb of Dublin, the family bought Torca Cottage in 1866 and resided there during summers until 1874. Shaw attributed his powers of imagination in part to having been removed at a young age from Dublin "to the heights of Dalkey Hill," where he watched splendid sunsets over Dublin and Killiney bays. The marked house survives in Torca Road midway up Dalkey Hill. After 1876 Shaw only saw Ireland on occasional visits.

(See Chapter 5, ENGLAND; also Chapter 6, LONDON.)

SWIFT, JONATHAN (1667–1745). Not only Ireland's greatest writer but probably the 18th century's foremost English-language prose stylist, Swift was of English ancestry and never let anyone forget it. He was born and died in **Dublin**, but little of the city he knew survives. His birthplace at the corner of Werburgh and Ship Streets (though some biographers dispute the claim) is long gone, but a tablet and bust mark the site.

BIRTHPLACE OF AN UNWILLING IRISHMAN. Jonathan Swift's birthplace no longer stands in what was once Hoey's Court in **Dublin**, but a marker identifies the site at Werburgh and Ship streets.

In 1713, angered and disappointed at his loss of position and power in London, he returned to Dublin to become Anglican dean of St. Patrick's Cathedral. There, between Sunday sermons and intense love affairs with Esther Johnson (his "Stella") and Esther Vanhomrigh ("Vanessa"), he wielded his fierce pen in some of the most lacerating satire ever written. "Night after night," wrote one critic, "the old churl sat by a snug fire in his splendid mansion and wrote hate letters to a world he chose to think had cheated him." This "splendid mansion" was, of course, the St. Patrick's Deanery, where he lived from 1713 and declined to violent insanity, restrained by his servants from self-destruction as he ran up and down the stairs in hyperactive frenzies. He died there. A part of Swift's Deanery was incorporated into the police station that now stands in Bride Street. Adjacent to it is the present Deanery. Built in 1781, it faces Upper Kevin Street and also occupies the original site. A few Swift relics may be seen on application to the house. The walled deanery garden planted by Swift (which he called "Naboth's Vineyard") stood near the southwest corner of the intersection of these streets.

Ordained to the Anglican priesthood in 1695, between long absences Swift became rector of the parish at **Laracor** in 1700 and resided there for 13 years. Northwest of the village church that replaced his own, portions survive of the glebe house where he wrote such tracts and satires as *An Argument Against Abolishing Christianity* (1708) and part of his *Journal to Stella* (1948). He held the appointment there for the rest of his life but seldom returned after 1713.

Swift spent many summers in **Virginia** as the guest of Rev. Thomas Sheridan at Quilca House, Sheridan's home, located about two miles northeast of the village off route T24. In this house Swift wrote the greater part of his satiric masterpiece *Gulliver's Travels* (1726). Later, Sheridan's grandson, playwright Richard Brinsley Sheridan, spent much of his boyhood there.

Celbridge Abbey was the home of Esther ("Vanessa") Vanhomrigh, who lived alone with her servants in this brown mansion built by her father. From about 1715 to 1723, when Swift abruptly ended their passionate affair, he rode there regularly to "drink her coffee," his euphemism for making love. She died there brokenhearted soon after his final enraged visit. The abbey is now occupied by the Hospitaller Brothers of St. John of God, who welcome interested visitors. Apart from the mansion's associations, its interior is a complex maze of corridors, odd woodwork and vaulted cellars replete with ghost tales. Noting "a gloom about the place," Susan and Thomas Cahill wrote, "it is a strange house—even for Ireland, a setting for actions never meant to bear the light of day." Celbridge Abbey stands south of the village on route L2. (Apply at St. Raphael's School across the road from the abbey for admittance.)

Swift tomb: St. Patrick's Cathedral, **Dublin**.

Exhibits: While he excoriated his native Ireland fully as much as he lambasted England for its Irish policies, Swift's sharpest daggers were always reserved for rich parasites and the aggressively stupid of whatever nationality. His personal generosity to common folk, on the other hand, was legendary; and though he chafed at his failure in politics and considered himself "like a poisoned rat in a hole" at St. Patrick's, Dubliners loved him for his reliable sedition ("burn everything from England but her coal," he advised) and championship of their rights. "The man who died mad," wrote the Cahills, "left his entire legacy for the first modern mental institution in Ireland." The 1746 St. Patrick's Hospital (usually known as "Swift's Hospital"), which he intended as his only memorial, still functions as a psychiatric center in Bow Lane West, James's Street, **Dublin**—though it no longer accepts patients without charge, as he stipulated.* The hospital displays an interesting collection of Swift relics which may be seen anytime.

Marsh's Library in St. Patrick's Close near the Deanery, founded in 1701 as Dublin's first public library, is one of the few buildings in modern Dublin that survive from Swift's day. It contains the main collection of Swift memorabilia including his annotated books, the oak table on which he wrote *Gulliver's Travels*, various manuscripts, and his death mask. (Open Monday 2:00—4:00, Wednesday—Friday 10:30—12:30, 2:00—4:00, Saturday 10:30—12:30; free.)

At St. Patrick's Cathedral in Patrick Street, Swift's plain wooden pulpit may be seen in the north transept along with his huge, black-leather chair. (Open daily.) Trinity College Library in College Park displays a few Swift relics in the Manuscript Room, notably his *Autobiographical Fragment*. (Open daily, 10:00—5:00; free.)

(See Chapter 5, ENGLAND; also Chapter 6, LONDON.)

WELLINGTON, ARTHUR WELLESLEY, DUKE OF (1769–1852). A native of **Dublin**, Britain's great military hero, conqueror of Napoleon at Waterloo, and later prime minister was born at Mornington House, 24 Upper Merrion Street. At last report the house bore no marker.

The country house of Wellington's father, the Earl of Mornington, was Dangan Castle. It lies now in ruins on route L25 a short distance south of **Trim**. Wellington spent most of his boyhood years there and attended the diocesan school in the town. The school building, the 1415 Talbot's Castle, was owned in 1717 by Esther Johnson (Jonathan Swift's "Stella") and briefly in 1718 by Swift himself (neither resided there; see the entry on Swift above). The stone building has since been modernized. Wellington resided in Dublingate Street during this period, where a pillar with his statue marks the site. Later (1790–95) he represented Trim in Parliament.

Exhibit: Tullynally Castle, formerly Pakenham Hall, located west of **Castlepollard** on route T10, displays a collection of Wellingtonian relics. This 17th-century mansion was the ancestral seat of Kitty Pakenham, Wellington's wife. (Open June—September, Sunday 2:30—6:00; admission.)

(See Chapter 3, PARIS; also Chapter 4, BELGIUM; also Chapter 5, ENGLAND; also Chapter 6, LONDON; also Chapter 8, SPAIN.)

WILDE, OSCAR (1854–1900). The poet and playwright, noted for his wit and exhibitionism, was born at 21 Westland Row in **Dublin**, his home for only his first year. From 1855 the family's city home was the imposing Georgian mansion at 1 Merrion Square.

Wilde's favorite boyhood home was Moytura House, built by his surgeon father Sir William Wilde as a country house in 1864. It is located about two miles from **Cong** near the mouth of the Lough Corrib.

(See Chapter 3, PARIS; also Chapter 5, ENGLAND; also Chapter 6, LONDON.)

---

*In bestowing this legacy, he wrote: "He gave the little wealth he had / To build a house for fools and mad; / To show, by one satiric touch, / No nation wanted it so much. . . ."

YEATS, WILLIAM BUTLER (1865–1939). One of the 20th century's most notable poets, Yeats—the son of noted painter John Butler Yeats—resided in several **Dublin** homes, though after years away from the city he did not establish himself there permanently until 1922. His birthplace, Georgeville, stands at 5 Sandymount Avenue, and was his home to the age of three. In 1883 the family moved into 10 Ashfield Terrace in the suburb of Harold's Cross and resided there until 1887. In 1922 Yeats bought the large Georgian house at 82 Merrion Square; it was his home until 1928. His next home (1928–32) was the top flat at 42 Fitzwilliam Square. Riversdale House in Willbrook, located in the southern suburb of Rathfarnham, was Yeats's last home from 1932.

The poet's summer residence from 1897 until about 1920 was Coole Park, the home of Augusta, Lady Gregory, playwright and director of the Abbey Theatre in Dublin. She lived there from 1880 until her death in 1932, and the house became a center of the Irish literary revival, hosting George Bernard Shaw, J. M. Synge, Sean O'Casey, John Masefield, Augustus John and—most regularly—Yeats, who worked in a room facing the lake of Coole. "The Wild Swans at Coole" (1919), one of his best-known poems, refers to his time there, as does much poetry of his "middle" period. In what Patrick Byrne called "an incredible act of vandalism," this beautiful house was demolished for its stone materials in 1941, as Yeats had forecast in "Coole Park, 1929." Surviving, however, are its garden walls and stable ruins plus the famed "Autograph Tree," a massive copper beech upon which Lady Gregory's noted guests carved their initials. It stands north of the house site. The grounds today are maintained by the Irish Forestry and Wild Life Service. Coole Park is located two and one-half miles northwest of **Gort** on route N18. (Open daily.) Near Gort (three miles northeast, signposted from route L11) stands Thoor Ballylee, a 16th-century derelict Norman tower bought by Yeats in 1916 from Lady Gregory and restored by him. He used it as a summer home from 1921 to 1929, writing there the poems in his volumes *The Tower* (1928) and *The Winding Stair* (1929). After his death the tower again became derelict, but it was restored by the Bord Failte Éireann and opened as a Yeats museum in 1965. The poet's original oak furniture, china, and first editions of his works may be viewed up the "narrow winding stair, a chamber arched with stone," repainted and preserved as they were when Yeats lived there with his wife, the spiritualist medium Georgie Hyde-Lees. (Open March—June, September—October, daily 10:00—6:00; July—August, daily 9:00—9:00; admission.)

Sligo, the home of Yeats's maternal grandparents, provided rich sources of legend and folklore for the poet, themes to which he returned even in old age. During the 1870s and 1880s he spent many periods at Merville, their large house on 60 acres in the southwest suburb of Magheraboy. Now crowded and overshadowed by urban structures, the residence survives as a part of Nazareth House, an institution for the orphaned and aged.

Yeats tomb: Drumcliff churchyard, **Drumcliff**.

Exhibits: "Yeats country" is the **Sligo** area; the poet mined this territory thoroughly for his mystical and symbolic imagery. The Sligo County Museum in Stephen Street displays an extensive Yeats collection, including letters, first editions, and other memorabilia. (Open Wednesday, Saturday 3:00—5:00; other times by request; free.) The adjacent County Library shows an art collection representing the work of Yeats's talented father, his brother Jack B. Yeats, sisters Susan and Elizabeth Yeats and niece Anne Yeats. (Open on request; free.) *The Yeats Country* (1965), by Sheelah Kirby, is an indispensable guidebook for any Yeats enthusiast in the Sligo area. Maps are also available at the County Museum. The Yeats International Summer School, held in Sligo each August, presents both scholarly and popular lectures, field trips, and plays and films relating to the Irish bard. (Contact The Yeats Society, Sligo, for information.)

(See Chapter 2, FRANCE; also Chapter 5, ENGLAND; also Chapter 6, LONDON.)

SCOTLAND

The Romans, who came as far north as modern Edinburgh in the first century, called the country Caledonia. Later, in 1018, Irish invaders (who were the original "Scots") and Norse invaders conquered the existing warrior kingdoms and native Celt and Pict tribes to establish the kingdom of Scotland. Wars led by William Wallace in 1297 and Robert Bruce in 1314 defeated English armies and maintained Scottish independence; the country was, in fact, never militarily conquered by England.

Until the Reformation, Scotland was strongly allied with France, an alliance which ceased with the end of the Scottish monarchy. The new Protestant doctrine brought the country into much closer cultural contact with England, enabling a union of the kingdoms. In 1603, a final conjunction of the crowns was achieved in the person of James VI, son of the executed Mary, Queen of Scots; he succeeded Elizabeth I on the British throne as James I. A century later, the 1707 Act of Union finalized the creation of Great Britain from the formerly separate countries of England, Scotland and Wales.

The clan system of the Scots, which probably originated in the sixth century, was based on family communities and groups of kinfolk. Clans contested with one another and with the kings who attempted to subjugate them until 1688, when the last clan battle occurred. The modern highland "clan cult" with its tartans, kilts, and piping survives as an antiquarian pursuit (albeit taken very seriously by participants), adding color and ceremony to festive occasions.

Cool and hilly Scotland occupies the northern 37 percent of Great Britain, including the Hebrides, Orkney, Shetland and numerous other islands. The southern uplands remain primarily agricultural, while the rugged granite highlands are sparsely populated. Glasgow, Scotland's largest city and Britain's foremost industrial complex, ranks twice as large as Edinburgh, the capital. About one-third of Scotland's population, approaching 5.5 million, centers in or near these cities.

The Scots, it has been said, share much in common with the Swiss, not in language or in racial heritage but in a certain "mountain psychology" which stems from a strong sense of independence and a strict Calvinistic, "this-worldly" heritage. No refuge for saints, Scotland gave birth to Presbyterianism in the fierce person of reformer-priest John Knox, forcing the abdication of its last exclusively Scottish monarch, the Catholic Mary.

As in Ireland, Wales and England, Scotland's most notable creators have been writers. Adam Smith reflected particularly Scottish values with his erudite formulation of laissez-faire economics, as direct an outgrowth of Calvinism as the work ethic itself. Yet behind Scotland's austere facade—

hustle, save and pray—exists another monotone: the drone of bagpipes, one of the rawest musical sounds on earth. Scotland's distinctive cultural elements, including the pipes and plaids, represent not only the shadow of old nationalistic aspirations but a modern quest for cultural identity, as well as nostalgia for a feisty Scotland that could not be taken for granted by its neighbors.

So anomalies exist. For example, the lowland "dialect Scots" writing of Robert Burns, a man whose character and writings hardly reflected the traditional Protestant virtues, began as a literary compensation for political defeats. Sir Walter Scott romanticized Scottish history in his lengthy *Waverley* series of novels. While Scott and Burns are the most memorialized Scots, James Boswell, Arthur Conan Doyle and Robert Louis Stevenson, though natives, ventured far from strictly Scottish subjects. Not to be forgotten is George Orwell, no Scotsman but an aloof Englishman who found a bleak Scottish island most conducive for writing a major work of the 20th century, *1984*.

BLAIR, ERIC ARTHUR. ("GEORGE ORWELL") (1903–1950). The last permanent home of the English author from 1946 was a remote stone farmhouse on the 30-mile-long Isle of Jura, one of the Inner Hebrides. Orwell was dying of tuberculosis and probably knew it when he rented Barnhill, built about 1900 and lacking a telephone and electricity. Still a relative unknown after a dozen books and numerous essays, he considered himself a literary failure when he began a race against death to write his last book, the chilling, best-selling portrait of the ultimate totalitarian state, *1984* (1949). (Orwell titled the book by simply reversing the last two digits of 1948, the year in which he wrote it.) The eight-room house where the writer, his adopted son, his sister, and a housekeeper lived until Orwell entered a sanatorium stands about seven miles north of **Ardlussa** at the end of a rutted, unpaved road (route A846) on the northern end of the island. During the year 1984 the desolate island became a literary-political shrine as hundreds of Orwell devotees sought this windswept corner of the world in order to honor his memory. As of 1984 there was no direct access from the mainland; the trip requires two ferry rides starting from the dock of Kinnacraig.

Orwell's home for most of the year 1949 was the private Cotswold Sanatorium at **Cranham**.

(See Chapter 3, PARIS; also Chapter 5, ENGLAND; also Chapter 6, LONDON.)

BOSWELL, JAMES (1740–1795). The devoted companion and biographer of Samuel Johnson was a native of **Edinburgh**. He was born in the fourth-floor rooms of a tenement that stood in Parliament Square, and which remained his home until 1749. Practicing law in the city during the 1760s and 1770s, Boswell occupied the former residence of philosopher David Hume at the eastern end of St. James's Court off the Lawnmarket, a house which was later destroyed by fire. Boswell was host to Johnson there in 1773. The only one of his city lodgings that survives is 15A Meadow Place, which he rented from an uncle.

The 17th-century family estate at **Auchinleck** came into Boswell's possession in 1782 after his father's death. Auchinleck House, which his family occupied until 1762, stands about three miles west of the village. Boswell himself never resided there after 1786, when he moved permanently to London.

Boswell tomb: Parish church, **Auchinleck**.

Exhibit: The **Auchinleck** Boswell Society maintains the Boswell Museum in the old parish church where his family worshipped. Located on Church Hill off route A76, it displays memorabilia and documents relating to the biographer. (Open Easter—September, Monday, Friday 6:30PM—8:00PM; other times by appointment with curator, 131 Main Street; Cummock 0290–20757; free.)

(See Chapter 6, LONDON.)

BURNS, ROBERT (1759–1796). Scotland's foremost poet, a native of **Alloway**, was born in a single-room thatched cottage that still survives. Rebuilt by his father from a clay hut in 1757, it remained Burns's home until 1764. Later, until

FIRST HOME OF SCOTLAND'S FOREMOST POET. Robert Burns was born in 1759 in this **Alloway** cottage built two years earlier by his father (the portion on the left). Much restored, it remains Scotland's foremost Burns museum among many.

1880, it was used as an ale-house. A museum at the rear of the Burns Cottage displays manuscripts, letters, songs he wrote, the family Bible and other relics. Poet John Keats wasn't much impressed with the place during his 1818 visit: "Oh, the flummery of birthplaces!" he wrote, a still often-valid lament of literary pilgrims everywhere. "It's enough to give a spirit the guts-ache." The Burns Cottage stands on route B7024 in the village. (Open April—mid-October, Monday—Saturday 9:00—7:00; June—August, daily 10:00—7:00; also March—May, September—October, Sunday 2:00—7:00; 0292-41215; admission.) In 1764 the family moved to Mount Oliphant Farm, located about two miles south on the same road.

From 1777 Burns lived with his parental family at Lochlea Farm, about three miles northwest of **Mauchline** off route B744, until his father's death in 1784. There he wrote some of the poems collected in his first book, *Poems Chiefly in the Scottish Dialect* (1786). From 1784 to 1789 the poet resided at Mossgiel, a rented farmhouse one mile north of Mauchline on the Tarbolton road, where he accomplished much of his best work. The house has been rebuilt on the site. Burns's first married home with Jean Armour Burns—the couple honeymooned in a rented room there in 1788—is now the Burns House Museum in Castle Street. Many relics of the poet are displayed. (Open daily 9:00—6:00; 0290-50213; admission.)

In 1781 and 1782 Burns studied flax dressing at **Irvine**, where he lived at 4 Glasgow Vennel. The house is marked.

In 1789 Burns leased Ellisland, a 100-acre farm located six miles northwest of **Dumfries** on route A76. He intended to improve the farm with new agricultural methods but failed to make it self-supporting, finally concluding in 1791 that farming was "an altogether ruinous business." He did produce some of his best-known works there, however, including his narrative poem *Tam O'Shanter* (1791). Personal relics associated with the poet are displayed, and scenes of many of his poems are signposted on the property. (Open daily, unrestricted times; Auldgirth 038774-426; free.)

Dumfries was the poet's home from 1791 until his death at his last residence, a two-story cottage in what is now Burns Street. In his study there he penned about 100 songs, among them "Auld Lang Syne" (1796). Now a museum, the Burns House displays books, manuscripts, personal relics, and memorabilia. Burns's bedroom remains furnished as it was on the day of his death. (Open April—June, September, Monday, Wednesday—Saturday 10:00—1:00, 2:00—5:00; July—August, Monday—Saturday 10:00—5:00, Sunday 2:00—5:00; October—March, Monday—Friday 2:00—4:30; 0387-5297; admission.)

Burns tomb: St. Michael's churchyard, **Dumfries**.

Exhibits: Judging from the number of Scottish exhibits devoted to Robert Burns memorabilia, one might conclude that the poet owned a lot more in the way of worldly goods than his numerous biographers would have us believe, but the word "memorabilia" covers multiple objects, of course, and in this case some of them are more directly relevant than others. Anyone seriously interested in viewing relics of the poet will soon sort out the exhibits that genuinely contribute to one's understanding of the man and writer from the "flummery" deplored by Keats.

In **Alloway** the Robert Burns Interpretation Centre presents audiovisual programs on the poet's life as well as exhibits. An annual highlight is the Burns Festival in mid-June, featuring special presentations and displays. (Open June, September, daily 10:00—6:00; July—August, daily 10:00—9:00; October—May, daily 10:00—5:00; 0292-43700; admission.) The nearby Burns Monument contains locks of the poet's hair and Highland Mary's Bibles. (Open same times as Burns Cottage, see above).

The Tam O'Shanter Museum in the High Street at **Ayr** is a former brewery to which Douglas Graham, on whom Burns based the title character of his poem, supplied grain. Burns portraits, prints and many small personal items belonging to the poet and his wife—including his cradle—are displayed. (Open April—September, Monday—Saturday 9:30—5:30; also June—August, Sunday 2:30—5:00; October—March, Monday—Saturday 12:00—4:00; 0292-69794; admission.)

The Burns Monument and Museum at Kay Park in **Kilmarnock**, where Burns's first volume of poetry was published, is a Victorian tower which has various manuscripts and first editions on display. (Open May—September by appointment with Curator of Dick Institute, Kilmarnock KAI 3BU; 0563-26401.)

In **Kirkoswald**, "Souter Johnnie's Cottage" belonged to cobbler John Davidson, a smuggler and Burns drinking companion who became "Souter Johnnie" in Burns's *Tam O'Shanter*. The thatched

18th-century cottage where Burns spent many hours swapping tall tales contains several pieces of original furniture, Davidson's reconstructed shop and, in the back garden, life-size detailed figures of Davidson and his friends. Literary historian Emilie C. Harting calls this cottage "a much more authentic slice of Burns's world" than the poet's "relatively bare" birthplace cottage in Alloway. It is owned by the National Trust for Scotland. (Open April 1—September 30, Sunday—Thursday, Saturday 12:00—5:00, other times by appointment; 06556–603; admission.)

In **Edinburgh**, Lady Stair's House in Lady Stair's Close off the Lawnmarket, a 1622 town house museum owned by the city, displays many literary relics of Burns, Sir Walter Scott and Robert Louis Stevenson (see the entries on Scott and Stevenson later in this section). Prints illustrating scenes from *Tam O'Shanter* and other Burns poems plus the poet's snuffboxes and sword stick are among the items exhibited. (Open June—September, Monday—Saturday 10:00—6:00; October—May, Monday—Saturday 10:00—5:00; 031–225–2424; free.)

The Globe Inn in **Dumfries**, Burns's favorite tavern, displays his chair and other relics.

Other collections of Burnsiana include exhibits at the Mitchell Library in North Street, **Glasgow**; and the Munson Burns Collection at the Central Library, Abbot Street, in **Dumfermline** (inquire locally for admission information).

BYRON, GEORGE GORDON, LORD (1788–1824).
As a child the English poet lived in **Aberdeen** with his mother at 64 Broad Street (now gone) from 1792 to 1798, the period when he attended the Old Grammar School.

Exhibit: The 1757 school building on Schoolhill is now the **Aberdeen** Art Gallery and Museums, displaying 16th- to 20th-century Scottish paintings and sculpture. (Open Monday—Saturday 10:00—5:00, except Thursday to 8:00, Sunday 2:00—5:00; 0224–26333; free.)

(See Chapter 1, SWITZERLAND; also Chapter 4, BELGIUM; also Chapter 5, ENGLAND; also Chapter 6, LONDON; also Chapter 8, GREECE, ITALY.)

CARLYLE, THOMAS (1795–1881).
The birthplace of the historian and essayist stands at **Ecclefechan** in the village's main street. Carlyle's father, a master mason, built this arched two-story house with his own hands in 1791, and his son lived there until 1806. Carlyle's birth room, now

furnished as a study, displays his cradle, traveling desk and manuscript letters. A number of original furnishings and domestic utensils owned by the family are also exhibited by the National Trust for Scotland. (Open April 1—October 31, Monday—Saturday 10:00—6:00; 05763–666; admission.)

After Carlyle's 1826 marriage to Jane Welsh, the couple lived at 21 Comely Bank in **Edinburgh** for two years. The house is marked with a tablet.

Jane Carlyle inherited a moorland farm at **Craigenputtock**, where the pair resided from 1828 to 1834. There Carlyle wrote his satiric *Sartor Resartus* (1833-34). The farm is located seven miles of Dunscore.

Carlyle tomb: Village cemetery, **Ecclefechan**.

Exhibit: At **Annan**, where Carlyle attended the Old Grammar School, the Moat House in the village displays memorabilia of his schooldays. (Inquire locally for admission information.)

(See Chapter 6, LONDON.)

CRUSOE, ROBINSON. See ALEXANDER SELKIRK.

DARWIN, CHARLES ROBERT (1809–1882).
The great English naturalist attended the University of **Edinburgh**, somewhat aimlessly preparing himself for the ministry before his epochal voyage on the *Beagle* and subsequent dedication of his life to science. With his brother Erasmus he lodged in fourth-floor rooms at 11 Lothian Street from 1825 to 1827.

(See Chapter 5, ENGLAND; also Chapter 6, LONDON.)

DOYLE, SIR ARTHUR CONAN (1859–1930).
The physician and author-creator of Sherlock Holmes was born at 11 Picardy Place in **Edinburgh**; the house was demolished in 1969. His family moved to various addresses in the city during his boyhood, among them 3 Sciennes Hill Place, which remained his home until 1876.

(See Chapter 1, SWITZERLAND; also Chapter 5, ENGLAND; also Chapter 6, LONDON.)

EDWARD VIII (1894–1972).
The brief monarch of Great Britain (1936), a man who had trained all his life to be king—and who, after his abdication for "the woman I love," became the duke of Windsor—spent much of his youth and young manhood at the royal highland residence of Balmoral near **Braemar**, where his parents, George V and Queen Mary, often resided. As king Edward made only one hurried visit there (see the entry of Victoria later in this section).

(See Chapter 2, FRANCE; also Chapter 3, PARIS, also Chapter 5, ENGLAND; also Chapter 6, LONDON.)

KNOX, JOHN (1505–1572). "He was a savage hater," wrote Antonia Fraser. "He saw himself as a heaven-sent preacher, whereas in fact he was a bold earthly revolutionary, who openly preached violence, and notoriously considered the death of an unjust ruler absolutely justified." The location of the Protestant reformer's birth site in **Haddington** remains uncertain, though biographers speculate that the house may have stood in either Gifford Road or Giffordgate.

At **St. Andrews** Castle, a ruined 13th-century stronghold, the fugitive heretic Knox joined other members of the outlawed faith in 1547. There for the first time he powerfully raised his voice against the papacy. Catholic forces of the Scottish regent reinforced by French troops soon seized the castle, and Knox was taken prisoner and served in the French galleys for almost two years. The castle ruins are now classified as an Ancient Monument, operated by the Scottish Development Department. (Open April—September, Monday—Saturday 9:30—7:00, Sunday 2:00—7:00; October—March, Monday—Saturday 9:30—4:00, Sunday 2:00—4:00; admission.) An earlier St. Andrews residence of Knox, during the 1530s and 1540s, was the 1512 St. Leonard's College. Its site and some of the old buildings are now occupied by St. Leonard's School for Girls at Abbey and South Streets. It was there that Knox, questioning certain church practices, began thinking like a reformer.

In **Edinburgh**, now the author of an inflammatory tract titled *First Blast of the Trumpet Against the Monstrous Regiment of Women* (1558), aimed primarily at his bewildered queen, the ex-Catholic priest ministered to the Reformed congregation at St. Giles's Cathedral from 1560. He lived in a 15th-century stone dwelling between the cathedral and Holyrood Palace in High Street, now the John Knox House Museum. Recent renovation has uncovered the original flooring in the Oak Room as well as a magnificent painted ceiling completed after Knox died here. Numerous memorabilia of the Presbyterian founder are exhibited. A model of the house is also on display, along with old prints and paintings showing its history and development. (Open Monday—Saturday 10:00—5:00; 031–556–6961; admission.)

THE JOHN KNOX HOUSE. This last home of the fierce reformer in **Edinburgh** has become a shrine devoted to the founder of Presbyterianism. The restored stone dwelling dates from the 15th century.

Knox tomb: Parliament Square, **Edinburgh**.

Exhibits: In **Edinburgh** St. Giles's Cathedral, where Knox thundered against Rome and the Catholic Mary, Queen of Scots (see the entry on Mary later in this section), has not been formally designated a cathedral since 1688, when it was Anglican. Officially, as the Presbyterian "mother church," it is known as the High Kirk of St. Giles. The present church, which was restored in the 19th century, dates from the 14th century. It was built on the site of a church first established in 984. Its tower, shaped like the crown of Scotland, stands at High Street and the Lawnmarket, not far from Knox's house. (Open daily; free.) Huntly House, a 1570 structure housing the City Museum at 142 Canongate, displays Knox's Psalter. (Open June—September, Monday—Saturday 10:00—6:00; October—May, Monday—Saturday 10:00—5:00; 031–225–2424; free.) In the National Museum of Antiquities at 1 Queen Street, may be seen Knox's wooden pulpit from St. Giles's. (Open Monday—Saturday

10:00—5:00, Sunday 2:00—5:00; 031-556-8921; free.)

(See Chapter 1, SWITZERLAND.)

LIVINGSTONE, DAVID (1813–1873). The famed missionary-explorer's birthplace stands in **Blantyre**. This 1775 mill tenement building housed 24 families, eight on each of three floors. The 14 x 10-foot room where Livingstone's parents and five children lived until 1827 is now part of an elaborate David Livingstone Centre, which displays memorabilia and personal relics along with an Africa Pavilion, showing modern African exhibits, and a Shuttle Row (Social History) museum. (Open Monday—Saturday 10:00—6:00, Sunday 2:00—6:00; 0698-823140; admission.)

DAIVD LIVINGSTONE'S BIRTHPLACE. The famed medical missionary to Africa was born in this massive, stuccoed-brick tenement building that housed 24 factory families in extremely crowded conditions. It is now part of a dressed-up museum complex that commemorates the **Blantyre** native.

Exhibit: St. Peter's Church in Francis Street, **Stornoway**, displays Livingstone's prayer book. (Open daily.)

(See Chapter 6, LONDON; also Chapter 8, PORTUGAL.)

MACBETH (?–1057). The character on whom Shakespeare built his tragedy actually did murder his cousin, King Duncan I, in 1040, and seize the Scottish throne, only to be slain himself by Duncan's son, Malcolm III, 17 years later. Contrary to the legends and chronicles used by Shakespeare, however, Macbeth was a fairly successful king of excellent qualities.

Nothing remains of his **Dingwall** birthplace except a few stones of a later 13th-century castle at the foot of Castle Street.

Where did Macbeth murder Duncan in 1040? Shakespeare places the location at **Inverness**, where the royal palace stood at Ault Castle Hill east of the present Castle Hill. The old castle was razed by Malcolm III soon after Macbeth's death. Other sources give the murder site as **Cawdor**, promised to Macbeth by the three witches on the "blasted heath." The oldest part of the present castle in this village dates only from the 14th century. It is the home of the present Earl of Cawdor. (Open May—September, daily 10:00—5:30; 06677-615; admission.) More likely than either of these sites was **Forres** Castle, now long gone from its site at the west end of High Street.

Probably Macbeth's main residence after becoming king was the ancient Scottish royal seat at **Scone**, where all of the Scottish kings until James I were crowned. Moot Hill, a solemn meeting place of Scottish royalty dating from the eighth century, rises in front of the 19th-century Scone Palace, incorporating parts of a 1580 palace that succeeded the ancient abbey and palace destroyed on this site by a Reformation mob in 1559. The "Stone of Scone" or "Stone of Destiny," on which the coronations took place, was removed by Edward I in 1297 to London, where it now lies beneath the coronation chair in Westminster Abbey. Scone Palace, seat of the Earl of Mansfield, displays French furniture, fine china, needlework and miscellaneous art objects but nothing directly relating to the historic site itself. (Open Easter—mid-October, Monday—Saturday 10:00—6:00, Sunday 2:00—6:00; 0738-52300; admission.)

Macbeth tomb (unmarked): Reilig Odhrain (St. Oran's Cemetery), **Iona**, Inner Hebrides.

MARY, QUEEN OF SCOTS (1542–1587). The daughter of Scotland's King James V and Mary of Guise, the successor to the Scottish throne at her birth, Mary Stuart was born in the northwest corner room of **Linlithgow** Palace. This palace, one of Scotland's most splendid fortified castles, was the traditional lying-in place of Scottish queens (James V himself had been born there) and it remained Mary's infant home until 1543. Edward I of England built the first tower at the southwest angle in 1302, a structure later incorporated into the palace that arose in the 15th century. Most of the present palace dates from the time of Mary's father, who vastly altered and enlarged it. The ornate quadrangle fountain in the courtyard was a 1538 wedding present from Mary's father to her mother and is said to have run with wine on that occasion. Mary's son (by Henry, Lord Darnley), who became British King James I in 1603, rebuilt the palace in 1618. In 1633 Charles I became the last monarch to stay there. The chamber where Mary was born is now roofless from a 1746 fire, as are many of the halls and rooms. Visitors may see the 94-foot-long great hall, the royal apartments and the chapel, among other portions of this grand ruin overlooking the town's lake. The castle is classified as an Ancient Monument. (Open April—September, Monday—Saturday 9:30—7:00, Sunday 2:00—7:00; October—March, Monday—Saturday 9:30—4:00, Sunday 2:00—4:00; admission.)

From 1543 until her 1548 departure to France as the intended child bride of the prince who would become the French King Francis II, Mary's home was **Stirling** Castle. It was here that at the age of nine months she was crowned Scottish queen in the Chapel Royal. A castle has stood on this site at least from the 12th century and possibly earlier, but most of the present buildings are fine examples of Renaissance architecture dating from the 15th and 16th centuries. Once considered the strongest castle in Scotland, Stirling was selected as the young queen's home because of fears that an attempt would be made by the English to abduct her. Much later, her son, James I, also spent his childhood here. He was crowned as James VI of Scotland in the castle in 1567; it ceased to be a royal residence when he also became king of England in 1603. A small round hole in the wall of "Queen Victoria's Lookout" on the northwest ramparts is said to have been made to enable the child Mary to look out. Upon her return to Scotland as the widowed queen of France in 1561, she resided here only occasionally. Castle buildings are arranged around lower and upper squares with

exhibits on excavations and various antiquities. The castle surmounts the town on a high escarpment in Upper Castle Hill. (Open January—April, November—December, Monday—Saturday 9:30—5:00, Sunday 12:30—4:30; May—October, Monday—Saturday 9:30—6:00, Sunday 11:00—6:00; admission.) On one side of the castle esplanade is a Scottish Landmark Centre which presents an audiovisual history of the castle's last 700 years. (Open March—October, daily 9:00—6:00; admission.)

At **Edinburgh** Castle in 1566 Mary gave birth to James I after a long, painful labor. A fortress existed on this site from the seventh century, though the 1076 St. Margaret's Chapel is now the oldest building in this high fortress on Castle Hill. It is a place that has experienced the full turbulence of Scottish history. Queen Mary's Apartments display furniture and period relics plus the tiny, curiously shaped room in which James was born. The castle also holds the historic crown regalia of Scotland plus the United Services Museum, Scotland's foremost military museum, and the Scottish National War Memorial. (Open May—October, Monday—Saturday 9:30—6:00, Sunday 11:00—6:00; November—April, Monday—Saturday 9:30—5:00, Sunday 12:30—4:30; admission.)

HOLYROODHOUSE PALACE. Mary, Queen of Scots made this historic seat of the Scottish monarchs her **Edinburgh** residence from 1561 to 1567. Her private apartments and audience chamber are displayed in the castle, which remains an official royal domicile.

Mary's foremost residence from 1561 until her forced abdication in 1567 was the Palace of Holyroodhouse, also in Edinburgh. In 1566 she witnessed the murder there of her secretary and alleged lover, David Rizzio, by a group of nobles.

Construction of the palace began about 1500 by Scottish King James IV, but most of it burned down in 1544 and was reconstructed. Oliver Cromwell occupied it briefly in 1650, and it was enlarged to its present dimensions during the reign of Charles II. In 1745 "Bonnie Prince Charlie," the Young Pretender, held court there. Though no sovereign has resided there for any length of time since James I left to ascend the English throne, most subsequent British monarchs have visited, and the palace still functions as the reigning sovereign's official Edinburgh residence. It remains best known, however, for its many associations with Mary Stuart. In 1565 she married her second husband, Lord Darnley, in the Chapel Royal (i.e., Holyrood Abbey, now ruins in the palace inner quadrangle). Two years later in the Picture Gallery, which now contains portraits of 111 Scottish kings (most of whose images are based on artistic imagination), she hastily married the Earl of Bothwell in a Protestant rite. The Historical Apartments display the rooms of Mary and Lord Darnley; the audience chamber here was the scene of her famous 1561 confrontation with John Knox (see the entry on Knox earlier in this section) and the murder of Rizzio. Rich tapestries and period furnishings decorate these rooms, witness to so much Scottish history and its reverberations across Britain and Europe. Holyroodhouse Palace stands at the east end of Canongate. (Open January—March, October 24—December, Monday—Saturday 9:30—4:30; March—October 23, Monday—Saturday 9:30—6:00, Sunday 11:00—5:15; 031-556-7371; admission.)

A number of other palace residences also served Mary during the adult years of her reign. **Falkland** Palace, now operated by the National Trust for Scotland, was a favorite royal hunting residence. Dating from the 12th century, it owes its present appearance to Mary's father, James V, who died there in 1542 shortly after being told of his daughter's birth. The royal apartments were located in the east wing, now ruins. Falkland's royal tennis court, dating from 1539, is Britain's oldest. Guided tours through palace and gardens proceed from the Visitor Centre. (Open April—October, Monday—Saturday 10:00—6:00, Sunday 2:00—6:00; 03375-397; admission.)

Craigmillar Castle, located east off Old Dalkeith Road southeast of **Edinburgh**, was one of Mary's favorite palaces. It is also the spot where, with or without her complicity, Darnley's 1567 murder was plotted—and where, later that year, she was

brought in a daze of horror after her surrender to Scottish rebels and Bothwell's desertion. In biographer Antonia Fraser's words, "For the first time she began to realize what the effect had been on the ordinary people of Scotland. . . of her reckless action in marrying her husband's assassin. To them she was now no longer their young and beautiful queen, but an adulteress. . . who had subsequently become the willing bride of a murderer." Craigmillar Castle dates from 1374 with 16th- and 17th-century additions. Period-furnished rooms may be viewed as well as the castle's strong wall defenses and a dungeon. (Open April—September, Monday—Wednesday, Saturday 9:30—7:00, Thursday 9:30—12:00, Sunday 2:00—7:00; October—March, as above except closes at 4:00; admission.)

At **Jedburgh** Mary Queen of Scots House in Queen Street displays exhibits relating to Mary, including letters and her enameled watch, which was recovered 200 years after she lost it in the "queen's mire" near Hermitage Castle in this area. Her personal communion service and death mask may not be authentic relics. Mary resided here in 1566 and fell violently ill on her return from Hermitage Castle, where she had visited the seriously wounded Bothwell. Her death seemed imminent, but she finally recovered because of—or despite—some rigorous "medical" treatment. It appears she had chosen the house because it was the only one in Jedburgh with indoor sanitation (probably anything but sanitary); the conditions may have contributed to her illness. (Open March—October, daily 10:00—5:30; 08356-3331; admission.)

Following her arrest in 1567, Mary was imprisoned for 11 months at Loch Leven Castle on Castle Island, where she suffered unsympathetic treatment as well as a miscarriage of twins. There also, by persuasion or force, she signed a deed of abdication in favor of her son, James VI. In May 1568 sympathizers finally accomplished her escape from the castle. (Sir Walter Scott's novel *The Abbot* [1820] describes this event.) In Mary's time the island in Loch Leven was smaller than today and the lake itself much larger. The tower where she lodged and parts of the wall date from the early 14th century. This castle, an Ancient Monument, is approached via ferry from **Kinross**. (Open April—September, Monday—Saturday 9:30—7:00, Sunday 2:00—7:00; ferry charge only.)

In borrowed clothes and shorn of her spectacular auburn hair, the fugitive queen chose flight to

England; there she was to remain imprisoned for 19 more years, and was finally to die on the scaffold. Her last, brief residence in Scotland was the 12th-century Cistercian Dundrennan Abbey, one of the country's most beautiful cloisters, where she wrote a final letter to Elizabeth I asking for sanctuary. She did not wait for a reply, however, before fleeing across the border. This abbey fell into ruin in the 17th century (it is now an Ancient Monument) and many of its stones were used for construction in the village of **Dundrennan**. (Open April—September, Monday—Saturday 9:30—7:00, Sunday 2:00—7:00; October—March, Monday—Saturday 9:30—4:00, Sunday 2:00—4:00; admission.)

Exhibits: As Antonia Fraser points out, many of the so-called execution relics which are displayed in Scotland and other places are of dubious authenticity, since Mary's English executioners took great care to destroy or confiscate every item of clothing, jewelry, and so on, that might possibly serve as "a holy relic to inspire devotion in years to come." Earlier authentic items do survive, however; they include many embroideries from Mary's expert hand (embroidery was an activity that grew to a virtual mania during her long years of captivity and enforced leisure) including pillows, bed hangings, chair covers, and quilts. These items are scattered throughout many European museums, and some also remain in private hands.

The 10th-century Traquair House, one mile south of **Innerleithen** on route B709—said to be the oldest continuously inhabited home in Scotland—was visited by Mary and Lord Darnley in 1566. Among its many historical treasures are one of those quilts embroidered by the imprisoned queen and the cradle of her son, James I. (Open Easter—October, daily 1:30—5:30; also July—August, from 10:30; 0896-830323; admission.)

The National Museum of Antiquities in **Edinburgh** also displays personal relics of the queen (see the entry on John Knox, *Exhibits*, earlier in this section); while the National Library of Scotland on George IV Bridge displays her last letter, written on the eve of her execution (open Monday—Friday 9:30—5:00, Saturday 9:30—1:00; free.)

In **Glasgow** the People's Palace on Glasgow Green exhibits the queen's purse and ring. (Open Monday—Saturday 10:00—5:00, Sunday 2:00—5:00; 041-554-0223; free.)

(See Chapter 2, FRANCE; also Chapter 3, PARIS; also Chapter 5, ENGLAND.)

ORWELL, GEORGE. See ERIC ARTHUR BLAIR.

RUSKIN, JOHN (1819–1900). The English art critic and historian spent numerous holidays as a boy with his parents in **Perth**, where their house stands marked at 10 Rose Terrace. In 1848 he married Euphemia Gray in her parental home, which had formerly belonged to Ruskin's grandparents (his grandfather had killed himself there). This house, now a home for senior citizens, also survives in the Bowerswell.

(See Chapter 5, ENGLAND; also Chapter 6, LONDON.)

SCOTT, SIR WALTER (1771–1832). Almost every European country has its leading Romantic novelist and poet, and Scott is Scotland's. A child of **Edinburgh**, Scott lived at his birthplace, a house that stood in College Wynd, until 1774. The approximate vicinity is marked by a tablet at 8 Chambers Street. From 1774 to 1797 the family resided at 25 George Square. After marrying Charlotte Carpenter in 1797, the couple lived at 108 George Street, then at 10 South Castle Street. In 1802 they moved into 39 Castle Street, which remained their Edinburgh home until 1826. Scott wrote most of his *Waverley* series of 32 novels and most of his best-known poetry at the latter address.

Located about five miles west of **Galashiels** is Ashiestiel, the house Scott rented from 1804 to 1812 while serving as sheriff of Selkirk. His first important work, *The Lay of the Last Minstrel* (1805), was published while he lived there, and there he also began his first novel, *Waverley* (1814). The house on Ashiestiel Hill overlooks the river on route 72, where the road turns northeast for Clovenfords.

Scott's last home, from 1812, was Abbotsford House, located about three miles west of **Melrose** on the Tweed. He bought the small farm called Cartleyhole, formerly owned by the monks of Melrose Abbey, and renamed it Abbotsford because it had been the monks' fording place across the river. Scott demolished the original farmhouse in 1822 and built the present mansion; the west wing and entrance lodge, however, were added after his death. Scott's house has been described as "mock baronial," an amalgam of turrets, gables and stylistic copies of miscellaneous Scottish palaces, chapels and cloisters. The rooms are still maintained by Scott descendants and are well preserved. They include his study, his 9,000-volume library, drawing room, armoury, and the dining room where he died after a long illness. Visitors may see many original furnishings, family Bibles and portraits, Scott's clothing and blunderbuss, plus his curious collection of weapons and historical exotica which includes such items as Napoleon's cloak clasp, Rob Roy's purse, a lock of Bonnie Prince Charlie's hair, and a bizarre portrait of the decapitated head of Mary, Queen of Scots. Scott entertained many literary visitors, including Washington Irving, Thomas Moore and William Wordsworth. His house and large estate eloquently reflect Scott the writer, as well as his boyhood dream of becoming a great border lord. When financial disaster overtook him in his later years, Scott's creditors gave him back the house they had prepared to claim for debts. (Open March 21—October, Monday—Saturday 10:00—5:00, Sunday 2:00—5:00; 0896—2043; admission.)

Scott tomb: Dryburgh Abbey, **Dryburgh**.

Exhibits: In **Edinburgh** more Scott relics are displayed in the National Museum of Antiquities and in Lady Stair's House; plus letters and papers at the National Library (see the entry on Robert Burns, *Exhibits*, earlier in this section). In Lady Stair's House may be seen Scott's tall, stand-up desk and his childhood rocking horse with its unequal footrests built to accommodate his lameness. The 1844 Scott Monument, a 200-foot spire forming a canopy over his statue, stands in East Princes Street Gardens. Niches display 64 figures of characters from his works. (Open April—September, Monday—Friday 9:00—6:00; October—March, Monday—Friday 9:00—3:00; admission.)

In **Selkirk** the 1803 Town Hall at Ettrick Terrace was formerly the courthouse where Scott performed his judicial duties as sheriff from 1804 to 1812. Relics of his association with the town are displayed. (Open mid-May—mid-September, Monday, Wednesday, Friday 2:00—4:45; also July—August, Tuesday, Thursday, same times; 0750—20096; free.) Bowhill, the 1795 mansion and seat of the Duke of Buccleuch, also displays Scott memorabilia. It lies two and one-half miles west of Selkirk off route A708. (Open May—June, September, Monday, Wednesday, Saturday 12:30—5:00, Sunday 2:00—6:00; July—August, Saturday—Thursday, same times; 0750—20732; admission.)

(See Chapter 5, ENGLAND.)

SELKIRK, ALEXANDER (1676–1720). The sailor and castaway, whose story was adapted by Daniel Defoe in his novel *Robinson Crusoe* (1719–20), was a native and lifelong resident (when not at sea) of **Largo**. A brawler and pirate, he was marooned by choice in 1705 from his ill-destined ship at Mas a Tierra Island, 400 miles off Chile, and there spent four years and four months in solitude, learning to capture goats for food and slowly mastering his environment. Finally back in Largo, his solitary habits proved addictive, and he made a cave for himself in the garden behind the family homestead. Eventually he went back to sea and died off the coast of Africa. His thatched cottage on the shoreline has been reconstructed on High Street, marked by a statue of Crusoe staring out to sea.

Exhibit: In **Edinburgh** at the National Museum of Antiquities may be seen a few Selkirk relics, including the coconut-shell drinking cup he fashioned during his island sojourn (see the entry on Robert Burns, *Exhibits*, earlier in this section.)

SMITH, ADAM (1723–1790). Founder of the classical school of economics, Smith was a native of **Kirkcaldy**. A plaque marks the site of his birthplace at 220 High Street, which was his home until 1737. Smith produced most of his influential treatise on laissez-faire economics, *The Wealth of Nations* (1776), there. The many-windowed house was demolished in 1844; a high wall and path on the property survive as Adam Smith's Close.

Smith's last home from 1778 was Panmure House at the foot of Panmure Close in the Canongate at **Edinburgh**. Smith died there. Built about 1691, the building later housed an iron foundry, then fell into ruin. It was restored in 1957.

Smith tomb: Canongate Church, **Edinburgh**.

STEVENSON, ROBERT LOUIS (1850–1894). A native of **Edinburgh**, the writer was born at 8 Howard Place. It was his home until 1853. Though once a Stevenson museum, this two-story stone house is no longer open to the public. From 1853 to 1857 the family resided at 1 Inverleith Terrace (now gone). They moved to 17 Heriot Row in 1857, and this pleasant house remained Stevenson's Edinburgh home until 1887, though he traveled frequently. A sickly child, Stevenson was often confined to his bed there, but during periods of health he would play in the gardens across the street from the house.

Another favorite boyhood home was The Manse, the rectory of his maternal grandfather in suburban Colinton. Much later Stevenson celebrated the house (which survives near the parish church) in his essay "The Manse."

BIRTHPLACE OF ROBERT LOUIS STEVENSON. Formerly a Stevenson museum, this dwelling at 8 Howard Place in **Edinburgh** has reverted to private ownership. Stevenson resided there with his parents for his first three years.

Swanston Cottage in the Swanston section of Edinburgh was the writer's frequent summer house from 1867 to 1881. The house on Swanston Road is now screened by trees in a neglected garden.

In **Braemar**, the house where Stevenson in 1881 began his novel *Treasure Island* (1883) stands opposite the Invercauld Festival Theatre.

Exhibits: Lady Stair's House in **Edinburgh** now contains the Stevenson exhibits formerly displayed at the author's birthplace. These include many letters, portraits and photographs, plus personal and family relics. More Stevenson letters and papers may be seen at the National Library. (See the entry on Robert Burns, *Exhibits*, earlier in this section.)

A still interesting if dated account of Stevenson's homes and travels is *On the Trail of Stevenson* (1915) by Clayton Hamilton.

(See Chapter 1, SWITZERLAND; also Chapter 2, FRANCE; also Chapter 5, ENGLAND.)

VICTORIA (1819–1901). Britain's queen from 1837 and her consort, Prince Albert, first visited Scotland in 1842, a year in which residual hostilily against England for the ill-fated Stuart monarchy still existed. Her decision to establish a highland residence, however, did much to assuage these lingering feelings and help unite Scotland and England in spirit as well as fact. In 1848 she leased, sight unseen, the 10,000-acre estate of Balmoral,

with its 1839 palace built by Sir Robert Gordon on the site of a 15th-century castle. Another 20,000 acres, mostly forest, were later acquired. The estate on the River Dee became a favorite resort of Prince Albert, who hunted deer and grouse there at every opportunity. Surrounded by moors, steep crags and dense woodland, Balmoral's splendid isolation also appealed to the queen, and the royal family spent weeks—and eventually months—there each year. A larger palace was soon required for their extensive retinue, however, and after Prince Albert bought the estate in 1852, work commenced on the present palace. This much larger towered and turreted structure with its thick granite walls arose some 100 yards north of the previous castle, which was then demolished. The family first occupied the new structure in 1855. After Prince Albert's death in 1861, Victoria continued to return each year for lengthy stays, the estate ("this dear Paradise") being closely linked in her mind with her beloved Albert, whom she continued to mourn in widow's weeds for 40 years. At Balmoral she relied heavily on her brusque Scottish factotum, John Brown, whose degree of intimacy with the queen has fueled historical gossip mongers for years. Most of her scholarly biographers wax highly indignant in the queen's defense or ignore the matter entirely. Yet if anyone could ever "boss" this tiny but imperious queen, certainly the rude, outspoken Brown was the one; his death in 1883 caused her weeks of grief. At Balmoral Victoria entertained many members of European royalty, most of whom were related to her, including Czar Nicholas II of Russia and the future German kaiser, Wilhelm II. She last resided at Balmoral for several weeks in 1900.

Each British sovereign since Victoria has also stayed at Balmoral, most of them frequently. George VI took greater interest in the estate than George V or Edward VII and further enlarged it; Elizabeth II—Victoria's great-great-granddaughter—has transformed Balmoral into a modern, self-supporting cattle and forestry enterprise. First and foremost, of course, it remains a vacation home; the royal family is usually in residence during late summer and autumn. The principal ground-floor rooms are grouped around a small courtyard. In the 68 x 25-foot ballroom may be seen an exhibit of Balmoral's Victorian history, with paintings, photographs and furnishings. Balmoral is located six miles northeast of **Braemar** on route 93. An interesting account of the castle is Ronald W. Clark's *Balmoral: Queen Victoria's Highland Home* (1981). (Open May—July, Monday—Saturday 10:00—5:00; 03384–334; admission.)

Other houses in the Balmoral vicinity used by Victoria include "Alt-na-Giubhsaich," a large shooting lodge which the couple named "The Hut" and used from 1849, located in the Glen Muick valley to the south; and Victoria's own "Glasallt Shiel," a sizable two-story dwelling on the west side of Loch Muick backed by the steep moor—she called it her "Widow's House." These places are accessible by marked track and trail off route 93.

Exhibit: Bowhill at **Selkirk** displays a few relics of the queen (see the entry on Sir Walter Scott, *Exhibits*, earlier in this section.)

(See Chapter 5, ENGLAND; also Chapter 6, LONDON.)

WALES

The smallest of Britain's three "countries," Wales occupies eight counties of western Britain—a rocky terrain of plateaus, peaks, and coastal plains, with a damp maritime climate. One-fifth of the total area has been classified as national park in order to preserve the country's rugged scenery and coasts. Some 70 percent of the population is to be found in the industrial coal-producing region of Glamorgan in south Wales. Cardiff, the capital, is also the largest city.

Celtic tribes conquered and absorbed the Iberian inhabitants of Wales in the late Bronze Age, while later Roman and Saxon invasions served to isolate rather than integrate this people. From Roman to medieval times, the Welsh (a Saxon designation, *Waelisc*, meaning "foreign") remained a law unto themselves, fiercely repelling the Saxons. Gryffyd ap Llewelyn had unified Wales as a single kingdom by 1063, but the Normans under William the Conqueror occupied the country only a few years later. Welsh guerrillas fought the Anglo-Normans for 200 years. British conquest was completed in 1282 by Edward I, who named his eldest son Prince of Wales, a title which has been handed down to British crown princes ever since. Wales and England finally came under one crown with the 1485 accession of Welsh Tudor Henry II, and the 1536 Act of Union completed the integration.

The Welsh population, now approaching three million, retains a strong sense of cultural independence. *Cymru* ("countryman"), the Welsh name for Wales, has come into more popular usage in recent years as a reflection of this concern. Both the Celtic tongue and brunet Iberian-Celtic features persist. While English is the main language, about a quarter of the population also speaks Welsh—a language whose impenetrable jungle of consonants is even more intimidating than Gaelic to the outsider.* Despite their wish to preserve a Welsh identity, however, voters in 1979 crushed a referendum that would have given them limited home-rule powers.

On the world stage, the country's two most notable figures were undoubtedly the statesman David Lloyd George, and the lyric poet Dylan Thomas, both 20th-century men (though Thomas himself, unlike Lloyd George, spoke no Welsh). Thomas's haunts, like James Joyce's in Dublin, have become informal shrines for platoons of English professors.

CARROLL, LEWIS. See CHARLES LUTWIDGE DODGSON below.

DODGSON, CHARLES LUTWIDGE. ("LEWIS CARROLL") (1832–1898). At what is now part of the Gogarth Abbey Hotel north of the Model Yacht Pond near the West Parade in **Llandudno**, the writer and mathematician wrote part of *Alice's Adventures in Wonderland* in 1864. Dodgson was vacationing with the family of Dean Liddell of Oxford, whose 10-year-old daughter Alice became the author's model for Alice in the story. The residence was then known as Pen Morfa. In the evenings there, Dodgson read aloud what he had written during the day to the assembled family and guests, who included Matthew Arnold and William E. Gladstone.

(See Chapter 5, ENGLAND.)

LAWRENCE, THOMAS EDWARD (1888–1935). The soldier and writer known as Lawrence of Arabia was born at **Tremadog** in a house called Gorphwyfsa ("Woodlands" or "Place of Rest"). It was his home only until 1889. Located on the Portmadog road just outside the

*The longest place name in Britain and probably in Europe identifies a village railroad station in north Wales: the 58-letter Llanfairpwllgwyngyllgogerychwyrndrobwllllantysiliogogogoch.

village, the marked house is now a mountaineering center.

(See Chapter 5, ENGLAND; also Chapter 6, LONDON.)

LLOYD GEORGE, DAVID (1863–1945). Born in England of Welsh parentage, the World War I prime minister always considered Wales his permanent home. Though his public career kept him mostly in London, he often returned, and finally died there. His childhood home (1864–77) was a two-story cottage called Highgate in **Llanystumdwy**, where he was raised by a shoemaker-Baptist preacher uncle. The cottage survives on route A497 east of the village center. Lloyd George's last home, Ty Newydd, a small farm of 37 acres which he bought in 1939, is also located between Llanystumdwy and Criccieth above the same route and is now the Lloyd George Memorial Museum. He lived here permanently after 1944 and died in the house. Relics and mementos include photographs and cartoons of the statesman. (Open Easter—September, Monday—Friday 10:00—5:00, Saturday—Sunday 2:00—5:00; 076671–2654; admission.)

Nearby **Criccieth** and its environs became Lloyd George's Welsh home for most of his life. He occupied several farms in the vicinity at various times. Mynydd Ednyfed, a 100-acre farm, belonged to his in-laws, and it became his first married home with Margaret Owen from 1888 to 1891. Richard Owen, his father-in-law, built Brynawel, a house on a hillside east of the village, for the couple in 1891; it was the first home of their own. When Owen's wife died in 1906, the couple sold Brynawel and moved next door to Owen's home, Lys Owen, where they lived until 1910.

Near **Mynydd Ednyfed** Lloyd George built his own large house, Brynawelon, in 1910, and Dame Margaret resided there until her death in 1941. Lloyd George himself seldom appeared at the house after his and his wife's 1925 separation. "Gradually he came to regard London as his base camp," wrote biographer Peter Rowland, "and while he never lost his love for Criccieth he tended, after a time, to go there more as a visitor. . . and less and less as one of its actual residents."

Lloyd George tomb: Lloyd George Mausoleum, **Criccieth**.

(See Chapter 5, ENGLAND; also Chapter 6, LONDON.)

NELSON, HORATIO, LORD (1758–1805).
Exhibit: In the Market Hall, Priory Street, **Monmouth**, the Monmouth Museum displays a fine collection of the admiral's relics, including letters, his swords, naval equipment, and a model of the Battle of Trafalgar. (Open Monday—Saturday 10:30—1:00, 2:00—5:00, Sunday 2:00—5:00; 0600–3519; admission.)

(See Chapter 5, ENGLAND; also Chapter 6, LONDON.)

RUSSELL, BERTRAND, LORD (1872–1970). A frequent resident of Wales from the 1940s, the English philosopher, mathematician, Nobel Prize winner and peace activist was born in a mansion called Ravenscroft in the village of **South Trellech**, his home until 1876. The 40-acre estate alongside the River Wye, which Russell revisited in 1953, is now known as Cleiddon Hall.

Russell lived from 1946 to 1949 in the altered and enlarged former village school, located about 200 yards downhill from the village of **Ffestiniog**. There, among other works, he wrote *The Faith of a Rationalist* (1947).

Russell's last home, from 1955, was Plas Penrhyn, a small Regency house with garden and orchard at **Penrhyndeudraeth** near Penrhyn Castle. There he accomplished his last writing, continued assaulting the conventional wisdoms of society as he had done all his life, and died at age 97. "I do so hate to leave this world," he said toward the last.

(See Chapter 3, PARIS; also Chapter 5, ENGLAND; also Chapter 6, LONDON.)

THOMAS, DYLAN (1914–1953). The poet's birthplace in **Swansea** at 5 Cwmdonkin Drive, a Victorian terrace house built just before his birth, remained his home until 1936, when he began receiving critical attention and moved to London.

Thomas's permanent home from 1949 was The Boathouse, a white slate-roofed cottage on the Taf estuary shore below the cliff in **Laugharne**, visible from the end of Cliff Road ("Dylan's Walk"). There, writing in his garden shed, he completed six poems—but his talent had, by this time, become a victim of his alcoholism. Benefactor Margaret Taylor bought The Boathouse for the use of Dylan and Caitlin Thomas, and they rented it from her for a nominal sum. An educational trust bought it from the poet's widow in 1974. Though Thomas always denied that Laugharne was the "Llareggyb" of *Under Milk Wood* (1954), his unfinished play for voices and probably his best-known work, the town is traditionally associated with the play, which is performed there during Laugharne's triennial Thomas festival.* (The Boathouse open Tuesday—Sunday; inquire locally for admission information.)

Thomas tomb: Parish Churchyard, **Laugharne**.

(See Chapter 5, ENGLAND; also Chapter 6, LONDON.)

*The 1971 film version of the play starring Richard Burton and Elizabeth Taylor used the town of **Fishguard** as the setting.

Chapter 8
Greece, Italy, Portugal, Spain

GREECE

To this ragged peninsula in Europe's southeastern corner must bow the whole of Western civilization for here was defined not only a value system but the scale of thought by which it is measured. Greece, synonym for civilization, gave the world a picture, albeit brief, of human possibilities that has never since been equaled.

The uniqueness of the Greek "golden age" lay in the fact that it marked one of the few occasions in world history when a portion of humankind behaved as if the very fact of birth conferred notable distinction, as if decency and self-respect were natural results of an uncringing joy of life. The Greeks of that period were somehow able to live as if questions of meaning were fully as vital as questions of survival. Compared with the Greek view of truth as not only good but inherently beautiful and worth the whole of a person's life to embrace, most world religions and philosophies have seemed negative, resigned, compulsively obsessed with how to cope; the Greeks taught how to live. If nothing else, history shows that the lessons mastered by the Greeks still rank among the most elusive to relearn in the quest for a decent society. No civilization since the Athenian democracy has found the wit, energy, and leadership to concentrate many of its resources on studying what it means to be human. How much easier it would be for us to rationalize and condone the conduct of peoples and nations had there been no

golden age of Greece. The fall of this Greece plunged the Western world into a dark-age spiritual abyss from which it has only rarely and briefly emerged. Both of the subsequent great flowerings of Western culture—Rome and the Renaissance—relied heavily on Greek models. If another such flowering of human aspiration should ever occur, it too would probably go back to the Greeks.

That golden age lasted briefly enough, only about 50 years (479–431 B.C.). It has probably been the most closely inspected and analyzed half-century of time ever known. Largely an Athenian phenomenon, it was guided and personified for 31 years by Pericles, a statesman with few peers in history. By sheer force of character and a genius for leadership, he held together a democracy that was so real and effective that all Western democracies since that time have seemed euphemistic imitations. Since the fifth century B.C. no nation has ever entrusted its affairs to its own citizenry to the same extent as the Athenian city-state. About 43,000 adult males formed the legislative body of Athens, and their votes were required for all affairs of state. With the death of Pericles, however, the golden key was lost—for the statesman himself, it turned out, had embodied the crucial wall between democracy and anarchy. Since the world seldom produces a Pericles, the prospects in Athens for a workable democracy that could transcend the abilities of its leader flickered out with his death. The great failure of Pericles, amidst all his accomplishments, lay in his blindness to the need for self-sustaining mechanisms, a system of checks and balances that would enable the Athenian democracy to survive without him. This failure may have resulted from his own touching democratic faith that people, once having seen the light, would surely act in their own best interests to preserve it.

Anyone who has studied Greek history can recognize telltale signs of weakness and decay in other nations. Thucydides (whom George Orwell must surely have read) described the process of degeneration he saw in Greece in a beacon signal of prose that has flashed warnings down the ages: "To fit in with the change of events, words, too, had to change their usual meanings. What used to be described as a thoughtless act of aggression was now regarded as the courage one would expect to find in a party member.... any idea of moderation was just an attempt to disguise one's unmanly character; ability to understand a question from all sides meant that one was totally unfitted for action. Fanatical enthusiasm was the mark of a real man, and to plot against an enemy behind his back was perfectly legitimate self-defense. Anyone who held violent opinions could always be trusted, and anyone who objected to them became a suspect.... As a result of these revolutions, there was a general deterioration of character throughout the Greek world."

Successions of ancient peoples and civilizations have passed across this land, leaving remnants of their works. The earliest Greeks we know anything about were the Minoans on the island of Crete, who flourished between 3000 and 1400 B.C. Mycenae was the center of another powerful civilization on the mainland about 1600 B.C. With the Dorian invasions in about 1100 B.C. tough warrior bands from the Danube Valley overran the entire peninsula as well as Crete. The Dorians founded colonies on the coast of Asia Minor in what is now Turkey; known as "Ionia," they became the next great center of Greek culture. Other colonies arose in southern Italy—the Latins named these encroachments "Magna Graecia" after a tribe they called the "Graeci," whence the name "Greece" originated—as well as on the French and Spanish coasts, and on the Black Sea.

The Greek city-state, arising in about the 10th century B.C., functioned as the main unit of Greek society for more than a thousand years. Several hundred of these miniature autonomous republics existed, forming alliances, fighting petty wars, cherishing their independence. The democratic city-state of Athens survived the Persian invasions of the fifth century B.C., finally routed Xerxes, and rebuilt itself as the powerful new center of thriving trade. But the Peloponnesian War (431–404 B.C.) against Sparta and other rivals stripped Athens of its power, wealth, and prestige along with its democracy. The "dangerous" intellectual climate of Athens was blamed for the defeat, and such lovers of truth as Socrates became feared enemies of the state. Too many of the initially most liberal and idealistic governments eventually restrain, imprison, or even execute their best people before enshrining them as heroes, and they usually do it for the same euphemistic reasons. Greece, unhappily, proved far from exceptional in this sordid convention.

From the Peloponnesian defeat until the 19th century, Greece existed as a pawn of world powers, yet at the same time it was "Hellenizing" its conquerors and making them emissaries of the classical ideals that no longer functioned in Greece itself. Macedonia, today a part of Greece, began the conquests, led by Philip of Macedon and Alexander the Great. Rome followed, adapting Greek ideals of art, architecture, and philosophy to the greatest European empire in history. Christianity launched itself from Jerusalem primarily by way of Greece, and the Byzantine Empire was predominantly Greek in language and culture. Yet while Greek mastery of creative thought and social commerce reigned supreme in the known world, Greece itself languished. The country remained under Latin political control until the Ottoman Turkish conquest in the 15th century. In 1821 the Greek War of Independence enlisted the sympathies of several European powers, whose combined navies defeated the Turkish fleet in 1827.

The modern nation of Greece, established by the major powers, was born in 1833. In 1863 it formed a constitutional monarchy headed by George I, a king imported from Denmark. His great-grandson, Constantine II, was deposed in 1967. A period of squalid dictatorship followed until the unsavory "colonels" were replaced by the present government—the Hellenic Republic—in 1973. Occupied by Axis troops during World War II, Greece also survived a devastating civil war and the threat of a Communist takeover during the late 1940s.

Greece's geography has always made the country difficult to unify. Its peninsula, 650 kilometers long, is made up of narrow valleys and plains split by mountain ranges. Some 400 islands make up one-fifth of the total land area, less than a quarter of which is arable—yet agriculture remains the dominant economic activity. Athens, the capital since 1834, contains about one-quarter of the national population of 9.2 million. Greece remains one of Europe's poorer nations, and is heavily reliant upon tourism. While Greek millionaire ship-owners have become exotic fixtures on the international celebrity scene, Greece itself remains a predominantly rural mountainscape of farm villages, olive groves, and sheepherders' huts.

In the modern, neon-lit city of Athens, "the relics of the past have more sense of life about them than the latest things," as Alexander Eliot writes. "Compare the Parthenon, for instance with the towering new Hilton Hotel. Both dominate the skyline: which one seems to be a hollow shell?" Acid pollution in those classical skies, however, is working rapid destruction on the ancient marble of the Acropolis so that the Parthenon itself, standing since 438 B.C., flakes and crumbles away as if, like the goddess of wisdom it enshrined, it is superfluous at last. Floodlit, facelifted, and touted in its grand aloofness like a freak show, it resists keen "preservation efforts," gracefully but insistently removing itself from the corrosive atmosphere of its present stage. As corroded, perhaps, have become the Olympic Games, begun in 776 B.C. at Olympia. Though they still provide a world athletic forum, their increasing degeneration into a political arena has considerably reduced their prestige for participating nations. No further demonstration is needed that, again, the 20th century is unequipped to emulate the Greek ideals.

The most profound legacy of Greece lies in its mighty words: the hero literature of Homer; the dramas of Aeschylus, Euripedes, Sophocles; the wisdom of the two greatest philosophers in history, Plato and Aristotle. Without St. Paul, writing in Greek to predominantly Greek communities, Christianity would have remained just another messianic sect in a Palestine that was full of them. In the modern age, Nikos Kazantzakis dared a sequel to Homer's *Odyssey*; he was probably the only writer in the world who could do so without presumption.

While museums of classical antiquities and archaeological research abound in Greece, very few house-museums exist, and there are no surviving homes of the great Greeks from the classical era. Even their specific sites or plots of ground have been buried and lost, and it is fortunate when we can localize them to the extent of identifying a city or village now ruined or capped by modern pavements. Thus, to a far greater degree than in other European countries, the home locations of noted Greeks must remain only vaguely defined within broad areas. In Athens, where most of them resided at various times, one must go to the old Athenian communal places where these figures spent so many of their waking hours—the Agora, the Theatre of Dionysos, the Lyceum, the Academy—to experience their "homes," places far more significant in terms of posterity than their unknown domestic arrangements.

Greek museums are noted for their often erratic and uncertain hours of admission; thus, even more than in most other European nations, the visitor should check locally and not rely too heavily on published information. Most excavated classical sites and many museums are under the general maintenance of the Greek Antiquities Service and the General Directorate of Antiquities and Restoration.

NOTE: The word *odhós* in the following pages is the Greek term for "street." The Greek language poses special problems regarding Romanized spellings of place names; virtually no two recent guidebooks agree on every aspect of such designations. Also, many places have two names: the local, often Slav or Albanian, name, and the ancient name which has now become official again. The preferred style in the following pages is to give, in most cases, only the latter designation according to at least one frequently used spelling.

AESCHYLUS (525–456 B.C.).

Exhibits: Greek drama first reached maturity with the works of Aeschylus, a native of **Eleusis**. Excavations of this seat of the "Eleusinian Mysteries," the secret cult of the goddess Demeter, have proceeded more or less continuously since 1882. Today visitors may walk among ruins of the great Telesterion, or Temple of Demeter, so familiar to the dramatist. Aeschylus narrowly escaped with his life when he inadvertently revealed some of the cult's mystical secrets in one of his plays; the work no longer exists. The excavations are located at the eastern foot and slopes of the Acropolis. (Excavations open summer, Monday, Wednesday—Saturday 8:30—2:30, Sunday 10:00—4:00; winter, Monday, Wednesday—Saturday 9:00—3:30, Sunday 10:00—4:00; admission.)

In **Athens** the great cathartic plays of Aeschylus, Aristophanes, Euripedes, and Sophocles were first seen and heard in the Theatre of Dionysos, the birthplace of European drama. Located at the southeast foot of the Acropolis, the huge structure held an audience of 17,000 in 67 tiers of wooden seats curved around a central orchestra; scholars, however, debate whether an actual stage was used at this period. Only a few traces exist of the actual theater known to Aeschylus. The present ruins largely represent a stone reconstruction dating from about 330 B.C. The Romans further altered the stage area, however, using old materials "so that the existing remains," wrote Stuart Rossiter, "present a puzzling conglomeration of the work of 750 years." Aeschylus wrote about 90 plays but only seven survive, including his masterpiece trilogy the *Oresteia* which was performed here in 458 B.C. The gateway to the theater excavations is approached from the Dion Areopaghitou. (Open Monday—Saturday 9:00—1:00, 3:30—5:30, Sunday 10:00—4:00; admission.)

(See ITALY in this chapter.)

ALEXANDER III, "THE GREAT" (356–323 B.C.). Probably the greatest general who ever lived, Alexander was a figure of startling paradoxes whom many in his own time believed to be a god (he may have believed it himself). "Alexander was truly immortal," wrote Vicki Goldberg. "We remember him now and seek him still. His empire lived on for centuries, even after its borders had crumbled: Indian gods acquired Greek postures and features, business in the Near East continued to be conducted in Greek, the New Testament was written in Alexander's native tongue." He was king of Macedonia at age 20, and ruler of a world empire at 30. When he died of a fever at 32, that empire stretched from Egypt to China, spanning most of the known world. Not the least of Alexander's achievements, however, was the unification of Greece.

This rather small, blond man was born in Pella, the capital of Macedonia and a city that probably deserves to rank with Jerusalem, Athens, and

A STONE MOSAIC PALACE FLOOR UNCOVERED IN MACEDONIA. While Alexander the Great probably never trod this particular floor in **Pella**, his birthplace and the Macedonian capital, this construction dates from about the time of his death and represents the royal milieu of his youth and education by Aristotle.

Rome for its fundamental importance in the history of civilization. For Pella became, through Alexander's conquests, the birthplace of Hellenism, the cornerstone for the later development of Near Eastern Christianity, and the foundation of the Byzantine Empire. After its decline from 148 B.C. and subsequent burial, the ancient city of Pella—a site of about four square kilometers in and adjacent to the modern **Nea Pella**—is slowly emerging again. Since 1957 archaeologists have unearthed broad streets lined with clay water pipes and stone sewers, ruined walls of palatial residences, and spectacular pebble-mosaic floors dating from about 300 B.C.; evidently the site also holds much more that has yet to be discovered. Thus far researchers have been unable to locate the Palace of Archelaos, which may have stood on the westerly acropolis of Pella's two hills. This royal palace, built about 400 B.C., was Alexander's birthplace and his residence through childhood. Raised by his ambitious mother, Olympias, and rarely seeing his warrior father, Philip II, Alexander was tutored by Aristotle (see the entry on Aristotle later in this section). He lived in the palace until 334 B.C., when, as king, he left Pella with a force of 35,000 foot soldiers and cavalry to conquer Persia. He never returned. A museum on the excavation site displays the superb floor mosaics as well as various objects that have been unearthed. (Site and museum open Monday, Wednesday—Saturday 9:00—1:00, 3:00—5:30, Sunday 10:00—4:00; admission.)

ARISTOPHANES (ca.450–ca.380 B.C.). "Home is everywhere a man can have a good time," according to a line in the dramatist's play *Plautus*. Aristophanes' masterpiece, *The Birds* (414 B.C.), defined "Cloudcuckooland" for all time as the favorite residence of politicians. The master of comedy in the Greek drama, a conservative whose plays fiercely satirized "permissive" Athenian society, and the grave solemnities of such playwrights as Euripedes, was a native of **Athens**. Beyond the fact that he was born somewhere in the heart of the ancient city, however, nothing is known of his specific residences. Indeed, except for the 11 surviving plays of the 40-odd that he wrote, little enough is known of his life.

A jest in his play, *The Knights*, implies that Aristophanes' family owned a country estate on the small, Athenian-conquered island of **Egina** in the Saronic Gulf, and ancient sources say that he spent most of his life there.

Exhibit: In **Athens** the plays of Aristophanes were frequently performed as comic relief after the performance of more "serious" plays in the Theatre of Dionysos (see the entry on Aeschylus, *Exhibits*, earlier in this section).

ARISTOTLE (ca. 384–322 B.C.). Aristotle mastered every field of learning known to the Greeks. Only a portion of his extensive writings (the treatises) have survived, but their influence on philosophy, science, medieval theology, and literary criticism was deep and profound. To his systematic mind we owe the beginnings of the scientific method, and the science of logic itself. Aristotle was a Macedonian, a native of Stagira, ruins of which lie near the present village of **Stagyra** on a by-road off route 16; a tourist pavilion is accessible for information on the ancient site. The philosopher returned here for several intervals during his life, the last time from about 340 to 335 B.C.

In 367 B.C. he went to **Athens**, where he enrolled in Plato's Academy (see the entry on Plato later in this section) and studied philosophy there for 20 years. Plato spoke of Aristotle's home as "the house of the reader" because of Aristotle's large collection of manuscripts for which he had spent large amounts of money. After periods of residence elsewhere, Aristotle returned to Athens in 334 B.C. and established his school, the Lyceum, in a rented building. Most of his teaching focused on biology and the natural sciences. Though students flocked to him, discipline was relaxed and much of the instruction informal as teacher and students shared a communal life and discoursed while strolling together up and down the Peripatos (walk—hence the later name "Peripatetic School"), which was used as a parade ground for athletes. Aristotle fled for his life in 323 B.C. when Athens rebelled against the Macedonian power. He never returned. On the modern map of Athens the Lyceum area spanned much of the present National Garden, extending beyond its western edge to the area of Xenofontos (Street). The Peripatos extended diagonally eastward from the vicinity of St.Paul's English Church in the Leofóros Amalías to a point about 70 meters off the southeast corner of the Greek Parliament Building in the Sindagma Square. Today, where Aristotle and his students walked, Athenians still enjoy the shady paths in the National Garden. (Open daily to sunset.)

At Pella (site adjacent to **Nea Pella**), from about 343 to 340 B.C., Aristotle resided (for at least part of that time) in the palace of Philip II of Macedon, who invited him there to tutor his undisciplined young son, Alexander, who would become the world conqueror Alexander the Great. The philosopher had his hands full with the fiery youth, probably teaching him Homer and the works of the dramatists, the staples of Greek education. Perhaps Alexander's habit of including botanists, geographers, and surveyors on his military expeditions derived from his sessions with the incessantly curious philosopher (see the entry on Alexander III earlier in this section).

In 323 B.C. Aristotle retired to **Halkida** (Chalcis), where he died. Disheartened at his fortunes, he may have ended his life by drinking hemlock. Few vestiges remain of this ancient city, which stood a short distance east of the present town. Some polygonal wall structures, present in Aristotle's lifetime, survive on the old Acropolis.

ATATÜRK, KEMAL (1881–1938). The Turkish soldier, statesman, and president Mustafa Kemal, who created the modern Turkish state and took the surname Atatürk ("Father of Turks"), was a native of **Thessaloníki**, a city under Turkish control until 1913. His birthplace, a red house adjacent to the Turkish consulate in Odhós Apostolou Pavlou, bears a marker.

BYRON, GEORGE GORDON, LORD
(1788–1824). The English Romantic poet lived twice in Greece: from 1809 to 1811, and during his last year. During the winter of 1809–10 he resided for 10 weeks in **Athens** at 11 Odhós Ayias Theklas, the home of an English widow whose 13-year-old daughter, Teresa Makris, he immortalized as the "Maid of Athens." This house has recently burned down. Later in Athens (1810–11), Byron lodged as a guest in the Capuchin Monastery, which stood at the west end of Odhós Lissikratous. Now a railed-in square, the site holds the fourth-century B.C. Choregic Monument of Lysikrates, a domed and columned marble structure that commemorated a musical contest of 334 B.C. The Capuchin monks used it as their library, and there Byron worked on his first cantos for *Childe Harold's Pilgrimage* (1812). The surrounding monastery itself burned down about 1823, and the ancient monument was restored in 1892.

Byron identified strongly with the Greek fight for independence from the Turks. In 1823 he left his friends and mistresses in Italy to engage himself directly in the struggle, but this he never did. Instead he settled for five months at **Metaxata** on the Ionian island of Cephalonia, arriving with no military experience but with chests full of gold, scarlet, and green uniforms and at least 10 swords. Greek factions courted his presence, not for these accoutrements or his literary reputation but for the £9,000 in cash he brought with him. The house he occupied in the village was demolished in 1953, but a marker on the gate identifies the site and the still-flourishing ivy he planted.

By the time he came to **Messolóngi**, his last home, most of his money was gone. His presence, however, could still inspire the patriots of the soon-besieged town. Byron resided there for four months before he died of a virulent fever, probably malaria. A memorial garden marks the site of his house in the Odhós Levidou; sources differ on whether the dwelling was destroyed during the town's defense in 1826 or during World War II.

Exhibits: The Gennadeion Library in the Dhinokratous, **Athens**, displays relics of Byron's activities in Greece. (Open Monday—Friday 9:00—2:00, 5:00—8:00, Saturday 9:00—2:00; free.)

In **Messolóngi** the Museum of the Revolution in the Plateia Botsari also exhibits memorabilia of the poet. (Inquire locally for admission information.)

(See ITALY in this chapter; also Chapter 1, SWITZERLAND; also Chapter 4, BELGIUM; also Chapter 5, ENGLAND; also Chapter 6, LONDON; also Chapter 7, SCOTLAND.)

CAESAR, JULIUS
(100–44 B.C.). In about 76 B.C. the Roman patrician who would become soldier, dictator, historian, and builder of the empire studied oratory under Apollonius Molo on the island of Rhodes. This was the famed School of Rhetoric established by Aeschines in the second century B.C. Its site is thought to be the ancient park of Rhodini, located about three kilometers south of **Rhodes** on route 95. Cato, Cicero and Lucretius also studied there. Plane trees, peacocks, and ponds adorn this site which heard the first speeches of some of history's greatest orators.

On the way to Rhodes, Caesar fell into the hands of pirates and was held for ransom about 40 days on the islet of **Pharmakousa**, which lies about 20 kilometers east of the Aegean island of Leros. He laughingly promised to crucify his captors, who admired his coolness and wit, as soon as he obtained his freedom. Immediately after his release he outfitted an expedition and promptly carried out his promise—then went on to Rhodes to study oratory.

(See ITALY in this chapter.)

CICERO, MARCUS TULLIUS
(106–43 B.C.). In 78 B.C. the patrician who would become Rome's greatest orator and one of its foremost statesman studied oratory at the School of Rhetoric in Rhodini, **Rhodes** (see the entry on Julius Caesar above).

Cicero also resided briefly in **Athens** (79 B.C.), **Thessaloníki** (58–57 B.C.), and the province of Epiros (48–47 B.C.), but none of his lodging sites have been identified.

(See ITALY in this chapter.)

EURIPEDES
(480?–406 B.C.). Eighteen tragedies survive of the 92 plays he wrote, works of profound psychological depth, but none of Euripedes' homes remain. His birthplace was the island of **Salamis** in the Saronic Gulf.

His childhood home stood at Phyla, a town site now occupied by **Alexandria City**, a northeastern suburb of Athens.

Some time around 440 B.C. or earlier he made his residence in **Athens** and there, until 408 B.C., wrote most if not all the plays that survive—*Alcestis, Medea, The Trojan Women, Orestes*, among others.

In 408 B.C. Euripedes moved to the court of King Archelaos in Pella, capital of Macedonia, near the modern **Nea Pella** (see the entry on Alexander III earlier in this section).

Euripedes tomb (unmarked): Site of Arethousa, **Rendina**.

HOMER (9th?–8th? century B.C.). The *Iliad* and the *Odyssey*—two cornerstones of Western literary tradition—expressed the ancient heroic ideal that formed the basis of classical education; their influence on today's culture, especially on our assumptions about human nature, is by no means negligible. Modern classical scholars are unable to clarify whether Homer was an actual Greek poet who wrote the two great books ascribed to him, or whether the works represent an oral literary tradition spanning several centuries. Nor has archaeology helped much in deciding whether Homer really lived. "The fact is," concludes the *Reader's Encyclopedia*, "that nothing whatever is known about Homer the man, including the crucial point of whether he existed."

The ancients, nevertheless, regarded Homer not only as a real person but as the greatest author who ever lived. Seven Greek cities claimed to have been his birthplace: Híos, Rhodes, Argos, Athens, and Salamis, plus Colophon and Smyrna (Izmir) which are located in the present nation of Turkey. Smyrna and Híos are generally regarded as the most probable sites, for whatever such probability is worth for a man whose existence is so questionable. At the northern outskirts of **Vrontádos** on the Aegean island of Híos facing Asia Minor, a cultic monument known as Homer's Stone marks the traditional spot where he taught and recited his poetic tales. "If indeed Homer was from Híos," wrote Peter Sheldon, "he was most likely born in the medieval village of **Pitios**" on the island; here his supposed house and olive grove may be visited. (Inquire locally for admission information.)

The village of **Volissós** over on the western side of the island was the home of the Homeridai, a clan who claimed descent from Homer.

Homer tomb (reputed): Mt. Pirgos, Plakoto, **Ios**.

Exhibits: Several modern authors have written "pilgrimage accounts" attempting to identify the sites and trace the voyages of Ulysses as presented in Homer's *Odyssey*. Such attempts, while presuming on rather thin evidence that Homer was vastly familiar with Aegean and Mediterranean geography, nevertheless provide entertaining armchair journeys as well as good excuses for maritime travel writers. Such accounts include Richard Halliburton's *The Glorious Adventure* (1927), Erich Lessing's *The Voyages of Ulysses* (1965) and Mauricio Obregón's *Ulysses Airborne* (1971).

JOHN, ST. (ca.9–ca.105). The self-designated "beloved disciple" of Jesus was the traditional author of the fourth and last to be written gospel (ca. 100) of the New Testament, the three epistles of John (ca.100), and the book of Revelation (ca.95). He was the only one of the Palestinian apostles about whom there was no widely accepted tradition of martyrdom (though Papias, a second-century Christian writer, reported him killed in Palestine before the year 70). According to legend he spent most of his later life in Ephesus (now Ayasoluk, Turkey), fled from the Emperor Domitian's persecution of Christians to the Greek island of Pátmos, later returned to Ephesus, and died there in his nineties. Most unbiased Biblical scholars believe, however, that the author of the gospel and the author of Revelation could not have been the same person; they point to enormous differences in style, vocabulary, and thought, and to the fact that the latter author does not identify himself either as the apostle or as the "beloved disciple." The King James Version calls this author "St. John the Divine."

Tradition states that St. John arrived on the Dodecanese island of Pátmos, either in flight or in chains, sometime during the last years of Domitian's reign (ca.90–95) and stayed until that emperor's death in 96. The Convent of the Apocalypse, a cell of the Monastery of St. John founded in 1088, overlooks **Skala**, the port and commercial center of the island. Located about two kilometers south of the town, on a hillside accessible by road and path, the convent's Cave of St. Anne is the once barren grotto ascribed by believers as the spot where St. John heard the voice of God through a crack in the cave roof, and dictated the book of Revelation to his disciple Prochoros. The cave is now heavily furnished with ornate fix-

WHERE ST. JOHN HEARD THE VOICE OF GOD. The island of Patmos is traditionally ascribed by Christian believers as the spot where the disciple experienced the visions recorded in the New Testament book of Revelatures. (Open Monday—Saturday 8:00—12:00, 3:00—6:00, Sunday 8:00—12:00; donation.)

tion. Towering over the harbor of **Skala**, the 11th-century Monastery of St. John shelters the grotto memorialized as the site of this "spiritual dictation."

KAZANTZAKIS, NIKOS (1885–1957). The central fact about any political or religious gospel is its intolerance of question or challenge, as Kazantzakis amply demonstrated. Like his ancient countryman Socrates, Greece's best-known modern writer was a truth seeker; he was greatly feared by the generals and archbishops because of his relentless challenges to orthodoxy. Unlike Socrates, however, Kazantzakis could not be silenced, though he was forced to spend much of his creative lifetime in other countries. Prolific novelist, poet, travel writer, translator, journalist, and revolutionary, Kazantzakis became a major literary voice of the 20th century through such works as *The Odyssey: A Modern Sequel* (1938), *Zorba the Greek* (1946) and *The Greek Passion* (1951). His birthplace in **Iráklio**, Crete, stands in the street named for him.

Kazantzakis tomb: Martinengo Bastion, **Iráklio**.

Exhibit: Room 9 of the Historical Museum of Crete, Lyssimachou Kalokerinou in **Iráklio**, displays the author's recreated study from Antibes, France, where he lived for many years. The collection includes his desk, books, photographs, letters, the original handwritten manuscript of *The Odyssey*, and various personal items. (Open Monday—Saturday 9:00—1:00, 3:00—5:30; admission.)

(See Chapter 2, FRANCE.)

MUSTAFA KEMAL. See KEMAL ATATÜRK.

PAUL, ST. (1 B.C.?–A.D. 67?). St. Paul's native language was probably Greek, the common tongue of Asia Minor where he was born and grew up. As the first Christian evangelist, he made three missionary journeys, the latter two of which brought him to Greece. His first Greek residence of any duration was in the year 49 at **Philippi**, now a largely abandoned site (except by French archaeologists) on route 66 about 16 kilometers northwest of Kavalla. Most of the visible ruins date from a somewhat later period than Paul's passage—the city he knew lies three to five meters below the present ground level. Accompanying Paul to Philippi were St. Luke, St. Silas and St. Timothy. This is where Paul and Silas were beaten and manacled or placed in stocks in an underground cell, then released by the timely intervention of an earthquake the next day. The site of this cell remains unknown, but the remains of an octagonal church, excavated east of the forum in the 1960s, were found to cover an earlier fourth-century basilican church dedicated to St. Paul; possibly it was erected either on the traditional site of this famous episode or on the site of Lydia's house, in which Paul stayed. The cell site claimed during the fifth century, on the other hand, was a crypt halfway up the terrace which diplays ruins of a building (labeled Basilica A by archaeologists) on the opposite side of the road. A frescoed chapel later crowned this site. Paul met great success at Philippi despite this interruption, and the church he established there was one of his favorite congregations. (Excavations and museum open daily; admission.)

At **Thessaloníki**, Paul, Silas and Timothy lodged (49–50) at the house of one Jason in the Jewish colony of the city, and Paul pursued his trade of tentmaker there in addition to preaching in the synagogue. One site vaguely associated with the apostle is the 14th-century Monastery of Vlatadon near the southwestern corner of the Acropolis wall, buildings which now house the Patriarchal Academy of Patristic Studies. St.Paul, it is said, preached from the clifftop here.

Paul visited **Corinth** three times, ca. 50, 55, and 58. "Somewhere on the plain of Corinth today," wrote H. V. Morton, "perhaps in a vineyard or beneath the courtyard of a whitewashed farm building, is the site of the house where Paul, Aquila and Priscilla settled down to make money for their daily needs; for Aquila also was a tentmaker." Silas and Timothy joined him later. This city was a thriving, cosmopolitan trade center, fairly new and as large as Athens in Paul's day. Its reputation as the wide-open "sin city" of the ancient world was notorious. In Corinth, where he founded a large and flourishing church, Paul lived for 18 months (50–52) and wrote his epistles I and II to the Thessalonians, whom he had recently left.

These letters are probably the earliest Pauline epistles as well as the earliest books of the New Testament. During his last visit to Corinth, Paul probably wrote his Epistle to the Romans and possibly his Epistle to the Galatians as well. Modern Corinth grew atop the Roman city, but a devastating earthquake in 1858 wiped it out; the city was later rebuilt on a nearby site. Excavated ruins of the ancient Roman agora where Paul worked and preached lie about five kilometers southwest of the present city between the mountain of Akro-Corinth and the sea. The American School of Classical Studies maintains ruins of this central portion of the city as well as a museum displaying recovered antiquities. The main entrance is via the Lechaion Road from the main Patras highway (route 8). (Excavations open Monday—Saturday 9:00-sunset, Sunday 10:00—1:00, 2:30—5:00; museum open summer, Monday—Saturday 8:00—1:00, 3:00—6:00, Sunday from 10:00; winter, Monday—Saturday 9:00—1:00, 2:30—5:00, Sunday from 10:00; admission.)

THE AGORA. These ruins of the community center and marketplace of ancient **Athens** mark the scene of St. Paul's preaching to the "men of Athens" as well as of the intricate conversations of Socrates. The Parthenon surmounts the Acropolis to the southeast.

Exhibits: During the year 51 in **Athens** Paul encountered philosophers of the Epicurean and Stoic schools and agreed to address them, which he did ("Ye men of Athens . . . ") on Mars' hill, delivering his sermon on "the unknown God." He spoke, it is believed, either from the rock or court of the Areopagus on the west slope of the Acropolis, approached via the Leofóros Apostolou Pavlou; or in the Stoa Basileios (Royal Portico), excavated remnants of which may be seen on the north side of the Agora. In the Agora itself, the outdoor assembly place and main square of the ancient city, St. Paul disputed daily with the curious Athenians. Excavations, conducted more or less continuously since the 1930s by the American School of Classical Studies, have revealed many details of this historic site which is located directly northwest of the Acropolis. Three entrances give access, from the northern, southern, and southwestern sides. The Agora Museum in the restored Stoa of Attalos (ca. 140 B.C.) displays numerous sculptures and miscellaneous items recovered from the area. (Grounds open summer, Monday—Saturday 8:00—7:00, Sunday 10:00—4:30; winter, Monday—Saturday 9:00—4:00, Sunday 10:00—4:30; museum open Monday—Saturday 9:00—4:00, Sunday 10:00—2:00; admission, except free on Thursday and Sunday.)

(See ITALY in this chapter.)

PERICLES (ca.495–429 B.C.).

Exhibits: The Age of Pericles was the glory of Greek classical culture. Ruler of the city-state of **Athens** and the Athenian Empire, builder of the Parthenon, statesman, supreme orator, and patron of arts and learning, Pericles finally lost his popularity and good name in an act of political opportunism—plunging Athens into war against Sparta in order, wrote Plutarch, "to make himself indispensable." Neither Pericles' homes nor precise knowledge of their sites survive, though his birthplace was probably his family's country house, which stood in the village suburb of Kholargos. A number of Athenian ruins, however, recall the scenes of his foremost activities.

Exhibits: The site of the Pnyx, the large, semicircular terrace where the Athenian citizen assembly (Ecclesia) met, lies exposed on the northeast slope of the Hill of the Pnyx almost directly west of the Acropolis. On this site Pericles delivered most of his rousing, brilliant speeches, giving oracular shape and form to the first great flowering of Western civilization. Most of the visible ruins of the Pnyx, however, date from about six centuries later and represent the fourth-century modifications of Lycurgus.

From a platform in the Kerameikos, the ancient cemetery district along the Ermou Avenue, Pericles addressed his famous Funeral Oration (440 B.C.) in tribute to the Athenian soldiers who died

in the Battle of Samos. Ruins of walls, tombs, gateways, and storehouses have been excavated on this site. (Open Monday, Wednesday—Saturday 9:00—3:30, Sunday 10:00—4:30; admission, except free on Sunday.)

PLATO (ca. 428–348 B.C.). One of the great triumvirate who laid the philosophical foundations of Western culture, the author of *The Republic*, young disciple of Socrates, and teacher of Aristotle was a native and virtual lifelong dweller in **Athens**. But the historical record of his life is almost a blank until his later years. Regarding *The Republic*, Kenneth Rexroth wrote, "the earliest critics pointed out that the community of *The Republic* is more school than state. So finally, we should think of the book as a founding manifesto or prospectus for Plato's Academy."

The only identifiable site that can in fact be linked with Plato today is that of the Academy, a sacred grove dating from before the sixth century B.C. Plato began his school of philosophy there in about 388 B.C. "The founding of the Academy," wrote A. E. Taylor, "is the turning point in Plato's life, and in some ways the most memorable event in the history of Western European science," for the Academy was, above all, a communal institute of science, concentrating on pure mathematics. Later called the "University of Athens," the Academy flourished for almost nine centuries. A church, the Ayios Trifon in Odhos Kolokinthou off route 8, marks the southern boundary of the Academy as revealed by 1966 excavations. Two main areas of old walls and pavements lie exposed in the vicinity of the Odhos Thenaias. Plato's own estate lay somewhere east of the Academy grounds and the hill of Kolonos, which begins in the vicinity of the Odhos Lenorman in today's western suburds of Athens.

Plato tomb (unmarked): Academy grounds, **Athens**.

SOCRATES (ca. 470–399 B.C.).

Exhibits: Though he left no writings of his own, Socrates' life and style of discourse ("the Socratic method") became known through the works of his disciple Plato (see the entry above). Socrates considered it his divine mission in life to question established assumptions, a process he accomplished through proposition, argument, hypothesis, and deduction. In striving to teach how to "know thyself," Socrates taught humanity to think objectively toward itself; thus in the marketplace of Athens was laid the foundation of modern Western culture. A self-proclaimed "gad-fly," Socrates' unkempt, grotesque appearance did not inspire the confidence of Athenians, for whom physical features reflected the state of the soul. Socrates was, in fact, ugly, with a pushed-in face, broad nose, and wide mouth. Well aware of his handicap, Socrates claimed that his face bore marks of the vices he would have had if he had not devoted himself to philosophy. A profoundly religious man, though uninterested in defining the nature of God or gods, he gathered a devoted group of young followers and refused to quit his discourses with them even when condemned to death for "impiety" and "corruption." Yet it was no tyrant but the vaunted democracy of Athens that condemned Socrates. In the words of William M. Taylor, "the culture that produced Socrates was no longer able to sustain him."

A native and virtual lifelong inhabitant of **Athens**, Socrates' main area of activity was, of course, the Agora or marketplace, where he mingled daily, engaging in conversation, posing simple-sounding questions, and drawing out unstated assumptions and exposing them to meticulous inspection. One specific place associated with him in the Agora is the excavated Stoa of Zeus Eleutherios, beneath the colonnade of which he is known to have discussed philosophy with his friends. Only foundation ruins remain. Another likely place is the Shop of the Cobbler Simon, which stood very near the surviving, inscribed Horos, or boundary stone. According to Diogenes Laertius, the philosopher often came to have his shoes repaired there and discoursed while waiting. It was Simon who first recorded the teachings of his vociferous customer. (See the entry on St. Paul *Exhibits*, earlier in this section.)

Socrates was tried by a jury of 501 citizens and condemned to death by a margin of 60. It was a judgment he could easily have amended or escaped by certain prescribed obsequious behavior, which he refused to follow. The site of this trial may well have been the Heliaia, largest and best known of the ancient Athenian law courts; its ruins lie in the southwestern portion of the Agora.

Socrates was imprisoned for a month before his execution and used the time to discourse as usual with his friends. Plato's dialogue *Phaedo* describes Socrates' last day. The so-called Prison of Socrates in the cliff face at the foot of Mouseion Hill, where Socrates supposedly spent his final weeks and died by drinking hemlock, has no proven connection with him. This rock dungeon consists of three rooms, one with a sloping ceiling. Today it is generally agreed that the actual prison stood somewhere in the southwestern portion of the Agora not far from the Heliaia.

SOPHOCLES (496–406 B.C.). One of the great triumvirate of Greek tragic dramatists, Sophocles wrote some 123 plays of which only seven survive. Periclean Athens preferred his works to those of Aeschylus and Euripedes. Sophocles was a native and lifelong resident of Kolonos Hippios, a hilltop village site which he used as the setting for his play *Oedipus at Colunus*. This village site, now enveloped by northwestern **Athens**, lies east of the Odhos Lenorman.

Exhibits: Sites associated with the playwright in **Athens** include ruins of the small shrine of the Amyneion, of which Sophocles held the priesthood; it is located on an ancient excavated road that leads south from the foot of the Areopagus west of the Acropolis (see the entry on St. Paul, *Exhibits*, earlier in this section). The dramas of Sophocles were presented in the Theatre of Dionysos (see the entry on Aeschylus, *Exhibits*, earlier in this section).

ITALY

All the numerous fountains of civilization that Europe has created and nurtured flowed from only two rich springs of human endeavor. From these two deep and marvelous sources every aspect of modern culture has fundamentally derived. The older source, of course, was Greece. But it was Italy—first from militaristic Rome as the hub of a world empire, then from the great Renaissance centers of art and learning—which not only defined the goals of Western political and cultural development but implanted the humanistic criteria by which we judge and observe the world.

At the time the Roman Empire *was* the world, anyone of a certain status who lived anywhere in that empire was a Roman citizen. Thus the span of Europe as well as parts of the Middle East and northern Africa were inhabited and controlled by peoples who, while they might never see Rome or Italy, could legitimately claim themselves to be Romans. This is not the place to analyze or even trace the growth, influence, and fall of Rome—subjects that have fueled lifetimes of scholarship. The final word on this mighty fountain of civilization will probably never be written, for each generation discovers new elements of its own psyche in ancient Rome. Today the Rome of the caesars lies mostly hidden beneath the pavements and buildings of the noisy, perpetual rush hour that is modern Rome. Only torn, ragged outcrops of old walls and floors, laid bare by excavation, intrude amid the frenzied traffic and smart shops. Like upthrust folds from a past geological age, they penetrate into modern Rome throughout the city. Down, too, into dank cellars or grottoes one must go to explore the former sun-washed center of the world, to rooms now needing lamps and flashlights to illumine the lingering traces of a confidence so vast, and brilliant that, from here, it reached to seize most of Europe.

As its imperial fortunes succumbed to outside invasions and inner corruption, and its secular power declined, the city gained a new kind of importance: as the center of an increasingly unmeek form of Christianity. Except during the medieval "Babylonian captivity" of the church in Avignon, France (1309–78), all popes since St. Peter have resided in Rome. The popes took to themselves many of the secular trappings of the defunct caesars, including terminology (e.g., "supreme pontiff"). Even today, the Vatican remains in some startling respects an administrative facsimile of the Palatine Hill—a stately shadow version of the Roman Empire.

Indeed, for most of its existence, the Vatican has been the center of secular as well as spiritual power, controlling much of Italy for centuries under the direct rule of the popes. As the most durable monarchical institution in the modern world, the papacy has never been less than significant as a geopolitical force.

At the same time, its moral authority has survived conspicuous immorality and some thoroughly bad men in a seat which has also held a number of saints and notable administrators—a record more or less paralleled in virtue, though for a shorter duration, by the Roman emperors. With rare exceptions (which include the first pope and the current one), most popes have been Italian by birth. The Western Christian church has, for most of its existence, looked as with one face toward Rome, as did ancient consuls and governors of the vast empire for ultimate authority.

The important scenes of the Italian panorama are several: the founding of the Roman Republic by the Latins in the eighth century B.C. and its expansion into an empire; that empire's flowering and decline; the feudal kingdoms of the Middle Ages; the burst of Renaissance creativity in the independent city-states, led by Florence and the brilliant court of Lorenzo de Medici; control by Spain, the Austrian Hapsburgs, and Napoleon; the *Risorgimento* ("resurgence") led by Garibaldi, Cavour, and Mazzini that led to a united Italy; the Fascist dictatorship of Mussolini, who represented a historically familiar type of Renaissance thug and is now regarded as bemusedly as a Borgia; and Italy's postwar recovery and modern industrial growth. Then, too, during the 19th century Italy became a kind of romantic Eden, an Arcadian nirvana for foreign travelers and expatriates from both East and West. Dostoevski, Goethe, Byron, Shelley, and the Brownings were only a few who established at least temporary homes in what they felt was a cultural atmosphere more conducive to the muses than their native lands.

The Italian paradox is well known. Surrounded by relics of the classical and Renaissance ages, Italians and their guests are never more than a stroll away from some reminder of past greatness. Yet on a daily level Italians probably dwell less in the past than most peoples who claim far shorter histories. Of all Europeans, Italians remain irrepressibly "here and now." The veneration of Rome is more of an import brought by history-conscious pilgrims than a product of the city itself. Though the church is Rome's main and most thriving "business," resident Romans are not particularly noted for any greater religiosity than elsewhere—indeed, they perhaps show less.

Italians are an outgoing, gregarious, extroverted people, creatures of crowds, not given to solitary pursuits or moody self-examination. A guilt-obsessed Italian Strindberg or Nietzsche is no more thinkable than a Swedish Cellini—or a German Mussolini, for that matter. Everything is "up front"; an Italian who is pleased, upset, loving, or disgusted does not make you guess at the feeling. Though Italy has produced great writers, including Dante, Petrarch, and Boccaccio, Italians have always warmed more to great talkers than writers. Oratory flourished in the marketplace, and the skill of swaying crowds is a necessary component of Italian political leadership. This has been true from the time of the great rostra speeches of Cicero and Julius Caesar, through the reformist thunderings of Savonarola in his Florentine pulpit, to the flamboyant posturings of Mussolini from his Palazzo Venezia balcony. For Italians, listening to oratory is far more than simply an ear experience, just as talking is never just a mouth exercise but an involvement of the entire body.

Italian listeners do not "weigh words" but measure the entire milieu that bathes and pulses sentences. Words are living creatures, and oratory is a caress or a slap, a volatile emotional transaction.

The modern nation of Italy is one of Europe's most recent; it dates only from 1861, with the kingdom of Sardinia as its nucleus. From that year until the Republic of Italy supplanted Mussolini's Fascist state and its aftermath in 1946, Italy was a constitutional monarchy led by kings of the House of Savoy. Political and economic chaos is rather more normal than exceptional in Italy. Nobody has ever been able to explain exactly how the Italian state and society function in the face of the individual near-anarchy that typically rules daily life. Regulations, to many Italians, amount to little more than challenging hurdles; order and system are precise on paper but hardly anywhere else (a fact that drove Italy's Axis partner Germany to fits of angry frustration during World War II); and bending the rules is a national art and science. Economic statistics are a cheerful shambles in Italy, about as sacred and reliable as alchemy. There is a separate, "moonlight" economy of tradespeople and merchants throughout Italy that has no connection with regular jobs and reportable income or with the official bureaucracy and tax structure; and it is this technically illegal, freelance economy that actually keeps Italy financially afloat. Everybody knows it, everybody deplores it, and everybody participates in it. Where, as in Italy, the exception so widely becomes the rule, certain conventions of anarchy result. Because the majority of people are anarchic in the same ways, Italy not only survives but in certain aspects and areas prospers. And since all authoritative explanations must be "official" ones, nobody can explain the phenomenon. Much of the charm of this unique method of "business through subversion" is that the resistance to official dogma—whether economic, political, or religious—does not appear sour, cynical, or resigned, but seems a positive engagement of people's talents. Hypocrisy is a readily embraced lifestyle, a marvelous conspiratorial game played against "them"—the bosses, top dogs, authority figures generally. Sad indeed would be the Italian spirit without these targets to outfox.

At bottom and despite the cultivated chaos of daily life, Italian society is probably as stable as any in Europe, for it rests on a monolithic structure: the family. The family is the Italian's first and dominant loyalty, paling by comparison his or her dedication to job, church, or country. "Family security," as Herbert Kubly writes, "makes Italians, even the poorest of them, one of the world's best-adjusted peoples and gives their nation a strength beyond anything that a political system could provide. It may also be one of the reasons why most Italians seem to have so little use for psychiatrists." The family is also supremely functional—there is always a cousin who knows somebody who owes a favor. This tightly meshed network of individual "connections" underlies the entire social structure in Italy and is vital to accomplishment of any sort.

Italian women have woven and continue to sustain the national fabric, keeping the home inviolate, cherishing the legal protections on marriage that other societies view as outmoded and severe. As Kubly states, "Italy is a land of illusions—all of them belonging to men. Italian women are hardcore realists who not only know but admit that a man who is disenfranchised from his fantasies is a sorry and ineffectual creature." One common male illusion is that of being God's gift to women, and male pursuit of any reasonably attractive female on any street in Italy is almost ritualistic in its form and expression. Yet Italian society cannot be defined as matriarchal; female suffrage dates only from 1948 and women's participation in the higher levels of government and industry is slight—except, as with many Italian definitions, in a conspiratorial, all-pervading sense. People who speak of the Italians as romantic often know little of Italy, for "romance requires sentiment," as Kubly states, "and sentiment is an Anglo-Saxonism not common in Italy." Personal relationships, whether between family, lovers, or friends, are rigidly structured on firmly nonromantic bases despite all the apparent emotional energy that goes into them. A person's place is well defined. Yet, withal, the poorest Italian peasant regards himself or herself as foremost a citizen of the world and does not hesitate to converse with anyone on the basis of that presumption.

This confident notion may have something to do with past glories, for no Italian ever forgets that this rocky finger of Europe not only mastered the known world but maintained its mastery for longer than any modern nation has existed. Today any call to Italian patriotism or national endeavor must necessarily invoke the Rome of the caesars if it is to have any hope of success. A large part of Mussolini's early success in reforming Italian economic life lay in his actor's ability to present himself as the legatee of imperial Rome.

The Italian peninsula is in many ways an island of the Mediterranean, cut off in the north by the Alps and surrounded on three sides by sea. The Apennine range extends almost the entire length, with the great Po River transversing the north. There are strong regional differences. The industrial north, with Italy's second-largest city, Milan, at its center, is the financial and creative hub of the country, as modern and fast-paced a city as any in Europe. Italy's great agricultural region covers the broad, northeastern plains of Emilia-Romagna. The mountainous Umbrian and Tuscan regions bridge north and south with orchard slopes and vineyards. South of these regions, one enters the *Mezzogiorno.* An area of chronic poverty, it is a rocky, often desolate landscape where human life seems cheap. Campania, Calabria, and the islands of Sicily and Sardinia constitute an area that has strongly resisted improvement through centuries of grinding wretchedness, though important gains have been made in the last several decades. These are lands that once held civilized centers of Greek and Norman culture, and the Holy Roman Empire courts of Frederick II. What happened to ravage and deplete them to such a dire extreme of poverty? Many authorities cite the region as a classical example of ecological disaster. Formerly heavily wooded, the slopes were denuded for fuel and quick cash crops. Topsoil, bereft of trees and other vegetation to anchor it, washed away; the bare clay land festered and bred malarial swamps; and sun and rain scourged the raw earth. As if in geological rage at this insult, eruptions of Vesuvius and Etna shook and buried cities, killing thousands. War and plunder added their toll. Communism thrives in such sinks, and the region has also long bred and exported violence in the persons of Mafia terrorists.

The list of notable Italians is long and distinguished, especially in the arts and sciences. The creative vigor of the Renaissance painters and sculptors alone—Leonardo, Michelangelo, Raphael, Botticelli, Titian, among others—places Italy at the apex of European art. Galileo and Marconi at once enlarged and condensed the world of their times by their mind-bending discoveries, as did global travelers Marco Polo and Christopher Columbus in different ways. Long rosters of Roman emperors and Catholic popes gave, in addition to many individual accomplishments, a sense of continuity and stability. The cynical political philosophy of Machiavelli, on the other hand, extends to our own time, giving most national governments much greater essential similarities than differences.

Italian cities and towns all have certain features in common. The piazza, or square, is a direct outgrowth of the Roman forum and in many communities serves much the same purpose as these ancient marketplaces and social centers. Residential or official buildings of moderate to large size are palazzos ("palaces"), though most of them are hardly "palatial" in the English sense of the word. A more exact correspondence is with the French word "hôtel," signifying a town house. The Italian villa is likewise similar to the French "château," which may or may not be a truly palatial country or suburban house.

Homes or portions thereof survive for most of the notables listed in the following pages, even for a surprising number of classical Romans. But travelers will find an often surprising municipal indifference to the marking of historic buildings or sites, an activity that one can usually take for granted in most other European nations. Thus one is pretty much left on one's own when seeking out precise spots where notable persons lived. As in Greece, many of the more ancient home sites cannot be localized to a satisfactory extent, and pilgrims must be content with a less explicit definition of "*site*" than normally applies in this book. Also, as in Greece, days and hours of museum admission are notoriously unreliable from one month and year to the next, so local checking is vital in planning visits.

Among specialized guidebooks, *A Christian's Guide to Rome* (1967) by S. G. A. Luff is interesting and useful.

AESCHYLUS (525–456 B.C.). The Greek dramatist visited the court of King Hieron twice—in about 471 and 458 B.C.—the second time leaving his bones there. Located in **Gela**, Sicily, only a few foundation ruins of the old city survive. According to hoary legend, Aeschylus died when an eagle, mistaking his bald head for a rock, dropped a tortoise on him.

Aeschylus tomb (unmarked): Ancient Necropolis (?), **Gela**.

(See GREECE in this chapter.)

AQUINAS, ST. THOMAS (1225–1274). A native of **Roccasecca**, this greatest of the medieval scholars was born in his family castle, that of the counts of Aquino, which towered above the town on a mountain crag. During a severe electrical storm, it is said, lightning struck the castle and killed Thomas's little sister, leaving the three-year-old boy unharmed. His mother, Theodora, believed him miraculously spared for some high destiny, which she foresaw as the abbot's seat of the nearby monastery in Monte Cassino—a role that would reunite the family lands and wealth with the abbey, which had held Roccasecca two centuries before. The castle, now ruins, is accessible on foot. In the village itself stands an old house with Gothic windows that is pointed out as another traditional childhood home of the saint.

At age five, the precocious young son was left at the Benedictine Abbey of Monte Cassino, a rich, powerful center of medieval learning, perched high above **Cassino**. There, until age 12, he was raised and rigidly trained in the classics by severe monks, who allowed no youngster to experience so unruly a period as childhood. Thomas appeared to be a humorless boy, however, temperamentally suited to the strict routines, and apparently never missed the lack of games and play. War disrupted this sober retreat in 1239 when the abbey was robbed and several monks were killed. Founded by St. Benedict in A.D. 529, the monastery underwent its greatest disaster on February 15, 1944, when more than 200 Allied bombers leveled it as a suspected German outpost ("Hill 516"), killing many refugees but hardly a German. "So conspicuous a landmark," wrote the German commander after the war, "would be quite unsuitable as an observation post"—an elementary point that somehow escaped the Allied strategists. German forces still held Cassino a month later. American General Mark W. Clark later described the bombing as "a tactical military mistake of the first magnitude," which enabled the Germans to turn the ruins into a major defensive fortress. The Italian government rebuilt the monastery after the war exactly as it had been, but its treasures—old manuscripts and chambers that had sheltered St. Thomas—were gone forever. Monte Cassino still attracts pilgrims, as it has for 14 centuries.

Aquinas spent most of his preparatory and final years in **Naples**, first as a novice monk, then as a master of theology who was renowned for his holiness and brilliant mind. In about 1244, when he entered the Dominican order despite his family's strenuous opposition—and again from 1272 to his death—Aquinas resided in the monastery adjacent to the Church of San Domenico Maggiore in the Largo San Domenico Maggiore.

The saint's cell is now a chapel, and his lecture room also survives. Aquinas completed his major philosophical treatise, the *Summa Theologica*, there. The head relic of the saint is visible on request. (Open daily.)

At **Orvieto**, where he taught from 1261 to 1265, he resided in the Convent of San Domenico and wrote the Office of the Feast of Corpus Christi to celebrate the Miracle of Bolsena, in which blood appeared on the host during a 1263 mass. The biretta and breviary of the saint are displayed in the adjacent Church of San Domenico, which was completed during his residence there. It stands in the Piazza Ventinove Marzo. (Open daily.)

The Monastery of Santa Sabina adjacent to the church in the Piazza Pietro d'Illiria, **Rome**, was Aquinas's residence from 1265 to 1267, and there he began writing the *Summa*. This basilican church, built in the fifth century and restored in 824 and 1216, is one of Rome's most beautiful churches and stands on the presumed site of the home of the martyred Roman matron, St. Sabina, where early Christians met. A room of this house has been excavated below the church floor. The rooms of St. Pius V and of St. Dominic may also be seen in the monastery. (Open daily.)

St. Thomas died in the 1187 Cistercian Abbey of **Fossanova**, where he had stopped while en route to the Council of Lyons. The room in which he died displays an altar and a sculpture by Bernini of the death scene; the latter does not provide a realistic effigy of the saint, who was an extremely heavy man. (Open daily.)

A good Italian-language guidebook for the Aquinas pilgrim is *Luoghi di San Tommaso* (1961), by P. Angelo Walz.

(See Chapter 3, PARIS; also Chapter 4, WEST GERMANY.)

ARCHIMEDES (ca. 287–212 B.C.). The most important scientist of antiquity, this Greek mathematician and inventor spent almost his entire life in the Sicilian Greek colony of **Syracuse**. There he formulated the principles of the lever, of quantitative analysis, and of integral calculus. He was probably best known in his own time as a military engineer, and developed many devices and engines of war; in the end they did not prevent Roman invasion of the city, however, or Archimedes' own death at the hands of a crazed soldier. Many excavations, especially in the Neapolis area of the city, have revealed portions of the Greek city familiar to Archimedes, but neither his home sites nor his tomb have yet been identified.

AUDEN, WYSTAN HUGH (1907–1973). The English-born poet resided during summers from 1948 to 1958 at **Forio** on the island of Ischia near Naples. Until 1953 he and his companion, Chester Kallman, rented a large house and garden at 14 Via Santa Lucia. Then from 1953 to 1958 they lived in the Quarto San Giovanni, Vico 4.

(See Chapter 1, AUSTRIA; also Chapter 5, ENGLAND.)

AUGUSTINE, ST. (354–430). "It is an astounding fact," wrote Charles Francis Potter, "that the Christianity of the last 1,500 years has been largely shaped by this one man." As the foremost theologian of Christian antiquity, Augustine developed the statement of doctrine that remains the cornerstone of orthodoxy for both Catholic and Protestant believers. His 22-book opus, *The City of God* (412–27), was written as a defense of doctrine against skeptics and hostile critics.

Augustine dwelled for most of his life in his native North Africa, but in 385 he underwent Christian conversion in **Milan**; the preaching of St. Ambrose, bishop of Milan, was a great influence and so was the energetic pushing of his mother, St. Monica. Augustine resided with his mother in a house with a garden at an unknown location. "As I walked about Milan," recalled the incomparable travel writer H. V. Morton in 1964, "I often wondered where the house with the garden had stood in which Augustine and Monica lived . . . what huge skyscraper, what block of flats, or what tramlines, now cover its site, and in what cellar below the modern level of the city is the spot, once a garden, where a man searching for God and haunted by Christ was eventually converted." The city was wiped out twice since this event, and burned and laid siege to many more times, so Augustine's footsteps are faint indeed in Milan.

In the Rome suburb of **Ostia Antica**, the residence of Augustine and his mother in 387 also remains unknown. St. Monica died there as they awaited embarkation back to Africa, an event described by Augustine in his *Confessions* (397–401). In *Ostia: Aspects of Roman City Life* (1981), however, Gustav Hermansen suggests that "of the excavated places in Ostia there is really only one which might fit St. Augustine's description of their hostel . . . the Insula di Bacco Fanciullo or its

neighbor Insula dei Dipinti." These excavated houses, originally of four stories, stand near the corner of the Via di Diana and the Via dei Dipinti. The large excavated area, exposed since 1907 and continuously enlarged, is approached by means of the Via Ostiense. Car lots provide parking outside the excavated streets and ruins, which must be covered on foot. (Open Tuesday—Sunday 9:00—6:00; admission.)

St. Augustine tomb (reputed): Church of San Pietro in Ciel d'Oro, **Pavia**.

Exhibits: The closest that one may approach St. Augustine in **Milan** today is via the places associated with the two most important people in his life, St. Ambrose and St. Monica. The Basilica of St. Ambrogio, built by the bishop from 379 to 386, is also his tomb, and his clothed skeleton, preserved here since his death in 397, may be seen in the crypt upon request. Most of the present church, located at the eastern end of the Via San Vittore, represents 9th- to 13th-century additions. (Open daily.)

The probable site of Augustine's baptism at Easter, 387, was the Basilica of St. Maria Maggiore, which stood until 1386 on the site of the present Milan cathedral in the Piazza del Duomo.

In **Rome** the Church of St. Agostino in the Via di Sant' Agostino contains the tomb of St. Monica, one of the best-known mothers in Christendom. This church, incidentally, was built of travertine plundered from the Colosseum. (Open daily.)

AUGUSTUS (63 B.C.–A.D. 14). Able and intelligent, this first and greatest Roman emperor (from 27 B.C. to his death) is associated with Rome's "golden age," that period of consolidation when Rome was the center of the known world in every conceivable way. The undisputed and self-aware master of that world, Augustus was a man of exceptionally high character, a benevolent, charitable ruler whose humane paganism looks refreshing when compared with the actions of many of the Christian emperors and popes who succeeded him in Rome. He was unusual among rulers in that day (and this) in his refusal to fear criticism, or to become alarmed or vindictive in the face of verbal insolence or challenge. More concerned with the realities than the trappings of power, he was not only a master statesman but probably the greatest mass psychologist of any leader in history.

Augustus was a native of **Rome**, the son of Octavius and Atia, and a grandnephew of Julius Caesar, who made him his adopted son and heir. The modest house where Augustus was born, and named Gaius Octavius Thurinus, stood on a lane called *ad Capita bubula*; it led southwest from the Colosseum up the Palatine Hill toward the Church of St. Bonaventura. Augustus, in contrast to later Roman emperors who crowded the Palatine with ornate palaces (the word "palace" derives from the Palatine), cultivated simple, unpretentious tastes in both living and ruling. In adulthood, according to Suetonius, "he lived at first near the Forum Romanum above the Stairs of the Ringmakers in a house which had belonged to the orator Calvus; afterwards, on the Palatine, but in the no less modest dwelling of Hortensius, which was remarkable neither for size nor elegance." This latter house, vacated by the orator Quintus Hortensius, was presented to Octavius (who assumed the title Augustus when he became emperor) by the Roman Senate in 36 B.C. This was after his defeat of Pompey in the Sicilian War, and the period of the Second Triumvirate when he shared Roman leadership with Mark Antony. Augustus continued to live there after becoming emperor. He enlarged the house and also bought the adjacent property. "For more than forty years," wrote Suetonius, "he used the same bedroom in winter and summer." Once each year, because of a dream, he would sit outside his door and beg alms from passersby. He kept a private "retired place" at the top of the house, says Suetonius, which he called "Syracuse." Most authorities believe that this residence survives as the so-called House of Augustus, now undergoing excavation between the Scalae Caci and the Temple of Apollo in the southwestern quarter of the Palatine. The west wing is thought to be the emperor's private quarters; interesting wall paintings have been uncovered in two of the rooms. Other rooms were apparently used for public ceremonies, and for libraries assembled by this well-read emperor. The excavation site may be visited by special permission from the Office of Excavations in the Antiquarium Forense, located in the east section of the Roman Forum. (Open Wednesday—Monday 9:30—12:30.)

Directly to the north is the House of Livia, discovered in 1869 and now believed to be the aforementioned property which Augustus added to his house (he had married Livia about 38 B.C.). Its masonry and notable murals date from the first century B.C. Livia's house "conveys better perhaps than anything else in the city what the home of a rich and cultivated Roman family was like

HOUSE OF LIVIA. On the Palatine Hill in **Rome**, the excavated courtyard of this first-century B.C. house, thought to be part of the dwelling of the Emperor Augustus, has been roofed by archaeologists. Rooms and faded wall frescoes indicate that the house was once the modest though elegant residence described by ancient biographers of Augustus.

just before the beginning of the Christian era," wrote Georgina Masson. The small, intimate rooms with their light, vivacious decorations contrast vividly with the imposing grandeur that one has come to expect of Roman ruins, especially on the Palatine. This house is shown by a custodian. Today, as they emerge from the burial of centuries, both houses still appear unimposing. In 1984 when the author visited them and stood in a passage of Livia's courtyard, no custodians or other visitors were present, and a profound, appropriate silence wrapped the ancient masonry. All Roman emperors from Augustus lived on the Palatine Hill, where Rome began. The Palatine is best approached from the north via the Roman Forum and the Clivus Palatinus. Since labels and markers are almost nonexistent on the Palatine, a good guidebook map is almost essential for identifying the various complex ruins and excavations. (Palatine Hill open Monday, Wednesday—Saturday 9:00—6:00, Sunday 9:00—1:00; admission.)

At **Prima Porta**, the junction of the Via Flaminia and the Via Tiberina about 12 kilometers north of Rome, stand ruins of the Villa of Livia, used as a country house by the imperial couple. A fine statue of Augustus, now in the Vatican, and frescoes were found here in 1863. According to Suetonius, this villa was called *ad gallinas*, from the story that when Livia first went to live there just before her marriage to Augustus, an eagle dropped a white hen (*gallina*) in her lap. The twig of bay held in its beak was planted and became the grove, so it is said, from which laurels were picked to crown the caesars. Frescoes from the sunken garden room of the villa, where the royal couple probably took refuge from the summer heat, were transferred in 1951 to the Roman National Museum in the Viale delle Terme di Diocleziano, **Rome**. The room, with its fruit and flower wall paintings, has been reconstructed on the museum's first floor as it was found in 1863. (Open Tuesday—Saturday 8:30—2:00, Sunday 9:00—1:00; admission.)

Augustus built one of his favorite palaces, the Villa Jovis, on the island of **Capri**. His successor Tiberius vastly enlarged this dwelling and retired there in A.D. 27, making Capri the virtual capital of the empire. Spectacular ruins of Tiberius' lavish villa surmount Monte Tiberio. (Open daily; admission.) Another possible Augustan palace site is that of the Villa Imperiale, also called the Damecuta Tower, in the island's northwestern corner. The so-called Gardens of Caesar, a terraced landscape established by Augustus near La Certosa, have survived all of his homes on the island.

Augustus tomb (site): Augusteum, **Rome**.

Exhibits: The Roman Empire was in a real sense the creation of this emperor, and its numerous tangible remnants in **Rome** itself and throughout Europe must all be considered memorials to Augustus. Specifically he was also a builder and beautifier of the city. Suetonius said that Augustus had found Rome "built of brick and left it in marble." One of his public works was the Temple of Julius Caesar in the Roman Forum (where Caesar's body was cremated in 44 B.C.) which was dedicated by Augustus in 29 B.C. This temple was also the site of his own funeral; his successor, Tiberius, spoke over his body on this occasion. (See the entry on Julius Caesar later in this section.)

(See SPAIN in this chapter.)

BERLIOZ, HECTOR (1803–1869). The French Romantic composer, a winner of the prestigious Prix de Rome in 1830, resided at the Villa Medici in **Rome** during the years 1831 and 1832 (see the entry on Galileo Galilei later in this section).

(See Chapter 2, FRANCE; also Chapter 3, PARIS; also Chapter 6, LONDON.)

BOCCACCIO, GIOVANNI (1313–1375). The rather obscure childhood of this Italian literary master led various biographers over the centuries to guess that he was either a native of Florence or Paris. Today, however, the general consensus is that he was born in **Certaldo** of unwed parents. The house which is thought to be his birthplace, located at 18 Via Boccaccio, is now a Boccaccio museum. Restored in 1823, the house was damaged by bombs during World War II; it has been rebuilt, and displays a library of Boccaccio's works, plus memorabilia, period furnishings, and utensils. (Ring next door as signposted for entry; free.) Certaldo was also the writer's last home, from 1361, but his address remains unknown.

HOUSE OF GIOVANNI BOCCACCIO. Rebuilt after bomb damage in World War II, this presumed birthplace of the writer in **Certaldo** now hosts a small museum devoted to his life and works.

Boccaccio spent much of his youth and working life in **Florence**. From 1341 to 1360, the period when he produced *The Decameron* (1351–53), he resided somewhere in the vicinity of the Church of San Piero Maggiore, now a ruin in the Piazza San Piero.

In **Naples**, where Boccaccio resided from about 1327 to 1341, the nearest point to which his address can be traced is the 13th-century Castel Nuovo vicinity in the Piazza del Municipio.

Boccaccio tomb: Church of St. Michael and St. James, **Certaldo**.

Exhibits: Boccaccio's will may be seen in the City Archive, Piccolomini Palace in the Via Banchi di Sotto, **Siena**. (Open Monday—Friday 9:30—1:00, Saturday 9:00—12:30; free.)

The traditional scene of the *Decameron* is the Villa Palmieri, located in the Viale Don Minzoni near the Piazza San Domenico, **Fiesole**.

BORGIA, CESARE (1476?–1507). The illegitimate son of Pope Alexander VI, Cesare was his father's chief tool in building the fortunes of the unscrupulous Borgia family. His mother, Vannoza de' Cattenei, was a longtime mistress of the cardinal who became Pope Alexander in 1492. The **Rome** birthplace of both Cesare and his sister Lucrezia Borgia (see the entry below) remains unknown, though some authorities think that the house at 27 Piazza Sforza Cesarini, corner of Via dei Banchi Vecchi, is a possibility since their mother was known to have lived there at a later date.

Cesare Borgia's residence from 1492 until his 1503 exile was the palace built for Cardinal Domenico della Rovere in 1480, which is located on the south side of the Via della Conciliazione in front of St. Peter's Square. Today known as the Penitenzieri Palace, it is occupied by the Penetentiaries, priests whose office it is to hear confessions in St. Peter's.

Briefly in 1503, after the death of his father, Borgia was imprisoned by Pope Julius II in the former Borgia Apartments at the Vatican Palace (see the entry on Lucrezia Borgia, *Exhibits*, below).

(See SPAIN in this chapter.)

BORGIA, LUCREZIA (1480–1519). Daughter of the infamous Pope Alexander VI and sister of Cesare Borgia, Lucrezia became a sacrificial marriage pawn in their ambitious political machinations. Despite her probably passive role, nobody ever accused her of standing absolutely above suspicion in the sordid domestic intrigues of the Borgias, though modern biographers discount much of the evil reputation that contemporary rumor and gossip attributed to her. Two of her marriages were annulled by her father, and her brother murdered her third husband. Attaching oneself to the Borgia family during the Renaissance would have been much like marrying into the Mafia today—a risky business. Later in life however, Lucrezia went far toward deflecting the unkind gossip surrounding her by becoming a notable patron of the arts.

Born in or near **Rome**, Lucrezia Borgia spent her early years in the house of her mother, Vanozza de' Cattenei, located in the Piazza Sforza Cesarini. This house, now called the Sforza Cesarini Palace at 282 Via dei Banchi Vecchi, was the longtime residence of Lucrezia's father, Cardinal Rodrigo Borgia, before he became pope. The north facade of the palace on the Corso Vittorio Emanuele side is a reconstruction, but inside is the original porticoed courtyard familiar to the Borgias; Rome travel writer Georgina Masson suggests evading "the watchful eye of the porter at No. 282" to see it. Later, until her marriage to Giovanni Sforza in 1493, Lucrezia Borgia resided with her cousin, Adriana de Mila Orsini, in the Orsini Palace of Santa Maria. This palace stood near the front of St. Peter's Basilica on the left side as one faces the steps.

When the stresses of being a Borgia became too much, Lucrezia usually retired to a convent (for women of the nobility, convents filled much the same function as psychiatric hospitals or sanitariums do for the middle class today). Lucrezia's favorite convent in Rome, where she lodged after the 1500 murder of Duke Alfonso, her second husband, was San Sisto Vecchio, the 13th-century residence of St. Dominic. It survives in the Piazzale Numa Pompilio.

In 1501 she married her fourth husband, Alfonso I, later the Duke of Ferrara, and resided in **Ferrara** from 1502. Though a political marriage like the others, the match turned out happily and no breath of scandal touched the duchess from that year. She set up a brilliant court, attracting learned scholars, poets, and artists from all over Italy, and became noted for her benefactions to education and charity. Her home was the magnificent 14th-century Estense Castle in the Piazza della Republica, a massive quadrilateral structure bounded by a moat and drawbridges. Altered in the 16th century, the castle now houses the University of Ferrara and provincial offices. In the rooms where Lucrezia Borgia hosted her own "university" of creative people, some ceiling paintings, frescoes, and marble decorations survive. (Guided tours daily, 9:00—12:00, 2:00—5:00; gratuity.)

Borgia tomb: Church of Corpus Domini, **Ferrara**.

Exhibits: In **Rome** any visitor intrigued by this redoubtable family must not miss the Borgia Apartments in the Apostolic Palace, the extreme southern portion of the Vatican Palace Museums. This was the private, six-room suite of Pope Alexander VI, father of Cesare, Lucrezia, and several other Borgias (though the entire apartments occupied the whole first floor of the Apostolic Palace). In room I of the apartments, Lucrezia Borgia's second husband, Duke Alfonso of Aragon, was smothered to death in 1500 by henchmen recruited by her brother Cesare; Alfonso was recovering at the time from wounds inflicted in a previous assassination attempt. Lucrezia rarely left him untended—but one night when she did, she returned to find him dead. Pope Alexander died in room XIII in 1503. In the same year Cesare Borgia was imprisoned by the new Pope Julius II in the room where Duke Alfonso was murdered. In the words of H. V. Morton, "Even in the Tower of London or Hampton Court one has the feeling that those who lived there have been long dead and have no further interest in the scenes of their earthly lives; but the Borgia rooms are haunted by uneasy spirits." Most of the floors, which are on curiously uneven levels, were reconstructed using copies of the original ceramic tiles in 1897. Today the cavernous Borgia rooms display notable frescoes of the family by Pinturicchio, done in 1492–94, as well as part of the Vatican Collection of Modern Religious Art. Originally built beside the first basilica of St. Peter in the sixth century, the Apostolic Palace was restored and enlarged in the 12th century and further elaborated several decades before Alexander's reign by Pope Nicholas V. (Open July 1—September 30, Monday—Friday 9:00—5:00, Saturday 9:00—2:00; October 1—June 30, Monday—Saturday 9:00—2:00; admission.)

In the museum of the Ambrosiana Library, Piazza Pio XI in **Milan**, may be seen a glass reliquary displaying a tress of Lucrezia Borgia's fine golden hair, upon which she lavished extraordinary care. This was the tress she sent as a keepsake to her lover, Pietro Cardinal Bembo, in about 1506. Before being enclosed, this relic enchanted Lord Byron who came here in 1816 to see it. He later boasted that he had stolen a strand of it (see the entry on Byron later in this section). (Open Sunday—Friday 10:00—12:00, 2:00—4:30, Saturday 10:00—12:00; admission.)

BOTTICELLI, SANDRO (1444?–1510). The Renaissance painter, born Alessandro di Filipepi, was a native and virtual lifelong resident of **Florence**. It is believed he was born at 28 Borgo Ognissanti, which was the rented family dwelling until 1458. In 1470 his father bought a house in the Via Nuovo, now part of the Via della Porcellana, and there the bachelor painter resided for the rest of his life. Botticelli maintained his studio on the same property, an unusual practice for artists of the time, and on this site produced most of his best-known works. His workshop, usually crowded with students and admirers, was viewed by some Florentines as "an academy for idlers with nothing better to do." Botticelli's neighbors included the parents of navigator Amerigo Vespucci. In 1494 Botticelli bought a country villa surrounded by vineyards and orchards on a hillside outside Florence; this plot of land provided wine, figs, and other fruit for the family. Some biographers believe Botticelli died at the villa. The house survives in the Via di Monte Oliveto in the suburb of Bellosguardo.

Botticelli tomb (unmarked): Church of the Ognissanti, **Florence**.

Exhibits: Botticelli's best-known works, including *Primavera* (ca. 1477) and the *Birth of Venus* (ca. 1485), are displayed in room 10 of the famed Uffizi Gallery in **Florence**. Other Botticelli paintings are also displayed there and in rooms 9 and 11. The Uffizi collection, housed in the 16th-century Uffizi Palace in the Piazza degli Uffizi, is Italy's most important art museum and one of the world's greatest. (Open Tuesday—Saturday 9:00—7:00, Sunday 9:00—1:00; 218341; admission, except free on Sunday.)

In **Rome** the Sistine Chapel in the Vatican Museums displays several religious paintings done by the artist there in 1481 and 1482 (see the entry on Michelangelo Buonarotti, *Exhibits*, later in this section).

BROWNING, ELIZABETH BARRETT (1806–1861).
BROWNING, ROBERT (1812–1889).

From 1847 until Elizabeth Barrett Browning's death, the English poets resided in **Florence** at a flat in the Casa Guidi, a 15th-century house marked by a tablet at 8 Piazza San Felice (corner of Via Maggio and Via Mazzetta). There Elizabeth wrote most of her *Sonnets from the Portuguese* (1850) and Robert also composed many poems. The couple raised their son Robert "Pen" Browning there (dressing him as a girl until age 13, when his mother died); and the only real cloud on their 16-year marriage was Elizabeth's interest, and Robert's disgust, in spiritualistic mediums and their trappings and rappings. After years of physical decline, the frail Elizabeth died there, and the anguished Robert returned with their son to England. The Casa Guidi, where the Brownings received many distinguished literary guests, still holds flats. Their apartment (rather dark chambers for someone suffering from tuberculosis) is now the Linguists' Club and contains nothing of the Brownings' own—except, as some might say, the very space in which they shared 14 years of their lives.* (Open 6:00p.m.—12:00; admission.)

In **Bagni di Lucca**, a health resort village where the Brownings vacationed from 1849 to 1853, Elizabeth worked on her *Sonnets from the Portuguese* at the Casa Tolomei, a marked villa in the main street.

The Brownings' occasional stays in **Rome** were not so pleasant, marred as they were by the fad for spiritualism that gripped both Rome and the fragile Elizabeth, and by Robert's desperate, solitary escapes into the city's nightlife and social round. In 1853 they lodged in a third-floor flat at the corner of the Via Bocca di Leone and the Vicolo del Lupo, now marked by a plaque, and returned there during winters and springs from 1858 to 1861. Angered by his wife's credulity, Browning wrote his poem "Mr. Sludge, the Medium" ("Now don't, Sir! Don't expose me! Just this once!") but never dared show it to Elizabeth.

Robert Browning's last lodging was the 17th-century Rezzónico Palace on the Grand Canal, **Venice**, approached on the landward side by the Fondamenta Rezzónico. Considered by many to be the most splendid patrician residence in the city, this majestic baroque palace had become the dwelling of "Pen" Browning, whose financially profitable marriage had enabled him to restore the building. The poet, who intended to spend his declining years with his son, did no actual writing there and in fact died only five weeks after taking up residence in the palace. The small, first-floor room where Browning died is arranged as it looked at the time but it is not often displayed to the public. Earlier (1879–80) the American painter James A. M. Whistler had occupied a room in the palace. The palace contains an exceptional collection of 18th-century paintings, furniture, and tapestries. (Open Monday—Saturday 9:00—12:30, 2:30—5:00, Sunday 9:00—12:30; admission, except free on Sunday.)

Elizabeth Barrett Browning tomb: English Cemetery, **Florence**.

Exhibit: The Municipal Museum in the 15th-century Loggia del Capitano, Via Regina Cornaro, at **Ásolo** displays memorabilia of Robert Browning's visits to the town, which he made the scene of his poetic drama *Pippa Passes* (1841). (Open daily, 9:00—12:00, 2:00—4:30; admission.)

(See Chapter 5, ENGLAND; also Chapter 6, LONDON.)

BYRON, GEORGE GORDON, LORD (1788–1824). The English poet resided and traveled widely in Italy from 1816 to 1823, enjoying a succession of villas, palaces, mistresses, and tight scrapes. Always straining to keep up with his own heroic self-image, Byron invariably succeeded in boring himself wherever he was, and constantly sought new scenes, activities, and women.

In **Venice** he stayed in 1816 at the house of a draper in the Frezzeria, a street leading off the Piazza di San Marco, and promptly took his landlord's wife, Marianna Segati, as his first Italian mistress. "Jealousy is not the order of the day in Venice," he found, "and daggers are out of fashion . . . It is very well known that almost all married women have a lover; but it is usual to keep up the forms, as in other nations." Byron stayed there at intervals until early 1818, producing one of his finest lyrics, "So we'll go no more a-roving." In 1818 he settled into one of the four 16th-century Mocenigo palaces on the Grand Canal. David

---

*Some houses of notable persons are more intriguing to modern visitors for their window views rather than for anything to be seen within. The Casa Guidi, facing the majestic Pitti Palace, is one such place. Elizabeth Browning, ever sympathetic to "causes," had Tuscan national aspirations in mind when she wrote her long poem *Casa Guidi Windows* (1851).

THE REZZÓNICO PALACE. In 1889, English poet Robert Browning died while lodging with his son in this Renaissance mansion facing the Grand Canal in **Venice**. The room he occupied is displayed as he left it.

Daiches described this period as "a life of studied debauchery with fluctuating mistresses, mostly from the poorer classes, Italian footmen and large numbers of Venetian parasites." Byron not only supported a large retinue of servants and hangers-on in the palace but also a sizable menagerie, including a fox, a wolf, dogs, monkeys, and birds. There he also began writing his masterpiece of self-satire, the epic *Don Juan* (1819–24). During his residence in this palace, Byron temporarily received his two-year-old daughter (by Claire Clairmont), and entertained Irish poet Thomas Moore. Byron lived there until 1819, when he met his last mistress, the 20-year-old Countess Teresa Guiccioli, wife of an aged nobleman.

Byron only stayed 23 days in **Rome** during the spring of 1817. "During that brief visit, most of which was spent on horseback," wrote H. V. Morton, "Byron wrote a more lasting impression of Rome [in Canto IV of *Childe Harold's Pilgrimage*, 1818] than many penned by those who have lived there all their lives." His unknown lodgings stood in the Piazza di Spagna somewhere near the final dwelling of John Keats (see *Exhibit* below).

In **Mira** Byron moved into the Villa La Mira, also known as the Villa Foscarini dei Carmini, in 1817, installing Marianna Segati there. Soon, however, he ousted her in favor of a baker's wife, the formidable Margherita Cogni whom he called "la Fornorina," who assertively took charge of the household. She was replaced after some violently emotional scenes in 1819 by the aforementioned Countess Guiccioli, who stayed until her husband arrived to demand his wife back. This villa, where Byron wrote the fourth canto of *Childe Harold*, is now occupied by the village post office.

In 1819 Byron followed the Guicciolis to their home in **Ravenna**, the Guiccioli Palace, where he was welcomed by all concerned. He settled into a rented suite at the palace as the countess's tacitly recognized lover, worked on *Don Juan*, and entertained his friend, poet Percy Bysshe Shelley. Byron lived at the palace until 1821. It stands at 54

Via Cavour northwest of the central Piazza del Popolo.

Byron established the countess and himself in the Lanfranchi Palace at **Pisa** in 1821 and 1822; for part of that period, the English essayist Leigh Hunt and his family, with whom Byron scrapped, also lived there. This 16th-century structure, now known as the Toscanelli Palace, stands on the River Arno at the corner of the Via delle Belle Torri and the Lungarno Medício. Byron was living there when Shelley drowned in June 1822.

Byron's final Italian home was the Casa Negroto, now called the Saluzzo Palace, at 1 Via Albaro in **Genoa**. He stayed there from September 1822 to July 1823 with the Hunts and the Countess Guiccioli. The latter by this time, wrote David Daiches, was "a mild habit rather than a passion." Byron, thirsting for action, left her that July in order to go to Greece and enlist in the struggle for independence against the Turks.

Exhibit: The Keats-Shelley Museum in **Rome** displays Byron relics along with those of Shelley, Leigh Hunt, and John Keats (see the entry on Keats later in this section).

(See GREECE in this chapter; also Chapter 1, SWITZERLAND; also Chapter 4, BELGIUM; also Chapter 5, ENGLAND; also Chapter 6, LONDON; also Chapter 7, SCOTLAND.)

CAESAR, JULIUS (100–44 B.C.). Sometimes called the greatest man of antiquity, the Roman conqueror of Gaul, reformer, orator, dictator, and military historian spent some 23 years of his life away from **Rome** in almost constant movement, leading armies and winning the far-flung domains that his grandnephew Augustus would consolidate into the Roman Empire. Indeed, from 80 to 44 B.C., Caesar lived in the city at intervals that only amounted to 13 years—"hardly more than enough to keep him from becoming a stranger in his native city," as one biographer wrote.

His patrician birthplace and home until 63 B.C. stood in the Subura district of the city, a low-lying area immediately northeast of the Roman Forum, traversed today by the Via Cavour. Elected *pontifex maximus* (supreme pontiff) in that year, he resided thenceforth in the Domus Publica. This residence in the Roman Forum was probably part of the House of the Vestals, the large rectangular structure that housed the six virgin priestesses of the goddess Vesta; it was rebuilt after the fire of Nero in A.D. 64. The outline and remnants of walls, pavements, and courtyards are visible in the cen-

tral part of the Forum along the Sacra Via. In 44 B.C., despite warnings and portents, Caesar emerged from the Domus Publica on the morning of March 15—the "Ides of March"—and journeyed to the Senate. There he was slain by a group of conspirators who feared that he wished to establish a hereditary monarchy. His body was carried back on a litter—"with one arm hanging down," wrote Suetonius—to his wife Calpurnia by three slaves. The Domus Publica probably stood on the Sacra Via almost directly across from the Regia. Now in ruins, the Regia was actually the official residence of the *pontifex maximus* but was too small for that purpose so was used as a working headquarters, or "office," by Caesar. Entrance to the Roman Forum is in the Via dei Fori Imperiali opposite the end of the Via Cavour. (Open Monday, Wednesday—Saturday 9:00—6:00, Sunday 9:00—1:00; admission.)

CAESAR'S CITY. Near this spot in the Forum, Julius Caesar resided with his wife Calpurnia and conducted his daily life in **Rome**. The covered excavation in the background is that of the Regia, Caesar's official residence. Further to the rear stand column ruins of the Temple of Castor.

Exhibits: The Forum of Caesar (Forum Julianum) was dedicated by Caesar in 46 B.C. to commemorate his victory at Pharsalus over Pompey. A statue of him as well as one of his paramour, the Egyptian queen Cleopatra, adorned the Temple of Venus Genetrix (see the entry on Cleopatra later in this section). Only ruins (excavated in 1932) remain of this first of the Imperial Fora. Entrance is by staircase near the Church of San Luca e Santa Martina in the Via del Tulliano.

Caesar was murdered in the Curia Pompei, where the Roman Senate met while awaiting completion of the new Curia Julia. A remnant of the Curia Pompei, its podium, survives behind one of the Republican temples in the Via di Torre Argentina. This hall or annex was part of the vast architectural complex of the Theatre of Pompey, erected in 55 B.C., and stood in its portico section east of the massive theater itself. Nothing else remains above ground of this structure. "If you wish to find the spot in Rome nearest to the place where Caesar fell," suggests H. V. Morton, "you would, curiously enough, find it on the steps of the Teatro Argentina," the 18th-century theater in the Largo Argentina. The Senate ordered the death chamber walled up, and it probably remained sealed for several centuries before falling to ruins. According to Suetonius, Caesar suffered 23 knife wounds, only one of which was fatal. He fell at the foot of Pompey's statue. Traditionally, this statue is the same one that was discovered in 1550 in the Via dei Leutari; it now stands in the General Council Chamber of the State Rooms in the 16th-century Spada Palace, seat of the Council of State in the Piazza di Capo di Ferro (open weekday afternoons by permission). Archaeologists, however, are convinced that this is not the same statue and does not represent Pompey. The actual statue may still exist somewhere beneath the modern pavements of Rome.

The site of Mark Antony's brief oration over Caesar's body was the Imperial Rostra, which stood in front of the Curia, the unfinished Senate House. The present brick Curia building in the Via della Curia, restored in 1937, dates from about A.D. 300, the reign of Diocletian, and was converted into the Church of St. Adriano in 638. The rostra itself, a 24 x 12-meter platform from which Caesar had spoken many times, now stands near the Arch of Septimius Severus, a short distance south of its original site. The Temple of Julius Caesar, begun in 42 B.C. and dedicated by Augustus in 29 B.C., marks the site of Caesar's cremation, an event which turned into a hysterical mob scene as people heaped anything at hand upon the pyre, even clothing. Only the central block of the podium and the round altar marking the cremation site survive. All of these places are located in the Roman Forum (see above).

Probably several thousand people obliviously cross the Rubicon daily on route 16. This small stream about 30 kilometers north of **Rimini** formed the border between Rome and Cisalpine Gaul. Caesar's armed advance in 49 B.C. was in defiance of the Roman Senate, which feared his power; it precipitated a 65-day civil war, at the end of which Caesar was master of Italy.

(See GREECE in this chapter.)

CARUSO, ENRICO (1873–1921). Christened Errico Caruso, and born in the slums of **Naples**, this operatic tenor was the eighteenth of 21 children. His birthplace, a decrepit stucco house, stood at 7 Via San Giovanello agli Otto Calli. Incompetent physicians deprived the world of this majestic voice in 1921 when they repeatedly misdiagnosed his acute condition and butchered him twice on operating tables. The medical victim was headed for yet another operation when he died in agonizing pain in the Hotel Vesuvio, 45 Via Partenope. Caruso laid in state there while thousands of admirers offered tribute.

Early in the century when Caruso first achieved renown, he acquired the Villa alle Panche at **Rifredi**, a suburb of Florence. Surrounded by olive groves, the house had a Moorish-style den in which the singer studied scores and rehearsed.

Though operatic engagements (especially in the United States) kept him away from Italy for long periods, he later bought a hilltop estate at **Lastra a Signa**, the 15th-century Villa Bellosguardo, where he retired during off-seasons. There, in 1919, an angry mob of peasant revolutionaries invaded his property taking stores of grain, wine, and olive oil that had been harvested from the estate. Caruso, who cared for little except his wife, children, and music, hardly bothered to protest.

Caruso's last residence of any duration, where he stayed for a month in 1921 and made rapid recovery until the doctors descended again, was the Hotel Vittoria, now the Excelsior Grand Hotel Vittoria, at 34 Piazza Tasso, in **Sorrento**. He and his wife occupied the entire first-floor.

Caruso tomb: Del Planto Cemetery, **Naples**.

CASANOVA, GIOVANNI GIACOMO (1725–1798). As one of the most famous libertines (or, at least, braggarts) in history, Casanova's name has become a synonym for a Lothario. He also made a life's work of "living in extravagance off the gullibility of the rich," wrote biographer John Masters. In his *History of My Life* (1826–38), Casanova records some 11 venereal attacks (almost one per volume) ranging from probable gonorrhea to a virulent case of herpes.* His reputed birthplace in **Venice** stands marked in the Campo San Samuele. In 1756 he was imprisoned in "the Leads" or "Piombi," cells so-called from their position beneath the leaden roof of the Doges' Palace, Piazzetta San Marco. This 12th-century castle, restored numerous times, housed the chief magistrates of the Venetian city-state until 1797. Today it functions as a notable art museum, and displays a lavish collection of paintings and sculpture of Venetian masters. The prison rooms are entered from the third floor. Casanova, held by the state inquisitors because of his failure to attend Mass, to observe Lent, and to invoke the devil's name when he cursed, escaped from his cell by digging to the roof with a sharpened bolt, then entering a lower chamber through a window.

After that the gentleman rogue traveled throughout Europe but usually lingered only long enough in any city to seduce a nun, cuckold a husband (or wife), or conduct an orgy—according to his own detailed account. He invariably "fell in love" with his sexual object, and his charm was apparently quite overwhelming. In **Rome** his 1743 lodging was the 17th-century Spanish Palace at 32 Piazza di Spagna. Worn out by 1785, he retired to Bohemia where he wrote his memoirs, and ended his career in dull celibacy as a castle librarian.

CELLINI, BENVENUTO (1500–1571). This sculptor, goldsmith, and rowdy hero of *The Autobiography of Benvenuto Cellini* (1730), one of the world's classic memoirs, was a native of **Florence** and never ceased trumpeting the fact. A talented artist of hair-trigger temper, he unapologetically recorded his life (up to 1566) as an incessant series of scrapes, duels, vast injustices, sweet revenges, and instances of triumphant upmanship. His birthplace and home until 1519 survives in the Via Chiara overlooking the Central Market. In

---

*He was, however, far from being the world's most rapacious lover. The authors of *The Intimate Sex Lives of Famous People* (1981) computed from his memoirs that "Casanova had a tenth the number of sex partners claimed by Sarah Bernhardt, Guy de Maupassant, Elvis Presley, Ninon de Lenclos, and others."

1545, upon his return from the court of Francis I in France, Cellini settled permanently in Florence under the patronage of Duke Cosimo I. Installed by the duke in a house of Cellini's own choosing "in a quarter much to my liking," the artist cleared the adjacent ground and built the workshop where he modeled and cast his magnificent *Perseus* (see *Exhibits* below), as well as crafted all of his later work. This house, where Cellini died, survives at 59 Via della Pergola.

During the years 1519 to 1540 Cellini based his activities in **Rome**. His lodging and studio, where he made his famous medallions for Pope Clement VII, stood in the Via Giulia, vicinity of the Via del Banco di San Spirito and the Via dei Banchi Vecchi. Several blocks southeast is the short street called Vicolo Cellini, said to be the scene of one of his numerous love affairs. In 1538 he was imprisoned by Pope Paul III, on the false charge of stealing jewels from the papal treasury, in the huge, circular Castel Sant' Angelo, originally the Mausoleum of Hadrian (see the entry on Hadrian later in this section). During the Middle Ages this multichambered tower became a citadel, fortress, papal castle, and prison. Cellini's cell still exists on the second floor, one of the small outer rooms facing the large space called the Courtyard of Alexander VI. Owing to his cultivated friendship with the warden, however, Cellini was given freedom of the castle and even crafted some small items there. The adventure of his escape by descending the tower wall on a rope of linen strips; his further scaling of the lower surrounding wall on the north side; and his fall resulting in a broken leg are told to great effect in his autobiography. He was soon recaptured, though, and returned to the castle. This time his incarceration was thoroughly unpleasant. "I was taken into a gloomy dungeon below the level of a garden, which swam with water and was full of big spiders and many venomous worms," he wrote. The artist endured some four months lying on a wet mattress in almost total darkness, with a broken leg, and with his teeth falling out because of malnourishment. In this condition he experienced ecstatic religious dreams and composed a long poem "in praise of my prison, relating in it all the accidents which had befallen me." Today these dungeon rooms are identified as the Historical Prisons, and under their floors numerous bones from prisoner burials have been found. Approached via a sloping passage from the Court of Alexander VI, they have been closed in recent years. Cellini was finally removed to his previous quarters in the castle and was soon released through the influence of friends in the papal court. Ironically, in 1527 Cellini had taken an active part in the defense of this besieged castle during the sack of Rome by the armies of Charles V, protecting the person of Pope Clement VII. Earlier Alexander VI, the Borgia pope, had often stayed in the luxurious papal apartments. Today the weight of history dwells heavily on this ancient structure, the scene of so much fear, despair, death, and contrasting opulence in the shape of the corrupt Renaissance papacy. It has been called "one of the most frightening buildings in the world." "One does not need to be psychic, or even unduly sensitive or fanciful," wrote one observer, "to feel that agony and suffering still cling to the dark corridors. . . . Compared with S. Angelo, the Tower of London is almost a happy place." Today the Castel Sant' Angelo, facing the Ponte Sant' Angelo across the Tiber, is a national military and artistic museum, and displays weapons, paintings, antiques, and tapestries. Of the former marble exterior, all that remains is Hadrian's immense brick core and the upper parts added during the Renaissance and later. The view of Rome from its topmost terrace (scene of the final act of Puccini's opera *Tosca*) is spectacular. (Open Tuesday—Saturday 9:00—1:00, Sunday 9:00—12:00; admission.)

Cellini tomb: Church of Santissima Annunziata, **Florence**.

Exhibits: The Uffizi Gallery in **Florence** displays the largest collection of Cellini works, including statues and scale models (see the entry on Sandro Botticelli earlier in this section). In the Loggia dei Lanzi, the 14th-century spacious structure at the west end of the Piazzale degli Uffizi, stands Cellini's bronze masterpiece *Perseus* (1554) with its intricate pedestal.

(See Chapter 3, PARIS.)

CHARLEMAGNE (742–814). In 800, the Frankish king was crowned as the first Holy Roman Emperor by Pope Leo III in St. Peter's Basilica, **Rome**. His residence during this momentous occasion may have been the early palace on the site of the present Apostolic Palace (see the entry on Lucrezia Borgia, *Exhibits*, earlier in this section). One source suggests that his palace may have stood on the site of the Campo Santo Teutonico on the opposite (south) side of St. Peter's Basilica, a spot now occupied by the Teutonic College.

(See Chapter 2, FRANCE; also Chapter 4, WEST GERMANY, THE NETHERLANDS.)

CICERO, MARCUS TULLIUS (106–43 B.C.). The Roman orator, statesman, and philosopher was born near **Arpino** on his family estate close to the junction of the Liri and Fibrenus rivers. Now long-gone, the villa erected by his grandfather probably stood toward the eastern side of the Fibrenus delta island called the Insula Arpinas, a location on route 82 about six and a half kilometers north of the town. The 11th-century monastery church of San Domenico stands less than 50 meters south of the actual villa site. Cicero returned here often throughout his life to relax and write, and his Platonic dialogue *De Legibus* is set on the estate, which he inherited. A century after his death, it was occupied by the poet Silius Italicus. Grant Showerman, in his *Momuments and Men of Ancient Rome* (1935), suggested that the nearby church and monastery "contain in their walls and floors so many fragments in the Roman villa style that it is entirely reasonable to suppose at least some of them were parts of the Cicero home."

In **Rome** Cicero's first home was probably located in the Carinae, an area of rising ground directly northeast of the Roman Forum, represented today by the Via Carine. Locations of Cicero's subsequent Roman homes remain unknown up to 62 B.C., but in that year he acquired a villa from Marcus Crassus on the northwest slope of the Palatine Hill (see the entry on Augustus earlier in this section). Pillaged and destoyed by fire in 58 B.C. when Cicero was temporarily banished, the villa was rebuilt the next year; Cicero continued to reside there, when in Rome, for the rest of his life. "In sight of almost the entire city is my home," he could say. Its site today is covered by later ruins.

In 75 B.C. Cicero began his political career as quaestor, or financial administrator, in the Sicilian town of Lilybaeum, the present site of **Marsala**. Excavations have revealed ruins of the ancient community in the Viale Piave. (Open daily, 9:00—12:00, 2:30—6:00; admission.)

Cicero owned a number of country villas, for essentially he preferred the solitude of his books and groves to the politically charged atmosphere of Rome. Though most of their general locations are known, few of the sites have been authentically narrowed to specific plots of ground. Near **Tusculum** he acquired a villa called the "Tusculaneum" about 68 B.C.; it was at this site, during a long retirement (47–44 B.C.), that he wrote the *Tusculan Disputations* and several other works. There is a so-called Villa of Cicero above the village, but its associations with the orator remain dubious.

Another summer villa stood in Antium, now **Anzio**, located somewhere on high ground northeast of the present city.

At **Formia** another so-called Villa of Cicero above the town apparently dates from a later period, though Cicero did reside in the vicinity, and complained of the lack of news from Rome in 59 B.C. The seaside Villa Rubino, privately owned, probably includes ruins of the actual dwelling. Cicero also lived at **Cumae**, an ancient Greek colony; at **Pompeii**, buried by Vesuvius in A.D. 79;* and at Puteoli, now **Pozzuoli**, where he acted as host to Julius Caesar in 45 B.C. The Emperor Hadrian's ashes were kept in the latter residence in A.D. 138 before their transference to Rome (see the entry on Hadrian later in this section).

Assassinated by order of a vindictive Mark Antony, the venerable statesman met his end at **Gaeta** not far from his villa at Formia. The nearby tower monument said to be Cicero's tomb may mark the spot where he was beheaded.

Cicero tomb (reputed): Appian Way (route 82), **Formia**.

Exhibits: Cicero was Rome's greatest orator in a city full of orators, and **Rome**, of course, was his dominant scene of activity, particularly the Forum and its vicinity. The Temple of Jupiter Stator ruins flanking the Via di San Bonaventura, founded in 294 B.C., was the site of Cicero's First Oration

Against Catiline, 63 B.C. His Second and Third orations were delivered from the Rostra in front of the Senate the same year. The Curia and Temple of Concord within the Roman Forum are other important Ciceronian sites. (See the entry on Julius Caesar earlier in this section.)

(See GREECE in this chapter).

CLEOPATRA (69–30 B.C.). "Age cannot wither her, nor custom stale her infinite variety"—thus Shakespeare described the Macedonian-descended queen of Egypt, reinstated on the Egyptian throne in 48 B.C. by Julius Caesar, who became her lover and father of her son Ptolemy XV (Caesarion). Cleopatra lived in **Rome** from 46 to 44 B.C., departing a month after Caesar's assassination (see the entry on Caesar earlier in this section). One traditional site of the villa in which Caesar installed her as his mistress—to the horror of Rome's conservatives and the delight of its gossips—is the large park of the Villa Doria Pamphilj, or Belrespiro, dating in its present design from 1650 and traversed by the Via Olimpica. This park is jointly maintained by the state and the Commune of Rome. (Open daily, sunrise to sunset.) Another possibility was a villa discovered in 1879 in the present grounds of the 16th-century Villa Farnesina in the Via della Lungara, though the excavated house's exact date remains a matter of controversy. Wall paintings and stuccoes from this house have been preserved (see *Exhibit* below).

Exhibit: Some **Rome** authorities believe that the

WHERE CHRISTOPHER COLUMBUS GREW UP. The future explorer of the New World was the son of a weaver in **Genoa**, but only foundation ruins of the Columbus dwelling survive in the Piazza Dante. The ivy-covered

structure at left in the first picture marks the house site, located very near the old city wall towers on the right. The second photograph shows the front of the same ruin, marked as the "House of Columbus."

aforementioned "Egyptianized" stuccoes and paintings may have decorated the villa often shared by Caesar and Cleopatra "across the Tiber" (naturally) from his home in the Forum with Calpurnia. These room decorations may be seen in first-floor rooms of the Roman National Museum (see the entry on Augustus earlier in this section).

COLUMBUS, CHRISTOPHER (1451–1506). "Columbus" is an anglicized version of the New World explorer's birth name, Christoforo Colombo. According to his foremost biographer, Samuel Eliot Morison, Columbus's **Genoa** birth site cannot be precisely fixed, but the vicinity was probably just inside the eastern gate of the old city, the Porta dell' Olivella, where the wool-weaving family lived until 1455; this quarter has been entirely rebuilt. Two stories of a former five-story dwelling marked as the House of Columbus where he grew up (1455–70) stands at 37 Vico di Morcento.

Exhibits: The Municipal Palace in the Via Garibaldi, **Genoa**, displays part of the explorer himself—fragments of his skeleton unearthed in Santo Domingo in 1877. Also on display are three of his letters. (Open daily, 9:00—12:00, 2:00—5:00; admission.) The 16th-century Bianco Palace at 11 Via Garibaldi also exhibits some Columbus letters. (Open Tuesday—Saturday 10:00—12:00, 2:00—6:00, Sunday 10:00—12:00; admission, except free on Sunday.)

(See SPAIN in this chapter.)

CONSTANTINE I, THE GREAT (272–337). The first Christian Roman emperor was probably a native of Naissus in Dacia (now Nish in Romania) and may not have even seen **Rome** until about the year 312, when he became emperor of the West and adopted Christianity. Constantine's efforts thenceforth were mainly concentrated in the eastern empire, where he became sole Roman emperor in 325. He apparently resided in the capital only in 312–13, 314–16, and during the summer of 326. During these periods he occupied the huge imperial palace at the center of the Palatine Hill, the Domus Augustana, built by Domitian in about A.D. 90 and elaborated, altered, and enlarged by succeeding emperors until the fall of Rome in the fifth century. These palace ruins cap the entire vast area of the hill summit. Treading these ancient floors and pavements, which lay at the very hub of the civilized world as it existed for six centuries, is an unforgettable experience for anyone who has felt the fascination of ancient Rome. It is

also mostly a solitary one, for the crowds of tourists that jam the Roman Forum below the hill do not usually come here in droves, and the silence, breezes, and sun lend a profound dignity to the grassy halls whose power once made the world tremble. (See the entry on Augustus earlier in this section.)

A PORTION OF THE DOMUS AUGUSTANA. Built by the Emperor Domitian, this massive complex of palaces on the Palatine Hill in **Rome** was also occupied by many of his successors, including Constantine I, Trajan, and Hadrian.

Exhibit: The Arch of Constantine, standing directly southwest of the Colosseum in the Via di San Gregorio, was erected in 315 to celebrate the emperor's final victory in 312 over his co-emperor Maxentius. It survives, probably thanks to the emperor's conversion, as the best-preserved monument of ancient **Rome**.

(See Chapter 4, WEST GERMANY; also Chapter 5, ENGLAND.)

COPERNICUS, NICOLAUS (1473–1543). The Polish astronomer displaced man from the center of the cosmos with his theory that the earth revolves around the sun—a vital development not only in astronomy but in scientific thought—and revolutionized theories of planetary motion. Copernicus spent about seven years studying in Italy before returning to his life's work in Poland. At **Bologna**, where he studied astronomy and Greek at the university from 1497 to 1501, he may have occupied lodgings with a professor in the Via San Giuseppe.

He studied medicine at the University of **Padua** (1501–03) and took his doctoral degree at **Ferrara** in 1503, but his lodging sites remain unknown.

Exhibit: The Astronomical and Copernicus Museum at 84 Viale Parco Mellini in **Rome** displays a collection of Copernicus memorabilia. (Inquire locally for admission information.)

DANTE ALIGHIERI (1265–1321). Italy's most famous poet and literary genius was a native of **Florence**. Tradition ascribes his birthplace as the site of the reconstructed house at 2 Via Dante Alighieri, the House of the Alighieris. He probably inherited the house in 1282 and resided there until his 1302 exile. Politically active but acid-witted and blunt-spoken, Dante made powerful enemies in Florence and was banished from the city on trumped-up charges of corruption and other crimes. Despite opportunities to do so, he never returned to Florence, and the rest of his life was indelibly marked by a profound love-hate attitude toward the city of his forebears. His weapons of dispute proved invincible in the long run, of course, for he immortalized his enemies by placing them in lower circles of "The Inferno," Part I of *The Divine Comedy* (1321), probably the greatest epic poem ever written. Today the "Casa di Dante," owned by the city, displays historical documents and Dante memorabilia. (Inquire locally for admission information.)

The last 19 years of the poet's life, except for a sojourn in Paris and his final residence in Ravenna, were mostly spent wandering throughout Italy, writing his masterpiece, and residing for various periods as the guest of friends and noble patrons. From 1302 to 1304, and again in 1316–17, he lived in **Verona**. Probably at least part of that period was spent at the Palace of the Governor, also called the Palace of the Scaligere, home of the ruling della Scala family for almost a century, now restored in its original 13th-century style and used for municipal offices. It is said that the nobles there sometimes made the poet a butt of practical jokes. This massive edifice stands at one end of the Piazza dei Signori.

The year 1306 found Dante in **Padua**, where he may have taught philosophy or composition. The Casa Carrarese, a marked dwelling in the Via San Lorenzo, is identified as his lodging.

Dante settled in **Ravenna** in 1317, residing there for the rest of his life under the patronage of the ruling Guido da Polenta. He first lived at the da Polenta palace, the Camera a Coronis, one wall of which remains with a marker. Later he was given a house of his own, the site of which has been much disputed and cannot be definitely stated. At these final lodgings Dante wrote the "Paradise" portion of his great poem.

Dante Tomb: Museum and Tomb of Dante, **Ravenna**.

Exhibits: Two Dante museums in **Ravenna**—the Museum and Tomb in the Via Dante and the Dante Museum in the Via Guido da Polenta—display memorabilia, manuscripts, editions, and relics of the poet. (Inquire locally for admission information.)

The Salviati Palace at 6 Via del Corso in **Florence** occupies the site of the Portinari houses where lived Beatrice Portinari, whom Dante idealized as his guide to Paradise in *The Divine Comedy*.

In **Rome** the 16th-century Firenze Palace houses the Dante Alighieri Society, which may be contacted for further information (see the entry on Galileo Galilei later in this section.)

(See Chapter 3, PARIS.)

DEBUSSY, CLAUDE-ACHILLE (1862–1918). The French composer, a winner of the prestigious Prix de **Rome** in 1885, resided from that year until 1887 at the Villa Medici. He called his room "the Etruscan tomb" in "that abominable villa," noting how its green walls "seemed to recede as one walked toward them" (see the entry on Galileo Galilei later in this section). Homesick for Paris during most of his stay, Debussy did not enjoy his period of study at Rome.

(See Chapter 2, FRANCE; also Chapter 3, PARIS; also Chapter 5, ENGLAND.)

DOSTOEVSKI, FEODOR MIKHAILOVICH (1821–1881). The Russian novelist came twice to **Florence**, the second time staying for two years (1867–69). In 1867 he and Anna Grigorievna Dostoevski stayed at the Swiss Pensione on the corner of the Via Tornabuoni and the Via della Vigna Nuova. An earlier resident there had been English novelist George Eliot (see the entry on Eliot below). The house bears a marker. In 1868 at 21 Piazza Pitti, Dostoevski wrote his novel *The Idiot* (1868).

(See Chapter 1, SWITZERLAND; also Chapter 4, EAST GERMANY, WEST GERMANY.)

ELIOT, GEORGE. See MARY ANN EVANS below.

EVANS, MARY ANN. ("GEORGE ELIOT") (1819–1880). At the Swiss Pensione in **Florence** the English writer and her lover, George Henry Lewes, resided for several months while she gathered material for her historical novel *Romola* (1863;

see the entry on Feodor Mikhailovich Dostoevski earlier in this section).

(See Chapter 1, SWITZERLAND; also Chapter 5, ENGLAND; also Chapter 6, LONDON.)

FRANCIS, ST., OF ASSISI (1182?–1226). The friar (never a priest) and founder of the mendicant Franciscan orders, one of the most joyous and nature-loving of saints, was a native of **Assisi**, and the town is full of bells, birds, and memorials to Francis. A 1616 church called Chiesa Nuova (New Church) in the southeast corner of the Piazza del

Comune stands on the supposed site of his birthplace, while a 13th-century oratory in an adjoining alley may be part of the house itself. The son of a prosperous cloth merchant, Francis was named Giovanni Francesco Bernardone. In 1205, after a brief career as a soldier, he dedicated himself to religion and a life of poverty. He began to preach and gathered a group of disciples; in 1209 he founded the Friars Minor order for men and in 1212 the Poor Clares for women.

The forest hermitage where Francis often retreated in order to meditate, and where he gathered his earliest followers, was an outlying area of caves and grottoes dug into the rock. During the 15th century the caves were made into enclosed cells below the present chapel and monastery of St. Bernard of Siena. Now known as the Eremo

THE HERMITAGE OF ST. FRANCIS. The mendicant founder of the Franciscan order, one of the church's most popular saints, gathered his band of followers at the Eremo delle Carceri near his native **Assisi**. The later Monastery of St. Bernard was erected over the original rock chambers and cells where the brotherhood had frequently retreated for meditation and acts of strenuous self-denial.

delle Carceri, the monastery stands about four kilometers east of the town on route N147. The saint's own cell with its granite slab for a bed may be seen—and outside, the ancient, now-braced oak tree beneath which he is said to have preached to the birds. (Open daily, 8:00—sunset; donation.)

One of the most important religious shrines in Italy, drawing some two million visitors annually, is Santa Maria degli Angeli, the 16th-century basilica built over the cell and oratory where Francis and his disciples conducted their daily lives. The white-stone Porziuncola Chapel that stands at the center of the nave was the original meeting place and spot chosen by Francis for his devotions. Not easy to imagine now is the former aspect of this place, a woodland clearing. The brothers built themselves rough, thatched huts in two lines on each side of the chapel. Within seven years, 12 disciples had grown to 5,000. Today's church floor probably covers only a part of the original encampment site. Relics of the saint may be seen in the Transito Chapel, built over the infirmary cell where St. Francis died. The Roseto Chapel rises over a cave used by the saint. The basilica stands about five kilometers south of town from the Porta San Pietro. (Open daily; donation.)

The Convent of San Damiano lies about one kilometer south of the Porto Nuova among olive and cypress trees. There in 1205 Francis took up his vows and, in 1212, founded this convent on the site of the rustic chapel where he prayed, and established St. Clare as its superior. She resided there until her death in 1253. In the garden, it is said, St. Francis composed his "Canticle of the Sun" (1225-26), one of the earliest poems in the Italian language. (Open daily, 8:00—12:30, 2:00—sunset; donation.)

About 40 kilometers southwest of **Rieti** on route N578 stands the Convent of Fonte Colombo, where Francis lodged and dictated the rules of his order in 1223. (Open daily; donation.)

It is said that the Monastery of **La Verna**, 26 kilometers east of Bibbiena on route N71, occupies a site given to Francis in 1213. There, after a 40-day fast in 1224, he received the wounds of the stigmata. The Stimmate Chapel inside the church portion supposedly marks the exact spot of this event. (Open daily; donation.)

In **Rome**, which Francis visited in 1219, the cell he occupied in the hospice of San Biagio is enclosed by the 1231 Church of San Francisco a Ripa in the Piazza San Francesco d'Assisi. Relics and a 13th-century painting of the saint are displayed. (Open daily; donation.)

St. Francis tomb: Basilica of San Francesco, **Assisi**.

GALILEO GALILEI (1564–1642). While Christianity has many martyrs, so does science, and scientists' worst persecutors have usually been churchmen. In 1983 the Roman Catholic church officially allowed that it may have made a major mistake in 1633 when it condemned the great founder of modern experimental physics for heresy because he insisted on the truth of the Copernican theory of a heliocentric solar system. Seldom has the church permitted itself to look so foolish for so long. Under threat of torture from the Inquisition, the infirm Galileo recanted his views, though of course he knew them to be right. The church dealt leniently with him for the "crime" involved, placing the aged astronomer under house arrest for the remainder of his life.

A native of **Pisa**, Galileo was born in a house that stood near the Porta Fiorentina; it was his home to about 1572. As a professor of mathematics at the University of Pisa from 1589 to 1591, he lived at what is now called the Domus Galileiana, 26 Via Santa Maria, which displays memorabilia of the scientist. (Inquire locally for admission information.)

In **Padua**, where he taught mathematics at the university from 1592 to 1610, he spent the 18 happiest years of his life. There he carried out his first astronomical experiments, invented the thermometer, improved the telescope and methods of observation, and observed sun spots and the moons of Jupiter, which gave visible proof of the Copernican theory.

Deeply religious but a forceful teacher and often sarcastic commentator on the opinions of ignorant authorities, Galileo abandoned teaching in 1610 to devote himself to further research in **Florence**. As the grand duke of Tuscany's "chief philosopher and mathematician," he produced his first defense of Copernicus, "Letters on the Sun Spots" (1613). His house at 19 Via della Costa di San Giorgio, where he lived until 1617 with his mistress Maria Gamba and their children, survives. Then from 1617 to 1631 he rented the Villa L'Ombrellino, which still stands in suburban Bellosguardo. Galileo's last home from 1631, where he lived as a virtual prisoner of the pope from 1633, was the Villa il Gioiello, his farm at 40-42 Via del Pian dei Giullari in suburban Pian de Giul-

THE DOMUS GALILEIANA. Galileo, the great scientist persecuted by the church for his astronomical observations and conclusions therefrom, lived in this Pisa dwelling at the end of the court during his professorship at the University of **Pisa**. Today it holds a Galileo museum.

lari, where a bust and inscription mark the house. He took this villa to be near his daughter Virginia, who was a nun at the adjacent Franciscan convent. Using subterfuge he managed to smuggle out his last great book, *Dialogues Concerning Two New Sciences* (1638), in small portions at a time for publication in countries less fearful of free inquiry. Blind and ailing, surrounded by household spies, he reserved scathing contempt for his papal censors, while welcoming students and admirers from all over Europe; English writers Thomas Hobbes and John Milton were among his famous visitors. This property is now undergoing restoration, and will be used as a center for the study of astronomy.

In 1633, summoned before the Inquisition of Pope Urban VIII in **Rome**, Galileo resided in the 16th-century Firenze Palace, seat of the Florentine Embassy, during his trial. It stands in the Piazza Firenze, Via Metastasio, and now houses the Dante Alighieri Society. The Villa Medici in the Viale della Trinita dei Monti, the Roman residence of the dukes of Tuscany, served as his usual lodging in the city between 1630 and 1633. Contrary

to the villa's inscription and most travel guides, however, Galileo was never held prisoner there (in fact, he was never officially "imprisoned" except for a few hours between his trial and sentencing in 1633). Built about 1544, the palace was bought by Cardinal Ferdinand de Medici in 1580 and passed to the grand dukes. The Spanish painter Velázquez also resided there in 1630 and 1650. Napoleon I purchased it in 1803, and since then it has housed the French Academy and winners of the Prix de Rome from the Paris Conservatory of Music. French composers who lodged there at various periods included Berlioz, Bizet, Charpentier, Debussy, Gounod, and Massenet (see the entries on Berlioz and Debussy earlier in this section). French students are still sent here from the École des Beaux-Arts in Paris for three years at government expense. Periodic art exhibitions are held in the villa itself, but the main feature is the unique Renaissance garden which is still laid out according to its original ground plan. (Inquire locally for admission information.)

Galileo tomb: Church of Santa Croce, **Florence**.

Exhibits: In **Pisa** the famed eight-story Leaning Tower, completed about 1350, leans almost five meters from the perpendicular and continues to increase its slant by 0.7 mm. each year. From its top in about 1585, Galileo reputedly dropped a cannonball and a bullet, which hit the ground almost simultaneously, demonstrating that falling bodies accelerate at the same rate independent of their weight. Modern scientists question whether he actually performed the experiment, though he certainly wrote about it, since his results have been impossible to reproduce. Galileo's basic theory was valid, but he did not take air resistance, which causes a differential rate of fall, into account. The Leaning Tower is located just east of the Pisa Cathedral. A spiral staircase of 294 steps leads to the top. (Open daily, 9:00—sunset; admission.)

The University Museum in the Via 8 Febbraio at **Padua** displays Galileo's chair and pulpit-like lectern of rough oak planks at which he taught for 18 years. (Open Monday—Saturday on application; gratuity.)

In **Florence** Galileo's telescope and other instruments are shown at the National Museum of the History of the Sciences and Natural History, 1 Piazza dei Giudici. (Open Monday—Saturday 10:00—1:00, 2:00—4:00, Sunday 9:30—12:30; admission.)

Galileo was tried and sentenced in the Dominican monastery adjoining the Church of Santa Maria sopra Minerva in the Piazza Minerva, **Rome**. A small museum (open on request) displays ecclesiastical items unrelated to Galileo. The painter Fra Angelico died there in 1455.

GARIBALDI, GUISEPPE (1807–1882). "A hundred years ago," wrote biographer Christopher Hibbert, "Garibaldi was, perhaps, the best-known name in the world." This soldier and creator of the unified Italian nation—the "father of his country"—is memorialized in street names, squares, and statues throughout Italy; and museums of the *Risorgimento* (resurgence), commemorating his patriotism and leadership, are found in most Italian cities and many smaller towns as well. He was born in an Italian portion of what is now southern France and later went to sea. Exiled from Italy for his nationalist agitation, he spent years as a soldier of fortune in South America before returning to lead his "thousand redshirts" in the conquest of Sicily and Naples, establishing Victor Emmanuel II of Sardinia as king of Italy.

Garibaldi's only Italian residence of long duration was the Casa Bianca, a stone bungalow he built in 1856 on the island of **Caprera**, which became his permanent home. He retired there for the last time in 1871; after 1878 he was confined to a wheelchair. The house is now a museum and displays original furnishings and memorabilia of the founder of modern Italy. (Inquire locally for admission information.)

Many villas and other domiciles throughout the country boast of sheltering the soldier-statesman for a night or brief interval during the period of struggle (1849–60) that led to a united Italy. Three of the more interesting ones include the following. "Garibaldi's Hut," where he hid as a fugitive from Austrian troops in 1849, is located in the Pineta di San Vitale off the Strada del Cimitero about seven kilometers south of **Ravenna**; the small cabin is a reconstruction of the original which burned down in 1911. The Villa Olmo, a 1780 dwelling which stands on Lake Como at **Como**, was the liberator's residence in 1859 when he fell in love with 18-year-old Giuseppina Raimondi, daughter of the owner. He married her there, unaware that her family had forced her into the marriage despite her protests. Garibaldi raged against the family when he found out, stormed away, and divorced her in 1880. The villa, now

used for exhibitions, stands in a large formal park approached by a lakeside path from the Via Puecher. (Inquire locally for admission information.) Garibaldi became dictator of Sicily in 1860 with his conquest of **Palermo**. His residence for most of that year was the 12th-century Royal Palace (Palazzo dei Normanni) in the Piazza del Parlamento, residence of all the Sicilian rulers and now the seat of the Sicilian Regional Assembly. The royal apartments on the top floor, where he resided, display mosaics and lavish decorations. (Open Monday, Friday—Saturday 9:00—12:30; admission.)

Garibaldi tomb: Casa Bianca, **Caprera**.

Exhibits: The Historical Museum in the Piazza XX Settembre, a 15th-century castle tower in **Lecco**, displays a Garibaldi collection; the Garibaldi Museum in the Ara dei Caduti, **Mentana**, also displays memorabilia. (Inquire locally for admission information.)

(See Chapter 2, FRANCE.)

GIOTTO (1267?–1337). The foremost Italian painter of the pre-Renaissance, a master of composition, and a skilled architect, Giotto was born Giotto di Bondone. He is often called the first modern painter. Information on his homes, unfortunately, is practically nonexistent. Tradition ascribes his birthplace to **Vespignano**, a tiny village 47 kilometers northeast of Florence. A marker on a tower ruin in the village probably does not indicate the authentic site; it is more likely to be a nearby hilltop farm site called Colle di Romagnano.

Florence became the painter's lifelong base, though his travels were frequent. During the first years of the 14th century, after his apprenticeship in the workshop of the painter Cimabue, he owned a house in the area of the Piazza Santa Maria Novello.

In **Naples**, where he lived from 1328 to 1333, he was employed by King Robert the Wise, a notable patron of artists. Giotto resided in the trapezoidal Castel Nuovo, the palace at 1 Piazza del Plebescito, which dates originally from 1280 but was largely reconstructed in 1450 and displays Renaissance interiors. Giotto's frescoes in the Palatine chapel there have been lost. (Open daily; admission.)

Giotto tomb: Cathedral of Santa Maria del Fiore, **Florence**.

Exhibit: Giotto's best-known works, the series of frescoes depicting the history of Christian redemption, painted from 1303 to 1305, adorn the Arena Chapel (Cappella degli Scrovegni) located in the Corso Garibaldi, in **Padua**. "Like true Italians," wrote H. V. Morton, Giotto's contemporaries "were fascinated by his ugliness. It is said that his friend Dante . . . sometimes sat in the chapel watching him swiftly transferring his pictures to the wet plaster, reflecting how odd it was that a man who could create such beauty should have created six children, each one as ugly as himself." Ribald Giotto had the perfect excuse, however. He told Dante, "I make my pictures by day and my babies by night." (Open Monday—Friday 9:30—12:30, 1:30—4:30, Saturday 9:30—12:30; admission.)

GOETHE, JOHANN WOLFGANG VON (1749–1832). The German poet, philosopher, and scientist traveled in Italy from 1786 to 1788, an experience he fully recorded in his *Italian Journey* (1816)—must reading for any Goethe seeker in Italy. He resided for most of that period in **Rome** at 18 Via del Corso, now the Goethe Museum operated by the Goethehaus in Frankfurt. Art works, editions, and photographs illustrate the writer's Italian experience. (Open Tuesday—Saturday 10:00—1:00, 4:00—7:00, Sunday 10:00—1:00; admission.)

(See Chapter 1, AUSTRIA, SWITZERLAND; also Chapter 3, FRANCE; also Chapter 4, EAST GERMANY, WEST GERMANY.)

GRECO, EL. See DOMÉNIKOS THEOTOKÓPOULOS.

GREGORY I, THE GREAT, ST. (ca. 540–604). After St. Peter himself, claimed by the Roman Catholic church as its first pope, St. Gregory may have been its greatest, most influential leader. He made the papacy a temporal power to be reckoned with, developed the absolutist system that endured through the Middle Ages, establishing church rules that still function today, and possibly originated the liturgical music known as Gregorian chant. He was also the last of the four officially acclaimed church fathers (after Saints Augustine, Ambrose, and Jerome). Son of a patrician family and a native of **Rome**, Gregory's traditional birth site is covered by the Church of San Gregorio Magno in the Piazza di San Gregorio. St. Gregory turned the family mansion into a Benedictine monastery and dedicated it to St. Andrew. A new church dedicated to St. Gregory arose

above these walls in the eighth century; it was rebuilt 10 centuries later as the present church on the site. In the original monastery, it is said, St. Gregory dispatched St. Augustine of Canterbury to convert England in 596. One knowledgeable observer writes that "there is probably no other site in Rome which would more richly repay excavation," for a search in 1890 revealed that Gregory's birthplace apparently remains largely intact beneath the present church. The baroque interior of the church contains several interesting chapels. St. Gregory's Chapel displays a magnificent 15th-century altar with reliefs depicting scenes from his life. An adjacent chamber is said to have been the saint's own cell, preserved from his original monastery and containing his stone bed plus (in notable contrast) his sculptured marble episcopal throne. The central Chapel of St. Andrew is believed to occupy the site of Gregory's oratory dedicated to this saint. In the Chapel of St. Barbara stands the table at which St. Gregory daily served meals to 12 poor men (one day an angel appeared, increasing the queue to a baker's dozen), and popes until 1870 repeated the custom, serving 13 pilgrims on Maundy Thursday of each year from this table. (Open daily; ring at adjacent convent.)

The first monk to ascend the papal throne, Gregory became the sixty-fourth pope in 590. His residence thenceforth was the Patriarchium on the site of the present Lateran Palace in the Piazza di Porta San Giovanni adjoining the Basilica of St. John Lateran. The original palace, given by Emperor Constantine I to Pope St. Melchiades in about 311, served as the official residence for popes until the papal move to Avignon in 1303. Damaged by fire in 1308, the palace was torn down in 1586 by Pope Sixtus V—an action that has been described as an unpardonable act of vandalism—and entirely reconstructed as the present Lateran Palace. Sixtus intended it as a papal summer palace, but it seldom served this purpose. The only surviving part of the Patriarchium is the Scala Santa, containing the Sancta Sanctorum (the private chapel of the popes) on the east side of the piazza (see the entry on Pontius Pilate later in this section). The Lateran Palace now holds offices of the Roman diocese, the Vicariate, and is not open to the public. The actual site of much of the original palace lies between the Scala Santa and the basilica. Many historic episodes of church history have occurred in these precincts.

An interesting model of the Patriarchium may

be seen in the Museum of Rome in the Piazza San Pantaleo. (Open Tuesday—Saturday 9:00—2:00, Sunday 9:00—1:00; also Tuesday, Thursday 5:00—8:00; admission.)

St. Gregory tomb: Clementine Chapel, St. Peter's Basilica, **Rome**.

HADRIAN (76–138). Imperial successor to his cousin, Trajan, in 117, Hadrian led the Roman Empire through a golden age marked by civil reform, consolidation, and ambitious building programs. He was the most traveled of the emperors, spending the greater part of his reign visiting outlying provinces of the empire, perfecting defenses, conferring, and suppressing revolts. Born in Spain, he first came to **Rome** at age 10 and received his education under the sponsorship of his guardian, Trajan. Locales of his early Roman homes remain unknown. After becoming emperor, however, he would have resided on the Palatine Hill in the huge palace complex begun by Domitian (see the entry on Constantine I earlier in this section).

One of the best preserved classical sites in Italy is that of Hadrian's Villa near **Tivoli**, about 30 kilometers west of Rome. Begun about the year 125 and incorporating a first-century-B.C. country house, the total land area on which the emperor constructed numerous buildings embraced some 11 kilometers in circumference. The land itself was owned by his wife, the Empress Sabina. As well as establishing a haven where he might devote his time to creative pursuits and end his days in "peaceful pomp," Hadrian's idea was to reproduce buildings on this property that had most impressed him during his extensive travels so that he might, in a sense, relive those travels. Accordingly he built duplicates of the Lyceum, Academy, and other buildings of Athens as well as structures he had seen elsewhere in Greece and Egypt. He even built a representation of Hades (which he had not seen but anticipated). The excavated buildings are grouped around four main structures: the Poikile, an Athenian reproduction; the Canopus, a replica of a sanctuary near Alexandria; the Academy, a complex of structures modeled on Plato's school in Athens; and the Imperial Palace, another extensive complex arranged around four peristyles including the central residence of Hadrian's "villa". Guest rooms, corridors, pavilions, fountains, libraries, baths, pools, and courtyards reveal the core of the most lavish estate in the Roman Empire. The circular building, cryptically called the Naval Theatre and enclosed by a

RUINS OF HADRIAN'S VILLA. One of Rome's greatest emperors built his vast country estate near **Tivoli** about A.D. 125, and the site has proven a rich mine of antiquities and works of art. Visitors who roam over the restorations and excavations come away with a renewed appreciation for Roman architectural and engineering skills as well as for an emperor who dreamed on such a lavish scale.

moat, contains a series of marble rooms that some authorities believe was Hadrian's personal studio where he withdrew to read, write, and paint. Hadrian's successors also used, modified, and abused the estate; barbarian invaders plundered it, and stonebuilders quarried it. The first excavations began during the Renaissance, but not until 1870, when the state acquired the site, did systematic archaeology begin. Hundreds of statues and works of art have been unearthed and shipped to museums all over Europe, and notable discoveries are still made. The subtle details of Hadrian's designs and the arrangements he made for his own and his guests' comfort and pleasure were manifested in such touches as a sunbathing beach with artificially heated sands. A museum on the site displays finds from recent excavations. At least half a day is needed for a cursory inspection of the restored buildings, excavated ruins, and extensive grounds. Hadrian's Villa is located about seven kilometers southwest of Tivoli from the Via Tiburtina. Tour buses from Rome depart from the Piazza della Repubblica at 20 minutes past the hour each day. (Open daily, 9:00—sunset; admission.)

Hadrian tomb (site): Castel Sant' Angelo, **Rome**.

Exhibit: Hadrian's most prominent memorial in **Rome** is the massive tomb he intended for himself and his family, the Castel Sant' Angelo or Hadrian's Mausoleum, now a national museum and one of the ancient city's best-known landmarks. Its appearance today gives only a truncated idea of its splendor when Hadrian's ashes were placed there. Its white marble facing, tiers of columns, and numerous statues, surmounted by an actual cypress forest on its roof, are all long gone; all that survives today is the core structure of this gigantic "wedding cake" designed by Hadrian himself about 130 and completed the year after his death. Ashes of his family members and of emperors Antoninus Pius, Marcus Aurelius, and Septimius Severus were also deposited and remained there until the Gothic sack of Rome in the fifth century. The stripped and modified mausoleum later served as an important defensive bastion, a papal refuge, and a prison where artist Benvenuto Cellini, among other unfortunates, was incarcerated on the whim of a pope. (See the entry on Cellini earlier in this section for admission information.)

(See SPAIN in this chapter.)

HEMINGWAY, ERNEST MILLER (1899–1961). The American author wrote his novel *Across the River and into the Trees* (1950) in **Torcello**, where he and his wife, Mary, stayed during the winter of 1948 in a village hotel, the Locanda Cipriani. It still hosts visitors in its five rooms.

(See SPAIN in this chapter; also Chapter 3, PARIS.)

IBSEN, HENRIK (1828–1906). During two lengthy periods in **Rome**, the Norwegian playwright created several of his best-known works. He wrote *Peer Gynt* (1867) at 55 Via Capo le Case, corner of Via Due Macelli, the apartment dwelling where he resided from 1864 to 1868. Much later (1880–85), he lived in a nearby apartment at 75 Via Capo le Case and there wrote *An Enemy of the People* (1882), and *The Wild Duck* (1884). Neither of these buildings survive.

Vacationing at **Sorrento** in the summer of 1881, Ibsen wrote *Ghosts* (1881) in the Hotel Imperial Tramontano, which still stands in the Via Vittorio Veneto.

(See Chapter 4, WEST GERMANY, NORWAY.)

IGNATIUS OF LOYOLA, ST. (1491–1556). The Spanish founder of the Jesuit order lived in **Venice** from 1535 to 1537. He and his devoted group of monks resided and ministered in the hospital attached to the Church of San Giovanni e Paolo, now the Ospedale Civile in the Calle Ospedaletto.

In **Rome** the saint's last home from 1544 was a house opposite the 1568 Church of Gesù, Rome's principal Jesuit church and the site of the smaller church he headed in his capacity of superior general of the Jesuit order. His private rooms have been incorporated into the Jesuit building now on this site, located off the Piazza del Gesù, and display numerous items associated with the saint and his militant order. Among such items is an altar at which he offered mass on the day he died in these rooms. (Open daily; admission.)

St. Ignatius tomb: Church of Gesù, **Rome**.

(See SPAIN in this chapter; also Chapter 3, PARIS.)

JAMES, HENRY (1843–1916). The American-English author loved **Florence** and often stayed at the Villa Mercedes in suburban Bellosguardo, which became a setting for his novel *The Portrait of a Lady* (1881).

James finished this novel in **Venice** at 4161 Riva degli Schiavoni. Years later he wrote *The Aspern Papers* (1888) during his stay at the 15th-century Gothic Barbaro Palace in the Rio del Orso. Among others entertained there by the Curtis family, who still own the mansion, were painters Claude Monet, John Singer Sargent, and James A. M. Whistler, and poet Robert Browning. James resided there several times as a guest.

(See Chapter 3, PARIS; also Chapter 5, ENGLAND; also Chapter 6, LONDON.)

JOHN XXIII (1881–1963). Probably the best-loved pope of modern times, noted for his reformist pontificate, ecumenical interests, and engaging personality, Angelo Giuseppe Roncalli was born the son of a peasant farmer in **Sotto il Monte**. His birthplace, a 300-year-old farmhouse, stands in the Via Bruscio on a corner of the central piazza of the village; it is a place of devoted pilgrimage by many besides Roman Catholics. The large Roncalli family occupied only a small portion of this sizable house, now owned by the Pontifical Institute of Foreign Missions, and resided there until 1887. The pope's birth room, a three-meter-square chamber on the second floor, displays several pieces of the family's humble furniture. (Open daily; admission.) From 1887 Roncalli's family home was "Colombera," an 18-room farmhouse on the edge of the village which is still occupied by Roncalli family members. Later, as archbishop and cardinal (1925–58), Roncalli maintained a summer villa called "the Camaitano," now known locally as "the Museum." Nuns of the Little Sisters of the Poor conduct tours through the house of Papa Giovanni, as Italians call him; gifts he received from all over the world, his various robes of office, and original furnishings are on display. (Open daily; admission.) Interesting preparation for a trip to Sotto il Monte is Kay Sullivan's *Journey of Love: A Pilgrimage to Pope John's Birthplace* (1966).

In **Bergamo**, where he served as secretary to Bishop Radini-Tedeschi from 1904 to 1914, Roncalli lived in the Bishop's Palace near the Piazza del Duomo.

As patriarch and bishop of **Venice** from 1953 to 1958, Roncalli renovated the 1830 Patriarchal Palace behind and adjacent to the Basilica of St. Mark in the famed Piazza San Marco. St. Pius X had also resided there before becoming pope in 1903.

Elected as 260th pope in 1958, John XXIII thenceforth occupied the papal apartments located on the top floor of the Apostolic Palace, **Rome**. These chambers, which have housed each pope since Pius X early in this century, are of course closed to the public. A tower on the Leonine Walls of Vatican City, just behind the Vatican railroad station, was adapted by this pope as a summer retreat.

Pope John also summered in the Papal Palace at **Castel Gandolfo**, as have other popes before and since. (See the entry on Pius XII later in this section.)

John XXIII tomb: Vatican Grottoes, St. Peter's Basilica, **Rome**.

(See Chapter 3, PARIS.)

JOYCE, JAMES (1882–1941). The self-exiled Irish writer spent several years in extremely impoverished circumstances with his family in **Trieste**, where he taught English in a Berlitz school but mainly relied on his brother Stanislaus for support. His addresses, all upper rooms and cheap flats, included 31 Via San Nicolo (1905–06), where he completed his short-story collection *Dubliners* (1914); 1 Via Santa Catarina (1907–09); 8 Via Vincenzo Scussa, where he began his novel *A Portait of the Artist as a Young Man* (1916); 32 Via Barriera Vecchia (1911–12); and 4 Via Donato Bramante (1912–15), where he began writing *Ulysses* (1922).

In **Rome** Joyce lived briefly and unhappily (1906–07) in fifth-floor rooms at 51 Via Monte Brianzo.

(See Chapter 1, SWITZERLAND; also Chapter 2, FRANCE; also Chapter 3, PARIS; also Chapter 7, IRELAND.)

KEATS, JOHN (1795–1821). The English poet came to Italy on medical advice in 1820, far too late to halt his advanced case of tuberculosis, and he died at his lodging in **Rome**. Now called the John Keats House, operated by the Keats-Shelley Memorial Association, it stands at 26 Piazza di Spagna. Keats, weak and leading what he called "a posthumous existence," roomed on the second floor there with his devoted friend, Joseph Severn, from November 1820 until his death the following February. Probably only the ceilings remain of the original rooms, which have been reconstructed. On display are the poet's death mask, an extensive library of works by and about Keats and Shelley, plus memorabilia of these poets and their friends, Lord Byron and Leigh Hunt (see the entries on Byron and Shelley in this section). (Open Monday—Friday 9:00—12:30, 2:30—5:00; admission.)

Keats tomb: Protestant Cemetery, **Rome**.

(See Chapter 6, LONDON.)

LAWRENCE, DAVID HERBERT (1885–1930). Unwelcome in his native England, this author (another whose death launched him into respectability) spent two periods in Italy during his final two decades of restless travel. In 1912 and 1913 he wrote his novel *Sons and Lovers* (1913) in the Villa Igéa on Lake Garda at **Gargnano**, where he resided with his mistress, Frieda von Richthofen (a cousin of the celebrated German aviator), whom he later married.

At the Fontana Vecchia, a villa marked by two cypresses in the Via Fontana Vecchia at **Taormina**, Sicily, the couple resided from 1920 to 1923 and Lawrence wrote *The Lost Girl* (1920), and *Sea and Sardinia* (1921).

The Lawrences rented the upper floor of the hilltop Villa Mirenda, located about 11 kilometers south of Florence at **San Paolo Mosciano**, in 1926 and stayed until 1928. Lawrence studied the ancient Etruscan culture there and wrote his best-known novel, *Lady Chatterley's Lover* (1928). Novelist Aldous Huxley, whose own *Point Counter Point* (1928) idealized Lawrence, was a visitor during this period.

(See Chapter 2, FRANCE; also Chapter 5, ENGLAND; also Chapter 6, LONDON.)

LEONARDO DA VINCI (1452–1519). As the greatest "Renaissance man" of all, Leonardo not only embodied the creative vigor of his own day; his technological ideas were centuries ahead of their time, as a look at some of his drawings and designs quickly show. The breadth of his genius embraced painting, sculpture, architecture, engineering, and science. He was a native of Anchiano, a tiny suburb of **Vinci**, where the stone house identified as his birthplace stands. Its external appearance remains unchanged, but a 1952 attempt to restore its interior was abandoned, wrote biographer Ritchie Calder, "because it had been altered so frequently in the intervening time as to remove all authentic evidence." The house belonged to his grandparents and was Leonardo's home to about 1467.

LEONARDO'S REPUTED BIRTHPLACE. The village of Anchiano near **Vinci** claims this stone dwelling as the first home of the prototypical "Renaissance man" of Europe.

Florence and the studio of sculptor-painter Andrea del Verrocchio became his home in about 1467. He apprenticed under the older artist until about 1477, then took lodgings of his own until 1482. Leonardo returned to Florence in 1500 and resided until 1506 in the monastery of the Servite order, attached to the Church of Santissima Annunziata in the piazza of that name. This was the period when he painted the portrait of Lisa del Giocondo, called the *Mona Lisa*, which hangs in the Louvre.

From 1513 to 1516, before leaving to make his last home in France, Leonardo resided in **Rome** at the Belvedere Pavilion of the Vatican Palace. Built by Pope Innocent VIII in about 1490, this northern extension of the palace now houses the Pio-Clementino Museum of classical sculpture, with galleries arranged around an octagonal courtyard, and the Egyptian Museum. (See the entry on Lucrezia Borgia, *Exhibits*, for admission information.)

Exhibits: The Vinciano Museum in the town castle at **Vinci** displays manuscripts, letters, and various mechanical devices and machines constructed from Leonardo's models and designs. (Open Monday—Saturday 9:30—12:00, 3:00—6:00, Sunday 10:00—12:00, 3:00—6:30; admission.)

Perhaps the world's best-known painting is Leonardo's *The Last Supper*, which has somehow survived the decomposition of his experimental pigments, numerous well-meaning but destructive attempts at restoration, war damage, air pollution, vibration, humidity, and mold. Leonardo painted it slowly and meticulously over a period of two years (1495–97), using a plastered and primered end wall of the Dominican refectory (dining hall) of the Monastery of Santa Maria delle Grazie in **Milan**. The painting had begun to fade and flake even before Leonardo's death, and six major restorations since 1726 have overpainted and darkened the mural. Today's visitors see only the ghost of Leonardo's original work, though his scheme remains intact. Since 1977 a painstaking restoration funded by the Olivetti Corporation has been in progress, stabilizing the old wall and cleaning away 500 years of accrued grime, glues, mold, and paint layers to arrive at Leonardo's own brilliant detail and color. Thus the current restoration is, in a sense, an excavation, though much of Leonardo's original painting will never be recovered. (Open April—October, Tuesday—Sunday 9:30—12:30, 2:30—5:30; November—March, Tuesday—Saturday 9:30—4:00, Sunday 9:30—12:30; admission, except free on Sunday.) The Ambrosian Library in the Piazza Pio XI displays a notable collection of Leonardo's drawings, designs, and notebooks. (Open Sunday—Friday 10:00—12:00, 2:00—4:30, Saturday 10:00—12:00; admission.) Models of machines and apparatus devised by Leonardo are shown in the Galleria Leonardesca of the Leonardo da Vinci Museum of Science and Technology in the Via

San Vittore. (Open Tuesday—Sunday 10:00—12:30, 2:30—11:00; admission.)

(See Chapter 2, FRANCE; also Chapter 3, PARIS.)

LISZT, FRANZ (1811–1886). The Hungarian composer and piano virtuoso made Italy his home from 1861 to 1870 and continued to reside there at intervals for the rest of his life. In **Rome** he took lodgings at 113 Via Sistina to be near his longime married mistress, the Polish Princess Carolyne von Sayn-Wittgenstein, who lived at 89 Via del Babuino surrounded by 14 busts of her lover. Liszt's ardor had, however, begun to cool, and he was relieved when her husband refused to grant a divorce, thus preventing the couple's marriage. He soon sought refuge from any further possibility of rash promises made in weak moments, by taking minor orders in the church (1865). The priestly garb of an abbé also provided a successful shield for further occasional affairs—for Liszt, though never married, was noted for his virtuosity with women as well as keyboards. (In the 1830s he had fathered three children by the French countess Marie d'Agoult.) During this period he occupied an apartment in the Vatican Palace near the Loggia of Raphael (see the entry on Raphael, *Exhibits*, later in this section).

From 1865 to 1870 Liszt's main dwelling was the top floor of the Villa d'Este, entered from the Piazza Trento in **Tivoli**, with its extensive gardens and fountains. He continued to use the estate as his Italian base from 1870 to 1886 and while there composed the third volume of his *Years of Pilgrimage* (1835–77), including the popular piece "Fountains of the Villa d'Este." Originally a Benedictine convent, this 16th-century villa became Italian government property in 1918. (Open May—October, Tuesday—Sunday 9:00—sunset; admission.)

(See Chapter 1, AUSTRIA, SWITZERLAND; also Chapter 3, PARIS; also Chapter 4, EAST GERMANY, WEST GERMANY.)

MACHIAVELLI, NICCOLÓ (1469–1527). The "ends justify means" school of philosophy is hardly a Renaissance creation, but this pragmatist was the first to apply it rigorously to politics. His most famous book, *The Prince* (1513), told aspiring rulers and politicians exactly how to succeed, and has been the basic bible for power brokers, bosses, dictators, and "motivators" ever since. Machiavelli, political philosopher and diplomat, was a native of **Florence**, resided there for most of his life, and learned well the lessons of political manipulation and intrigue. Probably his lifelong home—certainly his last dwelling from 1520, when he became official historiographer of the city—was the Casa Campigli, which stood at 16 Via de' Guicciardini. He died there.

Deprived of office by the Medici in 1512, Machiavelli retired in some bitterness to his farm estate in the village of Sant' Andrea in Percussina, a suburb of **San Casciano** about 17 kilometers south of Florence. He called his house "L'Albergaccio" ("the wretched hotel"), and until he left in 1520 he spent as little time there during the day as possible, preferring to engage in loud, angry card games at the local inn, "giving vent to this malice which is my fate." At night, however, he changed into his best clothes and sat down to write—*Discourses* (1517), *The Mandrake* (1518), and *The Art of War* (1520), in addition to *The Prince*. The privately owned house survives in pleasant wooded countryside on the main road through the village and is sometimes open to the public. (Inquire locally for admission information.) Wine from Machiavelli's vineyards may be bought nearby.

Machiavelli tomb: Church of Santa Croce, **Florence**.

MANN, THOMAS (1875–1955). In the **Rome** lodging of his brother Heinrich, a third-floor apartment in an old *palazzo* at 34 Torre Argentina, the German author began his first novel, *Buddenbrooks* (1900), in 1897. Mann had also resided there two years before.

(See Chapter 1, SWITZERLAND; also Chapter 4, WEST GERMANY.)

MARCONI, GUGLIELMO (1874–1937). The inventor of wireless telegraphy and the father of radio—a device he had to develop in England because of the disinterest of the Italian government—was a native of **Bologna**. His birthplace, the town house of his prosperous parents, is the Marescalchi Palace, a 17th-century mansion at 5 Via Quattro Novembre on the Piazza Roosevelt.

The place where in 1895 Marconi actually invented the wireless telegraph, albeit a primitive version, was the Villa Grifone at **Pontecchio**, a hilltop mansion originally owned by his grandparents. Marconi grew up there and returned at intervals until his later years. Despite his father's opposition to his early "tinkering," Marconi's spirited Irish mother provided two rooms at the top of the three-story house for a laboratory.

Years later, now an idolized hero of Italians and a world celebrity, Marconi returned after a long residence in England to make his last home in **Rome**, where he lent his immense prestige to the Fascist government of Mussolini. In his top-floor laboratory in a house called the Villa Sforza Cesarini on the Janiculum Hill, Marconi owned the only private radio in Italy in 1918. His final residence, from his second marriage in 1927, was the Bezzi-Scali Palace in the Via Condotti, the home of his in-laws. Marconi died there after a long physical decline.

Marconi tomb: Campo Santo, **Bologna**.

Exhibit: The Museum of Postal History and Telecommunications, at 11 Via Andreoli in **Rome**, displays the telegraphic apparatus used by Marconi in his epochal 1901 demonstration of long-distance transmission between Cornwall, England, and Newfoundland, Canada. (Open Tuesday—Sunday 9:00—1:00; admission.)

(See Chapter 5, ENGLAND; also Chapter 6, LONDON.)

MARCUS AURELIUS (121–180). Roman emperor from 161, eminent Stoic philosopher, a man of wide learning and gentle character yet fiercely opposed to the rising Christian sect which he viewed as dangerously seditious, Marcus Annius Verus, as he was born, was a native of **Rome**. His patrician family occupied a house on the Caelian Hill in the present vicinity of the Basilica of St. John Lateran, Piazza San Giovanni in Laterano, and there he grew up. In 138 he entered the imperial household on the Palatine Hill as the adopted son of Emperor Antoninus Pius. This household was the Palace of Tiberius, erected by that emperor in about the year 30. Its largely unexcavated site is covered by the 16th-century Farnese Gardens. The palace's west side faced the Clivus Victoriae. Later the emperors Domitian, Trajan, and Hadrian expanded the north side to the Nova Via. When Marcus Aurelius became emperor, he probably moved to the palatial Domus Augustana that Domitian had built on the hill's central summit, and this remained the Roman home of the emperor. (See the entries on Augustus, Constantine I, Hadrian, and Trajan in this section.)

A favorite country retreat of the emperor was the villa built by his predecessor at Lorium; nothing of the house remains on the present site of **Castel Di Guido**.

Exhibits: In **Rome** the famous bronze equestrian statue of this emperor in the Piazza del Campidolio dates from about 166 and is probably a reasonable likeness. It owes its survival—through centuries of religious vandalism of pagan monuments—to the fact that it was long thought to represent the Christian emperor Constantine I. It stood until 1538 in the Lateran Square near the emperor's birthplace. Traces of the original gilding remain on it; according to an old legend, when the statue again appears covered with gold, the end of the world is nigh.

The Roman equivalent of today's official medals of honor was a highly pictorial arch or column displaying relief sculptures of the lauded person's exploits. On the Column of Marcus Aurelius, erected shortly after the emperor's death, may be seen an ascending spiral of sculptured pictures commemorating his victorious struggles against the Germanic and Sarmatian tribes, actions that delayed the barbarian invasions of Rome for several centuries. Interior steps lead to the top of the 42-meter column. It stands in the Piazza Colonna, which for centuries was the center of the city. Permission to climb the tower may be obtained from the Ufficio del Comune, 3 Piazza Campitalli.

(See Chapter 1, AUSTRIA.)

MEDICI, LORENZO DE, 'THE MAGNIFICENT' (1449–1492). Most illustrious of the powerful family that governed **Florence** for two centuries and supplied cardinals, popes, and royalty to thrones throughout Italy and Europe, Lorenzo the Magnificent was a tyrannical ruler but also a lavish patron of the arts and an accomplished writer. A third-generation millionaire, he frankly admitted the reason for the family's financial dictatorship: "In Florence one can ill-live in the possession of wealth without control of the government." From 1444 until 1540 the family's chief residence was the Medici-Riccardi Palace at 1 Via Cavour. Inside this somewhat forbidding Renaissance palace, the Medici Museum now occupies the former private apartments of the family. Medici portraits, relics, and memorials, including Lorenzo's death mask, decorate the rooms they inhabited. The palace itself was not only the scene of Lorenzo's brilliant court but, for two years, the home of the young Michelangelo Buonarroti, whom the perceptive Lorenzo welcomed to his household. Michelangelo designed the ground-floor windows (see the entry on Michelangelo below). (Open Monday—Tuesday, Thursday—Saturday

9:00—1:00, Sunday 9:00—12:00; 217601; admission, except free on Sunday.)

A number of country villas were owned and frequently used by Lorenzo in the area immediately north of Florence. In the Viale G. Pieraccini at **Castello** stands the Medicea di Careggi, acquired by the Medici patriarch Cosimo the Elder in 1417; it was a favorite residence of Lorenzo's childhood, and another literary and artistic center of his court. Both Cosimo and his grandson Lorenzo died there. Later burned and looted, it was restored in the 16th century and again in the 19th. The villa now houses a nursing home. To visit this castellated mansion, apply to the hospital of Santa Maria Nuova in Florence.

Acquired by Lorenzo in 1477, the Villa di Castello, near **Sesto Fiorentino**, displays frescoes, fountains, and sculptures. It is now owned by the Accademia della Crusca. (Inquire locally for admission information.)

The Villa Medicea at **Poggio a Caiano**, bought and rebuilt by Lorenzo in 1485, also displays remarkable decorations and a pleasant park. It is the only surviving building for which he was personally responsible. (Gardens open daily, 8:30—sunset; admission.)

A favorite resort among the many Medici country houses was the Villa Medici, built in 1461; it is located between Maiano and **San Domenico Fiesole** in the Via Vecchia Fiesolana. (Open by owner's permission.)

Lorenzo de Medici tomb: Medici Chapels, **Florence**.

MICHELANGELO BUONARROTI (1475–1564). Probably the world's greatest creative genius in painting, sculpture, and architecture, Michelangelo was the son of a minor official and an invalid mother. His birthplace in the town of **Caprese Michelangelo**, where his father was temporary magistrate, survives at 3 Via del Castello, and is now the Michelangelo Museum and town hall. Memorabilia and period furnishings are displayed. (Inquire locally for admission information.)

Michelangelo seldom saw his parents during his first decade, being raised by his wet nurse and her stonecutter husband in **Settignano** (in later years he claimed he had absorbed his love of stone from his nurse's milk). The Villa Buonarroti, where Michelangelo spent his childhood, stands marked in the hillside village.

In about 1485 the youngster rejoined his parents in **Florence**, the city where he spent about half of his long lifetime. The family house, which belonged to an uncle, still stands on the southwest corner of the Via dei Bentaccordi and the Via dell' Anguillara. In 1490, combating the opposition of his father who thought the vocation of artist beneath the family dignity, Michelangelo attracted the attention of Florentine ruler Lorenzo de Medici. Lorenzo informally "adopted" the youngster and took him into his own splendid household, treating him as the prize that he was—much to the bewildered pleasure of the senior Buonarroti, who began to think that perhaps art was a fine occupation for his son after all. Michelangelo lived in the Medici-Riccardi Palace until Lorenzo's death in 1492. The 1574 Casino Medíceo in the Via Cavour, which today houses the law courts, occupies the site of the Medici Gardens; there Michelangelo studied and copied antique statuary from the Medici collection and from the sculpture academy of Giovanni di Bertoldo (see the entry on Lorenzo de Medici above). In 1503, following the completion of his statue *David*, the Opera del Duomo built Michelangelo a house and studio at the corner of the Borgo Pinti and the Via delle Colonne; he used it until 1505 and again during his last Florentine period (1516–34).

Michelangelo inspected and chose his materials as carefully as he worked them, and the famous quarry town of **Carrara**, known for its beautiful white marble which has been mined for more than 2,000 years from the Apuan Alp quarries nearby, was a frequent destination during his Florentine years. A house on the main square is identified as the lodging he used during these visits.

Michelangelo lived in **Rome** from 1534, occupying a house by himself at an unidentified location near the Markets of Trajan. An inventory of the house conducted the day after he died was short: an iron bedstead, a closet of clothes, a pony in the stable, and some 8,000 gold ducats tied up in handkerchiefs or placed inside jars.

Michelangelo tomb: Church of Santa Croce, **Florence**.

Exhibits: The Casa Buonarroti, a house Michelangelo built on the site of two earlier houses belonging to his family, is now the Michelangelo Museum at 70 Via Ghibellina in **Florence**. Michelangelo himself never lived there but gave the house to his nephew, and a grand-nephew later decorated it in the artist's honor. Today it is the foremost Michelangelo museum, and displays numerous examples of the painter's lesser works, as well as drawings, models, and exhibits on the artist and his difficult family. (Open Wednesday—Monday 9:00—1:00, 287630; admission.)

Michelangelo's works are scattered in art museums and churches throughout Italy. A few of his best-known paintings and sculptures include the following:

In **Florence** the Gallery of the Academy, at 60 Via Ricasoli, contains the original of his famous statue *David* (1501–03), along with other sculptures. (Open Tuesday—Saturday 9:00—2:00, Sunday 9:00—1:00; 214375; admission, except free on Sunday.)

In **Rome** the Church of San Pietro in Vincoli, in the piazza of that name, displays his majestic *Moses* (1544), which was originally intended as only a portion of the great unfinished tomb memorial for Pope Julius II. It is said that the artist spent six months in the quarries of Carrara (see above) searching for exactly the right block of marble; and that when the figure was completed he impulsively threw his hammer at the statue's bare knee commanding it to speak—the mark of the blow may be seen. (Open daily; donation.) Michelangelo's exquisite *Pieta* (1499), the only sculpture inscribed with his name, now stands behind protective glass in St. Peter's Basilica after 1972 damage (since repaired) caused by vandalism. (Open daily, 7:00—7:00; free.) In the famous Sistine Chapel of the Vatican Museums, Michelangelo's ceiling frescoes (1508–12) depict episodes from Genesis, while his fresco on the altar wall represents the *Last Judgment* (1534–41); they number among the great artistic treasures of the world. (For admission information, see the entry on Lucrezia Borgia, *Exhibits*, earlier in this section.)

MUSSOLINI, BENITO (1883–1945). "Not long ago," wrote one recent observer, "Mussolini seemed to be a modern phenomenon, but the truth is that he was a well-known historic type, and his terrible death proved that an Italian crowd, angry, can be as savage as its predecessors of the fourteenth century." It also proved that Italians were not nearly as tolerant toward a loser as were the Germans toward Adolf Hitler. A pompous, jut-jawed, strutting little man, Mussolini looks more comic than menacing in the old newsreels, and it is difficult for anyone except Italians to understand how he avoided being laughed off stage. First the cocky mentor, then the obsequious lackey of Hitler, Mussolini eventually decided to cast Italy's lot with the Nazi warlord, a decision that proved fateful for his country. As a dictator and warlord, Mussolini rapidly lost control of events after 1938, a fact that became painfully clear even to himself long before he was strung up by his heels in a Milan gas station.

Unlike Germany's rigorous postwar suppression of anything remotely suggestive of the Nazi leader, Italy exorcised much of its hatred of il *Duce* by the violence of his riddance. His birthplace, in **Predáppio**, a stone house where his father, an atheist and Socialist activist, ran a blacksmith shop, and his devoutly religious mother taught school, still stands. The family's two-room living quarters were on the second floor. By all accounts a pugnacious, rebellious youngster, Mussolini worked in the shop and absorbed intense political discussions between his father and village neighbors. Predáppio remained his home until 1901.

In 1910, after years of wandering, odd jobs, and increasing revolutionary involvement, Mussolini settled at **Forlì** with his common-law wife, Rachele Guidi, in two rented rooms at the Merenda Palace, Via Merenda.

Mussolini became editor of the Socialist newspaper *Avanti* in 1912, and the couple moved to a flat at 19 Via Castel Morrone in **Milan**. While living there he broke his Socialist connections and, in 1919, founded the Fascist party.

Becoming prime minister and Fascist dictator of Italy in 1922, Mussolini occupied a squalid third-floor apartment at 156 Via Rasella (the *Palazzo Tittoni*) in **Rome**. "There was no kitchen," wrote biographer Ivone Kirkpatrick, "and when he was at home any meals required were sent up by the landlord, who lived below." In 1929 he moved to the 40-room Villa Torlonia in the Via Nomentana, where he paid one lira in rent per year. This 35-acre estate remained his home until he was deposed in 1943. "His translation to these comparatively comfortable surroundings did not bring with it any change in his Spartan way of life," wrote Kirkpatrick. The only exception was the chance it gave him for more physical exercise; each morning he rode a horse about the grounds, jumping a few small hurdles. The Commune of Rome has acquired this property, and the grounds are now a public park. Extensive second- or third-century Jewish catacombs underlie the house and grounds. (Park open daily, 9:00—sunset.)

Shortly after Mussolini became prime minister, his native province of Forlì gave him a country mansion at **Rocca delle Caminate**. A restored hill-

THE VILLA TORLONIA, HOME OF *IL DUCE*. In **Rome** this 40-room mansion was Mussolini's residence from 1929 to 1943. His actual lifestyle, for all his love of pomp and display, was rather more spartan than the size of this house suggests. Servants wash his car in this 1934 photograph.

top feudal castle (Mussolini had often played in the prerestored ruins as a youngster), it became a frequent retreat and a depository for numerous gifts and awards. In time it came to resemble a museum more than a residence, and Mussolini apparently intended to leave it as a memorial of his regime. The castle suffered heavy damage and plunder during the war, and Rachele Mussolini sold it. The province of Forlì reacquired it, but there has been little restoration. It stands four kilometers northeast of Predáppio.

Following his humiliating arrest by King Victor Emmanuel III in 1943, Mussolini was shifted from place to place by a nervous military government and, in September, was finally lodged in the mountaintop Campo Imperatore Hotel at the Apennine ski resort of **Campo Imperatore**. He spent about a week there before his spectacular rescue by a German SS glider unit commanded by Otto Skorzeny. A day later he was in Germany.

Thoroughly demoralized and convinced of eventual Axis defeat, Mussolini nevertheless established his so-called Salo Republic in accordance with Hitler's wishes in October 1943. This puppet regime, heavily infiltrated and supervised by German officers, operated from various ministries scattered about the Lake Garda area. Mussolini's residence, chosen by the Germans, was the Villa Feltrinelli, a pink-marble house on the lakeshore about two kilometers north of **Gargnano** on the Gardesana Occidentale highway (route N45).

He established his office in the neighboring Villa delle Orsoline, "away from the noise, family squabbles, and petty intrigues of his home," wrote Kirkpatrick, "and there he spent the whole day in a pathetic attempt to maintain the appearance of governing." Mussolini lived there until April 1945.

From then until his capture and murder by Italian partisans, Mussolini's life was one of constant movement as he sought escape from the closing circle of Allied armies and civil insurrection. He stayed a week in the prefecture at **Milan**, located in the Corso Monforte, gathering the tattered remnants of Fascism about him. The German army surrender in Italy compelled his immediate flight; joined by his longtime mistress Clara Petacci, Mussolini decided to make a last defense in the rugged Valtellina area. At the prefecture in **Como** (Via Vittorio Emanuele) on April 25, he wrote a last letter to his wife. The next night, at the Hotel Miravalle in **Menaggio**, he awaited a troop detachment that never came. Joining a fleeing German convoy, he was captured in the public square at **Dongo**, where the convoy was halted for inspection. Mussolini's last lodging was a farmhouse in the village of **Bonzanigo** where, with Clara Petacci, he exhaustedly slept on April 28. There, the next day, Communist partisan Walter Audisio arrived, pretending a rescue mission; he hurried the couple to a waiting car, and drove them to their preselected execution spot (see *Exhibits* below).

Mussolini tomb: San Cassiano Cemetery, **Predáppio**.

Exhibits: The occasion of Mussolini's 1983 birth centennial did not pass ignored in Italy. While it was hardly "celebrated" in the usual centennial sense, new books, films, and recordings relating to the dictator and his regime were issued. **Predáppio**, his birthplace and the town where his widow, Rachele, operated a restaurant until her death in 1979, has become a shrine for the minority neoFascist Italian Social Movement and attracts thousands of visitors annually. To most Italians, however, Mussolini represents little more than a historical character beyond love or hate, along with Caesar, the Borgias, and the Medicis, and entitled like them to a place in the ruins—though some express nostalgia for *quello* ("that one") who "made the trains run on time." Many of Mussolini's practical accomplishments survive—the modern Italian transportation system which he virtually created, along with his slum clearance, drainage, and housing projects, for instance—but none of them overshadow the devastating results of his eagerness to lead Italy into war. On many occasions he privately voiced feelings of contempt for the Italian people.

Key places in his career include the hall in the Piazza San Sepolcro at **Milan**, the 1919 brithplace of the Fascist party; and in **Rome**, the 16th-century Chigi Palace at the corner of the Via del Corso and the Piazza Colonna, Mussolini's working quarters from 1922 to 1929. Also in Rome is the Venezia Palace, where he maintained his office from 1929 to 1943. From its balcony overlooking the Piazza di Venezia came those strutting poses and hoarse shouts that became so familiar to the world as Mussolini harangued crowds in the square (this spot is only a short distance north of the Roman Forum, where Caesar and Cicero spoke to crowds of equal size). Mussolini's office, the nerve center of Fascist Italy, occupied a cavernous chamber (the *Sala del Mappamondo*) on the second floor. Mussolini also installed his favorite mistress, Clara Petacci, in a third-floor apartment in the building. This Renaissance palace's history is intriguing for more reasons than its 14-year association with Mussolini, however. Begun in 1455 and finished a century later, it was built partly of stone from the Colosseum for the cardinal who later became Pope Paul II. It continued as a papal residence for a century. From 1797 to 1915 it was the Austrian Embassy. Its stately inner court may be viewed from its entrance at 49 Piazza di San Marco.

Mussolini's end was that of a Renaissance despot. He and his mistress met sudden death in front of a low stone wall in the village of **Giulino di Mezzegra** near Dongo. The wall fronts an estate known as the Villa Belmonte, and a small cross and flag at the site memorializes Clara Petacci.

Their bodies were taken to **Milan** and hung upside down like beef carcasses from the girders of a gas station in the Piazzale Loreto, where Italian mobs kicked at, spat, and urinated on the corpses. The present garage on the site has been reconstructed to obliterate all traces of the furious mob outburst.

NAPOLEON I (1769–1821). Of Italian ancestry, the French General Bonaparte (not yet emperor) invaded Italy in 1796, humbled the Vatican, and established the Cisalpine and Ligurian republics. Later he placed his brother, Joseph Bonaparte, and sisters, Élisa and Caroline, on various Italian thrones and crowned himself king of Italy.

The deposed emperor, brought to defeat in 1814 by a coalition of allied armies, spent his first period of exile (1814–15) on the Italian island of Elba. There the former ruler of Europe was granted the 10 x 30-kilometer island with full perpetual sovereignty over it and the title Emperor of the Isle of Elba. He reorganized the island government, drilled troops, and entertained visitors—but mainly he plotted his return to France. His principal residence was the Villetta dei Mulini, created from two old windmills overlooking the sea at **Portoferraio**. Today it displays memorabilia of his stay and his suite of rooms with their original furnishings. Napoleon's personal library was brought from the palace of Fontainebleu in France. (Open Tuesday—Saturday 9:00—1:30, Sunday 9:00—12:30; admission.) About four and a half kilometers west of the town stands the Villa di San Martino, which Napoleon used as a summer residence. Today it displays a Tuscan art collection. (Open same hours as Villetta dei Mulini; admission.) Napoleon slipped away from Elba in February 1815 to commence his ill-fated "Hundred Days" regime, which was finally ended by his crushing defeat at Waterloo.

Exhibits: Napoleon and his family are widely memorialized in Italy, not only because of their Italian ancestry but because Napoleon's reorganization of the Italian political map set the stage for Italy's final unification in the 19th century. Museums of Bonaparte relics and memorabilia include the following:

The Napoleonic Museum at 10 Piazza di Ponte Umberto in **Rome**, displays the collection of Bonaparte descendant Count Joseph Primoli; its 17 period rooms are heavy on pictorial matter, but also show robes of state, autographs, and the 1810 marriage contract of Napoleon and Princess Marie-Louise of Austria, his second wife. (Open Tuesday—Saturday 9:00—2:00, Tuesday and Thursday also 5:00—8:00, Sunday 9:00—12:30; admission.) Napoleon's redoubtable mother, Mme. Letizia Bonaparte Ramolino, died in 1836 at the Misciatelli Palace (formerly Bonaparte Palace), Piazza Venezia and Via del Corso, where she had lived since Napoleon's downfall at Waterloo.

For the following museums, inquire locally for admission information.

The Lombardi Museum, Viale Mariotti in **Parma**, displays a collection related to Empress Marie-Louise who, as Duchess of Parma, spent summers at the nearby Colorno Palace during Napoleon's long exile on St. Helena; she lived there with her lover, Count von Neipperg, and bore two children. Letters and wedding memorabilia are shown.

The Museum of the National Risorgimento, 23 Via Borgo Nuovo in **Milan**, displays regalia used by Napoleon in his 1805 coronation as king of Italy.

A Napoleonic Room in the Bezzi Palace in **Urbisaglia** also shows memorabilia of the emperor.

(See SPAIN in this chapter; also Chapter 1, AUSTRIA, SWITZERLAND; also Chapter 2, FRANCE; also Chapter 3, PARIS; also Chapter 4, EAST GERMANY, BELGIUM.)

NERO (37–68). Great-great-grandson of Augustus and great-grandson of Mark Antony, this Roman emperor began his career well but ended it as probably the most murderous and profligate of all the caesars. Raised in an intimidating atmosphere by the domineering Agrippina—a "stage mother" if ever there was one—he lived as emperor in perpetual fear of his life (as did most emperors), a fear that in his case developed into homicidal paranoia. Nero not only killed his mother, two wives, and many rivals and conspirators, either real or imaginary, but instituted the persecution of Christians. He probably did not, however, set the fire that destroyed much of Rome in the year 64.

A native of Antium, which is now **Anzio**, Nero built his own magnificent villa there, probably shortly after he became emperor in 54, and spent much time in it. According to the historian Tacitus, he was there when the devastating fire he allegedly set in Rome broke out in 64. Ruins of his villa survive near the promontory of Arco Muto in the broad avenue of the Riviera Mallozzi. Much fine statuary, now in Rome and Paris museums, has been excavated from this site.

In **Rome** Nero's first imperial palace was the Domus Transitoria on the Palatine Hill. Remnants of a marble pavement from this palace survive near the oval fountains of the Triclinium, or banqueting hall, near the central summit of the hill. Parts of the widespread complex also extend to the eastern section of the Roman Forum, where massive ruins of the Temple of Venus and Rome built by Hadrian in 121 now stand. Nero's palace was destroyed in the fire of 64 (see the entries on Augustus and Julius Caesar earlier in this section).

Nero promptly began construction of the largest, most lavish palace Rome has ever seen, the fabled Domus Aurea ("Golden House"), so-called because of its main facade of pure gold. The rebuilt Domus Transitoria portion on the Forum site of the Temple of Venus and Rome (see above) served as a vestibule to the new palace, which was actually a complex of many separate buildings and landscaped grounds spread over much of the Palatine, Caelian and Esquiline hills. A huge arc of property curved around the bowl of the later Colosseum site, a space which held a lake and extensive gardens. The total area encompassed at least 125 acres and perhaps as many as 375. Massive vaulted rooms, ivory ceilings, piped water and scents, colorful wall murals and frescoes, immense statuary, decorated halls, and elaborate courtyards arose and expanded for the emperor, who reputedly said of it all: "Good, now I can at last begin to live like a human being." Walled off from his enemies in this enormous city within a city, Nero indulged his favorite activities of singing (he had a fine bass voice), playing stringed instruments, and hosting endless nights of banquets and sybaritic orgies. His marvelous palace did not long outlive him. Succeeding emperors demolished and buried his buildings for their own palaces and projects (Vespasian drained Nero's lake on the site of the Colosseum in A.D. 72 to build that edifice). The magnificent statue of the Laocoön, now displayed in the Pio-Clementino Museum at the Vatican, was discovered in a burial chamber here in 1506. Today only a small northern portion of the Domus Aurea lies excavated and accessible; it is situated in the area of the Baths of Trajan on the Oppian Hill, one of the four Esquiline summits northeast of the Colosseum. The Baths, superimposed on these Domus ruins in about 100, create a somewhat confusing picture of the original layout even in this fragmented piece of the total complex. Entrance to the labyrinth of underground chambers and courtyards (which stood above ground, of course, when built) is gained from a guided descent below the high curved wall of the Bath ruins. The cavernous octagonal hall, and dark, cool passages once bathed in Roman sunlight, evoke varied reactions from visitors; some find them endlessly absorbing, others find them depressing and tomblike. Bring flashlights and binoculars in order to see the paintings that decorate some of the immensely high rooms. The Domus Aurea is approached on the Viale della Domus Aurea. (Open Tuesday—Sunday 9:00—1:00; admission.)

A HALL OF NERO'S DOMUS AUREA. In **Rome** remnants of the city's largest imperial palace, built by the sybaritic, bloodthirsty emperor in about A.D. 65, now lie mostly buried by the rubble of 19 centuries. This excavated corridor in the eastern wing of the "Golden House" shows some of the original wall paintings. Bring a flashlight if you tour these dark chambers; in Nero's day, they were flooded by sunlight.

"What an artist the world loses in me!" Nero mourned just before his death. His suicide was similar to Adolf Hitler's in its timing and desperation to avoid capture—in Nero's case, capture by rebellious legions who had finally had enough of his vindictive mania. He fled from the Domus Aurea to the villa of one of his aides, Phaon, and was pursued. Just before his would-be captors burst in the door, he plunged a knife into his throat and thence bled to death. This large villa, ruins of which remain, stood on the site of the private Casale Chiari several kilometers northeast of the city in the Via della Buffalotta, a short distance east of **Mentana**.

Nero founded the town of Sublaqueum, now **Subiaco**, to accommodate the workmen he employed to build another grandiose villa there; the grounds encompassed a large lake, now dried up. It is said that lightning once struck the banquet table at which he dined in the villa. Only traces of this house survive on the Ienne road above the town.

Nero tomb (site): Church of Santa Maria del Popolo, **Rome**.

NIGHTINGALE, FLORENCE (1820–1910). Named for **Florence**, the city of her birth, the English "lady with the lamp," the first professional nurse, and a major reformer of medical practice, was born at the 15th-century Villa La Colombaia in the Via Foscolo. She lived there with her family for about a year. Her fame was largely responsible for the revival of the name Florence for girls (though men as well as women had used it in earlier times).

(See Chapter 5, ENGLAND; also Chapter 6, LONDON.)

PAUL VI (1897–1978). The two hundred and sixty-first pope, elected in 1963, will probably remain best known for his encyclical *Humanae Vitae* (1968), which prohibited artificial methods of birth control for Catholics. He was born Giovanni Battista Montini at 14 Via Vantini in **Concesio**, his affluent family's summer home, and spent long periods there as a boy.

The Montini family town house, his home until his 1920 ordination, stands in the Via Santa Maria delle Grazie at **Brescia**.

As archbishop of **Milan** from 1954 to 1963, Montini resided in the 16th-century Archbishops' Palace in the Piazza Fontana.

Except for his Milanese period, Montini dwelled in **Rome** from 1920 until his death. From 1924 to 1954 he performed diplomatic duties in the Vatican secretariat of state. During the early part of that period (1928–33), he occupied a flat in the Via Terme delle Deciane. Later he occupied a Vatican apartment near his office in the San Damaso papal administration building, located in the northern angle of St. Peter's Colonnade and the Vatican Palace. As pope he inhabited the papal apartment in the Apostolic Palace and also the papal summer palace at **Castel Gandolfo** (see the entries on John XXIII and Pius XII in this section).

Paul VI tomb: Vatican Grottoes, St. Peter's Basilica, **Rome**.

PAUL, ST. (1 B.C.?–A.D. 67?). A Jew from Asia Minor, and the first Christian missionary-evangelist, Paul was also a Roman citizen by privilege of his family status in Tarsus. His parents were probably wealthy and influential, and—in the manner of Orthodox Jews—also trained their son to a trade, that of tent-making. Having appealed his imprisonment at Caesarea in Palestine to Caesar (i.e., Nero), he arrived in **Rome** about A.D. 62 as a prisoner of a centurion named Julius of the Augustan Cohort. He was received with marked courtesy and given the status of a prisoner on bail, free to live as he pleased under military supervision. According to St. Luke in his Acts of the Apostles (ca. 80), Paul dwelled for two years (62–64) "in his own hired house and received all that came in unto him," preaching and teaching, "no man forbidding him." Thus the "bonds" he often mentions at Rome were probably more figurative than real. A 10th-century tradition places Paul's "hired house" in the Via Lata, today the Via del Corso, the long street which connects the Venezia and Popolo piazzas, one of the modern city's most fashionable shopping areas. The traditional view is that Paul wrote his "captivity epistles" in this house: the New Testament books of Ephesians, Colossians, Philemon, and Philippians. "All that came in unto him" at Rome included St. Luke, St. Mark, and the slave Onesimus, subject of Paul's personal Epistle to Philemon. Following the disastrous fire of the year 64, which destroyed and damaged 10 of the city's 14 districts, a stunned Rome looked for scapegoats, and the Emperor Nero cleverly deflected public fury to the rising Christian sect. Thus began the first great persecution of the church, and Paul's "bonds" suddenly became very real. Church tradition states that he was jailed along with St. Peter for nine months in the Mamertine Prison before being executed on the same day as Peter in 67 (see the entry on St. Peter later in this section). In this prison Paul reputedly wrote his last letter, the Second Epistle to Timothy ("I have fought a good fight, I have finished my course, I have kept the faith").

St. Paul tomb (site): St. Paul's-without-the-Wall Basilica, **Rome**.

Exhibits: "The Rome of St. Paul," wrote H. V. Morton, "lies from thirty to sixty feet beneath living Rome. Its guardians are venerable monks, who grasp keys in their hands and lead the way down long flights of stone steps." Sites in **Rome** traditionally associated with the missionary include the home of his devoted friends and hosts, Aquila and Priscilla, probably the first gathering place (thus "church") of Christians in Rome. The fourth-century Church of Santa Prisca in the Via di Santa Prisca, Aventine Hill, overlies several reputed chambers of this house; it displays fourth-century frescoes and several statues of non-Christian deities. A small museum is attached. (Open on application; donation.)

The traditional site of St. Paul's martyrdom by beheading is the Abbey of the Three Fountains (*Abbazia delle Tre Fontane*), in the Via di Acque Salvie off the Via Laurentina—the third milestone south of the city from the Porta San Paolo, Paul's last walk in a lifetime of travels. (Open daily; donation.)

Two similarly titled books—*In the Steps of St. Paul* (1936) by H. V. Morton, and *In the Footsteps of St. Paul* (1977) by Wolfgang E. Pax—provide interesting addenda to our sparse knowledge of this saint and the many sites associated with him.

(See GREECE in this chapter.)

PETER, ST. (?–A.D. 67?). Most of St. Peter's **Rome**, like St. Paul's, lies far beneath the modern city. The Christian apostle considered by Roman Catholics as the first bishop of Rome (i.e., pope) from the year A.D. 42, and thus the founder of the church, nevertheless has many monuments in the modern city. Many of the sites and relics associated with St. Peter are backed by an extensive body of oral and written tradition; just how many of these "pieces and places" are genuinely authentic, however, greatly depends on the criteria for authenticity that one is willing to accept. If papal decree is judged the ultimate authority in these matters, there is no problem. By the different yardsticks used by secular archaeologists and historians, however, few of the attributed Petrine and Pauline sites can be verified as such. This doesn't necessarily mean they are *not* authentic—only that secular scholarship cannot establish them as historically genuine.

Two main traditional residence sites of the apostle exist in Rome. He supposedly lodged in the house of the Roman senator Cornelius Pudens (though some sources say this tradition, dating from the year 145, has been disproved). There are, at any rate, ruins of a first-century house beneath the Church of Santa Pudenziana, which was rebuilt on this long-hallowed site in the fourth century and several times later, notably in 1589. Excavations beneath the church were closed in 1970 because of flooding. The church itself, located in the Via Urbana, displays part of the wooden table on which some believe that St. Peter celebrated the Eucharist on this site. St. Paul reputedly frequented the house also, and it is said that St. Mark may have written the earliest of the four gospels there in about A.D. 66. (Open daily; donation.)

During the Roman persecution of Christians after A.D. 65, according to tradition, Peter was confined in the Tullianum, later called the Mamertine Prison (*San Pietro in Carcere*), along with St. Paul to await execution. This dungeon, originally a dank cistern, was entered only from a hole at the top. It lies in ancient sinister gloom beneath the Church of San Guiseppe dei Falegnami along the Via del Tor. (Open daily 9:00—12:30, 3:00—6:30; admission.)

St. Peter tomb (reputed): Vatican Necropolis, St. Peter's Basilica, **Rome**.

Exhibits: The Church of San Pietro in Vincoli in the piazza of that name, **Rome**, was originally built in 442. It was restored in 1475 to enshrine the two prison chains of St. Peter, said to have been recovered from the Tullianum (see above). They are held inside an elaborate tabernacle in a confessio below the high altar. (Open daily; donation.)

The Basilica of St. John Lateran, on the Piazza San Giovanni in Laterano, displays in its papal altar the greater part of the wooden altar table supposedly recovered from the Pudens house (see above), as well as the reputed head relics of Saints Peter and Paul. (Open daily; donation.) The site of St. Peter's crucifixion may have been a garden adjoining the Circus of Nero, the chariot race course that lies deep beneath the present Roman pavement directly south of St. Peter's Basilica. A small courtyard, the Piazza dei Protomartiri Romani, a portion of the Vatican Gardens directly south of the basilica wall, contains a pavement stone which marks the midpoint of the two pyramids that stood in the center of Nero's course, and is reputedly the spot where Peter died. In the mania of his homicidal zeal, it is said, Nero made a game of burning Christians in the circus, dressing himself

as a charioteer and running races around the track lighted by the tar-smeared flaming bodies.

PETRARCH (1304–1374). The poet occupied many Italian dwellings, but few of them survive. The house identified as his birthplace in **Arezzo**, at 22 Via dell' Orto, is probably not the actual dwelling where Francesco Petrarca was born and lived for his first year. Now the Accademia Petrarca, the 16th-century restored house displays early editions of his works. (Inquire locally for admission information.)

As a minor ecclesiastic in **Milan**, Petrarch resided from 1353 to 1358 in a house assigned to him by the archbishop on the north side of the Basilica of Sant' Ambrogio facing the church. This fourth-century basilica, enlarged in the ninth and eleventh centuries, stands in its own piazza. Petrarch's house is long gone.

Another canon's residence he occupied stood until the 16th century in the cathedral precincts of **Padua**, the Piazza del Duomo. Petrarch lived there in 1361 and 1362, and again from about 1367 to 1370.

In **Venice** he occupied a house—the towered Molin Palace—assigned to him by the Venetian Senate; it stood on the present site of the Casermo

LAST HOME OF PETRARCH. The poet built this stone house in 1369 at a village now called **Arqua Petrarca** and died there five years later. Possessions and memorabilia are displayed.

del Sepolcro in the Riva Degli Schiavoni, now a favorite promenade. It was his home from 1362 to 1367.

"Not more than ten miles away from Padua," wrote the poet, "I have built myself *una piccola, ma graziosa villetta*, surrounded by an olive grove and a vineyard which provide enough for my not numerous and modest family." This construction occurred in 1369 at a village northwest of Monsélice which is now called **Arquà Petrarca**. It was his last home. The wooden armchair in which the poet died is on display, together with a book chest, and various memorabilia. During the 18th and 19th centuries a visit to Petrarch's house was considered obligatory by many noted travelers, and a main feature here is the visitors' book which was signed by Mozart and Lord Byron among others. (Inquire locally for admission information.)

Petrarch tomb: Village church, **Arquà Petrarca**. (See Chapter 2, FRANCE.)

PILATE, PONTIUS (?–after A.D. 36). "For the past seventeen centuries," wrote New Testament scholar Paul L. Maier in his *Pontius Pilate* (1968), "Pilate has had an unusually bad press, and most tend to cloister him next to Judas Iscariot in mind and memory. This view seems unjustified, both by the practice of the early church in its crucial first three centuries, and, more importantly, by the sources themselves." The Roman functionary, governor of Judaea from A.D. 26 to 36, lives in history only because of his reluctant role in condemning Jesus to death. An early church father, Tertullian, claimed Pilate as "already a Christian in his conscience," and the Coptic Church canonized both Pilate and Procula, his wife, as saints. But until 1961, when a stone inscribed with his name was found in Caesarea, Pilate's very existence could not be epigraphically proven, although a large apocryphal literature did exist.

According to one tradition, Pilate was born in Caudium, an ancient site that lies northwest of the present village of **Montesarchio**. Certainly his ancestral home, that of the Samnite Pontii, if not his own birthplace stood in this mountainous vicinity.

Exhibit: In **Rome** the Scala Santa ("Holy Stairs") is the reputed staircase of Pilate's prefectural palace, brought from Jerusalem by St. Helena, the mother of Emperor Constantine I, and revered as the steps which Jesus descended after his condem-

nation. The 28 marble steps, protected by boards, may be ascended only by pilgrims on their knees. Once a part of the old Lateran Palace residence of the popes (see the entry on St. Gregory I earlier in this section), the staircase is now housed in the 1589 building opposite that palace in the Piazza di Porta San Giovanni. (Open daily; donation.)

PIUS XII (1876–1958). The scholarly, ascetic two hundred and fifty-ninth pope evoked more controversy than any pontiff of modern times by his failure to assert his immense influence and denounce Nazi atrocities against Jews before and during World War II, instead of remaining neutral. The Vatican state, of course, found itself surrounded by an Axis nation during those years. But despite the strong later defenses voiced on behalf of this pope's cautious decision in such circumstances, many Catholics and non-Catholics alike believed they might have expected something more than judicious diplomatic silence from "Christ's vicar" while the Holocaust raged. It was neither mankind's nor the church's finest hour. Such factors, however, will apparently have no bearing on the intricate canonical procedures of declaring Pius a saint, which continue; it is emphasized that he was a very holy man.

Eugenio Pacelli, son of a lawyer, was a native of **Rome**. His birthplace and home to age five, the Pediconi Palace where his family rented a third-floor flat, stands at 34 Via degli Orsini. From 1881 his family home was 19 Via della Vetrina. As papal secretary of state from 1929 to 1939, Cardinal Pacelli resided in a Vatican apartment in the Apostolic Palace. Upon his election as pope in 1939

RESIDENCE OF THE POPES. Towering above St. Peter's Square in **Rome** is a portion of the Apostolic Palace, private residence of all popes since Pius X.

he moved into the small papal suite on the third floor of this same palace, the private residence of all popes since St. Pius X in 1903. The Apostolic Palace stands almost directly north of the northern colonnade of St. Peter's Square.

The Papal Palace at **Castel Gandolfo**, a 1624 structure built on the site of the 12th-century Gandolfi castle, has been the summer residence of popes since its erection, except for the period 1870 to 1929. Pius XII did not use it during World War II, though the property is a Vatican rather than an Italian domain. The estate overlooks the volcanic Lake Albano at the northern entrance to the town. A special permit from the palace director must be obtained to visit this property, which contains a chapel, gardens, and the Vatican Observatory, as well as audience halls and residence suites.

Pius XII tomb: Vatican Grottoes, St. Peter's Basilica, **Rome**.

(See Chapter 4, EAST GERMANY.)

POLO, MARCO (1254–1324). "Marco Millions," as he was derisively nicknamed by fellow Venetians for the tales of Oriental marvels he brought back from the court of Kublai Khan in China, was one of the first great travel writers. His Asian journeys (1271–95) were probably the most extensive of any European's during the Middle Ages. A native of **Venice**, the merchant and his family occupied a large house in the passage now called Corte Seconda del Milion, where the site is marked. When Marco, his father, and his uncle, all long given up for lost, arrived back in Venice in 1295 their reception was at first hostile and disbelieving, then skeptical. Finally when they showed the rich clothing they had brought with them, and emptied the gems from the linings of the rags they had worn on their arrival, "Marco Millions" suddenly became a name to be reckoned with. Two Romanesque arches at number 5858 are apparently parts of the original house.

How very large the world was then. The immense Eastern empire described in *The Book of Marco Polo*, along with accounts of such Asian wonders as asbestos, burning coal, paper money, and block printing, was more mythical and obscure to Europeans in Polo's time than are the moon and its features today. Marco Polo dictated his famous book while held as a prisoner of war in **Genoa** (ca. 1298–99). His prison was the San Giorgio Palace in the Piazza Capricamento, a structure begun about 1260, enlarged in 1571, and since restored to 13th-century style. Today it houses the city harbor board and contains no specific reminders of Polo's stay there.

RABELAIS, FRANÇOIS (1494?–1553). The French writer and ex-monk lived in **Rome** from 1547 to 1549 and there finished the fourth book of his satiric opus *Gargantua and Pantagruel* (1532–64). Like its predecessors, this book was condemned by the Sorbonne for its attacks on the church. Rabelais dwelled under the patronage of Cardinal Jean du Bellay in the Piazza dei Santi Apostoli. Another lodging was the Osteria dell' Orso, located on the corner of the Piazza Ponte Umberto I and the Via di Monte Brianzo. Dating from 1460, this building was a hotel; Montaigne and Goethe numbered among its guests, as well as Rabelais. It is now a celebrated restaurant.

(See Chapter 2, FRANCE; also Chapter 3, PARIS.)

RAPHAEL (1483–1520). He was once regarded as the greatest of Italian Renaissance painters, but Raphael's reputation has declined in the 20th century. His birthplace in **Urbino** stands at 57 Via Raffaello Sanzio (Sanzio was his surname). Raphael lived there until 1497 and painted his first canvases in this house; his earliest surviving work, a *Madonna* fresco, adorns his birth room. Also exhibited in the courtyard is the stone on which he ground his colors. (Open daily, 9:00—1:00, 3:00—7:00; admission.)

The painter lived in **Florence** at intervals from 1504. One of his lodgings survives at 15 Via de' Ginori.

Raphael lived in **Rome** from 1508. The so-called House of Raphael, at 122–123 Via dei Coronari, was apparently never occupied by the painter but was bought by his executors as income property for the upkeep of his tomb. Raphael died in a house he bought in 1515; it stood in the Via della Conciliazione near St. Peter's Basilica. The Convertendi Palace, built in the 17th century and rebuilt in 1937, occupies the house site today.

Raphael tomb: Pantheon, **Rome**.

Exhibits: In **Florence** room II of the Pitti Gallery displays a collection of early works by the Renaissance master. The gallery is located in the famed 15th-century Pitti Palace in the Piazza Pitti. (Open Wednesday—Monday 9:30—4:00; admission, except free on Sunday.) The Uffizi Gallery, room 25, exhibits an important group of portraits by Raphael (see the entry on Sandro Botticelli, *Exhibits*, earlier in this section).

In **Rome** the Vatican Picture Gallery in the Vatican Museums displays several of Raphael's most famous paintings, including his last, *The Transfiguration* (1520), in room VIII. The painter's masterwork, however, is the series of frescoed rooms and arcades called the Stanze and Loggia of Raphael. Commissioned by Pope Julius II, this part of the Apostolic Palace, which constituted the official apartments of popes from Julius II to Gregory XIII, was almost wholly decorated by Raphael and his pupils from 1508 until the artist's death. Theological, classical, and historical subjects decorate these splendid walls, and represent the evolving genius and originality of the painter. (See the entry on Lucrezia Borgia, *Exhibits*, earlier in this section.)

ROSSINI, GIOACCHINO (1792–1868). A native of **Pesaro**, the prolific opera composer whose combined musical facility and later indolence fascinated and astonished his peers was born at 34 Via Rossini. It is now a Rossini museum and displays personal effects, pictures, and manuscripts. It was the composer's home until about 1802. (Open Monday—Saturday 10:00—12:00, 4:00—6:00, Sunday 10:00—12:00; 64452; admission.)

From 1802 to 1804 the Rossini family lived at 12 Via Eustachio Manfredi in **Lugo**, a suburb of Bologna.

From 1805 until about 1839 Rossini's family home was a second-floor flat in the Casa Gelmi, now called Casa Rossini, at 26 Strada Maggiore in **Bologna**. Though Rossini made his permanent home in Paris after 1824, he often revisited Italy. His later Bologna lodging (1846–51) was the Donzelli Palace.

In 1813 Rossini composed *Tancredi* at the 1570 Villa Pliniana, located on Lake Como east of the village of **Torno**. (Open mid-July—September, daily, 9:00—5:00; gratuity.)

Rossini composed his most famous opera, *The Barber of Seville*, in about 20 days in **Rome** in 1815; he lodged and wrote at the Pagliarini Palace, which stood in the Via de' Leutari near the Piazza Navona.

Rossini tomb: Church of Santa Croce, **Florence**.

Exhibits: The Rossini Foundation, 5 Piazza Olivieri in **Pesaro**, displays some of the composer's opera manuscripts, his spinet, and other mementos. (Apply to custodian; 30053; gratuity.)

In **Bologna** the Conservatorio G. B. Martini in the Piazza Rossini, where the composer studied from 1806 to 1810, displays his piano, a wig, and miscellaneous relics. (Open Monday—Saturday 9:00—1:00; admission.)

The Music Museum in the **Naples** Conservatory of Music, Via San Pietro a Majella, displays Rossini and Verdi manuscripts. (Inquire locally for admission information.)

(See Chapter 2, FRANCE; also Chapter 3, PARIS; also Chapter 6, LONDON.)

ROUSSEAU, JEAN-JACQUES (1712–1778). The French social philosopher first came into contact with political life and institutions when he accompanied the French ambassador to **Venice** in 1743. There, for about a year, he resided as the ambassador's secretary in the embassy building, which was the Surian Palace at 967 Fondamenta Cannaregio.

(See Chapter 1, SWITZERLAND; also Chapter 2, FRANCE; also Chapter 3, PARIS; also Chapter 5, ENGLAND.)

SAVONAROLA, GIROLAMO (1452–1498). The fiery dominican friar, reformer, and martyr was a native of **Ferrara**, which remained his home until 1475. His birthplace stands at 19 Via Savonarola facing the 1712 Church of San Girolamo.

From 1489 Savonarola's home was two cells, numbers 12 and 13, in the Monastery of San Marco in **Florence**. He became prior of the monastery in 1491. As his criticism of the excesses and immorality of Florentine life under the Medicis became more outspoken, he developed not only a devout following but also several powerful enemies, who finally gained the upper hand after he denounced the Borgia pope, Alexander VI. The former monastery is now the Museum of San Marco in the Piazza San Marco, and Savonarola's cells may be seen. Their contents include his wooden crucifix and rosary, his writing table and chair, a staff, and the Bible he inherited from his grandfather. The painter-monk Fra Angelico earlier spent six years in this monastery (1439–45), and the superb frescoes he painted during this period, notably *The Annunciation*, are worth a visit in themselves. Cosimo de Medici, patriarch of the great ruling family and patron of the monastery, also spent his final months in a monk's cell here (1464). (Open Tuesday—Saturday 9:00—2:00, Sunday 9:00—1:00; 210741; admission, except free on Sunday.)

Savonarola was imprisoned and tortured in 1498 in a tower cell at the Signoria, or Vecchio, Palace in the Piazza della Signoria. This 14th-century fortress, occupied by magistrates of the Florentine republic and later by Medici dukes, has been the seat of the municipal government since 1872. Many art works, in addition to Savonarola's "Alberghetto" cell may be seen. (Open Tuesday—Saturday 9:00—7:00, Sunday 8:00—1:00; admission, except free on Sunday.)

Exhibits: The main places associated with Savonarola in **Florence** include the huge Cathedral of Santa Maria del Fiore, the Piazza del Duomo, where Savonarola thundered against the corruption of church and state. In the Piazza della Signoria, Savonarola set a dangerous historical predecent in 1497 by becoming one of the first book-burners. Feverishly rousing the people to collect everything he deemed immoral throughout the city—pictures, rich clothing, cards, and dice as well as "lewd books"—he presided over the gigantic bonfires that consumed these "vanities." A year later, the bitter irony did not go unremarked as the deposed and excommunicated Savonarola died by hanging and burning on the same spot. In a frantic effort to prevent the populace from claiming saintly relics, authorities cast every vestige of his remains into the River Arno.

SHELLEY, PERCY BYSSHE (1792–1822). In 1818 the English poet and his wife, Mary Godwin Shelley, moved into the small Casa Bertini at 141 Viale Umberto in **Bagni di Lucca**, where they resided for several months, enjoying the mountain walks and forest bathing pools. The house is marked by a plaque.

A villa rented but never occupied by Shelley's friend, Lord Byron, at **Este** was taken by the Shelleys later in 1818. I Cappuccini, a former Capuchin monastery, is now known as the Villa De Kunkler, and is located behind the Este National Museum. Shelley worked on his lyric drama *Prome-*

theus Unbound (1820) there, and his daughter Clara died there of dysentery in September.

In **Rome**, where the poet lived during the spring of 1819, he continued work on *Prometheus Unbound*, occupying rooms in the Verospi Palace at 375 Via del Corso. The already grieving couple faced another death in June when their son, William, died there.

The Shelleys moved on to **Florence**, and resided in the Marino Palace, Via Valfonda, for six months (1819–20).

The greater part of their Italian stay was in **Pisa**, where they lived from 1820 to 1822. Shelley wrote some of his best-known shorter poetry here, including "The Cloud," "To a Skylark," "Ode to the West Wind," and "The Sensitive Plant." The couple resided longest at the "Three Palaces of the *Chiesa*," actually one building later known as the Scotto Palace, which now lies in ruins near the Ponte alla Fortezza in the Lungarno Galileo. Diagonally opposite across the River Arno stands the Toscanelli Palace, Lord Byron's residence at the time (see the entry on Byron earlier in this section).

The Casa Magni at **Lérici** became the poet's last home in 1822. It still stands on a small cape of the Gulf of Spézia a short distance north of the village. While returning there from Livorno by sea aboard the schooner *Don Juan*, on July 8, either a sudden storm or a larger boat swamped the schooner, and both Shelley and his friend Edward Williams drowned. The poet's body washed ashore 10 days later on the beach of Il Gombo south of **Viareggio**, and there his friends cremated him.

Shelley tomb: Protestant Cemetery, **Rome**.

Exhibit: See the entry on John Keats earlier in this section.

(See Chapter 1, SWITZERLAND; also Chapter 5, ENGLAND; also Chapter 6, LONDON.)

THEOTOKÓPOULOS, DOMÉNIKOS. ("EL GRECO") (1541–1614). The painter's Spanish nickname ("the Greek") represented his now-obscure Cretan origins. Though he produced most of his shimmering, mystical works in Spain, he resided in **Venice** from about 1560 to 1569. He apprenticed himself to the painter Titian and probably resided, for at least part of that period, in Titian's home and studio (see the entry on Titian below). El Greco's subsequent addresses in **Rome** (ca. 1569–77) remain unknown.

(See SPAIN in this chapter.)

TITIAN (ca. 1488–1576). The greatest of the Venetian Renaissance painters, Tiziano Vecelli, known as Titian, was born in **Pieve di Cadore**. Today his modest cottage birthplace, in the Piazza dell' Arsenale, is a museum which exhibits material on his long life and career. The house, which belonged to his grandparents and which was the artist's home to about 1497, held an inn during the 19th century. (Inquire locally for admission information.)

Titian resided chiefly in **Venice** for the rest of his life. He received his basic instruction in the workshop of Giovanni Bellini, which stood in the Piazza di Rialto. From the 1520s to about 1531 he inhabited a house which may have stood on the site of a modern tenement at 3024 Calle Ca' Lipoli.

In 1531 Titian rented an upper floor of the house he would occupy for the rest of his life, the Casa Grande. Built in 1527, the three-story dwelling with its adjacent barnlike studio was gradually taken over by the artist; he expanded its garden, and painted such works there as *Venus of Urbino* (1538–39), *Christ Before Pilate* (1543), and *Perseus and Andromeda* (1554–56). El Greco, the painter born in Crete who later went to Spain, probably studied and resided with Titian during the 1560s (see the entry on Doménikos Theotokópoulos above). The building, much altered over the centuries, stands at 5179-83 Fondamenta Cannaregio in the Campo Tiziano.

Titian tomb: Church of Santa Maria Gloriosa dei Frari, **Venice**.

Exhibits: Titian's works are scattered in numerous museums and churches all over Italy, with relatively few in **Venice**. One masterpiece that does remain there, however, is the *Annunciation* (1566). It may be seen in the Church of San Salvatore, Campo San Salvatore. (Open daily.)

Room 28 of the Uffizi Gallery in **Florence** is devoted to several of Titian's works, including the alluring *Venus of Urbino* (see the entry on Sandro Botticelli, *Exhibits*, earlier in this section).

TOSCANINI, ARTURO (1867–1957). The most widely known conductor of the 20th century was a native of **Parma**, where his birthplace stands at 13 Borgo Rodolfo Tanzi. The house was bought and given to the city by Toscanini's children on the occasion of their father's 1967 centennial. A later home where Toscanini lived with his grandparents (1870s) was 65 Strada dei Genovesi. From 1876 to 1883 he was a resident student cellist at the Conservatory of Music in the Strada Conservatorio, a building that has been modernized in recent years.

In 1911 Toscanini bought a 17th-century, three-story house at 20 Via Durini in **Milan**, which became his favorite residence and permanent home. Except for the World War II years, he spent portions of each year there even during his long conducting tenure in New York City. An elegant courtyard and wrought-iron balcony are distinctive features of the mansion.

Another favorite spot was the tiny Isola San Giovanni in the Gulf of Pallanza, Lake Maggiore, facing **Pallanza**. Toscanini first rented his summer villa there in 1932; later he bought the property and returned each year until 1939, then again from 1946 through the next decade. The Toscanini family still owns the villa.

Toscanini tomb: Monumentale Cemetery, **Milan**.

Exhibit: In **Milan**, the 1776 Teatro alla Scala in the Piazza della Scala, better known as La Scala, hosted Toscanini as chief operatic conductor from 1898 to 1907 and again from 1921 to 1929. The Theater Museum displays a collection of Toscanini batons, medals, and other memorabilia. (Open daily, 9:00—12:00, 2:00—6:00; admission.)

TRAJAN (53–117). One of **Rome**'s greatest builders and expanders of its empire, this Spanish-born emperor was the only one to be made an "honorary Christian." "St. Gregory the Great," recounts H. V. Morton, "touched by Trajan's compassion for the poor and for widows, asked God to open the gates of the Christian heaven to this good and compassionate pagan. And God, not too willingly, one gathers, answered St. Gregory's prayer, but stipulated that the saint must not make too many such requests." Trajan's home as emperor (98–117) would have been the palace complex on the Palatine Hill erected by Domitian (see the entry on Constantine I earlier in this section).

Trajan tomb (site): Trajan's Column, **Rome**.

Exhibits: The Forum of Trajan in **Rome**, the latest, most splendid, and northernmost of the Imperial Fora, was completed by Trajan's successor and adopted son, Hadrian (see the entry on Hadrian earlier in this section). Trajan's Column, the most conspicuous monument in the forum, stands directly northwest of these ruins. It arose in 113 as a tribute to Trajan's defeat of Dacia (now Romania); its spiral frieze details the exploits of his campaigns there in 102 and 106. Trajan's statue at the top was replaced in 1588 by the present one of St. Peter (there being limits, apparently, to "honorary Christianity"). The entrance to this rectangular forum may be reached from the column or from the Via Quattro Novembre.

(See SPAIN in this chapter.)

VELÁZQUEZ, DIEGO (1599–1660). The Spanish painter resided in **Rome** during 1630 and 1650 in the Villa Medici (see the entry on Galileo Galilei earlier in this section).

(See SPAIN in this chapter.)

VERDI, GUISEPPE (1813–1901). Master of vocal writing and dramatic effect as well as a supreme melodist, this opera composer shines brightest in Italy's galaxy of musical immortals. HIs humble birthplace in **Le Róncole**, near Busseto, was his family's inn and grocery shop. It was Verdi's home until 1826, and stands marked on the main street.

In 1848 Verdi purchased and remodeled the Villa Sant' Ágata about five kilometers north of **Busseto**, and this remained his lifelong home. His ancestors had been landowners and innkeepers in this area as early as 1650, so to Verdi this acquisition represented the restored fortunes of his family. Here the composer planted gardens and wrote most of his best-known operas—*Rigoletto* (1851), *Il Trovatore* (1852), *Aida* (1871), *Otello* (1887), and *Falstaff* (1893), among others. Today visitors to the villa may see portions of Verdi's operatic manuscripts, as well as his library, photographs, furnishings, piano, and a chamber containing the contents of the Milan hotel room in which he died. The house stands in a 50-acre park beside a lake. (Open summer, apply to caretaker; admission.)

In 1853 Verdi was a guest of his publisher, Ricordi, at the Villa Margherita, located just north of **Cadenabbia** on Lake Como, and there composed *La Traviata*.

The composer died at his frequent **Milan** residence, the Grand Hotel de Milan, 29 Via Manzoni. A six-day death watch took place as Verdi followers gathered outside the hotel after he suffered a stroke there in early 1901. This 90-room structure is still one of the city's most prestigious hotels.

After 1877 Verdi's frequent winter home was the Doria Pamphilj or Principe Palace, a 16th-century building in the Piazza Principe at **Genoa**. Part of the palace functions as an international seamen's center.

Verdi tomb: Casa di Riposa di Musicisti (Casa Verdi), **Milan**.

Exhibits: The Theater Museum in the La Scala opera house in **Milan** displays four pianos owned by Verdi, including his first, bought for him by his father in about 1826 and kept by the composer throughout his life. (See the entry on Arturo Toscanini, *Exhibit*, earlier in this section.)

In **Parma** the Institute of Verdi Studies, 57 Strada della Republica, displays Verdi letters along with a notable literary collection relating to the composer. (Open Monday—Friday 9:00—1:00, 3:00—7:30, Saturday 9:00—1:00; 26044; admission.)

The Conservatory of Music Museum in **Naples** also exhibits some Verdi manuscripts (see the entry on Gioacchino Rossini, *Exhibits*, earlier in this section).

VIRGIL (70–19 B.C.). "I sing of warfare and a man at war": thus begins Virgil's epic poem *The Aeneid*, one of the most influential masterpieces of Western literature. Greatest of the classical Roman poets, the "sage guide" of Dante, Publius Virgilius Maro was a native of Andes. Precisely where this village stood, however, is a question that has fueled generations of scholarly controversy. The two likeliest sites are a location between the villages of Carpenédolo and **Calvisano**; and the present village of **Piétole**, about eight kilometers southeast of Mantua. The consensus of opinion favors the latter site. As late as the 15th century, an old brick house on the hill between the parishes of Cerese and Piétole ("Mount Virgilius") was pointed out as the house of the poet. It is now long gone.

Virgil did not enjoy **Rome** as a residence and stayed there as infrequently as possible. Under the patronage of the statesman Maecenas, Virgil lived (54–50 B.C.) in a house that stood near the gardens of Maecenas on the southwestern slope of the Oppian Hill in the vicinity of the later Baths of Titus (ca. A.D. 80), of which scarcely anything remains. The Oppian Park, entered from the Via Labicana, now covers this area, which was also the heart of the Emperor Nero's great Domus Aurea (see the entry on Nero earlier in this section).

Virgil's most frequent and favorite Italian residence from about 49 B.C. was **Naples**, where he wrote the *Georgics* and *The Aeneid*. It is believed that he occupied a villa on the hilltop suburban site of Posilipo, perhaps inherited from his teacher Siro.

Virgil tomb (reputed): Strada di Piedigrotta, **Naples**.

VIVALDI, ANTONIO (1678–1741). A major influence on Bach, this innovative composer and priest spent almost his entire life in **Venice**, his native city. Called the "red priest" for the color of his hair, Vivaldi achieved moderate renown during his lifetime as a choir director and virtuoso violinist, but it was generations after his death that he became noted for his prolific compositions, especially his concertos. None of Vivaldi's early home sites can be identified. From 1704 to 1718 and again from 1735 to 1738, however, he probably resided at his place of employment, the girls' orphan asylum of the Ospedale della Pietà, where he first served as violin master, then concert master. Concerts at the Ospedale gained a wide reputation for vocal and instrumental excellence, despite the frequent antagonism of church authorities. The 1745 Church of Santa Maria della Pietà, in the Riva degli Schiavoni, occupies part of the orphanage site where most of these concerts were held. The church has been reopened after recent restoration.

Exhibit: Vivaldi manuscripts may be seen at the National University Library, 19 Via Po, in **Turin**. (Open summer, Monday—Friday 8:00—2:00, Saturday 8:00—12:00; winter, Monday—Friday 8:00—5:30, Saturday 8:00—12:00; 555064; free.)

(See Chapter 1, AUSTRIA.)

WAGNER, RICHARD (1813–1883). The German composer spent several brief periods in Italy. In **Venice**, during the winter of 1858–59, he wrote the second act of his opera *Tristan and Isolde* (1865) at the 15th-century Giustinian Palace on the Grand Canal adjacent to the Rezzónico Palace (see the entry on Robert Browning earlier in this section). Wagner died in the 16th-century Vendramin Calergi Palace, also on the Grand Canal, said to be the finest Lombardesque palace in Venice, a masterpiece of Renaissance architecture. He had come there in September 1882 "in search of the sun," rented 15 rooms in the palace, and immersed himself in writing an essay, *The Feminine Element in Humanity*, which rehashed the racial and

sexual bigotries that he never overcame. He died of a heart attack in his wife Cosima's arms in February. On the landward side, the palace is numbered 2400 Fondamenta Vendramin.

In **Palermo** Wagner spent the winter of 1881–82 at the Hotel des Palmes, now the Grande Albergo e Delle Palme at 398 Via Roma. There he completed his opera *Parsifal* (1882).

(See Chapter 1, AUSTRIA, SWITZERLAND; also Chapter 2, FRANCE; also Chapter 3, PARIS; also Chapter 4, EAST GERMANY, WEST GERMANY; also Chapter 6, LONDON.)

PORTUGAL

Europe's southwesternmost nation, which occupies a rim of the Iberian Peninsula, is also one of the Continent's oldest. It achieved independence from the Spanish kingdom of León-Castile in 1179. Before that the area had been dominated in turn by Carthage, Rome, and a succession of Vandal, Swabian, Visigothic, and finally Moorish regimes.

From the 12th century to our own, the Portuguese monarchy existed under four separate dynasties; the last king, Manuel II, was deposed in 1910. For 60 years of that period (1580–1640), Portugal and Spain were united under Hapsburg rule. Portuguese mariners, inspired by the geographical seminars of Prince Henry the Navigator (who himself never set foot beyond Tangier), led the vanguard of overseas exploration and colonization in the 15th century and extended Portugal's maritime empire to Africa, Asia, and South America. While Portugal gave up the last of her large colonies in 1975 with the granting of independence to Angola and Mozambique, the country's past influence—as disproportionate as England's to its size— is seen in the fact that some 100 million people in the world still speak Portuguese. About a tenth of this total lives in Portugal itself.

After the collapse of the monarchy, Portugal's First Republic became a dismal succession of weak presidents, military coups, and political instability. Strong-man Prime Minister António Salazar clamped tight control on the country in 1932. His dictatorial regime lasted until 1974 when it was overthrown by a bloodless coup. Chaos reigned for a time, but in 1976 a new constitution gave Portugal a modern Socialist-democratic state.

While political dissension and huge economic problems continue to trouble the Second Republic, Portugal seems determined to stay on its new-found liberal path, gradually acquiring a new self-image in the process—this one based on its present assets rather than on memories of its old imperialistic empire. Today the country leads the world in sardine fishing, and port wine production (as well as of cork for the wine bottles). It enjoys the fastest growing tourist industry in Europe. The capital of Lisbon, which has a population of almost two million, ranks as one of the world's loveliest seaport cities. (Next to Porto in size, the third largest Portuguese city is Paris, France, where some 500,000 temporary emigrants work at menial jobs to enable their final retirement in a homeland that has a chronic surplus of people over jobs.)

Historic Portugal remains most noted for its great seafarers, whose voyages enlarged the world beyond European conceptions. Vasco da Gama and Ferdinand Magellan were only two beneficiaries of Prince Henry's intrepid scholarship. Yet Portugal could have harvested even greater benefits in world exploration and the rewards therefrom had not the conservatism and caution of its rulers handed the big prizes to Spain. Christopher Columbus himself would have reaped riches and glory for Portugal if its shortsighted monarch had not rejected his schemes, causing him to seek Spanish sponsorship, for Columbus was a Lisbon resident of long duration (though his specific home site remains unknown). Magellan also had to first go to Spain in order to circumnavigate the globe.

While few intact homes of these mariners survive, Portugal displays many grand memorials to its famous sons in the form of statues and monuments.

FIELDING, HENRY (1707–1754). The English novelist, sent by physicians to Portugal because of his declining health, spent his last months and died in **Lisbon**. The exact location of the villa which he leased for a year in the suburb of Junqueira—and where he completed his final work, *The Journal of a Voyage to Lisbon* (1755)—remains unknown to biographers.

Fielding tomb: English Cemetery, **Lisbon**.

(See Chapter 5, ENGLAND; also Chapter 6, LONDON.)

GAMA, VASCO DA (ca. 1460–1524). The first navigator and colonist to reach India by rounding Africa and sailing east (1498), was a native of **Sines**. The town is now a tanker terminus and refinery center and has been described by one observer as "a sinister tubular jungle into which only the most intrepid traveler will want to penetrate." In about 1500 da Gama built himself a manor there, having taken possession of the whole district on the strength of a promise from Manuel I. Despite his vast honors and reputation, however, the explorer never received legal title to the land, and the landowners evicted him.

In **Évora**, to which he moved in about 1507, da Gama occupied a house in the Rua das Casas Pintadas. He decorated it with lavish paintings of beasts and Indians, gilded with scrollwork made of gold, it was said, that he brought from the East. This was apparently his last home. In 1536 it became part of the Court and Palace of the Inquisition, which stood on the northwest side of the Largo do Marquês de Marialva.

Da Gama tomb: Church of Santa Engrácia, **Lisbon**.

HENRY "THE NAVIGATOR," PRINCE (1394–1460). Son of King John I of Portugal and Queen Philippa of Lancaster, English daughter of John of Gaunt, Henry was not only a geographer but the sponsor of the great ocean voyages that made Portugal a dominant sea power. He was, in the words of Alan Villiers, a genius. "No swashbuckling seafaring man but a quiet scholar, he led the ascetic life of a monk; yet his imagination roamed the earth, and his determination changed the history of the world." Prince Henry was born in **Porto**, where the royal palace of his birth stood in the Rua da Alfândeg a Velha. The heavily restored and rebuilt structure, later used as the Customs House, now houses temporary exhibitions and the city archives.

In **Lisbon** the prince would have known intimately the royal residence, the Paco de Alcáçova. This Moorish palace, adapted and used by Portuguese kings until 1521, stood on the south side of the Moorish Castle of St. George (*Castelo de São Jorge*), the citadel that occupied the center of Phoenician and Roman Lisbon and which now lies in ruins. Later used as a prison, the castle retains its old terraces and towers, which command spectacular views of the city. Duck ponds now occupy the inner ruins of the residential palace.

After participating in four short crusades to North Africa, the mariner-scholar retired in 1419 to Portugal's (and Europe's) southwest coastal extremity and lived there for the rest of his life. He first occupied a small house in the village of **Raposeira**. Guadelupe Church, in which the prince worshipped, survives there.

From 1417 until his death, Prince Henry was grand master of the Order of Christ, whose great wealth supported many of the expeditions he sent out. Ruins of his palace lie adjacent to the 12th-century palatial Convent of Christ, at the crest of the hill above the town of **Tomar**; he probably occupied it frequently though for relatively brief periods.

Henry established his observatory and school of navigation at nearby **Sagres** in about 1420, creating what was really an ongoing seminar. Mathematicians, chart makers, astronomers, master mariners, and chroniclers came and went, each contributing new information on seas, tides, winds, and the coasts and lands that were being discovered on voyages down Africa's west coast. Though Henry's practical aims were to map sea routes, increase Portuguese trade, and extend Christianity, he also taught and accumulated geographical knowledge as a scholarly endeavor. The final result of his work was the establishment of ocean navigation as an exact science. Henry obtained royal concession of the entire bleak headland of Sagres in 1443 and began building the town which would act as host to his students and captains. Nothing remains of Henry's "school" on the neck of this windy peninsula except a circle of stones in the shape of a huge compass; they lie on a spot where he may have personally conducted classes in seamanship. Located on the grounds of a later fortress, this site, which fostered the great age of exploration, seems itself to be a prime candidate for exploration of the archaeological type. A film is shown (there is an English-language version) on the life of the great navigator. (Open daily; admission.)

Prince Henry's own solitary home, more fortress than palace, was the Vila do Infante, which he built on a desolate jut of rock about five kilometers west of Sagres toward Cape St. Vincent. Its entrance faced inland, and there the prince died. The English pirate Sir Francis Drake invaded the villa's thick stone walls in 1597 and sacked the house, and the devastating earthquake of 1755 further damaged it. Only ruins remain.

Prince Henry tomb: Church of Santa Engrácia, **Lisbon**.

Exhibits: In **Lisbon** the Naval Museum, Praça do Império in the Belem section of the city, displays the sword used by Prince Henry against the Moors in 1415; it is the one with which he was also knighted by his father. (Open Tuesday—Saturday 10:00—5:00, Sunday 11:00—6:00; admission.) Nearby, on the Avenida da India facing the river, stands the Padrão, a large stone monument which was erected in 1960 to commemorate Prince Henry and the age of Portuguese discovery. A mosaic map of the world as it was known to him decorates the base of the monument.

LIVINGSTONE, DAVID (1813–1873).
Exhibit: A few relics of the Scottish missionary-explorer, including his traveling-chair and telescope, are shown in the Geographical Society Museum at 100 Rua das Portas de Santo Antao in **Lisbon**. (Inquire locally for admission information.)

(See Chapter 6, LONDON; also Chapter 7, SCOTLAND.)

MAGELLAN, FERDINAND (ca. 1480–1521). Known as Fernao de Magalhaes in his native Portugal, the global circumnavigator was born in **Porto**, it is believed, but his family left few traces there or anywhere else in Portugal. Like Columbus before him, he left his homeland (1517) when royal support for his exploration plans was denied; and he too had better luck with the less shortsighted Spanish monarchy.

Before that, it is known, Magellan worked in **Lisbon** in the marine department of the royal government, probably in a building that stood somewhere along the Tagus River waterfront.

(See SPAIN in this chapter.)

SPAIN

"The Spaniard," writes Hugh Thomas, "is contradictory and inclined to go to extremes. He is either elaborately garrulous or gloomily silent, violently animated or coldly indifferent. He sees things as either black or white, heaven or hell, an agony or an ecstasy." And despite "the brilliant sunshine that constantly recalls the pure joy of living," says Thomas, the Spaniard "is morbidly preoccupied with the idea of death."

With the exception of Germany after World War II, probably no other European nation suffered such steep and drastic decline from major international standing as Spain. But the beginnings of Spain's decline came much earlier. From its 16th-century high point as the world's richest and most powerful country—when it controlled not only much of Europe but also the Philippines, most of Central and South America, and what became the southwestern United States—its own internal policies combined with merciless European geopolitics led it down a long road of divisiveness, economic chaos, and totalitarian dictatorship. That road has, at times, seemed an endless descent. Today, however, encouraging signs exist that Spain has "bottomed out" and is ready to seek more rational solutions to its age-old problems. As a new generation of leaders grapple with these problems and attempt to bring Spain into political and economic parity with its neighbors, the country's energy and determination for reform seems higher than it has for centuries. Nobody is more aware than the Spaniards themselves of their past greatness, their sad decline, and their present difficulties—subjects which are the source of endless analysis in the nation's press, social institutions, and streetcorner conversations. Not least among the causes of Spain's long trauma, many believe, is the fact of its extremely competitive regionalism, a situation which has been fostered by its mountainous geography. Most Spaniards identify themselves primarily as Galicians, Andalusians, Catalans, Castilians, and so on, rather than as Spaniards. National unity exists to a lesser extent than in any other European country, and it has been that way since Spain achieved its present borders in 1492. Spain's 13 regions remain highly diverse, not only in history and economic activity, but in speech, cultural ancestry, and general outlook on life. The Spain of Catalonia is not the Spain of Old Castile, as any traveler will discover; nor are "typically Spanish" flamenco dances strumming guitars, and picturesque donkeys representative of the country as a whole—that familiar "Spain" is mainly Andalusia.

"Spain, partly for climatic reasons," as Ian Robertson notes, "is almost a continent in herself." Chilly winds in the Gothic north contrast vividly with its sun-baked African south. In its peninsular isolation from the rest of Europe, separated from France by the jagged Pyrenees, Spain has also stood alone in other ways. The great cultural movements that have shaped much of modern Europe—the Protestant Reformation, 18th-century rationalism, the French and Industrial revolutions—largely bypassed Spain. The country is probably the most "un-European" of Continental nations, for the historic influence of its African

Moslem conquerors is almost impossible to overestimate, both in Spain's present culture and in the makeup of its population.

The original Spaniards, the Iberians (of whom the culturally distinct Basques may be descendants), probably settled the peninsula from North Africa in about 3000 B.C. Celtic invaders dominated the northern regions after 1000 B.C., and, Phoenician and Greek colonies introduced commerce, writing, the vine, and the olive. Carthage gave the land its name (*Span* or *Spania*, meaning "land of rabbits"). And from Carthaginian Spain came the great general Hannibal to challenge Roman rule of the world—an attempt that almost succeeded. Rome achieved mastery over the peninsula in the first century A.D., built large, thriving cities, and brought more actual unity to the country than it has enjoyed in most centuries since. Natives of Roman Spain included Trajan and Hadrian, two of the empire's most notable leaders. The Visigoths replaced Roman control in 411 and ruled Spain from Toledo until the early eighth century, by which time Spain had embraced Catholicism.

In 711 began a period of epochal importance. The Moors (Moslem inhabitants of Morocco), first invited by a politically beleaguered Visigothic king, swept across the entire peninsula in the space of seven years. Aflame with religious zeal, they not only spread the Moslem religion but created one of Europe's most humane and remarkable civilizations. Cultivating a high degree of literacy, establishing universities, introducing distinctive styles of architecture as well as new crops and industries, the Moors also gave a wide latitude of religious tolerance to their Christian subjects (a policy that Christians in like positions have usually found immensely difficult). While most of Spain remained under Moslem rule for more than three centuries, sporadic conflicts were almost continuous as Christian nobles and churchmen fought to regain their lost estates. They made decisive gains in the 11th century as the Moslem empire began to crumble from internal dissension; and in the 15th century proceeded to recapture the peninsula, finally conquering Granada, the last Moorish stronghold, in 1492. The 1469 marriage of Ferdinand and Isabella, meanwhile, united the kingdoms of Aragon and Castile, gave Spain its modern boundaries, and prepared the country for its emergence as a major world power. That zenith was reached during the reign of Philip II. But it was also during Philip's reign, in 1588, that England shattered the Armada, ending Spanish rule of the seas and ushering in four centuries of ill-advised military ventures, domestic conflicts, the establishment and overthrow of several monarchies, and declining international prestige.

Roman Catholicism, never less than powerful in Spain since its establishment as the state church in 589, found its most strenuously bigoted clergy in Spain. Ferdinand and Isabella, guided by Torquemada, established the notorious Inquisition in 1480 and Spain became the center of the Counter-Reformation—the world watchdog of Christendom, guarding the purity of doctrine and enforcing its will in Spain by torture and the stake. Led by the Jesuits, an aggressive, tightly disciplined corps of priests whose founder, St. Ignatius of Loyola, was a Basque, Spanish churchmen spread a militant brand of Christianity throughout Europe and the New World. Along with the rise of the nobility and the church as Spain's dominant ruling powers—and even as Columbus planted the Catholic flag in the New World in 1492—came a virulent anti-Semitism. It resulted in the expulsion of all Jews—the nation's professional trade class—from Spain. The collapse of the absolutist monarchy in 1808, Napoleon's placement of his brother Joseph on the Spanish throne, and the Duke of Wellington's 1814 victory over Bonapartist control marked stages in the decline of the once powerful nation. And subsequent restoration of the Bourbon monarchy did not halt the internal conflicts: traditionalists against liberal reformers, priests against a strongly populist anti-clericalism, outlying regions against centralized control from Madrid, a deprived working class against depraved, oblivious landowners. The army and the church functioned hand in glove as the real powers behind a succession of weak monarchs, while Spain's colonial empire dwindled and was all but gone by 1825; only the Philippines, Cuba, and Puerto Rico remained of its once vast dominions, and the American-contrived Spanish-American War took these. Anarchy and dictatorship held sway during much of the 20th century.

The culmination of Spain's bitter centuries of factionalism and misrule was its Civil War. This bloody conflict of 1936–39 provided a prolonged rehearsal for World War II as the German and Italian dictatorships rushed to support Gen. Francisco Franco's Fascist uprising, while the Soviet Union and Mexico lent halfhearted aid to the constitutional but hopelessly divided Republic. Franco's Nationalist victory represented the triumph of centralized power over regional autonomy, of the church against intellectual freedom, of the landowning class against the workers. The Falange became the only political party permitted in Spain; civil liberties were rigidly curtailed; and Franco, reliably backed by the army and church, became Spain's strongman. Wooed by both sides during World War II, Franco skillfully maintained a tightrope policy short of neutralism, first favoring the Axis, then the Allies. After the war he survived a period of international ostracism, a consequence of his wavering, and Spain was finally admitted to the United Nations in 1955. In the meantime his sordid regime was kept financially afloat by massive American aid and cold-war defense agreements which served to legitimize his autocracy. The law of succession, endorsed by national referendum in 1947, provided for a member of the royal family, which had been pushed aside in 1931, to succeed Franco. In 1969 the dictator named Prince Juan Carlos as his successor.

This Bourbon prince mounted the throne as Juan Carlos I in 1975 when Franco died. Political reform rapidly followed the accession of this popular constitutional monarch. The rigid press censorship ended in 1977, and that same year the first general election in 41 years brought a center-right coalition to power. The death penalty was abolished and divorce was legalized. In 1982 a Socialist majority won the national election and formed a government that has tried to distance itself as far as possible from the discredited Franco regime.

Spain's great literary master was Cervantes, whose immortal *Don Quixote* has been reprinted more often than any book except the Bible. Spain's creative genius has been most manifest, however, in the visual arts. Goya, El Greco, Velázquez, Picasso, Miró are only the foremost names in the artistic wealth that Spain has given the world. Chief plunderer but also colonizer of the New World, Spain is also well remembered for its explorers and *conquistadores*. After Portugal's cautious rejection of the daring schemes of such men as Columbus and Magellan, Spain not only welcomed their projects but reaped their glory. The great Magellan sailed from Spain to prove the world round, and the Italian-born Columbus opened the way for men such as Balboa, Cortés, and Pizarro to subdue large portions of the Americas for mineral wealth. The soldiers gave way in turn to generations of Spanish priests who labored to convert the robbed and vanquished American natives to a religion that claimed to abjure riches. Today both the Spanish language and Roman Catholicism are still dominant below the U.S. border, and testify to the effectiveness of Spain's historic conquests.

Spain's role has thus been large indeed, a profoundly mixed panoply of wealth, poverty, barbarism, courage, and genius. Both immoderate and immodest in most of its enterprises, the nation itself has not infrequently resembled that poignant man of La Mancha—riding forth on a sad horse to subdue the world with his sensible alter ego, Sancho Panza, providing rueful commentary and shaking his head.

With a population of about four of Spain's 37 million, Madrid, which was created the Spanish capital by Philip II in 1560, remains the capital and largest city. It is followed in size by Barcelona and Valencia.

Spanish museums are rapidly being modernized and increased in number. Most experienced travelers, however, agree that Spanish officialdom has much to learn about conventional European standards of museum display and public relations. The sometimes excessively custodial Patrimonio Nacional operates many of the larger, more important palaces; most of them admit only group tours, the pace of which often seems designed to remove visitors as soon as possible. Like most countries burdened by a totalitarian past, Spain lags in certain matters of public courtesy. Some of the older guidebooks are full of stern advice about standing your ground in Spain, not taking no for an answer from reluctant guides and custodians, and so on. However, since the situation is steadily improving, such strenuous guest-work is less called for today.

AUGUSTUS (63 B.C.–A.D. 14). The first Roman emperor made Hispania Tarraconensis the capital of a Spanish Roman province in 26 B.C. when he wintered there. Now known as **Tarragona**, the modern city contains only ruins of the numerous magnificent buildings he constructed. The Palace of Augustus, also called the Torreon de Pilatos from the fable that says Pontius Pilate once ruled here, is said to be part of the palace in which the emperor resided. It is located in the Bajada de Pilatos. The Emperor Hadrian also stayed here in A.D.

121 during one of his trips to the Spanish provinces.
(See ITALY in this chapter.)

BALBOA, VASCO NUÑEZ DE (1475?–1517). One biographer called Balboa "the most attractive and tragic figure in the Hispanic conquest of the New World." The first European to see the Pacific Ocean, which he named the "South Sea" and claimed for Spain in 1513, Balboa founded and governed the small colony of Darien in Panama. It was the first Spanish settlement in continental America. Four years later the explorer was executed on a trumped-up charge of treason.

Balboa was a native of **Jerez de los Caballeros**, where he was born into a patrician family. He probably lived in the town until he sailed for the New World in 1500. His birthplace, a small dwelling crusted with centuries of whitewash, stands at 10 Calle Cortés.

Exhibit: See the entry on Christopher Columbus, *Exhibits* (Seville).

BORGIA, CESARE (1476?–1507). The Italian Borgia family was Spanish in origin, with the surname *Borja*. In addition to Cesare, brutal soldier and infamous conspirator, it produced Popes Calixtus III and Alexander VI, the political pawn Lucrezia Borgia, and St. Francis Borgia. After Pope Alexander's death in 1503, his son Cesare was exiled to Spain by the succeeding Pope Julius II. From 1504 to 1506 he was imprisoned in the fortress of La Mota in **Medina del Campo**. This 15th-century brick and turreted castle, standing just east of the town, has been restored. Borgia escaped in 1506 but was soon killed in the siege of the castle at Viana.

Borgia tomb (site): Church of Santa Maria, **Viana**.
(See ITALY in this chapter.)

BOSCH, HIERONYMUS (1450–1516).
Exhibit: The Prado Museum in the Paseo del Prado, **Madrid**, displays three major altarpieces and several smaller paintings by this Dutch master, who is known in Spain as "El Bosco." (See the entry on Francisco de Goya, *Exhibits*, for admission information.)
(See Chapter 4, THE NETHERLANDS.)

CASALS, PABLO (1876–1973). Master cellist, composer, and conductor, Casals was born in

Vendrell, where his family occupied the two upper floors of the narrow stone house at 2 Calle Santa Ana. There the young prodigy began composing at age six or seven.

In **Barcelona** he lived with family friends in the Calle Nuevo de San Francisco while attending the Municipal School of Music (1887–92) at 7 Calle Lladó. From 1896 to 1900 he established his family and himself at 6 Plaza de Cataluna. Later, from 1919 to 1936, he made his permanent home base at 440 Avenida General Goded, where he founded the Casals Orchestra and stayed until official harassment made his life in Spain impossible. If Spain had no room for such native resources as Casals and Picasso under the Franco regime, however, France and the rest of the world eagerly embraced them both. Neither of these great artists ever returned to live in Spain after 1940 (see the entry on Picasso later in this section).

In **Madrid** Casals lived at 8 Calle de San Quintín with his mother and brothers while studying at the Madrid Conservatory (1893–95). They occupied the top floor of this 1845 building.

Casals built his summer home, the Villa Casals, on the Mediterranean beachfront at **San Salvador** in 1910 and resided there for lengthy periods each year until his exile. Since his childhood this village, located four kilometers south of Vendrell, had been the Casals family's summer haven. Casals renovated and enlarged his villa during the late 1920s, laid out extensive gardens and terraces, and entertained many of the world's foremost musicians and composers. In 1939, upon a brief return trip from a concert tour, he found the house crowded with Civil War refugees. The Franco government took possession of the house for a year, then turned it over to Casals's brother Lluís. It remains privately owned.

Casals tomb: Village cemetery, **Vendrell**.

(See Chapter 2, FRANCE; also Chapter 3, PARIS.)

CERVANTES SAAVEDRA, MIGUEL DE (1547–1616). Although some 10 other Spanish towns and cities have claimed to be his birthplace at various times, authorities generally agree that Spain's foremost writer and the world's first great novelist was a native of **Alcalá de Henares**. His birthplace stood at 48 Calle Mayor. The present house, a 1955 reconstruction, incorporates only the patio pillars and the well shaft of the original dwelling. Now a Cervantes museum, it displays period furnishings as well as books and documents relating to the novelist. (Inquire locally for admission information.) A contesting claim for his birth site is also made for a tablet-marked spot in the Calle de Santiago.

In **Esquivias** near Toledo, Cervantes married Catalina de Salazar in the still-existing church in 1584. The couple lived with the bride's parents until 1586, and again in 1602–03. The two-story house still stands in the village.

A "failed" writer, Cervantes worked as a minor bureaucrat. But he failed at his commissary and tax collection duties too. He spent brief periods in prison during the 1590s because, while he was perfectly honest, he couldn't keep his accounts straight. These cells included a site at 52 Calle de las Sierpes in **Seville**; and the surviving Town Hall in **Castro del Rio**, where his son was born.

Cervantes probably conceived and may have begun the first part of his great novel, *Don Quixote*

HOUSE OF CERVANTES. The author of *Don Quixote* probably wrote part of that great novel during his three years at 10–16 Calle del Rastro in **Valladolid**. The house is open to the public.

(1605), while imprisoned in 1597 at **Argamasilla de Alba** in the heart of the plain of La Mancha. He is said to have modeled his hero after a local nobleman, Don Rodrigo de Pacheco, whose portrait hangs in the parish church. The prison, called the Casa de Medrano, has been rebuilt on the site of the original.

In 1603 Cervantes occupied a dismal apartment in a house at 10–16 Calle del Rastro, off the Calle de Miguel Iscar in **Valladolid**. It was his home until 1606. He is believed to have written much of *Don Quixote* in this two and one-half story dwelling, which has been restored by the Hispanic Society of America. It now exhibits period furnishings and material illustrating the history of the house as well as the life and works of Cervantes. (Inquire locally for admission information.)

The poor and unknown writer's final residence in 1616 was a rented house that stood until 1833 at the corner of the Calle de León and the Calle de Cervantes in **Madrid**. Cervantes died there.

Cervantes tomb (unmarked): Trinitarian Convent, **Madrid**.

Exhibits: In the village of **El Tobosco**, various editions of Cervantes' novel and exhibits on life in Spain during his time are displayed in the House of Dulcinea, Don Quixote's lady love. (Inquire locally for admission information.)

CHOPIN, FRÉDÉRIC (1810–1849).
See GEORGE SAND.
(See Chapter 2, FRANCE; also Chapter 3, PARIS.)

CID, El. See RODRIGO DÍAZ.

COLUMBUS, CHRISTOPHER (1451–1506). He was Admiral of the Ocean Sea, and a sure way to antagonize Spaniards is to suggest that *Cristobal Colon*, as they call him, was not a native of Spain. Insistent claims for the explorer's Spanish birth have been made by generations of Spanish historians and nonscholars alike, despite general biographical consensus that the man credited with the discovery of the New World was Italian-born. Columbus certainly considered himself a Spaniard from his late 30s, though, and his four expeditions to the Americas were all sponsored by the Spanish government. Despite the ornate "tomb" in the Cathedral at Seville, however, his actual remains lie in Santo Domingo, Dominican Republic.

Columbus's first Spanish residence, in 1484, was the Franciscan Monastery of **La Rábida** near Seville. He left his young son, Diego, to be raised there while he sought the favor of the Catholic Monarchs for a dreamed-of enterprise—leading a sea expedition to "Asia." He returned to the monastery at intervals to see his son. In 1491, distraught after his idea had been rejected by Queen Isabella, he arrived there and prepared to go to France. Then came a summons from the queen: influenced by the prior of the monastery, she had decided to reverse her decision. Columbus returned to the monastery again in 1493 after his first voyage. A later resident was Hernando Cortés, one of Columbus's harsh successors in New Spain. The convent buildings, dating in part from the 14th century, were restored in 1892. Models of Columbus's ships and the room in which he lodged may be seen. (Open daily, 10:00—1:00, 4:00—7:00 donation.)

From 1484 to 1486, seeking to interest the University of **Salamanca** in his exploration schemes, Columbus resided at the 12th–century Dominican Monastery of San Esteban, located east by footbridge from the Calle San Pablo.

The explorer's subsequent movements and residences between voyages are difficult to trace. Often he followed the peripatetic court of his sovereigns, Ferdinand and Isabella, and he presumably lodged in the environs of whatever royal palace they happened to occupy during these periods (see the entry on Ferdinand II and Isabella I later in this section).

Arrested in Santo Domingo in 1500 for his dealings with rebellious natives, Columbus was brought back to Spain in chains. Suffering painfully from arthritis or perhaps rheumatic fever, he was lodged in the 1401 Carthusian Monastery of Las Cuevas in **Seville**. Soon released, he maintained residence there until 1502 while trying to reinstate his stripped honors and claims. The monastery later became his temporary tomb (1507–42). This complex of buildings, altered for use as pottery warehouses and workshops in 1841, is now known as the Cartuja. It is located west of the city and the Guadalquivir River, north of route 433. Restoration of some of the older buildings is planned.

Columbus's final return to Spain in 1504, after his unsuccessful fourth voyage, was a sad affair. Swollen and crippled, he made pathetic, imploring attempts to have his still-withheld claims validated but to no avail. He followed Ferdinand's court to **Valladolid** in 1506, then took to his deathbed at what is now the Columbus House-Museum in the Calle de Colón. A small exhibit of documents and maps is displayed. (Inquire locally for admission information.)

Exhibits: In **Seville** the Cathedral Museum in the Avenido Queipo de Llano exhibits the world-renowned Columbus Library, which houses the great explorer's manuscripts and books. Founded in 1552 by his son Fernando, the library also contains many other rare manuscripts and volumes. (Inquire locally for admission information.)

Also in Seville, the General Archives of the Indies in the Plaza del Triunfo displays a wealth of maps and documents (including letters signed by Columbus and Magellan) relating to New Spain. (Open Tuesday—Sunday 10:00—2:00; admission.)

A full-size replica of the explorer's 1492 flagship, the *Santa Maria*, may be seen at the Maritime Station in the harbor in **Barcelona**.

(See ITALY in this chapter.)

CORTÉS, HERNANDO (1485–1547). The conqueror of Mexico, one of Spain's most brutal and aggressive *conquistadores* (Mexico permits no statue of him to this day), was a native of **Medellín**. It was his home until 1504. His reputed birth site is marked by a stone tablet and a bench that was supposedly the door lintel of his home in the village.

During his first return to Spain (1528), Cortés lodged at the same Franciscan Monastery of **La Rábida** where Christopher Columbus had stayed some 35 years earlier (see the entry on Columbus above).

The conqueror made penance during his last years for the atrocities he had committed against the Aztecs, and he conceived the wish to die in Mexico. En route to his embarkation, he expired in the village of **Castilleja de la Cuesta** near Seville. A small 18th-century castle stands on the site of the Irlandesas Convent where he died. Located in the Calle Real, it has a small display of items relating to the Mexican conquest. (Inquire locally for admission information.)

Exhibit: See the entry on Christopher Columbus, *Exhibits* (Seville).

DÍAZ DE VIVAR, RODRIGO. ("EL CID") (ca. 1043–1099). Soldier of fortune and unabashed

opportunist in the battles between Castile and the Moors, El Cid's legendary exploits made him, in retrospect, a Spanish national hero and the prototypical cavalier. Folk epics, ballads, and Corneille's tragedy further amplified his legend. He "occupies in the heroic tradition of Spain," wrote Hugh Thomas, "the sort of place that King Arthur occupies in the tradition of England." Unlike the British warrior, though, there is no question that he really existed.

The village of **Vivar del Cid** near Burgos is the traditional site of his birth.

His longtime home from childhood, the Solar del Cid, stood in **Burgos**. The site of this ancestral mansion, a house demolished in 1771, is marked by a stone monument and two obelisks in the Calle de Fernán Gonzalez.

From 1081 to 1088 Díaz fought for the Moors against the Christian kings of Lérida and Aragon. His center of operations was probably La Aljafería, the Moslem palace completed in 1081 and now being restored, in **Zaragoza**. Used as a seat of the Inquisition, it was partially destroyed in 1809, then adapted for use as barracks, hospital, prison, and military installation. The original chapel as well as some original walls, ceilings, and decorative panels remain. The castle stands just east of the Plaza Portillo. (Open Monday—Saturday 11:00—1:30. 4:00—6:30, Sunday 11:00—1:30; admission.)

Exiled by the Castilian king, Alfonso VI, in 1081, Díaz retired briefly to the Monastery of **San Pedro de Cardeña**. Located 11 kilometers southeast of Burgos in the Castrillo del Val, it was built in 917. Díaz was buried there in 1099; a chapel was erected around his tomb in 1736. Though his remains were transferred to Burgos in 1919, the empty monument may still be seen. The hero's favorite horse, Babieca, was buried, it is said, outside the gates. An 11th-century tower and cloisters remain. Since 1950 the monastery has again belonged to its founding order, the Cistercians. (Open daily; donation.)

From 1094 until his death, Díaz ruled **Valencia**. His probable residence was the Moorish palace that stood on the present site of the 15th–century Lonja de la Seda (Silk Exchange) on the northeast side of the Plaza del Mercado.

Diaz tomb: Cathedral, **Burgos**.

Exhibit: In the cloisters of the **Burgos** Cathedral, Plaza de Santa María, may be seen the 1074 marriage contract between Díaz and Jimena, niece of

Alfonso VI. Also displayed is the fabled "Coffer of the Cid," an iron chest that he is said to have filled with sand then provided as surety for a loan from Burgos moneylenders. They never looked beneath the seal, trusting the knight's word that the chest was full of gold (the story doesn't explain why he would need a loan if he had all that gold). While it may not be authentic, the tale conveys El Cid's apparent lackadaisical attitude toward sacred oaths, an attitude that has charmed generations of anticlerical Spanish. (Open daily, 9:00—1:00, 3:00—7:00; admission.)

The reputed sword of El Cid, "La Tizona," may be seen at the Ejército (Army) Museum at 1 Méndez Núñez in **Madrid**. (Open Tuesday—Saturday 10:00—5:00, Sunday 10:00—1:30; 222—06—28; admission.)

DON JUAN. See MIGUEL DE MAÑARA.

FERDINAND II (1452–1516).
ISABELLA I (1451–1504).

The 1469 marriage of Ferdinand and Isabella joined the kingdoms of Aragon and Castile into a united Spain. The "Catholic Monarchs," as they are called, gave the country its first period—and one of its few—of able rule.

Son of King John II and Juana Enriquez of Aragon, Ferdinand was born in the Sada Palace in **Sos del Rey Católico**, an ancient walled village near Zaragoza. The palace, which still stands, was altered during the 17th century.

Until his marriage, Ferdinand's main residence would have been the castle of La Aljafería in **Zaragoza**, capital of Aragon (see the entry on Rodrigo Díaz earlier in this section). Both monarchs resided there during later visits, and their coats of arms are displayed in the Grand Staircase area.

In terms of activism and historical influence, Isabella was certainly Spain's (and possibly Europe's) greatest monarch. She inherited the kingdom of Castile and León from her half-brother, Henry IV, in 1474. The daughter of (another) John II and Isabella of Portugal, she was born in the Royal Palace in **Madrigal de las Altas Torres**. Later, as queen, she installed Ferdinand's illegitimate daughters here in order to keep them from marrying—a political move designed to thwart the possibility of later claimants through marriage to the Spanish throne. Remnants of the small palace are contained in the Augustinian convent, and the alcove in which the queen was born

may be seen. (Inquire locally for admission information.)

In nearby **Arévalo**, ruins of the brooding castle where Isabella resided with her mentally deranged mother from 1455 to about 1460 stand above the village. Parts of it are used for grain storage.

In **Ávila** she probably resided for a time (ca. 1460–62) at the Convent of Santa Ana, which survives at the northeastern edge of the city off the Avenida de Portugal. She came here again in 1468, seeking refuge from supporters who wanted to revolt and install her as queen when her brother Alfonso, the heir to Henry IV, died in suspicious circumstances.

Ferdinand and Isabella, distant cousins, met for the first time in 1469 only a few days before their marriage. The ceremony took place in the Palace of the Viveros in **Valladolid**, which stood on the present site of the 1562 Audiencia (Law Court).

According to tradition, the couple spent part of their honeymoon at the castle of **Fuensaldaña**, which still stands.

In the style of most European monarchs of their day, Ferdinand and Isabella were peripatetic rulers who traveled widely and often. In contrast to later times, the official center of power was not a permanent place but was invested in the persons of the monarchs themselves: thus, wherever they happened to be was, for the period of their presence, the actual "capital" of the country. Until their 1492 conquest of Granada, which drove the last of the Moors from Spain, the royal couple's main domiciles were Segovia, Seville, Toledo, and Córdoba.

The Alcázar in the Plaza del Alcázar, **Segovia**, overlooks the confluence of two rivers from a high bluff. The castle dates originally from Moorish or even Roman times and was enlarged in the 14th and 15th centuries. It was seriously damaged by fire in 1862. Its present appearance, except for the towers, dates mostly from a restoration begun in 1882. Paintings, weaponry, armor, and some of the medieval fixtures are on display. It was here in 1474, after a residence of several months, that Isabella learned of the death of Henry IV and was proclaimed queen of Castile and León. (Open daily, 10:00—7:30; admission.)

The Alcázar in the Plaza del Triunfo, **Seville**, arose on 11th-century Moorish foundations in 1366 and became the home of Spanish monarchs for almost seven centuries. Isabella built the chapel on the upper floor here, and the royal apartments, including Isabella's bedroom, display tile murals and wooden coffered ceilings. The couple's only son, Juan, was born there in 1478. Portuguese mariner Ferdinand Magellan lived there some 40 years later (see the entry on Magellan later in this section). (Open daily, 9:00—1:30, 4:30—7:00; admission.)

On the highest point of **Toledo**, the Alcázar, which had been built by Alfonso VI in 1085 on the site of a Roman fort, was rebuilt by Emperor Charles V, grandson of Ferdinand and Isabella, in the 16th century. Fires damaged and destroyed parts of it in 1710, 1810, and again in 1887. Dictator Francisco Franco lived there when it was a cadet school (see the entry on Franco later in this section), but a Civil War siege in 1936 left it in ruins. It has, however, been largely restored to its 16th-century appearance. The west facade dates from the reign of the Catholic Monarchs. Here the couple's daughter Juana ("the Mad"), mother of

Charles V, was born in 1479. The palace is approached from the Cuesta del Alcázar. (Open daily, 9:30—7:30; admission.)

Córdoba became the royal base for the war on Granada from 1485, and the 14th-century Alcázar in the Calle Amador de los Ríos was the monarchs' frequent domicile. Christopher Columbus first approached Ferdinand and Isabella here in 1486, seeking their support for his projected explorations (see the entry on Columbus earlier in this section). While Ferdinand at first rejected him out of hand, Isabella showed interest. The sailor hounded the couple from then until 1492 when Isabella, on the advice of her former confessor, reversed an earlier decision and gave the mariner full support—a decision that led in time to Spain's "golden age." (Open daily, 9:30—1:30, 5:00—8:00; admission.)

The year 1492 was also epochal in other ways. Not only did Columbus discover a New World

THE ALHAMBRA, SEAT OF MOORISH KINGS. After ousting its final defenders in 1492, Ferdinand and Isabella used this hilltop palace at **Granada** as a favorite retreat. Many of its features, such as the Court of the

Myrtles shown here, are exquisitely preserved. A bastion of the later Palace of Charles V towers incongruously behind the delicate restraint of Moorish pools and patios.

from which Spain would harvest abundantly, but Granada was won, ending the Moorish presence on the Continent. In that year, too, some 200,000 Jews, seen as a threat to the Catholic unity so highly valued by Isabella, were expelled from Spain. It was one of the queen's few shortsighted acts, wrote Hugh Thomas, depriving the country of "many of the people who formed the professional structure of the nation," and it ominously undermined Spain's increasing wealth and prosperity. In 1492 Ferdinand and Isabella, now at the height of their popularity, occupied the recently vacated Alhambra in **Granada**. Spain's outstanding architectural monument of its Moorish past, the Alhambra is not one building but a complex of structures built on the plateau above the city. The Alhambra dates mainly from the 14th century, though castles had occupied the site as early as the ninth century. Moorish rulers built and lavishly adorned its halls and courts; and here, with its surrender, they brought to an end one of Europe's most cultured and civilized dominions. Ferdinand and Isabella took intense interest in the palace complex: its acquisition represented the brightest jewel of their crowns. They repaired and strengthened the buildings, enjoying the spacious gardens and pavilions, and Isabella spent considerable time here, mainly in 1499, after the conquest. The building exteriors are deceptively simple and plain, but the delicacy of the interior ornamentation, the lacelike plaster and wood filigrees, the slender columns and arcades, give an overall impression of such fragility that one marvels at the fact of their survival. The Alhambra has, in fact, had some close calls. Charles V destroyed part of it to build his own massive (and massively incongruous) Renaissance castle in the heart of the Alhambra in 1526, and thus destroyed its stylistic unity. Two art museums occupy this grim, never finished palace. In 1812, after the Alhambra had suffered centuries of neglect, Napoleon's troops narrowly failed in their attempt to blow it up. American writer Washington Irving's *Legends of the Alhambra* (1832) romanticized and aroused interest in the dilapidated structures but it was not until 1862 that serious renovation attempts began. Today visitors see the Alhambra (or most parts of it) as it existed when the last of the Moorish kings ruled there. The Casa Real (Royal Palace) incorporated most of the main elements, including the Hall of the Ambassadors, the Court of the Lions, and the Hall of the Two Sisters. Irving resided for

three months of 1829 in the apartments of Charles V overlooking the Patio de Daraxa; the sadly derelict rooms are now undergoing restoration. The Alcazaba, the oldest part of the existing complex (ca. 1238), occupies the extreme western precipice of the hill. A Moorish citadel of which only exterior walls and towers remain, it affords a panoramic view of the surrounding plains and mountains—a sight which Ferdinand and Isabella must have viewed many times from this vantage. The Alhambra is entered via the Puerta Judiciaria, a 1348 gate tower, from the footpath of the Cuesta Empedrada; or, by car, at the Puerta de los Carros. (Open June—September, daily 9:00—7:00; October—May, daily 10:00—6:00; admission to buildings, grounds free.)

In 1485 Isabella gave birth to her second daughter who, as Catherine of Aragon, would become the first bride of England's Henry VIII in 1509. The birthplace was the 13th-century Archbishop's Palace in **Alcalá de Henares**; it now houses part of Spain's National Archives near the Puerta de Madrid.

In **Barcelona**, where the royal couple resided in 1492–93, they occupied the 14th-century Royal Palace in the Plaza del Rey. In its great hall, the Salón de Tinell, they received Columbus on his first return from America (1493). Purchased by the municipality in 1940 and restored, the palace also displays wall paintings from about 1300. (Inquire locally for admission information.)

Madrid became the primary royal residence in 1495. The palace where Ferdinand and Isabella resided, built by Henry IV about 1466 on the site of a previous Moorish castle, burned down in 1734. Its site is occupied by the present Royal Palace, begun in 1738, in the Plaza de Oriente (see the entry on Napoleon I later in this section). The Royal Armory in the palace displays swords of Ferdinand in room G21, and the Library exhibits missals that belonged to the pious couple (see the entry on Philip II, *Exhibits*, later in this section).

Another palace occasionally used by the monarchs was the Casa del Cordon, Avenida del Cid Campeador in **Burgos**. In this palace, which dates from 1482, the monarchs again hosted Columbus in 1496 after his second return from the New World. Their Hapsburg son-in-law, Philip I ("the Handsome"), the later King of Castile, died here in 1506. (Inquire locally for admission information.)

One of the queen's favorite retreats, the Dominican Convent of Santa María de la

Mejorada, survives in **Olmedo**. It is located on the northwestern edge of the town.

The Royal Palace in the center of **Aranjuez** is an 18th-century reconstruction of the original 14th-century palace on this site which the monarchs occasionally visited. Rococo salons are on display and there is a small museum which exhibits royal uniforms and period items. (Open daily, 10:00—1:00, 3:00—6:00; admission.)

Queen Isabella died in **Medina del Campo**, and the house in which she spent her last days and hours survives over an archway at the corner of the main plaza. Long used as a jail, the rooms are in derelict condition and remain barred to the public.

Ferdinand survived his wife by 12 years, and married Germaine de Foix, the young niece of Louis XII of France, in 1505. Though no longer king of Castile, he became regent for his insane daughter, Juana, in 1506 and thus continued to rule Spain until his death. He also continued to occupy most of the aforementioned palaces at various times. A decrepit old man, still trying desperately to father a son and heir (Germaine fed him a vile concoction containing bulls' testicles to restore his virility), he spent his last year in **Trujillo**. Standing above the town, the deserted, partly restored Moorish castle saw the final decline of this once-glorious monarchy as Ferdinand weakened (perhaps from his diet).

He died of a heart attack in **Madrigalejo**, a village near Guadalupe, while en route to La Serena.

Ferdinand and Isabella tombs: Capilla Real, **Granada**.

Exhibit: The sacristy of the Capilla Real, the royal chapel-mausoleum commissioned by the Catholic Monarchs in 1492 in **Granada**, displays several items of memorabilia relating to them. Among the exhibits are Isabella's crown and scepter, her mirror, embroideries she worked, and paintings from her private collection. Ferdinand's sword and banners used at the conquest of Granada may also be seen. The Capilla Real is located in the Plaza de la Lonja. (Open daily, 10:30—1:00, 4:00—7:00; admission.)

FRANCIS I (1494–1547). The Valois king of France, an eager warrior, suffered defeat in Italy at the Battle of Pavia (1525); he was imprisoned by Emperor Charles V in Spain until the Treaty of Madrid a year later. His probable place of confinement was the Tower of the Lujánes at 3 Plaza de la Villa, **Madrid**. The building was first restored in 1880. Now owned by the Royal Academy of Moral and Political Science, it contains the Hemeroteca Municipal, an outstanding newspaper library. (Open Monday—Friday 9:30—1:30, 4:30—8:30, Saturday 9:30—1:30; admission.) Francis was eventually removed to the Alcázar (see the entry on Napoleon I later in this section).

In the Calle Mayor, in **Illescas**, stands the house occupied by Francis in 1526 after his release from captivity.

(See Chapter 2, FRANCE; also Chapter 3, PARIS.)

FRANCO, FRANCISCO (1892–1975). While Franco brought a much-needed stability to Spain after decades of political turmoil, he did so at a terrible price in terms of human freedom. The soldier and 36-year dictator of Spain, who was courted by both Axis and Allied nations during World War II and later ostracized by the United Nations, nevertheless survived to become Spain's internationally accepted (if barely respected) leader. With the backing of the army and the powerful Roman Catholic Church, *el Caudillo*, as he was called, maintained tight control of every aspect of Spanish life. Leading the country backward into a pitiable state of fear and despair, he squelched its press, and filled its prisons with real and imagined opponents of his squalid regime.

A native of **El Ferrol** (later known as El Ferrol del Caudillo), Franco was born in a third-floor room at 134 Calle de Frutos Saavedra, a house bought by his grandfather in the 1850s. Franco and his parents inhabited the ground floor, and the house remained the parental home until his father died there in 1944. Franco himself left in 1907 but returned at intervals to visit his parents. Today the house displays relics of Franco the soldier; at the age of 33 he became Europe's youngest general since Napoleon. (Inquire locally for admission information.)

Franco received his military education at the Infantry Cadet School in **Toledo**. The famed Alcázar, which held the school from 1882 to 1936, was his residence from 1907 to 1910 (see the entry on Ferdinand II and Isabella I earlier in this section).

Franco achieved initial military fame in his campaigns (1920–26) against rebels in Spanish Morocco. From 1927 to 1931 he was director of the **Zaragoza** Military Academy, located in the Calle Nacional.

Though recent generations of Spaniards have been allowed to forget it, Franco was not a rebel leader at the outset of the anti-Republican insurgency: indeed, he mercilessly suppressed a 1934 antigovernment uprising, earning the nickname "Butcher." He finally joined anti-Republican plotters in 1936, took command of the insurgent forces, and received unstinting material support from Nazi Germany and Fascist Italy. During most of that fierce, bloody conflict, in which some 600,000 Spaniards died, Franco's home and headquarters (1937–39) was **Burgos**, specifically the Isla Palace in the Paseo de la Isla. Exhibits on his Civil War campaigns are displayed. (Inquire locally for admission information.)

From 1939 until his death, the pompous little dictator's residence was the village and moated palace of **El Pardo**, located 14 kilometers northwest of Madrid off route N4. His funeral Mass was also held there. A former royal dwelling, the present building dates from 1772. It stands on the site of a former palace completed in 1558 by Philip II (see the entry on Philip II later in this section), who used the surrounding wooded park as a royal hunting preserve. The present building was enlarged by Charles III and decorated by Charles IV and Ferdinand VII. The palace interior, it should be said, is much less elegant than its exterior. (Open to invited group tours; inquire locally for admission information.)

Franco tomb: Valley of the Fallen Monument, **Guadarrama**.

GARCÍA LORCA, FEDERICO (1898–1936). The poet and dramatist, a tragic victim of Fascist killers during the Civil War, is Spain's major 20th-century literary figure. A native of **Fuente Vaqueros**, a tiny village near Granada, García Lorca lived there only as an infant. His birthplace, a two-story, white-plastered brick house, survives inside a walled garden.

The son of a farmer, García Lorca grew up in a number of farm villages, including **Valderrubio**, **Vega de Zujaira**, and **Lanjarón**. In **San Vicente** the family spent vacations and holidays at "La Huerta de Vicente", a house bought by his father and still owned by the family in the Callejones de Gracia. García Lorca himself was last here in July 1936, a few weeks before his death.

In **Madrid** he lived for a decade (1919–29) in the famed Residencia de Estudiantes, 36 Calle San Marcos, a large apartment building where both formal and informal students were housed.

Painter Salvador Dali was a fellow resident there. García Lorca never married and often resided with his parents (1934–36) in the family apartment at 102 Calle Alcalá.

In August 1936, with his life in danger because of his well-known liberal sympathies, the poet hid from Falangist terrorists in the house of a politically conservative friend at 1 Calle del Angulo in **Granada**. There he was betrayed by an informer, arrested, and detained at the Civil Government building in the Calle de la Duquesa. Two days later he was shot at Viznar.

García Lorca tomb: Fuente Grande, **Viznar**.

GOYA Y LUCIENTES, FRANCISCO JOSÉ DE (1746–1828). One of Spain's greatest painters, Goya was born in **Fuendetodos**. His birthplace, a two-story, tile-roofed stone house, survives at 15 Calle de Alhóndiga. It remained his home until 1749. Period furnishings and personal memorabilia are displayed. (Inquire locally for admission information.)

In **Madrid**, from 1775 to about 1779, Goya lived with his wife, Josefa Bayeu, in a simple house at 66 Carrera de San Jerónimo. They then moved to 1 Calle del Desengaño, where they occupied a "handsome house" from 1779 to about 1819. Goya's last home in Spain was the "Quinta del Sordo," ("Deaf Man's Villa"). It stood on 65 acres along the Manzanares River, a long, low house where the now completely deaf painter lived from 1819 until he moved to France in 1824. There, during illness and despair, he painted the tortured murals known as the "Black paintings." Now a part of the branch railway, Goya Station, located west of the Paseo de la Ermita del Santo, is unrecognizable as a former dwelling.

Goya tomb: Church of San Antonio de la Florida, **Madrid**.

Exhibits: The foremost Goya collection is displayed in Spain's world-famous Prado Museum in the Paseo del Prado, **Madrid**. Room 55 contains his celebrated *Cartoons* (1776–91) for tapestries. Room 56A displays the "Black paintings" (see above), while the etchings entitled *Disasters of War* (1810–13), one of the most powerful antiwar indictments of all time, may be seen in room 53. Other Goya works, including the mysterious *Naked Maja* (ca. 1800), are exhibited in the Goya Rotunda, in room 32, and in room 10. (Open Tuesday—Saturday 10:00—6:00; Sunday 10:00—2:00; 230—34—39; admission, except free on Saturday.)

Other Goya canvases in Madrid may be seen at the Royal Academy of Belle Artes of San Fernando, 13 Calle Alcalá (inquire locally for admission information; 276—25—64); and at the Lázaro Galdiano Museum, 122 Calle Serrano. The *Conde de Miranda* (1777) displayed in the latter museum is the artist's first dated portrait (open daily, 9:15—1:45; 261—60—84; admission.)

The 1797 Church of San Antonio de la Florida has been the painter's tomb since 1919. It is now a Goya shrine, and is notable for the dome frescoes he painted in 1798. (Open Monday—Tuesday, Thursday—Saturday 11:00—1:30, 3:00—7:00, Sunday 11:00—1:30; 247—79—21; admission.)

(See Chapter 2, FRANCE.)

GRECO, EL. See DOMÉNIKOS THEO-TOKÓPOULOS.

HADRIAN (A.D. 78–138). Like his cousin and predecessor Trajan, Hadrian, one of Rome's greatest emperors, was a native of Italica. Formerly a prosperous Roman colony but now ruins in the Campos de Talca, it is located about one kilometer northwest of **Santiponce**. Hadrian lived there until about A.D. 86. Remnants of a forum, streets, mosaic floors, and an amphitheater remain. A small museum at the site entrance provides details on the excavations. (Open daily; admission.)

Also see the entry on Augustus earlier in this section.

(See ITALY in this chapter.)

HANNIBAL (247–183 B.C.). The Carthaginian general and would-be conqueror of Rome came to Spain in 237 B.C. with his father, the eminent Hamilcar Barca. It remained his home until he crossed the Alps in 218 B.C. to attack Italy. New Carthage, now **Cartagena**, became the center of Carthaginian power in Spain. The castle of the Barca family (who gave their name to the city of Barcelona) occupied the hill northeast of the Roman fort (now ruins) built on the city's highest point, the Castillo de la Concepcion. Puerta de la Serreta, the northern city gate, stands adjacent to the Barca palace site.

The 15th-century castle surmounting the town of **Játiva** is the traditional site of a previous castle where Hamilice, wife of Hannibal, bore a son during the latter's siege of Saguntum (now Sagunto) in 219 B.C.

HEMINGWAY, ERNEST MILLER (1899–1961). The American novelist, a bullfight aficionado as well as a major figure in 20th-century literature, loved Spain and spent numerous periods in the country. His first extended stay was in 1937–38, while living at **Madrid** with Martha Gellhorn in the Hotel Florida, his base for reporting the Spanish Civil War. His neighbors in the hotel included American writer John Dos Passos and French aviator-author Antoine de Saint-Exupéry. Hemingway made his own rooms available as a refuge for Spanish Loyalist fighters on leave. He also began his only play, *The Fifth Column* (1938), in these rooms. He returned to the hotel, which stood in the Plaza de Callao, briefly in 1953 during a visit. In the summer of 1954 he resided at the Palace Hotel at 7 Plaza de las Cortés. During Hemingway's last visit to Spain, in 1960, he shut himself for days in his suite at the Hotel Suecia, 4 Marqués de Casa Riera, worrying friends by his reclusive behavior; with hindsight, the episode seemed an ominous sign of the mental breakdown which was to cause him to take his own life a year later.

In **Pamplona**, where he liked to go in July to watch the traditional "running of the bulls" through the streets, he stayed (1959) in a small rented row house at 7 Calle San Fermín.

In **Churriana** near Málaga, Hemingway also stayed during intervals in 1959 and 1960 at the luxurious Hacienda de la Consula, the estate of his friend William Davis. Occupying a large corner room in the 1835 mansion, he celebrated his sixtieth birthday and worked on his last sustained piece of writing; ironically titled (in view of his increasing illness) "The Dangerous Summer," it was a long essay on bullfighters.

(See ITALY in this chapter; also Chapter 3, PARIS.)

IGNATIUS OF LOYOLA, ST. (1491–1556). Part of the birthplace of the Basque founder of the militant order of Jesuits, born Iñigo de Oñaz, stands in the Convent of the Sanctuary of **Loyola** in the Avenida de Loyola near Azpeitia. The Santa Casa, a portion of the tower house belonging to his prosperous family, displays personal relics of the saint. As a soldier in 1521, while convalescing from a severe leg wound received in the French siege of Pamplona, he began the introspective period of study that eventually led to the founding of the order. The present chapel on the second floor is the room he occupied during this period. Surrounded by buildings of the Jesuit College, the house also displays noteworthy decorations and reliefs illustrating the saint's life. A Jesuit radio station broadcasts from the basement. (Inquire locally for admission information.)

In **Manresa**, where he entered the Dominican convent in 1522, he began composing his *Spiritual Exercises* (1548) in the grotto immediately below the ruins of the 18th-century Church of San Ignacio. The 14th-century convent where he resided until 1523 still exists.

Exhibits: In **Pamplona** a brass plate in the sidewalk of the Avenida San Ignacio, near the Basilica of San Ignacio, marks the spot where Ignatius fell wounded in 1521.

The Church of the Jesuits in the Calle de Caspe, **Barcelona**, displays the sword which Ignatius left on the high altar of the Monastery of Montserrat in 1522 in order to symbolize his abandonment of military ambitions. (Open daily; donation.)

(See ITALY in this chapter; also Chapter 3, PARIS.)

ISABELLA I. See FERDINAND II.

LORCA, FEDERICO GARCÍA. See GARCÍA LORCA.

MAGELLAN, FERDINAND (ca. 1480–1521). The Portuguese circumnavigator of the globe enlisted the sponsorship of the Spanish king, Charles I (Emperor Charles V), in 1517 for a western voyage to the Portuguese Spice Islands (Moluccas). Earlier Magellan had sailed to the islands by the eastern route, via the Cape of Good Hope. Magellan organized the expedition in **Seville**. He maintained a headquarters on the Guadalquivir River front, probably within sight of the 1220 Torre del Oro, a tower battlement that was part of the wall of the Alcázar citadel. Magellan himself resided in the Alcázar during this period as the guest of the rich and influential Barbosa family, who were wardens of the palace (see the entry on Ferdinand II and Isabella I earlier in this section). Magellan married Beatriz Barbosa, daughter of the family, the same year (1517).

The voyage, from which Magellan himself was never to return, began on September 20, 1519, at **Sanlúcar de Barrameda**, in the Gulf of Cádiz, with five small ships and 280 men. The voyage also ended there three years later on September 6, 1522; only one ship and 18 survivors returned. Though there isn't much to see in this sun-baked little town today, the ocean front at Sanlúcar was the gathering point for seamen's families who bade farewell to their husbands and sons, many

for the last time, during the great age of exploration. Earlier, in 1498, Christopher Columbus had also departed from this point on his third voyage to America (see the entry on Columbus earlier in this section).

(See PORTUGAL in this chapter.)

MAÑARA, MIGUEL DE (1626–1679).
Exhibit: The legend of Don Juan, the inveterate rake, was first amplified and circulated by playwright Tirso de Molina. It has had numerous repercussions on European literature even into the 20th-century. Corneille and Molière built on the theme, as did Byron, Dumas, Goethe, Pushkin, and Shaw. Gluck, Mozart, and Richard Strauss used the legend for brilliant musical works. Mañara, the profligate noble of **Seville** who became the prototype for the Don Juan of music and story, eventually repented his wastrel ways and dissipated youth by entering the religious fraternity of the Caridad, an organization that provided Christian burial for executed criminals. He also paid for construction (1661–74) of the Hospital de la Caridad in the Calle Temprano. In the Chapter House may be seen a portrait of Mañara as well as his sword and death mask. (Open daily; donation.)

Mañara tomb: Chapel, Hospital de la Caridad, **Seville**.

MIRÓ, JOAN (1893–1983). A giant of Surrealism, "Miró was the last of the great modernist inventors," according to art critic Robert Hughes. His birthplace, a **Barcelona** apartment house, stands at 4 Pasaje del Credito, a small, gated street. The son of a goldsmith and watchmaker, Miró painted his first pictures there, and the address remained his Spanish base until 1950. In adulthood, he rented the floor above his parents' apartment, plus an attic studio which he kept until 1956. Miró rented his first studio in 1915 at 51 Baja San Pedro.

In 1911, near the village of **Montroig** south of Tarragona and close to the seacoast, Miró's father bought a farmhouse surrounded by several acres of olive trees and vineyards as a retreat where his son could recover from typhoid fever. Miró painted most of his early landscapes there. He commemorated the place in one of his most notable canvases, *The Farm* (1921–22), which novelist Ernest Hemingway bought. From about 1920 until 1956, Miró spent most summers there.

Miró always wished for ample studio space. After years of living and working in cramped apartments, his dream came true in 1956 when an architect friend, Josep Lluis Sert, built him a large, modern home and studio on the Balearic island of Mallorca (Majorca). He resided there for the rest of his long life, though ironically, the works he produced there are not considered among his most notable. The oceanfront estate is located in **Cala Mayor**, a short distance west of Palma de Mallorca. Miró bequeathed this property to the city of Palma, and it will probably be opened to the public as a museum at some future time.

Exhibit: The Joan Miró Foundation, Avenido del Estadio in the Montjuic section of **Barcelona**, displays the foremost collection of the artist's drawings, paintings, posters, sculpture, and weavings. (Open Monday—Saturday 11:00—8:00, Sunday 11:00—2:30; 319-19-08; admission.)

(See Chapter 3, PARIS.)

NAPOLEON I (1769–1821). At the height of the French emperor's power on the Continent, Spain rebelled against Napoleon's summary disposal of its king, Ferdinand VII, and his appointment of Joseph Bonaparte, his brother, in Ferdinand's place. Thus began the Peninsular War. Napoleon rushed to Spain in late 1808 with 180,000 men and temporarily stabilized the situation. In **Madrid**, where he resided at the Royal Palace until early 1809, he remarked to his brother, "You are better housed here than I at the Tuileries" (in Paris). Napoleon spent long periods in the palace silently studying the portrait of the long-dead Spanish monarch Philip II; "so long that the members of his suite," wrote Emil Ludwig, "watch in dumb amazement while the Emperor seems to be holding converse with the king." In 1812 the Duke of Wellington, having defeated Napoleon's troops in Spain as he would at Waterloo three years later, replaced Joseph Bonaparte as chief resident in the palace. Begun by Philip V in 1738 on the site of the previous palace occupied by Ferdinand and Isabella and Philip II, the present Royal Palace in the Plaza de Oriente was finished in 1764. A massive Renaissance neoclassical structure of 2,000 rooms (only 50 of which are open to visitors), the rococo interiors, royal apartments of Charles III, state dining room, throne room, and painting galleries are dominant features. The palace also serves the present restored monarchy as an official residence. (Open Monday—Saturday, 10:00—2:00,

4:00—7:00, Sunday 10:00—2:00, 248-74-04; admission.)

(See ITALY in this chapter; also Chapter 1, AUSTRIA, SWITZERLAND; also Chapter 2, FRANCE; also Chapter 3, PARIS; also Chapter 4, EAST GERMANY, BELGIUM.)

PHILIP II (1527–1598). The last of Spain's great monarchs, a Hapsburg, Philip inherited the world's most powerful nation as well as vast territories and possessions from his parents, Holy Roman Emperor Charles V and Isabella of Portugal. He married four times (his second wife, whom he rarely saw, was Mary I of England); waged Continental wars; and lost world naval supremacy when Sir Francis Drake defeated the Spanish Armada in 1588.

A native of **Valladolid**, Philip was born in what is now the provincial legislature building (*Diputación*), in the southeast corner of the Plaza de San Pablo. It dates from about 1500. This residence, say biographers, was the nearest to a permanent home that he enjoyed as a youth, since the royal court was a constantly moving establishment.

With his 1556 accession to the throne, Philip's lifestyle grew even more peripatetic. His residences included the alcázars and royal palaces of **Madrid** (his most frequent residence), **Toledo**, **Aranjuez**, and **Burgos** (see the entry on Ferdinand II and Isabella I and Napoleon I earlier in this section).

The hunting chateau in **Valsáin** was one of the monarch's favorite residences, and it was there, wrote biographer Edward Grierson, "that some of the most crucial decisions of the reign were taken." The chateau stood surrounded by an extensive royal forest, called "the Wood of Segovia" by the king. Burned in the 17th century, the chateau remains a neglected ruin.

Another frequent hunting lodge was **El Pardo** near Madrid; much later it became the residence of dictator Francisco Franco (see the entry on Franco earlier in this section). The present palace is a 1772 replacement of the 1543 chateau that Philip used and enlarged.

Philip II is most strongly identified with one of Spain's foremost historic treasures, the monastery and summer palace of the Escorial. Building began on a remote site northwest of Madrid in 1563 and was completed in 1584. Philip's pious objective was to create a monastery and royal mausoleum in gratitude for his 1557 victory over the French in

Flanders. He intended the palace to be simply an adjunct to the monastery of San Lorenzo del Escorial, but it became his most frequent residence after 1584. Here he dwelled as half-king, half-monk in almost monastic chambers inside the sumptous palace. They are among the rooms on display in the Royal Palace portion of the Escorial today. His whitewashed audience room with tilings and tapestries, the study where he received news of the Armada defeat, and the bedchamber where he died after weeks of agonizing illness ("Look at me and see how all the monarchies of the world end," were among his last words), may also be seen. The sedan chair in which he rode from Madrid to his deathbed, as well as other simple furnishings, are exhibited. Notable paintings and tapestries decorate the adjacent royal apartments which were used by succeeding generations of Spanish Hapsburgs and Bourbons until 1861, when the palace ceased to be used as a royal residence. Most of the art works which formerly hung throughout the palace are now grouped in the New Museums portion of the complex and make the Escorial one of Spain's foremost art museums. In the 40,000-volume library may be seen the missal used by Philip while concentrating on spiritual matters—as well as the large globe over which he pondered more earthly ambitions. Since 1885 the monastery has been occupied by the Augustinian order. The Escorial was designed in gridiron shape to symbolize the martyrdom of St. Lawrence, who was burned alive on a gridiron in A.D. 258. "It breathes the spirit of the Counter-Reformation," wrote one observer, an aspect also reflected in its granitic, fortress-like exterior. "The way in which the royal builder prescribed the most minute detail," wrote C. Justi, "his restless and omnipresent superintendence, his often niggling criticism . . . could not but paralyze the joy of creative energy," and the Escorial's resulting charm, "forming as it were a part of the landscape in which it is set," was apparently quite inadvertent. The rooms of architectural history in the basement of the Royal Palace display numerous designs, models, tools, and machines used in construction of this vast complex with its 120 miles of corridors, 80 staircases, almost 3,000 small windows, and 16 courtyards. The town of **El Escorial** has grown around the monastery-palace. (Monastery and palace open daily, 10:00—1:00, 3:00—7:00; admission; gardens and courtyards free).

During the 21-year building of the Escorial, Philip's residence was often what is now the clergy house in the nearby village of **Galapagar**.

Philip II tomb: Royal Pantheon, **El Escorial**.

Exhibit: Armor and ceremonial swords of this warrior-king are displayed in the Royal Armory in **Madrid** (see the entry on Ferdinand II and Isabella I, *Exhibits*, earlier in this section).

PICASSO, PABLO (1881–1973). The most renowned artist of the 20th century, this hugely versatile painter and sculptor was a native of **Málaga**. It remained his home until 1891. Picasso's birthplace survives at 16 Plaza de Merced.

From 1891 to 1895 the artist's family lived at 14 Calle Payo Gomez in **La Coruña**. Here José Ruiz Blasco, Picasso's father, renounced his own artistic efforts and gave his brushes and paints to his son—probably the most profound act of his life.

In **Barcelona**, the artist's home from 1895 at intervals to 1904, Picasso occupied several apartment and studio addresses. These included 4 Calle Llauder (1895); 3 Calle de la Merced (1896–97); 1 Calle de Escudillers Blancs (1899–1900, his "Modernist period"); and 28 Calle Comercio (1904), among others.

In **Madrid** he studied (1897–98) at the San Fernando Academy, now the Museum of the Academy of Bellas Artes at 13 Calle de Alcalá (see the entry on Francisco de Goya, *Exhibits*, earlier in this section). Later (1901) he lodged at 4 Calle Caballero de Gracia.

Exhibits: Picasso never resided permanently in Spain after 1904. Though the artist was a Spaniard, James A. Michener points out in *Iberia* (1968) that "Spaniards have never collected his work," and it was Paris that gave the artist his first recognition. Today, however, "Spain is desperately eager to reclaim this man as her son." Along with Pablo Casals and most of Spain's internationally known artists and intellectuals, Picasso regarded the Fascist Franco regime with loathing and contempt, and refused until his last years to sanction display of his works in the country.

In **Málaga**, his birthplace, the Museum of Bellas Artes in the Molina Larios displays a Picasso gallery containing early works. (Open Tuesday—Saturday 10:00—1:30, 5:00—8:00, Sunday 10:00—1:30; admission.)

The Picasso Museum at 15 Calle Montcada, in **Barcelona**, exhibits an important if hardly representative collection of works concentrating on the artist's early career (ca. 1889–1904). Picasso himself donated the collection to Barcelona in 1970 and it is housed in the 15th-century Aguilar Palace. (Open Monday 4:00—8:30, Tuesday—Saturday 9:30—1:30, 4:00—8:30, Sunday 9:30—1:30; 319–69–02; admission, except free on Sunday.)

The Cason del Buen Retiro at 13 Calle de Felipe IV, in **Madrid**, gratefully received and now displays one of Picasso's best-known paintings, the savage *Guernica* (1937), which laments the gratuitous terror-bombing of that Basque city in the Civil War. The painting was returned to Spain after restoration of the democracy in 1976, according to the artist's wishes. (Open Tuesday, Thursday—Saturday 10:00—5:00, Wednesday 3:00—9:00, Sunday 10:00—2:00; admission.)

(See Chapter 1, SWITZERLAND; also Chapter 2, FRANCE; also Chapter 3, PARIS.)

PIZARRO, FRANCISCO (1475?–1541). The ruthless conqueror of Peru was a native of **Trujillo**, where stands the baroque, three-story House of Pizarro (*Palacio Marqués de la Conquista*) in the Plaza Mayor. Never the actual residence of Francisco, this was the home of Hernando Pizarro, his half-brother, who, unlike Francisco, returned alive from South America. The large, stone family shield above a corner window is the most outstanding feature of the building.

Pizarro tomb: Church of Santa Maria de la Concepción, **Trujillo**.

Exhibit: The Royal Armory in **Madrid** displays a sword of Pizarro (see the entry on Ferdinand II and Isabella I, *Exhibits*, earlier in this section).

RUBENS, SIR PETER PAUL (1577–1640).

Exhibit: The Prado Museum in **Madrid** displays one of the world's largest collections of religious and allegorical canvases by the Flemish master (see the entry on Francisco de Goya, *Exhibits*, earlier in this section).

(See Chapter 4, WEST GERMANY, BELGIUM).

SAND, GEORGE (1804–1876). In 1838 the French novelist and her lover, composer Frédéric Chopin, came to the Balearic island of Mallorca (Majorca) in a fruitless attempt to mend Chopin's precarious health. Their residence of longest duration during a miserable rainy winter (they had ex-

pected a tropical paradise) was the 1399 Royal Carthusian Monastery in **Valldemosa**, from which the last monks had departed three years previously. The building was abandoned and derelict and the couple shared three frigid monastery cells. The villagers, meanwhile, frowned on the pair's illicit relationship, their refusal to attend church, and Sand's habit of wearing trousers and rolling and smoking cigarettes. Despite this period of "torture for him and torment for me," Sand wrote, she accomplished much: she collected notes for *A Winter in Majorca* and worked on her novel *Spiridion* (1838), took care of the ailing, anxious Chopin as well as her two children, and generally "held things together." Now restored, the old monastery occupies a spot of extraordinary pastoral beauty overlooking hills and flocks of sheep, views which were probably lost on the couple because of their excessive discomfort here. Memorabilia of their stay includes two pianos

REFUGE OF TWO LOVERS. But French novelist George Sand and composer Frédéric Chopin didn't enjoy much of their 1838 stay on the island of Majorca, where they came for Chopin's precarious health. The weather was freezing, the lovers squabbled, and villagers in **Valldemosa** looked askance at their illicit relationship and boycotted them. Their residence was this old Carthusian monastery, shown in a garden view.

reputedly used by Chopin, who worked at his Preludes and other works. (Open Monday—Saturday 9:30—1:30, 3:00—7:00; admission.)

(See ITALY in this chapter; also Chapter 2, FRANCE; also Chapter 3, PARIS.)

THEOTOKÓPOULOS, DOMÉNIKOS. ("EL GRECO") (1541–1614). Born in Crete, trained in Italy, El Greco ("The Greek") settled in **Toledo** in about 1577 and made it his permanent home. For 250 years after his death, the artist's intensely mystical distortions, elongated figures, and vivid contrasts of color and shadow marked him, wrote J. Carter Brown, "as an extravagant, even mad, painter who deserved little more than a footnote in history." Not until about 150 years ago did people begin taking a second look. "For us today," wrote Brown, "El Greco is one of the great prophets of modern art." He was also a highly learned man who wrote extensively on painting, sculpture, and architecture.

El Greco lived in the old Jewish quarter of the city, a section that afterward became a slum. About the time that interest in the artist was awakening, the area had become so dilapidated that most of it was soon demolished—but not before the Marques de la Vega Inclán bought one of the 16th-century houses (1905) and restored it as the Casa del Greco. The museum portion was subsequently enlarged and embellished with period furnishings and art works. "While these apartments are not the actual ones El Greco occupied," as biographer Pal Kelemen writes, "they give an atmosphere in which one can visualize the painter and his household." The El Greco paintings on display include *St. Francis and Brother Leo* (1600–05), and *View and Plan of Toledo* (1610–14). Among the few personal effects exhibited is the spinning wheel of his 37-year mistress, Doña Jerónima de las Cuevas. The House and Museum of El Greco are located in the Calle de Tránsito. (Open Monday 10:00—2:00, Tuesday—Saturday 10:00—2:00, 3:30—7:00; admission.) The site of the painter's actual dwelling from 1604 is located in the nearby park called the Paseo del Tránsito. There El Greco, his mistress, and their son occupied a lavish 24-room apartment in the palace of the Marqués de Villena overlooking the Tagus River gorge. The palace was torn down early in this century.

Exhibits: The spiritual heart of Spain was and is **Toledo**, which has been described as "an open-air

THE "HOUSE OF EL GRECO." Most biographers believe that the painter never lived in this **Toledo** dwelling. The restored, 16th-century residence does, however, display a fine art museum of El Greco's works.

gallery" of El Greco's works. His masterpiece, *Burial of the Count of Orgaz* (1586–88), hangs in the 14th-century Church of Santo Tomé, Calle Santo Tomé (open daily; admission). The Museum of Santa Cruz, located east of the Plaza de Zocodover, displays 22 of his paintings, including his 1613 *Altarpiece of the Assumption* (open daily, 10:00—7:00; admission).

(See ITALY in this chapter.)

TORQUEMADA, TOMÁS DE (1420–1498). The bloodthirsty "Himmler of the Counter-Reformation," a Dominican monk and confessor to Ferdinand and Isabella, Torquemada was made Grand Inquisitor by Pope Innocent VIII. It was he who organized the barbaric Spanish Inquisition, one of the most sordid instruments of church history, to root out Jews and supposed "heretics."

Probably a native of **Valladolid**, he took the Dominican habit in the Convent of San Pablo, still attached to the Church of San Pablo, Plaza de San Pablo, where he spent much of his youth.

Torquemada was stern prior of the Monastery of Santa Cruz in **Segovia** from 1452 to 1474. The monastery, restored in 1828 after a fire, lies along the Eresma River off the Ronda de Santa Lucia, at the northern edge of the city.

As Grand Inquisitor of the Roman Catholic Church and inquisitor general of Spain, Torquemada was a constant fixture at the movable court of Ferdinand and Isabella (see the entry on Ferdinand II and Isabella I earlier in this section), piously advising his monarchs on how best to burn heretics and expel the Jews from this supremely Christian kingdom. In **Granada** he is said to have occupied the 13th-century Moorish palace of Cuarto Real de Santo Domingo, one tower of which survives in the Plaza de los Campos Eliseos.

In 1482 this fierce policeman of the church began building the church and Royal Monastery of Santo Tomás, located in the Plaza de Granada in **Ávila**. He endowed the monastery and, from 1490 until his death, it was his chief residence, serving also as the main tribunal and prison for those who found themselves committed to his tender mercies. His monarchs sometimes spent vacations here and in 1497 buried their only son, Prince Juan, in the church. (Cloister open Monday—Saturday 10:00—1:00, 4:00—7:30; admission.)

Torquemada tomb: Church of Santo Tomás, **Ávila**.

TRAJAN (A.D. 53–117). Foremost soldier-builder of the Roman Empire, Marcus Ulpius Traianus was Spanish born. Though of Roman descent, he was the first Roman emperor born outside Italy. His birthplace—Italica, now a ruin near **Santiponce**—was also the birthplace of his successor Hadrian (see the entry on Hadrian earlier in this section).

(See ITALY in this chapter.)

VELÁZQUEZ, DIEGO (1599–1660). The highly influential court painter to Philip IV, mainly noted for his portraits, Velázquez anticipated Impressionism in his concern with the properties of light. His birthplace stood in the Calle de la Gorgoja, **Seville**, and was his home until 1610.

From 1622 he lived in **Madrid**, where he became court painter the following year, a position he maintained until his death. His last home, from 1655, was the Treasure House in the com-

pound of the Royal Palace; the two buildings were connected by a passage. Neither of them survives on the site of the present Royal Palace (see the entry on Napoleon I earlier in this section). The studio where he painted most of his numerous canvases of the royal family was in the former palace itself.

Exhibit: Paintings of Velázquez may be seen in many Spanish and other European museums, but the foremost collection is in the Prado Museum, **Madrid** (particularly room 12), which contains some of his best-known portraits and court scenes. (See the entry on Francisco de Goya, *Exhibits*, earlier in this section).

(See ITALY in this chapter.)

WELLINGTON, ARTHUR WELLESLEY, DUKE OF (1769–1852). The British conqueror of Napoleon first battled and defeated troops of the French emperor during the Peninsular War in Spain five years before Waterloo. It was in recognition of his Spanish successes that the Irish-born soldier was created a duke in 1814. He occupied various palaces and lodgings briefly during the years 1808 to 1814, while pursuing the French across the Iberian Peninsula. Probably his most significant abode was the Royal Palace in **Madrid**, which he occupied in 1812, replacing the French-imposed king, Joseph Bonaparte, as chief resident (see the entry on Napoleon I earlier in this section).

(See Chapter 3, PARIS; also Chapter 4, BELGIUM; also Chapter 5, ENGLAND; also Chapter 6, LONDON; also Chapter 7, IRELAND.)

NAME INDEX AND GAZETTEER

Listed here in approximately chronological order are all the known homes and residence sites for each noted person included in this book. Some listings are, however, more complete than others. As historians and biographers constantly add to our store of knowledge, many of these gaps can probably be filled. In the meantime, if you live in a house where someone notable has resided; if you know of such a house or site that isn't listed here; or even if you can supply a missing address for a known street; I invite your contribution of knowledge, c/o Facts On File Publications, 460 Park Avenue South, New York, NY 10016. Much of the present list has been compiled by means of such valuable cooperation and can likewise be improved.

KEY TO SYMBOLS AND ABBREVIATIONS
* Open to public visitation.
□ Extant dwelling but privately owned or occupied; not open to public visitation.
△ Site of dwelling, now vacant land or reoccupied by later structure.
X Site unknown.
Et seq. between two dates indicates that the house or site was occupied at irregular intervals between those dates; after one date only, it indicates occupation at irregular intervals for a lengthy but undetermined period from that date.
Exhibits are separately indexed only for pertinent locations not otherwise listed as residence locations.

ABÉLARD, PETER (1079–1142).
France, Le Pallet, la butte d'Abélard, Birthplace, 1079–95 △, 34
France, Paris, Abbaye Ste-Geneviève, 23 Rue Clovis, 1112–19, 1136 □, 79
———— 9 Quai aux Fleurs, 1118 △, 79
France, Laon, Benedictine Abbey, ca. 1113 □
France, St-Denis, Basilica of St-Denis, ca. 1120–23 □, 34
France, Soissons, St-Médard Abbey, Rue de Bouvines, 1121 △, 34
France, Nogent-sur-Seine, Abbey of the Paraclete, 1123–25 △, 34, 35
France, St-Gildas-de-Rhuys, St-Gildas de Rhuys Abbey, 1125–33 △, 35
France, Prissé, Chevigné Abbey, ca. 1137–39 □
France, Cluny, Abbey of Cluny, Rue Municipale, 1141 △, 35
France, Chalon-sur-Saône, Monastery of St-Marcel, 1142 △, 35
ADENAUER, KONRAD (1876–1967).
West Germany, Cologne, Birthplace, Balduinstrasse, 1876–? X, 130
———— Klosterstrasse, Lindenthal, 1904–06 X
———— Friedrich Schmitt Strasse, 1906–11 X
———— Max-Bruch-Strasse 6, 1911–33 △, 130

———— Kennedy-Ufer, 1944 △, 130
West Germany, Maria-Laach, Abbey, Laacher See, 1933–34 *, 131
East Germany, Neubabelsberg, 1934–35 X
West Germany, Bad Honnef-Rhöndorf, Konrad-Adenauer-Strasse 8a, 1935–67 *, 131
West Germany, Nister Mühle, 1944 X, 131
West Germany, Brauweiler, Brauweiler Prison, 1944–45 □, 131
West Germany, Bonn, Schaumburg Palace, Adenauer-Allee 139, 1949–63 □, 131
AESCHYLUS (525–456 B.C.).
Greece, Athens, Theatre of Dionysos, *Exhibit*, 309
Greece, Eleusis, Telesterion, *Exhibit*, 308
Italy, Gela, 471 B.C. 458 B.C. X, 319
ALEXANDER III, "THE GREAT" (356–323 B.C.).
Greece, Nea Pella, Palace of Archelaos, 356–34 B.C. X, 309
AMUNDSEN, ROALD (1872–1928).
Norway, Borge, Tomta, Birthplace, Highway 111, 1872 et seq. *, 172
Norway, Oslo, Little Uranienborg, Uranienborgveien 9, 1872–90 □ 172

Great Britain, London, 58 Queen Anne Street, 1851 ☐, 236

——— 10 Old Cavendish Street, 1852 △

——— 17 Old Cavendish Street, 1853 △

France, Paris, 4 Rue de Calais, 1856–69 ☐, 82

BERNADETTE OF LOURDES, ST. (1844–1879).

France, Lourdes, Boly Mill, Birthplace, Rue Bernadette-Soubirous, 1844 et seq. 1854 *, 36

France, Bartrès, 1840s, 1857–58 ☐, 36

France, Lourdes, Le Cachot, 15 Rue des Petits-Fossés, 1857–66 *, 36

France, Nevers, Convent of St-Gillard-de-Nevers, Rue St-Gildard, 1866–79 *, 36, 37

BERNHARDT, SARAH (1844–1923).

France, Paris, Birthplace (?), 5 Rue de l'École-de-Médicine, 1844–45 ☐, 82

——— 265 Rue St-Honoré, 1848, 1859–64 △, 82

——— 18 Rue Boileau, 1852–54 △

France, Versailles, Grandchamps Convent, 1854–59 △

France, Paris, Rue Duphot and Rue St-Honoré, 1864–68 X, 82

——— 16 Rue Auber, 1868–69 △, 82

——— Rue de Rome, 1869–76 X

——— Rue Fortuny and Avenue de Villiers, 1876–98 △, 82

France, Sauzon, Belle-Isle, route D25, 1887–1922 △, 37

France, Paris, 56 Boulevard Péreire, 1898–1923 △, 82

——— Théâtre Sarah Bernhardt, (Théâtre de la Ville), 2 Place du Châtelet, 1899 et seq. 1923 ☐, 82

BISMARCK, OTTO VON (1815–1898).

East Germany, Schönhausen, Birthplace, Bismarck Estate, 1815 et seq. 1898 △, 115

East Germany, East Berlin, Plamann Institute, Wilhelmstrasse 139, 1822–27 △

West Germany, Göttingen, Bürgerstrasse, 1832–33 ☐, 133

West Germany, Aachen, 1836–37 X

West Germany, Frankfurt am Main, Grosse Gallusstrasse 19, 1851–58 △, 134

East Germany, East Berlin, Reich Chancellery, Wilhelmstrasse 78, 1862–90 △, 115

West Germany, Aumühle-Friedrichsruh, Bismarck Museum, 1871 et seq. 1898 *, 133

West Germany, Hausen, Bismarck House, 1874 *, 133

BLAIR, ERIC ARTHUR. ("GEORGE ORWELL") (1903–1950).

Great Britain: England, Henley-on-Thames, Nutshell, Western Road, 1907–12 ☐, 186

——— Roselawn, Station Road, 1912–15 ☐, 186

——— 36 St. Mark's Road, 1915–17 ☐, 186

Great Britain, London, 23 Cromwell Crescent, 1917–18 ☐, 236

——— 23 Mall Chambers, 1918–21 ☐, 236

——— 10 Portobello Road, 1927 ☐, 236

Great Britain: England, Southwold, Queen Street, 1927–32 X, 186

France, Paris, 6 Rue du Pot de Fer, 1929 ☐, 83

Great Britain, London, The Hawthorns, Church Road, Hayes, 1932–33 ☐, 236

Great Britain: England, Southwold, Montague House, 36 High Street, 1932–33 ☐, 186

Great Britain, London, Warwick Mansions, Pond Street, South End Green, Hampstead, 1934–35 △, 236

——— 77 Parliament Road, 1935 ☐, 236

——— 50 Lawford Road, 1935–36 ☐, 236

Great Britain: England, Wallington, 1936–40 ☐, 186

Great Britain, London, 18 Dorset Chambers, Chagford Street, 1940–41 ☐, 236

——— 111 Langford Court, Abbey Road, 1941–42 ☐, 236

——— 101a Mortimer Crescent, Hampstead, 1942–44 ☐, 236

——— 27b Canonbury Square, 1944–46 ☐, 236

Great Britain: Scotland, Ardlussa, Barnhill, Isle of Jura, 1946–49 ☐, 292

Great Britain: Scotland, Cranham, Cotswold Sanatorium, 1949 ☐, 293

Great Britain, London, University College Hospital, Gower Street, 1949–50 ☐, 236

BLAKE, WILLIAM (1757–1827).

Great Britain, London, Birth site, 74 Broadwick Street, 1757–82, 1784–85 △, 236

——— 31 Great Queen Street, 1771–78 △, 236

——— 23 Green Street, 1782–84 △

——— 27 Broad Street, 1784–85 △

——— 28 Poland Street, 1785–93 △, 236

——— 13 Hercules Buildings, 1793–1800 △, 236

Great Britain: England, Felpham, Blake Cottage, 1800–03 ☐, 186

Great Britain, London, 17 South Molton Street, 1803–21 ☐, 237

——— 3 Fountain Court, 1821–27 △, 237

BLUEBEARD. See GILLES DE RAIS.

BOCCACCIO, GIOVANNI (1313–1375).

Italy, Certaldo, Birthplace, 18 Via Boccaccio, 1313–? △, *, 323

Italy, Naples, Vicinity, Piazza del Municipio, 1327–41 X, 324

Italy, Florence, Vicinity, Piazza San Piero, 1341–60 X, 324

BONHOEFFER, DIETRICH (1906–1945).

East Germany, West Berlin, Wangenstrasse 14, 1916–35 ☐, 115

West Germany, Tübingen, Igel Fraternity House, University of Tübingen campus, 1924–25 ☐, 134

West Germany, Friedrichsbrunn, 1913 et seq. X

West Germany, Finkenwalde, 1935–39 X

Spain, Barcelona, 1928–29 X

East Germany, Wedding, Oderbergerstrasse 61, 1932 ☐, 115

——— Marienburger Allee 43, 1936–43 ☐, 115

Great Britain, London, Manor Mount, Sydenham, 1933–35 ☐, 237

East Germany, East Berlin, Tegel Prison, Tegeler See, 1943–44 ☐, 115

——— Gestapo headquarters, Niederkirchnerstrasse 8, 1944–45 △, 115

West Germany, Flossenbürg, Flossenbürg Concentration Camp, 1945 △, *, 134

BORGIA, CESARE (1476?–1507).

Italy, Rome, Birthplace, 1476?–? X, 324

——— Penitenzieri Palace, Via della Conciliazione, 1492–1503 ☐, 324

——— Borgia Apartments, Apostolic Palace, Vatican City, 1503 *, 324

Italy, Perugia, Sapienza, 1489–91 X

Italy, Pisa, 1491–92 X

Italy, Spoleto, 1492 X

Spain, Medina del Campo, La Mota, 1504–06 ☐, 365

BORGIA, LUCREZIA (1480–1519).

Italy, Rome, Sforza Cesarini Palace, 282 Via dei Banchi Vecchi, 1480s ☐, 324

——— Palace of Santa Maria, St. Peter's Basilica vicinity, 1480s–93 △, 324

——— San Sisto Vecchio, Piazzale Numa Pompilio, 1500 ☐, 324

Italy, Ferrara, Estense Castle, Piazza della Republica, 1501–19 *, 324

BOSCH, HIERONYMUS (1450–1516).

The Netherlands, 's-Hertogenbosch, Birthplace, ca. 1450–1516 X, 161

The Netherlands, Oirschot, 1470s–1500s X, 161

Spain, Madrid, Prado Museum, *Exhibit*, Paseo del Prado, 365

BOSWELL, JAMES (1740–1795).

Great Britain: Scotland, Edinburgh, Birthplace, Parliament Square, 1740–49 △, 293

——— 15A Meadow Place, 1780s ☐, 293

Great Britain: Scotland, Auchinleck, Auchinleck House, 1740 et seq. 1786 ☐, 293

——— St. James's Court, 1760s–70s △, 293

Great Britain, London, 10 Downing Street, 1762 △, 237

——— Half Moon Street, 1768 X

——— Old Bond Street, 1769 X

GEOGRAPHICAL INDEX

This index refers only to places appearing in the narrative section of the book and excludes additional listings in the Name Index and Gazetteer.